WRITING EGYPT

Al-Maqrizi and his Historical Project

Nasser Rabbat

EDINBURGH
University Press

Edinburgh University Press is one of the leading university presses in the UK. We publish academic books and journals in our selected subject areas across the humanities and social sciences, combining cutting-edge scholarship with high editorial and production values to produce academic works of lasting importance. For more information visit our website: edinburghuniversitypress.com

Edinburgh University Press Ltd
The Tun—Holyrood Road
12 (2f) Jackson's Entry
Edinburgh EH8 8PJ

Typeset in EB Garamond by
Cheshire Typesetting Ltd, Cuddington, Cheshire, and
printed and bound in Great Britain

A CIP record for this book is available from the British Library

ISBN 978 1 3995 0281 8 (hardback)
ISBN 978 1 3995 0282 5 (paperback)
ISBN 978 1 3995 0283 2 (webready PDF)
ISBN 978 1 3995 0284 9 (epub)

WRITING EGYPT

Al-Maqrizi and his Historical Project

Contents

Preface

I did not know al-Maqrizi before my doctoral studies. Visiting Cairo in the summer of my first year on the PhD program, I spent many hot days touring the city's magnificent Mamluk monuments. I was smitten by their subtle elegance, composite geometry, and pronounced urban character. Upon my return to Cambridge, I decided that my dissertation topic would center on Mamluk Cairo.

For a seminar requiring a research paper on the architectural evolution of a monument, I picked al-Azhar Mosque, which has a long and glorious history. This is when I encountered al-Maqrizi for the first time, or more precisely his encyclopedic *Khitat*, the most comprehensive source on Cairo until the fifteenth century.

My focus on Cairo grew, and al-Maqrizi's work became indispensable to my research. In 1997–8, I began preparing a book on how medieval Arabic sources treated visual culture. Al-Maqrizi naturally constituted a good part of that study. But when I shared the unfinished manuscript with colleagues, Renata Holod recommended that al-Maqrizi deserved separate treatment. So was born the idea to write a book on him.

The project remained an idea for a couple of years. I gave a few presentations and published a few articles on al-Maqrizi's work. All along, I read all that al-Maqrizi wrote and all that was written about him. But I still had no access to the man himself, his life, worldviews, and motivations in devoting his adult life to history writing. Then, in 2002, Mahmoud al-Jalili published his family heirloom: a unique complete manuscript of al-Maqrizi's biographical dictionary, *Durar al-ʿUqud al-Farida fi-Tarajim al-Aʿyan al-Mufida*, which he had until then withheld from researchers.

To me, the *Durar* represented a qualitative leap. In it, al-Maqrizi not only collected the biographies of people whom he knew directly, including members of his family, teachers, friends, companions in his spiritual journey, rivals, patrons, and contemporary amirs and sultans, but also reported detailed stories about his dealings with them. The text thus opened a window into a more intimate knowledge of al-Maqrizi's feelings and musings about members of his social circle, offering an exceptional potential for a thorough biography of the man.

The *Durar*, however, also presented a challenge. I now had a treasure trove of material that required not only verification and cross-referencing, but also a reorientation of my research. I now had to plug the new knowledge of al-Maqrizi's sentiments, preoccupations, and views into the contextualization of his scholarly oeuvre to form a fuller treatment of his personality, methods of thinking and judging, and intellectual milieu. Consequently, the scope of the book widened and its human interest deepened.

A major aim of the book thus became to bring al-Maqrizi closer to us. He can no longer only be that traditional, if at times clearly idiosyncratic, author of chronicles and biographical dictionaries obscured by the passing of time and half-hidden behind the writing formula and conventions of his age. He now comes across as a sensitive and melancholy historian who not only records and preserves the memory of events, people, and places, but also reflects on the vagaries of life on both the personal and collective level. He also laments the growing immorality and the slackening of the established principles of religion among the Mamluk class as the main causes of the country's ruination (*kharab*), which permeates all of his writing, although it is most pronounced in the *Khitat* and the *Suluk*, the chronicle of his own times. To me, al-Maqrizi became first and foremost an opinionated witness of his age whose thoughts and quirks occupied me for a number of years, and which I try in this book to convey with all of their anxious worries, emotional charges, and ethical commitment.

The book has taken many years to complete, during which time I have accumulated so many debts to colleagues, friends, family members, and institutions that I will not be able to list them all. I hope that those among my inspirers who will read this book and don't find their name in the acknowledgments will forgive me and know that my gratitude to them is real even if absent here. My eternal thanks go to the late Leila Ibrahim, the "Maqrizi" of the twentieth century and my mentor in all things Cairene for many years. She, Irene "Renie" Bierman, and Margaret Ševčenko, were my three guardian angels, who, along with Oleg Grabar, left indelible marks on my scholarly persona and ways of seeing and writing about architecture. Renata Holod was the first to suggest that I write a book on al-Maqrizi. Patricia Crone rejected my first plan for a book and forced me to rethink my approach. Over the years, Hussah al-Sabah, Bruce Craig, Christian Velud, Timothy Mitchell, Charles Burroughs, Jeffrey Ravel, Edhem Eldem, Noha Forster, Gabriel Martinez-Gros, Roy Mottahedeh, Fahmida Suleman, William Granara, David Roxburgh, Nayel Shafei, Stefan Conermann, Bethany Walker, and Sarah Whiting invited me to the various platforms and programs they direct to speak about al-Maqrizi. Tarek Sweilem, Yusef Rakha, Courtney Lesoon, and Reza Daftarian read chapters and shared helpful comments. So did my anonymous reviewers, whose notes sharpened several arguments in the book.

Others gave advice, listened to my ideas, pointed to leads or sources, and encouraged me along the way. They include Dia' al-Din Chatty, Peri Bearman, Jere Bacharach, Gulru Necipoglu, James Wescoat, Heghnar Watenpaugh, Sibel Bozdogan, David Friedman, Stanford Anderson, Li Guo, Julien Loiseau, Heba Mostafa, Gul Kale, Aleksandar Sopov, Haggai Mazuz, Nezar AlSayyad, Reuven Amitai, Noah Gardiner, Judith Pfeiffer, Dana Sajdi, Ayman Fuad Sayyid, Patricia DeMartino, Erika Naginski, Jo Van Steenbergen, Sylvie Denoix, Doris Behrens-Abouseif, Dorothee Kreuzer, Abdelkader Al Ghouz, Gul Sen, Ruba Kanaan, Tarek Sabra, Barry Flood, Avinoam Shalem, Ayman al-Sayyad, Sara Galleti, Megan Reid, Evrim Binbas, Walid Saleh, Reem al-Shqour, Bernard O'Kane, Seif el-Rashidi, Kareem Ibrahim, and Ahmed el-Bindari. Of course, all infelicities and shortcomings of the book are my sole responsibility.

Fellowships, residencies, and memberships of scholarly groups and various institutions have supported the development of this book over time and provided sustaining environments. They are, in chronological order: the American Research Center in Egypt (ARCE); The Institute for Advanced Study, Princeton, N.J.; the Radical Reassessment of Arabic Art, Language and Literature (RRAALL) Group; the Misr Group; l'Institut du Monde Arabe (IMA), Paris; l'Institut Français d'Archéologie Orientale (IFAO), Cairo; the Radcliffe Institute for Advanced Study, Cambridge, M.A.; l'Institut d'études avancées de Paris; and the Annemarie Schimmel Kolleg, Bonn University, Bonn, Germany, where the book took its final shape. I am immensely grateful to all of them.

My partner Randa Shedid and son Kinan lived with the ghost of al-Maqrizi for many years, to the point at which asking "How is al-Maqrizi doing?" became a routine question in our household. My late mother, Nihad Kazoun, often urged me to finish the book so that she could read it before it was too late. Alas, it took me too long for her to see it published. Sorry Mom, I can now only dedicate it to your memory.

Short References to Frequently Cited Primary Sources

(For full citations, see Bibliography)

'Abd al-Basit al-Zahiri, *al-Mujma'*	'Abd al-Basit ibn Khalil ibn Shahin al-Zahiri, *al-Mujma' al-Mufanan.*
Al-'Ayni, *Iqd*	Al-'Ayni. *'Iqd al-Juman fi Tarikh Ahl al-Zaman*
Al-Buqa'i, *'Unwan al-Zaman*	Al-Buqa`i, *'Unwan al-Zaman bi-Tarajim al-Shuyukh wal-Aqran*
Al-Jawhari, *Inba'*	Al-Jawhari al-Ṣayrafi. *Inba' al-Hasr bi-Abna' al-'Asr*
Al-Jawhari, *Nuzhat*	Al-Jawhari al-Ṣayrafi. *Nuzhat al Nufus Wa-l-Abdan fi Tawarikh*
Al-Maqrizi, *Dhahab*	Al-Maqrizi, *al-Dhahab al-Masbuk fi Dhikr man Hajja min al-Khulafa' wa al-Muluk*
Al-Maqrizi, *Durar*	Al-Maqrizi. *Durar al-'Uqud al-Farida Fi Tarajim al-A'yan al-Mufida*, al-Jalili edition
Al-Maqrizi, *Ighathat*	Al-Maqrizi. *Ighathat al-Umma bi-kashf al-Ghumma*
Al-Maqrizi, *Itti'az*	Al-Maqrizi. *Itti'az al-Hunafa bi-Akhbar al-A'Imma al-Fatimiyyin al-Khulafa*
Al-Maqrizi, *Khitat1*	Al-Maqrizi. *Al-Mawa'iz wa-al-I'itbar fi Dhikr al-Khitat wa-al-Athar*. Bulaq edition
Al-Maqrizi, *Khitat2*	Al-Maqrizi. *Al-Mawa'iz wa-al-I'itbar fi Dhikr al-Khitat wa-al-Athar*. Sayyid edition
Al-Maqrizi, *Muqaffa*	Al-Maqrizi. *Kitab al-Muqaffa al-Kabir*
Al-Maqrizi, *Rasa'il*	Al-Maqrizi. *Rasa'il Al-Maqrizi*
Al-Maqrizi, *Suluk*	Al-Maqrizi. *Al-Suluk li-Ma'rifat Duwal al-Muluk*

Al-Qalqashandi, *Subh*	Al-Qalqashandi. *Subh al-A'sha fi-Sina'at al-Insha*
Al-Safadi, *Wafi*	Al-Safadi. *Kitab al-Wafi bi-al-Wafayat.*
Al-Sakhawi, *Daw'*	Al-Sakhawi. *Al-Daw' al-Lami' li-Ahl al-Qarn al-Tasi'*
Al-Sakhawi, *I'lan*	Al-Sakhawi. *Al-I'lan bi-al-Tawbikh li-man Dhamma al-Tarikh.*
Al-Sakhawi, *Tibr*	Al-Sakhawi. *Kitab al Tibr al-Masbuk fi Dhayl al-Suluk*
EI^{1}	*Encyclopaedia of Islam*, first edition
EI^{2}	*Encyclopaedia of Islam*, second edition
EI^{3}	*Encyclopaedia of Islam*, third edition
Ibn 'Abd-al-Zahir, *Rawd*	Ibn 'Abd-al-Zahir. *Al-Rawd al-Zahir fi-Tarikh al-Malik al-Zahir*
Ibn al-'Imad al-Hanbali, *Shadharat*	Al-Hanbali, Ibn al-'Imad. *Shadharat al-Dhahab fi Akhbar Man Dhahab*
Ibn al-Furat, *Tarikh*	Ibn al-Furat. *Tarikh al-Duwal wa-l-Muluk*
Ibn Duqmaq, *Intisar*	Ibn Duqmaq. *Al-Intisar li-Wasitat 'Aqd al-Amsar*
Ibn Duqmaq, *Jawhar*	Ibn Duqmaq. *Al-Jawhar al-Thamin fi-Siar al-Khulafa' wa-l-Muluk wa-l-Salatin*
Ibn Fadhl Allah, *Masalik*	Ibn Fadhl Allah al-'Umari. *Masalik al-Absar fi Mamalik al-Amsar*
Ibn Fahd, *Mu'jam*	Ibn Fahd, Najm al-Din Umar. *Mu'jam al-Shuyukh*
Ibn Hajar, *al-Durar al-Kamina*	Ibn Hajar. *al-Durar al-Kamina fi A'yan al-Mi'a al-Thamina*
Ibn Hajar, *Majma'*	Ibn Hajar. *Al-Majma' al-Mu'assis li al-Mu'jam al-Mufahris, Mashikhat Ibn Hajar*
Ibn Hajar, *Raf' al-Isr*	Ibn Hajar. *Raf' al-Isr 'an Qudat Misr*
Ibn Iyas, *Bada'i'*	Ibn Iyas. *Bada'i' al-Zuhur fi-Waqa'i' al-Duhur*
Ibn Iyas. *Nuzhat*	Ibn Iyas. *Nuzhat al-Umam fi'l-'Aja'ib wa'l-Hikam*
Ibn Qadi Shuhbah, *Tarikh*	Ibn Qadi Shuhbah. *Tarikh Ibn Qadi Shuhbah*

Ibn Shaddad, *Tarikh al-Zahir*	Ibn Shaddad. *Tarikh al-Malik al-Zahir*
Ibn Shahin al-Zahiri, *Zubdat*	Al-Zahiri, Khalil ibn Shahin. *Kitab Zubdat Kashf al-Mamlik wa Bayan al-Turuq wa-l-Masalik*
Ibn Taghri-Birdi, *Hawadith*	Ibn Taghri-Birdi. *Hawadith al-Duhur fi Mada al-Ayyam wa-al-Shuhur*
Ibn Taghri-Birdi, *Manhal*	Ibn Taghri-Birdi. *Al-Manhal al-Safi wa-al-Mustawfi ba'da al-Wafi*
Ibn Taghri-Birdi, *Nujum*	Ibn Taghri-Birdi. *Al-Nujum al-Zahira fi-Muluk Misr wa-l-Qahira*

Abbreviations

AAI	*Annales Islamologiques*
AUB	American University of Beirut
AUC	American University in Cairo
BEO	*Bulletin d'études orientales*
BSOAS	*Bulletin of the School of Oriental and African Studies*
BSROGE	*Bulletin de la Société Royale de Géographie d'Égypte*
IFAO	Institut français d'archéologie orientale
IFEAD	Institut français d'études arabes
IJIA	*International Journal of Islamic Architecture*
IJMES	*International Journal of Middle East Studies*
JAE	*Journal of Architectural Education*
JAH	*Journal of Art Historiography*
JAIS	*Journal of Arabic and Islamic Studies*
JAL	*Journal of Arabic Literature*
JARCE	*Journal of the American Research Center in Egypt*
JESHO	*Journal of the Economic and Social History of the Orient*
JOAS	*Journal of the American Oriental Society*
JRAS	*Journal of the Royal Asiatic Society*
JRASGBI	*The Journal of the Royal Asiatic Society of Great Britain and Ireland*
MEJ	*Middle East Journal*
MES	*Middle Eastern Studies*
MESAB	*Middle East Studies Association Bulletin*
MMA	*Majallat al-Mu'arrikh al-'Arabi*
MMAF	*Mémoires publiés par les Membres de la Mission Archéologique Française au Caire*
MMII	*Majallat al-Majma' al-'Ilmi al-'Iraqi*
MSR	*Mamluk Studies Review*
ROC	*Revue de l'Orient Chrétien*
SI	*Studia Islamica*
ZDMG	*Zeitschrift der Deutschen Morgenländischen Gesellschaft*

Notes on Transcription and Dates

Clarity is the overriding concern in the use of Arabic names, terms, and phrases. The transcription system used follows that of the *International Journal of Middle East Studies* (*IJMES*). Familiar geographical names such as Cairo, Damascus, and Aleppo are used in their common English form. Some Arabic words, phrases, or poetic quotations are reproduced in Arabic to convey the sound of the poetry or when the word has no immediate English equivalent. A simplified transliteration system is used whereby all transliteration of Arabic sounds is eliminated except for the *'ayn* (') and the *hamza* ('). This was done in agreement with the publisher as we felt that they encumber the non-specialist and are redundant to the specialist trained to read Arabic (or Persian). Dates are given in Common Era years; A.H. (Hijri) years are given only when required either by reference to an Islamic month, or as a direct quotation from an Arabic text which mentions a Hijri year. In all cases, A.H. is added after the Hijri date and the Common Era equivalent follows in parentheses. Primary sources used more than once are cited from the beginning in abbreviated form; the complete citation can be found in the List of Short References and the Bibliography. Books and articles cited only a few times are cited in full in the footnotes in which they first appear; they then appear in abbreviated form in subsequent citations.

Introduction: A Singular Mamluk Historian

Sometime in late 1413, Taqiyy al-Din Ahmad ibn ʿAli al-Maqrizi (1364–1442), a pious Egyptian scholar who had recently returned to Cairo from a long stay in Damascus, suffered what would appear to us today as a severe mid-life crisis. He had spent the previous twenty-six years of his life trying to navigate the treacherous waters of clientage in the pursuit of employment in the state administration or the religious establishment. This quest had left him both disillusioned and disgusted with the whole process of cultivating benefactors and overcoming rivals in the utterly corrupt and shifty Mamluk backstage politics. He had begun to contemplate a way out a few years earlier, but was still beholden to his circle of patrons and to the hope of attaining an office worthy of his knowledge and expertise. The momentous events of that year, however, gravely diminished both prospects. The sultan he had last served in an official capacity had been killed. His most powerful patron at court was executed a few months later. A clique of rising administrators tried to incriminate him after his patron's downfall. Desolate and indignant, he finally withdrew from the protracted and ultimately futile rat race. He retired to his family home in a venerable section of Cairo, where he spent the remainder of his life, thirty years in all, in almost total seclusion, except for infrequent visits to his fellow scholars and students and a number of extended sojourns to Mecca (*mujawarat*), where he seems to have found solace and scholarly recognition.

In his retreat, al-Maqrizi dedicated his time to studying, writing, and teaching history with a select group of students. His only companion in the house he inherited from his maternal grandfather was his daughter Fatima, whom he would lose in 1423 to the plague, after having lost the other members of his family earlier. He seems to have led a rather meager life with no steady employment or secure source of income. We know of only occasional, half-hearted, and mostly unsuccessful attempts at obtaining patronage and monetary rewards for some of his short treatises composed by commission. The outcome of his thirty-year labors, however, was an outstanding series of books and essays that aim to capture everything known about the history and geography of Egypt and the lives of its noteworthy citizens from the beginning of Islam up until his own time. Another writing project, which covers about a third of al-Maqrizi's scholarly output, was started later but ran parallel to the history of Egypt endeavor. It aimed to recount the exemplary life of the Prophet Muhammad and his family, and his prophetic lineage, ancestors, and descendants in two multi-volume compendia and several shorter treatises. An ardent devotional tone breathes in these books, which led some modern commentators to dub al-Maqrizi a sympathizer of the Household of the Prophet (Al al-Bayt), a trait which he shared with many pious ulama of the time who were, like him, otherwise committed Sunnis. If anything, al-Maqrizi was more strictly conservative than his peers, due to his background, upbringing, and intellectual inclinations.

Chief among al-Maqrizi's books is the *Kitab al-Mawaʿiz wa-l-Iʿtibar bi-Dhikr al-Khitat wa-l-Athar* [The Book of Moral Sermons and Lessons Derived from the Remembrance of Cities' Traces and Building Remains] abbreviated as the *Khitat*, and meaning more or less "urban settlements," the largest and most elaborate repository of topographic and historical information on Cairo and, to a lesser extent, other Egyptian cities up to its time. This masterpiece is also the first of al-Maqrizi's large historical oeuvres, which he may have started while still competing for official positions, and it is not even clear whether he completed it as intended before his death. He seems to have meant it as an act of preservation of urban memory at a time of crisis, and intended it to tell the entire history of Islamic Egypt through the history of its capital city, Cairo. He also seems to have realized the difficulty of including all the historical data he had collected, and was continuously expanding, in one book. He thus embarked on the more ambitious project of writing the comprehensive history of Egypt that netted a number of historical and biographical works all focused on the country, its rulers, and famous citizens. This included three comprehensive annals arranged in chronological order: the first on the early Islamic period (lost today), the second on the Fatimid period (tenth to twelfth century), and the third on the Ayyubids and the Mamluks up to al-Maqrizi's own time (1171–c. 1440). He supplemented the annals by concise works on various types of important players in the history of the country, such as the Arab tribes that migrated to Egypt before and after Islam and the viziers and the royal secretaries of the Islamic period (lost today). He also compiled a major multi-volume biographical dictionary, in which he wanted to group the biographies of all the important people who have lived in or visited Egypt since the Islamic conquest in the tradition of the prosopographies of al-Baghdadi and Ibn ʿAsakir, but appears to have died before its completion. His other, more intimate and shorter biographical dictionary, in which he listed the people he personally knew or who lived during his lifetime, remains incomplete by definition.

At a slightly later date, al-Maqrizi became engaged in writing the history of the Prophet Muhammad and his family, which included two connected multi-volume works on the Creation and on the descendants of the Prophet and a number of articles on various religious subjects such the history of the Ka'ba, the biographies of caliphs and kings who performed the Hajj, the dispute between the Umayyads and the Hashemites, and the story of a *sahabi* (companion of the Prophet) who was particularly venerated in Egypt. The large projects of history writing were interspersed with shorter treatises on diverse subjects, including a probing essay on famine and another on Islamic monetary history, two essays on Abyssinia and Hadhramaut, one on bees, and a strange article on the riddle of water, which can be seen as separate exercises of a solitary yet voraciously inquisitive man who may have wanted every now and then to take a break from the rather rigid program he imposed on himself.

Despite the quality and quantity of his historical works, al-Maqrizi's status as a major Mamluk historian was, and to a larger extent remains, open to interpretation and disagreement. To begin with, his contemporaries and immediate successors did not universally admire him, although most of them heavily depended on his writing. Many of his Mamluk biographers report that he was fascinated by and even engrossed in the study of history. They differ widely in judging his rank in that particularly rich period in prominent historians, with a few dubbing him "the dean of all historians" (*shaykh al-mu'arrikhin*), while many merely concede his immense historical knowledge. A few, however, dismiss him as irrelevant, or even worse, as a thief and a plagiarist, a particularly hypocritical accusation in a period in which many chroniclers simply copied from each other and compiled the work of their predecessors, and sometimes contemporaries, mostly without any attribution. The wide array of differing opinions about al-Maqrizi, however, points to his controversial personality as well as his sometimes hurtful bluntness, and possibly to enmities he accumulated during the time in which he was relentlessly competing for jobs and favors at the Mamluk court. Moreover, as will become clear in the course of this book, al-Maqrizi's writings may have been misunderstood by his contemporaries as they display a few idiosyncratic qualities, which flavor his narratives with features that we have come to appreciate more in our age of openly subjective and opinionated historical writing than they did then.

Indeed, in most of his writings, al-Maqrizi comes across as a historian with a clear ethical imperative in an intellectual milieu rife with history writing that seems by and large to have accepted a non-committal chronicling function. Here is a devout scholar who quit his public career at the prime age of forty-eight to devote himself completely to writing the history of his beloved country Egypt, whose irrevocable decline under the morally lax Mamluk rule he was somberly predicting and condemning. As the premier book of his historical oeuvre, the *Khitat* was all too evidently motivated less by professional ambition and more by personal responsibility and even intellectual anguish. In its subject matter, structure, and tone, this massive book reflects the defining period in al-Maqrizi's life with its intense and painful soul-searching and reckoning. It marks al-Maqrizi's transformation from a client to one or other among the Mamluk grandees to an independent, even aloof, historian with a critical stand. Even today, the book still comes across as a moving and challenging discursive oeuvre laced with political innuendos, sociocultural commentaries, nostalgic reminiscences, and grim proclamations. The same feelings echo in at least two of his other books, whose focus is the present and the recent past. The first is the third volume of his chronicle *al-Suluk li-Ma'rifat Duwal al-Muluk*, which covers the events he has witnessed directly in his adulthood and which stops only when he is no longer able to write. The second is his intimate biographical dictionary, *Durar al-'Uqud al-Farida fi Tarajim al-A'yan al-Mufida*, which contains the biographies of people he knew and dealt with and which he started compiling around the time he decided to retreat from public life. In this book al-Maqrizi offers a wide array of opinions, reflections, and personal details couched in his biographies of others.

But anger, melancholy, pessimism, angst, and relentless remembrance, all significant feelings that are rarely expressed in the medieval Arabic historical tradition, are not the primary qualities that make al-Maqrizi's writing so compelling. The primary quality, rather, is his perception of the role of the historian. This is so cogently captured in a statement attributed to him by his nemesis al-Sakhawi in his *al-'I'lan bi al-Tawbikh li man Dhamma al-Tarikh*, where the latter gathered a series of definitions of history by his peers past and present (which will be contextualized later). Al-Maqrizi is supposed to have said, "The person who writes the history [of his time] is tallying the days [i.e. time itself] on the days of his life (*hasaba al-ayyam 'ala 'umrihi*), and the one who writes the events of his time is making later generations witness his own age (*ashhada 'asruhu man lam yakun min ahl 'asrihi*). The historian in this brief statement is transcending his routine function of recording the events of his time to become part and parcel of what he is reporting, not as a participant, which he may or may not be, but as witness (*shahid*), a word that in Arabic carries traces of moral obligation. He becomes the embodiment of these events, which he transmits to his readers, especially those who come after him, through his description, his comprehension of what he is reporting, and his reaction to it, all of course expressed through language. But his subjectivity, or more precisely his personal judgment, is not suppressed or buried under layers of (artificially) cleansing semantic tools, such as coded and tailored professional language, methods of verification, or detachment from what is being reported, as the strict definition of a medieval historian would have us believe. It is instead enmeshed in his narrative so that what he knows, interprets, feels, or judges is recognized and conveyed as his own.

Yet, this is not the image that comes across from the modern critical literature on al-Maqrizi. Nor do the idiosyncratic qualities of his writing inform contemporary judgments of the man and his oeuvre. True, he has been considered the most accomplished historian of Mamluk Cairo. His annals and biographical compositions have been praised from as early as the beginning of the nineteenth century for their breadth, and for having preserved older material, some of which would have been lost to us otherwise. They have been also admired for offering the most spirited eyewitness testimony we have of the Mamluk sultanate in the first half of the fifteenth century. His *Khitat* book in particular has been described as the single most important and influential source for the study of the history of Cairo in the medieval period. This, in my opinion, is an understatement, for the book is not merely a mine of invaluable historical material; it is above all a unique exploration into history writing through the chronicling of settlements, buildings, and ruins. It historicizes, and to an astonishing degree personalizes, writing on the city as a human artifact. In fact, the *Khitat* may be regarded as one of the first, if not the first, truly interpretive histories of a city anywhere to have come down to us from the medieval period.

Al-Maqrizi was among the first Egyptian historians to become known outside of Egypt. His *Khitat* was translated into Ottoman Turkish and partially incorporated into a new history of Egypt not long after the Ottoman conquest of Egypt in 1517. Selections from his writings have been translated into various European languages and commented upon from at least the middle of the eighteenth century. His *Khitat*, first published in its entirety in 1853–4 in Bulaq, has been consulted by many generations of Orientalist students of Islamic history in general and of Egypt and Cairo in particular. The twentieth century saw multiple attempts at systematic and scholarly editing of his vast body of work, an effort that continues until the present, especially with the reissuing of his *Khitat* and his Fatimid history book, *Iti'azz al-Hunafa bi-Akhbar al-A'imma al-Fatimiyyin al-Khulafa*, by Ayman Fu'ad Sayyid in 2003 and 2012 respectively, and the even more ambitious Bibliotheca Maqriziana project undertaken by Brill under the direction of Frédéric Bauden, whose ultimate aim is to publish his entire oeuvre in thorough critical editions. The bulk of his shorter treatises, too, have been edited and published, many in recent years and some in more than one edition of varying merit. Some of these epistles, especially the controversial or polemical ones, have been translated into various languages and incorporated into larger debates about the history of the Mamluk Sultanate (1250–1517), under whose rule al-Maqrizi lived all of his life, or the family of the Prophet, of whose exalted status al-Maqrizi was a passionate partisan.

Al-Maqrizi himself, however, has remained up until the late twentieth century an unknown historical entity save for a few conventional biographical entries dating his birth and death and listing his teachers, works, and students. More recently, two extensive biographical books were published in Arabic, in addition to a number of studies in European languages. Several essays on al-Maqrizi the scholar, his work, and his views and possible inclinations and biases were conveniently gathered in a special issue of *Mamluk Studies Review* in 2003. More critical material is being published piecemeal since 2000 in an ongoing series of articles by Frédéric Bauden based on his analysis of an unpublished autograph manuscript of al-Maqrizi's collected references and source material. In one of these articles, Bauden, following a number of Mamlukists before him, questions the reliability of al-Maqrizi's historical data in light of a nasty accusation of plagiarism alleged by his contemporary antagonist, al-Sakhawi, and presents conclusive evidence of al-Maqrizi's direct copying from a colleague (a subject that will be discussed later). Yet, with all of this juicy material, no one has attempted a full personal and intellectual biography of this most intriguing and controversial of Mamluk historians, who, moreover, is still the one most cited despite the palpable antagonism heaped upon him in recent Western scholarship.

The present book tells al-Maqrizi's life story as it can be gleaned from the wealth of primary source material available, a good part of which, especially his own *Durar al-'Uqud al-Farida*, has not been put to that use before. Weaving biography with the historiographical analysis of his oeuvre, the book aims to re-present al-Maqrizi both as a man of his age who nonetheless forged a distinct and unique scholarly persona and as a historian with an exhaustive, structured, and principled historical project. His project was to follow the history of Egypt over time through annals, biographies, and short treatises with circumscribed scope. This grand plan began with, evolved along with, and culminated in the *Khitat*, which al-Maqrizi was continuously enlarging, revising, and redacting until shortly before his death. Other annalistic compendia and prosopographies came in sequentially to classify and amplify the various facets of Egyptian history and to better structure the vast amount of material al-Maqrizi gathered about them over the years. But the major import of the *Khitat* was that it represented the pivot around which the rest of the historical works revolved. It embodied the conclusion of their cumulative narratives and illustrated in an almost visual way the changing fate of Egypt, and Cairo, until the irreparable damage (in al-Maqrizi's opinion) that befell them under the Mamluks of his time, which he blamed on their immoral and unjust rule. This was his critical stance, as it were, conceived and presented from within the epistemological framework of a medieval Muslim thinker: in other words, pre-humanist, inherently teleological, and ultimately moralizing.

In our age of hardened positions regarding the interpretation of Islamic history and its documenters, al-Maqrizi comes across as a pure product of the most devout context in Mamluk Cairo who nonetheless reveals a significant degree of individuality, passion, and criticality that are rarely associated with the typical image of a member of the ulama then or now. This book will try to explain how and why.

PART 1

THE LIFE OF AL-MAQRIZI

CHAPTER 1

The Formative Years

Today, it is all too common to view any author's oeuvre in the light of their circumstances and psychological, emotional, and intellectual conditions and proclivities. Background, upbringing, successes and failures, and all the other experiences are seen as fundamental building blocks in shaping, understanding, and explaining an author's oeuvre. So established has this mode of inquiry become that it has spread from its original application to creative pursuits to permeate the study of all literary and scholarly forms, even those social sciences that have traditionally claimed to be governed by rules of objectivity, empiricism, and scholarly detachment immune to the tendencies of personality and circumstances. This development is a direct outcome of two of modern culture's foremost post-Freudian psychosociological foundations. One is the belief in the primacy of individual motivations and inhibitions in determining the scope and orientation of one's life and work.[1] The second is the mania for memorializing, which translates into a society-wide effort

[1] The outburst of biographies in our times is proof enough of our contemporary culture's fascination with the individual and the individual psyche as historical agents. A recent development, the collection and republishing of obituaries from newspapers, shows how far has this obsession gone. See Marvin Siegel, ed., *The New York Times Book of Obituaries and Farewells. A Celebration of Unusual Lives* (New York: William Morrow, 1997), or the ongoing series of *Daily Telegraph* obituaries books, collected and edited by Hugh Massingberd and published by Macmillan: *A Celebration of Eccentric Lives* (1995); *Heroes and Adventurers* (1996); *Entertainers* (1997); or even Jane O'Boyle's more pertinently titled *Cool Dead People: Obituaries of Folks We Wish We'd Met a Little Sooner* (New York: Plume, 2001) and, more recently, Keith Colquhoun and Ann Wroe, *The Economist Book of Obituaries* (New York: Bloomberg Press, 2008) or *The Obits: The New York Times Annual 2012* ed. William McDonald (New York: Workman, 2012). In the same vein, genealogical research has become a major pursuit in the US, with specialized magazines, companies, websites, and web search engines all serving the large number of Americans engaged in family history research. An editorial in *Ancestry* magazine (July–August 2001) cites a poll that put their number at 60 percent of the population. This mostly web-based occupation has gained the scholarly cachet of approval in 2001 through the National Endowment for the Humanities (NEH)'s production of "My History Is America's History" guidebook and its sponsorship of many related scholarly conferences and meetings. For references to NEH activities in this domain, see NEH's family history website (http://www.myhistory.org).

to preserve every shred of memory of those outstanding individuals deemed worthy of remembrance and celebration by the nation, if not by everyone.[2]

Medieval cultures were less emphatic on both counts. Record keeping was far more restricted in range and magnitude and far more arduous and time-consuming than it is today. Medieval scholars had different and less pronounced attitudes toward individuality, authorship, immortality, and remembrance, all concerns that underwent a phenomenal shift in significance in modern times.[3] This observation has been made about both the Western and Islamic worlds. Medieval Islamic scholars, like their Western peers, maintained a relatively inconspicuous presence in their writing, though in varying degrees depending on the genre. They followed established scholarly and literary etiquettes that tended to conceal personal touches behind ready-made narrative structures and elaborate prose techniques. Their personas, however, came with distinct sensibilities, codes, and textual strategies specific to their religious and sociocultural values.[4] On the whole, they shared with the rest

[2] The pioneering study of Maurice Halbwachs, *The Collective Memory* trans. Francis J. Ditter Jr. and Vida Yazidi Ditter (New York: Harper Colophon Books, 1980), 22–87, which was first published in French in 1950, set the stage for the slew of studies on the manifestations of this collective memory. For the monumental aspect of memory preservation, the first scholarly study of the memory cult is, of course, Alois Riegl, *Der Moderne Denkmalkultus, sein Wesen, seine Entstehung* (Vienna; Leipzig: W. Braumüller, 1903), ed. and trans. by Kurt Forster and Diane Ghirardo as "The Modern Cult of Monuments: Its Character and its Origin," *Oppositions* 25 (Fall 1982): 20–51. A more recent sweeping study is David Lowenthal, *Possessed by the Past. The Heritage Crusade and the Spoils of History* (London: Viking, 1997).

[3] On the slow process of change from a muffled to a clear voice of the individual in Western literature, cf. Philippe Ariés and Georges Duby, eds., *A History of Private Life: Revelations of the Medieval World*, Arthur Goldhammer, trans. (Cambridge, M.A.: Harvard University Press, 1988), particularly Danielle Régnier-Bohler, "Imagining the Self. Exploring Literature," 373–82, and Philippe Braunstein, "Toward Intimacy: The Fourteenth and Fifteenth Centuries," 536–56.

[4] This problem has generated a heated debate in Islamic studies, not devoid of a political agenda, about the cultural difficulties of writing about people's lives, whether in the first person or the third, in the premodern Islamic world. For a collection of essays generally skeptical about the existence of true autobiography in Islamic literature, see Martin Kramer, ed. *Middle Eastern Lives: The Practice of Biography and Self-Narrative* [proceedings of a conference sponsored by the Moshe Dayan Center for Middle Eastern and African Studies] (Syracuse, N.Y.: Syracuse University Press, 1991). A collection that sheds light on the genre of autobiography in medieval Islamic literature is Dwight Reynolds, ed. *Interpreting the self: Autobiography in the Arabic Literary Tradition* (Berkeley: University of California Press, 2001). See also the essays in Mary Ann Fay, ed. *Autobiography and the Construction of Identity and Community in the Middle East* (New York: Palgrave, 2001), especially the methodological discussion of Virginia Aksan, "The Question of Writing Premodern Biographies of the Middle East," 191–200. For the Mamluk period see the remarks of Stephan Conermann, "Ibn Tulun (d. 955/1548): Life and Works," *MSR* 8/1 (2004), 115–40, reprinted in his *Mamlukica: Studies on the History and Society of the Mamluk Period* (Bonn: Bonn University Press and V&R Unipress, 2013), 229–36; Mohammad Gharaibeh, "Narrative Strategies in

of their society a fatalistic outlook on life, an inherent disinterest in causality, individual will, and responsibility in explaining events and occurrences. Most of their reporting stopped short of searching for reasons or explanations, and usually ended instead with a variation on an equivocal expression, such as "*wa li-Allah al-amr min qabl wa min ba'd* (It is God's will before and after)," or "*wa Allah a'lam* (God only knows)."[5] Thus, any attempt to read the motives, inhibitions, opinions, and ideals of a medieval Islamic scholar by examining his writing has to take those particularities and limitations into account. It also has to decode the textual and verbal impersonal methods to uncover their established modes of signification and their encoded expressive messages.[6]

This is not to say that readers in the medieval Islamic world did not perceive any relationship between an author's intellectual and emotional disposition and his oeuvre. Quite the opposite; but they saw that relationship less in terms of the author's character, feelings, and choices, and more in terms of his family background, religious and scholarly affiliations, direct and indirect teachers, and professional positions and patrons. In other words, the work of an author was thought to be defined more by his social and intellectual circle than by his personality, preferences, or eccentricities, even when those were noted and occasionally commented upon. The good reputation of an author, and therefore his subsequent commemoration in history books, depended fundamentally on how closely he adhered to, and rose within, the established norms of his social class or professional group. At least, this is the impression we receive from reading any number of *kutub al-tarajim* (biographical dictionaries), the most extensive and most reliable source of information we have on distinguished individuals and social groups in premodern Islamic societies. These collections, which peaked in the Mamluk period for a variety of reasons, are among the most common of medieval historical genres. They record, mainly, the lives of ulama from various *madhahib*, Sufis

---

Biographical Dictionaries: The *ad-Durar al-Kamina* of Ibn Hagar al-'Asqalani—a Case Study," in *Mamluk Historiography Revisited—Narratological Perspectives*, Stephan Conermann, ed. (Bonn: Bonn University Press and V&R Unipress, 2018), 51–75. See also Ethan L. Menchinger, *The First of the Modern Ottomans: The Intellectual History of Ahmed Vasıf* (Cambridge: Cambridge University Press, 2017), 1–12, for a perceptive discussion of the interconnection between biography and history in the Ottoman context, a slightly later period than the one covered by this book, and one that is much better recorded.

[5] Shakir Mustafa, *al-Tarikh al-'Arabi wa-l-Mu'arrikhun: Dirasa fi Tatawwur 'Ilm al-Tarikh wa-Rijaluhu fi-l-Islam*, 4 vols. (Beirut: Dar al-'Ilm li'l Malayin, 1978–93), 2: 83–5.

[6] There is also the ever-present impediment of the loss of most records, not just on an individual, or class of individuals, but even on an entire era, which is more widespread in the Islamic world than the West. Michael Chamberlain, *Knowledge and Social Practice in Medieval Damascus, 1190–1350* (New York: Cambridge University Press, 1994), 5–7, noticed the disparity between the huge number of records kept in medieval Europe and the scarce remnants in the Islamic world, and the research and methodological implications of that disparity.

from all orders, and literati (*udaba'*), followed by sultans, amirs, and bureaucrats, in addition to some odd categories such as idiots (*mughaffalin*), misers (*bukhala'*), and blind people, and, very rarely, women.[7]

Most medieval biographers used standard formulas to present their subjects, thus limiting the range of personal traits they could include. They nonetheless managed at times to be quite expressive by manipulating and nuancing the exact rhetorical and narrative devices within the confines of their otherwise conventionally circumscribed text. A typical entry presents a more or less consistent set of facts about the biographee (*mutarjam lahu*): his (or, very rarely, her) full name, titles, and lineage, dates of death and birth (if known), and family connections. This is supplemented by specific information that depends on his profession, so that for a *'alim*, for instance, the biography includes his education and teachers/masters (*shuyukh*), books read and memorized, *ijazat* (licenses) obtained, employment history, quotations from poetry if he had composed any, reputation among peers, and, in conclusion, a doxology. With few exceptions, medieval biographers tended to leave out personal or anecdotal details about the biographee, not because they were uninteresting, but because they did not help define the individual within his scholarly, military, or social milieu, which is what the biographical genre was intended to do in the first place.[8] The few biographers who routinely included anecdotes, both real and invented, seem to have used them as encoded messages about the scholarly qualities or moral standards of their subject—both defining aspects of the individual scholar in medieval Islamic etiquette.[9] Anecdotes, it appears,

[7] On biographical dictionaries in the Islamic tradition, with an emphasis on the Arabic branch, see H. A. R. Gibb, "Islamic Biographical Literature, " in B. Lewis and P. M. Holt, eds., *Historians of the Middle East* (Oxford: Oxford University Press, 1962), 54–8; Franz Rosenthal, *A History of Muslim Historiography* (Leiden: Brill, 2nd edn., 1968), 100–6; Carl Petry, *The Civilian Elite of Cairo in the Later Middle Ages* (Princeton, N.J.: Princeton University Press, 1981), 5–14; Tarif Khalidi, *Arabic Historical Thought in the Classical Period* (New York: Cambridge University Press, 1994), 200–10; Konrad Hirschler, "Studying Mamluk Historiography. From Source-Criticism to the Cultural Turn," in Stephan Conermann, ed. *Ubi sumus? Quo vademus? Mamluk Studies—State of the Art* (Bonn: V&R Unipress, Bonn University Press, 2013), 159–86, esp. 170–80, where he emphasizes the dynamic evolution of biographical dictionaries during the Ayyubid-Mamluk period.

[8] Chamberlain, *Knowledge*, argues that these prosopographies should be seen more as registers of the practices by which the influential social classes manipulated power. Fedwa Malti-Douglas, "*Mentalités* and Marginality: Blindness and Mamluk Civilization," in C. E. Bosworth, et al. *Essays in Honor of Benard Lewis: The Islamic World from Classical to Modern Times* (Princeton: Darwin Press, 1989), 211–37, makes an interesting and innovative use of a subset of the medieval biographical dictionaries, but stresses nonetheless their usefulness for understanding the mentality of an entire category rather than individuals. See also Mohammad Gharaibeh, "Narrative Strategies," 59–67 for a comparative analysis of one person's biography in two dictionaries with the aim of uncovering the author's agenda.

[9] See Nimrud Hurvitz, "Biographies and Mild Asceticism: A Study of Islamic Moral

provided a free space within the codified structure of the genre for praise and criticism, which allow us to know more not only about the subject of the biography but also about the biographer himself and his relationship to his subject (if he knew him personally), or to his social group, such as his *ʿaqida* (doctrine), *madhhab* (sect), or racial, ethnic, or religious origin.

Sources on al-Maqrizi's Life

Contrary to the frequent complaints about the scarcity of information available on the personal lives of medieval Muslim scholars, we know a good deal about al-Maqrizi. This is not because he wrote his own autobiography as a few of his peers did.[10] He did not. In fact, he did not even write a *mashikhat*, a list of his teachers and the *ijazat* he received from them, the medieval Islamic equivalent of the curriculum vitae, though this was the norm for scholars of his caliber in his time. Throughout his historical texts, however, al-Maqrizi offers juicy snippets about himself in spontaneous statements, giving his own reaction to an event he had witnessed, or his whereabouts when another event occurred. His authorial voice becomes even more personal and at times confessional in the invaluable biographical dictionary, *Durar al-ʿUqud al-Farida fi Tarajim al-Aʿyan al-Mufida*, which, he states in the introduction, he started compiling after he had reached fifty years of age to preserve the memory of people he knew and loved and had started to lose. The date would be around 816/1413 (an important date in al-Maqrizi's life).[11] He was still working on the book less than a year before his death.[12]

Imagination," *SI* 85, 1 (February 1997): 41–65, for a discussion of these issues in the context of an analysis of the biography of Ahmad ibn Hanbal.

[10] Conermann, "Ibn Tulun," 232–6, compares the structures of four Mamluk ulama autobiographies that show the common thread and personal touches in them.

[11] The book was, strangely, published three times in the span of ten years. The first edition was in two volumes and edited by Muhammad Kamal al-Din ʿIzz al-Din (Beirut: ʿAlam al-Kutub, 1992). The second edition of the same manuscript was by ʿAdnan Darwish and Muhammad al-Masri (Damascus: Ministry of Culture, 1995). These two editions were both based on a severely incomplete autograph manuscript preserved in the library of Ghota (Ar. 270), which contains only 330 biographical entries of the letter *alif* and a few under the letter *ʿayn* out of the total 1473 biographies in the complete manuscript. Shortly thereafter, the reluctant owner of the only known complete manuscript of the *Durar*, Mahmoud al-Jalili, was convinced by the publisher in Dar al-Gharb al-Islami to have his valuable manuscript published. Released in 2002 in four volumes complete with profuse notations by al-Jalili, whose family in Mosul, Iraq, had owned the manuscript since at least 1225 A.H./1810 C.E., as indicated by the autograph of his ancestor ʿUthman b. Sulayman Pasha al-Jalili al-Mosuli on the cover page. This book uses this last, complete edition.

[12] The last entry in the manuscript of the *Durar* is the biography of Abu al-Hasan b. al-Sayrafi

Many of al-Maqrizi's subjects were family members, teachers, patrons, colleagues, or competitors. Others were simply friends and acquaintances. A few were important contemporary figures who had died after his own birth. Since their lives fell within the span of al-Maqrizi's own life, which formed the chronological framework of his book, they qualified to be included in the dictionary regardless of whether he knew them or not. In all his biographical entries, but especially in those of his close relatives and friends, al-Maqrizi enlivens his accounts with anecdotes revealing how intimately he knew them. He includes casual conversations he had with them, stories they told him, poetry they recited to him, and reflections about the way their lives had turned out, and even dreams they had had and had reported to him while they were alive, or dreams al-Maqrizi had in which they visited him after their passing, both of which sources of meaning and are taken seriously by the author.[13]

Through these recollections, al-Maqrizi offers a lively and uninhibited image of himself and of his social milieu as more than just that of a scholar/historian. From his writings, we learn more about al-Maqrizi than the usual lists of *shuyukh*, books read, *ijazat* obtained, books composed, patrons, colleagues, and *manasib*s (official appointments). He actually displays the quintessential qualities of first-person narrative and provides glimpses of his experiences, feelings, beliefs, and reflections, which are invaluable for assessing who he was and how his life informed his worldviews and scholarly output. In fact, what al-Maqrizi presents in his *Durar* is a multifaceted autobiographical text spread over a large number of biographies of others and replete with musings on intellectual, moral, and paranormal issues, as well as cozy revelations about himself and his opinions about people and events approaching the tone of a personal diary, even though he meant the book to be read by others, as is clear from his introduction. This kind of openness is quite rare in Islamic prosopographical writing in general, and even rarer in Mamluk biographical dictionaries, which tend to read more like lists of professional résumés. In fact, any comparison of the biographical entries of the same person in al-Maqrizi's *Durar* and in other contemporary Mamluk biographical dictionary, such as the books of his contemporaries Ibn Hajar

al-Dimashqi, who died in Damascus on Monday [*sic*] 11 of Ramadan 844/February 3, 1441, less than a year before al-Maqrizi's death on the 16 of Ramadan 845/January 28, 1442.

13 On the role of dreams in Islamic history, see Gustave E. von Grunebaum, "Introduction: The Cultural Function of the Dream as Illustrated by Classical Islam," and Toufic Fahd, "the Dream in Medieval Islamic Society," in *The Dream and Human Societies*, Gustave E. von Grunebaum and Roger Caillois, eds. (Berkeley: University of California Press, 1966), 3–22, 351–63; Nile Green, "The Religious and Cultural Roles of Dreams and Visions in Islam," *JRAS* 13, 3 (2003): 287–313; Dwight Reynolds, "Symbolic Narratives of Self: Dreams in Medieval Arabic Autobiographies," in *On Fiction and Adab in Medieval Arabic Literature* Philip Kennedy, ed. (Wiesbaden: Harrassowitz, 2005), 261–86.

and al-Sakhawi, reveals an unabashedly intimate, subjective, and emotional side to al-Maqrizi's narrative.[14] Nor does al-Maqrizi try to hide his subjectivity in the *Durar*, especially in the biographies of those closest to him. This was definitely a selective modification on his part, because he takes on a serious and staid narrative demeanor that conforms with the standard of the time as regards the entries on the grandees and scholars he did not know personally.[15]

This is not all we have on al-Maqrizi's life. As a leading and controversial historian in fifteenth-century Cairo, al-Maqrizi elicited strong opinions among the many colleagues who knew him, and even from some who did not know him. Some regarded him as a friend and peer. Others were his students, the disciples of his students, but also the students of his competitors and opponents. Still others were simply rivals or even downright adversaries with known or hidden grudges against him. Many wrote relatively substantial biographies of al-Maqrizi in which they tried to maintain the guarded decorum that was considered a must at the time.[16] The mood and cadence of their texts, however, betray the intensity of their feelings toward al-Maqrizi and to a large extent reflect the nature of their relationship to him. His admirers emphasize his personal wit and easy demeanor as well as his scholarly qualities and religious virtues. They differ in judging his eminence as a historian, but agree that he belonged to the highest rank of the profession. His detractors

[14] The only other Mamluk historian who infuses his writing with the personal in a similar fashion is Shihab al-Din Abu Shama (1203–67), in his *al-Dhayl 'ala-al-Rawdatayn* M. Zahed al-Kawthari, ed. (Cairo: Dar al-Kutub al-Malikiyya, 1947), which is a chronicle of Damascus during the author's lifetime, interspersed with events in his personal life and reflections on them written with an unusual degree of chattiness and candor. See Louis Pouzet, "Abu Šama (599–665/1203–68) et La Société Damascaine de Son Temps," *Bulletin d'études orientales* 37–8 (1985–6), 115–26; Joseph E. Lowry, "Time, Form and Self: The Autobiography of Abu Shama," *Edebiyat* 7, 2 (Autumn 1996): 313–25.

[15] A similarly conventional tone pervades the entries in al-Maqrizi's other large biographical dictionary *al-Muqaffa*, where he attempted to gather the biographies of all the important people who lived in, visited, studied in, or died in Egypt, an immense undertaking which he consciously modeled after al-Khatib al-Baghdadi's *Tarikh Baghdad* or Ibn 'Asakir's *Tarikh Dimashq*, which he never completed and of which it is said that it would have ended up filling eighty volumes had he finished it.

[16] A partial list of his Mamluk biographers includes Ibn Taghri-Birdi, *Nujum*, 15: 225–6; idem, *Manhal*, 1: 415–20; idem, *Hawadith*, 1: 63–8; Ibn Hajar, *Majma'*, 3: 58–60; idem, *Inba'*, 9: 170–2, which Maqrizi seems to have read before his death; al-'Ayni, *'Iqd*, 574; al-Sakhawi, *Daw'*, 2: 21–5; idem, *Tibr*, 1: 70–8, same as *Daw'* with at least one crucial difference about al-Maqrizi's genealogy; Ibn Fahd, *Mu'jam*, 63–7; 'Abd al-Basit al-Zahiri, *al-Mujma'*, 1: 469–75; al-Buqa'i, *'Unwan al-Zaman*, 1: 109–10; al-Jawhari, *Nuzhat*, 4: 242–4; Ibn al-'Imad al-Hanbali, *Shadharat*, 7: 254–5, copied from ibn Taghri-Birdi; Ibn Iyas, *Bada'i'*, 2: 231–2; Muhammad ibn 'Ali al-Shawkani, *al-Badr al-Tali' bi Mahasin man ba'd al-Qarn al-Sabi'*, 2 vols. (Cairo: Dar al-Sa'ada, 1930), 1: 79–81, adapts most of his information from al-Sakhawi and Ibn Hajar, but questions the motivation of the former to attack al-Maqrizi.

question his accuracy, rigor, sincerity, and authorial integrity, and write disdainfully about his interest in divination, numerology, and geomancy, in which he seems to have excelled indeed. These divergent assessments allow us to add further color to the portrait we can glean from the personal details revealed in the *Durar*, especially with the hints they divulge about some of the more ambiguous aspects of al-Maqrizi's genealogy, character, scholarship, and career. Through a modern and interpretive lens, this chapter and the next aim to reconstruct the life of al-Maqrizi using both his many autobiographical statements, dispersed over his full oeuvre but especially present in the biographies of his relatives, teachers, friends, and acquaintances in the *Durar*, and the reports of his contemporary and later Mamluk biographers. This first chapter covers the childhood, family, and teachers of al-Maqrizi, as well as the much-debated question of his genealogy and how it might have shaped his views about the history of Egypt.

A Family of Scholars

Taqiyy al-Din Ahmad ibn ʻAli ibn ʻAbd al-Qadir al-Maqrizi was born in Cairo to a family of learning on both sides. He never provided, in any of his own writings, the exact year of his birth, stating only that he was born sometime after 760/1360. Judging from internal evidence and from several biographies written about him, he was most likely born in 766/1364.[17] Al-Maqrizi grew up in the house of his maternal grandfather Ibn al-Sa'igh al-Hanafi in the venerable neighborhood of Harat al-Burjuwan at the heart of Fatimid Cairo, behind the late Ottoman mosque and *sabil-kuttab* of Suleiman Agha al-Silahdar (built 1839). He seems to have lived there all his life.[18] This was a house of learning and scholarship where students were received at night on a regular basis for *qira'at* (canonical readings of the Qur'an) lessons under the supervision of his grandfather. Almost everybody in his immediate family was involved in some form of religious learning (*ʻilm*), despite the difference in *madhhab* between his paternal and maternal sides.

[17] Al-Sakhawi, *Daw'*, 2: 21; idem, *Tibr*, 1: 71.

[18] This can be deduced from the lists of neighbors in Harat Burjuwan listed in the *Durar*, whose dates of death cover the 35-year period from 774/1372 to 809/1406, even though al-Maqrizi mentions in the biography of Jamal al-Din al-Inbabi (al-Maqrizi, *Durar*, 3: 560–1) that he lived on the Nile in the thoroughfare of Jazriat al-Fil (Elephant Island) in the year 795/1394, a period in which al-Maqrizi was moving up in the ranks of the Mamluk administration, see Al-Jalili, *Durar*, Introduction, 21. For the location of the house, see Hasan ʻAbd al-Wahab, "Hawl Dar al-Maqrizi," in *Dirasat ʻan al-Maqrizi*, Muhammad Mustafa Ziyada et al., eds. (Cairo: Egyptian Historical Society, 1971), 75–9.

Al-Maqrizi's father, 'Ali, was a Hanbali scribe (*katib*) who studied hadith and excelled in some epistolary sciences such as composition and mathematics.[19] He worked and lived in Damascus before moving to Cairo, where he occupied a few minor positions in the judiciary and the viceregency before rising in the administration by becoming an administrator attached to the great amir Aqtamur al-Hanbali, the powerful viceregent of the sultanate between 777 and 779 (1376–8).[20] 'Ali married al-Maqrizi's mother, Asma', in Rajab 735/April 1364. The couple resided in her family house and had, in addition to our historian, two more sons, Muhammad and Hassan, about whom we know nothing except their names and the fact that Muhammad studied the Qur'an as a child.[21] The father seems to have played a small role in al-Maqrizi's upbringing. He died when al-Maqrizi was less than fourteen years of age in 25 Ramadan 779/ January 25, 1378, having not yet turned fifty. His work connections, however, seem to have benefited his son, for in his *Durar* al-Maqrizi credits at least twelve of his father's friends with influential roles in his education or early career.[22] The son also insists on his father's piety in the very brief biography he penned, recalling that his mother had said that, in the fourteen years of their marriage, 'Ali never missed the late-night prayers except when he was sick.

Al-Maqrizi's paternal grandfather, 'Abd al-Qadir al-Maqrizi, who died on the 28 Rabi' al-Awal 732/ December 29, 1331, many years before his grandson's birth, was born in Baalbek. He traveled around Bilad al-Sham, Egypt, and the Hijaz seeking to learn with the major scholars and hadith transmitters (*muhaddithin*) of his age before finally settling down in Damascus, where he became a well-known Hanbali scholar and *muhaddith*. Aside from heading a premier Damascene institution, the Dar al-Hadith al-Baha'iyya (named after al-Baha' ibn 'Asakir of the famous Damascene scholarly family), he also held some posts in the judiciary and administration.[23]

19 On the father, see al-Maqrizi, *Suluk*, 3, 1: 326; idem, *Durar*, 2: 517; Ibn Hajar, *Inba'*, 1: 166; Muhammad Kamal al-Din 'Izz al-Din, *al-Maqrizi Mu'arrikhan* (Beirut: 'Alam al-Kutub, 1990), 18. Al-Maqrizi's brothers are: Nasir al-Din Muhammad (772/1371–822/1419) (see al-Maqrizi, *Suluk*, 4, 1: 514) and Hasan. Anne F. Broadbridge, "Academic Rivalry and the Patronage System in Fifteenth-Century Egypt: al-'Ayni, al-Maqrizi, and Ibn Hajar al-'Asqalani," *MSR* 3 (1999): 85–107, 86, mistakenly puts the father's death in 886/1384 (following a convoluted sentence in Ibn Hajar, *Inba'*, 9: 171 and al-Sakhawi *Daw'*, 1: 22) and makes him a Shafi'i.

20 Al-Jalili, *Durar*, Introduction, 15; Ibn Taghri-Birdi, *Nujum*, 11: 191.

21 Al-Maqrizi, *Durar*, 3; 145, in the biography of Muhammad b. Ahmad al-Hijazi, a teacher of boys, who taught Muhammad the Qur'an. Hasan, who is not mentioned again after the first reference to his name, might be the child that al-Maqrizi's mother lost, as stated in her biography in *Durar*, 1: 395.

22 Al-Jalili, *Durar*, Introduction, 14–20.

23 On the grandfather, see al-Safadi, *Wafi*, 19: 42–3; Ibn Hajar, *al-Durar al-Kamina*, 2: 391;

Al-Maqrizi's paternal grandmother was also a scholar in Damascus according to her grandchild. In his *Durar*, al-Maqrizi once mentions his grandmother by her first name and patronym, Zaynab bint al-Kamal, but does not give us her full *nisba*. This causes some confusion as there seem to have been more than one Zaynab bint al-Kamal. In the biography of Burhan al-Din Ibn Jamaʿa (725/1325–790/1389), a famous scholar who went on to become a first-rate Shafiʿi judge in the Mamluk sultanate and who was a friend of al-Maqrizi's father, al-Maqrizi lists Zaynab bint al-Kamal among Ibn Jamaʿa's teachers. A few pages later in the same biography, al-Maqrizi reports a conversation with Ibn Jamaʿa, in which he told him that he had studied the *al-Muwatta'* of Ibn Malik, the famous compendium of *fiqh*, with his (al-Maqrizi's) "paternal grandmother" Zaynab b. al-Kamal.[24] Among the other biographers of Burhan al-Din Ibn Jamaʿa, only one, Ibn Qadi Shuhba, lists the famous hadith scholar Zaynab bint al-Kamal among his biographee's teachers, but he does not say that she was al-Maqrizi's grandmother, although Ibn Qadi Shuhba knew al-Maqrizi personally.[25] A Zaynab bint al-Kamal was indeed a famous hadith transmitter in Damascus and is mentioned many times in the *Durar* and the *Muqaffa* as a teacher of various scholars whom al-Maqrizi knew, but not once does he say again that she was the same person as his grandmother.[26] Other scholars provide more biographical information on her that complicates the matter further. Ibn Hajar, quoting from al-Dhahabi, states her full name as Zaynab bint al-Kamal Ahmad b. ʿAbd al-Rahim b. ʿAbd al-Wahid b. Ahmad al-Maqdisiyya and says that she was born in Damascus in 646/1249, more than a hundred years before al-Maqrizi's birth, and died on 19 Jamada al-Awla 740/22 November 1339 without ever being married.[27] Other biographies of Zaynab bint al-Kamal raise further problems of chronology and correspondence with the life dates of al-Maqrizi's grandfather, her purported husband.[28]

al-Maqrizi, *Suluk*, 2, 1: 365; idem, *Durar*, 2: 517 where a report on the death of ʿAbd al-Qadir, the grandfather, is affixed to the beginning of the father's short biography, and reportedly copied directly from al-Safadi's *Muʿjam* even though the text does not appear in the printed edition of *Wafi*; ʿIzz al-Din, *al-Maqrizi Mu'arrikhan*, 25–7; Ibn Taghri-Birdi, *Manhal*, 7: 324.

24 Al-Maqrizi, *Durar*, 1: 86 and 91; Jalili, *Durar*, Intro, 17; ʿIzz al-Din, *al-Maqrizi wa-Kitabuhu*, 1: 160.

25 On Ibn Jamaʿa, see al-Maqrizi, *Suluk*, 3, 2: 586; Ibn Hajar, *Inbaʿ*, 2: 292–4; Ibn Taghri-Birdi, *Manhal*, 1: 97–8. The only bio to mention Zaynab bint al-Kamal is Ibn Qadi Shuhbah, *Tarikh*, 1: 248.

26 Al-Maqrizi, *Durar*, 1: 88, 92, 159, 161; 2: 177, 199, 203, 232; idem, *Muqaffa*, 1: 45, 4: 439; 5: 46, 7: 61.

27 Ibn Hajar, *al-Durar al-Kamina*, 2: 117–18; Shams al-Din al-Dhahabi, *Muʿjam al-Shuyukh*, Muhammad Habib al-Hailai, 2 vols. (Ta'if, Saudi Arabia: Maktabat al-Siddiq, 1988), 1: 248.

28 Al-Safadi, *Wafi*, 15: 68, says that he studied with her in Damascus in 729/1329; al-Subki, *Tabaqat al-Shafiʿyya al-Kubra*, M. M. al-Tanahi and Abd al-Fattah M. al-Huluw, eds.,

Were there two Zaynabs b. al-Kamal? Could al-Dhahabi have been wrong in his statement that she had no children? Could the editors of the various editions of al-Maqrizi's *Durar*, already based on two different manuscripts, have made the same mistake? Unfortunately, until more biographical evidence comes to light, al-Maqrizi's grandmother will have to remain a possible hadith teacher named Zaynab bint al-Kamal, but not necessarily the famous Zaynab bint al-Kamal.

Al-Maqrizi provides a relatively long biography of another member of his family who contributed to his education and life experience. This is his mother's uncle, the judge Taj al-Din Isma'il b. Ahmad b. 'Abd al-Wahab al-Makhzumi al-Hanafi (c. 720/1320–12 Rabiʿ al-Akhar 803/November 30, 1400).[29] Al-Makhzumi held second-tier posts in Cairo such as substituting for the city's *muhtasib* (a position that al-Maqrizi himself would occupy three times) and for his patron and close friend, the Hanafi chief judge Ibn al-Turkmani. Al-Maqrizi reports several pieces of advice that he received from his grand uncle, some of which are presented as part of the uncle's role as a tutor to al-Maqrizi when he was young. Some reflect al-Makhzumi's life choices, such as his dislike of women, which led to his never being married. He told al-Maqrizi that someone he had loved in his youth died after he had had a dream where an unknown person recited a verse predicting the death of the beloved. He also claimed that his father warned him against marriage. He, in his turn, reacted unfavorably to al-Maqrizi's decision to buy a slave girl as a concubine. Al-Maqrizi also mentions several fantastic happenstances that his uncle, who seems to have been an accomplished raconteur just like his great nephew, experienced during his travels around Egypt or heard from a whole gamut of people ranging from his own father to a boatman on the Nile.

Even al-Maqrizi's male servant, Muhammad b. Abi Bakr b. Muhammad al-Suʿudi (born around 750/1349; date of death unknown), receives a copious biography, not as his servant but as someone who benefited him with his knowledge and shared with him the love of poetry and strange tales with moral

---

10 vols. (Cairo: Hajar, 2nd edn., 1992), 1: 147 states that he was present during a lesson by Zaynab bint al-Kamal in Rabiʿ al-Awwal 740/ September 1339, when she was already ninety years old, which makes it difficult to see her as the wife of al-Maqrizi's grandfather 'Abd al-Qadir, who died in Damascus in 1331 aged around sixty, according to al-Safadi and al-Maqrizi himself quoting al-Safadi (i.e. his alleged wife would have been twenty-five years older than him).

[29] Al-Maqrizi, *Durar*, 1: 415–18; al-Sakhawi, *Daw'*, 2: 290. Another member of al-Maqrizi's family who earned an entry in a biographical dictionary is the husband of his maternal aunt, Badr al-Din Hasan b. 'Abdallah al-Qabbani, who studied religious sciences as a young man, but left the life of *'ilm* to work as a weigh man (*qabbani*), although he seems to have played a leading role among his ulama peers during their formative years, see Ibn Hajar, *Inba'*, 9: 145–6.

lessons embedded in them. But mostly, al-Maqrizi reports several poems that al-Su'udi recited to him on various occasions, some of which appear to be of his own composition.[30] Many of the poems quoted, especially those of al-Su'udi, revolve around the themes of neglect, desertion, repudiation, and forgiveness, themes usually associated with lovers' lamentations, and might be read in that sense if we did not know the context in which they are reproduced. But in this case they serve as poetic background to what appears to have been a troubled relationship between master and servant, for al-Su'udi recites one such lamentation every time al-Maqrizi disavowed him. The relationship soured to the point, so al-Maqrizi tersely tells us at the beginning of the biography, where, after al-Su'udi had served him for years, he repudiated him for an unspecified reason, so that the servant took refuge with another master and, in 806/1403–4, left al-Maqrizi, who no longer heard of him again.

The first tutor and the most important figure in the early education of al-Maqrizi was his maternal grandfather, Shams al-Din Muhammad ibn 'Abd al-Rahman, Ibn al-Sa'igh al-Hanafi (c. 710/1310–11 Sha'ban 776/January 15, 1375). One of the most prominent Hanafi jurists in Cairo, he held a series of prestigious judicial posts and composed a number of philological, grammatical, and exegetical books.[31] He was well-respected among the great scholars of Cairo at the time, which permitted him to introduce his young grandson to the teaching circles of many among them. Under his tutelage, al-Maqrizi received the traditional education available to boys of his background with its focus on Qur'anic studies, hadith, Arabic grammar, literature, and *fiqh*. The grandfather, however, died too early to have left a lasting influence on al-Maqrizi, at least in matters of *madhahb*. The grandson, who was taught by Ibn al-Sa'igh in the Hanafi *madhhab*, switched to the Shafi'i *madhhab* as an adult and even became a steady detractor of the Hanafis. In the copious and admiring biography he devoted to Ibn al-Sa'igh in his *Durar*, al-Maqrizi strangely fails to mention that he was his grandfather, despite taking the time to list the titles of forty-eight of his treatises on grammatical, literary, and legal issues before delving into reproducing nineteen samples of his poetry.[32] Much of the poetry cited in the *Durar* is not produced elsewhere, suggesting

[30] Al-Maqrizi, *Durar*, 3: 202–5; al-Sakhawi, *Daw'*, 7: 196, abridged from the *Durar*.

[31] Al-Maqrizi, *Durar*, 3: 254–60; idem, *Suluk*, 3, 1: 92, 198, 245, and 4: 1107, chronicles the last stages of the career of his grandfather, which he personally witnessed; 'Izz al-Din, *al-Maqrizi Mu'arrikhan*, 27–32. Other biographies of Ibn al-Sa'igh are: al-Safadi, *Wafi*, 3: 244; Ibn Hajar, *Inba'*, 1: 95–6; idem, *al-Durar al-Kamina*, 3: 499–500.

[32] He also does not mention that his grandfather left a substantial fortune, as reported by Ibn Hajar, *al-Durar al-Kamina*, 3: 500. This may have supported his descendants, including al-Maqrizi, although his share would have been small since he did have a maternal uncle, Qawiyy al-Din Muhammad (al-Maqrizi, *Durar*, 1: 394), who would have inherited the largest share.

that al-Maqrizi might have had access to the private papers of his grandfather. One distich is worth quoting here as it reveals the grandfather's strong 'Alid sympathies, which we know al-Maqrizi shared, albeit less vocally, as it was his habit to be careful in disclosing his devotion. Ibn al-Sa'igh says:

دعني وعشق علي　　فالعشق أعلا المناهج
وفي علـي دخـول　　وعـــايبوه خـــوارج

> Leave me to my devotion (*'ishq*) to 'Ali
> For devotion is the highest of ranks
>
> In 'Ali there is an entry (into the faith?)
> And his detractors are the deserters (*khawarij*)[33]

Al-Maqrizi's biography of his maternal grandfather concludes with a story his father told him about a dream he had had of Ibn al-Sa'igh (i.e. his father-in-law) after his death, even though al-Maqrizi here again fails to mention the family relation. The father asked the grandfather, "How did God treat you?," to which the deceased answered with a verse that I could not source confirming God's mercy for those who repent.[34] This report is asserted with the utmost seriousness as a plausible exchange between the living and the dead, a recurrent component of al-Maqrizi's reporting about the people he knew and those who predeceased him. He was not alone in believing in the possibility of communication with the dead: in fact, such paranormal verbal exchange in "good" (*hasan*) dreams was a staple of Islamic narratives and historical reports from the times of the Prophet onward, though by the fifteenth century it had lost some of its currency.[35] Al-Maqrizi's proclivity to use dreams in his narratives was scornfully noted by many of his contemporaries, who stressed his interest in the sciences of the occult and divination, questioning his historical gravitas or accusing him of using his divination skills to endear himself to patrons and colleagues. Many of these detractors, however, were not immune to believing in magic, numerology, geomancy, and the role of dreams in

[33] The contrast between entering and exiting or deserting is highlighted by the possibility of homographic reading of *khawarij* as simple outsiders or deserters or as the actual group who deserted the camp of Ali in his struggle with the Umayyads.

[34] Ibn Hajar, *al-Durar al-Kamina*, 3: 499, reports the same dream story on the authority of Badr al-Din al-Zarakshi (1345–92), one of the most authoritative scholars of the time, which lends the story more weight than if it were reported only on the authority of a grandson speaking of his grandfather.

[35] For a recent analysis of the role of dreams in the mission and revelation of the Prophet and how this became a model for pious Muslims in the medieval period, see Elizabeth Sirriyeh, *Dreams and Visions in the World of Islam* (London: I. B. Tauris, 2015), 32–102; see also the discussion of Marshall Hodgson, *The Venture of Islam: Conscience and History in a World Civilization* 3 vols. (Chicago: University of Chicago Press, 1974), 2: 466; Henry Corbin, "The Visionary Dream in Islamic Spirituality," in *The Dream and Human Societies*, 381–408.

understanding the world, as we will see.[36] In fact, dreams and their interpretations were essential tools of understanding and representing the world in Mamluk historiography, as they were in most premodern cultures.[37]

The Loving Presence of Women in al-Maqrizi's Life

Al-Maqrizi is one of only a few scholars of his time to express in writing distinct tender feelings toward the women in his life, most especially his mother.[38] His great affection for his mother is clear from the unusually extensive and detailed biographical entry he devotes to her in his *Durar*.[39] Asma' bint Ibn al-Sa'igh al-Hanafi was born in Cairo on the 21 Rajab 747/ 7 November 1346 and died there on 12 Rabiʿ al-Awal 800/December 3, 1397. She was married three times, her first marriage being when she was twelve years old to a Najm

[36] One of the most complicated dreams is told about Ibn Hajar, the staid scholar and friend of al-Maqrizi, in the biography written by his adoring student al-Buqaʿi. The dream is a complex one seen by a Mamluk amir who supposedly did not know Ibn Hajar, yet saw him leading a prayer in a mosque where the body of the prophet was in an exposed coffin. Ibn Hajar and another judge took from inside the shroud of the prophet six jasmines, before Ibn Hajar engaged the [dead] prophet in a conversation. The entire dream is presented as a proof of the blessedness of Ibn Hajar and as a means of absolving him of an accusation in front of the sultan, one of the fundamental functions of dreams at the time, see al-Buqaʿi, *ʿUnwan al-Zaman*, 1: 162–5.

[37] On the role of dreams in Mamluk historical narratives, see Yehoshua Frenkel, "Dream Accounts in the Chronicles of the Mamluk Period," in Louise Marlow, ed. *Dreaming Across Boundaries: The Interpretation of Dreams in Islamic Lands* (Cambridge, M.A.: Harvard University Press, 2008), 202–20.

[38] To my knowledge, the only other scholar of the period to speak extensively, openly, and kindlily about the womenfolk in his life—in this case, his wife—is Abu Shama, *al-Dhayl ʿala-al-Rawdatayn*, 196–8, where he produces a 46-verse panegyric for his wife Sitt al-ʿArab. See also the special issue of *Annales Islamologiques* entitled Histoire de Famille and guest-edited by Julien Loiseau, especially Yossef Rapoport, "Ibn Ḥağar al-ʿAsqalānī, His Wife, Her Slave-Girl: Romantic Triangles and Polygamy in 15th Century Cairo", *AI* 47 (2013): 327–53, and René Guérin du Grandlaunay, "Le milieu familial de Šams al-Dīn al-Saḫāwī. Quelques aspects d'une lecture autobiographique," *AI* 47 (2013): 283–306. See also the four articles on the representation of women in the Mamluk period published in *MSR* 21 (2018): Mirella Cassarino, "Between Function and Fiction: The Representation of Women in al-Ibshīhī's al-Mustaṭraf," 1–20; Antonella Ghersetti, "The Representation of Slave Girls in a Physiognomic Text of the Fourteenth Century," 21–46; Pernilla Myrne, "Women and Men in Al-Suyūṭī's Guides to Sex and Marriage," 47–68; and Daniela Rodica Firanescu, "Medieval Arabic Islam and the Culture of Gender: Feminine Voices in al-Suyūṭī's Literature on Sex and Marriage," 69–86.

[39] Al-Maqrizi, *Durar*, 1: 394–7; Ibn Hajar, *Inbaʿ*, 2: 33, mentions the biography written by al-Maqrizi of his mother and calls it "*jayyida*" [good]. Ibn Hajar is also the source for her death date. It is very unusual to have such detailed dates for women in the medieval biographical dictionaries.

al-Din al-Muhallabi, about whom we know nothing but the name reported by her son.[40] After her first husband left her she married al-Maqrizi's father in Muharram 765/October 1363, and had three sons with him: Ahmad, Muhammad, and Hasan. Following the death of al-Maqrizi's father in 1378, his mother married the third, unnamed husband and had an unnamed son by him. Clearly al-Maqrizi did not care much for this third husband or his half-brother, as he included neither of their names in his mother's biography. The disregard may be a delayed reaction to a youthful resentment over what had befallen him as an adolescent when his mother had remarried after his father's death.

Be that as it may, al-Maqrizi palpably adored his mother. Her portrayal in the *Durar*, though proper and prim as befitting the image of a pious Muslim woman of her status as a daughter of a known judge and scholar and mother of a famous scholar, betrays deep filial affection and admiration. Al-Maqrizi stresses her piety, devotion, strict adherence to religious rules, knowledge, and stoicism, qualities that he himself was drawn to by temperament and by training and will repeatedly praise in other influential figures in his life. But in his telling, his mother went the extra mile in her religiosity and forbearance. She uncomplainingly endured hardships such as the loss of a son (perhaps his brother Hasan, who is mentioned nowhere other than when al-Maqrizi reports his name, or his unnamed half-brother), surgery on her eyelids, without anesthetics of course, and a fever lasting years that was finally the cause of her death. All along, she always completed her night prayer, fasted Mondays and Thursdays, and read litanies and sections of the Qur'an daily. So pious was she that when she went on Hajj, she left with the early caravanserai of Rajab (*Rajabiyya*) so that she could spend extra time in the Holy Cities. She also told her son that she had "never shown her face to an outsider [*ajnabi*]," implying that she always wore a face-veil (*niqab*), even when she went to visit the tomb of her father, for, according to her, "spirits stay around their tombs." This ultra-orthodoxy, although colored by popular beliefs in the world of spirits, corresponds with the self-image of her staid scholarly son, who proudly states that his mother was "unequalled in her time [in piety]."

Al-Maqrizi's relationship with his mother was not only visibly intimate, it also appear to have been formative on more than one level. On her own terms, Asma' played important roles in his intellectual and emotional formation. Though not a scholar, she seems to have been somewhat more educated than women were commonly permitted to be at the time.[41] In her biography,

[40] Ibn Hajar, *Inba'*, 1: 214, calls him al-Ramli, which may mean that his family was from al-Ramla in Palestine.

[41] For an analysis of the limits of women's education in the Mamluk period, see Jonathan Berkey, "Women and Islamic Education in the Mamluk Period," in *Women in Middle*

al-Maqrizi includes a few details that reveal more original aspects of her personality: she liked to intone tender Sufi love poetry, which she claimed to have learned from her father, Ibn al-Sa'igh, who was after all a notable teacher. She was also a storehouse of popular wisdom, vernacular medical recipes, and incredible happenstances, some of which she asserted she had witnessed personally. Her son reports many of these supernatural or prescient events and dreams, and never doubts their truthfulness.[42] He even draws *'ibar* (moral lessons) from them, a theme that recurs in many biographies in the *Durar*. Seeking the moral messages in happenstances and historical events alike underlines all of al-Maqrizi's writing, not just the more or less chatty biographies of his teachers, family members, and acquaintances. In fact, the pattern of *'ibar* forms the backbone of his reasoning on the importance of historical writing in general, a rationale that was shared by all pious medieval Muslim historians, including those who were otherwise critical of the occult sciences.[43] Al-Maqrizi's biography of his mother highlights how supernatural phenomena informed his thinking about mundane as well as serious things from the earliest stages of his life.

Though not as elaborately as in the entry for his mother, al-Maqrizi also writes of his wife Safra (سفرى) in the *Durar*. Safra bint 'Umar bint 'Abd al-'Aziz al-Baghdadi was born in Cairo in 770/1370 and married al-Maqrizi when she was twelve and he was about fifteen, on the 15 of Shawwal 782/January 12, 1381.[44]

Eastern History: Shifting Boundaries in Sex and Gender, ed. Nikki Keddie and Beth Baron (New Haven: CT: Yale University Press, 1991), 143–57.

[42] One story about his mother that does not appear in al-Maqrizi's biography of her is cited in al-Maqrizi, *Suluk*, 4, 3: 1106; al-Jawhari, *Nuzhat*, 4: 61, on the authority of al-Maqrizi. In this story, al-Maqrizi justifies a punishment that befell the family of a certain Abu Hurayra in 842/1439, by quoting his mother who had heard her father, the famous Ibn al-Sa'igh al-Hanafi, say that God addressed David as such: "O David, I Am the Worshipped God, I punish grandchildren for the sins of their grandparents." The moral of the story, says al-Maqrizi, is that the family of Abu Hurayra are paying for the harm their grandfather Abu Imama Muhammad ibn al-Naqqash had caused to a Muhammad ibn al-Hirmas more than eighty years earlier. On a similarly complicated story related to the Imam Ahmad b. Hanbal, see Michael Cooperson, "Probability, Plausibility, and 'Spiritual Communication' in Classical Arabic Biography," in Kennedy, *On Fiction and Adab*, 69–84.

[43] His views of the moral function of historical inquiry, which will be analyzed later, are introduced in his preface to the *Khitat* 1: 4, and more elaborately recorded in his large book, *al-Khabar 'an al-Bashar*, which deals with the universal cosmology and Arab history and genealogies until the mission of Muhammad, see al-Maqrizi, *Kitab al-Khabar 'an al-Bashr fi Ansab al-'Arab wa Nasab Sayyid al-Bashar* 8 vols., Khaled Ahmad al-Malla al-Suwaydi and 'Arif 'Abd al-Ghani, eds. (Beirut: al-Dar al-'Arabiyya lil Mawsu'at, 2013), 1: 53–4, 141–56; 'Izz al-Din, *al-Maqrizi Mu'arrikhan*, 63, 215–16, published the preface from the copy of the autograph ms. Tunis National Library, no. 3558. For the widespread view of history as a moral lesson, see Khalidi, *Historical Thought*, 216–19.

[44] Al-Maqrizi, *Durar*, 2: 98–9.

She gave birth to her first son, Muhammad, in 786/1384, before, al-Maqrizi reports, he divorced her in Ramadan of the same year, without any explanation. He took her in again less than two years later in 1386, again without any explanation. He tells us that on the night of his remarriage, he had a dream in which someone recited two poetical verses, that he understood to mean that Safra would live with him for only two more years, although that inference is not easily decipherable in the poetry.[45] Safra indeed died two years later after having giving birth to a second son, Abu Hashim 'Ali.[46] Al-Maqrizi recalls the anxiety he felt during her death sickness through his favorite medium, dreams and poetry quotation. This time, though, he quoted a known poet, Abu Dhu'ayb al-Hadhali, who lived during the time of the Prophet and wrote a famous poem mourning five of his sons who had died during one year of the plague, from which the one sorrowful verse is lifted. Dreams remained the medium of communication and expression after Safra's death, as al-Maqrizi recounts how he saw her in a dream in her burial garment after she had died and asked her, "Do you receive what I send you [of prayer]?" She answered positively and thanked him profusely. He promised her in the dream to meet soon (which of course did not happen). He outlived her by more than fifty years, although he does not seem to have ever remarried, though he had at least one concubine. Al-Maqrizi concludes the biography of Safra with another mournful poetic quotation from another famous poet of the time of the Prophet, al-Nabigha al-Ja'di, that amounts to a love lamentation, albeit stated circuitously as might be expected of the solemn and prudent al-Maqrizi.[47]

[45] Those two verses are quoted in several historical books from the Mamluk period, where al-Maqrizi could have read them. See, for instance, Ibn Manzur, *Mukhtasar Tarikh Dimashq l-Ibn 'Asakir* Ruhiyya al-Nahhas, M. Muti' al-Hafiz, et al., eds. 29 vols. (Damascus: Dar al-Fikr, 1984–90), 27: 34–6; Ibn Kathir, *al-Bidaya wal-Nihaya* 'Ali Shiri, ed. 14 vols. (Beirut: Dar Ihya' al-Turath al-'Arabi, 1988), 10: 238–9. The poet is apparently unknown although the verses appear in relation to a tragic love story that unfolded in the *majlis* of the 'Abbasid Caliph Haroun al-Rashid.

[46] Al-Maqrizi, *Durar*, 3: 132, in the highly approving biography of Shams al-Din al-Ja'bari the Dream-Interpreter, al-Maqrizi tells of a dream he had that was interpreted by al-Ja'bari as foretelling the birth of his son Abu Hashim 'Ali. But he dates the birth differently from in the biography of Safra where he provides a full date and he gives a different name for her grandfather.

[47] The two distichs were sung in two memorable instances in Arabic history. The first is when al-Walid ibn Yazid, the libertine Umayyad caliph, invited the famous singer of Madina, Ma'bad, to visit him in one of his palaces, identified by Robert W. Hamilton, "Khirbet al-Mafjar: The Bath Hall Reconsidered," *Levant* 10 (1978): 126–38, as Khirbet al-Mafjar near Jericho, where he witnessed the prodigious decadence of the caliph. The second instance was at the court of al-Amin ibn Haroun al-Rashid when a slave girl sang the poetry inadvertently right before the deposition and killing of al-Amin, see Abu al-Faraj al-Isfahani, *Kitab al-Aghani*, 25 vols., Ihsan 'Abbas et al. eds. (Beirut: Dar Sader, 2008), 1: 16–17.

The one other woman mentioned in the *Durar* with whom al-Maqrizi had a conjugal relation after Safra is a slave girl with the unusual-sounding name Soul or Sol (سول).[48] In the brief but tender biography he penned of her he informs us that she was a slave girl raised and educated in the house of Sultan Barquq.[49] In 799/1398, when she was fifteen years old, al-Maqrizi says, "the circumstances dictated that she was to be sold," so he bought her as a virgin to be his concubine. How a scholar could buy a slave from the sultan's household is unclear, but this might have been a favor granted to al-Maqrizi by Sultan Barquq, because this was the same year in which al-Maqrizi became very close to the sultan, and even attended his *majlis* as a *nadim* (boon companion). Soul stayed with al-Maqrizi for an unspecified number of years and may have borne him his daughter Fatima, who is mentioned only when she died years later and is not named among Safra's children. Al-Maqrizi states, without specifying a reason, that he lost Soul (*kharajat min yadi*) to an unnamed new master/consort who took her to Mecca, where she had several children and became known for her decency and goodness.[50] He reports her death and burial in the renowned public cemetery in Mecca, al-Muʿalat, in Safar 824/February 1421, some years after they parted ways.[51] Bizarre as it may seem in view of the customs of the time, this suggests that al-Maqrizi kept in touch either with Soul or with her new master after he had lost her, or that he was following her news, both possibilities indicative of a rapport that transcended the formal master/consort relationship that joined the two for some time.[52] It

48 I am not sure of the origin of the name and whether it is Turkish or Circassian. The only possible meanings I have found in medieval Turkish (sol: left, as is today) and (söl: the juice of the meat/lymph) do not fit as proper names, unless she has acquired the name "left" as omen as was customary in Turkish-speaking cultures. See Sir Gerard Clauson, *An Etymological Dictionary of Pre-Thirteenth Century Turkish* (Oxford: Clarendon Press, 1972), 824.

49 Al-Maqrizi, *Durar*, 2: 114–15; there is an abridged biography of Soul copied from al-Maqrizi in al-Sakhawi, *Daw'*, 12: 66–7.

50 Al-Maqrizi, *Durar*, 2: 262, speaks of a slave girl that he purchased at an unspecified date for concubinage (*tassarri*), but his mother's uncle Taj al-Din al-Makhzumi warned him against having children from slave girls. The woman could have been Soul herself. In the Introduction to al-Maqrizi, *Mukhtasar al-Kamil fi al-Duʿafa wa-ʿIlal al-Hadith li-Ibn Adi*, dated 795/1392, ed. Ayman ibn Arif Dimashqi (Cairo: Maktabat al-Sunna, 1994), 39, al-Maqrizi speaks of his children, but does not give their number, their names, or the names of their mothers.

51 Might the year that he lost Soul be the same as the one when he repudiated his servant al-Suʿudi (806/1403–4)? This was a difficult year which al-Maqrizi claimed to be the beginning of the deterioration of the Sultanate and the city, as we will see. He also may have been experiencing some financial difficulties at that time, after having lost his influence at court following the death of his one true patron among the Mamluk sultans of his time, Barquq.

52 Compare this story of a master/slave girl relationship with the story of al-Maqrizi's friend Ibn Hajar's sly relationship with his wife's slave girl, Khass Turk, see Rapoport, "Ibn Hajar al-ʿAsqalani, 327–51.

is possible that Soul was the last woman in al-Maqrizi's life, for he otherwise has nothing to say about other wives or concubines in all of his writing.

From Soul, al-Maqrizi's intellectual gain seems to have been direct and palpable, for it centered on specific skills and knowledge. He praises Soul's learning and says that he has benefited from her knowledge and *adab*, especially in writing (or calligraphy, *kitaba* in the text) and geomancy (*darb al-raml*, lit. reading the future in the sand),[53] a skill for which al-Maqrizi became widely known and for which he garnered both praise and derision. Even his tender affection for Soul finds its expression in poetic quotation, as is his habit, and in reference to geomancy, probably because this pursuit brought them closer. Al Maqrizi says that Soul sang him four verses, three of which were composed by the Ayyubid poet Baha' al-Din Zuhair, famous for his lyrical lines favored by singers.[54] They say:

تعلمت ضرب الرمل لما هجرتهم   لعلي أرى شكلاً يدل على الوصل
فصـــادفني فيـــه بيـــاض وحمرة   فعـــاينتهـــا في وجنة سلبت عقلي
وقالـــوا طـريقاً، قلت يرب للقـــا   وقالوا اجتمـــاعاً قلت يرب للشمل
وقالـــوا نقـــي الخد ذاك معـــذبي   يجور على ضعفي ويسعى على قتلي

> I learned *darb al-raml* after I left them; maybe I can see a form that signals a reunion
>
> I found in it whiteness and redness, which I had noticed in a cheek that stole my mind
>
> They said it is a path, I said O God may it be toward an encounter; they said it is a meeting, I said O God may it be a reunion
>
> They said the one with the pure cheek is my tormentor who takes advantage of my weakness and seeks my elimination

The fourth distich, which I could not source, replaces the fourth verse in Zuhair's original poem and evokes a theme familiar in Arabic love poetry (*ghazal*) about the fatal effect of passion. The fourth distich in Zuhair's original is closer in theme to *darb al-raml*, and it is perplexing that al-Maqrizi substitutes it with the torture-of-love verse. Moreover, there are numerous deviations in al-Maqrizi's quotation from the original, which nonetheless

[53] The term "geomancy" comes from medieval Latin *geomantia*, first used in Spain in the twelfth century as a translation of the Arabic name *'ilm al-raml* ("the science of sand"), see Emily Savage-Smith, "Geomancy", *The Oxford Encyclopedia of the Modern Islamic World*, 4 vols. J. L. Esposito, ed. (New York: Oxford University Press, 1995), 53–5.

[54] Al-Baha' Zuhair, *Diwan al-Baha' Zuhair*, Muhammad Abu al-Fadl Ibrahim and Muhammad Taher al-Gabalawi, eds. (Cairo: Dar al-Ma'arif, 1977), 221–2; on his life see Sa'ida Muhammad Ramadan, *Baha'al-Din Zuhair al-Hijazi al-Makki al-Qusi, Hayatuhu wa Shi'ruhu* (Cairo: Dar al-Ma'arif, 1982).

manage to keep the meter and the rhyme without changing the meaning, except in one crucial place. Zuhair's first hemistich reads "I learned *darb al-raml* after you left us [*hajartum*, second person plural]," whereas al-Maqrizi's is stated in the first person (*hajartuhum*), implying that the speaker is the deserter (i.e. Soul in this instance), who is supposed to have recited the verses to al-Maqrizi. Did al-Maqrizi modify the poetry on purpose to express his feelings of longing or were his sources confused? Is it possible that the verses were indeed recited by Soul to him after she had transferred to another master as is implied by the desertion theme? Were the two in love, and were they forced apart for reasons beyond their control? Could there have been a correspondence between the two after their separation through which she sent him these verses? All of these options seem possible and could be read in the poem as al-Maqrizi modified it. Bounded by the norms of his time and status, however, our historian does not clarify any of these points, but relies instead on the double-entendre implied in the verses. Unfortunately, a reunion does not seem to have taken place since Soul died far away in Mecca in the possession of the other, unnamed master, although we do not know if al-Maqrizi managed to meet her before her death in Mecca. Alas, this is unlikely so far as the data we possess can tell. Al-Maqrizi, who visited Mecca seven times for Hajj or *mujawara* during his life, was absent from the city between 790/1388, nine years before acquiring Soul, and 825/1422, more than a year after her passing.[55] Still, an acute sense of loss pervades Soul's short biography with its enigmatic end, accentuating the impression that al-Maqrizi's old age was indeed marred by loneliness.

Alas, the departure of Soul was not to be al-Maqrizi's last tragic loss. He seems to have also lost his two sons by Safra, Muhammad and 'Ali, who cease to appear in his writing after the brief mentions of their birth and education. Al-Maqrizi does not report the dates of their passing. But they certainly died before him, because his nephew Muhammad, who otherwise could not be a legal heir in the presence of sons, inherited from him, as evidenced by Muhammad's signature of ownership on the cover of some of al-Maqrizi's autograph manuscripts.[56] His last known child, a daughter named Fatima, whose mother is unnamed but might have been Soul, died in Rabi' I, 826/

[55] Ibn Fahd, *Mu'jam*, 65.

[56] One manuscript that Muhammad al-Maqrizi owned is the autographed first volume of *Suluk*, held in the library of Yeni Mosque (Yeni Cami Kütüphanesi held in the Sülemaniye) in Istanbul, # 887. His name appears immediately following the title on the cover page with the verb *malakahu* ("owns it"). A copy of the page is published in al-Maqrizi, *Suluk*, 1: 2; Frédéric Bauden, "Maqriziana IX: Should al-Maqrizi Be Thrown out with the Bath Water? The Question of His Plagiarism of al-Awhadi's Khitat and the Documentary Evidence," *MSR* 14 (2010), 215, note 159, lists the holograph's manuscripts of al-Maqrizi on which his nephew's mark of ownership appears.

March 1423, almost twenty years before her father.[57] She appears to have been the last member of his immediate family. Al-Maqrizi seems to have lived alone for almost twenty years after her passing and the desertion of his long-time servant Muhammad al-Su'udi.

A Solid Scholarly Formation

As we have seen, al-Maqrizi's first formal teacher was his grandfather Ibn al-Sa'igh, who not only personally taught him but also introduced him to many top scholars of the time. Ibn al-Sa'igh used to hold study and discussion sessions in the family house in Harat al-Burjuwan, where, as a boy, al-Maqrizi was exposed to his first lessons of *fiqh*, hadith, history, language, and other usual topics of study for a pupil of his class and background. He appears to have also attended classes from a young age in madrasas near his house, such as the Madrasa al-Zahiriyya (of Baybars, which was removed in the late nineteenth century; only its portal still stands) on the main thoroughfare in Fatimid Cairo, not very far from Harat al-Burjuwan.[58] In the same entry, al-Maqrizi offers another aspect of his budding personality as he reports that in his early years of studentship, he was so shy as to refrain from speaking in class, so his teacher al-Tajir al-Hanafi exhorted him to overcome his shyness by quoting what appears to be a popular saying cited in the colloquial "Who does not jump in the water cannot learn to swim."[59] Al-Maqrizi also mentions another teacher, Muhammad b. Hasan b. 'Ali al-Bayjuri al-Shafi'i (d. 827/1424), whom he calls *mu'adibi* (my tutor), a term that is usually reserved for teachers of the first stage of learning who supervise their students' memorization of the Qur'an and the acquisition of reading and writing skills.[60] Al-Bayjuri appears to have been a scholar of some renown who taught hadith, especially from the most canonical Sahih al-Bukhari, in Cairo.[61] Al-Maqrizi managed to achieve scholastically what was expected of a boy of his stature and family background: he memorized the Qur'an at the age of seven and received several *ijazat* by that early age from a number of notable scholars, most of them hadith transmitters, undoubtedly with the help of his grandfather.[62]

57 Al-Maqrizi, *Suluk*, 4, 2: 651.

58 Al-Maqrizi, *Durar*, 1: 132 reports the name of the madrasa in the biography of Zayn al-Din Abi Bakr al-Tajir al-Hanafi (d. 805/1402), who held his lessons there. Other biographies of al-Tajir al-Hanafi in Ibn Hajar, *Inba'*, 5: 97; al-Sakhawi, *Daw'*, 11: 79.

59 Ibid.

60 Al-Maqrizi, *Durar*, 3: 37.

61 Ibn Hajar, *Majma'*, 3, 1: 300–1, also read a book of hadith with al-Bayjuri; al-Sakhawi, *Daw'*, 11: 194.

62 Ibn Fahd, *Mu'jam*, 65, mentions three scholars who gave al-Maqrizi their *ijazas* when

This was only the beginning of a distinguished scholarly career, for al-Maqrizi went on to learn from some of the most famous teachers of his time and later to become a venerable teacher with his own students and disciples. All in all, he claims to have studied with or received *ijaza* from more than six hundred *shaykhs* (teachers, in this instance) in Cairo, Damascus, and Mecca, a number that evidently includes all those he had heard lecturing, even if only once, or those from whom he received an *ijaza* without ever meeting them. The extant roll of his *shaykh*s, though much less than six hundred, is an impressive collection of thirty-nine names of scholars, according to Muhammad Kamal 'Izz al-Din, who collated his list from Ibn Taghri-Birdi, Ibn-Fahd, and al-Sakhawi.[63] Al-Sakhawi, however, as is his habit, questions the validity of two important names on the list: Muhammad b. 'Ali b. Yusuf 'Ali al-Harawi, who died in 781/1379 in Cairo, when al-Maqrizi was thirteen years old; and Ibn Kathir, who died in Damascus in 1373 when al-Maqrizi was only seven.[64] Al-Sakhawi's casting doubt on the basis of age is debatable, as it appears that bringing very young children to the lessons of famous scholars was a common practice in the period. In the case of al-Harawi in particular, the evidence for al-Maqrizi reading the book *Fadhl al-Khayl* (On the Merits of Horses) by the *hafiz* Sharaf al-Din al-Dimyati (613/1217–705/1305) and directly transmitting it from him is conclusive. First, al-Harawi was a neighbor of al-Maqrizi's family in Harat Burjuwan and may have been one of his grandfather's companions in the *majalis* that the boy al-Maqrizi attended. He may also have been sent to study with him at a very early age. In this, he does not seem to have been alone: Ibn Fahd names two children who studied *Fadhl al-Khayl* with al-Harawi in Cairo around the same time as al-Maqrizi.[65] Second—and this will take us to the end of al-Maqrizi's life—Ibn Taghri-Birdi states that he attended a series of *sama'* (recitations) of al-Maqrizi's reading of *Fadl al-Khayl* after al-Harawi's transmission, the last of them at the end of Sha'ban 845/beginning of January 1442, that is, two weeks before the death of al-Maqrizi. This last recitation was performed by Qutb al-Din al-Khudayri, who studied with al-Maqrizi in his later years, in the

---

he was five in 771/1370. Al-Maqrizi in his *Durar* mentions thirteen, see al-Jalili, *Durar*, Introduction, 1: 25–6.

[63] For the full roster see 'Izz al-Din, *al-Maqrizi Mu'arrikhan*, 34–42.

[64] Al-Sakhawi, *Daw'*, 2: 23. Al-Maqrizi, *Durar*, 1: 401 says that he studied hadith with Ibn Kathir after he lost his eyesight toward the end of his life; On al-Harawi, al-Maqrizi, *Durar*, 3: 192–3 mentions that they were neighbors and that he studied the book *Fadhl al-Khayl* with him. This book will be read at al-Maqrizi's house at the end of his life.

[65] The first is Yunis b. Husayn al-Zubayri (born c. 755/1355), Ibn Fahd, *Mu'jam*, 302; The second is 'A'isha b. 'Ali al-Kinani al-'Asqalani of the Nasrallah family whom al-Maqrizi will befriend, born in 761/1360 in Cairo, who attended al-Harawi's reading of *Fadhl al-Khayl* in 769/1367–8 when she was seven years old, idem, *Mu'jam*, 323.

latter's Harat al-Burjuwan house, presumably because al-Maqrizi was too sick to do the reading himself.[66]

Ibn Taghri-Birdi's testimony is corroborated by a manuscript of *Fadhl al-Khayl*, which was in the *waqf* of the Madrasa al-Ahmadiyya in Aleppo (built in 1165/1751), as its *ex libris* inscription is stamped on several pages.[67] The last pages of the manuscript seem to have been damaged by water, so it is impossible to find out the date of copying or the name of the copyist, usually stated at the end colophon, which has totally faded.[68] Yet the title page and pages 1 and 2 of the manuscript contain long and partially damaged texts of *sama'* reports written lengthwise on the outer margins that nonetheless allow us to ascertain that all three *sama'* were led by al-Maqrizi in his house at Harat al-Burjuwan (miswritten as Amir Juwan in two of the three). None of the three texts is in al-Maqrizi's handwriting, which is to be expected as he was the *musammi'* (the reciter) and someone else must have been recording the session. All three reports have lost their first lines where the *musammi'* is identified, but the attestation on page 1 of the manuscript still retains faded traces of that first line where three words are readable, "the historian of his age [two words' space] 'Ali," (*mu'arrikh 'asruhu ... 'Ali*), undoubtedly al-Maqrizi himself.[69]

66 Ibn Taghri-Birdi, *Manhal*, 7: 372–3, drops this remark in the biography of al-Dimyati, the author of *Fadhl al-Khayl*; idem, *Hawadith*, 1: 67; idem, *Nujum*, 8: 219. On the relationship between al-Maqrizi and al-Khudayri, see Ibn Fahd, *Mu'jam*, 389–90. Al-Khudayri read the autograph manuscript of *al-Muqaffa* (Leiden, MS. Or. 14533) and commented on folio 170 v. "Thank be to God, has read this bundle till this page asking for God's granting long life to its author the servant of God Muhammad b. Muhammad b. al-Khudayri, the Damascene, the Shafi'ite and copied from it and benefited from its content in the month of Sha'ban 844," exactly a year before he did the reading of *Fadhl al-Khayl*; see Ayman Fu'ad Sayyid, *al-Kitab al-'Arabi al-Makhtut wa 'Ilm al-Makhtutat* 2 vols. (Cairo: al-Dar al-Misriyya al-Lubnaniyya, 1997), 1: 342–3. Sayyid also notes that al-Khudayri, who arrived in Cairo in 843/1439 at the age of twenty-two, composed a treatise, *al-Iktisab fi Talkhis al-Ansab*, which he finished on the 12 of Shawwal 844/March 6, 1441, and of which the autograph manuscript is in the Abbasi Library in Basra, Iraq, with many comments by al-Maqrizi and Ibn Hajar. Al-Khudayri studied with both of them in Cairo.

67 The manuscript is published at http://majles.alukah.net/t125927/, with the entire manuscript accessible through the link http://ge.tt/api/1/files/4AMdDNJ1/0/blob?download (last accessed February 10, 2016). The title page, reproduced at http://majles.alukah.net/imgcache/2014/02/836.jpg, contains various attestations of reading of different dates, the most noticeable of which is al-Sakhawi's, which appears on the upper right corner without a date, and one *sama'* that goes back to the fourteenth century, and seven attestations of ownership (*tamalluk*), many of which belong to the tenth-century Hegire and seem to have been deliberately erased. Two *tamalluk* attestations below the title block have their dates preserved, one dating to 979/1571, and the other to 927/1520, and one or two have been erased deliberately.

68 Reproduced at http://majles.alukah.net/imgcache/2014/02/835.jpg

69 The two *sama'* at al-Maqrizi's house are on pp. 1–2 and are written perpendicularly to the

The *sama'* text begins with the customary format, "I read all of this book in front of the *shaykh*, *al-imam*, the master scholar, the historian," then the line is effaced. The second line says "has heard it *al-Shaykh*, the traveler [*al-rahhala*], Najm al-Din Muhammad known as 'Umar ibn Fahd al-Hashimi al-Makki," who was al-Maqrizi's disciple and companion in Mecca and Cairo. His name is followed by several others, each credited with the amount of text he or she heard (there is a woman in the group), until the fifth line where the name of Nasir al-Din Muhammad b. Muhammad b. 'Ali b. 'Abd al-Qadir al-Maqrizi appears with the identification that he is the nephew of the *musammi'*. The last two lines have lost their last two words. But the tenth line reads "on Wednesday the sixth of Jamada I and the last [session] on Wednesday the thirteenth of Jamada I" [no date, but the only year in the last ten years before the death of al-Maqrizi in which the two dates correspond to Wednesday is 838/1434]. The eleventh line reads "of the *musammi'* in the Harat Burjuwan in Cairo the Guarded and then he gave us his *ijaza*," which could only be a reference to the house where the recitation took place.[70] This *sama'* text unequivocally proves the established authority of al-Maqrizi in transmitting the version of *Kitab Fadhl al-Khayl* he learned from al-Harawi, raising serious doubts about the objectivity of al-Sakhawi's questioning of that authority, especially since his own signature appears on the title page, definitely written at a date later than the date of al-Maqrizi's *sama'* since al-Sakhawi would have been less than seven years old at the time. The *sama'* also confirms that Ibn Fahd and al-Maqrizi's nephew Muhammad were among the students who studied hadith with him, as did Ibn Taghri-Birdi, who attended the later *sama'* of the same book marked on page 1.

Mahmoud al-Jalili offers a longer list of al-Maqrizi's teachers than the one 'Izz al-Din gleaned from Ibn Taghri-Birdi, Ibn-Fahd, and al-Sakhawi.[71] Al-Jalili extracted it from the *Durar*, and divided the names of the *shuyukh*s into three different groups: one of those with whom al-Maqrizi studied for a long period, which has fourteen names, a second for those he learned from

---

title and are reproduced at http://majles.alukah.net/imgcache/2014/02/834.jpg. The report on page 1 records the completion of the *sama'* over four sessions, the last of which is dated to the end of Sha'ban 845/beginning of January 1442, the same date affixed by Ibn Taghri Birdi in his *Manhal*. The report on page 2 also records the completion of the *sama'* over four sessions, but the date in unreadable.

70 Below the text, another three-liner with the signature of the copyist appears identifying him as 'Abd al-Rahman b. Ahmad b. Isma'il ibn al-Qalqashandi (817/1414–871/1467), the shafi'ite *faqih* who was close to Ibn Taghri-Birdi and who later rose in the scholarly world. On al-Qalqashandi, the nephew of the famous uber-*katib* and historian, see Ibn Taghri-Birdi, *Nujum*, 13: 187; al-Sakhawi, *Daw'*, 4: 59.

71 Al-Jalili, *Durar*, Introduction, 21–7.

or listen to hadith recitations with, which amounts to twenty names, and a third for those with whom he studied in Mecca, which contains ten names. In addition to these forty-four teachers, al-Jalili identified twenty-five other individuals who granted al-Maqrizi *ijazat*, including those who did this when he was still a child, some of whom should in this context be considered fully-fledged teachers. This considerably increases the number of al-Maqrizi's known teachers and provides some context for his interaction with many of them. Between this list and the one provided by Ibn Fahd, which states the books al-Maqrizi studied with the teachers listed, we can form a fairly good idea about al-Maqrizi's learning experience, even though this image does not amount to what we can achieve for other contemporary scholars who wrote their own *mashikhat* (sing. *mashyakha*), like Ibn Hajar and Ibn Fahd, both of whom listed al-Maqrizi among their *shuyukh*. For Ibn Hajar, however, al-Maqrizi was expectedly one of the *aqran* (peers or equivalents), with whom he does not seem to have studied any book in particular, although he mentions *Fadhl al-Khayl*, and that he had consulted one of al-Maqrizi's books on the history of Cairo, although he misnames it as *al-Ightibat bi-Ahwal al-Fustat* instead of *'Iqd Jawahir al-Asfat fi Tarikh Madinat al-Fustat*, the correct title.[72]

From the extensive list of teachers, it becomes clear that al-Maqrizi studied hadith with some of the best *muhaddithin* (hadith transmitters) of his time. Notable among them are al-Siraj ibn al-Mulaqqin (723/1323–804/1401), one of the most prolific authors of religious treatises of his time,[73] the Shafi'ite chief judge al-Siraj al-Balqini (724/1324–805/1402),[74] the earlier Shafi'ite chief judge al-Burhan ibn Jama'a (725/1325–790/1388), who was a friend of al-Maqrizi's father,[75] the famous *hafiz* (memorizer of hadith) 'Izz al-Din ibn al-Kuwayk (715/1315–790/1388), who was a neighbor in Harat al-Burjuwan and taught al-Maqrizi hadith and grammar, but also the popular literary book *Maqamat al-Hariri* (*Assemblies of al-Hariri*), which was used as a textbook for rhetoric.[76] Al-Maqrizi also studied hadith in Mecca during his *mujawarat*,

[72] Ibn Hajar, *Majma'*, 3: 60; idem, *Raf' al-Isr*, 3, acknowledges in his Introduction his debt to al-Maqrizi in compiling his book on the judges of Egypt, which indicates that he must have read more books of al-Maqrizi on the history of Egypt. Al-Maqrizi, *Durar*, 1: 194–202, on the other hand, writes an extensive biography of Ibn Hajar, complete with *shuyukh*, positions, books read, books composed, and titles, and gives many indications that he read many of Ibn Hajar's works.

[73] Al-Maqrizi, *Durar*, 2: 429–31, who calls him the greatest and most dignified of his teachers; Ibn Hajar, *Majma'*, 2: 311–19, who has a rather negative opinion of al-Siraj as someone who wrote on every religious science even if he did not know it; al-Sakhawi, *Daw'*, 6: 100–5.

[74] Al-Maqrizi, *Durar*, 2: 431–6; Ibn Hajar, *Majma'*, 2: 294–311, who also evinces negative criticism of his treatises and especially of his poetry; al-Sakhawi, *Daw'*, 6: 85–90.

[75] Al-Maqrizi, *Durar*, 1: 85–92.

[76] Al-Maqrizi, *Durar*, 3: 55–6.

especially during the first and the second ones in 783/1382 and 787/1386 when he was in his twenties, before he began to teach hadith himself there in his later *mujawarat* in the 830s/1430s, when he was in his late sixties and early seventies.[77]

In his adulthood, al-Maqrizi showed interest in various non-religious sciences such as calculus, which he studied with the vizier Sharaf al-Din Muhammad al-Damamini (d. 803/1401).[78] He learned about various astronomical sciences such as *'ilm al-miqat*, which encompasses astronomical timekeeping and the determination of prayer and fasting times, *'ilm al-zij*, or the tabulation of the positions of the moon, sun, and the planets and stars, and the astrolabe, the most elaborate instrument for astronomical calculations, from Nur al-Din al-Buwayti al-Hasib (720/1320–799/1397), who seems to have been an eccentric individual.[79] Al-Maqrizi also appears to have taken some interest in medicine, which he learned about from the physicians he befriended, although he shows more interest in the wondrous cures that he reports on their authority and less interest in the practice of medicine.[80] Al-Maqrizi also showed considerable curiosity about mechanical devices built by his contemporaries, such as water clocks and waterwheels.[81] He also evinces a noticeable curiosity in the fine arts and crafts in general, although his interest does not seem to have led to his seeking the appropriate knowl-

[77] In Mecca, he studied with many *muhaddiths*, including Jamal al-Din al-Amyuti (d. 1388), *Durar*, 1: 100–1, Zayn al-Din ibn al-Tabari (d. 1413), *Durar*, 3: 396–7, and Ibn Sukkar (d. 1399), *Durar*, 3: 43–4. He is said to have copied and read his book on the life of the Prophet, *Imta' al-Asma'* in Mecca in one of his last *mujawarat*, 838/1435 or 839/1436, Ibn Taghri-Birdi, *Manhal*, 1: 418.

[78] Al-Maqrizi, *Durar*, 3: 75–6. Muhammad al-Damamini served as *muhtasib* during the same time frame in which al-Maqrizi served in the same position, which may be how they knew each other.

[79] Al-Maqrizi, *Durar* 2: 520–1; Ibn Hajar, *Inba'*, 3: 353.

[80] Although there are a number of biographies of physicians in the *Durar*, al-Maqrizi only explicitly states that he learned medicine from one of them: Siraj al-Din al-Bahaduri al-Hanafi (762/1360–834/1431), *Durar*, 2: 441–2. On the other hand, al-Maqrizi reports a number of times about prescriptions suggested to him by a number of his physician friends, including *al-Ra'is* (Chief Physician) 'Ala' al-Din Ibn Saghir (715/1315–796/1394), who cured al-Maqrizi of a pain in his chest and back, among other instances of successful prescriptions, *Durar*, 2: 468–9. At times, he focuses on the marvelous cures reported by physician friends which he did not witness, such as a story about a person suffering from chronic diarrhea recounted by Shams al-Din ibn Muhammad al-Saghir, *Durar*, 3: 439–40.

[81] For instance, al-Maqrizi, *Durar*, 2: 526 reports at length on the work of 'Ala' al-Din Ibn al-Shatir, including how he made an astronomical sphere that emits words in Syriac (?) in Damascus, without having seen it himself. He learned about it from his own teacher of astronomy, al-Buwayti al-Hasib. This Ibn al-Shatir was a second cousin of the famous astronomer, also named 'Ala' al-Din Ibn al-Shatir, but with the title al-Kabir (The Elder), who died in Damascus before al-Maqrizi's birth.

edge about them, a shortcoming that he shared with most of the ulama of his time.[82]

Al-Maqrizi evinced a serious interest in the sciences of the occult, especially geomancy and other forms of divination, which were related to the astronomical sciences he pursued, as well as *'ilm al-harf* (science of letters), in which one makes predictions from numerical values and particular arrangements of letters.[83] In fact, al-Maqrizi seems to have studied both kinds of science, astronomy and astrology, with the same teachers sometimes, and to have practiced geomancy himself. Al-'Ayni, who was a formidable rival of al-Maqrizi in both the pursuit of positions and history writing, was clearly disdainful when he stated, in the obituary he wrote of al-Maqrizi, that he "practiced history, divination, and geomancy," implying that he was not a true historian.[84] This is a strange and hypocritical insinuation coming from al-'Ayni since he himself had extensively used divination, *hisab al-tali'* (horoscope), and *'ilm al-harf* in the two sycophantic encomia he successively wrote for the two sultans al-Mu'ayyad Shaykh (r. 1412–21) and al-Zahir Tatar (r. four months in 1421 after usurping the throne from al-Mu'ayyad's son).[85]

Al-'Ayni's spiteful statement did not escape the attention of later commentators. Ibn Taghri-Birdi remarked: "one should not heed the opinion of peers (*aqran*) about their peers, as for the dispute between the two of them, it is well known, may God have mercy on them both."[86] The later Mamluk historian 'Abd al-Basit b. Khalil b. Shahin al-Zahiri takes strong exception to Ibn Taghri-Birdi's opinion, probably because he looked down on him,

[82] One instance is his reporting on the work of Jamal al-Din al-Maghribi al-Susi (d. 1400), who was famous for his thin paper-making and his miniaturist writing, al-Maqrizi, *Durar*, 2: 345. Another is his reporting on several paintings in his *Khitat2*, 4: 288–90. I treated this general condition in an article "*'Ajib* and *Gharib*: Artistic Perception in Medieval Arabic Sources," *The Medieval History Journal* 9, 1 (2006): 99–113, in which I noted al-Maqrizi's curiosity about painting and his inability to describe the foreshadowing and foregrounding techniques in paintings that he describes.

[83] Al-Maqrizi, *Durar*, 3: 479, states that he learned *'ilm al-harf* from one of the renowned practitioners, Muhanna b. Hasan al-Baghdadi. Al-Sakhawi, *Daw'*, 2: 24, lists geomancy, *miqat*, the Astrolabe, and *zayarja* (divination devices or techniques that use relationships between letters and sentences and their numerical values) as one list of both astronomical and astrological sciences that al-Maqrizi knew.

[84] Al-'Ayni, *'Iqd*, 2: 574.

[85] Al-'Ayni, *al-Sayf al-Muhannad fi Sirat al-Malik al-Mu'ayyad*, Fahim Muhammad Shaltut, ed. (Cairo: Dar al-Katib al-'Arabi, 1967), 33–9, 59–62, 105 and the horoscope and the divination table, 306–7; idem, *al-Rawḍ al-Zahir fi Sirat al-Malik al-Zahir Tatar* Hans Ernst, ed. (Cairo: Dar Ihya' al-Kutub al-'Arabiyya, 1962), 7–12, 38–40, where he predicts that the sultan will rule for a long time, but he was to die in a couple of months. These two short books have the same structure and aim and seem to have been meant as a ticket for al-'Ayni to the court of these two sultans.

[86] Ibn Taghri-Birdi, *Hawadith*, 1: 64.

but offers something revealing about al-Maqrizi that may help us to understand the general opinion about geomancy at the time. ʿAbd al-Basit emphasizes, first, that peers know better about their peers, hence their judgment is accepted, especially since it is well-known that al-Maqrizi knew and practiced geomancy. He then says, "there is nothing dishonorable about geomancy and it does not belittle his achievements as a historian."[87]

Geomancy was definitely part of al-Maqrizi's pursuit of knowledge. Al-Sakhawi offers another instance in which al-Maqrizi is supposed to have read the *taliʿ* (horoscope) of another key figure, Ibn Khaldun, whom al-Sakhawi also passionately disliked. Al-Maqrizi predicted the time of Ibn Khaldun's appointment to the office of chief judge, which happened as he projected, and that was considered a marvel.[88] Al-Maqrizi, however, does not report this event anywhere in his writing, although he wrote extensively and intimately on his relationship with Ibn Khaldun in many of his historical works. He even mentions several occasions when Ibn Khaldun told him of marvels he had witnessed on his travels or divination procedures he was able to verify. In fact, in his own writing, al-Maqrizi never admits to practicing divination techniques, although he is very clear about having studied them with the best teachers available to him. This is puzzling, because al-Maqrizi never refrains from reporting divinations and dreams and volunteering their interpretation, or from citing strange and fantastic stories, which he uses both in his historical writings and his biographies as facts complementing, animating, and driving his narrative. At times it seems that, more than with any of his contemporaries, wonders, marvels, and dreams form the core of the Maqrizian biographical narrative, not only its ornament or riveting enhancement. This is especially evident in the entries on people with whom al-Maqrizi had a long and intimate relationship, such as those on his mother and wife, but also that on his foremost teacher Ibn Khaldun, to whom he devoted one of the longest and most admiring biographies in his *Durar*.

Ibn Khaldun: Teacher and Interlocutor

Indeed, Ibn Khaldun, although a relatively latecomer into al-Maqrizi's life, was one of the most influential figures in his education and, most probably, in the formulation of his worldviews and methods, even though the arrogant Ibn Khaldun never mentions al-Maqrizi in his writings. The two must have met shortly after Ibn Khaldun's arrival in Cairo in January 1383, even though

[87] ʿAbd al-Basit al-Zahiri, *al-Mujmaʿ*, 1: 473–4.

[88] Al-Sakhawi, *Daw'*, 2: 24.

we do not know how and where.[89] In his biographical note on a distant relative of his, Najm al-Dīn al-Bahi al-Hanbali, al-Maqrizi mentions that they both read a book with Ibn Khaldun, *al-Jumal fī l-Mantiq* by Afdal al-Din al-Khunaji (1194–1248), a short but very popular treatise on logic.[90] In his *Muqaddima*, Ibn Khaldun comments that the teachers of the East (i.e. Egypt and Syria) depended on that book in his day.[91] Al-Maqrizi also mentions that al-Bahi al-Ḥanbalī was related to his grandfather, Ibn al-Sa'igh al-Hanafi. This suggests that the two young students, al-Bahi and al-Maqrizi, may have been introduced to Ibn Khaldun by a friend of al-Maqrizi's late grandfather, as Ibn al-Ṣa'igh had enjoyed the support of an influential network from among the major ulama of Cairo, any of whom could have recommended al-Maqrizi to Ibn Khaldun, the new star teacher in Cairo. Be that as it may, al-Maqrizi, a young man of around eighteen years of age with a traditional ulama education, seems to have fast become a regular in the circle of Ibn Khaldun and to have benefited from his knowledge on many topics. It is clear from the contexts of several passages that al-Maqrizi directly copied from the master's dictation, or the many recorded discussions he had with him or with others in his circle of acolytes, bearing dates spanning more than ten years, that the relationship between the two men was long-lasting.[92] It may in fact have lasted until the end of Ibn Khaldun's life. Al Maqrizi more than once states that Ibn Khaldun told him that a new city would grow around the funerary *khanqah* built for Sultan Barqūq by his son Faraj between 1400 and 1411.[93] This prediction could not have happened before 1400 when the site was first selected for the *khanqah*, only six years before the death of Ibn Khaldun in 1406.

Al-Maqrizi's high esteem for his *shaykh*, as he repeatedly calls him, and admiration for his ideas come across very clearly in the extensive biography he wrote of Ibn Khaldun in his *Durar*, which he closes with a sigh: "May God have mercy on his soul, how much I have benefited from him."[94] Though

[89] Ibn Tawit al-Tanji, *Al-Taʿrif bi-Ibn Khaldun*, 246; Walter Fischel, *Ibn Khaldun in Egypt; His Public Functions and his Historical Research, 1382–1406; a Study in Islamic Historiography* (Berkeley: University of California Press, 1967), 18.

[90] Al-Maqrizi, *Durar*, 3: 88–9.

[91] Ibn Khaldun, *al-Muqaddima* Abdessalam M. Cheddadi, ed., 5 vols. (Casablanca: Bayt al-Funun wal-ʿUlum wal-Adab, Khizanat Ibn Khaldun, 2005), 3: 95, mentions al-Khunaji and his three books and their popularity in the East. On al-Khunaji and his book, see Khaled el-Rouayheb, "al-Khūnajī, Afḍal al-Dīn," *Encyclopaedia of Islam III*, ed. Gudrun Krämer, Denis Matringe, John Nawas and Everett Rowson. Brill Online, 2012, http://referenceworks.brillonline.com/entries/encyclopaedia-of-islam-3/al-khunaji-afdal-al-din-COM_24187 (last accessed May 15, 2012).

[92] Examples in al-Maqrizi, *Khitat2*, 1: 130, 3: 605–6, 4, 2: 921.

[93] Ibid., 4, 2: 921.

[94] Al-Maqrizi, *Durar*, 2: 383–410. The biography was published initially by Mahmud al-Jalili, "Tarjamat Ibn Khaldun li-l-Maqrizi," *MMII* 13 (1965): 215–42.

exuberantly complimentary, the biography is in no way overly glorifying. Most of its factual information is in fact summarized from Ibn Khaldun's own autobiography that appears in his *Ta'rif*, proving that al-Maqrizi read that book. Its second part, though, offers a series of stories brimming with popular wisdom, vernacular beliefs, and incredible happenings and wonders, told directly by Ibn Khaldun to al-Maqrizi, which sheds some light on the nature and depth of the relationship between the two men and reveals some usually overlooked common aspects in their characters.

Robert Irwin, who did not use al-Maqrizi's biography of Ibn Khaldun, reviewed the two men's reaction to various methods of divination and tried to understand the impact of that system of belief on their work. He concluded that al-Maqrizi was more prone to supernatural explanations than the more sober and empirical Ibn Khaldun, which was evidently the case.[95] Yet a fair number of the stories told about Ibn Khaldun by al-Maqrizi reveal that both men shared an interest in the power of the supernatural, especially when transmitted via prophecies, visions, and dreams, as a means of explaining the world no less important than observation and experience.[96] Although the stories are only recounted by al-Maqrizi, they put a different spin on the skepticism Ibn Khaldun purportedly reserved for most supernatural phenomena and divination.[97]

Al-Maqrizi could not have invented these stories, as most of them involve ruling figures from North Africa and Spain with whom Ibn Khaldun

[95] Robert Irwin, "al-Maqrizi and Ibn Khaldun, Historians of the Unseen," *MSR* 7, 2 (2003): 223–8.

[96] See especially al-Maqrizi, *Durar*, 2: 409–10, where al-Maqrizi reports the stories of two dreams told to Ibn Khaldun by the Merinid sultan Abu 'Inan Faris (r. 1348–58), then adds a comment by Ibn Khaldun that "the proof of a true dream is that the person would wake up right after seeing it and would remember it."

[97] This revision of Ibn Khaldun's attitude toward divination is bolstered by the praiseful biography of Ibn Khaldun by a contemporary and fellow Andalusian, Isma'il b. Yusuf b. al-Ahmar, who served at the court of Ibn 'Inan with him, see Isma'il b. Yusuf b. al-Ahmar, *Nathir Fara'id al-Juman fi Nazm Fuhul al-Zaman*, Muhammad Radwan al-Daya, ed. (Beirut: Dar al-Thaqafa, 1967), 297–310, esp. 298, which reports that "he [Ibn Khaldun] is well versed in the study of logic and *'ilm al-nujum* [the science of the stars (divination)] and whatever is related to theoretical sciences." The story that al-Maqrizi took his horoscope of course acquires a certain plausibility in light of this report. Ibn al-Ahmar's biography of Ibn Khaldun was written before the latter moved to Egypt. The issue is definitely larger than whether Ibn Khaldun believed in the occult sciences, for he is usually quoted in his rational debunking of occult in his *Muqqadima*. This uncritical attitude is changing with more scholarly examination of both Ibn Khaldun's actual position and latter commentators' use of his purported rejection of the occult as a shining example of medieval Islamic rationalism, see Matthew Melvin-Koushki, "In Defense of Geomancy: Šaraf al-Dīn Yazdī Rebuts Ibn Ḫaldūn's Critique of the Occult Sciences," *Arabica* 64, 3/4 (2017): 346–403, esp. 370–84.

worked directly during his long administrative career there. The context of the stories' retelling and their content suggest that Ibn Khaldun represented an important source of information for al-Maqrizi, who took advantage of the first-hand knowledge he gained on regions that he never visited in his historical writing. He included extensive biographies of near-contemporary Maghribi rulers in his *Durar* and recorded the events of their reigns in the *Suluk*, his contemporary history book, with a level of detail that is unmatched by any of his Egyptian peers.[98] Two of the reports in particular deserve to be mentioned as they concern real historical events that al-Maqrizi could not have known about even if he had access to written chronicles from the Maghreb. They must have come from the mouth of an eyewitness like Ibn Khaldun who had direct and intimate access to the two sultans/narrators. The first is ascribed to the Nasrid king of Granada Muhammad b. Yusuf (Muhammad V, r. 1354–9, 1362–91), whom Ibn Khaldun served twice, first for almost three years (1362–5) and then for less than a year in 1374. The sultan tells Ibn Khaldun the story of the struggle between Pedro the Cruel of Castille (r. 1334–69), whom al-Maqrizi names Butra, and his bastard brother Henry of Trastámara, called al-Qumt [Count], as he supposedly heard it from Pedro himself. Although the report is infused with at least two far-fetched incidents meant to weave God's mercy on the Andalusian Muslims into the narrative in the Maqrizian fashion, the story is correct in all its major details.[99]

The second story starts with the Merinid sultan Abu al-Hasan (r. 1331–51), who reportedly learned about the discovery of the Canary Islands from Genovese sailors he met in Ceuta. Abu al-Hasan acquired from the Genovese two natives who ultimately learned Arabic and informed him about their islands and their people. Then his son and successor sultan Abu 'Inan (r. 1348–58), whom Ibn Khaldun served between 1352 and 1357, sent the captain of his fleet with one fully loaded *ghurab* (frigate) to conquer the Canaries. But the captain returned without reaching the islands, which angered the sultan, who questioned his officer in the presence of Ibn Khaldun. Again, this story corresponds in dates and circumstances with the actual European re-discovery of the Canaries, which saw many adventurers, both Europeans and Maghribis, landing there between the 1330s and 1405 when the Castilians finally conquered and annexed the archipelago.[100] The story in fact reveals an otherwise unknown episode in the struggle between the Iberian Christians and Moroccan Muslims to dominate the sea and the coasts of southern Spain and

[98] Cf. al-Maqrizi, *Durar*, 1: 117, 121 (the biography of the sultan Abū Salim the Merinid), 1: 307, and 1: 375 (the biography of the sultan Abū l-'Abbas the Merinid).

[99] Al-Maqrizi, *Durar*, 2: 405.

[100] Al-Maqrizi, *Durar*, 2: 406–7.

Morocco, a competition that by the late fourteenth century tilted strongly toward the Iberians.[101]

Inserted between the two stories in the *Durar* is a short remark pertaining directly to the métier of the historian, which united the master and his disciple. Ibn Khaldun advises al-Maqrizi that one rule of thumb for establishing the veracity of a genealogy is to count a hundred years for every three generations so that one can estimate the length of time if the dates are missing, or the number of generations if the genealogy is incomplete. After all, al-Maqrizi and Ibn Khaldun may have talked about history when they met, not just knowledge of the future, as Irwin surmises.[102]

This is further suggested by a short passage in the *Durar* on the *Muqaddima* of his master, for which al-Maqrizi reserves his highest praise. After stating that Ibn Khaldun authored the marvelous book titled *'Unwan al-'Ibar wa-Diwan al-Mubtada' wal-Khabar fi-Tarikh al-'Arab wal-Barbar* [*sic*], al-Maqrizi says:

> Nothing like it [the *Muqaddima*] has been written before and it would be difficult for anyone to try to achieve something like it in the future . . . It is the cream of knowledge and sciences and the creation of sound minds and intellects. It informs about the essence [*kunh*] of things and tells about the reality [*haqiqa*] of events and happenings, as if it is expressing the condition [*hal*] of being and revealing the origin [*asl*] of everything in existence in a style which is brighter than a strand of pearl and purer than water fanned by a zephyr.[103]

This passage has often been dismissed as rhymed prose and verbal acrobatics that do not reveal any real understanding of Ibn Khaldun's interpretation of the movement of history on the part of al-Maqrizi.[104] Some modern historians have even quoted the guileful reports of al-Maqrizi's contemporary detrac-

[101] John Mercer, "The Canary Islanders in Western Mediterranean Politics," *African Affairs* 78, 311 (April 1979): 159–76.

[102] Irwin, "al-Maqrizi and Ibn Khaldun," 230.

[103] Al-Maqrizi, *Durar*, 2: 403.

[104] Only a few modern historians went further than stating the pedagogical and collegial connection or the shared involvement in geomancy to detect a certain intellectual affinity between the Khaldunian notions of history's cyclical pattern and the method and structure of several of al-Maqrizi's historical treatises, cf. Anne F. Broadbridge, "Royal Authority, Justice, and Order in Society: The Influence of Ibn Khaldun on the Writings of al-Maqrizi and Ibn Taghribirdi," *MSR* 7, 2 (2003): 231–45; Sabri Jarrar, "Al-Maqrizi's Reinvention of Egyptian Historiography," *The Cairo Heritage: Essays in Honor of Laila Ali Ibrahim*, Doris Behrens-Abouseif, ed. (Cairo: AUC Press, 2000), 30–53; Cengiz Tomar, "Between Myth and Reality: Approaches to Ibn Khaldun in the Arab World," *Asian Journal of Social Science* 36, 3/4 (2008): 590–611, esp. 592–4, where he states the influence of Ibn Khaldun on al-Maqrizi's work with little analysis.

tors accusing him of having misunderstood the *Muqaddima*.[105] These same detractors brazenly cite al-Maqrizi's testifying to the *Muqaddima*'s uniqueness, while at the same time they doubt that uniqueness without apparently having read the book. In fact, a cursory review of the contemporary and near-contemporary biographies of Ibn Khaldun reveals that hardly anyone beside al-Maqrizi was familiar enough with the text of the *Muqaddima* to comment on its content or arguments.[106]

Leaving hyperbole aside, there is in this passage much that intimates a different understanding of the way history moves from what is usually expected of an allegedly teleological and traditional mind. The *Muqaddima* was indeed the cream of the knowledge available to a Muslim scholar in the fourteenth century, and it did call for the exercise of reason in evaluating things and events, as al-Maqrizi observes. But more to the point, al-Maqrizi's coupling of the two pairs of correlative terms *kunh* and *haqiqa* and *hal* and *asl* in the phrase "it informs about the essence [*kunh*] of things and tells about the reality [*haqiqat*] of events and happenings, as if it is expressing the condition [*hal*] of being and revealing the origin [*asl*] of everything in existence" may be a recognition of the need to consider the structural or intrinsic as well as the contingent in all that is examined. This is, in fact, a first step in moving from the certainty of belief to the possibility of history and the unpredictability of human action that is reported and analyzed. If al-Maqrizi meant what he seems to be saying, then there is no doubt that he has learned a great deal from the *Muqaddima*, especially from the analytical and historiographical aspects of its argument about the writing of history, if not from the Khaldunian structure of the cyclical evolution of human societies.[107] Of course, there is no way of verifying how much of the *Muqaddima* al-Maqrizi read, although he had ample time to read the whole text during the years he spent in the company of Ibn Khaldun. It is even possible that the two men discussed the book together as it evolved from its first draft completed in Qal'at ibn Salama in Algeria, since Ibn Khaldun seems to have continued working on it in Cairo until 1404, many years after al-Maqrizi had become his student and then his colleague.[108]

A weightier indication of al-Maqrizi's understanding of the conceptual core of the *Muqaddima*, however, emerges from the analysis of a number

[105] Ibn Hajar, *Inba'*, 5: 331; idem, *Raf' al-Isr*, 2: 348; al-Sakhawi, *Daw'*, 4: 148.

[106] The only exception is the Egyptian *faqih* Ibn 'Ammar (1367–1440), who wrote two lines quoted in al-Sakhawi's biography of Ibn Khaldun (*Daw'*, 4: 149). For a collection of contemporary biographies of Ibn Khaldun, see 'Abd al-Rahman Badawi, *Mu'alafat Ibn* Khaldun (Cairo: al-Majlis al-A'la lil-Thaqafa, 2nd edn., 2006), 253–310.

[107] For a succinct analysis of the *Muqaddima*'s structure, see Ibn Khaldun, *al-Muqaddima*, "Introduction" by Abdessalam M. Cheddadi, XXII–L.

[108] Irwin, "al-Maqrizi and Ibn Khaldun," 230; Cheddadi, *Muqaddima*, XXXV.

of his thematic treatises, such as his early essay on the economic crisis and the famine of 806/1403–4, *Ighathat al-Umma bi-Kashf al-Ghumma*, and his analysis of the rivalry between the Umayyads and the Abbasids, *al-Niza' wal-Takhasum fima bayn Bani Ummaya wa-Bani Hashim*, which will be discussed further in Chapter 3.[109] But his analytical acumen is most conspicuously evident in the structure and argument of the *Khitat*, which suggests that Ibn Khaldun's conceptualization of history may have provided al-Maqrizi with the theoretical framework he needed to rationalize and organize his feelings of attachment to Cairo and Egypt and of loathing toward those who caused its decline. Ibn Khaldun seems to have influenced al-Maqrizi's thinking in two ways: analytical, that is, looking for causes and effects behind events and appearances; and interpretive, that is, seeing in the urban and architectural history of the city a reflection of the underlying cycle of the ups and downs of civilization. In the *Khitat*, as I argue in Chapter 4, al-Maqrizi was the first person to apply his master's theory of the cyclical movement of history (which Ibn Khaldun himself did not apply in his *'Ibar*) to a concrete example—the city of Cairo—and to draw from it how the decline he observed in Egypt would resolve.

A Glorious Lineage?

Despite the relative openness that we can observe in al-Maqrizi's presentation of the biographies of his parents, grandparents and other relatives, he seems to have deliberately kept his genealogy somewhat obscure. In the prefaces of most of his books, where he lists his lineage as was the custom at the time, he deliberately stops short at the ninth or tenth forefather, 'Abd al-Samad or Tamim respectively, names that on the surface do not ring any bells.[110] He

[109] M. Mustafa Ziyada, "Tarikh Hayat al-Maqrizi," in *Dirasat 'an al-Maqrizi*, 13–22; Gaston Wiet, "Le Traité des famines de Maqrizi," *JESHO* 5, 1 (February 1962): 1–90; Adel Allouche, *Mamluk Economics: A Study and Translation of al-Maqrizi's Ighathat al-Ummah bi-Kashf al-Ghummah* (Salt Lake City: University of Utah Press, 1994), 4–7; C. E. Bosworth, "al-Maqrizi's Exposition of the Formative Period in Islamic History and its Cosmic Significance: The *Kitab al-Niza' wa-al-Takhasum*," in *Islam: Past Influence and Present Challenge: In Honour of William Montgomery Watt*, ed. A. T. Welsh and P. Cachia (Edinburgh, 1979), 93–104, reprinted in idem, *Medieval Arabic Culture and Administration* (London, 1982) as no. XI; Anouar Louca, "Pèlerinage à trois voix: lecture d'un texte de Maqrizi," *Arabica* 36 (1989): 93–108, esp. 107–8; Tomar, "Between Myth and Reality: Approaches to Ibn Khaldun in the Arab World," 592–4.

[110] For al-Maqrizi's own presentation of his genealogy in the preface of his books, see *al-Mawa'iz wa-l-I'tibar bi-Dhikr al-Khitat wa-l-Athar*, 2 vols. (Bulaq, Cairo: al-Matba'a al-Amiriyya, 1853), 1: 4, where he stops at his great-grandfather; *al-Suluk li-Ma'rifat Duwal al-Muluk*, ed. Muhammad Mustafa Zyada et al., 4 vols. (Cairo: Dar al-Kutub, 1934–72),

does the same thing in the biographical notices he penned for his father and grandfather.[111] He is said to have intentionally limited his lineage, though he could have extended it by two or three more names to a very glorious ancestor, al-Muʿizz li-Din Allah (r. 953–75), the first Fatimid caliph in Egypt and the founder of al-Qahira, or to an even more illustrious forebear, ʿAli ibn Abi Talib, the Prophet's cousin, son-in-law, fourth successor and first Imam for all the Shiʿite sects, including the Fatimids, of course.[112] Ibn Hajar al-ʿAsqalani, who was, at least publicly, sympathetic to al-Maqrizi, reports that his friend had once deleted all the names before his tenth ancestor in the copy of one of his books copied by an unnamed Meccan student of his (who is most probably Najm al-Din ʿUmar b. Fahd, who will be discussed below).[113] On another occasion, al-Maqrizi kept his answer to Ibn Hajar vague, when the latter asked him point blank to verify a report by the biographer Ibn Rafiʿ al-Sallami (d. 1372) about al-Maqrizi's grandfather's Ansari (a descendant of a Medinese companion of the Prophet) origin. Al-Maqrizi merely questioned the authority of the biographer, but neither confirmed nor rejected his claim.[114] Why he did this is not explained by Ibn Hajar, although it is not too difficult to guess. Al-Maqrizi was probably divided between accepting the opportunity to attach himself to an extremely prestigious and safe, though false, pedigree (i.e. the Ansari genealogy) and revealing that his real pedigree, at least in his belief, was even more glorious, but doctrinally perilous in Sunni Mamluk Egypt.

The Meccan scholar Najm al-Din ʿUmar b. Fahd (1409–80) explains this dilemma in his *Muʿjam al-Shuyukh*, where he lists al-Maqrizi as his thirtieth *shaykh*, to whom he seems to have been quite close and with whom he had

---

1, 1: 22, and *Durar* (Damascus edition), 1: 47, with the ten names stopping at the name of Tamim, the father of ʿAbd al-Samad, who is in fact the grandson of the Caliph al-Muʿizz according to al-Sakhawi's longer chain.

111 The same line appears in al-Maqrizi obituary of his grandfather ʿAbd al-Qadir in *Suluk*, 2, 2: 365, and his father ʿAli in ibid., 3, 1: 326.

112 Ibn Taghri-Birdi, *Nujum*, 15: 490 and Ibn Hajar, *Majmaʿ*, 3: 59, enumerate the forefathers of al-Maqrizi back to the eighth ancestor, ʿAbd al-Samad, and say that they have copied it from al-Maqrizi himself. Ibn Taghri-Birdi then adds that al-Maqrizi's nephew, Nasir al-Din Muhammad, dictated his uncle's genealogy after his death and brought it up to ʿAli ibn Abi Talib through the Fatimid caliphs. The same report appears in al-Jawhari, *Nuzhat*, 4: 244.

113 Ibn Hajar, *Inbaʾ*, 4: 188; ʿAbd al-Basit al-Zahiri, *al-Mujmaʿ*, 1: 472, copies the story.

114 Ibn Hajar, *al-Durar al-Kamina*, 2: 238; *Inbaʾ*, 9: 172; al-Jawhari, *Nuzhat*, 4: 242 distorts the report he is copying from Ibn Hajar to the point of making it impossible to understand. ʿUmar Tadmuri, the modern editor of ʿAbd al-Basit al-Zahiri, *al-Mujmaʿ*, 1: 472, note 3, notices that Ibn Rafiʿ's *al-Wafiyyat* does not include a biography of al-Maqrizi's grandfather, who died in 732 A.H., whereas Ibn Rafiʿ's book starts in 736 A.H. Ibn Hajar might have seen a note by Ibn Rafiʿ that was not included in *al-Wafiyyat*, or else he was mistaken in the attribution.

spent a significant amount of time in both Mecca and Cairo.[115] Ibn Fahd states that he had seen in the handwriting of al-Maqrizi a report about one of his ancestors (might it be the grandfather of the previous story?) explaining that he claimed to be an Ansari as a means of hiding his true identity. The ancestor said that, when asked by a nagging interlocutor why he did so, he responded that he meant that he belonged to Ansar Allah (the supporters of God), in reference to the Qur'anic verse "O ye who believe! Be ye helpers of God [*Ansar Allah*]" (al-Saff 61: 14), a learned and rhetorical way of avoiding the issue. Ibn Fahd also mentions another deflection ascribed to a still unnamed ancestor of al-Maqrizi's who answered the question about his genealogy by calling himself al-Bahili (of the known Bahila Arabic tribe). When asked again by a cynical listener, he answered, "I meant that I am of the Ahl al-Mubahala [People of the Cursing Exchange]," in reference to the episode in the lifetime of Prophet Muhammad when he debated with the Christians of Najran using the process of *mubahala*, that is, disputation with a prayer to God to damn the wrongful side (Qur'an, Al-'Imran 3: 61).[116] This episode in the mission of the Prophet Muhammad, recorded by all the early Islamic sources besides the Qur'anic reference, has occupied many an Islamic exegete, and it is especially used by Shi'ite interpreters to emphasize the preeminence of Ahl al-Bayt (the People of the Prophet's Household), since the verse mentions the Prophet and his people and their wives and sons as one side of this exchange, and since the Prophet apparently brought 'Ali, his daughter Fatima, and his two grandsons al-Hasan and al-Husayn to the actual encounter with the Najrani Christians.[117] In ascribing that answer to al-Maqrizi's ancestor, our reporter must have been aware of the hidden dimension of the claim: the alleged ancestor is artfully claiming descent from the Prophet in clarifying an answer that was purportedly aimed at just hiding such heritage, a tactic that al-Maqrizi deploys in his own writing about his genealogy and his criticism of his contemporaries.

Whether intentionally or inadvertently, Ibn Fahd also clarifies another ambiguous point about al-Maqrizi: his surname (*nisba*), which he recasts as a possible reference to a Fatimid connection. The name "Maqrizi" is said

[115] Ibn Fahd, *Mu'jam*, 63–4.

[116] Ibid. The Qur'anic verse in Yusuf Ali's interpretation: "If any one disputes in this matter with thee, now after (full) knowledge hath come to thee, say: 'Come! let us gather together, – our sons and your sons, our women and your women, ourselves and yourselves: Then let us earnestly pray, and invoke the curse of Allah (*nabtahil*) on those who lie!'"

[117] Louis Massignon, *La Mubahala de Medine et l'hyperdulie de Fatima*, in Louis Massignon, *Parole donnée* (Paris: Éditions du Seuil, 1983), 147–67; Sidney H. Griffith, *The Church in the Shadow of the Mosque: Christians and Muslims in the World of Islam* (Princeton: Princeton University Press, 2010), 160–2; Muhammad Javad Reza'i and Mahdi Dasht Bozorgi, "A Study of the Verse of Mubahalah," *Journal of Shi'a Islamic Studies* 2, 1 (2009): 69–83.

by all of his other biographers to be toponymic and to refer to a neighborhood in Baalbek, in today's Lebanon, Harat al-Maqariza, whence his family came, although no one seems to have verified this story or the existence of this neighborhood.[118] Ibn Fahd again provides an explanation consistent with the other measures of *taqiyya* (prudence or concealment) taken by al-Maqrizi's ancestors to hide their Fatimid origin. He quotes from a text in the first person by al-Maqrizi, which is otherwise unavailable, in which our historian explains that his fifth ancestor Muhammad ibn Tamim (who probably lived around the time of the fall of the Fatimids) settled in the neighborhood of al-Maqariza in Baalbek so that he could "protect his descendants by providing them with a toponymic place of origin that will hide their genealogy for fear of being killed."[119] He then recites a verse about muddling one's traces so that they are undecipherable and continues with the two reports on the explanations of the two false genealogies mentioned above, to enigmatically conclude with a Qur'anic verse on the invincibility of the will of God (Al-Rum, 30: 6). These three instances provide ample corroboration of the reasons for which al-Maqrizi was reluctant to reveal his true Fatimid pedigree except to his close friends. Further examples will reinforce this interpretation.

There is no Harat al-Maqariza in Baalbek today, and it is quite difficult to verify whether such a name existed in al-Maqrizi's time. Gamal al-Din al-Shayyal, the modern editor of *Itti'az al-Hunafa bi-Akhbar al-A'imma al-Fatimiyyin al-Khulafa*, raises the possibility that the family gave its name to the *hara* (neighborhood) rather than the other way round, which is common in other examples.[120] Still, the name "Maqrizi" itself is rather strange, and its Arabic etymology strenuous at best. The tripartite root q-r-z means to grasp dirt with the tip of the fingers, but it is difficult to deduce from it the meaning of "Maqrizi" as a third form of exaggeration of the verbal noun m-q-r-z, that may indicate either an attribute of q-r-z or the name of a profession related to that action.[121] But if we agree that the family may have given its name to the *hara* instead of the other way round, there is another possible explanation

[118] Ibn Hajar, *Majma'*, 3: 58, says that a great-grandfather of al-Maqrizi, Ibrahim b. Muhammad, settled in Baalbek in the Harat al-Maqariza, but does not say when or from where he came.

[119] Ibn Fahd, *Mu'jam*, 63. The name of the ancestor is not correct, though: one name in the chain, Ibrahim, is missing between Muhammad and Tamim. Ibn Hajar in the previous footnote has the right name.

[120] Al-Maqrizi, *Itti'az al-Hunafa*, 1: 11.

[121] Al-Fayruzabadi, *al-Qamus al-Muhit* (Cairo: Bulaq Press, 1856), 2: 193; Ibn Manzur, *Lisan al-'Arab* (Beirut: Dar Sader, 1968), 5: 394. A wild suggestion would be that there is a connection between geomancy as *darb al-raml*, literally the beating of sand, and *taqriz*, the clenching of dirt.

offered by the sources, which, although speculative and depending only on one report from a questionable informant, would still insinuate the connection of al-Maqrizi to a Fatimid pedigree.

There is a little-known Roman-Berber city in the western desert of Libya, which boasts of a number of third-century CE mausoleums.[122] According to the eleventh-century geographer al-Bakri the city was still inhabited in the eleventh century and possibly later by Berber tribes, especially the Hawwara.[123] It is known today as Ghirza, a Berber designation, and the name's Arabic transliteration, Qirza, قرزة, may have provided the toponymic reference of the name "Maqrizi," although neither al-Maqrizi nor any of his biographers seem to be aware of that city. A strange story, attributed to Muhammad b. Ahmad al-Furriyani (1378–c. 1444), a friend and companion of al-Maqrizi's from Tunis, may reflect echoes of a possible attribution of al-Maqrizi to Ghirza or to a Berber origin, which would indirectly corroborate a Fatimid connection through marriage.[124] Ibn Fahd reported that al-Furriyani, in a written report, stated that he had read, in an unnamed text detailing the progeny of Imam 'Ali ibn Abi Taleb, that al-Maqrizi descended from a Berber emir from the Kitama tribe named Ibn Amaqriz, who married his daughter to a descendant of the Fatimid caliph al-Mu'izz stemming from his son, the Great Amir 'Uqayl, named 'Abd al-Samad, a name that appears twice in the genealogical chain listed by all the biographers of al-Maqrizi as the seventh and the ninth ancestors. The story is full of unverifiable details and gives the appearance of a fictive tale, especially since the majority of Mamluk scholars, except for al-Maqrizi and apparently Ibn Fahd, considered al-Furriyani a "liar" and an untrustworthy fabricator of biographical information and of historical reports. Al-Maqrizi, however, never doubted him in the many reports he ascribes to him in his various books, although he was severely criticized for this (more about al-Furriyani later).[125] Nevertheless, the story, regardless of

[122] Olwen Brogan and David Smith, "The Roman Frontier Settlement at Ghirza: An Interim Report," *Journal of Roman Studies* 47 (1957): 173–84, report Fatimid coins found at the site of Ghirza; G. R. D. King, "Islamic Archaeology in Libya, 1969–1989," *Libyan Studies* 20 (1989): 193–207.

[123] Abu 'Ubayd al-Bakri al-Andalusi (1030–94), *Kitab al-Masalik wal Mamalik*, 2 vols., Adrian van Leeuwen and André Ferré, eds. (Carthage: Bayt al-Hikma, 1992), 2: 660, writes about Qirza/Kirza that it was a stone statue on an outcrop that was still adored by the Berber tribes living in its vicinity, who sought its intervention to cure their maladies and augment their wealth, probably a reference to one of the antique temples in the city with its idol.

[124] Biographies of al-Furriyani in al-Maqrizi, *Durar*, 3: 146–7; Ibn Hajar, *Inba'*, 9: 226–8; al-Sakhawi, *Daw'*, 7: 67; Ibn al-'Imad al-Hanbali, *Shadharat*, 7: 261. See also Ahmed el-Bahi, "Feriana (Furriyana) à l'époque médiévale: questions de toponyme," *Actes du 5ème colloque international sur l'histoire des steppes tunisiennes*, Fathi Bejaoui, ed. (Tunis: Institut National du Patrimoine, 2008), 249–58. I am indebted to Iheb Guermazi for this reference.

[125] Noah Gardiner, "Esotericism in a manuscript culture: Aḥmad al-Būnī and his readers

its actual veracity, sheds light on a thorny issue concerning the genealogy of al-Maqrizi and offers a more plausible explanation for the unusual name "Maqrizi" than an elusive neighborhood in Baalbek, a point already noted by a later Mamluk historian.[126]

Despite his deliberate obfuscation of his lineage in the introductions to his books, al-Maqrizi selectively evinces pride in it in different ways. In a biography he penned of his neighbor, colleague, and competitor after his death, Shihab al-Din al-Awhadi (761/1360–811/1408), al-Maqrizi says that al-Awhadi shared with him a small autographed *diwan* (anthology) of his poetry and cites several examples of tender moral stanzas, some of which are quoted by other biographers of al-Awhadi. Al-Maqrizi then approvingly volunteers a number of panegyrical stanzas ostensibly written to him by al-Awhadi, in one of which the latter candidly and unapologetically exhorts him to take pride in his noble Fatimid pedigree (*al-nasab al-sharif al-fatimi*). Then in the second verse of that stanza, al-Awhadi says, "If you recount a complimentary story about them [i.e the Fatimids] and are confronted by a detractor, then trace yourself back to al-Hakimi [al-Hakim; the "i" is added for the rhyme]," advice that al-Maqrizi never publicly followed though he reported many praiseworthy qualities of the Fatimids and was often disparaged for that by many of his contemporaries. In another stanza, al-Awhadi calls al-Maqrizi the scion of the caliphs (*ibn al-khala'if*) and the buttress of our age (*'adid 'asrana*),

---

through the Mamlūk period," PhD diss. University of Michigan (2014), 250–1 and figure 15, discovered a remark in the handwriting of Ibn Hajar on the margins of the page of a holograph copy of al-Maqrizi's *Muqaffa* (Leiden MS or. 14.533, fol. 87) in which al-Maqrizi wrote the biography of Ahmad al-Buni. Ibn Hajar's hasty remark changes the impression we have about his opinion of his friend al-Maqrizi. Ibn Hajar said: "In this biography is that which is baseless and irresponsible, such as would be too lengthy to explain. The short version is that the name of the man mentioned and the name of his father mentioned here, his date of birth, date of death, travels, shaykhs, and many of his attributes—there's no truth to any of that. The author of this book learned that from something written for him from memory by our friend Abū 'Abd Allāh al-Furriyānī, and al-Maqrīzī took it from him on good faith. I warned the author about this, but he did not come to his senses. This biography shows that whoever places confidence in it is doing so out of ignorance of the reports of the people. And God is the helper." This is a very strong rebuke of al-Maqrizi, the like of which does not appear in the biographies Ibn Hajar wrote of his friend, where he praises his historical knowledge, and recalls, or more correctly presages, al-Sakhawi's diatribe. I thank Noah Gardiner for the reference. The unreliability of al-Furriyani may have been treated in Frédéric Bauden, "Al-Maqrizi, Ibn Ḥajar and the Man Who Pretended to Be the Sufyānī: An Insight into Source Criticism in the Late Mamlūk Period" (28th Congress of the Union Européenne des Arabisants et Islamisants, Università di Palermo, 2016), but I was not given access to this unpublished text.

126 'Abd al-Basit al-Zahiri, *al-Mujma'*, 1: 475, cites an abbreviated version of the story, compares it to the reference to the neighborhood in Baalbek, and concludes that the Berber ascription "might be more correct."

suggesting a patronage relationship between the two men.[127] These laudatory lines appear nowhere else in either al-Awhadi's or al-Maqrizi's various biographies, even though both Ibn Hajar and al-Sakhawi read *al-Durar* and used it extensively in their own biographical dictionaries, and more revealingly in redacting the biography of al-Awhadi and al-Maqrizi himself, where al-Sakhawi at least could have used the panegyric to further scorn al-Maqrizi.[128] The fact that al-Maqrizi is the only one who speaks of a *diwan* of poetry by al-Awhadi that he claims to have read and critiqued may indicate that Ibn Hajar and al-Sakhawi did not have firsthand access to al-Awhadi's writing, a point that will become important in the discussion of al-Maqrizi's appropriation of al-Awhadi's *khitat*. That al-Maqrizi uses al-Awhadi's purported poetry in his praise can only be explained as an implicit admission of his own Fatimid pedigree, even though it is couched in someone else's words, a tactic that was repeatedly used by al-Maqrizi for other purposes, not just to assert his glorious lineage.

All the evidence cited thus far does not amount to a verifiable genealogy. The question is crucial, as it bears on the alleged biases of al-Maqrizi in his writing about the Fatimids. The Fatimid historian Paul Walker, for instance, suggests that al-Maqrizi may have believed in his Fatimid pedigree at the beginning of his career (although al-Maqrizi copied al-Awhadi's stanza in his fifties), but as he researched the history of the Fatimids to complete his *Itti'az al-Hunafa*, he must have discovered the impossibility of such a lineage.[129] According to Walker, the eldest son of the Fatimid caliph al-Mu'izz, who is supposed to be the ancestral link between al-Maqrizi and the Fatimids, was impotent. Moreover, al-Maqrizi knew this and articulated it in his biography of Tamim in his major biographical dictionary *al-Muqaffa al-Kabir*.[130] The genealogy that Walker cites by al-Sakhawi, however, does not include Tamim as an ancestor of al-Maqrizi.[131] It connects al-Maqrizi to al-Mu'izz through a certain 'Ubayd, whom Walker was unable to identify. Thus, he considers it a mistake and suggests that the first descendant in this genealogical chain should be Tamim instead, as recorded in the other biography by al-Sakhawi,

127 Al-Maqrizi, *Durar*, 1: 185–90, the poetry on page 187. Al-Maqrizi has a shorter biography of al-Awhadi in *Muqaffa*, 1: 513–14, in which he does not mention anything about their relationship, but the text in the manuscript is distorted by a sentence most probably added by the copyist, for it mentions al-Maqrizi doing a final copy of the draft of *khitat* left by al-Awhadi, a subject that we will return to.

128 See al-Awhadi's biographies in Ibn Hajar, *Inba'*, 6: 112–13; idem, *Majma'*, 3: 38–9; al-Sakhawi, *Daw'*, 1: 358–9; Ibn al-'Imad al-Hanbali, *Shadharat*, 7: 89–90.

129 Paul Walker, "al-Maqrizi and the Fatimids," *MSR* 7, 2 (2003): 87–8.

130 Al-Maqrizi, *Muqaffa*, 2: 588–9.

131 Al-Sakhawi, *Tibr*, 1: 70–1. Tamim, on the other hand, is listed in the other biography that he wrote of al-Maqrizi, al-Sakhawi, *Daw'*, 2: 21.

and proceeds to refute the entire genealogy. Walker does not raise the possibility that the spelling of ʻUbayd may have been a typo, especially since one of al-Muʻizz's four documented sons is named ʻUqayl.[132] In fact, Ibn Fahd, in his biographical entry on al-Maqrizi, lists his master's full lineage all the way up to ʻAli ibn Abi Taleb via al-Husayn, his second son and the great martyr of Shiʻism, and through ʻUqayl the son of the first Fatimid Caliph al-Muʻizz, who was the twelfth ancestor of al-Maqrizi.[133]

This, of course, does not address the other problem that Paul Walker raises about the interruption in the Fatimid lineage imposed by Salah al-Din al-Ayyubi. In a cruel attempt to eradicate the Fatimid line, he separated the members of the caliphal family by gender—and incarcerated them so that they did not reproduce. The implication here is that there were no descendants of the Fatimids to take refuge in Baalbek. But we are not certain that Salah al-Din managed to round up all the members of the Fatimid dynasty, especially those of them who had been separated from the ruling line for generations as appears to be the case with al-Maqrizi's pedigree, most of whose names succeeding ʻUqayl are otherwise unmentioned in the historic sources until al-Maqrizi's grandfather ʻAbd al-Qadir.[134] Here again Ibn Fahd is our best guide to verifying the plausibility and the acceptability, if not the veracity, of al-Maqrizi's lineage. As a Hashemite and ʻAlid, or a descendant of ʻAli, Ibn Fahd had some authority in acknowledging other ʻAlids, a fairly regulated and strictly guarded process of authentication until today.[135] Moreover, Ibn

[132] It is very plausible for an uninformed copyist to write ʻUqayl as ʻUbayd (although this is a point that requires checking of the actual manuscript to settle). The genealogy in *al-Tibr al-Masbuk* is quite perplexing, not only for the possibility of a typo in spelling ʻUbayd but also for al-Sakhawi's apparent acceptance of the genealogy of the Fatimids back to ʻAli b. Abi Taleb, as Walker noted. It is clearly sloppily copied from a source other than that of Ibn Fahd, for al-Muʻizz is qualified in al-Sakhawi's version as *amir al-mu'minin*, a title that only believers in the Fatimids' right to rule would have accepted, and al-Sakhawi was definitely not one of them. The same genealogy is repeated by modern commentators on Islamic sites. See, for example, Multaqa Ahl al-Hadith (Assembly of Hadith Students), http://www.ahlalhdeeth.com/vb/archive/index.php/t-154175, and the website of al-Imam al-Ajurri for Islamic law, http://www.ajurry.com/vb/showthread.php?t=1623 (last accessed November 24, 2015).

[133] Ibn Fahd, *Muʻjam*, 63–4; Sibt Ibn al-ʻAjami, *Kunuz al-Dhahab fi Tarikh Halab*, 2 vols., Shawqi Shaʻath and Faleh Bakkour, eds. (Aleppo: Dar al-Qalam, 1996), 2: 267, copies the story of the Berber Amir Amaqriz in his biography of al-Maqrizi, but inserts into it the full genealogical chain of al-Maqrizi up to ʻAli b. Abi Taleb as it appears in Ibn Fahd's *Muʻjam*. Sibt Ibn al-ʻAjami is probably copying from Ibn Fahd, who was one of his teachers of hadith.

[134] Other examples cited by Walker, "al-Maqrizi and the Fatimids," 88, note 17.

[135] Ibn Fahd was an acknowledged descendant of ʻAli through ʻAli's younger son, Muhammad (Ibn al-Hanafiyya). The genealogy of Ibn Fahd *père*, Muhammad, to ʻAli, appears in al-Maqrizi, *Durar*, 3: 385–6, which states that Muhammad and his son Omar read

Fahd was living in Mecca away from the religious politics of Cairo and under an 'Alid Shi'ite ruling family, the Hasanid Sharifs, who flaunted the same ancestry to 'Ali through his eldest son Hasan, albeit carefully when it came to dealing with the zealously Sunni Mamluks.[136] Had the 'Alid genealogy of al-Maqrizi been in doubt, Ibn Fahd would have been the first to note it.

Even in Cairo, al-Maqrizi's Fatimid genealogy seems to have been conceded by some of his biographers, albeit grudgingly and in roundabout ways. Ibn Hajar, ostensibly al-Maqrizi's most impartial biographer, is our source for the story of al-Maqrizi erasing the names of his ancestors beyond the tenth and up to al-Mu'izz, to which ascription he adds *Allahu a'lam* (God only knows). In filling the gap in the line of succession, Ibn Hajar makes the mistake of deriving al-Maqrizi's line from Tamim, the impotent son of al-Mu'izz instead of 'Uqayl, the son recorded by Ibn Fahd.[137] Elsewhere, Ibn Hajar persists in his mistake of attribution by calling al-Maqrizi "al-Tamimi" (the descendant of Tamim, probably referring to the son of al-Mu'izz, not to the seventh or the ninth ancestors of al-Maqrizi, both of whom were also named Tamim).[138] This may have been Ibn Hajar's way of ascribing his friend to the Fatimids without having to state this openly. He also reports that Nasir al-Din Muhammad, al-Maqrizi's brother, told him that he had checked with his brother for his source about his Fatimid pedigree, and the reply was that al-Maqrizi's father took him to al-Hakim Mosque in Cairo one day and said, "Son, this is the mosque of your ancestor."[139] Al-Sakhawi, al-Maqrizi's most acrimonious detractor, copies the same story, but adds an indignant remark

al-Maqrizi's book *Imta' al-'Asma' bi-ma lil Rasul min al-Abna' wal Akhwal wal Hafada wal Mata'* in Mecca in 834/1432. Al-Sakhawi, *Daw'*, 9: 281–3, lists a shorter genealogy of this Ibn Fahd *père*, whom he knew well and whose funeral in Mecca he attended, but refers thereafter to the biography of his father, where he lists the full line-up to 'Ali b. Abi Taleb, ibid., 9: 231. On the control of the genealogies of Ahl al-Bayt, see Kazuo Marimoto, "Keeping the Prophet's Family Alive: Profile of a Genealogical Discipline," in Sarah Bowen Savant and Helena de Felipe, eds., *Genealogy and Knowledge in Muslim Societies. Understanding the Past* (Edinburgh: Edinburgh University Press and Aga Khan University, 2014), 11–23; Teresa Bernheimer, "Genealogy, Marriage, and the Drawing of Boundaries among the 'Alids (8th–12th centuries)," in Kazuo Morimoto, ed., *Sayyids and Sharifs in Muslim Societies. The Living Links to the Prophet* (London: Routledge, 2012), 75–91.

136 On the Hasanid Sharifs and their long hold on Mecca, see art. "Makka," by A. J. Wensinck [C. E. Bosworth] in *EI²*, 6: 148–51, and art. "Hashimids" by G. Rentz in *EI²*, 3: 262–3.

137 Ibn Hajar, *Inba'*, 9: 172. This may be the source of the mistake made by al-Sakhawi and then Paul Walker in according al-Maqrizi a descendant of Tamim b. al-Mu'izz, even though Ibn Hajar credits the erased long chain to a Meccan student of al-Maqrizi's, who most probably was Ibn Fahd. Ibn Fahd's reported chain of al-Maqrizi's lineage critically differs from what Ibn Hajar attributes to him.

138 Ibn Hajar, *Raf' al-Isr*, 1: 2, in a complimentary remark on his friend al-Maqrizi in his introduction.

139 Ibn Hajar, *Inba'*, 9: 172; idem, *al-Durar al-Kamina*, 3: 5. Ibn Hajar offers no comment here.

that seems to have been meant to show either how gullible al-Maqrizi was or how unsubstantiated his claim was of a Fatimid ancestry. The skepticism, nevertheless, does not seem to have prevented al-Sakhawi from adding the titles "al-Husayni" (descendant of al-Husayn) and "al-'Ubaydi" (descendant of 'Ubayd Allah, the founder of the Fatimid dynasty in Tunis) to al-Maqrizi's list of surnames, a tacit admission of the Fatimid lineage even though al-Sakhawi here does not bring the chain of ancestors up to al-Mu'izz as he does in *al-Tibr al-Masbuk*. He also notes that, although al-Maqrizi did not go beyond his ninth ancestor, 'Abd al-Samad b. Tamim, in his own prefaces, he used to "reveal more than that to those he trusted." Al-Sakhawi then continues by saying "then I saw what indicates that he adapted this pedigree from al-Furriyani, infamous for his lying, so God knows (what the truth is)," undoubtedly echoing the antagonistic opinion his revered master, Ibn Hajar, had of al-Furriyani (and of those who copied from him like al-Maqrizi).[140] Ibn Taghri-Birdi, who was al-Maqrizi's close student and follower, traces his master's genealogical line only to the eighth ancestor, 'Abd al-Samad, in the three obituaries he wrote in his *Hawadith al-Duhur*, *al-Manhal al-Safi*, and *al-Nujum*. He adds in *al-Nujum*, however, that al-Maqrizi's nephew, Nasir al-Din Muhammad (who seems to have had the same name and honorific title as his father),[141] dictated his full genealogy after his uncle's death and brought it all the way up to 'Ali b. Abi Taleb through the Fatimid caliphs.[142] Clearly then, al-Maqrizi was not the only member of his family who believed in having a Fatimid ancestry, since Ibn Hajar and Ibn Taghri-Birdi are directly quoting two other family members to that effect.

It seems, then, that al-Maqrizi maneuvered his Fatimid pedigree, of which he was obviously very proud, as an open secret with a margin of deniability (as we say today).[143] The caution was justifiable in the context of the competitive

140 Al-Sakhawi, *Daw'*, 2: 23.

141 See Al-Sakhawi, *Daw'*, 9: 150 for a brief bio of the nephew Mohammad that lists al-Awhadi, al-Maqrizi's neighbor and colleague, among his teachers, which may indicate that they all lived together in the family house in Harat Burjuwan.

142 Ibn Taghri-Birdi, *Nujum*, 15: 225.

143 In that al-Maqrizi, who was obviously proud of his genealogy, had to act differently from another Mamluk historian who had a royal ancestor, Ibn Tulun al-Salihi of Damascus (1475–1546), who was a descendant of Khamarawieh b. Ahmad b. Tulun, the rulers of Egypt in the second half of the ninth century. Ibn Tulun lists his genealogy up to the famous Ibn Tulun in his *al-Fulk al-Mashhun fi Ahwal Muhammad ibn Tulun* (Damascus, Maktabat al-Qudsi wa Budayr, 1929–30), 6. Ibn Tulun was so proud of his ancestry that he penned two opuscules on his illustrious eponymous ancestor: *al-'Uqud al-Lu'lu'iyya fi al-Dawla al-Tuluniyya* and *Hur al-'Uyun fi Tarikh Ibn Tulun*. He also bought a copy of al-Balawi, *Sirat Ahmad ibn Tulun* and gifted it to the Madrasa al-'Umariyya, the most famous Hanbali madrasa in al-Salihiyya north of Damascus. See Najiyya 'Abdallah Ibrahim and Nada 'Abd al-Razzaq al-Jilawi, "al-Sira al-Zatiyya wal 'Ilmiyya li-Ibn Tulun Shams al-Din

and even cutthroat scholarly milieu which he and his colleagues navigated in Cairo. A public assertion of his Fatimid (i.e. Isma'ili) ancestry, which was abhorred in the almost totally Sunni Mamluk Egypt, could have ruined his carefully constructed career as a solid Sunni Shafi'ite *'alim*, and perhaps also as a private citizen. Even without any solid confirmation of a Fatimid connection, al-Sakhawi, in his maliciously and underhandedly disparaging biography of al-Maqrizi, uses the derogatory patronymic al-'Ubaydi, that is, descendant of 'Ubayd Allah, the first in the Fatimid line to claim descent from the Prophet's daughter Fatima in 906.[144] "Al-'Ubaydiyyun" was indeed a spiteful title adopted by all Sunni commentators in Mamluk Egypt who rejected the Fatimids' claim of descent from the Prophet through Fatima and 'Ali. The same title is still used today by Islamist historians who adhere to their predecessors' rejection of the Fatimids' claim of Prophetic lineage. Moreover, the term does not seem to have lost any of its negative connotations.[145]

Al-Maqrizi's Representation of the Fatimids

It is very plausible that al-Maqrizi's flattering portrayal of the Fatimids and their achievements in his writing was partly animated by his belief that he was their descendant, though this was not the only reason, as we will see later.[146]

Muhammad b. 'Ali al-Dimashqi al-Salihi," *Majallat Kuliyyat al-Tarbiya lil Banat* 26, 4 (2015): 1057–75, https://www.iasj.net/iasj?func=fulltext&aId=117237 (last accessed June 20, 2019).

144 Al-Sakhawi, *Daw'*, 2: 21, idem, *Tibr*, 21. There is a whiff of professional jealousy toward al-Maqrizi in al-Sakhawi's preface to his *Tibr*, which is effectively a continuation (*dhayl*, lit. tail) to al-Maqrizi's *Suluk* ordered by the Great Amir Yashbak min Mahdi. That order and the way al-Sakhawi responds to it in his preface suggest that Yashbak considered al-Maqrizi as the equivalent of a master to al-Sakhawi.

145 For a review of the debates over the Fatimid lineage in medieval and contemporary writing, see Michael Brett, *The Rise of the Fatimids: The World of the Mediterranean and the Middle East in the Tenth Century* c.e. (Leiden: Brill, 2001), 29–49; Farhad Daftari, *Ismaili Literature: A Bibliography of Sources and Studies* (London: I. B. Tauris, 2004), 84–103. Uncertainty about the Fatimids' claim of Prophetic lineage still dominates the debate, and will probably never be historically resolved, see Luke Yarbrough, "Medieval Sunni historians on Fatimid policy and non-Muslim influence," *Journal of Medieval History* 45, 3 (2019): 331–46.

146 Shakir Mustafa, *Tarikh*, 2: 148, raises this possibility as well, but Sayyid, *Musawwadat*, Introduction, 45, does not seem to think that it was the case. See also my "Who Was al-Maqrizi? A Biographical Sketch," *MSR* 7, 2 (2003): 1–19; idem, "al-Maqrīzī's Connection to the Fatimids," in *The Study of Shi'i Islam: History, Theology, and Law*, Farhad Daftari and Gurdofarid Miskinzoda, eds. (London: I. B. Tauris; Institute of Ismaili Studies, 2014), 67–75. See also Shainool Jiwa, *The Founder of Cairo: The Fatimid Imam-Caliph al-Mu'izz and his Era: An English Translation of the Text on al-Mu'izz from Idris 'Imad al-Din's*

Especially commendatory is his elucidation of the Fatimid Caliphate in his *Khitat*, and his description of the many spectacular structures and the order and decorum it established in Cairo and in Egypt in general, which occupies almost a third of the compendium.[147] He, however, does not heed al-Awhadi's exhortation to outwardly "trace his ancestry" to the Fatimids in any of these sections. Instead, he takes on something almost as daring: he mounts a fervent defense of the authenticity of the Fatimids' lineage back to Fatima, the daughter of the Prophet. Such an assertion amounts to recognizing them as the rightful caliphs for anyone who considers descent from the Prophet as the primary condition for any claim to the caliphate. Although a prophetic lineage was a requirement for rule professed by many Islamic religious authorities beyond the Isma'ilis, it did not, of course, include the Sunni scholarly establishment in the Mamluk sultanate. Mamluk ulama had long accepted a more expansive definition of kinship with the Prophet that privileges the Abbasids, the descendants of the Prophet's uncle, even when many ulama personally evinced a love of Al al-Bayt (the 'Alids), as we saw in the case of al-Maqrizi's grandfather Ibn al-Sai'gh.[148]

Al-Maqrizi was thus breaching two anathemas in his defense of the Fatimids: tracing their line back to the Prophet and accepting their legal right to rule. But he was very careful not to support or advocate their doctrine, which was seen as bordering on the heretical in Sunni Mamluk Egypt. This comes across clearly in the long review of the genealogy of the Fatimids with which he prefaces his *Itti'az al-Hunafa*, which he then offers in summary form in his *Khitat*.[149] In that text, al-Maqrizi presents all the reports on

---

'Uyun al-Akhbar (London: I. B. Tauris, 2009), 25–8; idem, *Towards a Shi'i Mediterranean Empire: Fatimid Egypt and the Founding of Cairo, The Reign of the Imam-Caliph al-Mu'izz from al-Maqrizi's Itti'az al-hunafa' bi-akhbar al-Ai'mma al-Fatimiyyin al-Khulafa* (London: I. B. Tauris, 2009), 32–47. The main instances of Fatimid praises in al-Maqrizi's oeuvre are the Fatimid section of his *Khitat*, the biography of al-Mahdi in al-Maqrizi, *Kitab al-muqaffa al-kabir*, 8 vols., Muhammad Ya'lawi, ed. (Beirut: Dar al-Gharb al-Islami, 1991), 4: 523–70, and the *Itti'az*.

147 Al-Maqrizi, *Khitat2*, 2: 172–307, 342–608.

148 The re-establishment of an Abbasid Caliphate in Cairo by the Mamluks after the fall of Baghdad to the Mongols in 1258 elicited many reflections among the Mamluk ulama on the role of the Caliph and the Caliphate, see Mona Hassan, *Longing for the Lost Caliphate: A Transregional History* (Princeton: Princeton University Press, 2016), 99–140; Mustafa Banister, '"Naught Remains to the Caliph but his Title": Revisiting Abbasid Authority in Mamluk Cairo,' *MSR* 18 (2014–15): 219–45.

149 Al-Maqrizi, *Itti'az*, 1: 15–54, where he logically argues the truth of their lineage and lists prominent scholars, such as Ibn Khaldun, who accepted it. Idem, *Khitat1*, 1: 348–9, is a summary of the *Itti'az*'s discussion. For a translation and discussion of the relevant passages see Jiwa, *Towards a Shi'i*, 44–7. Another Mamluk historian who accepts their claim is Ibn 'Abd al-Zahir, *al-Rawda al-Bahiyya fi Khitat al-Qahira al-Mu'izziyya*, ed. Ayman Fu'ad

their genealogy in detail, both those approving of it and those denying it. He, however, takes the added precaution of stating at the beginning of every denial he cites that he "disagrees with it" (*bara'a*, lit. "claim innocence of"), a way of emphasizing both his objectivity (i.e. citing those with whom he disagrees) and his personal opinion. Starting with Ibn Hazm al-Andalusi, whom he otherwise revered, al-Maqrizi disagrees with his denial of the Fatimids' genealogical claim and tries to explain that rejection as a function of it having been generated in al-Andalus, where Ibn Hazm grew up in the court of the Umayyads in Cordoba, who were the political and ideological opponents of the Fatimids.[150] Al-Maqrizi then enumerates a few other sources that rejected the Fatimids' claim to Prophetic genealogy, such as Ibn al-Nadim in *al-Fihrist*, who cites a tenth-century *sharif* from Damascus, Akhu Muhsin, the author of a rebuttal of the Fatimids' pedigree that al-Maqrizi read, took *bara'a* from, and reproachfully quoted.[151]

Al-Maqrizi then approvingly records the arguments of two major historians in favor of the Fatimids, Ibn al-Athir, whom he quotes extensively, and Ibn Khaldun. He summarizes Ibn Khaldun's long and historically careful defense of the authenticity of the Fatimids' genealogy, an opinion that earned Ibn Khaldun many curses from his contemporary Mamluk biographers.[152] Finally, al-Maqrizi challenges his reader directly:

> if [you] were untarnished by intolerance and bias to reflect on the aforementioned statements of those who deny the Fatimid Prophetic genealogy so that he can see for himself how arbitrary they are and how much fabrication has permeated them. You would then realize that these statements cannot be accepted by those whose judgment is sound and who can notice their spuriousness, for it has been proven that God would not aid those who use deception to divert people from His way.[153]

This strong statement is daringly put forth at a time when the learned consensus in Sunni Egypt was that the Fatimids were impostors who had

---

Sayyid (Cairo: al-Dar al-'Arabiyya li-l-Kitab, 1996), 6–7. Other Mamluk historians who deny their lineage: Ibn Taghri-Birdi, *Nujum*, 4: 69–112; Abu Hamid al Qudsi, *Kitab Duwal al-Islam al-Sharifah al-Bahiyah: wa-Dhikr ma Zahara li Min Hikam Allah al-Khafiyah fi Jalb Ta'ifat al-Atrak ila al-Diyar al-Misriyah*, Ulrich Haarmann and Subhi Labib, eds. (Beirut: al-Sharika al-Muttahida, 1997), 12–15.

150 Al-Maqrizi, *Itti'az*, 1: 15–16.

151 Al-Maqrizi, *Itti'az*, 1: 22–34. On Akhu Muhsin, see Brett, *The Rise of the Fatimids*, 42–6, where he analyzes the origin and peregrinations of his account traced back to Ibn Rizam and calls it a "parody" of Isma'ili stories. Al-Maqrizi, *Itti'az*, 1: 38, vehemently rejects the story of Ibn Badis in his *Tarikh Ifriqiyya wa al-Gharb*, which traces the Fatimids to a Jewish origin.

152 Al-Maqrizi, *Itti'az*, 1: 44–52.

153 Al-Maqrizi, *Itti'az*, 1: 52–4.

descended from a minor preacher with a suspect lineage, ʿUbayd Allah, "the fifth descendant of Maymun al-Qaddah ibn Daysan, the Manichean."[154] It is this lineage that the term "ʿUbaydiyyun" invokes when used by the Mamluk ulama to reject the Fatimids' association with the Prophet's daughter.

Al-Maqrizi's plea to his reader to accept the Fatimids' prophetic genealogy did not go unnoticed. On the margin of the page of the main manuscript used for the modern edition of *ittiʿaz*, in which he reports Imami traditions on the rise of the Fatimids, a remark states that "al-Maqrizi—God Forgiveness be upon him—is not to blame for mounting this defense of the Fatimids because his lineage goes back to them."[155] The fifteenth-century commentator then presses on with a stock historical argument to refute al-Maqrizi's assertion that God does not aid liars: "there were examples in history, such as Bukhtanasar (Nebukadnezar II) in the olden days and the Mongols and Tamerlane in the near past, in addition to the Umayyads who dominated the People of the House of the Prophet." Nor was the tacit knowledge of his lineage confined to his contemporaries. Later scholars also mention al-Maqrizi's purported Fatimid pedigree when commenting on his apparent bias toward them. Muhammad b. ʿAli al-Shawkani, a famous Yemeni scholar from the eighteenth century, writes an entry on al-Maqrizi in his biographical dictionary, which he mostly adapted from Ibn Hajar and al-Sakhawi. But he adds a personal note, saying "I wondered why al-Maqrizi was full of praise for the ʿUbaydiyyun in his *Khitat* since he was of a different *madhahb* from theirs, until I learned about his claim of descent from them so I concluded that he was inspired to list the achievements of his ancestors."[156] Al-Maqrizi is also explicitly criticized in the biographical notice on Ibn Khaldun written by al-Sakhawi.[157] Not only does he denounce Ibn Khaldun for accepting the ʿAlid lineage of the Fatimids, but al-Sakhawi goes on to mock al-Maqrizi's naivété in having written a glorifying biography of his *shaykh* without realizing that Ibn Khaldun used the Fatimid claim to retroactively smear the

[154] Ibid. The Maymunid genealogy is discussed in the same section.

[155] Al-Maqrizi, *Ittiʿaz*, 1: 54, no. 2; 1: 31, identifies the copyist, who copied his text from an autographed version in 884/1479, as an Azharite (as his *nisba* indicates), Muhammad ibn Ahmad al-Gizi al-Shafiʿi al-Azhari.

[156] Al-Shawkani, *al-Badr al-Taliʿ*, 80. Questions about al-Maqrizi's *madhhab* and his Fatimid lineage continue to occupy Islamic scholars today, who are as perplexed as his contemporaries by how he could reconcile his doctrinal beliefs with his Fatimid lineage and his defense of their claims of belonging to Al al-Bayt; cf. the discussion of the prolific Saudi Shaykh Nasir b. Muhammad al-Ahmad on his website, https://alahmad.com/view/40 (last accessed July 27, 2017).

[157] Al-Sakhawi, *Daw'*, 4: 147–8; idem, *Iʿlan*, 94. If there is any truth to the claim, it may be seen to suggest that al-Maqrizi's belief in his Fatimid ancestry animated his biographical writing as well.

reputation of their great ancestor, ʿAli ibn Abi Talib, whom, al-Sakhawi alleges, he hated.[158]

Finally, al-Maqrizi's title, *Ittiʿaz al-Hunafa bi-Akhbar al-Aʾimma al-Fatimiyyin al-Khulafa*, itself amounts to another bold public declaration of his belief in their genuineness as descendants of the Prophet. In the first clause, he is inviting his readers, whom he calls *hunafa* (sing. *hanif*), to draw lessons (*mawaʿiz*, same as the title of the *Khitat*) from the history of the Fatimids. But his use of the term *hunafa* is motivated by more than the necessity of rhyme. It is probably intentional and significant. A *hanif*, in the general sense accepted in the medieval period, is a believer in the original and true religion, that is, someone who predates the sectarian division that prompted the Sunnis to vehemently denigrate both the Ismaʿili doctrine and the genealogical claim of the Fatimids.[159] But the most significant part of the title is the second clause, since it strongly emphasizes the Fatimids' privilege as both *khulafa* (caliphs) and *aʾimma* (imams) of the Islamic community, that is, the supreme rightful leaders of the community in both the theological/judicial and institutional senses.[160]

This is not the same as saying that al-Maqrizi believed in the Ismaʿili doctrine of the Fatimids, for he most certainly did not. None of his biographers, including the most malicious among them such as al-ʿAyni and al-Sakhawi, accuses him of such a transgression, although they heap all sorts of petty doctrinal failings on him such as believing in charms and magic, having Zahiri leanings but not really understanding the *madhhab*, and displaying strong animosity toward the Hanafis. The remark that al-Maqrizi himself tacks onto his exposé of the Fatimids' dogma in his *Musawaddat* of the *Khitat* is critical in understanding the difference between believing in the Fatimids' glorious pedigree and accepting their dogma. In the text, al-Maqrizi distances himself (*yatabarraʾ baraʾa*; asserts distance) from the Ismaʿili doctrine he is about to explain, as he did in reporting the accounts denigrating the Fatimids genealogy in the *Ittiʿaz*.[161] It is curious that the note of *baraʾa* does not appear in

158 Ibn Hajar, *Rafʿ al-Isr*, 2: 343–8, in his biography of Ibn Khaldun uses another excuse for al-Maqrizi's fascination with the *Muqaddima* by attributing it to Ibn Khaldun's mastery of rhymed prose and other verbal acrobatics. He also criticizes Ibn Khaldun's acceptance of the Fatimid lineage in his *Inbaʾ*, 5: 331, though not in his entry in *Majmaʿ*, 3: 157–60.

159 On the meaning and development of the term, see art. "Hanif," by W. Montgomery Watt in *EI*^{2}, 3: 165–6; on the historical evolution of the term from pre-Islam to the Qur'an and later, see Frederick Mathewson Denny, "Some Religio-Communal Terms and Concepts in the Qur'an," *Numen* 24, 1 (April 1977): 26–34.

160 On the meaning and development of the Imamate, see art. "Imama," by W. Madlung in *EI*^{2}, 3: 1163–9; on the Caliphate, see art. "Khilafa, the History of the Institution" and "Khilafa, In Political Theory," by D. Sourdel and A. K. S. Lambton respectively, in *EI*^{2}, 4: 937–50.

161 Sayyid, *Musawwadat*, Introduction, 45, and p. 94 of the text.

the published copy of the *Khitat*, which is based on later redactions of the book, although the *da'wa* section is copied in its entirety from the text of the *Musawaddat*.[162] This is probably due to the transformation that al-Maqrizi underwent in the period between the date of the draft and that of the last redaction of the *Khitat*. By the later date, which was toward the end of his life, al-Maqrizi may have felt that he no longer needed to assert the solidity of his Shafi'i Sunni creed since he no longer was interested in competing for public positions or patronage. The defense of the Fatimid genealogy, however, appears in both *Musawaddat* and *Khitat* as well as in the *Itti'az*, underscoring al-Maqrizi's strong conviction in its truthfulness throughout his life. In fact, al-Maqrizi seems to have held strong convictions from the beginning of his career. The circumstances of its end, abrupt and precarious as we will see in the following chapter, and the general gloomy mood he consequently fell into only sharpened his convictions and allowed him to be more assertive about them in his writing and in his general comportment.

[162] Al-Maqrizi, *Khitat1*, 1: 348–9, 393–5, in which the same exposé is presented.

CHAPTER 2

Career, Moral Crisis, and Withdrawal

When the Mamluks came to power in 1250, Cairo was still a city struggling to define its territorial boundaries and reassert its supremacy in the region after a chaotic century in which Jerusalem, Damascus, Aleppo, and other smaller cities rose to competitive positions under rival amirs of the Ayyubid clan or crusading princes. In less than a century, the Mamluks managed to transform the city not only into the undisputed capital of their formidable military empire, but also into the foremost Islamic metropolis of its time. In a building fury, sultans and amirs sponsored splendid mosques, madrasas, *ribat*s, *khanqah*s, and mausoleums, endowing them as institutions of learning and Sufi piety. These structures lined up the major thoroughfares of the city, competing with one another to attract scholars and students or *shaykhs* and disciples. By the middle of the fourteenth century, Cairo had become the premier intellectual center of the Islamic world, a position that it managed to maintain for a couple of centuries.[1]

The profusion of wealth and the excellence of institutions of learning in Mamluk Cairo attracted and sustained a large number of well-educated and motivated students and scholars who flocked to the city from all over Egypt as well as from faraway places such as Syria, Anatolia, Iran, Central Asia, India, al-Andalus, West Africa, and the Maghreb.[2] Not unlike our

[1] For an analysis of the growth of Cairo under the Ayyubids and early Mamluks see my *The Citadel of Cairo: A New Interpretation of Royal Mamluk Architecture* (Leiden: E. J. Brill, 1995), esp. 50–89, and 229–43; see also Viktoria Meinecke-Berg, "Quellen zu Topographie und Baugeschichte in Kairo unter Sultan an-Nasir b. Qala'un," *ZDMG*, supplement 3 (1977): 539–50; John Alden Williams, "Urbanization and Monument Construction in Mamluk Cairo," *Muqarnas* 2 (1984): 33–45. On the long-term effect of Mamluk urbanism, see the incisive analysis of Jean-Claude Garcin, "Outsiders in the City," in Behrens-Abouseif, *The Cairo Heritage*, 7–15.

[2] For an analysis of Cairo's education institutions in the Mamluk period, see Jonathan Berkey, *The Transmission of Knowledge in Medieval Cairo: A Social History of Islamic Education* (Princeton: Princeton University Press, 1992), 6–9, 21–43; Carl Petry, "Scholastic Stasis in Medieval Islam Reconsidered: Mamluk Patronage in Cairo," *Poetics Today* 14, 2 (1993): 323–48, especially his summation of the situation on p. 324, quoted in Jo Van Steenbergen, *Caliphate and Kingship in a Fifteenth-century Literary History of Muslim Leadership*

modern-day top-notch university cities, Cairo offered its scholarly émigrés a myriad opportunities. Some came specifically to study with a famous professor who had established his seat of teaching in Cairo. Others hoped to profit from the abundant *waqfs* that supported the livelihood of teachers and students there.[3] Still others were simply lured by the bountiful employment possibilities for all types of academic and religious professionals in well-endowed Mamluk religious institutions as well as in the Mamluk administration, which engaged a sizeable number of ulama in addition to the usual *kuttab* (sing. *katib*, scribe) who received their training at the *diwan al-insha'* (literally the "bureau of composition" or the chancery).[4] Better scholars who had proven their academic mettle publishing and teaching elsewhere were invited to assume prestigious positions in one or more of Cairo's premier madrasas or in one of the four judiciary structures established by the Mamluks to represent the four Sunni *madhahib*. Still others stopped on their way to the Hajj to consult with their peers or to participate in scholarly activities, but found themselves staying in the city for many years, and sometimes for life.[5]

---

and Pilgrimage. A Critical Edition, Annotated Translation, and Study of al-Maqrizi's al-Dhahab al-Masbuk fi Dhikr man Ḥajja min al-Khulafa' wa-l-Muluk (Leiden: Brill, 2016), 19; Petry, "Educational Institutions as Depicted in the Biographical Literature of Mamluk Cairo: The Debate over Prestige and Venue," *Medieval Prosopography* 23 (2002): 101–23. George Makdisi, *The Rise of Humanism in Classical Islam and the Christian West* (Edinburgh: Edinburgh University Press, 1990), passim, presents one of the most thorough discussions of the types of knowledge and kinds of settings available to medieval Islamic "humanists" (to use Makdisi's term).

3 One of the most comprehensive studies of *waqf* in Mamluk Egypt remains Muhammad M. Amin, *Al-Awqaf wa-l-Hayyat al-Ijtima'iyya fi-Misr. 684–923 A.H./ 1250–1517 A.D.* (Cairo: Dar al-Nahda al-'Arabiyya, 1980); see also my "Perception of Architecture in Mamluk Sources," *MSR* 6 (2002): 155–76.

4 The *diwan al-insha'* was an important department in the Mamluk administration. Its role was to produce official documents from letters of appointment to correspondence with foreign rulers. The chancery followed strict protocols that were collected in several chancery manuals that provided instructions, examples, and templates on how to prepare documents, along with copious description of state administration. The head of the chancery was known as the *sahib diwan al-insha'* (director of the chancery) and also as *katib al-sirr* (lit. clerk of secret affairs, or private secretary). An executive position was added to the chancery in the late Bahri period for a high Mamluk officer called the *dawadar* (literally, the inkwell holder), but functioned more like supervisor of state affairs. See Reuven Amitai, "Egypt: 4. Late Medieval (including Syria: Ayyubid, Mamluk)," in *The Encyclopedia of Empire*, 4 vols. 1st edition N. Dalziel and J. M. MacKenzie eds. (London: John Wiley, 2016), 2: 779–86; Anne F. Broadbridge, "Diplomatic Conventions in the Mamluk Sultanate," *AI* 41 (2007): 98–107 for a discussion of Mamluk chancery manuals; Joseph H. Escovitz, "Vocational Patterns of the Scribes of the Mamluk Chancery," *Arabica* 23 (1976): 42–62.

5 Petry, *Civilian Elite*, offers one of the most comprehensive and quantitatively robust studies of medieval Muslim scholars; Jonathan Berkey, "Mamluks and the World of Higher

This created a vigorous intellectual atmosphere in Cairo, the like of which was rarely seen elsewhere in the medieval period. Due primarily to the dynamic Mamluk system of patronage, the city rose to the position of a cultural mecca whose scholarly and literary output in the fourteenth and fifteenth centuries far exceeded the production of any other Islamic metropolis of the time such as Damascus, Tabriz, Delhi, Samarkand, Fez, or Granada. In fact, many of the famous scholars who contributed to building the reputation of these and other Islamic cities as intellectual centers had lived and studied in Cairo for a portion of their lives. The tradition lived on until very recently, albeit on a much reduced scale and in somewhat antiquated fashion, in al-Azhar University. Located in the historic heart of Cairo, al-Azhar became a premier institution of Sunni learning under the Mamluks, was expanded and endowed with several annexed madrasas by them, and was still a choice destination for missionaries and religious scholars from all over the world well into the twentieth century.[6]

This was the milieu in which al-Maqrizi moved, benefiting especially from his maternal grandfather's scholarly and professional status and his network of ulama and officials. He also profited from his father's network in the Mamluk chancery, which consisted of middle-rank administrators and *kuttab* (clerks). Mahmud al-Jalili counted sixteen individuals that al-Maqrizi identified as friends of either his father or grandfather (or both), who stepped in after the passing of both men to help him when he was still an inexperienced adolescent.[7] Some of these friends were entrusted with the financial affairs of the family after the death of its two providers.[8] Others patronized al-Maqrizi as he took his first steps in the Mamluk administration, which he joined in 786/1384 after having tried his hand at a few inconsequential and minor religious posts. His first major patron was the *katib al-sirr* (privy secretary) Muhammad b. ʿAli b. Fadhlallah (d. 1393, of the famous Fadhlallah family of administrators), whose father, the *katib al-sirr* ʿAli b. Yahya, was

---

Education in Medieval Cairo, 1250–1517," in *Modes de transmission de la culture réligieuse en Islam*, Hassan Elboudrari, ed. (Cairo: IFAO, 1993), 93–116.

[6] For an assessment of the rise and continuous importance of al-Azhar, see my study "Al-Azhar Mosque: An Architectural Chronicle of Cairo's History," *Muqarnas* 13 (1996): 45–67.

[7] Al-Jalili, *Durar*, Introduction, 1: 32–3, 37–9. Al-Jalili missed at least one more benefactor who was a friend of al-Maqrizi's father, Fath al-Din Muhammad b. ʿAqil al-ʿAqili al-Qurashi al-Misri, *Durar*, 3: 51.

[8] Al-Maqrizi, *Durar*, 3: 99, in the biography of Taqiy al-Din al-Dajawi al-Shafiʿi, who was the executor of his grandfather's inheritance; idem, *Durar*, 3: 469 mentions, in the biography of the *muhadditha* Maryam b. Ahmad, that she was the sister of Shams al-Din Muhammad, the *khatib* of the Mosque of Amir Shaikho, who was a friend of al-Maqrizi's father and an executor of his grandfather's inheritance as well; idem, *Durar*, 2: 427–8, where al-Maqrizi says that ʿUmar b. ʿAbd al-Muhsin al-ʿAmiri was the executor of the inheritance of al-Maqrizi's father.

the patron of both al-Maqrizi's father and grandfather.[9] Yet, despite his reliance on family contacts, al-Maqrizi displayed a streak of independence when launching his own professional career, a trait that was to both help him maintain his integrity while pursuing patronage in the treacherous environment of the Mamluk administration and to earn him several detractors and enemies among his peers.

Reconstructing the trajectory of al-Maqrizi's career from his first chancery appointment to his withdrawal from the competition game, this chapter examines his religious stance, professional formation, interaction with patrons and peers, intellectual maturation, and disillusionment with the Mamluk system. It then analyzes the background and motivations behind his decision to retreat to his family home and dedicate the rest of his life, almost thirty years, to history writing.

A Question of *Madhhab*

In 786/1384, when he was barely twenty years old, al-Maqrizi decided to switch to the Shafi'i *madhhab* and to abandon both the Hanbali *madhhab* of his forefathers and the Hanafi one of his maternal grandfather, in which he had been formally instructed. Changing his *madhhab*, while not unusual in itself, was not a casual decision. It could be interpreted in two ways, which are not necessarily mutually exclusive. First, it may have been a sign of a self-righteous and individualistic—even, perhaps, a bit rebellious— personality in the making. Changing his *madhhab* may have represented to al-Maqrizi a chance to reject his forebears' teaching and authority, and therefore a liberatory act on the way to self-fulfillment as an independently-minded scholar. He was in fact known later in life for his partiality against, even exaggerated antipathy toward, the Hanafi *madhhab*. Alternatively, the switch may have been a calculated professional move since the Shafi'i *madhhab* was dominant in Egypt. The Hanbali *madhhab* was practically unknown and usually associated with Syrian or Hijazi scholars, while the Hanafi *madhhab* was primarily followed by the Turks.[10] This may indeed be what Ibn Hajar meant when he

[9] Al-Maqrizi, *Durar*, 3: 66–7, provides a laudatory biography of Ibn Fadhlallah.

[10] What makes the switch even more curious is that al-Maqrizi could have benefited from substantial Mamluk patronage had he remained a Hanafi (and a grandson of a famous Hanafi judge), for the late fourteenth century witnessed a movement of conversion from Shafi'ism to Hanafism among the ulama of Egypt prompted by a number of great Mamluk amirs who were staunch promoters of their Hanafi *madhhab*. The most active among these amirs was the famous Yalbugha al-'Umari (d. 1367), who established many positions in the judiciary and madrasa teaching for Hanafis. See Jo Van Steenbergen, "The Amir Yalbughā al-Khāṣṣakī, the Qalāwūnid Sultanate, and the Cultural Matrix of Mamlūk Society: A Reassessment of

commented that "when al-Maqrizi became aware and competent (*tayaqqaza wa nabuha*), he switched to Shafi'ism."[11] The two verbs, both denoting gradual alertness gained with age, may have been chosen by Ibn Hajar to indicate that the young and pragmatic al-Maqrizi consciously planned the switch to secure a career in the Shafi'i-dominated scholarly milieu of Cairo, which he embarked upon shortly after.[12] Al-Maqrizi says nothing about the switch. Ibn Taghri-Birdi, however, claims that he heard him mention a specific incident that prompted it, but refrains from revealing it in the laudatory biography he penned of his master.[13]

A telling detail mentioned by al-Maqrizi's biographers, however, suggests that the reason for the switch to Shafi'ism was more fundamental: al-Maqrizi was embracing a different doctrinal position rather than merely rebelling against the *madhhab* of his grandfather. To that end, the switch may even have been only a first step in the direction of a more conservative exegetical stand than the one proffered by either Shafi'ism or Hanafism. It might in fact have hidden a more decisive move toward espousing the Zahiri *madhhab*, by then an uncommon school of jurisprudence in Egypt.[14] Although unacknowledged by al-Maqrizi, this shift was noted by all his contemporary biographers. His prejudice against the Hanafis, according to Ibn Hajar, al-Sakhawi, Ibn Fahd, and Ibn Taghri-Birdi, was motivated by his leaning toward the Zahiri *madhhab*. While al-Sakhawi and Ibn Fahd echo Ibn Hajar's snide remark that al-Maqrizi "did not know the [Zahiri] *madhhab*,"[15] Ibn Taghri-Birdi is more understanding. He elaborates:

> People ascribed al-Maqrizi to the Zahiri *madhhab*, but only God knows his inner belief, although he exceedingly revered Ibn Hazm al-Andalusi. There is nothing

Mamlūk Politics in the 1360s," *JOAS*, 131, 3 (July–September 2011): 438–41; also Leonor Fernandes, "Mamluk Politics and Education: The Evidence from Two Fourteenth Century Waqfiyya," *AI* 23 (1987): 87–98, esp. 90–5. Al-Maqrizi himself noted this phenomenon and attributed it to the work of Yalbugha, al-Maqrizi, *Khitat2*, 4: 44.

11 Ibn Hajar, *Majma'*, 59.

12 Sayyid, *Musawwadat*, Introduction, 39, favors this interpretation.

13 Ibn Taghri-Birdi, *Manhal*, 1: 394; idem, *Nujum*, 15: 491. The exceedingly long biography that al-Maqrizi penned of Imam al-Shafi'i in his *muqaffa*, 5: 309–419, though incomplete as published and composed mainly of older reports collated from different sources, reveals his unconditional admiration for the Imam.

14 The same happened with the poet Badr al-Din al-Bashtaki (d. 830/1427), who was a Hanafi, switched to Shafi'ism and became a follower of Ibn Hazm's *madhhab* according to al-Maqrizi, *Durar*, 3: 81. Al-Maqrizi says that he "accompanied [al-Bashtaki] for a while," and quotes many samples of his poetry, then he adds in his obituary in *Suluk*, 4: 1599, "May God have mercy on him, I have been distraught by his demise. He has not been succeeded by anyone like him."

15 Al-Sakhawi, *Daw'*, 2: 22, copying his master Ibn Hajar, *Inba'*, 9: 170.

wrong in admiring the writing of Ibn Hazm for he was a *hafiz* [memorizer] and a ʿalim whose learning cannot be denied even if he was a Zahiri.[16]

The Zahiri *madhhab*, founded by Dawud b. ʿAli b. Khalaf al-Isfahani (d. 883) and named after its founder's insistence on admitting only the apparent (*zahir*) meaning of the Qu'ran and hadith, upheld a strict, literalist approach to interpretation and to legal speculation and opposed all other *madhahib*, but especially the Malikis and Hanafis, on basic interpretive issues.[17] The *madhhab* gained a following in Iraq and al-Andalus and was later codified by the Andalusian polymath Ibn Hazm (994–1064), who is considered its second founder, but it never attained the same kind of theological synthesis achieved by other Sunni *madhahib*. Although it never took root in Egypt and Syria, it was alarming enough for the Mamluk ulama to evince an unmistakable enmity toward the adherents of the Zahiri *madhhab*. The fundamentalist challenges it posed to the established theological and jurisprudential *madhabib*s in the past were still felt in fourteenth-century Cairo. Today, the *madhhab* lives only as an intellectual reference or a school of thought favored by a few traditionalist thinkers among the *ahl al-sunna* and *ahl al-hadith*, especially in Saudi Arabia.[18]

Al-Maqrizi himself says nothing about his anti-Hanafi stance. His hostile feelings, however, are discernible in the favorable biographies he writes of Shafiʿis who resisted what they regarded as lax Hanafi legal practices and in the biographies of Hanafi judges suspected of corruption or of currying favor with the rulers.[19] As for his Zahiri leanings, al-Maqrizi is even more ambiguous. He never directly admits his belief in the *madhhab*, even though he reveals a strong Zahiri perspective in his *Khitat*. At the end of a section in which he discusses the various Islamic sects, he unequivocally declares his commitment to a creed that shares with the Zahiri *madhhab* its strict adherence to the literalist reading of the Qur'an and the Hadith.[20] Slightly reworked from Ibn Hazm's *al-Fasl fi al-Milal wa-al-Ahwa' wa-al-Nihal* without any change in its Zahiri

[16] Ibn Taghri-Birdi, *Manhal*, 1: 396; also ibid., 2: 88, where he accuses his revered teacher al-Maqrizi of favoring al-Burhan simply because he was a Zahiri.

[17] On Zahirism, see art. "al-Zahiriyya," by R. Strothmann in *EI*[1], 8: 1192–3; and art. "Dawud b. ʿAli b. Khaalaf," by P. Voorhoeve in *EI*[2], 2: 182–3; and art. "Ibn Hazm," by R. Aenaldez in *EI*[2], 3: 790–9; Ignaz Goldziher, *The Zahiris: Their Doctrine and Their History. A Contribution to the History of Islamic Theology*, Wolfgang Behn, trans. and ed. (Leiden: Brill 1971), 40–62.

[18] Cf. http://www.aldahereyah.net/forums (last accessed August 21, 2009). For an instructive discussion about the Zahiris today and whether they constitute a *madhhab*, see http://www.ahlalhdeeth.com/vb/archive/index.php/t-175688.html (last accessed May 9, 2016).

[19] Al-Maqrizi, *Durar*, 1: 106–9, the biography of Burhan al-Din al-Waʿiz, who faced a Hanafi conspiracy but was saved by the Shafiʿi chief judge.

[20] Al-Maqrizi, *Khitat2*, 4: 449–50. This section is quoted in toto and discussed in Chapter 3.

emphasis, this statement offers the clearest proof of al-Maqrizi's Zahirism despite the doubts of his contemporaries.[21] Furthermore, al-Maqrizi often identifies with well-known Zahiris of the past, such as the famous grammarian Abu Hayyan al-Andalusi (1256–1344), whom he describes as follows: "He was Zahiri in *madhhab*, partial to Abi Muhammad 'Ali ibn Ahmad ibn Sa'id ibn Hazm, leaning toward the *madhhab* of Imam al-Shafi'i, and he revered Taqiyy al-Din Ahmab ibn Taymiyya [the Hanbali controversial scholar of fourteenth-century Damascus] and concurred with his opinion"—a description that could have applied to al-Maqrizi himself.[22] He was also very close to many contemporary Zahiris, or at least to individuals who are identified in the Mamluk sources as Zahiris because of their bias toward the writing of Ibn Hazm or their traditionalist views.[23] Moreover, he is full of praise for them as righteous individuals, "following the true path of Islam," as he says on more than one occasion.[24] He admires their fervent struggle for justice and truth, equanimity, self-restraint, and chastity, as is apparent from the biographical entries on various Zahiris in his *Durar* and *Suluk*.[25] These same qualities characterized the *madhhab*'s codifier Ibn Hazm, whom al-Maqrizi revered, and were ascribed to al-Maqrizi himself later in life, following his withdrawal from the competition for public posts.

But what seems to have truly attracted him to Zahirism was not only the moral rectitude of its founders and followers. Nor was it its theological puritanism, an intellectual stance that had lost most of its potency by the end of the fourteenth century.[26] It was probably what can nowadays be termed the "militant" spirit that some of its last organized groups deployed in the face of the religiously corrupt Mamluk regime. This spirit rose to the

[21] Ibn Hazm, *al-Fasl fi al-Milal wa-al-Ahwa' wa-al-Nihal* 5 vols., Muhammad Ibrahim Nasr and Abdul-Rahman 'Amira, eds. (Beirut: Dar al-Jil, 1996), 2: 274–5.

[22] Al-Maqrizi, *Muqaffa*, 7: 505.

[23] Ibn Taghri-Birdi, *Manhal*, 2: 113, reports that al-Maqrizi said of a Shihab al-Din al-Ashmuni al-Nahawi (1348–1407) "that he was a Zahiri then turned against them," and then al-Maqrizi said "I accompanied him for some years," implying that that was when al-Ashmuni was still a Zahiri; see al-Maqrizi, *Durar*, 1: 365. Al-Maqrizi also reports of Abu Bakr al-Hashimi al-Husayni (d. 815/1412) that he was a Zahiri and a client of Fath Allah *katib al-sirr*, al-Maqrizi's most important patron, *Durar*, 1: 158–60.

[24] See, for example, al-Maqrizi, *Durar*, 1: 149–51, in the biography of his teacher al-'Imad al-Hanbali; idem, *Durar*, 1: 158, in the biography of the Sharif and *muhaddith* Abu Bakr al-Hashimi.

[25] Al-Maqrizi admired moral rectitude wherever he encountered it. See, for instance, his report in *Khitat*, 2: 279–80, where he praises the steadfastness of the Shafi'i judge al-Minawwi, who betrays Zahiri leanings in his discourse, in upholding what he considers right.

[26] See the discussion on the confusion about Zahirism in Mamluk sources in Lutz Wiederhold, "Legal-Religious Elite, Temporal Authority, and the Caliphate in Mamluk Society: Conclusions Drawn from the Examination of a Zahiri Revolt in Damascus," *IJMES* 31, 2 (May 1999): 203–35, esp. 204–6.

surface in the so-called "Zahiri Revolt" of 788/1386, an event that greatly impressed al-Maqrizi (who switched to Shafi'im around the same time), at least if we judge from the glowing image he paints in his *Durar* of its leader, the rather obscure Zahiri shaykh Ahmad ibn Muhammad ibn Isma'il ibn al-Burhan (1353–1406).[27] Ibn al-Burhan foolishly and tenaciously organized this doomed uprising against Sultan Barquq and the Mamluks. He claimed to have had supporters among the Mamluk amirs and the Arab Bedouins of Syria. The uprising failed nonetheless because of a betrayal; three of its organizers were caught and jailed at the Citadel of Damascus awaiting to be sent to Cairo. When Ibn al-Burhan and his co-conspirators were brought in chains in front of Sultan Barquq for questioning, a gripping exchange took place that al-Maqrizi approvingly records in his *Durar*.[28] Sultan Barquq calmly asked about the reasons for the revolt, to which Ibn al-Burhan replied that the Mamluks did not satisfy the strict Islamic prerequisites to rule: they were not descendants of Quraysh, the tribe of the Prophet, and they instituted several un-Islamic practices, chief among them the unlawful levying of tariffs (*mukus*).[29] Barquq, however, was primarily interested in knowing

[27] Al-Maqrizi, *Durar*, 1: 297–303. Al-Maqrizi, *Suluk*, 3, 2: 554, offers a compact report on the revolt, and in *Suluk*, 4, 1: 23 produces a brief obituary of Ibn al-Burhan which carries the same positive assessment; Ibn al-Furat, *Tarikh al-Duwal wa-l-Muluk*, vol. 9, pt. 1, ed. K. Zurayk (Beirut: American University Press, 1936), 7, gives a report on the "Syrian *fuqaha'*," meaning Ibn al-Burhan and company working as chained prisoners in a royal building project for a week, then they were unchained.

[28] Al-Maqrizi, *Durar*, 1: 298–9. He is the only historian to record this exchange.

[29] An interesting comparison could be made with the way a scholar criticized power in premodern China. One well-published case is that of the intellectual Zeng Jing and the Qing emperor Yongzheng (r. 1722–35), turned into a historical novel by Jonathan Spence, *Treason by the Book* (London and New York: Penguin, 2001). Zeng Jing, a failed degree candidate, attempted in October 1728 to incite the Governor-general of Shaanxi-Sichuan to rebellion. He gave a long list of accusations against Yongzheng. This triggered a series of investigations, which captured the attention of Yongzheng, who was eager to make his ascent to the throne seem legitimate. Highly concerned with the implications of the case, Yongzheng pressed his officials to collect all the information they could about the conspirators given up by Zhang, chief among them Zeng, who seemed to be the main plotter. The emperor wanted to understand what had influenced Zeng, where he acquired his ideas and, when his ideas were based on rumors about Yongzheng himself, where the rumors had come from. The investigation, which took several months, involved dozens of arrests, careful examinations of private libraries and the investigative skills of the highest-ranking officials in three of China's provincial capitals. Eventually Yongzheng chose to place primary blame for the anti-Qing discontent on a formerly revered Confucian scholar named Lu Liuliang, already dead. Having so decided, Yongzheng then engaged in a long correspondence with the imprisoned Zeng to convince him that his unfavorable view of Manchu rule was unjustified. A version of the correspondence between the emperor and the would-be traitor, including Zeng's initial accusations and the emperor's rejoinders, was published under the title "Awakening from Delusion" and made mandatory reading throughout the country.

who among the mamluks supported the revolt, so he sent the prisoners to be tortured. After three years of severe imprisonment and forced labor, they were finally released on 8 Rabiʿ al-Awwal/March 7, 1389 (al-Maqrizi records the exact date). Ibn al-Burhan, "impoverished" and "emotionally broken" (أقام على مضض من الحياة وضيق من العيش), maintained his integrity and strong beliefs throughout his imprisonment and questioning by the Sultan and after his release to a life of obscurity up until his death.

Al-Maqrizi's impassioned and detailed description of the "Zahiri Revolt" as he reports it in Ibn al-Burhan's biography substantially differs from other Mamluk historians' reports.[30] His is the only one that goes deep into the exegetical roots of the revolt to justify it rather than just passing them over to speak of the intrigues that led to its failure as does Ibn Qadi Shuhbah, the other main source for the revolt.[31] Furthermore, Ibn Qadi Shuhbah uses the term *fitna* (sedition), a disapproving legal term, to describe the revolt, whereas al-Maqrizi variably calls it *al-daʿwa* (the summoning, like the clandestine *daʿwa* of the ʿAlids or the Ismaʿilis), or the more radical *muharabat muluk al-ʿasr* (fighting the kings of the time). Al-Maqrizi also shows that Ibn al-Burhan had prepared for the revolt for some time, for he states that the latter traveled for two years around Syria trying to convince people to "return to the Word of God and the *sunna* of his Prophet, to obey Quraysh, and to fight the kings of the time who usurped the rule (i.e. the Mamluks)."[32]

Al-Maqrizi seems to have heard the full story of the revolt from Ibn al-Burhan himself, for he speaks of a very intimate relationship with the man and his family and of many sessions spent studying with him and copying his dictations on religious issues. He even states that he copied Ibn al-Burhan's treatise on the conditions of righteous rulership, *Tariq a-Istiqama li-Maʿrifat al-Imama* (The Right Path to Knowing the Imamate), and verified the text with him. This incendiary short treatise was written in Aleppo in 787/1385, probably while Ibn al-Burhan was garnering support for his revolt in Syria.[33]

30 For other historians' reports see Ibn Taghri-Birdi, *Manhal*, 2: 87–9, who says that al-Maqrizi exaggerated in his praise of al-Burhan because he was a Zahiri; Ibn Hajar, *Inbaʾ*, 2: 232–4, where he offers a positive opinion of Ibn al-Burhan's knowledge and states that he attended his funeral with seven other people, the same number reported by al-Maqrizi; Ibn Hajar, *Majmaʿ*, 3: 73–5; al-Sakhawi, *Dawʾ*, 2: 96–8.

31 Ibn Qadi Shuhbah, *Tarikh*, 1: 89–91, 186–9, 269; Wiederhold, "Zahiri Revolt," 209–16, bases his reconstruction of the revolt on Ibn Qadi Shuhbah. It is revealing that al-Maqrizi, unlike Ibn Qadi Shuhbah, never uses the word *fitna* (sedition) in his description.

32 Al-Maqrizi, *Durar*, 1: 297.

33 The treatise was edited and published by ʿAqil Jasim Dahsh and ʿAbd al-Hadi ʿAbd al-Rahman al-Shawi in the *Kufa Studies Center Journal* 1, 55 (2019): 115–76, https://www.iasj.net/iasj/article/176522 (last accessed January 23, 2021). The editors did not know who the author was and ascribed it to a Shiʿite Imam Abi Hashem (which is the real patro-

Written in the form of a discourse, its content, ranting against the infractions of the Mamluk rulers and debunking all excuses for their behavior, was likened to a political manifesto by Walid Saleh, who seems to have been the first to have identified its real author and connected it to the leader of the "Zahiri Revolt."[34]

Ibn al-Burhan must have had a significant effect on al-Maqrizi. In a cryptic sentence in his *Durar* entry on Ibn al-Burhan, al-Maqrizi describes him as "one of three men whom God has graced me with in ways that I hope to be blessed for" (أحد الثلاثة الذين نفعني الله بهم نفعاً أرجو بركته), implying that his gains from Ibn al-Burhan were of the ethical and possibly mystical kind. This sentence may be pointing toward a master–disciple relationship in a *sufi* sense, that is, Ibn al-Burhan leading al-Maqrizi on the way of true knowledge. But it is probably also an admission that Ibn al-Burhan, along with the two other unnamed individuals, offered al-Maqrizi a model of rectitude, which he was consciously trying to follow in his own life. The two other individuals, both Zahiris as well, are identified by al-Maqrizi in the *Durar*. The first is ʻAli b. ʻUmar b. al-Rukn al-Khawarizmi (d. Safar 806/August 1403), a Sufi descendant of a Mamluk soldier in the corps of al-Halaqa who gave up his *iqtaʻ* and left Egypt for Syria after the revolt of Ibn al-Burhan for fear of repercussions. Al-Maqrizi explicitly names him as one of the three who taught him the most.[35] The third may have been Ahmad b. ʻAli al-Qassar (718–800/1318–97), also a Sufi and a Zahiri, whom al-Maqrizi accompanied for many years and learned extensively from, presumably in all manners of asceticism. He quotes al-Qassar describing the ulama of his time as *qutta' tariq* (lit. highway robbers), an indication of al-Maqrizi's awareness of the rapacity that plagued his professional class. Al-Maqrizi also says that when he read the New Testament later in life (presumably after the death of al-Qassar) he discovered that the description

---

nymic of Ibn al-Burhan) as the author was listed in the late manuscript they used (copied in 1157/1744), with the place and date of composition as Aleppo 1385. The editors guessed that the author had concealed his full name because of the radical nature of his treatise's content. The manuscript used by the editors is preserved in the library of Riyadh University under the number 216.9 and is available online at https://ia600207.us.archive.org/12/items/Maktotat_KSU/0296.pdf (last accessed January 23, 2021).

34 Walid Saleh gave several lectures on his discovery and his reading of the treatise in the context of Mamluk political writing under the title "A Rebel and His Treatise: On Revolutionary Religious Language in a Medieval Society," He generously shared the text of his lecture with me. He calls Ibn al-Burhan "a revolutionary activist, an ideologue, and a visionary man." More importantly for this book, Saleh states that "al-Maqrizi was not only writing the biography of a rebel, he was writing the biography of a raped land. The biography of Ibn al-Burhan by al-Maqrizi was a damnation of a system he saw rotten to the bone." This is a perceptive remark that applies to the entire project of history writing of al-Maqrizi.

35 Al-Maqrizi, *Durar*, 2: 471–2. Ibn Hajar, *Inba'*, 5: 178, adds that Ibn al-Khawarizmi read the books of Ibn Hazm and revealed his Zahirism.

is based on a verse in Matthew, 23:13, which recounts the hypocrisy of the teachers of the law and Pharisees, a strong indication that al-Maqrizi not only read the Scriptures but was also able to detect references to them in inferences he heard from his teacher.[36] Thus, al-Maqrizi's reported leaning toward the Zahiris, and Ibn al-Burhan in particular, may have been motivated by his respect for their fortitude as committed individuals and his approval of their firm opposition to the Mamluks on religious grounds as well as his adherence to their religious interpretations.

This observation endows al-Maqrizi's passionate support of the "Zahiri Revolt" with a more pronounced understanding, and obviously appreciation, of its motivations and aims. Though he was not necessarily a fully confirmed Zahiri, he wove the principles of Zahirism, which he obviously knew well, into his complex set of religious beliefs. These beliefs, though not uncommon at the time, may appear somewhat paradoxical to our modern eyes accustomed to a palpable Sunni–Shi'i sectarian division and expecting from the doctors of the law a clear adherence to a specific *madhhab*. First, al-Maqrizi, a pious and strict Shafi'i *'alim*, seems to have harbored strong 'Alid sympathies throughout his life, which in and by itself was not an unusual feeling among members of his ulama class at the time. However, al-Maqrizi's sympathies were on the whole more tangible and vocal, as he expressed them as written statements in many of his treatises and even built historical arguments around them. This is well illustrated by his acceptance of the Imamate of the Fatimids in his *Itti'az al-Hunafa'* where he admitted their claim to be the progeny of the Prophet, not only because he believed them to be his own ancestors. What his defense of the Fatimids hints at, moreover, comes across more clearly in other tractates focusing on the *Al al-Bayt*, especially his *al-Niza' wa al-Takhasum fima Bayn Bani-Umayya wa Bani-Hashim* (Book of Contention and Strife Concerning the Relations between the Umayyads and the Hashimites).[37] In this undated short work, which seems to belong to his early career, al-Maqrizi was trying to make metahistorical sense of the apparent failure of the 'Alids, the Bani Hashim of his title, to keep what was their divinely-ordained birthright, namely the caliphate (and of course the imamate from a Shi'i perspective). After analyzing the circumstances of the conflict between the Umayyads and the Hashimites (both Abbasids, or

[36] Al-Maqrizi, *Durar*, 1: 206–7.

[37] First ed. and trans. in 1888 as al-Maqrizi, *Kitab al-Niza' wa-al-takhasum fi-ma bayna Bani Umayyah wa-Bani Hashim, Kampfe und Streitigkeiten zwischen den Banu Umajja und den Banu Hasim; eine Abhandlung von Takijj ad-Din al-Makrizijj*, ed. Geerhardus Vos (Vienna and Strasbourg, 1888). Several Arabic re-editions followed but they did not add much. For an English translation and commentary, see Clifford Edmund Bosworth, ed. and trans., *al-Maqrizi's 'Book of Contention and Strife Concerning the Relations between the Banu Umayya and the Banu Hashim'* (Manchester: Manchester University Press, 1983).

descendants of the Prophet's uncle al-'Abbas, and 'Alids), he comes down squarely on the side of the 'Alids. He assumes the same stance in other similar treatises where the 'Alids are unambiguously identified as the God-appointed rulers and guides of the Islamic community.[38] This opinion, which al-Maqrizi seems to have steadfastly held throughout his life, might have further animated his passionate support for the "Zahiri Revolt" against Barquq, for the revolt's main demand was the installation of a Qurayshi caliph, though not specifically an 'Alid one, in fulfillment of a strict interpretation of orthodox Islamic tenets.

But it is quite revealing that neither his explicit 'Alid leanings nor his excited verbal empathy with the "Zahiri Revolt" prevented al-Maqrizi from pursuing his career in the religious and administrative branches of the Mamluk regime, a regime which glaringly lacked the legitimacy of a Qurayshi lineage. This implicit contradiction was never picked up on by his biographers, simply because his collaboration with and seeking patronage within the Mamluk system were very ordinary at the time. Almost every other scholar eagerly pursued Mamluk patronage, despite the collectively held intellectual and religious resentment of the Mamluks themselves.[39] What distinguishes al-Maqrizi from the average Sunni *'alim* of his ilk is his anxious and manifest sympathy for militant religious movements, such as the 'Alid cause and the "Zahiri Revolt," aimed at redressing the wrong they perceived at the top of the ruling system in the Islamic world. Never mind that both causes ultimately failed. What matters is that al-Maqrizi, in his reporting and his analysis, displays an honest sense of justice and objection to deviation from the proper Islamic way

[38] On al-Maqrizi's pro-'Alid sympathy see Clifford Edmund Bosworth, "Al-Maqrizi's Epistle 'Concerning What Has Come Down to us About the Banu Umayya and the Banu l-'Abbas,'" in Wadad Kadi, ed., *Studia Arabica and Islamica: Festshrift for Ihsan 'Abbas* (Beirut, 1981), 39–45; idem, "al-Maqrizi's Exposition of the Formative Period in Islamic History and its Cosmic Significance: The *Kitab al-Niza' wa al-Takhasum*," in *Islam: Past Influence and Present Challenge. In Honour of William Montgomery Watt*, A. T. Welsh and P. Cachia, eds. (Edinburgh: Edinburgh University Press, 1979) 93–104. Reprinted in idem, *Medieval Arabic Culture and Administration* (London: Variorum Reprints, 1982) as nos. IX and XI respectively.

[39] On the subject of the ulama's relationship with mamluks, see the two pioneering articles by Ulrich Haarmann, "Arabic in Speech, Turkish in Lineage: Mamluks and their Sons in the Intellectual life of Fourteenth-Century Egypt and Syria," *Journal of Semitic Studies* 33 (1988): 81–114; idem, "Rather the Injustice of the Turks than the Righteousness of the Arabs—Changing 'Ulama' Attitudes Towards Mamluk Rule in the Late Fifteenth-Century," *SI* 68 (1989): 61–79. See also Chamberlain, *Knowledge*, 37–54, 57–113, which discusses the development of these practices among the ulama as a class in thirteenth- to fourteenth-century Damascus. See also my "Representing the Mamluks in Mamluk Historical Writing," in *The Historiography of Islamic Egypt, c. 950–1800*, Hugh Kennedy, ed. (Leiden: E. J. Brill, 2000), 59–75; reprinted in my *Mamluk History Through Architecture: Building, Culture, and Politics in Mamluk Egypt and Syria* (London: I. B. Tauris, 2010), 12–19.

as he saw it. This is not to say that he was personally and explicitly involved in any actual political or socioreligious actions. He obviously was not. Instead, he strictly confined his contention to his writing, most of which is many years subsequent to the events themselves. This is possibly another sign of that same personality trait that he had exhibited earlier against his family's *madhhab*: opportunistic acquiescence on the surface accompanied by quiet, passionate, and indirect resistance; that is, to protest by proxy what he perceived as unjust but did not have the audacity to actively oppose. This trait allowed him to maintain his professional standing at the Mamluk court throughout his early adulthood when he was actively competing for official positions. But it gave way to his true feelings in his writing, where al-Maqrizi expressed his opinions about his contemporaries with tactless bluntness, primarily in his *Durar*, but also in the *Suluk*. He is full of praise for those he considered pious and just and quite unrelentingly judgmental of those he saw as lacking in moral rectitude. That apparently imprudent irreverence caused his student and on-and-off admirer Ibn Taghri-Birdi to bitterly criticize what he rightly perceived as the fickleness of al-Maqrizi in judging Mamluk sultans and amirs, even those who had been his steadfast or occasional benefactors.[40]

Building a Career

With his restless and anxious personality and exacting opinions, al-Maqrizi entered the competitive Mamluk administration around the same time he switched his *madhhab*. He had a meteoric but relatively short public career, which was over when he was still in his prime at around forty-eight years of age. Yet at the beginning of his career the young Taqiyy al-Din was as immersed in the competition for patronage and *manasib* (salaried positions) as any of his peers. He began as a *muwaqqi'* (literally, the "signer" responsible for filling in the titles at the end of official documents) at the *diwan al-insha'* at the Citadel of Cairo, perhaps following the example of his late father, but more probably just because of his father's connections among the *kuttab* class. He first served under the *katib al-sirr* (private secretary of the sultan) Muhammad ibn 'Ali of the famous *kuttab* family of the ibn Fadhl Allah (d. 796/1393), whose father 'Alaa' al-Din Ibn Fadhl Allah had been a *katib al-sirr* before him as well as the patron of both al-Maqrizi's father and his maternal

[40] Ibn Taghri-Birdi, *Nujum*, 11: 290, rebuking al-Maqrizi's negative opinion of Barquq, 13: 151–3, of Faraj ibn Barquq, 13: 171, and of Yalbugha al-Salimi, who was a capricious benefactor of al-Maqrizi's. Ibn Taghri-Birdi refers the reader to his other rebuttals, in Barquq's and Faraj's obituaries, *Nujum*, 14: 109–10, in Tatar's obituary, 14: 198–201, 207, in al-Mu'ayyad's obit, 14: 245, and in Barsbay's, 14: 310–11.

grandfather. Al-Maqrizi does not specify the exact date at which he began working in the chancery.[41] Ibn Fadhl Allah (*the younger*, as it were) served as the *katib al-sirr* twice: first between 769/1367 and 784/1382 and secondly under Sultan Barquq from 786/1385 till his untimely death in 796/1394 with a one-year interruption (792–3/1391). Al-Maqrizi states in his *Durar* that, when Ibn Fadhl Allah was appointed *katib al-sirr* for the second time, he was summoned from his family home to meet the sultan without any warning and that al-Maqrizi, who was present at the house visiting Ibn Fadhl Allah's brother Hamza, accompanied him to the citadel on the 7th of Rajab 786/ January 17, 1385. Al-Maqrizi was not yet twenty at that date. Could that have been the date of his first appointment under Ibn Fadhl Allah? It is difficult to ascertain, especially since al-Maqrizi says in the biography of Fath al-Din al-Sa'di al-Judhami (1338–88) that he went up to the citadel when Fath al-Din was appointed *katib al-sirr* in 784/1382 because he was working at the chancery then and thus was expected to ride in the entourage of the new boss. This may suggest that al-Maqrizi started his career during Ibn Fadhl Allah's first tenure as *katib al-sirr*, most probably not long before the latter's dismissal in Shawwal 784/December 1382, when al-Maqrizi was not yet seventeen years of age. Al-Maqrizi continued to work in the chancery under 'Alaa' al-Din Hamza b. 'Ali (d. 797/1395), the brother of Ibn Fadhl Allah *the younger*, who substituted for his brother in his secretarial position.[42] Al-Maqrizi, who lists among his treatises a book entitled *Khulaṣat al-tibr fī akhbar kuttab al-sirr* on the Egyptian *kuttab al-sirr*, which is unfortunately still lost, praises their days as unequalled and irreplaceable, but does not explicitly compare the two brothers to any other *katib al-sirr*.[43]

The last scions of the Ibn Fadhl Allah family were not the only backers at the highest levels of the administration that al-Maqrizi had at the beginning of his career. He also benefited from the support of Shams al-Din Ibrahim ibn 'Abdallah Katib Arlan (or Arnan), a Coptic convert and an old friend and colleague of al-Maqrizi's father who served as vizier under Sultan Barquq from 1383 until his death in 1387. Al-Maqrizi does not report a clientage relationship with Katib Arlan similar to the one he had with the two Ibn Fadhl Allahs. He only states that he used to visit him frequently and that the vizier used to take care of him, but he does not specify in what capacity or to what end.[44] The vizier, by most opinions, was one of the best viziers in that troubled

[41] Al-Maqrizi, *Khitat1*, 2: 225; *Durar*, 3: 67.

[42] Al-Maqrizi, *Durar*, 2: 49.

[43] Al-Maqrizi, *Khitat2*, 3: 204. On the date of that book, see Frédéric Bauden, "Maqriziana XIII: An Exchange of Correspondence between al-Maqrīzī and al-Qalqashandī," in *Developing Perspectives in Mamluk History: Essays in Honor of Amalia Levanoni*, Yuval Ben-Bassat, ed. (Leiden: Brill, 2017), 216–17 and notes.

[44] Ibid., 1: 105–6. Other biographical notices for Katib Arlan are in al-Maqrizi, *Suluk*, 3: 312;

period: austere, principled, honest, and devoted to his work. Al-Maqrizi, who gives a detailed account of Katib Arlan's career under Barquq, is full of praise for him, although he notes at the end that the vizier was reputed to have kept to his Christian faith in private, an accusation that is occasionally leveled in Mamluk chronicles at Coptic *kuttab* who were sometimes forced to convert in order to keep their high positions but would remain suspect as to their adherence to their new faith.[45] Al-Maqrizi, probably not wanting to come across as supporting the allegation, attributes it to someone "who knew the private life of the vizier," ending his report with a revealing comment, "*khafafa Allahu ʿanhu* [May God lighten his (punishment)]."[46] This indicates that al-Maqrizi believed the charge against Katib Arlan, as Christians in the traditional Islamic belief cannot attain total salvation and will therefore have to endure punishment in the hereafter, but he nonetheless thought well enough of the vizier to ask for God's mercy on him.

We do not know when al-Maqrizi left the chancery. Mahmoud al-Jalili asserts in his notes that al-Maqrizi continued to work with the *kuttab al-sirr* throughout his career, which al-Jalili estimates to have spanned fifty years of intermittent employment.[47] His evidence is that al-Maqrizi was a companion to many of the *kuttab al-sirr* of his time, beginning with the two Ibn Fadhl Allahs, then Fath Allah al-Tabrizi, followed by Badr al-Din ibn Muzhir, and finally the two members of al-Barizi family, Nasir al-Din and his son Kamal al-Din, who succeeded one another in the *kitabat al-sirr* from 815 to 856, with the latter of them dying more than fourteen years after al-Maqrizi's death.[48] Al-Maqrizi, while reporting on his close connections with all these *kuttab al-sirr*, and sometimes stating that he benefited from them, never says that he

Ibn Hajar, *Inbaʾ*, 1: 338–9; Ibn Taghri-Birdi, *Manhal*, 1: 74–6; Ibn Qadi Shuhba, *Tarikh*, 1: 224–5.

[45] Donald P. Little, "Coptic Conversion to Islam under the Bahrī Mamlūks, 692–755/1293–1354," *BSOAS* 39 (1976): 555; see also Donald Richards, "The Coptic Bureaucracy under the Mamluks," *Colloque International sur l'histoire du Caire, 27 mars–5 avril 1969* (Cairo: Ministry of Culture, 1972), 373–81. Tamer el-Leithy "Coptic Culture and Conversion in Medieval Cairo, 1293–1524 A.D.," PhD. diss., Princeton University, 2005, is still unpublished. It explores the patterns of conversion among the Coptic *kuttab* during the Mamluk period; Shaun O'Sullivan, "Coptic Conversion and the Islamization of Egypt," *MSR* 10, 2 (2006): 65–79, reviews the evidence about conversion in Egypt in general and adds interesting factors to explain its history, but does not deal with the conversion of Coptic *kuttab* per se.

[46] Al-Maqrizi, *Durar*, 1: 106.

[47] Al-Maqrizi, *Durar*, Jalili's notes, 4: 43–52, esp. 51–2.

[48] See Al-Maqrizi, *Durar*, 3: 115–17 for Nasir al-Din, about whom al-Maqrizi says that he accompanied him for many years and benefited a lot from him. See ibid., 3: 247–8 for the incomplete biography of the son Kamal al-Din, who outlived al-Maqrizi, and whose biography is amended on the margin of the manuscript, possibly by the copyist.

worked with any of them. In fact, we could infer from al-Maqrizi's notes on all these high officials that they were close to him as both friends and patrons, some more so than others, that they might have helped him or assigned him a few tasks, but that he did not work under their supervision in the chancery. Thus, al-Maqrizi most probably left the chancery for unknown reasons after the death of his last chief there, 'Alaa' al-Din Hamza Ibn Fadhl Allah, in 797/1395, as he does not mention working there after that date. But he remained active in the circles of patronage in the Mamluk court and was cultivating connections with high officials and amirs, and possibly with Sultan Barquq himself, in the pursuit of higher positions in the administration or the religious sector. His efforts were soon to splendidly succeed, at least for a short while. After a momentary lull between 1395 and 1399, during which we do not know how al-Maqrizi was earning his living, he suddenly became the *muhtasib* (usually translated as "market supervisor") of Cairo on Rajab 11, 801/March 19, 1399, at the relatively young age of thirty-five, only months before Sultan al-Zahir Barquq's death (Shawwal 15, 801/June 20, 1399).[49]

Quest for Patrons

The attainment of such a coveted post as the *muhtasib*, who effectively supervised adherence to the religiously-sanctioned civic rules in the city, must have been the culmination of years of maneuvering and clientage to a number of influential individuals in the Mamluk ruling class. But we know little about it. In addition to his connections in the chancery, which seem to have remained strong after he left it, al-Maqrizi befriended a few of the highest-ranking amirs and administrators, one or more of whom apparently introduced him to Sultan Barquq. He describes these relationships in his *Durar*, and more succinctly in the chronicles of his *Suluk*, in a rather neutral and sometime haughtily judgmental language. He also briefly reports on how he met each of them and what he gained from his relationship with them in general terms, never connecting any one individual to any particular service. This quest for patrons was not unique to al-Maqrizi: most chroniclers who occupied high positions in the Mamluk administration had to maintain an obsequious

[49] Al-Maqrizi, *Suluk*, 3, 3: 969; Ibn Hajar, *Inba'*, 2: 43, 54; Ibn Taghri-Birdi, *Nujum*, 5: 592, 6: 32; Jere Bacharach, "Circassian Mamluk Historians and the Quantitative Economic Data," *JARCE* 12 (1975): 77; Ahmad 'Abd al-Raziq, "La hisba et le muhtasib en Égypte au temps des Mamluks," *AI* 13 (1977): 148–53; Allouche, *Mamluk Economics*, 3–4. On the development of the office of *hisba* in the Mamluk period, see Jonathan Berkey, "The *muḥtasib*s of Cairo under the Mamluks: Toward an Understanding of an Islamic Institution," in *The Mamluks in Egyptian and Syrian Politics and Society*, Michael Winter and Amalia Levanoni, eds. (Leiden: Brill, 2004), 254–5.

clientage to their Mamluk patrons even though they seem to have felt superior to them as religious scholars and, at the same time, feared their change of heart or their wrath, which could be extremely humiliating and even at times deadly.[50] What distinguishes al-Maqrizi from his peers is the candor with which he criticizes the amirs he knew in his *Durar*, and, later on in the last volume of his *Suluk*, the vehemence, with something of a bitter taste, that he directs at the sultans who ruled during his adult life.[51] Al-Maqrizi, in fact, more than any other contemporary biographers such as Ibn Hajar and al-Sakhawi, uses adherence to the tenets of Islamic law as the litmus test in his judgment of those amirs and sultans, irrespective of how much they might have benefited him. [52] The moral contradiction inherent in al-Maqrizi's seeking the protection of the same amirs as those he verbally castigated was not lost on him or on his biographers, who sometime took him to task for it. It was also to trouble him long enough before he finally decided to quit the race for positions, abandon caution in his writing, and unleash his direct and unrestrained criticism on the Mamluks, as we will see.

Almost all the important amirs who supported al-Maqrizi belonged to the two reigns of Barquq and his son Faraj b. Barquq, spanning the years 1382 to 1411, which are the years in which al-Maqrizi was active in the competition for *manasib*.[53] They all occupied pivotal positions at court at one point or another during that long period, although they almost all died a violent death, a fate not uncommon for ambitious Mamluk amirs. Sudun al-Fakhri al-Shaykhuni (d. 798/1396), who reached the high position of vicegerent (*na'ib al-saltana*) under Barquq, is the only one among them who died of old age at his home in Cairo after he had resigned his position and returned his *iqta'* to the state treasure.[54] Al-Maqrizi states that he befriended him and praises his piety, chastity, and observance of Islamic requirements. He even ascribes to his good influence the moral restraint that Sultan Barquq exhibited at the beginning of his reign and which he dropped after the death of Sudun. But al-Maqrizi does not mention any services rendered by the amir to him. He also notes the amir's simplemindedness, which other commentators emphasized

50 Haarmann, "Rather the Injustice," 61–77; Rabbat, "Representing the Mamluks in Mamluk Historical Writing," 66–72.

51 Donald Little, "A Comparison of al-Maqrizi and al-'Ayni as Historians of Contemporary Events," *MSR* 7, 2 (2003): 205–15.

52 Compare, for instance, the biographies of Sudun al-Fakhri and Yalbugha al-Salimi in al-Maqrizi's *Durar* and *Suluk* with Ibn Hajar's *Inba'*, and al-Sakahwi's *Daw'*, below.

53 Van Steenbergen, *Caliphate and Kingship*, 1, 1: 21–5, sees in al-Maqrizi's inability to adjust to deep changes in the state's structure after Faraj and to attract new patrons another reason for his ultimate withdrawal in despair.

54 For his biography, see al-Maqrizi, *Durar*, 2: 100–1; Ibn Hajar, *Inba'*, 3: 303; Ibn Taghri-Birdi, *Nujum*: 12: 151.

more strongly than he does, and which prompted a satirist, Ibn Makanis, to compose a parody on him. Amir Yalbugha al-Salimi (d. 811/1408), who occupied various high posts under Sultan Faraj b. Barquq, was sent to prison in Damietta and Alexandria three times during his bumpy career, and was strangled in his cell at the age of thirty-seven. Al-Maqrizi says that he accompanied Yalbugha at home and in travel and that the amir venerated him. But he omits any specific mention of patronage.[55] Sudun al-Zahiri (d. 803/1401), *amir akhur* under Barquq and the governor of Damascus in the early days of Faraj, died under torture in Damascus after Tamerlane had arrested him in Aleppo.[56] Al-Maqrizi, who notes the amir's reputation for violent reaction and ruthlessness, says that he accompanied him for a while without having to experience any improper behavior from him. He hints, however, that Sudun, "with the help of God," provided him with favors and authority, perhaps implying help in acquiring a *mansib*, but he does not elaborate further. Yashbak al-Sha'bani *al-atabiki* was a clever power broker during the reigns of both Barquq and his son Faraj until he sided with the wrong faction in 810/1407 and lost his life in the adventure.[57] Al-Maqrizi may have met him through his master Ibn Khaldun, who was close to the amir, and, if we are to believe al-Sakhawi, became so close to him so that the amir entrusted him with some of his gold when he was anticipating arrest and confiscation. Al-Maqrizi, however, does not mention any connection to Yashbak in either his *Durar* or his *Suluk*. This casts some doubt on al-Sakhawi's report, given how malicious he can be, especially apropos al-Maqrizi, and the fact that

[55] For his biography, see al-Maqrizi, *Durar*, 3: 543–9, where he praises his piety, knowledge of Islamic sciences, and, especially, his resolution and dedication; Ibn Hajar, *Inba'*, 6: 133; Ibn Taghri-Birdi, *Nujum*: 13: 171; al-Sakhawi, *Daw'*, 10: 289. He is remembered as the amir who built the minaret and the *mihrab* in the Fatimid al-Aqmar Mosque in 1397, see Doris Behrens-Abouseif, "The Façade of the Aqmar Mosque in the Context of Fatimid Ceremonial," *Muqarnas* 9 (1992): 29–38. He also tried to stabilize the fiscal policy of the sultanate and to counter the spread of the Venetian ducats in the markets of Cairo by striking a new Dinar in 803/1401, which became known as al-Dinar al-Salimi, and which was withdrawn from circulation after his assassination, see Jere L. Bacharach, "The Dinar Versus the Ducat," *IJMES*, 4 (1973): 77–96, p. 85. Hasebe Fumihiko wrote at least two articles in Japanese on the career of Yalbugha al-Salimi that are unfortunately not accessible to me, "Yalbugha al-Salimi—Koki Mamluk-cho ustadar no shogai (1)" (The Career of Yalbugha al-Salimi al-Ustadar [1]), *Keio Gijuku Daigaku Gengo Bunka Kenkyujo Kiyo* (*Reports of the Keio Institute of Cultural and Linguistic Studies*) 33 (2001): 147–59; "Yalbugha al-Salimi al-Ustadar no shogai (2)" (The Career of Yalbugha al-Salimi al-Ustadar [2]), *Keio Gijuku Daigaku Gengo Bunka Kenkyujo Kiyo* (*Reports of the Keio Institute of Cultural and Linguistic Studies*) 35 (2003): 133–45.

[56] For his biography see al-Maqrizi, *Durar*, 2: 101–3; idem, *Suluk*, 3: 1072; al-Sakhawi, *Daw'*, 3: 285.

[57] For his biography see al-Sakhawi, *Daw'*, 10: 278–9; Ibn Taghri-Birdi, *Manhal*, 4: 313–19; Broadbridge, "Academic Rivalry," 88.

al-Maqrizi usually reveals his patrons among the Mamluk amirs, even those of whom he disapproves.[58] The last important amir was Shaykh al-Safawi *amir majlis*, a rather little-known but influential amir, well-educated and conversant in various scholarly and artistic pursuits.[59] He appears as patron to many young and promising ulama in late fourteenth-century Cairo, including al-Maqrizi. He is depicted as a bon-vivant with a pronounced taste for pederasty, singing, music, and comedies (*masakhir*), all of which may have contributed to his demise and ultimate death in prison. His specific service to al-Maqrizi remains unclear.[60] The only amir al-Maqrizi reports meeting after he had quit the competition for *manasib* and retired to his home is Amir Janibek al-Ashrafi (d. 831/1428), the *dawadar* ("inkwell holder," the amir who manages state affairs) of Sultan Barsbay.[61] Al-Maqrizi met him during his pilgrimage in 825/1422 and preached to him repeatedly, presumably against the abuses of power and in favor of a stricter adherence to the tenets of Islam. The amir, according to al-Maqrizi, wanted to meet with him in Cairo, but the latter avoided this because of his dislike of Janibek, a feeling that he expressed toward almost all Mamluk grandees after his withdrawal from public life. In this avoidance of the amir's entreaty to meet, the reader can sense that al-Maqrizi is no longer willing to run after patronage whenever the opportunity presents itself, even though he clearly has not categorically renounced the practice if the potential patron was to his liking.

At the beginning of his career, al-Maqrizi was thus eager to cultivate as many contacts with power brokers at court as possible with little manifest concern for their moral corruption, which he nonetheless sometime reported. He seems, however, to have depended primarily on individuals in the chancery who were friends of his father and/or maternal grandfather. This is

58 Al-Sakhawi, *Daw'*, 2: 22; Ibn Taghri-Birdi, who offers an elaborate obituary of Yashbak, does not mention any relationship between the amir and al-Maqrizi, which weakens al-Sakhawi's allegation.

59 For Shaykh al-Safawi, see al-Maqrizi, *Durar*, 2: 124–5, which offers an incomplete biography that starts with a sentence implying a text preceding it and covers only the last few months of the amir's life; Ibn Taghri-Birdi, *Manhal*, 6: 312–14; idem, *Nujum*, 13: 8; al-Sakhawi, *Daw'*, 3: 308.

60 Al-Maqrizi, *Durar*, 1: 247–8, the biography of Ahmad Saru Sayyidina, a Turkish ascetic close to many amirs, including Shaykh al-Safawi, who introduced him to al-Maqrizi. The conversations al-Maqrizi has with him reveal that al-Maqrizi's information about the amir comes through Ahmad Saru, not directly from the amir. This may be because al-Maqrizi did not speak Turkish or may be an indication that he was not so close to the amir after all.

61 For his biography, see al-Maqrizi, *Durar*, 1: 571–2; Ibn Hajar, *Inba'*, 8: 153; al-Sakhawi, *Daw'*, 3: 54. Another amir whom al-Maqrizi seems to have continued to see until his death is Baktimur al-Sa'di (d. 831/1428), about whom he says only good things and adds that he learned from him how Faraj ibn Barquq was killed because he was his companion, *Durar*, 1: 488.

how he met Amir Shaykh al-Safawi relatively early in his ascendancy in the *manasib*. He was presented to him by an otherwise little-known Hanafi *faqih* of *awlad al-nas* background, Ahmad ibn Kundughdi, who had been the son of a close friend of al-Maqrizi's father and a friend of al-Maqrizi himself.[62] But Ibn Kundughdi, who was very well-connected at the court of Barquq, may have played a more important role in al-Maqrizi's career than just having introduced him to an amir. Al-Maqrizi and Ibn Hajar both tell us that Ibn Kundughdi had become a *nadim* of Barquq at the end of the sultan's life, to the point where he used to sleep in his palace, probably on account of his Mamluk origin. Ibn Kundughdi may have reached that standing thanks to the same Shaykh al-Safawi, as noted by al-ʿAyni, who was himself a client of the same amir.[63] Ibn Kundughdi thus had unrestricted access to Barquq and was likely al-Maqrizi's conduit to the sultan as well, although al-Maqrizi is silent on this subject. In fact, al-Maqrizi reports that Barquq turned against Ibn Kundughdi just before his death. He also adds that Ibn Kundughdi was accused of having given the sultan permission to drink wine (*nabidh*) in accordance with his Hanafi *madhhab* (a clear jab at the *madhhab* he was accused of disparaging). Al-Maqrizi says that he confronted Ibn Kundughdi with the allegation and that the latter did not deny it. Nonetheless, al-Maqrizi ends his short biography by stating that Ibn Kundughdi was one of the most intelligent and honorable people. Still, his indignation at the allowance of *nabidh* is credible, of course: al-Maqrizi always displays this kind of probity vis-à-vis any violation of Islamic law, even though his resentment in this instance is directed at the facilitator not the actual offender (i.e. the sultan). In this, there might be a tinge of residual competitiveness with Ibn Kundughdi, who actually snatched a royal mission from al-Maqrizi years later during the reign of Faraj b. Barquq, as well as a certain meekness, for, according to Ibn Taghri Birdi, al-Maqrizi himself achieved the same status of *nadim* to Barquq toward the end of the sultan's life.[64] This might have been the prelude to acquiring the *mansib* of *muhtasib*, which is usually assigned by the sultan. The circumstances of al-Maqrizi's life support such an inference, for it is at that point in time that he acquired Soul, the slave girl educated in the house of Barquq, as his concubine, probably as a gift from the sultan to his *nadim*. Al-Maqrizi himself says nothing about his relationship to Barquq, although his unusually high opinion of the sultan, in most instances but not in the obituary he wrote of him, may imply deferential treatment based on a clientage

[62] For his biography, see al-Maqrizi, *Durar*, 1: 328–9; Ibn Hajar, *Inbaʾ*, 5: 227–8; idem, *Majmaʿ*, 3: 64; Ibn Taghri-Birdi, *Manhal*, 2: 64–5; al-Sakhawi, *Dawʾ*, 2: 64–5; Ibn al-ʿImad al-Hanbali, *Shadharat*, 7: 61–2, who copies al-Maqrizi.

[63] Al-Sakhawi, *Dawʾ*, 2: 65 and Ibn Taghri-Birdi, *Manhal*, 6: 314 both quote al-ʿAyni, who says that he had summarized two books for the amir, one in *fiqh* and the other in dogma (*ʿaqida*).

[64] Ibn Taghri-Birdi, *Nujum*, 14: 270, 15: 89.

connection. Other biographers of al-Maqrizi only state that he had been in the entourage of Barquq and later of his son Faraj, but in what capacity, they do not specify.[65]

The most capable and lasting of al-Maqrizi's patrons appears to have been the *katib al-sirr* of both sultans Barquq and Faraj, Fath Allah b. Mu'tasim Fath al-Din al-Isra'ili al-Dawoodi al-Tabrizi (759/1358–5 Rabi' al-Awal 816/ June 5, 1413), whose influence at court had risen just before the time al-Maqrizi was appointed to the *hisba*.[66] Fath Allah, who hailed from a wealthy Jewish family from Tabriz, Iran, came to Cairo as a young boy with his father and sister to join his physician grandfather Nafis and uncle Badi', who were both key physicians in the Mamluk capital. The grandfather and his two sons had come to Cairo in 754/1354, where the grandfather later converted to Islam at the hands of Sultan Hasan b. al-Nasir Muhammad and became his physician. Mu'tasim, instead, returned to Tabriz for a while, where his son Fath Allah was born, before coming back to Cairo with his family. In Cairo, Fath Allah followed in the footsteps of his grandfather and uncle and became a physician of note and a *faqih* in the Hanafi *madhabb*. There, he met Amir Shaykh al-Safawi at the house of the latter's former Mamluk master, Baybugha al-Sabiqi. But when Amir Shaykh moved to the service of Sultan Barquq, he took Fath Allah under his patronage and married him to his mother (a rare occurrence in the Mamluk context, where mamluks are supposed to have no family members from back home).[67] Equipped with this recent Mamluk kinship and his talent both as a physician and as a shrewd advisor, Fath Allah soon landed the positions of personal physician of the sultan and head of physicians (*ra'is al-atibba'*) in Cairo after the death of his uncle Badi' ibn Nafis. Shortly afterwards, he was named *katib al-sirr* on 10 Jumada I, 801/January 18, 1399, two months before al-Maqrizi's own appointment to the *hisba*. He remained in that position for the next fourteen years, weathering the transition from Barquq's reign to his son Faraj's with one painful and testing interruption in 808/1405. He returned to the position after that interruption and retained it against all odds until the end of Faraj's chaotic reign and his assassination in Muharram 814/May 1411. But, after a triumphant beginning under al-Mu'ayyad Shaykh as a sort of *éminence grise* who helped plot the removal and elimination of Faraj and the dismissal of the Abbasid Caliph al-Musta'in Billah from his short-lived interim sultanate, he was unexpectedly

[65] Ibn Fahd, *Mu'jam*, 63; Ibn Hajar, *Inba'*, 2: 43, 54; al-Sakhawi, *Daw'*, 2: 22.

[66] For Fath Allah's career dates, see Bernadette Martel-Thoumian, *Les civils et l'administration dans l'état militaire Mamluk. IXe/XVe siècle* (Damascus: IFEAD, 1991), 451.

[67] For the biography of Fath Allah, see al-Maqrizi, *Durar*, 3: 8–16; idem, *Khitat*, 2: 62–3; Ibn Hajar, *Inba'*, 7: 137–9; idem, *Dhayl al-Durar al-Kamina*, 231–2; al-Sakhawi, *Daw'*, 6: 165–6; Doris Behrens-Abouseif, *Fath Allah and Abu Zakariyya: Physicians under the Mamluks*, Supplement aux *AI*; cahier no. 10 (Cairo: IFAO, 1987), 20–1.

imprisoned, tortured repeatedly, and later executed on 5 Rabiʿ al-Awwal 816/ June 5, 1413.

It is probably through his son-in-law Shaykh al-Safawi that Fath Allah met and befriended al-Maqrizi, who states in his *Durar* that he had accompanied him for more than thirty years, apparently even when Fath Allah was traveling.[68] This statement locates the beginning of the relationship between the two men at the beginning of al-Maqrizi's career in the 1380s. Although al-Maqrizi never specifies the nature of the relationship, the contexts in which Fath Allah's name pops up in the *Durar* and *Suluk* suggest an intimate and close connection of mutual respect and even a camaraderie between the two men, and apparently a clientage on al-Maqrizi's part. Al-ʿAyni, however, implies a different kind of association between the two men, which is not altogether complimentary to al-Maqrizi. He disparagingly brands al-Maqrizi as one of Fath Allah's clients and his private diviner and geomancer, an accusation that echoes al-Sakhawi's claim about a similar connection between al-Maqrizi and Ibn Khaldun, which, despite the rancor that motivated it, may reflect a true pattern in al-Maqrizi's relationships with his patrons/friends.[69]

The *Hisba* Saga

Among all the powerful patrons who may have supported al-Maqrizi at one point or another in his career, only Yashbak al-Shaʿbani and Fath Allah were secure enough in their positions in 1399 to have been capable of helping him obtain the *hisba*. The others were in no position themselves to promote him at court. Shaykh al-Safawi, who might have been the first to bring al-Maqrizi to the attention of the sultan, languished in prison at Marqab in Syria before he died there in Rabiʿ II 801/December 1398.[70] Ahmad ibn Kundughdi, according to al-Maqrizi, was banned from court toward the end of Barquq's reign because of his perceived transgression, although he

[68] Al-Maqrizi, *Durar*, 3: 15, quoted in Fath Allah's biography by Ibn Hajar, *Inba'*, 7: 138–9, Ibn Taghri-Birdi, *Manhal*, 4: 315–16, and al-Sakhawi, *Daw'*, 6: 165, who copies Ibn Hajar verbatim. Ibn Hajar, *Inba'*, 7: 99, speaks of a certain Musa ibn Saʿid al-Misri, who was a client of Fath Allah and who gained a few posts in Damascus because of that relationship. Musa is also identified as a fellow of al-Maqrizi's, probably in the entourage of Fath Allah.

[69] Al-ʿAyni, *ʿIqd*, 28; al-Sakhawi, *Daw'*, 2: 24. Al-Maqrizi never directly claims to be a geomancer, but he shows an inordinate interest in the practice, even though his factual information has been considered weak and sometimes invented, see Gardiner, "Esotericism in a Manuscript Culture," 241–61. He occasionally shows his knowledge in astrology, as when he explained to Amin al-Din al-Humsi al-Ansari the astrological meaning of a relief the latter saw on the gate of Palmyra that had an eagle holding a crab with ten legs (which does not seem to have survived), *Durar*, 3: 74.

[70] Ibn Taghri-Birdi, *Manhal*, 6: 312–14; al-Sakhawi, *Daw'*, 3: 308.

was brought back in during Faraj's reign, which may throw some doubt on al-Maqrizi's report and leave Ibn Kundughdi as the possible conduit to the sultan.[71] Ibn Khaldun, who could have played a role as a recommender at least, was also relatively remote from court when al-Maqrizi received his appointment. In fact, both al-Maqrizi and Ibn Khaldun might have enjoyed the support of the same patron, for Ibn Khaldun himself was reassigned to the post of chief Maliki judge on 15 Ramadan 801/May 21, 1399, two months after al-Maqrizi's appointment.[72] It is even possible that al-Maqrizi himself was the cause of Ibn Khaldun's return to the chief judgeship, perhaps as a reciprocation of his teacher's previous courtesy. If Ibn Taghri Birdi's assertion that al-Maqrizi had become a *nadim* to Sultan Barquq is true, then he was indeed in a position to put in a good word for his revered master, although Ibn Khaldun was famously too haughty to have acknowledged such a service.

Al-Maqrizi was displaced from the *hisba* on 1 Dhu al-Hijja, 801/August 4, 1399, less than two months after the death of Barquq, which entailed a total reconfiguration of the power structure according to the pattern of the time. Al-Maqrizi's replacement was his would-be nemesis Badr al-Din al-ʿAyni (1360–1451), who enjoyed the patronage of a troika of influential amirs. One of them, Jakam, had become a commanding figure in the early days of Barquq's son and successor, Faraj, and was decidedly the one who promoted al-ʿAyni to the *hisba* post.[73] Al-Maqrizi, however, did not disappear from the scene. He quickly readjusted his standing at the court of Faraj ibn Barquq, and returned to the position of *muhtasib* twice for very short intervals in the next five years, although he is very reticent about mentioning them in his writing. The first was between Jamada I and Shaʿban 802/January and April 1400, when he dislodged al-ʿAyni, who did not let the event pass without firing a snide remark against his rival.[74] Al-Maqrizi then lost the position to a certain Jamal al-Din al-Tanbadi, a regular in the position of *hisba* who paid for it according

[71] Al-Maqrizi, *Durar*, 2: 107. The transgression is that he gave Barquq a Hanafi legal opinion allowing the drinking of *nabidh* (wine or unfermented grape juice?), which is obviously forbidden by all *madhahib*, for *nabidh*, see Ibn Manzur, *Lisan al-ʿArab*, 5: 48. We obviously see here another sign of al-Maqrizi's disdain for Hanafi *fiqh*.

[72] Al-Maqrizi, *Durar*, 2: 396–7. It is interesting to note that al-Maqrizi says that Ibn Khaldun came back to his chief judgeship without any help. In 807/1405, they were appointed within two months of each other, Ibn Khaldun first in 11 Shaʿban/12 February, and al-Maqrizi in 22 Shawwal/April 23. They lost their positions within five days of one another, al-Maqrizi on the 21 Dhu al-Qiʿda/May 21 and Ibn Khaldun on 26 Dhu al-Qiʿda/26 May, see al-Jawhari, *Nuzhat*, 2: 200–1.

[73] Al-Maqrizi, *Suluk*, 3: 970; Ibn Taghri-Birdi, *Nujum*, 15: 287; al-Jawhari, *Nuzhat*, 2: 20; al-Sakhawi, *Daw'*, 10: 132; Broadbridge, "Academic Rivalry," 90.

[74] Al-Maqrizi, *Suluk*, 3: 999; al-Jawhari, *Nuzhat*, 2: 45–6, 57; ʿAbd al-Raziq, "Hisba," 131–2, 149–50.

to al-Maqrizi, which was not a rare occurrence.[75] The last tenure of *hisba* for al-Maqrizi was for less than a month, between Shawwal and Dhu al-Qiʿda 807/April and May 1405, when he came back to the post, apparently against his volition and after he had excused himself in front of the sultan three times, "to no avail" as he puts it.[76] He suffered during that brief tenure, because of the continuous struggle between the young sultan and his supporters in Cairo on the one hand and the three major amirs, Jakam, Yashbak, and Shaykh al-Mahmudi, who had divided Syria among them, on the other. This led to further monetary muddling, aggravated by Amir Yalbugha al-Salimi's ostensible regulatory reforms, and financial abuse, aimed at collecting funds for a punitive campaign against the rebellious amirs, in which al-Maqrizi was forced to participate. We do not know how he finally managed to leave his position, for he fails to report the date of his dismissal in his *Suluk*, noted by other historians, despite reporting the dismissal of Ibn Khaldun five days later.[77]

That al-Maqrizi and Ibn Khaldun were appointed to their respective positions of *muhtasib* and Maliki chief judge twice within a few days of each other (in 1399 and 1405) and dismissed in the same week may have been a coincidence. But it may also indicate that the two men belonged to the same faction or "community of interest" at court since their fates there rose and fell together. They may have benefited from the patronage of the same amir, or more than one amir, with Fath Allah as a possible constant supporter, although we have no indication that Fath Allah and Ibn Khaldun had any particular relationship.

Muhtasib was to be al-Maqrizi's last real administrative position, except for an unverifiable political assignment that never materialized and a number of shorter, mostly religious, appointments later. Al-Maqrizi says in passing that he was nominated by Sultan Faraj in 807/1404 for an embassy to Timur (Tamerlane), but the embassy went instead to one of his earlier patrons, and by then probably competitor, Ahmad ibn Kundughdi, who actually died in Aleppo before reaching Timur in Rabiʿ al-Awwal 807/September 1404.[78] Otherwise, al-Maqrizi seems to have drifted through a succession of minor jobs in the teaching circuit of Cairo's mosques and madrasas in the early 1400s.[79]

75 Al-Maqrizi, *Suluk*, 3: 1013.

76 Ibid., 3: 1155; Ibn Qadi Shuhbah, *Tarikh*, 3: 414.

77 Al-Maqrizi, *Suluk*, 3: 1157; Ibn Qadi Shuhbah, *Tarikh*, 3: 416 and al-Jawhari, *Nuzhat*, 2: 201, report the date of al-Maqrizi's removal.

78 Al-Maqrizi, *Durar*, 1: 329; ʿIzz al-Din, *al-Maqrizi wa-Kitabuhu*, 2: 379; other biographers of Ibn Kundughdi, who report the story of his incomplete embassy, do not mention al-Maqrizi's nomination, except for Ibn Taghri-Birdi, *Manhal*, 2: 64–5, who actually copies al-Maqrizi's report.

79 Al-Sakhawi, *Daw'*, 2: 22; idem, *Daw'*, 5: 164, puts a date on the position at the ʿAmru

Al-Sakhawi mentions several undated posts in Cairo: *niyabat al-hukm* (assistant to a chief judge), preaching in the mosque of ʿAmru ibn al-ʿAs, and the Madrasa of Sultan Hasan, and leading the prayers in the al-Hakim Mosque as well as supervising its *waqf*, and, later after 1421, and much more problematically, he lists the position of substituting for Muhibb al-Din b. Nasrallah in teaching hadith in the mosque of al-Muʿayyad Shaykh, to which we will return. Ibn Fahd, who was much closer to al-Maqrizi, only lists the two posts at the mosque of ʿAmru ibn al-ʿAs and the al-Hakim Mosque.[80] Al-Maqrizi himself only indirectly mentions acquiring the position of preaching at the mosque of ʿAmru in 805/1403, probably immediately after he was dismissed from the *hisba* for the second time, but does not specify how long he held it.[81] In his *Suluk* and his *Khitat*, however, al-Maqrizi displays an inordinate interest in reporting the happenings in both al-Hakim and al-Muʿayyad mosques, such as appointments, repairs, and expenditure, which may reflect his involvement in their affairs.

The *hisba* experience definitely had its positive effects on the formation of the future historian of Cairo. It furthered his familiarity with the streets and buildings of the city he lived in and loved, as the job involved touring the streets and neighborhoods and checking the old and new structures for their compliance with the building codes, property rights, and privacy according to Islamic law. It introduced him to official data on the city, its markets, and its major buildings as found in the chancery or *waqf* documents, to which he had full access, as is clear from the lengthy quotations from such documents in his later writing. It also helped him gain firsthand knowledge of market dynamics and price fluctuations in Mamluk Cairo, and to directly observe all sorts of hoarding and extortion practices adopted by corrupt Mamluk amirs, administrators, and merchants.

The practical knowledge of the state's structure and the city's functioning that al-Maqrizi acquired during his service as a *muhtasib* directly marked the scope and tone of his early sociohistorical writing. This is especially evident in his two short and important treatises on famine and money. He composed the first, *Ighathat al-Ummah bi-Kashf al-Ghummah*, in 1405, immediately after the third *hisba* appointment and as a reflection on the famine that had hit Cairo the year before (806/July 1403–July 1404). He probably wrote the second treatise, *Shudhur al-ʿUqud fi-Dhikr al-Nuqud*, in 818/1415 in response

mosque, 805/1403, which corresponds to al-Maqrizi's date.

80 Ibn Fahd, *Muʿjam*, 65.

81 Al-Maqrizi, *Durar*, 2: 512, in the biography of Nur al-Din al-Adami al-Shafiʿi, who substituted for al-Maqrizi in leading the prayers in the mosque. The biography is repeated in ibid., 2: 550–1, without the mention of the mosque of ʿAmru. Ibid., 3: 90–1, in the biography of Sharaf al-Din Abu al-Fadhl al-Maqdisi, who also substituted for al-Maqrizi in leading the prayers.

to the financial reforms that al-Mu'ayyad Shaykh initiated but never completed. His experience at the *hisba* was also to inform the development of his thinking toward launching the greatest project of his career as a historian less than a decade later: to write a comprehensive history of the ups and downs of the Egyptian metropolis during the Islamic period, both to preserve the memory of its architecture and urban development and as a backdrop to stressing its sorry state during his lifetime and condemning the perpetrators of its degradation among the ruling Mamluks and their operatives. The end result of this project was the *Khitat*, the one book that he worked on until shortly before his death in 1442, without really completing it as he had planned it, as discussed below.

Rivalry with Badr al-Din al-ʻAyni

The experience at the *hisba* seems to have had its socially and psychologically harmful effects as well. Competition over this lucrative office incurred the animosity of some powerful players in the Mamluk administration. Chief among them was Badr al-Din al-ʻAyni, who himself managed to occupy the office of *muhtasib* seven times during the period 1399–1443.[82] Al-Maqrizi must have known al-ʻAyni from earlier encounters, as both had been clients of Shaykh al-Safawi. But al-ʻAyni went on to collect a series of very powerful patrons, including the three successive sultans al-Mu'ayyad Shaykh, Tatar, and Barsbay. While al-Maqrizi's success at court was rather modest after Barquq and, possibly, his son Faraj, al-ʻAyni remained at the highest level of the Mamluk administration until his death in 1451.[83] The hostility between the two men seems to have begun after al-ʻAyni succeeded al-Maqrizi in 1399 for his first term as *muhtasib*, and grew further when al-Maqrizi in his turn displaced al-ʻAyni in 1400. Their rivalry lasted until the death of al-Maqrizi and colored their opinions of one another to the bitter end.[84] This was pri-

[82] For al-ʻAyni, see al-Maqrizi, *Durar*, 3: 467–8; al-Sakhawi, *Daw'*, 10: 131–5, mentions the notice on al-ʻAyni in *Durar*; Ibn Iyas, *Bada'iʻ*, 2: 292–3; Laila Ibrahim and Bernard O'Kane, "The Madrasa of Badr al-Din al-ʻAyni and its Tiled Mihrab," *AI* 24 (1988): 253–68, esp. 253–4; art. "al-ʻAyni," by W. Marçais, EI^2, 1: 790–1.

[83] Al-ʻAyni indicates that his first contact with Barquq dates to 795/1393 when the sultan gave him ten thousand dirham to perform the Hajj in the name of Amir Sudun al-Tarantay, who had died and left more than a million dirham, most of which went to the sultan, *al-Sultan Barquq min khilal Makhtut ʻIqd al-Juman fi Tarikh Ahl al-Zaman*, Iman Umar Shukri, ed. (Cairo: Madbuli, 2003), 369. Ibid., 460, al-ʻAyni says that he composed for the Dawadar Qulmatay al-ʻUthmani, who died in 800/1398, two religious books, perhaps as a way of cultivating his patronage.

[84] Ibn Taghri-Birdi, *Nujum*, 16: 9, in the biography of al-ʻAyni.

marily expressed elliptically in their writing.

The two men were definitely recognized as the top historians of their time. They were both aware of each other's work, even though they rarely quoted each other, and may have been competing in gathering information for their chronicles that covered the same time frame: *Suluk* for al-Maqrizi and *'Iqd al-Juman fi-Tarikh Ahl al-Zaman* for al-'Ayni.[85] Al-'Ayni was so close to the center of power that he had the opportunity to read (and simultaneously translate into Turkish) his history book to Sultan Barsbay, who, according to Ibn Taghri-Birdi, said, "Without al-'Ayni our religion would not have been good, and we would not have been able to manage our kingdom."[86] The sultan, probably in recognition of al-'Ayni's erudition, appointed him Hanafi chief judge in 829/1426. Al-Maqrizi, at that same time, was decidedly shunned from court. That, however, did not prevent Ibn Taghri-Birdi, a student of both men who thought highly of the pair, to assert in his obituary of al-Maqrizi that he was "hands down the dean of all historians."[87]

This apparently was not only Ibn Taghri-Birdi's opinion. Al-Maqrizi's reputation seems to have gone beyond Egypt and the Mamluk Empire to reach the Timurid Empire. In Muharram of 833/ October 1429, an envoy from Shah Rukh's court arrived in Cairo with a request for two books: *Fath al-Bari bi-Sharh al-Bukhari*, the famous hadith exegesis of Ibn Hajar al-'Asqalani, and al-Maqrizi's *Suluk* in history. This was a great honor, and al-'Ayni must have been quite irritated at having been passed over in favor of al-Maqrizi, for he neglected to mention that the *Suluk* had been requested by Shah Rukh, although he went into some detail describing the gifts Shah Rukh sent to the Mamluk Sultan Barsbay on that same occasion in his chron-

[85] Al-Maqrizi, *Durar*, 3: 468, lists al-'Ayni's major works without any comment. See the discussion of the two chronicles' shared sources, similarities, and differences in Sami Massoud, *The Chronicles and Annalistic Sources of the Early Mamluk Circassian Period* (Leiden: Brill, 2007), 151–62. In his conclusion, 192, Massoud, who calls al-Maqrizi "one of the foremost ideologues of the state decline under the Circassians," notices that his criticisms of Barquq in the *Suluk* are uniquely his and cannot be traced to his source, Ibn al-Furat.

[86] Ibn Taghri-Birdi, *Nujum*, 15: 110; al-'Ayni was noted for his fluency in both Arabic and Turkish, which he may have learned in his youth in 'Ayntab (Gaziantep in Turkey today). Still, in the dignified custom of the time he published his book only in Arabic, and apparently never recorded his Turkish translation despite the broadened audience such a translation would have provided, not to mention rewards from powerful Mamluk patrons. The book was finally translated into Turkish three centuries later in Istanbul by a committee of thirty scholars as part of a large project of translation sponsored by the enlightened vizier Damad İbrahim Pasha (vizier 1718–30), which indicates its continuous importance at least from the Turkish point of view, see Salim Aydüz, "Bilimsel Faaliyetler Açısından Lâle Devri," in Mustafa Armağan (ed.), *İstanbul Armağanı: Lâle Devri* (İstanbul, 2000), 159–93; for the committtees, see Çelebizâde İsmail Âsım Efendi, *Târih-i Râşid ve Zeyli*, ed. Abdülkadir Özcan et al. (İstanbul, 2013) vol. 3, 1484–5.

[87] Ibn Taghri-Birdi, *Nujum*, 14: 150; 15: 189.

icle.[88] Nor does al-ʿAyni mention *Fath al-Bari*, by his other rival Ibn Hajar, as the other work requested by Shah Rukh. A request for books was definitely seen as a reflection of their authors' excellence and renown. At least this is what al-Sakhawi implies when he remarks that although al-ʿAyni's hadith exegesis was copious and elaborate, it was not as excellent as the *Fath al-Bari* of his teacher Ibn Hajar, to be requested by "Muluk al-Atraf [Kings of the Peripheries]" (as al-Sakhawi cosmocentrically calls them), definitely referring to the Shah Rukh episode.[89] The manipulation of these reports is clearly motivated by the fierce competition that marked the relationship between scholars. Al-Maqrizi and his student Ibn Taghri-Birdi are rather evenhanded in that regard. They list both the *al-Suluk* and *Fath al-Bari* books as those requested by Shah Rukh.[90] Al-Maqrizi very courteously puts Ibn Hajar's book first and passes on the report with no comment on the merit of his own book, perhaps a calculated performance of his magnanimity. But al-Maqrizi's consideration was not even reciprocated by his friend Ibn Hajar. He too fails to mention that al-Maqrizi's *Suluk* was requested, although he proudly says that he set up three volumes of his *Fath al-Bari* to be sent to Shah Rukh.[91]

Al-ʿAyni overstepped the boundary of civility in his dealing with al-Maqrizi a few times. His contemptuous remarks on al-Maqrizi's preoccupation with divination and geomancy, for instance, do not quite square with his own use of astrological forecasts to predict the longevity and prosperity of the two sultans, al-Muʿayyad Shaykh and al-Zahir Tatar, for whom he penned two almost identical sycophantic encomia.[92] The same could be said about

88 Al-ʿAyni, *ʿIqd al-Juman*, Qarmut selections, 371; Broadbridge, "Academic Rivalry," 103–4.

89 Al-Sakhawi, *Daw'*, 10: 134.

90 Al-Maqrizi, *Suluk*, 4: 818; Ibn Taghri-Birdi, *Nujum*, 14: 170; al-Jawhari, *Nuzhat*, 3: 178.

91 Ibn Hajar, *Inba'*, 8: 194. Hasan Habashi, the editor of the second edition of Ibn Hajar, *Inba'*, noted that Ibn Hajar neglected also to mention that Barsbay refused to fulfill any of Shah Rukh's request, which included sending a *kiswa* to the Kaʿba and doing work in Mecca, which means that the books may never have reached Shah Rukh, see Ibn Hajar, *Inba'* (Habashi edition), 3: 434, no. 2. The episode is noted in a few modern works, cf. Everett Jenkins Jr., *The Muslim Diaspora: A Comprehensive Reference to the Spread of Islam in Asia, Africa, Europe and the Americas, 570–1799*, Vol. 1, 570–1500 (Jefferson, N.C.: McFarland, 2000), 296.

92 Al-ʿAyni, in his *ʿIqd al-Juman*, denigrates al-Maqrizi for his involvement in divination at least two times: once in his biography of Fath Allah and once in his biography of al-Maqrizi himself (ʿAyni, *al-Sultan Barquq*, 484 in reporting the appointment of Fath Allah as secretary of the privy). For al-ʿAyni's use of the same means, see his *al-Sayf al-Muhannad fi Sirat al-Malik al-Mu'ayyad Shaykh al-Mahmudi*, Fahim M. Shaltut, ed. (Cairo: Maktabah al-Arabiyah, 1966), 306–37, where he affixes a zodiac diagram purporting to predict the prosperity of al-Mu'ayyad's reign, and another table foreseeing who will rule in Egypt that he copied from a "trustworthy diviner"; for an analysis of the content of the two encomia for al-Zahir Tatar and al-Mu'ayyad Shaykh, see P. M. Holt, "Literary Offerings: A Genre of Courtly Literature," in Thomas Philipp and Ulrich Haarmaan, eds., *The Mamluks*

his denunciation of al-Maqrizi for having exaggerated Fath Allah's pedigree by linking him to King David, when al-'Ayni himself invented a whole new tribal lineage for al-Mu'ayyad Shaykh to aggrandize his status, when it would have been practically impossible to trace the lineage of any one mamluk to more than his father.[93] Al-'Ayni was also the only historian to have accused al-Maqrizi of corruption, when he reported how al-Maqrizi was the only *na'ib al-hisba* willing to accept the *hisba* position after he himself had renounced it, allegedly in protest at the unjust practices of Amir Sudun, the Dawadar al-Kabir (the equivalent of Chief of Staff), who was trying to force merchants to buy confiscated cereal at arbitrarily set prices, a dubious practice called *tarh* in the sources.[94] The incident, however, may have been more complex than al-'Ayni wants us to believe. Amir Sudun had been appointed to his influential office only two days before al-'Ayni's resignation (14 Jamada al-Awla 802/ January 12, 1400) as part of a major check-up among the magnates of the sultanate. The confiscated goods belonged to an amir of the *ancien régime* who was on the run, and al-'Ayni may have just been a victim of the administrative realignment that ensued from the political change at the highest level, as was customary in that tumultuous period. The allegation against al-Maqrizi is therefore at least exaggerated if not altogether unjustifiable, given the testimony of all other commentators, including the hostile al-Sakhawi, about the integrity and morality al-Maqrizi displayed during his governmental service. Al-'Ayni, moreover, shows the degree of his hatred toward al-Maqrizi by calling him a *la'im* (wicked or ignoble), a degrading term that al-Maqrizi himself never uses to describe any of his opponents among the ulama, regardless of their violations or his feelings toward them.[95] Al-Maqrizi says nothing personal about al-'Ayni when he reports the same incident of *hisba*. But he seems to have kept a bitter taste of the baseness involved in al-Ayni's retelling in particular and in his seeking and holding public office in general, that will show up later in his behavior and writing.

His response to al-'Ayni's provocations came in the form of a number of reports in his *Suluk* and *Durar*, which, as expected from this mild-mannered and prudent historian, used omission and circumspection rather than asser-

---

in Egyptian Politics and Society (Cambridge: Cambridge University Press, 1998), 3–16, esp. 8–12.

[93] See Al-'Ayni, *al-Sayf al-Muhannad*, 5, for a rhymed Persian encomium that uses all astrological signs. His elaborate, and highly fanciful, genealogy of the Turks and Mongols ends up in the tribe of al-Mu'ayyad, which he ascribes to the Ghassanids, hence Arab, in a known twist to assign to the Turks in general an Arabic lineage, 22–30.

[94] Al-Jawhari, *Nuzhat*, 2: 45–6. See also 'Abd al-Raziq, "Hisba," 131–2; Bacharach, "Circassian Mamluk Historians," 78.

[95] Al-Jawhari, *Nuzhat*, 2: 46, no. 1. The editor cites al-'Ayni's condemnation of al-Maqrizi from the still-unpublished part of his history, *'Iqd al-Juman*, part 25, folio 99–100.

tion to imply al-ʿAyni's callousness and injustice.[96] For instance, al-Maqrizi records an event that he calls *shanʿa'* (outrageous), in an entry describing the economic hardships in Dhu al-Hijja 828/November 1425. Al-ʿAyni, who was then the *muhtasib*, was harassed on his way to the citadel by a mob of riff-raff (*ruʿaʿ* and *harafish*) angry at his handling of bread prices. He went straight to the sultan and complained about the threats of stoning he received, which prompted the sultan to exact a severe and unjustified punishment on a number of ostensible instigators, including beating and cutting off of noses and ears. Al-Maqrizi goes on to indirectly register his empathy with those punished by saying that "men's hearts were alienated by this and tongues were loosed with imprecations."[97] Ibn Taghri-Birdi, when reporting the same incident years later, noted that al-Maqrizi omitted to mention that the mob indeed stoned al-ʿAyni on his way to the Citadel, which would have justified his decision to report them to the sultan out of fear for his life. Ibn Taghri-Birdi wryly comments that "al-Maqrizi aimed at exaggerating the defamation of al-ʿAyni because of the long-standing hostility between the two."[98] Al-Maqrizi followed up with another report in Safar 829/January 1426, in which he analyzes the causes of an artificial rise in the prices of staple cereals. He blames this partly on the ignorance of the *muhtasib* of the time, al-Shashmani, who was unfamiliar with the *hisba* principles (probably because he was a Mamuk amir), but notes also that the crisis may have been a late consequence of al-ʿAyni's policies as *muhtasib*, for he was too lenient with the greedy merchants, allowing them to manipulate prices to make the most gain.[99] This is the extent of al-Maqrizi's direct criticism of al-ʿAyni: moderate, civil, and roundabout, standing in stark contrast to his biting and straightforward condemnation of contemporary Mamluk sultans and amirs, which fills his *Khitat* and the later parts of his *Suluk*. Thus, his obviously sore and harsh remarks regarding unjust rulers around him acquire extra pungency when set against his relatively mild, discreet, and ostensibly impartial way of registering reproaches against his equals and competitors, of which al-ʿAyni's episode is a typical, albeit drawn-out and personally felt, example.

[96] Another possible sign of this tactic is al Maqrizi's overlooking of the Madrasa of Badr al-Din al-ʿAyni (completed c. 1428) in the roster of Cairene madrasas in his *Khitat*, although he must have seen it being built while he was redacting the book, Ibrahim and O'Kane, "The Madrasa of al-ʿAyni," 254–5.

[97] Al-Maqrizi, *Suluk*, 4: 698; idem, *Durar*, 1: 468, in the biography of Sultan Barsbay; Ibn Taghri-Birdi, *Nujum*, 14: 117–18; Broadbridge, "Academic Rivalry," 99–102.

[98] Ibn Taghri-Birdi, *Nujum*, 14: 281–2.

[99] Al-Maqrizi, *Suluk*, 4: 710–11.

The Damascus Interlude

Al-Maqrizi did not, however, break away from the morally and personally exacting cycle of patronage immediately after his *hisba* debacle. He seems to have remained a client of Fath Allah, who succeeded in retaining his power and position as *katib al-sirr* under Faraj, except for a few months' hiatus (26 Rabiʿ I-7 Dhu al-Hijja, 808/September 21, 1405–May 26, 1406) in which he was disastrously out of favor with the sultan and some of his great amirs. Al-Maqrizi traveled in Fath Allah's entourage while accompanying the sultan on his journeys to Syria during the tumultuous and ultimately disastrous period of repeated droughts and plague pandemics, frequent amirial dissensions, and bloody internecine fights between 1407 and 1412. In his *Suluk* and *Durar*, he several times mentions that he was with Fath Allah in the entourage of Sultan Faraj in Syria. The first was in 812/1409, when al-Maqrizi assisted Fath Allah (in no official capacity) during the tricky negotiations between the sultan and Amir Shaykh al-Mahmudi (later Sultan al-Mu'ayyad Shaykh), who rebelled against the sultan and was planning to declare himself a sultan. The second time was in Muharram 815/April 1412, when the insurgence of Amir Shaykh and his collaborators flared up again and led eventually to the murder of Sultan Faraj, in which Fath Allah played a pivotal part.[100]

According to Ibn Fahd, al-Maqrizi lived in Damascus for unknown lengths of time on at least four occasions between 810/1407 and 815/1412, when he came with Fath Allah.[101] It is not clear whether he was alone or with his children.[102] He appears to have served in a few religious offices there as a substitute for Fath Allah during the relatively long visit of 813/1410. These included supervision of the *waqf*s of Bimaristan al-Nuri (hospital of Nur

[100] Al-Maqrizi, *Suluk*, 4: 100, 105, where he says that he was with Fath Allah during his negotiations with Amir Shaykh in Shawbak; see also idem, *Durar*, 1: 366 and 3: 13–14, where he states that he often traveled with Fath Allah; ibid., 1: 368 and ʿIzz al-Din, *al-Maqrizi wa-Kitabuhu*, 2: 437 in the biography of Shihab al-Din al-Husbani, where al-Maqrizi mentions that he met him at the *majlis* of Fath Allah when the former came as an envoy for the Amir Shaykh in 808/1406.

[101] Ibn Fahd, *Muʿjam*, 66, says that al-Maqrizi came with the sultan in 810 and went back to Cairo with him, then came again to Damascus in 812, and again in 813 when he substituted for Fath Allah in a few positions, then came back again in 814 and stayed in the city until the killing of Faraj. Al-Maqrizi, *Durar*, 1: 154, in the biography of Taqqiy al-Din al-Kinani, Qadi al-Zabadani, only states that the *qadi* accompanied him during his visits to Damascus between 810 and 815.

[102] If his sons Muhammad and ʿAli had still been alive, they would have been young adults by then (at least 19 and 16 respectively). Fatima may have been younger and still at home. Al-Maqrizi most probably lost Soul before these sojourns in Damascus and does not seem to have taken another wife. He is totally silent about women in his life after the bizarre Soul episode.

al-Din, built 1154) and Dar al-Hadith al-Qalanisiyya (built 1329), and teaching in the Madrasa al-Iqbaliyya (built 1203) and the Dar al-Hadith al-Ashrafiyya (built 1232).[103] While in Damascus, al-Maqrizi might have also ingratiated himself with Amir al-Mu'ayyad Shaykh, the fickle *na'ib* of Damascus for Faraj, when the amir was operating in and around Damascus in the early 1410s. But here the sources are extremely laconic. The only evidence we have is a report in al-Maqrizi's *Suluk* that he received the supervision of the *waqf* of the Madrasa al-Qalanisiyya in Damascus, a post normally given to the chief Shafi'i judge of the city as part of a larger package, on 19 Shawwal 811/March 7, 1409.[104] The very same day, Amir Shaykh received his appointment as Faraj's governor in Damascus.[105] The decree (*taqlid*) for the appointment was issued from the chancery in Cairo, where al-Maqrizi appears to have been living then. It is unlikely, therefore, that Shaikh, who was in Damascus at that time, was responsible for al-Maqrizi's position.

Al-Maqrizi probably owed this position to the goodwill of his friend and protector Fath Allah, who was instrumental in securing the governorship of Damascus for Amir Shaykh in return for a respite in the constant challenges to the throne of Sultan Faraj that he instigated with other amirs. Fath Allah, who was then at the zenith of his influence as a powerbroker, might have been behind the offer that al-Maqrizi appears to have received to become the Shafi'i chief judge of Damascus, which would have been the highest position al-Maqrizi would have attained had he accepted. But although he himself does not say anything about such an offer, both al-Sakhawi and Ibn Taghri-Birdi report that Sultan Faraj offered the prestigious *mansib* to al-Maqrizi more than once but that he refused to accept it.[106] Why, they do not say. The supervision of al-Qalanisiyya's *waqf* may have been a compromise between the desire of the patron to set his client up in a powerful position and al-Maqrizi's hesitation in assuming such a demanding responsibility in a city not his own.

We know that al-Maqrizi was in the company of Fath Allah at the camp of Sultan Faraj in the fateful month of Muharram 815/April 1412. He took

[103] Ibn Fahd, *Mu'jam*, 66; Al-Sakhawi, *Daw'*, 2: 22, mention several posts that al-Maqrizi occupied in Damascus that I could not verify in other sources. They differ in the Madrasa al-Iqbaliyya, which Ibn Fahd replaces with the Madrasa al-Aminiyya. Al-Maqrizi only speaks of his administration of al-Qalanisiyya.

[104] Al-Maqrizi, *Suluk*, 4: 83–4. Al-Maqrizi is very specific in indicating that Ibn Hajji, who was appointed chief Shafi'i judge that day, took all the posts that were usually granted to the holder of his new position except for the supervision of the *waqf* of the Madrasa al-Qalanisiyya, which was given to al-Maqrizi.

[105] Ibid. This reinforces the reports copied by Ibn Taghri-Birdi, *Manhal*, 1: 417, that al-Maqrizi was offered the position of Shafi'i chief judge in Damascus in the early days of the sultanate of Faraj b. Barquq, but refused it.

[106] Ibn Taghri-Birdi, *Manhal*, 1: 396; al-Sakhawi, *Daw'*, 2: 22.

the side of his patron Fath Allah when the latter fell out with the sultan who had insulted him publicly and declared that he was plotting with the sultan's enemies, accusations that turned out to be quite true. Al-Maqrizi, sensing his patron's waning loyalty to the sultan, expressed some uneasiness about Fath Allah's capriciousness and his exploitation of his wide network of connections to conspire against the sultan. In fact, Fath Allah, and al-Maqrizi with him most probably, along with the Abbasid caliph and other ulama in the entourage of the sultan, switched camp and joined the rebellious amirs, Shaykh and Nawruz al-Hafizi, after they had dealt the sultan a serious defeat near Damascus on the 13 of Muharram 815/24 April 1412.[107] Faraj took refuge in the citadel of Damascus and the race to the sultan's office began. Fath Allah cunningly managed to convince the amirs who were themselves suspicious of each other to settle on the caliph al-Musta'in Billah as sultan—a first in the Mamluk period—the next day. This complicated conspiracy on the part of Fath Allah seems to have aimed at nothing less than replacing the sultan with the caliph and therefore undermining the Mamluk system altogether.[108] The scheme must have titillated most of the ulama, who had never truly accepted the Mamluk system as fully legitimate under Islamic law, even though they were clearly aware that the sultanate of the caliph was only a transitional arrangement until the great amirs resolved their differences and settled on a sultan from among themselves.[109] Some of the ulama also expressed some qualms about reneging on their oath to a sitting sultan, a doubt that faded

[107] Al-Maqrizi, *Suluk*, 6: 318.

[108] See al-Maqrizi, *Suluk*, 6: 319–25, for the details of the last week in the life of Faraj and the role of Fath Allah in destroying his reign; Ibn Taghri-Birdi, *Nujum*, 13: 94–108, tells the same story more or less, but with details that he gleaned from his sister, who was Faraj's wife, and his father, the dying governor of Damascus who died during that campaign. Ibn Taghri-Birdi, however, takes a different stand vis-à-vis the killing of Faraj that reflects his Mamluk leanings and upbringing.

[109] This is painfully clear in a poem composed by Ibn Hajar al-'Asqalani on the occasion of the entry of al-Musta'in Billah as sultan into Cairo in Rabi' al-Akhir 815/July 1412. In it Ibn Hajar says openly, "The status of the family of the Prophet is back to its rightful place after much neglect," and then continues "Thanks be to God who has elevated His religion after it was retreating, and eliminated the injustice that had hurt every turbaned one (ulama) of all creeds," showing the receptiveness of his class to the change and their expected benefit from it. But he is well aware of the precariousness of the new arrangement, for he continues with the line "Don't deny al-Musta'in in his ascendancy to the throne after rejection and overlooking," because he already knew that the amirs were about to revert to the established system of rule:

رجعت مكانة آل عم المصطفى   لمحلـها بعد طـول تنـاس
فالحـمـد لله المـعز لدينـــه   من بعد ماقد كان في إبلاس
وأزال ظلمــاً عم كل معـمـم   من سائر الأنواع والأجنـاس
لاتتنكـروا للمسـتعين رئاسـة   في الملك بعد الجحود الناسي

with the killing of Sultan Faraj on 16 Safar 815/May 28, 1412. Even though he never says it openly, al-Maqrizi seems to have been at the heart of the action during that delicate period of uncertainty, for he reports the events of the movements of the sultan, the amirs, and their Mamluk factions in and around Damascus in the language of an eyewitness. He does not voice a definite opinion with or against Sultan Faraj's removal then killing, even though he is very disdainful of him. After reporting his death, he describes him as the most "ill-fated of the Muslim rulers [*ash'am muluk al-Islam*], who has destroyed the land of Egypt and Syria with his crooked policies." He then (exaggeratedly) lists all the calamities that befell the sultanate during his reign from the invasion of Tamerlane to the mismanagement and corruption of the state affairs, uneven monetary policy (about which al-Maqrizi had very strict views), the wasteful expenditure on court pomp and useless campaigns, and the elimination of large numbers of amirs and mamluks of al-Zahir Barquq on flimsy suspicions. The result was the ruination (*kharab*) of every district in Egypt from Alexandria to Aswan, according to the scornful al-Maqrizi. He ends his list with the sultan's behavioral infractions, which infuriate him the most, like excessive drinking, debauchery, and, most offensive of all to our pious historian, the sacrilegious disregard of the name of God and mockery of Him and His prophets, which the young and impertinent sultan was known to have often committed.[110]

The Beginning of Estrangement

Al-Maqrizi seems to have left Damascus shortly after the killing of Faraj with Fath Allah in the entourage of the Caliph al-Musta'in Billah, who had been appointed sultan, and Amir Shaykh, who was soon to remove the caliph and become Sultan al-Mu'ayyad Shaykh.[111] Those dramatic and quickly evolving

---

The poem is quoted in *toto* in Jalal al-Din al-Suyuti (1445–1505), *Tarikh al-Khulafa'*, Muhammad Muhiyy al-Din 'Abd al-Hamid, ed. (Cairo: Dar al-Sa'ada, 1952): 506–8, cited in Ibn Taghri-Birdi, *Nujum*, 13: 150, note 2.

110 Al-Maqrizi, *Suluk*, 4: 225–8; Ibn Taghri-Birdi, *Nujum*, 13: 108–10, disapprovingly copies the text of al-Maqrizi in its totality then adds "this is pure folly," commenting on al-Maqrizi's overstatements and saying that he could have responded to all of al-Maqrizi's accusations, but abstained for fear of "unnecessary excess and boredom."

111 Al-Maqrizi never specifies the date of his return. His equal coverage of events in both Damascus and Cairo in 815/1412 and 816/1413 after Faraj's killing and Shaykh's return to Cairo (*Suluk*, 4, 1: 228–54) suggests that he was either still in Damascus until early 816 or was in touch with informants at the highest levels of the Mamluk administration, which is the more probable explanation, as Ibn Fahd tells us that al-Maqrizi returned to Cairo in the summer of 1412.

events were to have both an immediate and a long-term impact on al-Maqrizi's career, due primarily to his association with Fath Allah and his heightened sense of integrity respectively. The *katib al-sirr* seems at first to have managed to weather the changes and to maintain his position at the court of the caliph/sultan al-Musta'in Billah while Amir Shaykh was maneuvering his ascendancy to the throne. To achieve that goal, Shaykh was treading very carefully as he needed to work on three fronts at the same time. He had to remove the supporters among the Mamluk amirs of both the slain sultan Faraj b. Barquq and his partner-in-crime Amir Nawruz, who had taken control of Syria, and replace them with his own trusted Mamluk amirs, as well as to finesse the ejection of the caliph from the sultanate. Fath Allah artfully helped him in all three tasks, even though he had started slowly but systematically to lose his privileges in the inner circles of power, probably with Shaykh's tacit assistance, as he wanted to free himself from the architect of his long-drawn scheme to become sultan, and possibly also as a delayed payback for past offenses.[112]

Less than two months after acceding to the throne in Sha'ban 815/November 1412, al-Mu'ayyad Shaykh dismissed Fath Allah from the position of *katib al-sirr* and arrested him on 9 Shawwal 815/January 12, 1413 along with his supporters and protégés, of whom al-Maqrizi was definitely prominent. Although al-Maqrizi does not say anything about his own detention, Ibn Fahd gives some details that hint at his *shaykh*'s close escape from arrest. He writes, "Jamal al-Din al-Ustadar [*sic*; the correct name is Badr al-Din Hasan b. Muhibb al-Din al-Ustadar] resented the closeness of al-Maqrizi to Fath Allah and managed to hurt him in the early days of al-Mu'ayyad Shaykh's sultanate. He was aided by the Hanafi chief-judge Sadr al-Din al-Adami but God saved al-Maqrizi," with no further explanation.[113] Al-Maqrizi says nothing about this, but his opinion of both Badr al-Din al-Ustadar and the judge al-Adami

[112] First, Shaykh, who had appointed himself Amir Kabir (Great Amir) and *atabek*, stripped Fath Allah of the prestigious function of reading petitions at court in September 1412, which slightly lowered his standing among the administrators. Then, a month later, Fath Allah lost a case against the heirs of his former nemesis Jamal al-Din al-Ustadar and was forced to return some of the confiscated properties to them. See al-Maqrizi, *Suluk*, 4: 241–2; Ibn Taghri-Birdi, *Nujum*, 13: 154, but he does not report the event of the reversal of Jamal al-Din's confiscation. Al-Maqrizi, *Durar*, 3: 13–14, tells us that there was some friction between Fath Allah and Amir Shaykh during the negotiations with Sultan Faraj in 1409 and 1410. He also reports on Fath Allah's frequent change of sides and accuses him of betraying his oath.

[113] Ibn Fahd, *Mu'jam*, 66, makes the mistake of attributing the revenge to Jamal al-Din al-Ustadar, who had been executed in 812/1409 and had been a patron of al-Maqrizi instead of Badr al-Din Hassan b. Muhibb al-Din, who was the *ustadar* at that point in time and who played a major role in eliminating Fath Allah. The heirs of Jamal al-Din al-Ustadar were also instrumental in the downfall of Fath Allah.

is quite harsh and his condemnation unsparing, perhaps as a residue of the bitterness he felt about their conspiracy against him.[114]

Meanwhile, Fath Allah endured an agonizing six-months' imprisonment, during which he was tortured for three months to reveal the locations of his hidden wealth. In his *Suluk*, al-Maqrizi records in painful detail the ordeal of his patron, who was finally strangled in his prison on 6 Rabiʿ al-Awwal 816/June 6, 1413. This cold-blooded crime was unusual even for the brutal standards of the time, for incarceration then execution of high officials after the confiscation of their wealth was generally swift. This episode must have been especially distressing for al-Maqrizi, not only because Fath Allah was a dependable and resourceful patron but also because he was a faithful friend for more than thirty years, as is evident from the numerous reports of intimate and casual interactions between the two men.[115] The event also hastened al-Maqrizi's desire to withdraw from the *manasib* race in disgust and despair. His aversion may have been amplified by the cruelty of the crime against Fath Allah, which culminated with the Sultan banning the people from attending his funeral and from praying over him. Prohibiting attendance at Fath Allah's funeral was indeed extraordinary.[116] Praying over the deceased was a serious religious obligation, which someone like al-Maqrizi dutifully upheld and which sultans rarely, if ever, obstructed. His despair at ever attaining a high position at court or in the administration that he felt worthy of became even more pronounced after the killing of Fath Allah, although it might have taken al-Maqrizi some time to realize it. His futile flirtation with political power had come to a decided end.

The violent death of Fath Allah was the last straw in a series of demoralizing losses that al-Maqrizi suffered between 807/1405 after his last *hisba* stint and 815/1412 when he reached fifty years of age according to the Hegira calendar. In that relatively short period, he tried his hand at several religious positions in Cairo but did not last in any of them. He traveled in the prestigious company of Fath Allah and Sultan Faraj to Damascus on at least three and maybe four occasions, the last of which was long enough for him to assume a

[114] See al-Maqrizi, *Durar*, 2: 454–8 for the biography of al-Adami; idem, *Suluk*, 4: 598–9 for a brief note on Badr al-Din al-Ustadar. He also reports in some detail the conspiracy of Badr al-Din al-Ustadar and the judge al-Adami, along with the secretary of al-Mu'ayyad Shaykh, Nasir al-Din b. al-Barizi, against Fath Allah, but says nothing about himself, in his description of the fate of the Madrasa of Jamal al-Din al-Ustadar under al-Mu'ayyad Shaykh, al-Maqrizi, *Khitat2*, 4: 645–7; idem, *Suluk*, 4: 174–5.

[115] Al-Maqrizi, *Suluk*, 4, 1: 242, 248, 252, 256, 259, and 4, 2: 1012, recalls his great achievements thirty years after his killing on the occasion of the rise of Badr al-Din ibn Nasrallah to the position of the sultan's secretary in 840/1437; Ibn Hajar, *Inba'*, 7: 137–9, gives much shorter reports.

[116] Ibn Hajar, *Inba'*, 7: 104, shows real disbelief in reporting it.

few temporary positions there, but did not manage to establish himself in the city of his father. He witnessed the disintegration of the network of patrons he had managed to maintain at the royal court after the death of Sultan Barquq, and failed (or was reluctant) to establish a new network among the new generation of powerful Mamluk amirs. Finally, he lost many of his family members, teachers, patrons and colleagues, as he so melancholically states in the Introduction to his *Durar*:

> By the time I had reached my fiftieth birthday, I had lost many of my loved ones and people close to me. I was sad at their passing and my life has become unbearable without their presence. So I consoled myself by remembering them, and substituted the pleasure of seeing them with the collection of their biographies (فعزيت النفس عن لقائهم بتذكارهم وعوضتها مشاهدتهم باستماع أخبارهم) in this book, which I called *Durar al-'Uqud al-Farida fi Tarajim al-A'yan al-Mufida*, which is in fact the recollection of those I loved and the remembrance of the times I had with my teachers and friends. I ask God to cool their burial places and make their slumber easy till the Day of Judgment, and to reunite me with them in the abode of His Glory and to grant me and them life in His heaven with all the pious ones for eternity.[117]

The despondency evident in this sentence is magnified in a pedestrian poem of his own composition that he affixes below the introduction, in which he further expresses his grief at the loss of his loved ones (including probably his children, as he uses the Arabic verb *thakal*, ثكل, which usually indicates the loss of children), his loneliness after their departing, and his missing the advice of those who cared for him or who lent him their stature (*wa-la munjidun bil-jah bihi qadri ya'lu* ولا منجد بالجاه به قدري يعلو) (probably his departed patrons?). He then moves on to state that he is no longer interested in entertainment and in gatherings, and that he instead has become engrossed in learning and in writing. The plainness of the poem is offset by its immediacy, sincerity, and descriptive move from sadness and melancholy to a focus on his pursuit of scholarship, both as a learner and an author, a fair description of the transformation that al-Maqrizi was actually undergoing during that time, which would land him away from the corridors of power and in retreat at his house for the next thirty years. These would be the years in which he will produce the bulk of his historical work. But the actual withdrawal appears to have taken more time to materialize, during which al-Maqrizi was still trying to gain favor at court or from powerful administrators by writing short essays in response to their requests. How long this irresolution lasted is not clear.

His rapport with al-Mu'ayyad Shaykh after his accession—provided that there was a direct one in the first place—is a case in point. It appears to have

[117] Al-Maqrizi, *Durar*, 1: 61–2.

been uneven and to have quickly deteriorated to the point that al-Maqrizi seems to have stopped appearing at court altogether fairly early during al-Mu'ayyad's reign. He might have been shunned by the sultan for his connection to Fath Allah, a banishment that was to last for the remaining thirty years of his life and under several sultans. He also might have retreated on his own, depending on how we interpret the hints he gives about himself in the *Durar* and *Suluk*, but also the seeming contradictory statements of his detractor al-Sakhawi, his student Ibn Fahd, and his other student and sometime impassioned admirer/sometime sly critic, Ibn Taghri-Birdi. None of the three, however, notes precisely when al-Maqrizi withdrew from public life or how and why this took place. Al-Maqrizi himself never confronts the subject head on. In various biographies in his *Durar*, and to a lesser extent in the last part of his *Suluk*, he offers in passing a combination of reasons that may have contributed to his overall disgust with the ruling system in general: unyielding disapproval of the un-Islamic behavior of contemporary Mamluk sultans and great amirs; moral indignation at the corruption at court and in the administration and religious *manasib*; concern about the manipulation of the financial system; warning of the decay of the agricultural basis of the economy and the ruin of his city of Cairo and other cities. To these should be added more personal reasons, such as his tiredness with the rivalry and degradation inherent in the race for office, and despair at ever managing to secure a high enough position through his patrons despite his repeated attempts and his firm belief in his outstanding qualifications.

Ibn Taghri-Birdi, on the other hand, repeatedly presents an explanation for al-Maqrizi's withdrawal in several comments in his *Nujum* on his master's writing that underhandedly emphasizes the last two factors while overlooking the others. He, does not, however, bring up the subject in his three biographical entries on al-Maqrizi in his two chronicles, *Nujum* and *Hawadith*, or in his biographical dictionary *al-Manhal al-Safi*.[118] In the chronicle part of his *Nujum*, he more than once says that al-Maqrizi was denied access to the sultans after Barquq and deprived of their patronage despite his various attempts otherwise. In commenting on al-Maqrizi's assessment of Sultan Tatar's career (r. 824/1421), for instance, Ibn Taghri Birdi says, "I can excuse his errors in what he had reproduced, because he was isolated from the court and was collecting his information on the Turks [i.e. the Mamluks] from simple soldiers [*ahad*]. He therefore was committing many mistakes, which I corrected for him."[119] Later on in the same chronicle, Ibn Taghri Birdi offers a

[118] Sami G. Massoud, "Al-Maqrizi as a Historian of the Reign of Barquq," *MSR* 7, 2 (2003): 119–36, esp. 134–5, suggests that Ibn Taghri-Birdi "might have been engaged in a low-level work of demolition of al-Maqrizi's reputation."

[119] Ibn Taghri-Birdi, *Nujum*, 14: 200–1; he repeats the same accusation against Ibn Hajar, idem, *Nujum*, 14: 242.

more elaborate appraisal of al-Maqrizi's erratic relationship with the Mamluk sultans when he discusses al-Maqrizi's harsh opinion of Sultan Barsbay:

> Shaykh Taqyyi al-Din, God Have mercy on him, (for he was writing after his death) had certain aberrations for which he was well known, though he is to be forgiven for this; for he was one of those I have met who were perfect in their vocation; he was the historian of his time whom no one could come near; I say this despite my knowledge of the other historians/ulama who were his contemporaries. With all that, he was removed from court [regime: *dawla*]. No sultan was bringing him near to himself, although he was a pleasant conversationalist and an agreeable companion. Al-Malik al-Zahir Barquq brought him near, made him a boon companion (*nadim*) and appointed him market supervisor of Cairo toward the end of his reign. But when al-Malik al-Zahir died, he [al-Maqrizi] had no success with those who succeeded Barquq. They kept him away without any favor. So he began to track down their immorality and venality. And one who does evil cannot take offense. But al-Maqrizi was honest with himself, pious, and giving. It was once asked of a poet, "Till when will you praise and scorn?" He answered, "As long as the well-doer does good and the ill-doer does wrong."[120]

This statement may appear at first sight to confirm that al-Maqrizi's criticism of the sultans was no more than retaliation for their disregard of him, overlaid with Ibn Taghri-Birdi's known bragging about his knowledge of the inner working of the sultanate, his having been the son of a Great Amir, and his fluency in Turkish.[121] Both advantages were of course unavailable to al-Maqrizi. But the statement may as well be read as proof that al-Maqrizi's criticism was genuine and even courageous. For although it is true that he seems to have lost access to the royal court after Barquq (or possibly Faraj b. Barquq), he did not allow his beneficial relationship with these two sultans, or with high officials at their court, to fully color his opinion or to tamper with his criticism of their actions, even though he was less scathing in his evaluation of Barquq's shortcomings during his second reign than he was of those of their successors, including Faraj b. Barquq.[122] In fact, al-Maqrizi

[120] Ibid., 15: 89; trans. into English in Ibn Taghri-Birdi, "History of Egypt 1382–1467 (Part IV: 1427–1438)," William Popper, trans. in *University of California Publications in Semitic Philology* (Berkeley and Los Angeles: University of California Press, 1958) 18: 143; also Broadbridge, "Academic Rivalry," 92–4.

[121] Because of his pomposity and propensity to correct his peers' interpretation of Turkish words, Ibn Taghri-Birdi was put down by many chroniclers, see al-Jawhari, *Inba' al-Hasr*, 175–82, but the two were academic rivals in more than one way. For a modern and different assessment of Ibn Taghri-Birdi's scholarship and his efforts to counter the biases against the Turks in Mamluk historiography, see Irmeli Preho, "Ibn Taghrībirdī's Voice," *Studia Orientalia 114, Travelling through Time: Essays in Honour of Kaj Öhrnberg*, S. Akar, J. Hämeen-Anttila and I. Nokso-Koivisto, eds. (2013): 135–45.

[122] As noted by Ibn Taghri-Birdi again, "Shaikh Taqiyy al-Din was guilty of well-known

was most unsparing of al-Ashraf Barsbay (r. 825/1422–841/1438), the sultan during whose reign he wrote the bulk of his *Suluk*. Barsbay could have punished him severely for his affront, for he was known for his viciousness and cruelty, especially toward the end of his life.[123] Al-Maqrizi does not seem to have taken any precaution, though: his book seems to have been read by his contemporaries during Barsbay's reign, any of whom could have reported its content to the sultan.[124] This reinforces the view that al-Maqrizi's harsh stance came out of religious and moral conviction more than bitterness and that his mounting rebuke was based on observation of how affairs of state were further deteriorating from one corrupt reign to the next, as they indeed seem to have been.[125] Undoubtedly, though, al-Maqrizi was becoming gloomier and less *mansib*-motivated in his writing as he grew older and lonelier with the loss of his last family member, his daughter Fatima, in 1423, and perhaps also the loss of Soul, who died in Mecca in 1421, even if he had not seen her for many years before that.[126]

---

inconsistencies; he said now this and now that . . . And my statement that the Shaikh sometimes praises Barquq and sometimes blames him rests on the fact that when the author was friendly with al-Malik al-Zahir during his second sultanate and al-Zahir made him the object of his beneficence, he went to extremes in praising him in several passages of his works, and forgot this earlier statement of his and others similar to it; it escaped his notice that he should have changed this earlier account, for, as the proverb runs, 'Who praises and blames is as though he lied twice,'" Ibn Taghri-Birdi, *Nujum*, 11: 290–1; idem, *The History of Egypt*, trans. Popper, 13: 44–5; Massoud, "Al-Maqrizi as a Historian of the Reign of Barquq," 131–2. As we will see, al-Maqrizi was not consistent in his criticism of all the sultans he knew. The explanation lies in *why* he was critical, not in who he criticized, or as Ibn Taghri-Birdi himself said, he "was honest with himself."

123 Al-Maqrizi, *Suluk*, 4: 1033, 1048. The most infamous incident was when Barsbay, shortly before his death in 1438, cut his two doctors, al-'Afif and Khadr, in half (*wassat*) because he was frustrated with the failure of their treatment to cure his illness. Al-Maqrizi, *Suluk*, 4: 1041–2, provides a vividly horrific description of the execution.

124 Ibn Fahd and Ibn Hajar state that they have read it. Ahmad Darrag, *L'Égypte sous le Régne de Barsbay 825–841/1422–1438* (Damascus: Institut Français de Damas, 1961), 432–5, notes the different opinions about Barsbay held by contemporary historians, and that al-Maqrizi's was the harsher and least restrained.

125 In his relentless debunking of his master's criticism of the Mamluk sultans, Ibn Taghri-Birdi, *Nujum*, 11: 290–1, disagrees with al-Maqrizi, who complains about Sultan Barquq's acquisition of beautiful mamluks and slave girls (despite the fact that al-Maqrizi himself acquired Soul from Barquq's *harem*) by reminding his reader that al-Nasir Muhammad, whom al-Maqrizi revered as a great sultan, was excessive in his purchase of beautiful slave girls and that he bought a number of young mamluks for the highest of prices and made them *khassaki*s and amirs and married them to his daughters to keep them around him.

126 Irwin, "al-Maqrizi and Ibn Khaldun," puts too much emphasis on al-Maqrizi's pessimism.

Last Attempts at Finding Patronage?

Al-Sakhawi is the only source to provide concrete information on al-Maqrizi's alleged continuing service in some official capacity during the reign of al-Mu'ayyad Shaykh, which was understood by some modern scholars to mean that al-Maqrizi retained a public role until at least 823/1420, a year before the death of al-Mu'ayyad.[127] Al-Sakhawi's information, however, has to be treated with caution for at least two reasons. First, it might simply be wrong, for it is not reported by other biographers such as Ibn Fahd and Ibn Taghri-Birdi, who were closer and had direct access to the man during his lifetime and who, as admirers, had no reason to hide any of his professional achievements. Second, and perhaps more likely, al-Sakhawi was biased against al-Maqrizi in ways that exceed his typical haughty and spiteful presentation of his biographees. The causes for that excessive belittling range from pure jealousy, as can be detected in al-Sakhawi's introduction of *al-Tibr al-Masbuk fi-Dhayl al-Suluk*, to deriding al-Maqrizi's association with Ibn Khaldun and his more colorful religious leanings.[128] Assigning al-Maqrizi positions that he did not hold after he had quit the *manasib* race may have been a way of implicitly questioning the sincerity of his decision and perhaps even his integrity.

The most problematic, yet easily refutable, report is al-Sakhawi's mention that al-Maqrizi succeeded Muhibb al-Din Ahmad ibn Nasrallah al-Baghdadi to the position of hadith teaching at the Mosque of al-Mu'ayyad Shaykh (al-Mu'ayyidiyya), "when the latter became the teacher of the Hanbali *madhhab* at the same institution."[129] If it were correct, this would be proof that al-Maqrizi continued to receive royal patronage under al-Mu'ayyad Shaykh, for the position of teacher at al-Mu'ayyadiyya would have required the sultan's approval. But this report is not supported by any other source,

[127] Sayyid, *Musawwadat*, Introduction, 43; Zuhair Humaidan, ed. and commentator, "Introduction," *Min Kitab al-Mawa'iz wa-al-I'tibār bi-Dhikr al-Khiṭaṭ wa-al-Athar al-Ma'ruf bi-al-Khiṭaṭ al-Maqriziyya* 4 vols. (Damascus: Ministry of Culture, 1987), 1: 12–13; Sa'id 'Abd al-Fattah 'Ashur, "Adwa' Jadidah 'alá al-Mu'arrikh Ahmad ibn 'Ali al-Maqrizi wa-Kitabatihi," *'Alam al-Fikr* 14, 2 (1983): 453–98, esp. 468.

[128] Al-Sakhawi, *Tibr*, 21. For al-Sakhawi's mocking of the relationship between Ibn Khaldun and al-Maqrizi, see al-Sakhawi, *Daw'*, 2: 24; for the biography of al-Maqrizi see ibid., 4: 147–8; for the biography of Ibn Khaldun see idem, *al-I'lan bi-al-Tawbikh li-man Dhamma al-Tarikh* (Damascus: al-Qudsi, 1930), 94.

[129] Al-Sakhawi, *Daw'*, 2: 22. Sayyid, *Musawwadat*, Introduction, 43, accepts al-Sakhawi's claim in the *Daw'* without fixing a date and duration for the position and postulates as late a date as 1421 for al-Maqrizi's withdrawal from public life. 'Izz al-Din, *Maqrizi*, 43, and Broadbridge, "Academic Rivalry," 87–8, state that other sources did not mention this post. I doubt this late date and the entire reference of al-Sakhawi, who was manifestly hostile to al-Maqrizi.

although all other historians, al-Maqrizi included, mention the appointment of al-Muhibb to the Hanbali chair at al-Mu'ayyidiyya, which was then the premier teaching institution in Cairo, on the 16 Muharram, 823/ February 1, 1420. He replaced 'Izz al-Din al-Baghdadi, who had held that position since the madrasa was first opened in Jamada I, 822/June 1419. Muhibb al-Din remained in that position until his death on 15 Jamada I, 844/October 12, 1440, after which the teaching position passed on to a certain al-'Izz al-Kinani.[130] Furthermore, there is no indication that Muhibb al-Din taught hadith at the same institution before his appointment to the Hanbali chair. In fact, al-Maqrizi tells us that the initial teacher of hadith at al-Mu'ayyadiyya was none other than his old nemesis, Badr al-Din al-'Ayni.[131] Al-Maqrizi, furthermore, mentions neither Muhibb al-Din nor himself in connection with the hadith post in his extensive entry on al-Mu'ayyadiyya in the *Khitat*, where he lists all the office holders in the mosque during his time, or in his many references to al-Mu'ayyadiyya in the *Suluk*.[132] Al-Sakhawi himself states, in his entry on al-'Ayni in his *Daw'*, that he taught hadith in al-Mu'ayyadiyya from its inauguration until his death in 855/1451, more than nine years after al-Maqrizi's death, which clearly obviates the report of al-Maqrizi's occupying the same position.[133] Even if al-Sakhawi meant that al-Maqrizi intermittently substituted for Muhibb al-Din in his actual Hanbali chair in an informal arrangement between the two men, as was the habit among ulama, this would still not be correct, for the simple reason that al-Maqrizi was not a Hanbali scholar, a prerequisite for the position. This, however, does not imply that al-Maqrizi had no connection to the Nasrallahs, the scholarly Hanbali family to which Muhibb al-Din belonged and which prospered in religious and administrative circles in Mamluk Egypt in the first half of the fifteenth century (1403–62).[134] Three members of the family—Muhibb al-Din, his brother the vizier Badr al-Din Hasan, and his nephew the multi-talented official Salah al-Din Muhammad—who held high administrative and religious positions under al-Mu'ayyad Shaykh were all

[130] See al-Maqrizi, *Suluk*, 4: 520, for Muhibb al-Din's appointment and 493 for the first round of appointments; also Ibn Hajar *Inba'*, 7: 375; Ibn Taghri-Birdi, *Nujum*, 14: 93; al-Jawhari, *Nuzhat*, 2: 465; al-Sakhawi, *Daw'*, 2: 238, for the statement that Muhibb al-Din remained in the position until his death, which obviously contradicts the assertion that al-Maqrizi occupied that place.

[131] Al-Maqrizi, *Khitat2*, 4, 1: 346, but he neglects to report the appointment in *Suluk*, 4: 496, where he otherwise tracks the employment development in al-Mu'ayyadiyya. See also Ibn Hajar, *Inba'*, 3: 201.

[132] Al-Maqrizi, *Khitat2*, 4, 1: 334–47; idem, *Suluk*, 4, 1: 479, 493, 496, 520, 526, 541, 533; 4, 2: 597, 660–1, 680.

[133] Al-Sakhawi, *Daw'*, 10: 134–5.

[134] On the clan of the Nasrallahs, see Martel-Thoumian, *Civils et l'administration*, 213–25.

friends of al-Maqrizi and may have occasionally provided him with some support.[135]

Al-Sakhawi casually adds another intriguing detail, which was copied by many commentators on al-Maqrizi without being checked. In the *Daw*, al-Sakhawi reports that al-Maqrizi "versified the biography [*qarada sirat*] al-Mu'ayyad of Ibn Nahid."[136] This was construed as another attempt on al-Maqrizi's part to bring his skills to the sultan's attention, even though neither al-Maqrizi nor Ibn Taghri-Birdi mentions a versified *sirat* of al-Mu'ayyad in their lists of al-Maqrizi's oeuvre. The story, however, is much simpler. The printed version of al-Sakhawi's text has a typo. The verb in question should have been written with a Zha' ظ as *qarraza* قرظ which means "to endorse poetically," or "to write a blurb," a well-known practice among the literati in Mamluk Egypt.[137] The poet Shams al-Din Muhammad ibn Nahid (c. 757/1356–841/1438), who made his living in Cairo by writing panegyrics for famous ulama and high officials, composed a *sirat* of al-Mu'ayyad Shaykh in 819/1416, even though it is not evident that the sultan saw it.[138] Ibn Nahid naggingly sought endorsement of it from fellow scholars and religious figures, many of whom appear to have obliged, and their *taqariz* (pl. of *taqriz*) have been preserved as a collection.[139] Al-Maqrizi appears as one of at least sixteen scholars and notable officials whose *taqariz* are gathered in this collection, which included Ibn Hajar, al-'Ayni, and al-Maqrizi's friend and possible

135 Al-Maqrizi, *Suluk*, 4: 1231–2, gives a cordial biography of Muhibb al-Din; ibid., 4: 1063, uncommonly expresses his sadness at the death of Salah al-Din Muhammad, the nephew of Muhibb al-Din and a high administrator who was close to the sultan. Al-Sakhawi, *Daw'*, 2: 233–9, gives a mixed account, but asserts on p. 238 that al-Maqrizi befriended Muhibb al-Din after his arrival from Baghdad. Ibn Taghri-Birdi, *Hawadith*, 1: 66–7, speaks about a certain degree of intimacy between the Nasrallahs and al-Maqrizi, which allowed the latter to occupy the center of their *majlis* and to speak his mind freely in their presence, although "they were a haughty family."

136 Al-Sakhawi, *Daw'*, 2: 23.

137 Franz Rosenthal, "'Blurbs' (*taqrīẓ*) from Fourteenth-Century Egypt," *Oriens* 27–8 (1981): 177–8; Amalia Levanoni, "A Supplementary Source for the Study of Mamluk Social History: The *Taqārīz*," *Arabica* 60 (2013): 146–77.

138 See al-Maqrizi, *Durar*, 3: 379–80, for a brief and rather dismissive note on Ibn Nahid; al-Sakhawi, *al-I'lan bi-al-Tawbikh*, 77; idem, *Daw'*, 10: 67, copies the biography by al-Maqrizi but adds the details about the Sīrat al-Mu'ayyad. For a detailed discussion of the text, see Amalia Levanoni, "'Sīrat al-Mu'ayyad Shaykh' by Ibn Nāhid," in *Texts, Documents and Artefacts: Islamic Studies in Honour of D. S. Richards*, ed. Chase Robinson (Leiden: Brill, 2003), 211–33. For the edited *sirat*, see Rudolf Vesely, "Ibn Nāhiḍ's As-Sīra aš-Šaykhīya (Eine Lebensgeschichte des Sultans al-Mu'ayyad Šaykh): Ein Beitrag zur *Sīra*-Literatur," *Archiv Orientalni* 67 (1999): 149–220.

139 Amalia Levanoni, "Who Were the 'Salt of the Earth' in Fifteenth-Century Egypt?" *MSR* 14 (2010): 63–83, esp. 63–4, and notes 6 and 7.

patron the chief judge Jalal al-Din al-Bilqini.[140] This is quite an impressive list of endorsers, which contains some of the best-known ulama and officials of the period, who all moved in the same circles. They seem to have indulged in this exercise either as a practical joke on the hapless Ibn Nahid, who was of much lower scholarly and social standing than any of his endorsers, or as a form of soft competition in which each of them tried to show his poetic prowess.[141] One thing is certain, however: this was no way to win favor with the sultan for al-Maqrizi or any of his other colleagues.

There is some indication, however, that al-Maqrizi may have written or dedicated his own work to Sultan al-Mu'ayyad Shaykh. Two of his short treatises, *Shudhur al-'Uqud fi Dhikr al-Nuqud* (Pearls of the Divine Ordinances Concerning Money) and *al-Dhahab al-Masbuk fi Dhikr man Hajja min al-Khulafa' wa al-Muluk* (The Book of Molded Gold in Evoking the Accounts of the Caliphs and Kings who Performed the Ḥajj), may have been composed for al-Mu'ayyad, whether by direct order or not is not known. The evidence, though circumstantial, warrants careful examination. The first treatise, *Shudhur al-'Uqud*, was certainly written during the reign of al-Mu'ayyad, who is mentioned as the reigning sultan throughout the text. The most direct evidence is the dates, Shawwal 817/January 1415 and 24 Safar 818/May 5, 1415, which appear in the text where al-Maqrizi speaks approvingly about the silver *dirhams* minted and imposed by al-Mu'ayyad during that period.[142] He then

[140] Al-Sakhawi, *I'lan*, 43; idem, *Daw'*, 10: 67, says that a number of people put the *sirat* into verse; in his entry on al-'Ayni, ibid., 10: 135, he says that al-'Ayni too versified the *sirat* of al-Mu'ayyad by Ibn Nahid; see ibid., 4: 111 for al-Bilqini versification; idem, *Tibr*, 84–5 records how Ibn Nahid specifically sought an endorsement from a certain Shams al-Din al-Sufi al-Shadhli. The versification of Ibn Nahid's *sirat* became a kind of competition between the scholars of the period to show off their competence in poetic composition. Levanoni, "Salt of the Earth," 66–74, counted 21 scholars, to whom we can add al-'Ayni and Ibn Katib al-Samsara (al-Maqrizi, *Durar*, 3: 151; al-Sakhawi, *Daw'*, 8: 113), making a list of 23 scholars and clerks who knew each other.

[141] Amalia Levanoni, "Salt of the Earth," largely reads in the endorsements the mockery by upper-class scholars of a parvenu. It is possible, however, to detect a competitive edge in the fact that all these scholars accepted writing *taqariz* after the first two of them, who held powerful *manasib*, had agreed to do this.

[142] The treatise has been edited and published several times. The last publication, edited by Muhammad 'Abd al-Sattar 'Uthman, discusses the date and purpose of the treatise; it is the one used here. For the date, see al-Maqrizi, *Shudhur al-'Uqud fi Dhikr al-Nuqud*, ed. Muhammad 'Abd al-Sattar Uthman (Cairo: Dar al-Ma'arif, 1990), 149. The final verification and redaction of the book took place in Ramadhan 841/March 1438, as stated by al-Maqrizi himself on the margin of the last page in an autographed manuscript, ibid., 12–13 and figs. Also stated by A. Sylvestre de Sacy in his translation, "Traité des monnaies musulmanes, traduction de l'arabe de Makrisi," quoted in Bacharach, "Circassian Mamluk Historians," 77, n. 23. We now know that al-Maqrizi redacted a series of his opuscules at that date, probably for final publication. He did not change the titles of the

compares al-Mu'ayyad's move to the precedent established by the Umayyad caliph ʿAbd al-Malik ibn Marwan (r. 683–703), who was the first Muslim ruler to mint an Islamic-designed *dirham*, and lists a number of religiously meritorious motives behind al-Mu'ayyad's decision to issue his silver *dirham*. After this conventional eulogy, al-Maqrizi goes on to recommend a number of policy decisions in order to establish the preeminence of the Mu'ayyadi Dirham and to stabilize its exchange rate against the various golden dinars in use. He prays to God that the Sultan al-Mu'ayyad implement these policy decisions through the mediation of an unnamed individual, referred to only as *al-safara al-karima* (the noble intermediary), who must be the one to have commissioned the treatise from al-Maqrizi. He repeats the same appeal to the same unnamed intermediary at the end of the book, and then closes the text with a few invocations addressed to the probable patron, which add no clue as to his identity or rank.[143]

Al-Mu'ayyad was indeed facing a severe economic crisis in the years 817–19/1415–16. His response to its monetary aspect was rather inconclusive, but he did move slowly toward instituting his own silver *dirham* as the basis for monetary exchanges, exactly as al-Maqrizi recommends in his treatise. His argument was based on the Islamic principle that only gold and silver should be used as currency. The implementation of the Mu'ayyadi Dirham came in stages, which spanned the period between Rabiʿ II and Ramadhan 819/May and October 1416.[144] This gives us the plausible timeframe within which al-Maqrizi's book was composed: Safar 818/May 1415 to Ramadhan 819/October 1416. As for the patron for whom the book was composed, it was ultimately al-Mu'ayyad himself, although it is not clear whether al-Maqrizi presented the book to him directly or through an intermediary. In the introduction, al-Maqrizi speaks of an *amr ʿali* (high order) which was issued requesting the composition of a short work on Islamic monies.[145] The adjective *ʿali* suggests a sultanian order, which al-Maqrizi was obeying, thus implying a direct contact between the author and the sultan. The repeated references to *al-safara al-karima*, or the "honorable embassy," on the other hand, favor the presence of an intermediary between al-Maqrizi and al-Mu'ayyad. Here, the sequence of events in 818/1415 provides a possible candidate: the Chief Shafiʿi Judge Jalal al-Din al-Bilqini, who was appointed by al-Mu'ayyad in Safar 818/May 1415 to consider the question of monetary

---

addressees, on purpose, as he intended the treatise on money to be presented to another royal patron.

143 Al-Maqrizi, *Shudhur*, 151–3, 159–62.

144 Detailed coverage, almost on a day-to-day basis, is in al-Maqrizi, *Suluk*, 4: 304–8, 311, 312, 318, 354, 360, 363, 366; less detailed in Ibn Hajar, *Inba'* (Habashi edition), 3: 38, 54, 91, 100. Ibn Taghri-Birdi does not mention the entire event.

145 Al-Maqrizi, *Shudhur*, 104.

policy.[146] He was in attendance at all the subsequent meetings held by the sultan to discuss the issue and may have asked al-Maqrizi to write an essay on Islamic monetary history as a way of bringing in the weight of normative religious history to the new policies.[147] There is no direct proof of this hypothesis, but al-Bilqini is reported by al-Sakhawi to have approvingly turned in public to al-Maqrizi for a historical question, which was considered an acknowledgment of al-Maqrizi's preeminence in historical knowledge.[148] Al-Maqrizi, on the other hand, had only favorable qualities to ascribe to al-Bilqini in the obituary he penned of him in his *Suluk*, which he closes with the highest form of appreciation, that he "was one of those who embellish the age [ممن يتجمل بهم الوقت (*miman yatajamal bihum al-waqt*)]."[149]

The second opuscule, *al-Dhahab al-Masbuk*, is a short thematic work on Muslim rulers who had performed the Hajj, from the Prophet Muhammad down to and including the cancelled Hajj of the Bahri Mamluk Sultan al-Ashraf Sha'ban in 778/1377, who was assassinated en route to Mecca. Jamal al-Din al-Shayyal, the book's first editor, notes that it was composed for an unnamed patron whom al-Maqrizi calls *al-Maqqar al-Makhdum* (المقر المخدوم).[150] *Maqqar* was an honorific title whose status deteriorated over the Mamluk period according to al-Qalqashandi, our main source on Mamluk protocol. It was used primarily for sultans during the early Bahri period, but depreciated in the Burji/Circassian period, to be given only to great amirs and sometimes to high administrators.[151] *Al-Makhdum*, or "the one to whom service is due," is a formulaic title frequently used to address patrons in the Ayyubid and Mamluk periods. It does not carry any special

146 Al-Maqrizi, *Suluk*, 4: 307; the appointment is not clearly stated in Ibn Hajar, *Inba'* (Habashi edition), 3: 54, although al-Bilqini is mentioned as expressing reservations about the sultan's intended policy.

147 John Meloy, "The Merits of Economic History: Re-Reading al-Maqrizi's *Ighathah* and *Shudhur*," *MSR* 7, 2 (2003): 183–203, p. 197 calls it "monetary history as *fada'il*," or religious merits; see also Clément Onimus, "Réforme des monnaies et spéculation dans le sultanat mamlouk au début du IXe/ /XVe siècle: al-Maqrizi et la question de la responsabilité de l'élite mamlouk dans l'instabilité monétaire," *Arabica* 64, 2 (2017): 213–36.

148 Al-Sakhawi, *al-I'lan bi-al-Tawbikh*, 43–4.

149 On al-Bilqini, see al-Maqrizi, *Suluk*, 4: 599–600; Ibn Taghri-Birdi, *Nujum*, 14: 237; Ibn Hajar, *Inba'*, 7: 440; idem, *Majma'*, 3: 154–6; al-Sakhawi, *Daw'*, 4: 106–13.

150 Al-Maqrizi, *al-Dhahab al-Masbuk fi Dhikr man Hajja min al-Khulafa' wa al-Muluk* ed. Jamal al-Din Shayyal (Cairo: Maktabat al-Khanji, 1955), introduction, 24–5, text, 2–3. A new edition and translation, accompanied with a substantial analytical and interpretive essay, is Jo Van Steenbergen, *Caliphate and Kingship*. I thank the author for providing me with a copy of the analytical part of his study before its publication.

151 On *maqqar*, see al-Qalqashandi, *Subh*, 5: 494–5; Hasan al-Basha, *al-Alqab al-Islamiyya fi al-Tarikh wa al-Watha'iq wa al-Athar* (Cairo, Maktabat al-Nahda al-Misriyya, 1957), 489–95 for a discussion of the devolution of the title *Maqqar* in the Mamluk protocol.

titular value. Al-Shayyal concludes that the book must have been written for a great Mamluk amir.

However, the book's title, theme, and introduction favor its dedication to a sultan rather than an amir. First, the book is a survey of all the caliphs, kings, and sultans who performed the Hajj up until the end of the eighth century Hegire/fourteenth century. To have composed it for a great amir may have been impertinent on the part both of the amir and his client, for it could be construed as a sign of dangerous aspirations to the throne, especially in that troublesome period when many revolts were initiated by dissatisfied great amirs. Second, al-Maqrizi's Introduction contains a few expressions that could not have been addressed to anyone but a ruling monarch. For instance, he speaks of capturing enemies and enviers, or about adding glory and territory (*'izz wa mulk*) to his patron's. These actions are exclusively royal; amirs were supposed to assist their sovereign in acquiring new territory, but never to claim any in their own names.[152]

The final clue that this work was most certainly written for the audience of the ruling sultan comes from the events of al-Mu'ayyad's reign. In Jamada I, 821/June 1418, on his seventh year on the throne, al-Mu'ayyad announced his intention to perform the Hajj. He was to be the first Mamluk sultan since al-Ashraf Sha'ban (1363–78) to perform the Hajj while in office. However, this would not be al-Mu'ayyad's first Hajj, as he had previously served as Amir al-Hajj (Leader of the Egyptian Caravan to the Hajj) in the last year of Barquq's reign and then subsequently led the caravan after the sultan's death in Shawwal 801/June 1399.[153] Al-Mu'ayyad sent to the amirs of Hijaz to prepare what was needed, and spent the next few months preparing camels and provisions for the voyage. On the 20 of Rajab/August 23, he paraded in the streets of Cairo with the Mamluks assigned to accompany him, camels, and the presents to be taken to the ruling families in the Holy Cities, and everyone was convinced that he was serious about his publicized intention. On the same day, and after the parade, he received disturbing news about a major attack on the northeastern frontiers of Syria, which put him off going on the Hajj. He immediately began preparation for a military campaign to

[152] Al-Maqrizi, *Dhahab*, 1–2.

[153] Al-Maqrizi, *Durar*, 2: 126, in the unusually long, detailed, and incomplete biography of al-Mu'ayyad that al-Maqrizi wrote (63 pages), in which he tracked down Shaykh's early life, his ascent in the Mamluk system and his adventures in Syria; he stops it abruptly just before the accession of Caliph al-Musta'in to the sultanate. The detailed reporting of Shaykh's movements in Syria suggests that al-Maqrizi was writing the entry while in Damascus, which is supported by the fact that he never came back to finish it after the return of Shaykh to Cairo and his accession to the sultanate, although he clearly was working on other biographies up until the end of his life.

Syria.[154] Al-Maqrizi, in his Introduction, says precisely: "it has become known that the noble intent [*al-'azm al-sharif* العزم الشريف] to perform the Hajj has become strong."[155] Nowhere in the text does he mention that the intent has turned to action, thus making it possible to postulate that the book was composed as a response to an intention.[156] Dates appearing in the text also support the ascription of the book to al-Mu'ayyad's aborted Hajj episode. The last date al-Maqrizi mentions in the body of the text is 815/1412, when the *khutba* was said in the name of the Egyptian Abbasid caliph/sultan, al-Musta'in bi-Allah, in Mecca, which immediately predates the accession of al-Mu'ayyad to the throne.[157] This must be the *terminus a quo* for the composition of the book.

Al-Maqrizi, thus, may have written this short treatise when al-Mu'ayyad's preparations for the Hajj were made public in June 1418, but was unfortunate enough to see his hopes of reward for it dashed with the sudden and unpredictable cancellation of the trip in August. That he used the title *maqqar* to address his patron may indicate that Mamluk titulature was more fluid than al-Qalqashandi implies in his strict manual in his *Subh al-A'sha*. It may also mean that al-Maqrizi was either ignorant of the protocol, a rather farfetched possibility, or deliberately negligent in using the proper title to address the sultan in his typical passive insubordination and assertion of autonomy. The last possible explanation is that al-Maqrizi did not want to ascribe the treatise to a single patron, in the hope of rededicating it to another royal patron, a practice that we observe in other fields of artistic production in the Mamluk period.[158] The title *maqqar* alone, however, cannot invalidate the identification of the book's patron as al-Mu'ayyad, and the circumstantial evidence supports that ascription. Al-Mu'ayyad's cancelation of his intended Hajj may have thwarted al-Maqrizi's attempt to regain access to the sultan through his erudition and reinforced his resolution to quit the useless rat race. It is difficult

154 Al-Maqrizi, *Suluk*, 4: 444, 458–9; Ibn Taghri-Birdi, *Nujum*, 14: 66–7; al-Jawhari, *Nuzhat*, 413–15.

155 Al-Maqrizi, *Dhahab*, 2. *Sharif* is an adjective that is normally applied only to the sultan's actions or attributes, which reinforces the proposition that the book was written for al-Mu'ayyad.

156 Van Steenbergen, *Caliphate and Kingship*, 27–36, weighs all the evidence for the dates and patrons of the treatise and comes down on the side of al-Mu'ayyad and 1418, although he suggests that al-Maqrizi might have reworked the text later to present it to other potential patrons, a hypothesis that I do not support.

157 Ibid., 62. Al-Shayyal, the earlier book editor, in his introduction on page 25, mistakenly accepts the date of redaction (Dhu al-Qi'da 841/May 1438) as the book's composition date. Al-Maqrizi redacted many of his treatises in Dhu al-Qi'da 841.

158 Thus, we sometimes have generic titles on metalwork, ceramic, textile, and enameled and gilded glass lamps, probably in the hope of widening the buyers' base, see Bethany J. Walker, "Ceramic Evidence for Political Transformations in Early Mamluk Egypt," *MSR* 8, 1 (2004): 68–70.

to ascertain whether he used the treatise again as a tool to seek patronage later in life, as suggested by some of the book's editors. However, al-Maqrizi returned to this text later and reproduced a "pre-publication draft" of it in Dhu al-Qiʿda 841/May 1438, as indicated on the colophon of the oldest extant manuscript of the *Tibr*.[159]

Al-Maqrizi's inconclusive and eventually ill-fated relationship with al-Mu'ayyad Shaykh is reflected in the diverse remarks on the sultan and his rule in his two more historical books, the *Khitat* and *Suluk*. In his chronicling of the sultan's actions during his reign, he sometimes comes across as apologetic, and even as downright flattering at other times. The flattery is especially palpable in his observations on the bonhomie, modesty, and heartfelt piety of the sultan in the face of natural disasters such as drought and pestilence, which plagued most of his rule.[160] However, his tone changes to antagonistic in the short biographical note he wrote of al-Mu'ayyad when he reported the sultan's death in his *Suluk*.[161] He begins by listing the sultan's good qualities, such as courage, fearlessness, and, especially, compliance with Islamic law and respect for the ulama (an obvious concern for all Mamluk ulama/historians). But he then quickly shifts to a litany of failings such as avarice, irascibility, envy, obscenity, and abuse. He finishes his obituary by blaming al-Mu'ayyad for perpetrating injustices and causing destruction and misery, especially during his governorships in Tripoli and Damascus, but also throughout his reign.

These religiously argued and observation-based indictments—which appear to varying degrees of intensity in all of al-Maqrizi's assessments of the sultans of his days from Barquq to Barsbay—do not preclude the possibility that al-Maqrizi tried to ingratiate himself with al-Mu'ayyad or to directly seek employment under him, especially at the beginning of his reign.[162] In fact, the short positive reports in the *Suluk* may have been intended as a means of

[159] Van Steenbergen, *Caliphate and Kingship*, 1–7 proves that the *Tibr* manuscript, included it in a codex containing sixteen of al-Maqrizi's treatises and preserved in the Library of the University of Leiden, which were copied between 840 and 841/1437–8 as indicated in the dates on the colophons of the various treatises and verified by al-Maqrizi, was copied from an earlier yet lost autograph draft. This may be the one he initially wrote for al-Mu'ayyad, or another version which he developed for unknown reasons, and possibly unknown patrons, in the intervening years.

[160] Al-Maqrizi, *Suluk*, 4: 531–2, on the penitence of the sultan in public on two occasions; p. 534, on an example of al-Mu'ayyad's rejection of popular beliefs when they contradict orthodoxy, even when he is the beneficiary of the belief.

[161] Al-Maqrizi, *Suluk*, 4: 550–1; Ibn Iyas, *Bada'iʿ*, 2: 62, confirms al-Maqrizi's hostility toward al-Mu'ayyad.

[162] Here again we have Ibn Taghri-Birdi, *Nujum*, 14: 110, claiming that he can debunk all of al-Maqrizi's accusations against al-Mu'ayyad, but that he will refrain from doing so, so that he does not waste time and paper.

preserving some sort of an open channel with the sultan and his court. One remark in particular throws light on how al-Maqrizi may have been mentally trying to justify his continuous attempt to work for the sultan while condemning the excesses and abuses of his government. When commenting on a statement by al-Mu'ayyad that implies his humbleness before God, al-Maqrizi observes that if the sultan "had been assisted by better lieutenants and courtiers, he could have effected positive deeds; instead, he had been surrounded by bold profligates and wretched swindlers," very strong accusations indeed, expressed in atypical language.[163] Can we read in this invariably and universally evoked apology for despots a lamentation for his removal from court? Or maybe even a plea for his restoration to service? Subconsciously perhaps, although his actual bids to gain the sultan's attention were clearly unsuccessful, as suggested by the fate of the two treatises he probably composed for him. Beside the unattested and paltry job of substitute hadith teaching at al-Mu'ayyadiyya, al-Maqrizi is not recorded as having taken up any official position, religious or administrative, under al-Mu'ayyad Shaykh or any of his successors.

This disappointment, which tentatively expresses itself in the chronicling of al-Mu'ayyad Shaykh, will eventually translate into al-Maqrizi's breaking all measures of caution and consideration in reporting the failings of the succeeding Mamluk rulers. Al-Maqrizi hit that turning point sometime during al-Mu'ayyad's reign, probably before the inauguration of al-Mu'yyadiyya in 1420, when he seems to have finally decided to withdraw in despair at ever reconciling his moral indignation with his ambition to reach a high position. This inference is based on the change of tone in his *Suluk* text. The mixed reports on al-Mu'ayyad, with their alternation between his good and bad habits and attributes, are followed by the Maqrizian trademark criticism by proxy, where he reports negative opinions of al-Mu'ayyad on the authority of others, such as Amir Nawruz, the sometime ally/sometime enemy of al-Mu'ayyad.[164] This is succeeded by al-Maqrizi's resolutely negative feelings at the end of al-Mu'ayyad's obituary. From then on, he will unleash his unmitigated hostility toward al-Mu'ayyad's successors, especially Barsbay, where—as noted by Ibn Taghri-Birdi—he "leaves no room for reconciliation or rapprochement."[165]

[163] Al-Maqrizi, *Suluk*, 4: 487–8.

[164] As reported by Ibn Hajar, *Inba'*, 7: 163 in his biography of Amir Nawruz.

[165] This is where Ibn Taghri-Birdi's repeated remarks on al-Maqrizi's hostility toward Barsbay gain their full meaning, see *Nujum*, 14: 200–1, 245, 310–11; 15: 109–10.

Withdrawal

Although al-Maqrizi's alienation from the treacherous milieu of sultans and courtiers did not come to full expression until midway through the reign of al-Mu'ayyad, its causes seem to have been accumulating over his years of service under Barquq and Faraj. The first signs of weariness surfaced when he repeatedly turned down Sultan Faraj's offer of the coveted *mansib* of the Shafi'i chief judge of Damascus. Al-Maqrizi's refusal may be ascribed to the traditional pious ulama's fear of inadvertently committing injustice while holding the position of judge, a fear that al-Maqrizi explicitly exhibits when he singles out accepting the judgeship of the Hanbalis as the only sin of his friend and patron al-Muhibb ibn Nasrallah.[166] But this was not the only sign of the shift in his thinking. A passage in his *Durar* reveals his leaning toward *zuhd*, the "mild asceticism" professed by a number of ulama in the medieval period, who followed a venerated tradition starting with the Imam Ahmad ibn Hanbal in the ninth century.[167] Al-Maqrizi says that he tried to convince a judge and colleague in Damascus to "quit seeking favors of the amirs if he is really sincere about his renunciation of worldly gains."[168] The passage carries a tone of self-reflection that may indicate that al-Maqrizi himself was going through that transformation at the time.

This is how we can understand al-Maqrizi's moral quandary after the execution of his trusted patron Fath Allah. His unsuccessful attempts to gain access to al-Mu'ayyad during the first half of his reign by dedicating several works to him or through the ineffectual intercession of other patrons, such as the Nasrallahs or the chief judge al-Bilqini, represented the end of an era for him. Soon thereafter, he would take his final decision and quit both court and courtiers, but not without a bitter feeling that will show in his writing.

This feeling of despondency is amply displayed in the introduction to *al-Suluk li-Ma'rifat Duwal al-Muluk*, which suggests that Maqrizi started this book when he was still wavering between self-imposed isolation and another trial at court. This suggestion is supported by the evidence we have about the start date for the composition of the book: al-Maqrizi embarked on it late in life after he had finished his two earlier histories of al-Fustat and of the Fatimids and parts of his large biographical dictionary *al-Muqaffa*.[169] On the first page of the autographed manuscript of the *Suluk*, al-Maqrizi

166 Al-Maqrizi, *Suluk*, 4: 1232.

167 Hurvitz, "Biographies and Mild Asceticism," 48–52; L. Kihnberg, "What is Meant by Zuhd?" *SI* 61 (1985): 27.

168 Al-Maqrizi, *Durar*, 2: 60. This may be contrasted with what Ibn Taghri-Birdi, *Nujum*, 15: 189, says about his master's forced withdrawal from court. The truth is probably a combination of both impulses.

169 Al-Maqrizi, *Suluk*, 1: 9.

unambiguously, and on two parts of the page, poured out his heart to his reader. The first passage, which is written below the title, seems to be directed to himself as an incantation. It says:

> May God save you from requesting the reimbursement for a good deed you have rendered and a payment for a favor you have offered, and may He not abase your hand below that for whom it was above, and may He protect you from a passing glory and an exigent living. May God keep you alive as long as life is beautiful by your presence and may He take you if death was better for you, after a long life and high eminence. May He conclude your deeds with kindness and allow you to reach in this life your hopes and guide your unsteady way, and may He rectify your predicament in the hereafter. He is the All-hearing, the Magnanimous, and the Granter [of wishes].[170]

This revealing invocation conveys the author's contradictory feelings: hope and despair, pride and dejection, love of life and an admission of the inevitability of death. These sentiments reflect the circumstances that al-Maqrizi found himself in during and immediately after the reign of al-Mu'ayyad Shaykh. He was banished from court, lonely after the death of Soul in 1421 and Fatima in 1423, yet still full of self-esteem and the will to contribute to public life. The passage should thus be dated to the period of the first composition of the book, which must have been completed in its first draft before 1428, when it was requested by Shah Rukh. At the bottom of the same cover page, there is another passage in al-Maqrizi's hand, written longitudinally in the middle of the page between two other unrelated informational passages. This short passage must have been added at a later date, not only because of its odd position on the page, but also because of the strong feeling of resignation it bespeaks. In it, al-Maqrizi declares:

> I have been afflicted with such a bad fortune, that whenever it goes up, it immediately comes down, and whenever it stands up, it inevitably falls down, and whenever it goes straight, it surely bows down again, and whenever it runs smoothly, it at once encounters obstacles, and whenever it becomes alert, it soon sleeps again . . . [Then there follow two verses.]
>
> By your life, I do not lack a banner of glory
> Nor did the horse tire of competing
> Instead, I am afflicted with a bad fortune
> Just like a beautiful woman is afflicted with divorce
>
> لعمرك ما عدمت لواء مجدٍ ولا كَلَّ الجوادُ عن السباقِ
> ولكني بُليت بحظ سوءٍ كما تُبلى المليحة بالطلاقِ

[170] Ibid., 1, 1: 3 and see facing page for a photographic reproduction of the autographed manuscript's cover page (Istanbul, Yekki Cami, # 887).

Here we find the extreme expression of melancholy that must have overtaken al-Maqrizi after he realized the futility of his repeated attempts to gain the sultan's favor or to grab another public position. He thus reverts to his belief in the supernatural—fortune or luck—to explain his failure. The insertion of the *dubayt* poetic quatrain at the end, however, attests that he did not lose his self-esteem: he still thinks of himself as able and worthy. He only resigns himself to his fate in order to concentrate fully on his scholarly and ascetic pursuits.

To this point in time should be dated his final retreat to his family home in Harat al-Burjuwan.[171] He was to spend the rest of his life studying, writing, and teaching in almost total seclusion, except for rare visits to his fellow ulama and students, and for at least three Hajjs (pilgrimages) and *mujawara* (living in proximity to the Ka'ba) in Mecca between 1430 and 1435.[172] He wrote his *Khitat* book and completed most of his long historical treatises during these thirty-plus years, but we have no fixed dates for any of them. The *Khitat*, however, was the first book he tackled. As such, it was closely connected with this defining period in his life, with its intense and painful soul-searching and reckoning. It marked his transformation from a client to one or other among the Mamluk grandees to an independent, even aloof, scholar and historian and a pessimistic observer recognizing the corrupt structure of power but not knowing what to do about it except to chide its perpetrators.[173] These strong yet ultimately desperate feelings of disillusionment inevitably seeped into the

171 He seems to have been the only heir to his maternal grandfather Ibn al-Sa'igh, who left a sizeable fortune according to Ibn Hajar, *Inba'*, 1: 96.

172 Ibn Taghri-Birdi, *Manhal*, 1: 397, Sakhawi, *Daw'*, 2: 24 mentions only a *mujawara*; Jawhari, *Nuzhat*, 3: 219, 367, quotes al-Maqrizi in the years 834/1431 and 840/1437 respectively as having been in the Hajj; Ibn Taghri-Birdi, *Nujum*, 14: 355, quotes him in 835/1432, which may mean that he stayed in Mecca for a whole year. Al-Maqrizi, *Durar*, 2: 336–7, in the biography of the Sufi 'Abdallah ibn Muhammad ibn Burayk al-Hadhrami al-Yamani, reports that he met him during his *mujawara* in Mecca in 839/1436 and read a portion of *Sahih Muslim* with him; Ibn Fahd, *Mu'jam*, 65, lists seven pilgrimages, many of them coupled with *mujawarat*, the first three when al-Maqrizi was a young man, 803/1401, 807/1405, and 809/1407, followed by a pause of sixteen years, then another four pilgrimages and *mujawarat* in 825/1422, 834/1431, 838/1435, and a long *mujawara* and Hajj in 839–40/1436–7.

173 There are certain personality traits and attitudes of al-Maqrizi that eerily parallel those of a later historian who was associated with Egypt for part of his life, the Ottoman scholar Mustafa 'Ali of Gallipoli (1541–1600), who retreated to his native city Gallipoli toward the end of his life (1593) to write reflective poetry and begin the composition of his chef-d'oeuvre *Künh ü-Ahbar* (*Essence of History*). For a review of these final years, see Cornell Fleischer, *Bureaucrat and Intellectual in the Ottoman Empire Book: The Historian Mustafa Ali (1541–1600)* (Princeton: Princeton University Press, 1986), 143–87. See the sensitive analysis of his personality in Ulrich Haarmann, "Plight of the Self-Appointed Genius: Muṣṭafā 'Ālī," *Arabica* 38, 1 (March 1991): 73–86.

structure and tone of the *Khitat*. They amplified al-Maqrizi's observations on the state of the city and gave them a personal dimension. Corruption, decline, and ruination (*kharab*) are frequently mentioned in the book, especially in the sections dealing with the condition of Cairo and its *khitat* during al-Maqrizi's lifetime, the same time period as that covered by the *Suluk*.

Death

Al-Maqrizi died in Ramadan 845/ January–February 1442 after a protracted but unnamed illness. His biographers dispute the exact date of his death, none of them managing to record the correct day of the week on which he died.[174] This is further evidence of his relative isolation from his milieu at the end of his life. His biographers might not have learned of his death until some time after it occurred, or they might not have bothered to check the correct date, as Ibn Taghri-Birdi pungently claims al-ʿAyni did. Al-Maqrizi was buried without any elaborate funeral in the Sufi Baybarsiyya cemetery outside the Bab al-Nasr north of Cairo in a simple tomb.[175] A large burial ground in the Mamluk period, the Sufi cemetery was the final resting place of many ulama of the period, including al-Maqrizi's revered teacher Ibn Khaldun.[176] Unfortunately, their tombs have been lost. After several alterations to the area north of the Fatimid walls of Cairo in the twentieth and the early twenty-first century that left the cemetery exposed to encroachment, it was stealthily removed in 2001 without any attempt to preserve the tombs of the great ulama buried there.[177]

The anonymity of al-Maqrizi's burial place is an indication that his *zuhd* was real, since he does not seem to have provided a specific place for his interment, as was the habit with distinguished members of the ulama class in medieval Egypt. His *zuhd* seems also to have been acknowledged by his peers,

[174] Ibn Hajar, *Inba'*, 9: 172, places it on Thursday 26 of Ramadan (the correct day is Wednesday); Ibn Taghri-Birdi, *Nujum*, 15: 490, and *Manhal*, 1: 399; al-Sakhawi, *Daw'*, 2: 25, put it on Thursday 16 Ramadan (the correct day is Sunday), whereas al-ʿAyni, *'Iqd*, Qarmut edition, 547, carelessly—as noted by Ibn Taghri-Birdi—put it on Thursday 29 Shaʿban, although he was at least correct in the day of the week. Al-Jawhari, *Nuzhat*, 4: 343–4, reports Ibn Hajar's and al-Ayni's dates, but favors Ibn Hajar's in accordance with his master (whom he later on will denigrate), Ibn Taghri-Birdi, although Ibn Taghri-Birdi's date is different from Ibn Hajar's.

[175] This was probably a section of the main cemetery of Bab al-Nasr, see al-Maqrizi, *Khitat2*, 2: 271–2, 4: 918–19; ʿAli Pasha Mubarak, *al-Khitat al-Tawfiqiyya al-Jadida*, 20 vols. (Cairo: Bulaq, 1888–9), 2: 71; Ibn Taghri-Birdi, *Nujum*, 10: 336, no. 1.

[176] Al-Maqrizi, *Durar*, 2: 398; al-Sakhawi, *Daw'*, 10: 146.

[177] Galila el-Kadi and Alain Bonnamy, *Architecture for the Dead: Cairo's Medieval Necropolis* (Cairo: AUC Press, 2007), 284–97.

at least by those Sufis responsible for allowing his burial in the Baybarsiyya cemetery. The simplicity of his entombment becomes even more poignant when contrasted with the pomp of that of his old competitor al-ʿAyni, who had taken the trouble to build himself a sumptuous mausoleum (*qubba*) in his madrasa, which he had constructed next to his house adjacent to al-Azhar Mosque. The *qubba* is lavishly decorated; the prayer hall next to it had a *mihrab* covered with colored tile mosaic (destroyed in an unauthorized restoration in the early 1980s), which was uncommon in Cairo. Layla Ibrahim and Bernard O'Kane proved that the tile work is copied from older Anatolian madrasas and was most probably done by Karamanid craftsmen, indicating that al-ʿAyni had maintained contact with his native ʿAyntab and that he wanted to assert his "Turkishness" through the use of a recognizable Anatolian decoration.[178] The mausoleum was further embellished by a gilded wooden dome ordered specially by Sultan al-Mu'ayyad Shaykh as an unusual sign of favoritism. The sultan al-Mu'ayyad also provided some income in his *waqf* for the Madrasa of al-ʿAyni, another clear sign of favoritism to a member of the ulama class.[179] The same al-Mu'ayyad seems to have shunned al-Maqrizi, who ultimately resolved to quit the quest for patronage and turn away from the court and its intrigues.

[178] Ibrahim and O'Kane, "Madrasa of al-ʿAyni," 267; Mubarak, *al-Khitat al-Tawfiqiyya*, 6: 10.

[179] Al-ʿAyni, *ʿIqd*, 110 (*Awqaf* 938q: Waqf of Sultan al-Mu'ayyad Shaykh. Dated 12 Rajab, 823/1420, lines 331–41). The Egyptian Ministry of Culture restored al-ʿAyni's Madrasa in 2002 and turned it into a center of creativity for children.

PART 2

THE WRITINGS OF AL-MAQRIZI

CHAPTER 3

Harvest of a Lifetime

Al-Maqrizi was "hands-down the *shaykh* (chief or dean) of the historians of his generation," if not of the entire fifteenth-century Mamluk history writing, which was one of the richest and most elaborate Islamic historical traditions.[1] This is not so only because of the volume of his historical writing or the variety of topics he covered. It is also because his was an exhaustive, structured, and principled historical project with clear ethical messages pursued in an intellectual milieu replete with history writing that seems by and large to have accepted a non-committal chronicling function.[2] In contrast, al-Maqrizi consciously and unabashedly wrote history in a personal, sentimental, and moralizing fashion. He allowed his biases, beliefs, feelings, and political and religious views to inform both his narrative and the reader who might be interested in identifying the motives behind what he/she is reading. He even explicitly addressed his reader whenever he was presenting a contentious issue or a controversial interpretation, such as when he defended the genealogy of the Fatimids, to ask for his/her unbiased weighing of the evidence before forming an opinion. That he was obsessively focused on Egypt or that his message appears to have been unduly pessimistic or puritanical does not diminish the power and uniqueness of his project. On the contrary, they add to it certain distinctive traits, such as an uncompromising ethical stand, pronounced love of country, and melancholy, which are otherwise rarely expressed in the chronicles of the time. Such qualities make the study of al-Maqrizi and his historical oeuvre all the more fascinating and timely.

Al-Maqrizi was also one of the very few eminent scholars of his age who could be termed a "professional" historian, essentially devoting himself to history writing. Unlike the work of other comparable ulama/historians such as Ibn Hajar, al-ʿAyni, or, later, al-Sakhawi, whose main scholarly output

[1] Stated in different forms on various occasions by Ibn Taghri-Birdi, *Nujum*, 14: 150; 15: 89; 15: 490.

[2] Shakir Mustafa, *Tarikh*, 3: 82–4, calls this *al-taqlid al-sukuni* (static tradition), marked by "the surrender to the rushing of events whichever way they develop and the avoidance of any negative judgment of people or events regardless of their gravity."

was in *fiqh*, *hadith*, or *tafsir* and who wrote history on the side as it were, al-Maqrizi's oeuvre is primarily historical, even when his topic is related to religion. In that he resembles his master Ibn Khaldun, his student Ibn Taghri-Birdi, and the trio of lesser-known and socially modest contemporary historians, Ibn Duqmaq, Ibn al-Furat, and al-Awhadi, whose output is almost exclusively historical. Al-Maqrizi distinguishes himself from them (of course with the exception of Ibn Khaldun) by maintaining his standing as a *'alim* whose religious erudition was amply demonstrated in his parallel project of covering the *sira* of the Prophet in several multi-volume works and in his more specialized treatises on various legal, devotional, economic, or geographical subjects, which span his career of more than forty years of writing. But even in these shorter treatises, his approach is basically historical, discussing and judging the issues in a chronological order in which the model of the Prophet and of his companions offers a solid foundation for bringing the historical argument down to his own time and context. This rather fundamentalist frame of presentation, however, did not prevent al-Maqrizi from exploring causality and taking contextual circumstances into account in assessing historical events. He was a firm believer in the teleological Islamic divine scheme of history that has a beginning, a trajectory, and a preordained end according to the projections of the Qur'an and the Hadith. He accepted paranormal phenomena, wonders, and thaumaturgy as influential factors in the flow of events. Yet, he is one of the few historians of the time to have upheld a critical stance vis-à-vis the events he was reporting, conceived and presented from within the epistemological framework of a medieval Muslim thinker: in other words, pre-humanist, inherently deterministic, and ultimately moralistic. In that regard he is not very different from his revered teacher Ibn Khaldun, even though he might have been more emotional and more attentive to quotidian and personal details.[3]

Al-Maqrizi's historical project thus deserves a more careful look than it has received so far, one that can transcend the biases of our rationalizing and thoroughly secularized and psychologized conception of history to try to understand the import of history in his own time and his contribution to it. To do this, we need to take into account both the evolution of the discipline of history in Islamic thought in relation to, and under the umbrella of, the religious sciences and the religious, intellectual, and emotional con-

[3] Hayden White, "Ibn Khaldun in World Philosophy of History (Review Article)," *Comparative Studies in Society and History* 2 (1959–60): 110–25, accused Ibn Khaldun of adopting a similar metaphysical framework totally ignoring the cultural milieu within which the two men were thinking and theorizing. For a more nuanced understanding see Briton Cooper Busch, "Divine Intervention in the 'Muqaddimah' of Ibn Khaldūn," *History of Religions* 7, 4 (May 1968): 317–29; also Irwin, "al-Maqrizi and Ibn Khaldun," 229–30; idem, *Ibn Khaldun: An Intellectual Biography* (Princeton: Princeton University Press, 2018), 19.

ditions under which al-Maqrizi wrote history. For here is a devout scholar who quit his public career at the prime age of forty-eight to devote himself completely to writing the history of his beloved country Egypt, whose irrevocable decline under the morally lax Mamluk rule he was somberly predicting and loudly condemning. He followed this massive undertaking with another historical project, the life of the Prophet and the history of his household (Al al-Bayt), which, though secondary in comparison to the Egypt project, is equally important for understanding his beliefs, motivations, and ethical message. Unlike his Egypt project, which spans more than thirty years and at least six interrelated, large, multi-volume books and a number of shorter treatises, the prophetic history project was all too evidently motivated less by professional ambition and more by personal piety and intellectual and religious responsibility. On the whole, the two projects embody the intense and painful soul-searching and reckoning that al-Maqrizi experienced as he went through a conscious transformation from a typical competitor in the *manasib* race and a client to one or other among the Mamluk grandees to a fiercely independent and resolutely outspoken historian with a critical stance that is both pessimistic and religiously committed.

A Tentative Inventory of al-Maqrizi's Works

Despite the great interest in al-Maqrizi, both during his time and in recent scholarship, we still lack a definitive list of his works. We do not even know for sure whether he was able to complete some of his most famous books as he had originally planned them. This confusion is primarily due to the fact that, unlike his peers such as Ibn Hajar, Ibn Fahd, or al-Sakhawi, al-Maqrizi did not pen a list of his compositions during his lifetime, nor did he write a *mashikhat* of his teachers. One possible reason may be that he shared the humility that marked some of the ulama of the time, who avoided boasting of their scholarly accomplishments or academic genealogies, although he did not lack self-esteem, and even a bit of pride, as is clear from the reflective comments he wrote on the covers of some of his holographs, or what he made his biographees say about him in his *Durar*. Another reason may be that he did not have the time to do it, as he was contemplating his life's work shortly before his death, when he was struggling with his fatal illness, for we know that he was redacting, correcting, and collecting many of his short opuscules in 1439 and 1440, perhaps as a prelude to finalizing all of his works. But we know that he actually died with a number of his large compendia, such as the *Khitat* and *al-Muqaffa al-Kabir* or *Majma' al-Fara'id*, still in progress and many new essays still in draft form. We also know that he was still adding new material to many of them, as revealed by the fact that he was still inserting loose sheets (called *tayyarat* in Arabic, literary meaning "flying") between the pages of his autograph manuscripts or adding entries in the margins of his final, fair drafts up until shortly before his death.[4] Furthermore, the fact that we are still discovering manuscripts of al-Maqrizi's work, some of which are holographs, means that we still might unearth some of the missing works or parts of the incomplete works and adjust the list of his complete oeuvre.[5]

The situation is exacerbated by the conflicting reports about al-Maqrizi's oeuvre in the biographies written by his contemporaries. Three of them, al-Sakhawi, Ibn Taghri-Birdi, and Ibn Fahd, compiled lists of his works, but none of them attempted a definitive one. Al-Sakhawi and Ibn Taghri-Birdi enumerate twenty-eight and twenty-three titles respectively and add that they

[4] Ayman Fu'ad Sayyid, "Remarques sur la composition des Hitat de Maqrizi d'après un manuscrits autographe," in *Hommages à la mémoire de Serge Sauneron, 1927–1976, II: Égypte post-pharaonique* (Cairo: IFAO, 1979), 231–58; Jan Just Witkam, "Les autographes d'al-Maqrizi," in *Le manuscrit arabe et la codicologie*, ed. Ahmed-Chouqui Binebine (Rabat: Publications de la Faculté des Lettres et des Sciences Humaines, 1994), 89–98, esp. 94; Frédéric Bauden, "Maqriziana II: Discovery of an Autograph Manuscript of al-Maqrizi: Towards a Better Understanding of His Working Method, Analysis," *MSR* 12, 1 (2008): 51–118, esp. 91–3; idem, "Vers une archéologie du savoir en Islam: la méthode de travail d'al-Maqrizi, historien du XVe siècle," *Comptes rendus des séances de l'Académie des Inscriptions et Belles-Lettres* 153, 1 (2009): 97–110; idem, "Maqriziana X. Al-Maqrizi and His al-Tarih al-Kabir al-Muqaffa li-Miṣr. Part 1: An Inquiry into the History of the Work," *Studies in Islamic Historiography: Essays in Honour of Professor Donald P. Little*, Sami G. Massoud, ed. (Leiden: Brill, 2020), 70–1.

[5] See, for instance, Jan Just Witkam, "Reflections on al-Maqrizi's Biographical Dictionary," in *History and Islamic Civilization: Essays in Honour of Ayman Fu'ad Sayyid*, Obada Kohela, ed. (Cairo: al-Dar al-Misriyya al-Lubnaniyya, 2014), 93–114, where he tracks down the information we have on *al-Muqaffa al-Kabir*; Frédéric Bauden, "Maqriziana I: Discovery of an Autograph Manuscript of al-Maqrizi: Towards a Better Understanding of His Working Method, Description: Section 1," *MSR* 7 (2003): 21–68; idem, "Maqriziana I: Discovery of an Autograph Manuscript of al-Maqrizi: Towards a Better Understanding of His Working Method, Description: Section 2," *MSR* 10, 2 (2006): 81–139; idem, "Maqriziana II," offers an exhaustive analysis of the codex MS 2232 at the Liège library (whose provenance is shrouded in mystery and which may have been looted by the French in Algeria, though Bauden refrains from going into this possibility), *Maqriziana* I, 1, 28, and Bauden, "De la codicologie à l'archéologie du savoir. Le cas particulier du carnet de notes de l'historien égyptien al-Maqrizi (m. 845/1442)," in *Le livre au fil de ses pages, actes de la 14e journée d'étude du Réseau des Médiévistes belges de Langue française*, Renaud Adam and Alain Marchandisse, eds., *Archives et Bibliothèques de Belgique= Archief en Bibliotheekwezen in Belgie* Numéro Spécial 87 (2009): 31–3, which is a collection of excerpts from the sources that al-Maqrizi used in his writing: appendix I, 115–16 lists all the autograph manuscripts of al-Maqrizi; Noah Gardiner with Frédéric Bauden, "A recently discovered holograph fair copy of al-Maqrizi's *al-Mawāʿiz wa-al-iʿtibār fī dhikr al-khitat wa-al-āthār*: University of Michigan Islamic MS 605," *Journal of Islamic Manuscripts* 2 (2011): 123–31, on the 2010 discovery of a hitherto unknown manuscript of al-Maqrizi's *Khitat*, which raises the numbers of autograph manuscripts to twenty-four.

have overlooked some more.[6] Between them, al-Sakhawi and Ibn Taghri-Birdi share twenty-two titles, and both overlook the important treatise on famine and economic crisis, *Ighathat al-Umma bi-Kashf al-Ghumma*, one of al-Maqrizi's earliest original compositions, and the short essay on *dhikr*, *Hirs al-Nufus al-Fadhila 'ala Baqa' al-Dhikr*. Ibn Taghri Birdi alone lists the opuscule on bees, *Nihal 'Ibar al-Nahal*, whereas al-Sakhawi has five titles that do not appear in Ibn Taghri-Birdi's list. They include two short treatises that are known and published, *al-Ishara wa al-Ima' ila Hall Lughz al-Ma'* (Pointing and Hinting at the Solution of the Riddle of Water) and *al-Ishara wa al I'lam bi Bina' al-Ka'ba wa al-Bayt al-Haram* (Showing and Informing about the Construction of the Ka'ba and the Sanctified House), to which he adds its abridgment, *Dhikr Bina' al-Ka'ba wal-Bayt al-Haram*, which brings his count to twenty-eight. He also lists five other missing titles, one of which is the versification of Ibn Nahid's *sirat* al-Mu'ayyad, already proven to be no more than an appraisal among many contributed by the famous scholars of the time in Chapter 2. The four others, *Majma' al-Fara'id wa Manba' al-Fawa'id* (The Compendium of Rarities and the Source of Benefits), *al-Akhbar 'an al-A'zar* (Reports on Circumcision), *Shari' al-Najat* (Path to Salvation), and *'Iqd Jawahir al-Asfat fi Tarikh Madinat al-Fustat*, are missing today. But we have internal references from al-Maqrizi's own writing about the occasion on which he wrote them, even though we have no references to their content in later scholarship.[7] Missing too are two books of unknown length that al-Maqrizi alone mentions in his *Khitat*, one on the viziers of Egypt, *Talqih al-'Uqul wal-Ara' fi Tanqih Akhbar al-Jullat al-Wuzara'*,[8] and the other on the *kuttab al-sirr*, *Khulasat al-Tibr fi Akhbar*

[6] Al-Sakhawi, *Daw'*, 2: 22–3; Ibn Taghri-Birdi, *Manhal*, 1: 397–8.

[7] Al-Maqrizi, *Suluk*, 4: 913, reports that he composed this treatise on the occasion of the circumcision of sultan Barsbay's son, Jamal al-Din Yusuf (r. 841–2/1438), in mid-Sha'ban 837/ late March 1434; Van Steenbergen, *Caliphate and Kingship*, 29. Al-Maqrizi, *Dhahab*, 33–4, where he informs his readers that he responded to criticism of the book by Ibn Hazm, the reviver of the Zahiri *madhhab*, on the last Hajj of the Prophet in his own *Shari' al-Najat*, even though Ibn Hazm has no book on the pilgrimage of the Prophet but has written an essay on the *Sira* of the Prophet, *al-Risala al-Kamiliyya fi al-Sira al-Nabawiyya*, which might be the work al-Maqrizi meant. Al-Sakhawi, *Daw'*, 1: 258, says that *Shari' al-Najat* "comprises everything about the disputes among people over the basic tenets of their religions and their branches, with the elucidation of their proofs and the designation of the correct ones," which may be a Maqrizian version of Ibn Hazm's *al-Fasl fi al-Milal*, which we know al-Maqrizi read and quoted in his *Khitat*, as we will see later. Al-Sakhawi's reference to *Shari' al-Najat* thus suggests a book of an encyclopedic nature rather than a short treatise.

[8] Al-Maqrizi, *Khitat2*, 2: 452, 3: 723. Sayyid also mentions the holograph draft of al-Maqrizi kept at Bibliotheca Alexandrina (#2125d), where he lists several biographies of viziers, including a list of the Seljuk viziers, which Sayyid thinks formed a draft for his planned and missing book *Talqih al-'Uqul*, al-Maqrizi, *Khitat2*, Indexes, 6: 23.

Kuttab al-Sirr.[9] Ibn Fahd, who would have had better knowledge of his master's work, as he seems to have spent a considerable amount of time with him during his pilgrimages and *mujawarat* in Mecca in the last few years of his life, only lists the major oeuvres, amounting to eight.[10]

Al-Sakhawi says that he read a note by al-Maqrizi himself stating that his compilations exceeded 200 large volumes (*mujalladat*), which is a difficult statement to interpret since many of al-Maqrizi's historical works consisted of several volumes each and since Ibn Taghri Birdi and Ibn Fahd, who report on the subject, differ as to the number of volumes they assign to each title.[11] Ibn Taghri Birdi reports that *al-Khabar 'an al-Bashar* comprises four volumes and one volume as introduction; Ibn Fahd counts two volumes only. Ibn Taghri Birdi assigns three volumes to *Durar al-'Uqud al-Farida*, Ibn Fahd four, whereas the only complete manuscript of the book that has survived and that was copied in 878/1473 in Cairo, twenty-eight years after the death of al-Maqrizi, is composed of two volumes only. The two biographers agree that *Imta' al-Asma' bima lil-Rasul min al-Abna' wa al-Akhwal wa al-Hafada wa al-Mita'* covered six volumes, and that the missing *'Iqd Jawahir al-Asfat fi Tarikh Madinat al-Fustat* and the *Itti'az al-Hunafa bi-Akhbar al-A'imma al-Fatimiyyin al-Khulafa* each covered one volume. *Suluk* encompassed five volumes according to Ibn Fahd, whereas the incomplete *Muqaffa* comprised sixteen volumes, that is, one fifth of the eighty volumes al-Maqrizi is said to have projected it to cover had it been completed as planned. The total that these two biographers account for is almost forty volumes. If we add to this the short treatises and consider each one a volume, and add the eighty missing volumes of the enormous compendium *Majma' al-Fara'id wa Manba' al-Fawa'id*, of which al-Maqrizi is said to have made a fair copy, then the total of his *mujalladat* would approach 150 volumes, a very impressive output indeed, if still at great variance with the 200 volumes reported by al-Sakhawi.

The uncertainty about al-Maqrizi's complete oeuvre was compounded by developments after his death. Since he does not seem to have left any children behind to preserve his legacy, his library, which of course included all autograph manuscripts he was working on, was most probably passed on to the only known surviving member of his family, his nephew Nasir al-Din Muhammad, whose signature appears on the frontispiece of the autograph

[9] Al-Maqrizi, *Khitat2*, 3: 204.

[10] Ibn Fahd, *Mu'jam*, 64, lists eight titles, which are those of the major historical books minus one: *al-Bayan wa al-I'rab amman Dakhala Misr min al-A'rab*, a short, incomplete treatise on the Arabic tribes that moved to Egypt, that complements his multi-title history of Islamic Egypt. Ibn Fahd does not list *al-Khabar 'an al-Bashar* by title; instead he calls it *al-Madkhal* (the introduction) to the larger compendium on everything related to the life of the Prophet, *Imta' al-Asma'*.

[11] Ibn Taghri-Birdi, *Manhal*, 1: 397–8; Ibn Fahd, *Mu'jam*, 66.

manuscript of the *Suluk*, with some works finding their way into the hands of some of his scholar friends like Ibn Hajar, who clearly obtained al-Maqrizi's incomplete *al-Muqaffa al-Kabir*, to which he added several entries that al-Maqrizi had left blank.[12] Al-Maqrizi's popularity, however, was substantial enough in the remainder of the Mamluk period for copyists to copy his manuscripts and for patrons to commission continuations on his chronicle *al-Suluk*, even if at least one of these continuators, al-Sakhawi, says that he had done so begrudgingly and in deference to the order from his patron the Great Amir Yashbak min Mahdi.[13] The *Khitat* in particular appears to have garnered a wide readership, to judge from the abridgments made of it or the manuscripts of the book preserved in libraries around the world, and these are only the fraction that survived the vagaries of time. Their numbers are constantly rising as new manuscripts are discovered that had lain unidentified or combined with other titles of other authors during one of the transactions that led to their final acquisition by their current repositories. Gaston Wiet, for instance, counted 174 full or partial copies of the *Khitat* dating from al-Maqrizi's own time and well into the sixteenth and seventeenth centuries when he started his translation project in 1911, and had to abort it in 1927 because he was continuously discovering more manuscripts which would have necessitated a team of researchers to carry on the translation.[14] Frederic Bauden in 2014 reports the number of manuscripts preserved in libraries across the world to have reached more than 250.[15]

At present, the list of al-Maqrizi's known and verifiable works comprises thirty-seven titles and several abridgments of works by other authors (*mukhtasarat*, sg. *mukhtasar*).[16] They range in length from multi-volume biographical dictionaries, devotional histories of the Prophet Muhammad and his family, or historical chronicles of the major dynasties that ruled Islamic Egypt to a number of shorter treatises, more like articles, treating of various subjects. Most of the long historical oeuvres, seven in total, are published, some more than once, although a few of them were imperfectly edited and without any critical collating of their various known manuscripts.

12 Witkam, "Les autographes d'al-Maqrizi," 95–6.

13 Al-Sakhawi, *Tibr*, 1: 37–38, where he criticizes al-Maqrizi in a very convoluted way even though he admits to having been commissioned, in fact ordered, to write a continuation of his *Suluk*; see also Ibn Taghri-Birdi, *Manhal*, 1: 418.

14 Sayyid, *Musawwadat*, Introduction, 94; al-Maqrizi, *Khitat2*, Introduction, 5: 12–13.

15 Frederick Bauden, "Taqi al-Din Ahmad b. ʿAli al-Maqrīzī", *Medieval Muslim Historians and the Franks in the Levant*, Alex Mallett, ed. (Leiden: Brill, 2014), 171–2.

16 Al-Maqrizi, *Ittiʿaz*, Introduction, 1: 13–22; al-Shayyal, "Mu'allafat al-Maqrizi al-Saghira," in *Dirasat ʿan al-Maqrizi*, 23–4; Sayyid, *Musawwadat*, 45–64, and Izz al-Din, *al-Maqrizi Mu'arrikhan*, 51–80, list and analyze al-Maqrizi's works; Bauden, "al-Maqrizi", 167–96; Van Steenbergen, *Caliphate and Kingship*, 27–8.

They comprise two historical chronicles on Egypt, *Itti'az al-Hunafa* on the Fatimids and *al-Suluk* on the Ayyubids and the Mamluks down to al-Maqrizi's death, his incomplete big biographical dictionary, *al-Muqaffa al-Kabir*, his more intimate dictionary of the people of his time, *Durar*, and the *Khitat*, his most influential book. To this list should be added his short treatise on the Arab tribes of Egypt, *al-Bayan wa-l I'rab 'amman Dakhal Misr min al-A'rab*, and his still-missing book on al-Fustat, the first Islamic capital of Egypt, *'Iqd Jawahir al-Asfat fi Tarikh Madinat al-Fustat*. The two other large compendia are *al-Khabar 'an al-Bashar*, a universal history of humanity from Adam down to the Prophet Muhammad (published in eight volumes), which Ibn Fahd calls *al-Madkhal* (the introduction) to the larger compendium on everything related to the life of the Prophet, *Imta' al-Asma' bima lil-Rasul min al-Abna' wa al-Akhwal wa al-Hafada wa al-Mata'*, amounting in its recently published edition to fifteen volumes.[17] To these large compendia should be added the *Kitab Mujama' al-Fara'id wa Manba' al-Fawa'id*, which is said by al-Sakhawi to have been planned as an inclusive encyclopedia of more than a hundred *mujalladat* comprising all *'aqli* (rational, i.e. philosophical and scientific) and *naqli* (transmitted, i.e. religious) knowledge. Al-Sakhawi reports that al-Maqrizi completed only eighty volumes of this ambitious compilation before his death, and those are still missing.[18]

The known and available titles of al-Maqrizi's treatises are twenty-eight in total. All have been published, some more than once, but almost all are still awaiting professional editions.[19] These article-like opuscules underscore al-Maqrizi's odd interests in a wide scope of topics, ranging from singing, *Izalat al-Ta'ab wa al-'Ana' fi Ma'rifat Hal al-Ghina'* (Removing Fatigue and Exhaustion in Knowing the Explication of Singing), to the history of the Ka'ba, *al-Ishara wa al-I'lam bi Bina' al-Ka'ba wa al-Bayt al-Haram* (Showing and Informing about the Construction of the Ka'ba and the Sanctified House), which was most probably written in Mecca and abridged as *Dhikr Bina' al-Ka'ba wal-Bayt al-Haram*, to a number of linguistic riddles, such as *al-Ishara wa al-Ima' ila Hall Lughz al-Ma'*, to some biographical or theological opinions. There are several treatises on religious topics: four on the issue of *tawhid* (the belief in God's uniqueness), two on the struggle between the Umayyads and the clan of the Prophet's, the

[17] Al-Maqrizi, *Imta' al-Asma' bima lil-Rasul min al-Abna' wa al-Akhwal wa al-Hafada wa al-Mata '*, 15 vols., Muhammad 'Abd al-Hamid al-Namisi, ed. (Beirut: Dar al-Kutub al-Ilmiyya, 1999).

[18] Al-Sakhawi, *Daw'*, 2: 23–4.

[19] Al-Maqrizi, *Rasa'il al-Maqrizi*, Ramadan al-Safanawi Badri and Ahmad Mustafa Qasim, eds. (Cairo: Dar al-Hadith, 1998), assembles eleven articles, many of which have been published before.

Hashmites, which highlight al-Maqrizi's partisanship toward the Al al-Bayt, and two (or three) opuscules on the praise of Al al-Bayt, a topic that reappears in many of al-Maqrizi's compositions, including of course the large compendium *Imta' al-Asma'*. There is also one essay on the tricky question of inheritance from a Companion of the Prophet in Palestine, *Daw' al-Sari li-Ma'rifat Khabar Tamim al-Dari*,[20] and another on the rulers of Islam who performed the Hajj, *al-Dhahab al-Masbuk bi-Dhikr man Hajja min al-Khulafa' wa al-Muluk*.[21] Two more tractates appear to have been composed in Mecca with mostly oral material on faraway lands acquired during his *mujawara* there: one on Hadhramaut in Southern Yemen, *al-Turfa al-Ghariba fi Akhbar Hadhramut al-'Ajiba*, and the other on the Muslim rulers in Abyssinia, *Kitab al-Ilmam bi-Akhbar man bi-Ard al-Habasha min Muluk al-Islam*.[22] To those should be added the treatise on bees, *Nihal 'Ibar al-Nahal*, and the one on minerals, *al-Maqasid al-Saniyya li Ma'rifat al-Ajsam al-Ma'daniyya*.[23]

Notebooks and Abridgments: A Window into al-Maqrizi's Sourcing Method

Al-Maqrizi was a voracious reader of history, geography, and *adab* books, if we are to judge from his various citations from a wide variety of sources, which have been remarkably preserved in a number of notebooks and drafts. The most important of these notebooks is the Liège Manuscript (MS 2232), a collection of 205 folios which covers the period from 811 A.H. (1408) to 831 A.H. (1427) and possibly later, perhaps the most active period in al-Maqrizi's writing career. Frédéric Bauden has devoted a great deal of effort and time to painstakingly explore the Liège Manuscript in search of al-Maqrizi's "working method," in a series of ongoing numbered publications collectively titled

[20] A new annotated and translated edition of the book was published by Yehoshua Frenkel, *Daw' al-Sari li-Ma'rifat Habar Tamim al-Dari. On Tamim al-Dari and his Waqf in Hebron* (Leiden: Brill, 2014) as Vol. 2 of the Bibliotheca Maqriziana.

[21] Van Steenbergen, *Caliphate and Kingship*, as Vol. 3 of the Bibliotheca Maqriziana.

[22] Franz-Christoph Muth, "A Globe-Trotter from Maghrib in al-Maqrizi's Booklet on Ethiopia: A Footnote from Some Arabic Sources," *Afrique & histoire*, 4, 2 (2005): 125–6, argues that although al-Maqrizi claims that he composed this book during his *mujawara* in Meccan in 1435, most of the first two sections of the book are taken from Ibn Fadhl Allah al-'Umari's *Masalik al-Absar fi Mamlik al-Amsar*. Al-Maqrizi's use of Ibn Fadhl Allah was more extensive than this copying, as we will see.

[23] A new annotated and translated edition of the book was published by Fabian Käs, Al-Maqrizi's *Traktat Uber Die Mineralien: Kitāb al-Maqāṣid al-Saniyyah li-Ma'rifat al-Ağsām al-Ma'diniyyah* (Leiden: Brill, 2016) as Vol. 4 of the Bibliotheca Maqriziana.

Maqriziana.[24] There is another known notebook of al-Maqrizi in the library of Alexandria, consisting of fifty-three folios, which has not yet received any systematic study.[25] Notebooks like these, which have rarely reached us, reveal valuable information on an author's method of reading, collecting, extracting data, arranging it, abridging it, and ultimately reusing it in his own compositions.

Bauden has found in the notebook digests of various sources that al-Maqrizi used in his own books: Ibn Abi Usaybu'a, *'Uyun al-Anba' fi Tabaqat al-Attiba'*, the most important biographical dictionary on physicians; Ibn 'Abd al-Hakam, *Kitab Futuh Misr wa-Akhbaruha*, the earliest book we have on the Islamic conquest of Egypt and its early Islamic history; and Waki', *Kitab al-Dananir wa-l Darahim* (which Ibn al-Nadim calls, in his *Fihrist*, *Kitab al-Sarf wa-l Naqd wa-l Sikka*, which is probably more accurate). Al-Maqrizi also copied several texts from several historical sources, such as the encyclopedic biographical dictionary of Ibn Aybak al-Safadi, *al-Wafi bi-l Wafiyyat*; the lost chronicle of Musa ibn al-Ma'mun on his father, the famous Fatimid vizier al-Ma'mun al-Bata'ihi (r. 1121–5); Ibn Nazif al-Hamawi's history of the Ayybid, *al-Tarikh al-Mansuri*; Ibn Sa'id al-Maghribi's indispensable history, *al-Mugharrib fi-Hulyy al-Maghrib*; the geographical encyclopedia of Ibn Fadhl Allah al-'Umari, *Masalik al-Absar fi Mamalik al-Amsar*; and many other books from which al-Maqrizi copied texts that varied in length from small citation to full section.[26] Al-Maqrizi seems to have been adding more citations over time, sometimes by inserting new loose pages, and at other times by writing on the margins or in the empty space above or below already copied texts. Bauden, and Ayman Fu'ad Sayyid in his copious introductions to the several books of al-Maqrizi he has edited in recent years, have furthered our understanding of al-Maqrizi's methods of sourcing beyond the straightforward listing of his sources, a topic that is still being debated in scholarly circles, which we will further tackle in what follows.[27]

[24] Bauden, "Maqriziana I," 21, and "Maqriziana II," 76–104; there are so far, as far as I can ascertain, eleven articles with the title "Maqriziana." They are numbered in Roman numerals from I to XIV and published over the period of as many years with three missing numbers: 3, 5, and 6. Idem, "Review of *al-Mawa'iz wa-al-I'tibār fī Dhikr al-Khitat wa-al-Athār*. Edited by Ayman Fu'ad Sayyid. Vols. 1–2," *MSR* 11–2 (2007): 172–3, shows a great determination to maintain the pace of detailed and exhaustive analysis that he initiated in his Maqriziana series. Ayman Fu'ad Sayyid provides a summary description of the Liège Manuscript (MS 2232) in al-Maqrizi, *Khitat2*, 5: 19–22.

[25] Bibliotheca Alexandrina, ms. Ta'rīh, 2125 D (formerly at al-Maktaba al-Baladiyya). Sayyid provides a summary description of its contents in al-Maqrizi, *Khitat2*, 5: 22–4, which indicates that most of its material is biographical notices. Bauden, "Vers une archéologie," 101, n. 7, and "Maqriziana II," 74, only mentions it in passing.

[26] Bauden, "Maqriziana II," 80–2.

[27] Bauden, "Maqriziana IX," 159–232, establishes that nineteen leaves in the handwriting of

One example that illuminates how al-Maqrizi handled his source material is his writing on Tamerlane, who not only was his contemporary, but al-Maqrizi might have been with the Egyptian army that retreated from Damascus upon Tamerlane's attack in January 1401, or he might have even stayed behind with other ulama such as Ibn Khaldun when Tamerlane took the city. Yet al-Maqrizi does not say anything personal about Tamerlane. Instead, he depends on other contemporary authors to present an elaborate and rather neutral biography of the conqueror in his *Durar*, as well as detailed reports on Tamerlane's invasion of Syria in 803/1400 in his *Suluk*.[28] His major source for both texts is the book of his contemporary Ibn 'Arabshah (1392–1450) on Tamerlane, *'Aja'ib al-Maqdur fi Nawa'ib Taymur*, from which he copies substantial material, sometime verbatim, especially in the section on Tamerlane's early life. He does not specifically state that his biography depends on Ibn 'Arabshah's. But, at the same time, he says, in his entry on Ibn 'Arabshah in his *Durar*, that Ibn 'Arabshah showed him his book on Tamerlane, which he promptly proceeded to abridge because the original was composed in a rhyming style and was filled with poetry quotations (which it is).[29] That digest is missing today, but it most probably formed the basis of Tamerlane's biography in the *Durar*, where al-Maqrizi twice quotes Ibn 'Arabshah in two reports, and even identifies Ibn 'Arabshah as the author of the *sira* of Tamerlane without mentioning his digest of it.[30] He also supplements Tamerlane's biography by quoting sources that do not appear in Ibn 'Arabshah's book, possibly as a way of muddling the issue of copying, as many of his detractors would have claimed, or simply to diversify his sources. Most prominently, he cites four oral reports from Ibn Khaldun toward the end of the biography, two of which are about events that happened outside Damascus when Ibn Khaldun was in the company of Tamerlane, which of course lends the biography an aura of authenticity.[31]

---

al-Awhadi, al-Maqrizi's neighbor, colleague and posthumous competitor, are attached with alterations and erasures to al-Maqrizi's draft of his *Khitat* in an effort to prove that al-Maqrizi's book is nothing but a plagiarized rendering of the draft of *Khitat* by al-Awhadi (761/1361–811/1408), as suggested by al-Sakhawi, *Daw'*, 3: 358–9, and idem, *al-I'lan bi-al-Tawbikh*, 266.

[28] Al-Maqrizi, *Durar*, 1: 501–59; idem, *Suluk*, 3: 1044–53.

[29] Al-Maqrizi, *Durar*, 1: 287–8. Al-Maqrizi is full of praise for the book and for its metered prose and its abundance of information. Al-Sakhawi, *Daw'*, 1: 126–7, offers a more detailed admiring biography of Ibn 'Arabshah, although he copies al-Maqrizi's biography as well and mentions that al-Maqrizi made the digest of the book on Tamerlane.

[30] Al-Maqrizi, *Durar*, 1: 499, in the biography of Tokhtamish (d. 1406), a contemporary khan of Tamerlane who unified the White Horde and Blue Horde and died fighting Tamerlane, and 1: 558 at the end of Tamerlane's biography, where he cites a story reported by Ibn 'Arabshah on the authority of a certain Mahmud al-Khawarizmi, a *faqih* in the service of Tamerlane.

[31] Ibid., 1: 551, 552, 554, 555.

The biography of Tamerlane begins to elucidate al-Maqrizi's tactics of reworking copied texts to make them his own, which was not unusual behavior for his time. He almost always offers an indirect admission of copying by quoting the author from whom he is copying in reports that add information to the material copied, although he rarely indicates what he is copying straight from that same author, especially in the case of a contemporary. He also supplements the copied texts with information from other sources so as to enrich it and widen its scope. In the case of Ibn 'Arabshah, for instance, al-Maqrizi begins with a review of the history of Turks and Mongols, starting with their founding kings down to Tamerlane, that does not exist in Ibn 'Arabshah's book and ends with the direct quotations from Ibn Khaldun. He rearranges the material he copied to fit his chronological order and cleans it of excessive assonance, although he sometimes keeps the phraseology and even the exact words of Ibn 'Arabshah.

But in this particular case, al-Maqrizi poses a riddle that makes the question of attribution even more complicated. In his short biography of his contemporary friend, neighbor, and sometime competitor Ibn Duqmaq in the *Durar*, he ascribes to himself an authentic account of Tamerlane's conquest of Aleppo that was copied verbatim not only by Ibn Duqmaq, but also by Ibn al-Furat, the other contemporary historian to have chronicled the same period.[32] There have been in Mamluk as well as recent historiographic scholarship repeated accusations leveled at al-Maqrizi and other prominent historians of the time, such as al-'Ayni, of specifically lifting historical material from Ibn al-Furat, and other less known historians of the time, without acknowledgment.[33] Al-Maqrizi here politely reverses the accusation. He states not only that Ibn Duqmaq (and after him Ibn al-Furat) copied his account, but that they penned the same expression, "a witness that I cannot mistrust told me," as he had used in his report as an indication of a first-hand account in

[32] Ibid., 1: 102. The Damascene historian Ibn Qadi Shuhbah (1377–1448), the author of another history of the Burji period, who read and commented on the manuscript of al-Maqrizi's *Durar*, questioned al-Maqrizi's allegation in the margin. His negative tone is not surprising since he is the author of two selections from Ibn al-Furat and Ibn Duqmaq, who, moreover, formed his main sources, in addition to al-Maqrizi himself, for the material on Egypt in his history *al-Dhayl*, see David C. Reisman, "A Holograph MS of Ibn Qadi Shuhbah's '*Dhayl*,'" *MSR* 2 (1998): 19–45. See also Bauden, "Maqriziana II," 105–6, for a translation of the section in *Durar* on Ibn Duqmaq and a discussion in a different direction.

[33] The most detailed account of al-Maqrizi's "borrowing" without attribution from Ibn al-Furat is Fozia Bora, "A Mamluk Historian's Holograph: Messages from a Musawwada of Ta'rīkh," *Journal of Islamic Manuscripts* 3 (2012) 119–53; but see also Reuven Amitai, "Al-Maqrizi as a Historian of the Early Mamluk Sultanate (or: Is al-Maqrizi an Unrecognized Historiographical Villain?)," *MSR* 7, 2 (2003): 99–118; Frédéric Bauden, "al-Maqrizi," *Encyclopedia of the Medieval Chronicle*, R. G. Dunphy ed. (Leiden: 2010), 1074; Massoud, *Chronicles and Annalistic Sources*, 49–50, 112–15.

theirs, as if they were the eyewitnesses, when it was al-Maqrizi.[34] Al-Maqrizi, however, does not call Ibn Duqmaq a thief as al-Sakhawi had him, or as many contemporary historians are doing these days, probably because he was a well-mannered individual who generally refrained from diatribes against other ulama, although of course he was famous for his angry denunciations of contemporary Mamluk sultans. Instead, he blames this (mis)appropriation of his text on a milder character fault of Ibn Duqmaq's: his carelessness (*ghafla*), which had ostensibly put him in worse situations in his professional life than the embarrassment of usurping someone else's text. Al-Maqrizi also hastens to add a number of praiseworthy qualities of Ibn Duqmaq and to proclaim him a friend and colleague. But polite as he may be, al-Maqrizi's remark suggests that he either did not hold Ibn Duqmaq in high esteem or else believed—and wanted us to know—that his drafts had provided the original source of some of Ibn Duqmaq's historical writing.

There is another source that al-Maqrizi summarizes in his notebook that deserves a deeper look for what it would contribute to our understanding of al-Maqrizi's use of sources, especially original Fatimid sources, for which he is sometimes our only authority. The abridgment also sheds some light on al-Maqrizi's interest in Fatimid history and *da'wa* (mission), which may have been induced by his belief in his Fatimid genealogy, since hardly any contemporary Mamluk historians shared that interest. The source is the theosophical opus of the famous Isma'ili *da'i* (missionary) Hamid al-Din Ahmad b. 'Abdallah al-Kirmani (flourished 996–1021) *Rahat al-'Aql* (Peace of Mind, or Comfort of Reason). An influential treatise on Isma'ili doctrines and beliefs in the time of Caliph al-Hakim (r. 996–1021), this book was written in defense of the Caliph and as a corrective to the exaggerations of other *du'at* (plural of *da'i*) who cast al-Hakim as divine. Al-Maqrizi chose seven lines from different places in the book and inserted them in the leftover space below his digest of Ibn Abi Usaybu'a's *'Uyun al-Anba' fi Tabaqat al-Attiba'* in his notebook.[35]

[34] The circle is completed by Ibn Hajar al-'Asqalani, who, in his introduction to his *Inbā'*, 1: 2–3, lists his sources for his historical chronicle of his own times as Ibn al-Furat and Ibn Duqmaq, from whom he is "copying most of what he is writing," and Ibn Hajji (d. 1413), al-Maqrizi, Shaykh al-Haram al-Fasi (1373–1429), and al-Afqahasi (d. 1420). Then he says that he compared the chronicle of Ibn Duqmaq to the history of al-'Ayni [*'Iqd al-Juman*], but discovered that he was copying Ibn Duqmaq so extensively that he would copy the grammatical mistakes and would attribute to himself witnessing events in the first person, as Ibn Duqmaq does in his original, at a time when al-'Ayni was still in his native 'Ayntab and could not have witnessed the events in Cairo. Ibn Hajar adds also a revealing remark when he says, "I will not busy myself in following his [al-'Ayni's] mistakes, yet I still copied from him events that he would attend and that we would be absent from," most probably a reference to al-'Ayni's closeness to the circles of Mamluk power and his first-hand reporting of that. Al-Sakhawi, *Daw'*, 1: 145, repeats the accusation of his master Ibn Hajar.

[35] Bauden, "Maqriziana I," 81–3; "Maqriziana II," 66, thoroughly analyzes the excerpts from

These lines are extracted from various pages in the book and rearranged as if to summarize the whole book from al-Maqrizi's perspective, suggesting that he was not copying from a secondary source but reading the original and extracting from it what he deemed important, although we still do not know whether he ever used this abridgment in any of his own books.[36]

But what this abridgment reinforces is al-Maqrizi's claim that he had access to original Fatimid sources, although, with the exception of al-Kirmani, he does not reveal the names of the authors or the titles of the books on Fatimid beliefs he used in his own books. He instead says, at the end of his copious explanation of the Fatimid Isma'ili *da'wa* in his *Khitat*, "this is the sum [*hasil*] of the knowledge of the *da'i*; they have many compilations in these subjects from which I summarized," without further elaboration.[37] It is not clear who the *da'i* in question here is, but it is evident from the text that it is not al-Kirmani, which suggests that al-Maqrizi had access to more theological Isma'ili sources than *Rahat al-'Aql*. His reticence about listing his sources may be typical, but it could also be motivated by other concerns. This is intimated by the revealing statement with which he ends his exposé on the Fatimid *da'wa*, "they have many more testimonies that I am refraining from citing, for there is enough in what I have quoted here for anyone who reasons [*liman 'aqala*]."[38] The same type of statement and qualifiers is used in al-Maqrizi's *Itti'az* and is addressed directly to the alert and unbiased reader.[39] This mixture of scholarly indignation and caution, which al-Maqrizi displays in several other places, may explain his reluctance to reveal his Fatimid doctrinal sources. He was careful lest he should be accused of being pro-Fatimid, or worse still, of being a closet Isma'ili in a staunch Sunni learned environment.[40] The same worries must have instigated his concealment of his Fatimid genealogy, the most candid admission of which he buried in a poetry quotation by his friend al-Awhadi or shared with his trusted student Ibn Fahd. A Fatimid

Kirmani; in "Maqriziana II," 65, Bauden inserts a picture of the page in the notebook showing the arrangement of the text.

36 Ibid. Bauden notes that there is no mention of al-Kirmani in al-Maqrizi's extant book, but that a biography of al-Kirmani may have been written in the missing part of *al-Muqaffa* since this abridgment has all the elements needed for a brief biography.

37 Al-Maqrizi, *Khitat2*, 2: 308–20. Bauden, "Maqriziana I," 83, noticed that al-Maqrizi did not use this sentence after briefly describing the Fatimid *da'wa* in the *Musawwadat* (p. 106), which suggests that he had access to more Fatimid source between the composition of the *Musawwadat* and the draft of the book that reached us.

38 Al-Maqrizi, *Khitat2*, 2: 320.

39 Al-Maqrizi, *Itti'az*, 1: 54. See also the translated passage from *Itti'az* and the related discussion in Paul Walker, "al-Maqrizi and the Fatimids," 89–92.

40 As we have seen in Chapter 1, he was accused by Ibn Hajar, al-Shawkani, and even the contemporary Saudi Shaykh Nasir ibn Muhammad al-Ahmad of being naively pro-Fatimid because of his belief in his Fatimid ancestry.

connection may explain how al-Maqrizi had access to original Fatimid theological sources. He may have known other hidden descendants of the Fatimids, who gave him access to the Fatimid sources in their libraries, since we know that Fatimid doctrinal books had been destroyed or burned after the fall of the Fatimids and that no copies of them existed in the known Mamluk collections of the time in Cairo.[41]

There is still an important point to elucidate in discussing al-Maqrizi's very short summary of *Rahat al-ʿAql*. This is the difficulty inherent in dealing with this complex gnostic and philosophical text, which requires an advanced level of specialized knowledge. Symbolically arranged in the scheme of a city with seven ramparts or chapters each containing many pathways or sections, the book treats complicated theosophical, theological, cosmological, and esoteric questions, which are not easy to grasp even for followers of the doctrine or for modern scholars.[42] The problem would have been even more acute for a Sunni *ʿalim* in Mamluk Egypt, who not only lacked the terminological and conceptual tools to appreciate the language of al-Kirmani and other likeminded esoteric authors, but also moved in an environment that actively denounced such writings as heretical. Yet al-Maqrizi managed to go through the book and to extract from it what he felt was significant. But what is really revealing is how al-Maqrizi redacted and rearranged his extracts.[43]

It is possible that al-Maqrizi was simply eliminating from the obtuse text of al-Kirmani what he could not understand of Ismaʿili theological notions or could not accept due to his fundamentalist beliefs. But an analysis of the short summary text suggests that he deliberately cleansed the sentences that he lifted from various sections of the book of obscure or polysemic clauses, and reworked them to present the book's thesis in a manner acceptable to the Sunni doctrinal consensus of the Mamluk period. This is especially clear in the last sentence of the extract. Al-Maqrizi adds to the first clause the word *sharʿi* (derived from sharia), and to the second *min al-sunan* (of the traditions), so that his sentence reads, "every sharia command or tradition of traditions

[41] Farhad Daftary, *The Ismaʿilis: Their History and Doctrines* (Cambridge: Cambridge University Press, 1990), 274–5, shows that small Ismaʿili communities survived in Upper Egypt, possibly into the time of al-Maqrizi, who might have preserved some of the sect's books.

[42] Paul Walker, *Hamid al-Din al-Kirmani: Ismaili Thought in the Age of al-Hakim* (London: I. B. Tauris, 1999), 104–17, 131–2. An Arabic Ismaʿili website, *Muntada al-Hiwar al-Mutahaddir al-Ismaʿili* (the Forum of Civilized Ismaʿili Dialogue), advises its reader not to read al-Kirmani's *Rahat al-ʿAql* "because in many of its concepts, the book depends on unpublished treatises that are not available for consultation, which makes it difficult to understand the concept as presented by al-Kirmani," http://readz.top-me.com/t190-topic (last accessed July 24, 2017).

[43] Bauden, "Maqriziana II," 65–7 reconstructs the process of lifting, rearranging, and redacting from the original *Rahat al-ʿAql*.

(*sunna min al-sunnan*) has an influence in the soul where its positive effect can be seen and, if (this command is) abandoned, the harm caused will show negatively in the soul إن كل أمر شرعي أو سنة من السنن فإن له في النفس بإثباته قوة يبين أثرها فيها وبتركه مضرة يظهر شره عليها."[44] With these additions, al-Maqrizi changed the more general, and more philosophical, original meaning of the sentence, which could be read as "in every matter and every tradition (not exclusively Islamic)," to a more religiously confined and specific meaning focusing on divine law and prophetic traditions.

Furthermore, the sentence that al-Maqrizi quotes is consciously taken out of its context in the original, where al-Kirmani explains what he means by sharia, which is very different from what a Sunni understanding of the term would be. In the sentence immediately preceding the quoted sentence, al-Kirmani assets that sharia has a *zahir* (ظاهر tangible, apparent) and a *batin* (باطن inherent, inner) aspect which is accessible only to the *nutaqa'* (نطقاء sing. *natiq*, speaker), *awsiyya'* (أوصياء sing. *wasi*, representative), and *a'imma* (أئمة sing. *imam*), the three categories of selected deliverers and carriers of divine revelation according to Ismaili doctrine.[45] Al-Maqrizi was aware of this Ismaili cosmological scheme based on the meaning of the number seven, as evidenced in his exposé on the *da'wa* in the *Khitat*, but he chose to ignore it here and to present the quoted sentence as if it were about sharia in the Sunni sense. He also stops short at presenting the topic of the book in his abridgment at "the description of the field studying God's uniqueness (*bayan 'ilm al-tawhid*)," a legitimate Sunni scholarly pursuit, without explaining al-Kirmani's understanding of the term, which extends the divine authority to the imams. Did al-Maqrizi do this on purpose? It is difficult to answer this question either way.[46] But from reviewing his exposés in many of his books of contentious doctrinal issues in Islam, and from his reviews of the various sects that branched out of the core Sunni or Shi'i belief systems, it becomes clear that he was not a lazy, negligent, or compliant historian. He was quite cognizant of the divisions and differences in interpretations and even belief systems among the various Islamic sects of the past and of his own time. He was in fact trying, sometimes successfully and sometimes less so, to understand how and

44 Bauden, "Maqriziana II," 65; the photo shows that al-Maqrizi added the word *shar'i* on the right margin and *min al-sunnan* above the word *sunna* between the lines as an afterthought that probably aims to confine the effect of the sentence to religious commands. I also differ in my reading from Bauden, who reads the first word as *darr*, meaning harm, whereas I prefer *amr*, meaning command.

45 Al-Kirmani, *Rahat al-'Aql*, Muhammad Kamil Hussein and Muhammad Mustafa Hilmi eds. (Cairo: Dar al-Fikr al-'Arabi, 1953), 101–2.

46 Paul Walker, "al-Maqrizi and the Fatimids," 89, ponders the same question. Although al-Maqrizi emphatically stresses his belief in the *zahir* of the religion in his declaration of his creed, analyzed below.

why Islam fragmented into the various schools and sects he was documenting, and, perhaps more important, how doctrinal unity could be achieved again, even though the extent of his questioning and advocacy was perforce limited by his education and by the dominant conservative views of his time.

Seen from this perspective, al-Maqrizi comes across as a critical historian who was trying to historicize Islam and to explain how its denominational off-shoots quarreled over the issue of interpreting or refraining from interpreting the foundational exegetical texts, primarily the Qur'an and the records of the life and traditions of the Prophet, his descendants, and his direct companions. This comes across very clearly in his summary opinion at the end of his long exposé of Islamic divergent sects in his *Khitat*.[47] The passage deserves to be quoted in full, for, besides very strongly indicating al-Maqrizi's Zahirism, it reveals an open-minded historical reasoning in treating such a polemical topic as the sects in Islam. Al-Maqrizi writes:

> The truth that admits no doubt is that the religion of God is manifest [*zahir*, exoteric] with no hidden meaning [*batin*], an essence with no secret underneath it. It is required in its totality of everyone with no exemption. The Prophet did not hide a single word of the sharia, and has not revealed to any of his close relations, including his wife and cousin [i.e. 'A'isha and 'Ali b. Abi Talib] something of the sharia that he has hid from others. He had no secret, no symbol, and no hidden meaning separate from what he preached. Had he concealed anything, he would have deviated from his divinely ordained mission, and whoever says that is an unbeliever according to the consensus of the *umma*.[48]
>
> The origin of every heresy is the distance from the discourse of the forebears [*salaf*] and the deviation from the belief of the first generation of Muslims. Thus the *qadari* [believer in predestination] exaggerated in his belief so as to make the servant of God a creator of his deeds, and the *jabri* [believer in divine compulsion] exaggerated in his belief in return so as to deny the servant of God any reason or choice, and so did the *mu'attil* [denier of divine attributes] so as to strip God of his perfection and transcendence [*tanzih*], and the *mushabbih* [believer in divine nearness to human attributes] so as to reduce God to a human being, and the *murji'* [believer in deferred judgment] eliminated punishment, while the *mu'tazilite* would perpetuate penance. The *nasibi* [those who profess hatred toward Al al-Bayt] exaggerated in denying the imamate of 'Ali, whereas *al-ghulat* [extremists among the Shi'a] made him divine. The Sunni overstated the priority of Abu

[47] Al-Maqrizi, *Khitat2*, 4: 400–50. In note 6, the section about pre-Islamic religion is mostly a summary of Muhammad ibn 'Abd al-Karim al-Shahrastani, *Kitab al-Milal wa-l Nihal*, 2 vols., Muhammad b. Fath-Allah Badran, ed. (Cairo: Anglo-Egyptian Library, 1956), 2: 62–127. Part of the book is trans. as *Muslim Sects and Divisions. The Section on Muslim Sects in Kitab al-Milal wa 'l-Nihal* A. K. Kazi and J. G. Flynn, trans. (London: Kegan Paul, 1984; reprint, New York: Routledge, 2013).

[48] This section is copied from Ibn Hazm, *al-Fasl fi al-Milal* with slight edits that do not diminish the stress on the Zahiri creed, see Ibn Hazm, *al-Fasl fi al-Milal*, 2: 274–5.

Bakr whereas the *rafidhi* [denier of early caliphs] pushed him back to the point of making him an infidel.

The scope of opinion [*zann*] is vast and the order of delusion [*wahm*] is prevalent (وميدان الظن واسع وحكم الوهم غالب). Thus, conjectures clashed and delusions escalated. Each group pushed its belief with utmost evil and tenacity and transgression and corruption to an extreme. They hated and cursed each other, took properties from each other, killed each other. They sought support in their aggression from empires and kings. Those who overstated an issue should have competed with the others in getting close to that issue instead of going to the extreme opposite end, since opinions are not that far off of each other, but they insisted on what we have exposed of hostility and separation {but they will not cease to differ. Except whom your Lord has given mercy} [Qur'an, Hud 11: end of 118–beginning of 119].[49]

In this short and dense text, al-Maqrizi sums up his opinion on the status of the Islamic nation and offers a simple and logical remedy to its doctrinal problem that has a hint of humanism, or at least a willingness to accept the possibility of both difference and rapprochement among divergent sects. He begins, as appropriate for a *'alim* of his stature, by stating his own creed, which proffers what appears to be an uncompromising Zahiri affirmation, taken almost verbatim from Ibn Hazm, and a rejection of esotericism in all its forms, carefully attributing it to the majority opinion of the Sunni community even though it has a very traditionalist salafist tinge.

Affirming his creed allows al-Maqrizi to frame his argument about the causes of fragmentation in a historically verifiable yet clearly salafist tenor. Spinoff sects came about because of deviation from the teaching of the *salaf*, *al-sadr al-awwal* (i.e. the Prophet and his companions). But despite the accusation of deliberate deviation from the true teaching, al-Maqrizi does not explicitly excommunicate any of the sectarian groups he has listed. Instead, he de facto accepts them, although he does not condone them or accept their dogmas. He weighs things logically and asserts that the possibility of erring, which he calls opinion and delusion, is wide open. This is what leads to dispute and hatred. He therefore does not lay the blame on any one group, but invites all sects to practice moderation and even to attempt to understand the other's opinion, or at least to debate with an eye to rapprochement. This is because he sees similarities in the process of forming opinions that stem from the wide-open field of interpretation. He is, in a way, advocating a search for the common ground among the various sects, even though he ends with a statement taken from two verses of the Qur'an that recognizes the inevitability of quarreling except when God wishes otherwise: that is, he reverts at the

[49] Al-Maqrizi, *Khitatz*, 4: 449–50; al-Maqrizi does not seem to be paraphrasing anyone else in this text despite the fact that he was copying Ibn Hazm in the preceding assertion of his creed.

end to the core Ash'arite belief in the divine plan for humanity.[50] But he does not do this before having laid down an almost hermeneutical discourse on the history of Islamic fragmentation that searches for explanations and causes in the actions and temperaments of people. Throughout, al-Maqrizi is also aware of the political underpinnings of religious disputes and of the role political powers (kings and empires) play in deepening the disagreements and in using violence to impose a certain dogma. This perception will repeatedly inform his analyses of specific cases in Islamic history, especially in his discussion of the Fatimid Caliphate in the *Itti'az* and his polemical tract on the dispute between the Umayyads and the Hashemites, *al-Niza' wa al-Takhasum fi ma bayn Bani Umayya wa Bani Hashim*.

The Beginnings: From Abridger to Author

In the tradition of his time, al-Maqrizi began his career as a promising religious scholar with an abridgment of a major book on the critique of hadith transmitters (*al-jarh wa al-ta'dil*) by the famous *hafiz* 'Abd Allah Ibn 'Adi (277/891–365/976) entitled *Mukhtasar al-Kamil fi al-Du'afa wa-'Ilal al-Hadith li-Ibn 'Adi*. The autographed manuscript of the book is dated to the beginning of the year 795/1392.[51] This is the first known book of al-Maqrizi, who was twenty-eight years of age at the time, married with at least two children and probably employed in some unsatisfactory religious capacity in various Cairene madrasas and mosques with possibly still some connection to the chancery. He might have made the abridgment as a textbook for his students in some of these madrasas, but we do not know for sure.[52] The

[50] Al-Maqrizi's Ash'arism is in doubt. He is fully aware that the dominance of the Ash'arite creed in his own time has become almost absolute and that "whoever denies it will be executed," as he states a few lines before the text quoted here, in a manner that could be interpreted as either favorable or disdainful; al-Maqrizi, *Khitat2*, 4: 446. A discussion of al-Maqrizi's belief on the website of the Saudi Shaikh Nasir ibn Muhammad al-Ahmad is still inconclusive about al-Maqrizi's creed, https://alahmad.com/view/40 (last accessed August 1, 2017).

[51] See al-Maqrizi, *Mukhtasar al-Kamil fi al-Du'afa wa-'Ilal al-Hadith li-Ibn Adi*, Ayman ibn Arif al-Dimashqi, ed. (Cairo: Maktabat al-Sunna, 1994), 36 for a copy of the frontispiece of the autographed manuscript, and 39–41 for the text. The last digit of the date on the autographed copy of the book (Mulla Murad Lib., Istanbul 569) is smeared. It is a 4, a 5, or a 6. But al-Maqrizi says that he finished it on Sunday at the beginning of the year, which corresponds to 1 Muharram 795/November 17, 1392. See also the discussion in Bauden, "Maqriziana II," 78–9.

[52] Sayyid, *Musawwadat*, 62, postulates that al-Maqrizi might have used his *Mukhtasar* while teaching hadith at the Madrasa of Sultan Hasan and later at al-Mu'ayyadiyya. His teaching in either madrasa is, of course, not corroborated by the sources.

author's introduction reveals a conservative, dedicated, and youthful persona clinging to the religious ideals he had read about and believed. Its opening passage shows that al-Maqrizi was preoccupied with the purity of his and his children's ways as devout and rather traditionalist Muslims. It also reveals that he was from the beginning of his career wary of the injustice of rulers and the temptations of religious innovations, as a budding Zahiri might be. It reads:

> O God, lead me and my children on the voyage of truth, and guide me and them to the correct side of that which has been argued over of religion, and direct us to the ways of virtue, and shelter us under the umbrage of right guidance, and multiply your blessings on us, and make us preachers to what has been neglected of Your Religion and forgotten of the tradition [*sunnat*] of Your Prophet, and keepers of what has been abandoned of the laws of Islam and forfeited of the rules of the allowed and the forbidden [*al-halal wa al-haram*], and keep me and my children away from the unjust rulers, and turn me and them away from the doctrines of the inventors, and avert our hearts from the creed of the relinquishers [of a religious tenet], and purify our tongues and hearings from the nonsense of the ignorant, You are The One with exalted grace . . .[53]

We do not know for sure what al-Maqrizi composed after this abridgment. But some of his other short religious or historico-religious treatises or abridgments may date back to this early period. For instance, he completed the digest of three treatises by al-Hafiz Muhammad b. Nasr al-Marwazi (202–94/818–907) on the accepted traditions in the performance of different types of prayer, *Kitab Qiyam al-Layl*, *Kitab Qiyam Ramadhan*, and *Kitab al-Witr*, on Thursday 23 Jamada II, 807/December 27, 1404.[54] This date falls in the lull between his second and third appointments to the *hisba*, when he was still immersed in the competition for positions during the reign of Faraj b. Barquq while probably teaching in some Cairene madrasa or preaching in one or more mosques as a means of support. A third early abridgment is the selections (*muntaqa*) of Ibn Muyassar's *Akhbar Misr*, whose surviving manuscript contains only the second volume. This volume, chronicling the Fatimid and the post-Fatimid period down to the year before the author's death in 677/1278–9, was completed by al-Maqrizi on 24 Rabiʿ II, 814/15 August 1411, as indicated in its colophon.[55] This is a tricky date in terms of

[53] Al-Maqrizi, *Mukhtasar al-Kamil*, 40 (my translation).

[54] Al-Maqrizi, *Mukhtasar Qiyam al-Layl wa Qiyam Ramadhan wa Kitab al-Witr lil Imam Abi ʿAbdallah Muhammad b. Nasr al-Marwazi* (Faysalabad, Pakistan: Hadith Academy, 1988), 341; Bauden, "Maqriziana II," 79. Al-Maqrizi's abridgment was published several times in Pakistan, in 1902, 1969, and, finally, in 1988, and republished as an offset edition in Beirut 1983, whereas the last treatise, *Kitab al-Witr*, was edited by Muhammad A. ʿAshur and Jamal ʿA. al-Kumi (Cairo: Dar al-Iʿtisam, 1993).

[55] Al-Maqrizi, *al-Muntaqa min Akhbar Misr li ibn Muyassar*, also *Choix de passages de la*

establishing the place of production, for al-Maqrizi was frequently traveling between Cairo and Damascus during this period with the *katib al-sirr* Fath Allah in the entourage of Sultan Faraj b. Barquq, who was desperately trying to secure his rule and quell dissension by his amirs in Syria. Al-Maqrizi, as we saw, mentions his presence in Syria during that period in the *Suluk* a few times but does not specify the dates or lengths of his stays. He says in passing in the biography of Taqiyy al-Din, the judge of Zabadani, that "I came to Damascus between 810/1407 and 815/1412," but does not add any details.[56] By extrapolating from the dates of the trips of the sultan to Damascus, and by assuming that al-Maqrizi was in the company of Fath Allah all the time, however, we can estimate that he spent around twenty-two months in Damascus over at least three visits in five years. Producing Ibn Muyassar's selections in Damascus was thus quite possible.

Evidently, summarizing Ibn Muyassar's book was not the first work of a historical nature undertaken by al-Maqrizi. We know that he had taken a great interest in the history of Egypt from early on in his scholarly life and had even composed a few historical treatises before his sojourns in Damascus. The earliest evidence we have of his historical studies are his signatures, which start to appear from as early as 803/1400 on several covers of primary sources that he consulted and that he will use in his own works. One such example is his signature on the surviving fortieth volume of the immense history of al-Musabbihi (977–1029), *Akhbār Miṣr*, at the Escorial Library in Spain, which constitutes one of al-Maqrizi main sources for his writing on the Fatimids in the *Khitat* and the *Itti'az*.[57] Al-Maqrizi's signature appears on the upper left margin of the cover folio and is dated to 807/1404 (although

chronique d'Égypte d'Ibn Muyassar, Ayman Fu'ad Sayyid, ed. (Cairo: IFAO, 1981), 1; Bauden, "Maqriziana II," 79–80, notices that although al-Maqrizi calls the résumé *al-Muntaqa min Akhbar Misr li ibn Muyassar*, he nonetheless includes material from two other sources that he relied upon in his Fatimid history. This may suggest that this résumé is more of a notebook and not intended for publication like the abridgments of Ibn 'Adi and al-Marwazi.

56 Al-Maqrizi, *Durar*, 1: 154. But he does give at least one reference to a trip from Cairo to Damascus and back, which covered a bit more than a year between 810/1407 and Dhi al-Qi'da 811/March 1409, *Durar*, 3: 433–4, the biography of Muhammad ibn 'Ali ibn Khatib Zar'.

57 The volume was published twice in Cairo: the historic part was edited by Ayman Fu'ad Sayyid and Thierry Bianquis as *al-Juz' al-arba'un min Akhbar Misr lil-Musabbihi* (Cairo: IFAO, 1978); followed by the literary section of the same volume edited by Husayn Nassar (Cairo: IFAO, 1984). The second edition, which contains both sections, titled *Akhbar Misr fi Sanatayn (414–415)*, was edited by William G. Millward (Cairo: General Egyptian Book Organization, 1980). Both editors noted the two signatures of al-Awhadi and al-Maqrizi. On al-Maqrizi's copying from al-Musabbihi, see Sayyid and Bianquis, *al-Juz'*, Sayyid introduction, T. In his introduction to Sayyid, *Musawwadat*, 86, Sayyid noted that most of what al-Maqrizi copied of al-Musabbihi in that draft is on the margins or in *tayyarat*, which suggests that he came upon al-Musabihhi's book late in his composition.

the number is effaced and could be one rather than seven).[58] Another signature that appears on the upper right margin is al-Awhadi's, and is dated to 803/1400. This is a pattern that will recur several times, and it poses interesting questions about the habits of borrowing and reading by these two historians, as well as the third neighbor Ibn Duqmaq, whose signature shares theirs on some other sources. But what is interesting for now is that al-Maqrizi seems to have read whatever was available of al-Musabbihi's grand work seven years before he made the selections of Ibn Muyassar's history, which was a continuation (*dhayl*) on al-Musabbihi's history, as indicated in its full title, *al-Tarikh al-Kabir 'ala al-Sinin dhayyala bihi 'ala Kitab al-Musabbihi*.[59] This suggests that al-Maqrizi was for a long time immersing himself in reading about the Fatimids and collecting and redacting primary sources in preparation for his two major contributions on that little-studied dynasty, the first part of the *Khitat* and the *Itti'az*.[60]

Another major source on which we have a signature of al-Maqrizi is the manuscript of the Egyptian section of *al-Mughrib fi-Hula al-Maghrib* by six Andalusian authors, the last being Ibn Sa'id al-Maghribi, a book that he will use extensively in his later historical work on Egypt.[61] Al-Maqrizi's signature appears with the same formula and the same date, "has benefited from it praying for it owner Ahmad b. 'Ali al-Maqrizi in the year 803/1400," on the two preserved volumes of the same set, Volume 4 in Cairo's Dar al-Kutub and Volume 6, which was in a private library in Balsafura, Suhag, in Egypt before it was transferred to Dar al-Kutub.[62] Al-Awhadi signed both volumes' covers, as well on the lower right corner, and dated his signature 802/1399. This time Ibn Duqmaq's signature shares the cover page on the upper right

[58] The cover of the manuscript of El Escorial, MS 534, fol. 132a is published in Sayyid and Bianquis as *al-Juz' al-arba'un*, fig. 1. Millward, *Akhbar Misr*, 11, reads it as one; it is difficult to decide from the published photo if it is seven or one. See also Bauden, "Maqriziana II," 118.

[59] For a succinct discussion of the relationship between the two works see Michael Brett, "Review of *Choix de passages de la chronique d'Égypte d'Ibn Muyassar Tāǧ ad-Dīn Muḥ. b. 'Alī b. Yūsuf b. Ǧalab Rāǧib m. 677 H.*, sélection faite par Taqiyy ad-Dīn Aḥmad b. 'Alī al-Maqrizi en l'année 814 H. by Ayman Fu'ad Sayyid," *JRASGBI* 2 (1983), 293–5.

[60] Millward, *Akhbar Misr*, Appendices A and B, 237–52, prints sections of the *Itti'az* and the *Khitat* copied from al-Musabbihi.

[61] Zaki Muhammad Hasan, "Introduction," to Ibn Sa'id al-Maghribi, *al-Mughrib fi-Hula al-Maghrib: al-Juz' al-Awwal min al-Qism al-Khaṣṣ bi-Misr [al-Ightibaṭ fi Ḥula Madinat al-Fusṭaṭ]*, Shawqi Dhayf et al. eds. (Cairo: Fu'ad al-Awwal University, 1953), 49–50, discusses al-Maqrizi's use of *al-Mughrib*; Bauden, "Maqriziana II," 74–6.

[62] Hasan, "Introduction," to Ibn Sa'id al-Maghribi, *al-Mughrib [al-Ightibaṭ]*, 62; the Balsafura manuscript has, in addition to the signatures of al-Safadi and the three historians, that of the famous *faqih*, *adib*, and historian al-Suyuti (1445–1505); al-Maqrizi, *Khitat2*, 1: 114°; Bauden, "Maqriziana II," 118.

hand of Volume 4, with gratitude to the owner but without a date. This important holograph manuscript was written by Ibn Sa'id between 645 and 647 (1247–9) for his friend and patron Ibn Abi Jarada, known as Ibn al-'Adim (1192–1262), the famous biographer and historian of Aleppo, presumably in Aleppo where it was preserved in Ibn al-'Adim's library. The copy belonged later to another famous early Mamluk biographer and historian, Ibn Aybak al-Safadi (1297–1363), who signed his name on the cover of Volume 4 as "has read it and selected from it its owner Khalil b. Aybak b. 'Abdallah al-Safadi," without a date.[63] We do not know when or where Ibn Aybak acquired the book.

Ayman Fu'ad Sayyid has noted that this manuscript must have ended in Cairo for the three neighbors/historians to be able to read it, sign it, and offer gratitude to its owner. But he did not know who that owner might be after al-Safadi.[64] Al-Safadi might have brought the book with him to Cairo when he assumed his position in the chancery there at the beginning of his career and then sold it or gifted it when he left to take up his series of chancery positions in various Syrian cities before dying in Damascus in 764/1363.[65] We know that this particular manuscript, or at least parts of it according to al-Sakhawi, ended up as part of al-Mu'ayyad Shaykh's *waqf* on his mosque in Cairo, which was constructed between 818 and 824/1415 and 1421, for his *waqf* mark appears on many of its folios.[66] But the three historians must have read the book in someone else's library since the two signatures of al-Awhadi and al-Maqrizi predate the mosque's construction, and since Ibn Duqmaq died in 809/1407, which is a *terminus ante quem* for his signature and more than ten years before the book moved to the Mosque of al-Mu'ayyad. Who was that owner? Perusing the facsimile of the cover folio, I discovered a signature tucked under al-Maqrizi's signature, which has been neglected by other

[63] The first to publish the facsimile of the manuscript cover (fol. 1a, Cairo, Dar al-Kutub MS 103 Tarikh Mim) was Bernhard Moritz, *Arabic Paleography: A Collection of Arabic Texts from the First Century of the Hidjra till the Year 1000* (Cairo: Khedivial Library, 1905), 167; reprinted in Hasan, "Introduction" to Ibn Sa'id al-Maghribi, *al-Mughrib [al-Ightibaṭ]*, 69; al-Maqrizi, *Suluk*, 1: 961. See also Sayyid, *Musawwadat*, Introduction, 74–6; Bauden, "Maqriziana II," 75, 118.

[64] Al-Maqrizi, *Khitat2*, 1: 114˚.

[65] On Ibn Aybak's biography, see al-Maqrizi, *Suluk*, 3: 87, *Durar*, 2: 77–8; Ibn Hajar, *al-Durar al-Kamina*, 2: 208.

[66] Hasan, "Introduction" to Ibn Sa'id al-Maghribi, *al-Mughrib [al-Ightibaṭ]*, 58–60, discusses the circumstances of recovering the dispersed parts of the manuscripts from the Mosque of al-Mu'ayyad and elsewhere in Egypt and mentions that parts of the endowed manuscript may have been taken from the Mosque before 1827 when the reformer legist and Shaykh al-Azhar Hasan al-'Attar (1766–1835) read it in the mosque and noted that parts of it are missing. Al-Sakhawi, *I'lan*, 132, mentions that parts of the book were in al-Mu'ayyad Mosque in the year 902/1492.

commentators.[67] It reads, "Has read it and the preceding volumes Fath Allah in the year 80 [the last digit is unclear]."[68] Could that be the same Fath Allah, the *katib al-sirr* who was al-Maqrizi's main patron for a long time? Could he have been the owner of the manuscript (or the last owner of the manuscript) between al-Safadi and the date of its acquisition for al-Mu'ayyad's *waqf*?

Circumstantial evidence strongly supports this possibility. First, Fath Allah was not a common name at the time, and there is only one Fath Allah in al-Maqrizi's *Durar*, the *katib al-sirr*. Second, Fath Allah was a voracious reader in various fields of knowledge, especially, according to al-Maqrizi, "toward the end of his life as he diligently read books of hadith and *athar* [opinions of the Companions of the Prophet] and books of disputations on exegetical matters."[69] Third and most pertinently, Ibn Khatib al-Nasiriyya (774–843/1373–1439), who was a known judge and historian from Aleppo and who knew Fath Allah and al-Maqrizi personally, said that Fath Allah "collected precious books."[70] Was al-Safadi's copy of *al-Mughrib fi-Hula al-Maghrib* one of Fath Allah's books? This is more than plausible, and it solves the question of how the three historians read the book. Al-Maqrizi definitely had access to Fath Allah's library, and he might have introduced the two other historians, al-Awhadi and Ibn Duqmaq, to his patron and his library since the three were neighbors and friends and were, as al-Maqrizi reports in his *Durar*, exchanging notes and borrowing notebooks and drafts from each other.

Moreover, ascribing al-Safadi's copy of *al-Mughrib fi-Hula al-Maghrib* to Fath Allah's library in the early fifteenth century helps to explain how the book ended up in the *waqf* of al-Mu'ayyad Shaykh. As we have seen in Chapter 2, al-Mu'ayyad forced Fath Allah, under torture, to relinquish all of his properties in 1413, including those that had already been made into *waqf*, and to re-endow them to the sons of al-Mu'ayyad (even though Fath Allah's house was returned to his heirs after the passing of al-Mu'ayyad).[71] This is one possible route for al-Safadi's book to have passed from the ownership of Fath Allah to the *waqf* of al-Mu'ayyad Shaykh, and thus Fath Allah may be the owner to whom the gratitude of al-Maqrizi and Ibn Duqmaq is addressed on the cover folio of *al-Mughrib fi-Hula al-Maghrib*.

There are several other signatures of al-Maqrizi on other sources that were important for his work. Most notable are his signatures on several draft

[67] Hasan, "Introduction" to Ibn Sa'id al-Maghribi, *al-Mughrib [al-Ightibaṭ]*, 59, notes the signature but does not recognize Fath Allah.

[68] Ibid. puts the date at 810/1407–8.

[69] Al-Maqrizi, *Durar*, 3: 16.

[70] Ibn Khatib al-Nasiriyya is quoted in the entry on Fath Allah in al-Sakhawi, *Daw'*, 6: 166. On Ibn Khatib al-Nasiriyya, see al-Maqrizi, *Durar*, 2: 552.

[71] Al-Maqrizi, *Durar*, 3: 15; idem, *Khitat2*, 3: 203; Behrens-Abouseif, *Fath Allah and Abu Zakariyya*, 21.

volumes of Ibn al-Furat's *Tarikh* between 818 and 819 (1415–16), which he consulted in someone else's library after the death of its author as the dedication ("with gratitude to its owner") indicates, and from which he copied extensively in his *Suluk* without attribution.[72] Another set of signatures appear on Ibn Fadhl Allah al-'Umari's *Masalik al-Absar fi Mamlik al-Amsar*, which date to 831/1428, at the height of al-Maqrizi's writing spree; he depended heavily on its material on geography and cosmology and early Mamluk Cairo for his *Khitat.*[73] The third significant signature shows on Ibn al-Khatib's *al-Ihata fi Akhbar Ghurnata*, and is dated to 808/1406.[74] This date corresponds to the year of Ibn Khaldun's death, in whose biography in the *Durar* al-Maqrizi directly quotes from Ibn al-Khatib's *al-Ihata.*[75] Ibn al-Khatib is also the source of much information on Andalusian figures that appear in al-Maqrizi's *Durar*. But the manuscript of *al-Ihata* on which al-Maqrizi put his signature is now lost. The signature is reported by al-Maqqari (1578–1632) in his *Nafh al-Tib min Ghusn al-Andalus al-Ratib wa Zikr Waziraha Lisan al-Din Ibn al-Khatib*, whose second part is an extended biography of Ibn al-Khatib. In describing the fair copy of Ibn al-Khatib's *al-Ihata*, which he sent during his lifetime as a *waqf* to the *khanqah* of Sa'id al-Su'ada' in Cairo, al-Maqqari noted a number of signatures of Maghrebi and Egyptian ulama on the cover folio of Volume 4, including those of Ibn Hajar, al-Suyuti, Ibn Duqmaq, and al-Maqrizi, whose familiar dedication is quoted in full: "Has selected from this book while sending gratitude to its owner Ahmad b. 'Ali al-Maqrizi in the month of Rabi' [*sic*] of the year 808."[76]

It is clear from the frequent appearance of the signatures of al-Maqrizi, al-Awhadi, and Ibn Duqmaq on the same books that these three neighbors were interested in the same topics, perhaps competitively, which will translate into the three of them composing books on the *khitat* and history of Egypt. It is also clear that they were not wealthy enough to own their own copies of the sources they needed for their own historical compositions. They were thus borrowing them, sometime one after the other, from private libraries, like that of Fath Allah, or reading them in endowed libraries of madrasas

[72] In addition to Bora, Amitai, and Bauden, who recently analyzed al-Maqrizi's copying from Ibn al-Furat, see Little, *Mamluk Historiography*, 76–8, where he pinpointed the sections of Ibn al-Furat most heavily used by al-Maqrizi as the ones covering the late thirteenth century. We know of course from Ibn Hajar that he and al-'Ayni too copied from Ibn al-Furat.

[73] Al-Maqrizi, *Khitat2*, 1: 198, no. 2. The text of the signature is slightly different from the usual formula in that it says "selected from it with gratitude to its lender," instead of owner.

[74] Bauden, "Maqriziana II," 117–18, for all the signatures.

[75] Al-Maqrizi, *Durar*, 2: 386, 398, 403.

[76] The book has been edited and published several times. For this reference, see al-Maqqari, *Nafh al-Tib min Ghusn al-Andalus al-Ratib wa Zikr Waziraha Lisan al-Din Ibn al-Khatib* 8 vols., Ihsan 'Abbas, ed. (Beirut: Dar Sader, 1968, 2nd edn., 1997), 7: 106.

and *khanqhas*, like the Khanqah of Sa'id al-Su'ada'.[77] Moreover, the dates of the signatures show that the three neighbors took up their interest in history at almost the same time, toward the last decade of the thirteenth and the first years of the fourteenth century. Al-Maqrizi, who was the youngest of the three, may have been influenced by his two neighbors, since many of their signatures preceded his, but his work in the administration and his three appointments to the *hisba* may have had equal, if not greater, impact on his decision to turn to history writing and on the orientation of his investigations and the ethical aims he would persistently brandish in almost all his work. Similarly, the *mihna* (usually translated as "crisis")[78] of the year 806/1403–4 might have been the catalyst that compelled al-Maqrizi to take up history writing as a means of understanding and commenting on the depressing events he was witnessing, and to search for ways to critique their perpetrators and remedy their effects.[79]

Indeed, al-Maqrizi seems to have begun his vocation as a historian soon after his stint in the Mamluk administration as a *muhtasib* for the third time. His first historical essay appears to have been his treatise on the severe economic crisis of 806/1403–4, *Ighathat al-Umma bi-kashf al-Ghumma*, which establishes the anxious tone and anticipates the analytical method of his later *Khitat*. In the *Ighathat*, he begins by describing the famines in Egypt, especially that caused by the *mihna* of 806, which he had just witnessed and which affected him tremendously. But he quickly moves to his real concern and the root cause of the famines in his view, the *ghala'* (price inflation). In the second part of the book, he analyzes the causes of inflation from his viewpoint, which include the corruption and negligence of the rulers, the capricious increase in land levies coupled with recurring natural catastrophes that devastated the agricultural system sustaining the economy of Egypt, and the mounting dependence on copper *fulus* (the smallest currency denomination), which causes artificial inflation, a complaint to which al-Maqrizi will devote another treatise in a couple of years, *Shudhur al-'Uqud fi-Dhikr*

[77] Frédéric Bauden, "Vers une archéologie," 104–6, notes that the development of a quotation from al-Safadi's *al-Wafi bil-Wafiyyat* from an abridgment to its final appearance in the *Khitat* suggests that al-Maqrizi no longer had access to the original source when he redacted his *Khitat*.

[78] Al-Maqrizi uses several terms to describe the "806 crisis." They are *mihna*, *bala'*, and *ahdath*. *Ahdath* is the most neutral as it simply means "events." *Mihna* and *bala'*, the first derived from the root "to test" [by God], the second from "to torment" [also by God], have fatalistic connotations and Qur'anic references, a point that reinforces the need to understand al-Maqrizi's narrative in its pious, religiously defined context.

[79] A full analysis of the effect of 806 on al-Maqrizi is Julien Loiseau, "Les événements de l'année 806. Ou comment al-Maqrizi a pensé une rupture majeure dans l'histoire de l'Égypte," *Médiévales* 64 (Spring 2013): 119–34.

al-Nuqud.[80] His solution is what would be expected from this pious and traditionalist thinker trained primarily in *fiqh* and hadith, whose botched administrative experience must have created a bitter taste in his mouth: the return to sharia economic rules, the reenactment of justice, the elimination of corruption, and monetary reform according to Islamic tradition, which upheld gold and silver as the only acceptable currency, or what Meloy has brilliantly called "monetary *sunnah*."[81]

Al-Maqrizi finished redacting and correcting his treatise "in one night of the month of Muharram 808/July 1405," two months after his last and painful dismissal from the *hisba*, which suggests that this may have been a raw and angry reaction to the erratic economic measures in which he forcibly took part when he was appointed to the *hisba* position against his will, as he laments.[82] But Adel Allouche, using internal textual evidence, argues that the date of completion must be pushed later by a few months to after Jumada I 808/October–November 1405.[83] This is important because the new date allowed John Meloy to see in the *Ighathat* not just a rudimentary economic history or the religious exhortation of an indignant ex-*muhtasib* and budding historian, but a policy recommendation for a potential new royal patron who might reappoint him to the *hisba*.[84] This royal patron is supposed to have been the boy sultan ʿAbd al-ʿAziz b. Barquq, who reigned for a little more than two months (September 20–November 28, 1405)[85] when his brother Faraj b. Barquq decided to go into hiding in exasperation at the internecine fighting troubling his sultanate, before coming out again and resuming his throne. This is a weak probability, partly because ʿAbd al-ʿAziz was a pubescent boy who ruled for a very short period, but also because the recommendatory tone of the text, and the formula al-Maqrizi uses to address his reader, appear to be speaking more to an equal rather than to a royal figure.[86] Addressing the reader directly is indeed a

[80] Loiseau, "Les événements," 122–7; Meloy, "Economic History," 191–7.

[81] Ibid., 189.

[82] Al-Maqrizi, *Ighathat al-Umma bi-kashf al-Ghumma, aw Tarikh al-Majaʿat fi Misr*, Badr al-Din al-Sibaʿi, ed. (Homs, Syria: Dar Ibn al-Walid, 1957), 87; Wiet, "Traité des famines," 1. As we saw, al-Maqrizi, *Suluk*, 3: 1155, vocally complained about this third appointment to the *hisba*.

[83] Adel Allouche, trans. and ed., *Mamluk Economics: A Study and Translation of al-Maqrizi's Ighathat al-Ummah bi-Kashf al-Ghummah* (Salt Lake City: University of Utah Press, 1994), 6–7.

[84] Allouche, *Mamluk Economics*, 3; Meloy, "Economic History," 189–90.

[85] Al-Maqrizi, *Suluk*, 4: 1, and 9, for the dates of ʿAbd al-ʿAziz's reign, whereas Meloy extends his reign to five months.

[86] Two examples of address from Allouche, *Ighathat*, show that al-Maqrizi is not using the traditional protocol to address a royal patron. On page 77, he begins with, "Know—may God grant you eternal happiness and felicity." On page 80, he says, "Know—may God guide you to your own righteousness and inspire you to follow the straight paths of your

textual device for emphasis that al-Maqrizi often employs, even when no particular person is meant, such as when he spoke directly to his reader in *Itti'az* to persuade him/her of the validity of his (controversial) argument about the genealogy of the Fatimids. When he intends to address his exposé to a royal patron (or would-be patron), al-Maqrizi uses more specifically laudatory locutions, respecting the strict protocol observed in the Mamluk chancery, such as he does in his monetary history treatise, *Shudhur al-'Uqud*, and his essay on the rulers of Islam who performed the Hajj, *al-Dhahab al-Masbuk*, both of which might have been addressed to Sultan al-Mu'ayyad Shaykh at the beginning of his reign when al-Maqrizi may still have been hopeful of having a public role.[87] Had he meant the *Ighathat* as a direct message to a royal patron, he would have used different and more protocol-observing titles of address, and he would most probably have addressed it to Faraj b. Barquq himself while he was still on his throne, since al-Maqrizi still had access to him through his patron Fath Allah, and possibly other patrons.

Al-Maqrizi continued to compile short historical/religious tractates during his long stays in Damascus before 1412, where he accompanied Fath Allah in some unspecified capacity in the entourage of Sultan Faraj. His name appears on a short essay on the difference between the *sufi* creed of unionism (*tawhid*) and apostasy, *Kitab al-Bayan al-Mufid fi al-Farq bayn al-Tawhid wa al-Talhid*, on the 3rd of Rajab 813/1st November 1410, completed in the Khanqah Khatun outside Damascus.[88] But it is not clear whether he copied or compiled this short treatise, for the copyist of the manuscript, a certain Ahmad b. Husayn al-'Abbasi, who penned it in 896/1490, states in the colophon that al-Maqrizi copied the text from the composition of an unnamed person who had finished it in 702/1302.[89] To this period also may belong an earlier version of al-Maqrizi's epistle on the rivalry between the Umayyads and the Abbasids, *al-Niza' wa al-Takhasum*, which he reedited in its final form in Shawwal 841/March–April 1438, when he was collating and editing

fellow humans."

[87] See discussion in Chapter 2.

[88] According to the editor of the treatise, there is a note indicating that the text was completed on the 3rd of Rajab 813/ November 1, 1410 in the Khanqah Khatun outside Damascus, see Georges C. Anawati, "Un aspect de la lutte contre l'hérésie au XVème siècle d'aprés un inédit attribué à Maqrizi," in *Colloque International sur l'Histoire du Caire*, 23–31. On the Khanqah Khatun, built by 'Ismat al-Din Khatun bint Unur (d. 1186), the wife of both Nur al-Din and Salah al-Din, outside Damascus to the west near al-Sharaf, see Abd al-Qadir al-Nu'aymi, *Kitab al-Daris fi Tarikh al-Madaris* 2 vols., Ibrahim Shams al-Din, ed. (Beirut: Dar al-Kutub al-'Ilmiyya, 1990), 2: 113–14. It is not clear why al-Maqrizi stayed there.

[89] Anawati, "Un aspect de la lute," 24; Fu'ad Sayyid et al., *Fihrist al-Makhtutat al-Musawwara, Ma'had al-Makhtutat al-'Arabiyya*, 3 vols. (Cairo: Dar al-Riyadh, 1954–60), 1: 119, column 2. Al-Maktaba al-Shamila ascribes the same title to the Syrian historian Ibn Habib (1310–77), http://shamela.ws/browse.php/book-5678/page-43532 (last accessed August 10, 2017).

fair copies of many of his treatises.[90] But this is still only a possibility at the current state of our knowledge. Furthermore, the treatise on money, *Shudhur al-'Uqud*, which picks up the question of the proper Islamic currency where the *Ighathat* left off, was completed in Shawwal 818/December 1415, as stated in the colophon of an original manuscript, and, as we discussed in Chapter 2, may have been composed to gain favor with al-Mu'ayyad Shaykh.[91]

To this period also his intimate biographical dictionary *Durar* should be dated, for al-Maqrizi states that he started it when he had reached his fiftieth year, which in the Hegira calendar is 816/1413–14. This was a period of grief and disenchantment for him, having just lost his most trustworthy patron Fath Allah to the cruelty of the sultan and the machination of his enemies, in addition to having been on the verge of being arrested himself as a companion of Fath Allah, if we are to trust Ibn Fahd's report on the whole debacle. It was also a transitional period professionally, for al-Maqrizi came back to Cairo from Damascus without any promise of a position or clear employment. His hitting the age of fifty and finding himself bereft of friends, supporters, and gainful employment is sorrowfully conveyed in the introduction to the *Durar* and in the accompanying poem he composed for the occasion.[92] His decision to quit the competition for positions and to retreat to his house and devote himself to writing becomes all the more understandable when all these detrimental circumstances are factored in. The poem, in particular, although quite sentimental, lists all the causes of his melancholy. But it is its last three distiches that clearly announce what al-Maqrizi has resolved to do to counter this downturn in his life. He is going to study and write; or, to quote the three distiches in toto:

> My pastime and occupation have become—thank God—the pursuit of knowledge, which keeps me always busy. Sometimes my pen is writing down beneficial material, whose correctness is attested both by revelation and by reason. And at other times, I memorize *'ilm*, which lifts my spirit up and brings me solace.[93]

وصار بحمد الله شغلي وشاغلي فوائد علم لست من شغلها أخلو
فطوراً يراعي كاتب لفوائد بصحتها قد جاءنا النقل والعقل
وآونة للعلم صدري جامع فتزكو به نفسي وعن همها تسلو

[90] Bosworth, *Book of Contention and Strife*, Introduction; Paul Cobb, "Al-Maqrizi, Hashimism, and the Early Caliphates," *MSR* 7, 2 (2003): 71–2. The book was reedited by al-Maqrizi in Shawwal 841/March–April 1438, as he notes on the autographed manuscript in Leiden (no. 1888); Witkam, "Les autographes d'al-Maqrizi," 91–2.

[91] See Meloy, "Economic History," 197–202; Witkam, "Reflections on al-Maqrizi," 112, for a photo of the colophon-like attestation of al-Maqrizi of the date of final redaction of *Shudhur*, Ramadan 841/March 1438, in MS Leiden Or. 560, f 22b.

[92] See Chapter 2.

[93] Al-Maqrizi, *Durar*, 1: 62.

From the testimonies of his contemporary biographers, both admirers and detractors, al-Maqrizi seems to have conformed to this regimen for the rest of his life, even during his extended *mujawarat* in Mecca.

The Concept of Kharab: Looking Back as Method

Al-Maqrizi may have begun thinking about writing a history of Egypt from as early as 803/1400, when he started to read available sources on the country's history, as indicated by his signature on Ibn Sa'id's book. The *mihna* of 806/1403–4 and its grave repercussions provided the impetus for him to try his hand at history writing, whereas his extensive *hisba* experience and his dismissal from that position in 807/1405 engendered the thematic frame for his inquiry. The *Ighathat* seems to have constituted a first exercise in that direction, focused as it is on the history of famines, mismanagement, and monetary history, and possibly meant as a policy recommendation. But the strong feelings that animated this rather short treatise reappear in more elaborate ways in the *Khitat*, and in much sharper and explicit bouts of denigration in the biographies of the early Burji sultans, from Barquq to Barsbay, in the *Durar*, as well as in the chronicling of their reigns in the last volume of the *Suluk*, which al-Maqrizi continued working on almost until the end of his life. The themes too—corruption, neglect of sharia, negation of traditions, exploitation of power, devastation of agricultural land, monetary irregularities, low Nile flooding, plague, and dangerous inflation—which al-Maqrizi identified as the causes of the misery and suffering he witnessed in the calamitous *mihna* of 806 weigh heavily on his diagnosis of the fate of his city during his lifetime in the second halves of both his *Khitat* and his *Suluk*.[94] In the *Khitat*, though, they seem to steer his analysis toward the gloomily predicted *kharab* (ruination) of Egypt, whereas in the *Ighathat* they were primarily offered as explanations for the exceptional rise in prices (*ghala'*) in 806 and the two years following without any prediction of irrevocable ruin.[95]

[94] A key sentence appears in al-Maqrizi, *Suluk*, 3: 1135, in which he states, in the middle of his description of the calamities befalling Egypt, that he "used to hear in the past that Egypt will be stricken by price rise [*ghala'*, super-inflation in today's parlance], displacement [*jala'*], and annihilation [*fana'*], and we witnessed all of that in the years 806 to 808 (1403–6), in which more than two thirds of the country's population perished and the majority of its villages were destroyed." Regardless of the ostensible numerical exaggeration, this statement strongly suggests that that period was pivotal for al-Maqrizi as he deliberated his decision to document and analyze the history of Egypt.

[95] Loiseau, "Les événements," 122–7, offers a detailed and critical analysis of al-Maqrizi's frame of analysis in the *Ighathat* and how they connect with the *Khitat*. Idem, *Reconstruire la Maison du sultan, 1350–1450: ruine et décomposition de l'ordre urbain au Caire*, 2 vols.

This significant development may reflect the change of mood and circumstances of al-Maqrizi between the writing of the *Igathat*, a one-shot treatise penned by an angry yet hopeful ex-*muhtasib* with a view to influencing policy or regaining an administrative advantage, and that of the *Khitat*, an accretive exercise in nostalgic and pessimistic urban history that occupied the disillusioned al-Maqrizi for the second half of his life. Unfortunately, though, al-Maqrizi does not say anything about the conceptual relationship between the *Igathat* and the *Khitat*. Nor does he manage to complete a fully-fledged discussion on *kharab*, which he announces as the final section of the *Khitat* in his introduction and refers to several times in the narrative, such that we are able to fully assess the maturation of the concept in his mind.[96] Instead we have a few short and hard-to-date discussions of *kharab* in the *Khitat*, in addition to dispersed mantra-like mentions of the term in the narrative of the *Khitat* and *Suluk*, and also in a few biographies in the *Durar* of contemporary sultans, amirs, and high administrators.[97] The first chronologically among these discussions is a well-structured sketch on *kharab* in the middle of the *Musawwadat* published by Sayyid in 1995, where al-Maqrizi attempts a first compilation of the material he had been collecting on *Khitat* for some time.[98] Al-Maqrizi here provides a compact and interrelated list of all the causes separately enumerated in the *Ighathat*, followed by an eschatological prediction about the destruction of Cairo ascribed to the enigmatic master Sufi Ibn ʿArabi, and reportedly explained to al-Maqrizi by none other than his admired Zahiri guide, Ibn al-Burhan. Then, in the published text of the *Khitat*, redacted a decade or two later, the *Musawwadat* report is split into a section on the causes of *kharab* that does not add much to the *Musawwadat* text, and an independent section on the eschatological prediction of *kharab* where al-Maqrizi claims to have seen the treatise that explains Ibn ʿArabi's prophecy himself and dispenses altogether with the testimony of Ibn

(Cairo: IFAO, 2010), 1: 19, calls al-Maqrizi's *Khitat* "autopsie de la ruine" (the dissection of ruins).

96 Al-Maqrizi, *Khitat2*, 1: 244, 299; 3: 721; 4: 178, 756; Loiseau, "Les événements," 128, note 28 enumerates the instances of *kharab* in al-Maqrizi's *Khitat*, *Suluk*, and *Durar*. The fact that the section on *kharab* does not exist even though al-Maqrizi refers to it repeatedly is a strong argument in support of the incompleteness of the *Khitat* as it has reached us, rather than an indication of al-Maqrizi's change of mind as he was writing his book to dispense with that section. See al-Maqrizi, *Khitat2*, 3: 692–4.

97 Loiseau, "Les événements," 131–2 offers a French translation of al-Nasir Faraj ibn Barquq's biography in al-Maqrizi, *Suluk*, 4: 225–8, one of the most vituperative condemnation of a sultan's role in the *kharab*. I have collected twenty-four mentions of *kharab* in *Khitat1* (1: 60–1, 110–11, 128, 184, 227, 265, 305. 361, 365, 372–3, 405; 2: 98, 105, 119. 120. 132–8, 223, 232, 280, 283, 296, 311) and eight mentions in the last two volumes of *Suluk* (3: 1124, 1127, 1135, 1149, 1155, 1157, 1167, 1168, 4: 29), and this is a partial list.

98 Sayyid, *Musawwadat*, 62–3.

al-Burhan.[99] A third, inchoate analysis, *min asbab al-kharab* (some causes of ruination), is appended to the end of Sayyid's recent edition of the *Khitat*.[100] It concentrates on the direct pillaging of people's properties and belongings in rural Egypt by the Mamluks following the depletion of the treasury during the reign of Faraj b. Barquq because of Tamerlane's devastation and the ensuing infighting between the sultan and his amirs in Syria, but ends abruptly with an incomplete story on the forced selling (*tarh*) of confiscated honey to the merchants of Cairo. This text may have constituted a kernel of the missing section on the analysis of *kharab* since it basically elaborates on one of the factors previously tallied in the *Ighathat* and the *musawwadat* of the *Khitat*—direct plundering—and gives it historical causes.

Another short, and perhaps more perceptive, analysis of the causes of ruination has not been included in the list of excursuses on *kharab* in al-Maqrizi's *Khitat*. It is a passage in the description of the *tibaq* (barracks) of the young Mamluks in the Citadel of Cairo, where al-Maqrizi characteristically digresses to describe the changes from the strict system that governed their training in the Bahri period to the slackening of rules and traditions under Barquq and, especially, his son Faraj. Al-Maqrizi nostalgically opines:

> Mamluks used to be bought at a young age and were put through rigorous training and a thorough religious education before they were manumitted and enlisted in the army. That is why they were skillful and thoughtful leaders who managed a great empire and fought for the cause of Islam. The system was relaxed under Barquq, who allowed his mamluks to live in the city and to socialize with the local population through marriage and business transactions. It deteriorated even further under Faraj b. Barquq, when new mamluks were brought at a fairly advanced age, after their character had already been formed, and were no longer required to undergo an extensive religious education before their manumission. Consequently, the sultanian mamluks became the lowest of people, the most undignified and greedy, and the most ignorant in worldly matters and in religion. They became more lustful than monkeys, more ravenous than rats, and more harmful than wolves. No wonder then that the land of Egypt and Sham was ruined [*kharubat*] from the Nile to the Euphrates because of the venality in assigning governing positions, the exploitation of governors, and the depravity of those in charge [i.e. the Mamluk ruling class].[101]

[99] See al-Maqrizi, *Khitat2*, 2: 225 for the first section and *Khitat2*, 2: 241–2 for the second.

[100] Al-Maqrizi, *Khitat2*, 4: 1087–8; Sayyid states that he is adding it from the *Musawwadat*, but I could not find it in the *Musawwadat*, published by him as well. Loiseau, "Les événements," 128–9.

[101] Al-Maqrizi, *Khitat2*, 3: 692–4; see also Ibn Taghri-Birdi, *Nujum*, 7: 328–9, where he deplores the changes in the Mamluk army structure from the time of Qalawun and describes the mamluks of his time as "holding their buttocks in the water and their nose in the sky" (meaning that they were both impotent and arrogant). There is a tendency among

It is in this passage that al-Maqrizi works out the most important underlying causes for the *kharab* that he is trying throughout his *Khitat* to articulate. The natural and external causes that heavily contributed to the sorry state of affairs he has observed in his adulthood are of lesser concern, and some of them, as noted by Loiseau, go unnoticed.[102] It is the incremental political corrosion that he is after, and in the *Khitat* (but also the series of chronicles covering the history of Islamic Egypt) he was able to take a longer view on history that allowed him to understand better how a country and its glorious capital, so blessed and so resilient against past calamities, had succumbed to the then-current irreversible *kharab* that he was so bitterly lamenting. From its first tentative appearance in the *Ighathat* to its becoming the leitmotiv of the historical review of Cairo, and Egypt, in the *Khitat* and elsewhere, the notion of *kharab* played a central role in the development of al-Maqrizi's thinking about the Mamluk rule of his time and its effect on his city and country.[103] It also represented one of the strongest impulses that drove him to conceive of his large project of the history of [Islamic] Egypt. This inference not only suggests that the writing of the *Khitat* came on the heel of the *Ighathat*, but that the two of them belonged to a conceptual continuum that runs through al-Maqrizi's entire history-of-Egypt project, which he kept on restructuring, reshaping and broadening until the end of his life as more and more source material accumulated and as the sharpening of his observations and reflections made him realize the need to treat certain specific subjects or periods separately. Throughout, al-Maqrizi maintained control over the growing project not only by arranging its components chronologically or distinguishing them thematically, but also by devising a system of cross-referencing that connected the parts together while allowing him to assign a piece of information or a narrative its proper place in the overall project spread over several specialized treatises and compendia.[104]

---

the Burji historians to idealize the Bahri period, but as David Ayalon ("Harb," *EI*^{2}, 3: 189) remarks, "this tendency is by no means without foundation."

102 Loiseau, "Les événements," 129.

103 Loiseau, *Reconstruire la maison*, 1: 25–7, offers an interesting analysis of the etymology and semantic field of the term as understood by al-Maqrizi and equally theorizes *kharab* as the concept that allows al-Maqrizi to imbue his material with an emotional charge of nostalgia. Loiseau then launches an elaborate investigation into the presence of *kharab* in official documents of the period (mainly *waqfs*) to propose a reconstitution of the urban order in the city of Cairo in the second half of the Burji period on a smaller and less monumental scale while incorporating ruination in that order, a phenomenon that still haunts the city today.

104 Numerous examples appear throughout al-Maqrizi's texts where he refers to one or the other of his books for further information or discussion. But one of the most elaborate examples of cross-referencing is his reporting on his patron and friend *katib al-sirr* Fath Allah. In his biographical notice on Fath Allah in al-Maqrizi, *Khitat2*, 3: 204, he says, "I have covered his life in more detail in my book, *Durar al-'Uqud al-Farida* and in my

The History of Egypt: An Integrated Project

The thesis advanced here is that al-Maqrizi conceived of his project to write the history of Egypt primarily out of concern for the corruption of the Mamluk regime and the consequent ruination of the country and the city he had observed for years of public service, which culminated in his highly informative experience as *muhtasib*. The scope and tone of the project were informed by his personal views and emotions, sense of belonging, education, professional disappointments and aspirations, and scholarly competition, but especially by his strict religious leanings, which saw in the past a desired ideal to recover. As such, al-Maqrizi's project was retrospective in nature, that is, it looked at the past not only as a way of understanding the present, but also as a tool for rebuking the present's excesses and lamenting its actors' deviation from the right path. Having been reading relevant historical sources and collecting data for a number of years, starting at least in 803/1400, potentially in competition with his neighbors Ibn Duqmaq and al-Awhadi, and having accumulated an administrative experience that educated him in questions of politics, economy, and urban development, al-Maqrizi was probably considering what format to use when the *mihna* of 806 jolted him into setting down his thoughts on paper. The *Ighathat* was the first salvo, aimed at showing his knowledge, testing his hypotheses and methods, and expressing his indignation at the divergences from sound economic policies of his time. The next step was the *Khitat*, although it is not totally clear when he began composing the book.

The question is further complicated by the revival of al-Sakhawi's accusation against al-Maqrizi of scholarly theft that Frédéric Bauden so resolutely argued in minute detail. He proved without any doubt that al-Maqrizi incorporated at least nineteen leaves of data in the handwriting of his neighbor al-Awhadi in the first draft of his *Khitat*, without any attribution, and sometime erased words that might reveal the original author (but not always, as Bauden himself proves) and replaced them with his own words. That this was intentional is not in question. Al-Maqrizi himself admitted it in his biography of al-Awhadi, where he says "God helped me with drafts in his handwriting on the *khitat* of Cairo, which I incorporated in my compendium entitled *Kitab al-Mawa'iz wa-l Athar fi-Dhikr al-Khitat wa-l Athar*."[105] Bauden, channeling al-Sakhawi, wants us to see al-Maqrizi as a deliberate plagiarist,

[missing] *Khulasat al-Tibr fi Akhbar Kuttab al-Sirr*." He then says, in *Durar*, 3: 16, "He has a magnificent house and a mausoleum outside Cairo, I recorded them in the *Khitat*, and I mentioned him in my *al-Muqaffa*." Al-Maqrizi thus cross-references Fath Allah's material four times across four of his books. See also Bauden, "Maqriziana X," 94–6, 113.

105 Al-Maqrizi, *Durar*, 1: 186.

and he might be right to accuse him of that, despite al-Maqrizi's admission of having used al-Awhadi's material and Bauden's uncovering of similar cases of possible incorporation without attribution by both Ibn Hajar and his student and acolyte al-Sakhawi, the two accusers of al-Maqrizi.[106] But for our purpose here, the more important question is whether al-Maqrizi's acquisition of al-Awhadi's drafts and possible fair copy of some of his *khitat* material after his death in 811/1408 was behind his decision to write his own *Khitat* or not. Another, concomitant, question is how much of al-Maqrizi's *Khitat*'s material, structure, and, especially, purpose can be attributed to al-Awhadi's material and how much of it stems from al-Maqrizi's own thinking and circumstances. There are no definite answers to either question, and the issue will be dealt with in more detail in the section below on the *Khitat*. Here, the first question will be considered in light of what we know about al-Maqrizi's life and scholarly development.

Bauden does prodigious work in tracking down the inconsistencies between the texts incorporated by al-Maqrizi and those rewritten by him to reconstruct his (clearly unsuccessful) method of hiding the traces of his plagiarism. He does not fully address the question of what effect, if any, that plagiarism had on al-Maqrizi's overall project of writing a *khitat* book, except in stating that al-Maqrizi "did not begin working on the *Khitat* prior to al-Awhadi's death."[107] However, he uses internal textual evidence to firmly establish the possible dates of composition of the two surviving draft volumes as between 811/1408 and 818/1415, and then narrows the range down to 814/1411–818/1415.[108] These dates will now have to be taken as the earliest dates of composition of the *Khitat*. The most important is of course 811/1408, the date of al-Awhadi's death and the passing of his papers to al-Maqrizi in ways that are unknown to us but that did not seem objectionable to his contemporaries, not even al-Sakhawi. Bauden sees this date as the *terminus post quem*, which may be true for the writing of the surviving draft. But that does not mean that al-Maqrizi did not think about writing a *khitat* book before that date. Bauden's external evidence to the contrary work both ways. First, that al-Maqrizi produced a treatise on economic history, the *Ighathat*, in 808/1405, indicates that he was working on historical material pertinent to Egypt some years before the death of al-Awhadi. Moreover, although

106 See Bauden, "Maqriziana IX," 216–17, for Ibn Hajar, 219 for al-Sakhawi.

107 Bauden, "Maqriziana IX," 208, repeated again in 218, although he cautions that "there is insufficient evidence to prove this view."

108 Bauden, "Maqriziana IX," 204–9; he then narrows the range in idem, "Maqriziana XII: Evaluating the Sources for the Fatimid Period: Ibn al-Ma'mūn al-Baṭā'iḥī's History and Its Use by al-Maqrīzī (with a Critical Edition of His Résumé for the Years 501–515 A.H.)," in *Islamic and Fatimid Studies in Honor of Paul E. Walker*, Bruce D. Craig ed. (Chicago: Middle East Documentation Center, 2010), 57.

produced urgently and quickly, the treatise contains elaborate historical data that must have required time to collect and organize. Second, al-Maqrizi's trips to Damascus between 810/1407 and 815/1412, which we have established to have been less than two years in total out of the five years, would not have hindered the beginning of a book on the *khitat*, especially since we know that al-Maqrizi might have finished the abridgment of Ibn Muyassar during that period. Third, and perhaps most important, al-Maqrizi's signature on sources he read and selected from on the history of Egypt from 1400 to 1406, that is, prior to the crucial 811/1408 date, provide strong circumstantial evidence that his intention and preparation to write such a book predate his acquisition of al-Awhadi's draft and may have to do more with his concurrent experience as a *muhtasib*, which allowed him first-hand knowledge of both the layout of the city and the working of its institutions.[109]

Yet, although the conceptualization and active collection of material for the *Khitat* may have started before and intensified after the completion of the *Ighathat* in 1405, it was probably not until al-Maqrizi decided to retreat to his family home in 1415 that he had the time and space necessary to undertake the actual writing of the book.[110] At that time he had been reading relevant historical sources for a number of years, had accumulated an administrative experience that educated him in questions of politics, economy, and urban development, and had composed a number of treatises, at least three of which, the *Ighathat*, *Shudhur al-ʿUqud*, and possibly *al-Nizaʿ wa al-Takhasum*, were historical in method and in argumentation. Indeed, he was now ready to embark on the project of his life. And he did. Between 1415 and his death in 1442, al-Maqrizi wrote two sets of interconnected long historical oeuvres, one on Egypt's history and another on the Prophet's life. This last project may have stemmed from an intensification of religious piety, which al-Maqrizi experienced toward the end of his life and which took him to Mecca for at least three Hajjs and two extended *mujawarat* in the span of six years from 834/1431 to 839–40/1436–7.[111]

Toward the end of his life, he returned to composing or redacting short treatises, some apparently on commission from some unknown patrons, while others were written in Mecca while he was living there. The Meccan treatises deal with subjects about which al-Maqrizi was able to collect information

109 See Bauden, "Maqriziana IX," 204–5, and 178, note 51, for a list of al-Awhadi's signatures on books' covers, and 210–11, but there is no mention of al-Maqrizi's similar if slightly later dates as argued in this chapter. Bauden also does not take al-Maqrizi's experience as a *muhtasib* into account as a possible impetus behind the decision to compose a *khitat* book.

110 That is why I lean toward the early date for the first draft of the *Khitat*, of the range suggested by Sayyid to be between 811/1408 and 818/1415 (i.e. between al-Awhadi's death and al-Maqrizi's final decision to retreat to his home and devote himself to writing).

111 Ibn Fahd, *Muʿjam*, 65.

from pilgrims and visitors to the Holy City during the frequent visits and stays he effected there toward the end of his life. They include his treatise on the Muslim rulers of Abyssinia, *al-Ilmam bi-Akhbar man bi-Ard al-Habasha min Muluk al-Islam*, and the one on Hadhramut, *al-Turfa al-Ghariba fi Akhbar Hadhramut al-'Ajiba*, both compiled in Mecca in 839/1435–6.[112] Another bout of writing occurred in Cairo in the year 841/1437–8. The treatise on metals, *al-Maqasid al-Saniyya li Ma'rifat al-Ajsam al-Ma'daniyya*, was written in its final form in Shawwal 841/ March–April 1438, and at least two other treatises were compiled, or perhaps just finalized, in the next month of Dhu al-Qi'da 841/April–May 1438: a treatise in praise of the Prophet's family, *Nabza 'ala 'Izam Qadr Ahl al-Bayt*, and his book on Hajj in Islam, *al-Dhahab al-Masbuk*, composed initially for al-Mu'ayyad Shaykh in 821/1418.[113] But it was the project of writing the history of Egypt, exemplified in the *Khitat* and the *Suluk*, that stayed with him until the end of his life.

112 Al-Maqrizi *Durar*, 2: 336–7, in the biography of the Sufi 'Abdallah b. Muhammad b. Burayk al-Hadhrami al-Yamani, reports that he met him during his *mujawara* in Mecca in 839/1436 and read a portion of *Sahih Muslim* with him. Al-Maqrizi adds that he learned things or wonders from him that he included in a section of his treatise on Hadhramut, which means either that the treatise was a late work or that he was still working on it and revising it toward the end of his life.

113 Al-Shayyal, "Mu'allafat al-Maqrizi al-Saghira," 26–7; idem, Introduction to al-Maqrizi, *Ittiaz*, 1: 13–17; idem, Introduction to al-Maqrizi, *Dhahab*, 24–5.

CHAPTER 4

The *Khitat*: History and Belonging

Al-Maqrizi's considerable historical oeuvre on Islamic Egypt appears to us today to have been systematically structured to cover every aspect of its history from the perspective of a medieval Muslim scholar: its annals, important and remarkable people, tribes, cities, countryside, the Nile, and deserts, wonders and religious merits, glorious days and gloomy ones, and its changing relationships to its larger Islamic and world context. This large set of topics, each treated under its specific title or titles written over more than thirty-five years, was nonetheless intertwined with the writing of the *Khitat*, which was al-Maqrizi's first true introduction to history writing after a small number of short, exhortative or advisory treatises. The separate titles proceeded in an almost chronological order, from the pre-Islamic history to the contemporary affairs of the country, in a manner that seems to have reflected the stages of the *Khitat*'s gestation. This rationalized and long project was interspersed with shorter treatises, which can be seen as the separate exercises of a solitary man who may have wanted every now and then to take a break from the rather rigid writing program he imposed on himself. They may also have been commissioned by kind patrons as means of providing indirect financial support to the otherwise impoverished and proud scholar. This at least appears to be the case with one of al-Maqrizi's most unusual treatises, *al-Ishara wa al-Ima' ila Hall Lughz al-Ma'*, completed on the 14th of Muharram 823/30 January 1420, during the early part of his retreat, in which he mentions that he composed it in compliance with the *al-ishara al-karima* (noble wish), although he does not say anything about the identity of that patron, or any possible patron of any of his other treatises for that matter.[1] Given the date of the treatise, however, this patron was most probably one of the powerful Nasrallah trio, Muhibb al-Din, Badr al-Din, and Salah al-Din, all of whom are mentioned repeatedly and appreciatively by al-Maqrizi in his *Suluk*.[2]

[1] Al-Maqrizi, *Rasail al-Maqrizi, al-Ishara wa al-Ima' ila Hall Lughz al-Ma'*, 267.

[2] Al-Sakhawi, *Daw'*, 2: 238, Ibn Taghri-Birdi, *Hawadith*, 1: 66–7. It may not have been a total coincidence that al-Maqrizi completed this riddle two days before Muhibb al-Din,

Al-Maqrizi was already a seasoned administrator and a known scholar with a number of short treatises to his credit when he decided to withdraw from public life and devote himself entirely to history writing. He probably began contemplating the composition of a *Khitat* book before his withdrawal, in which he thought to review the entire history and geography of Egypt through the history and topography of its capital city, Cairo, and, to a lesser extent, other Egyptian cities, as well as its Nile, wonders, and what he could glean of its ancient history.[3] Writing the book turned out to be an intensive and prolonged labor of love, for he often came back to it, adding, correcting, amending, and restructuring throughout the second half of his life, and it is clear from internal textual clues as well as from the material evidence of *tayyarat* in the autographed volumes of the book in our possession that he did not complete it as intended before his death.[4]

Al-Maqrizi also seems to have realized the difficulty of preserving the focus of the book strictly on *khitat* (i.e. the urban topography and related topics), while at the same time expanding its scope to include all the historical data on dynasties, sects, tribes, and people of Egypt he collected and wished to treat. He thus embarked on his parallel historical project that moved in two complementary directions, annalistic and biographical, while he was slowly working on the *khitat* and in conjunction with these distinct books. Although he never states it outwardly, al-Maqrizi composed his separate chronicles on each of the major phases of Egyptian Islamic history after he had begun the treatment of that same period in his *Khitat*. He used these specialized chronicles to supplement the limited historical sections in the *Khitat* and to expand on historical material that could not be fitted into a *khitat* format. He compiled his three huge annals, which he seems to have arranged in chronological order: *'Iqd Jawahir al-Asfat fi Tarikh Madinat al-Fustat* on the early Islamic period (lost today), *Itti'az al-Hunafa bi-Akhbar al-A'imma al-Fatimiyyin al-Khulafa* on the Fatimid period, and the indispensable *al-Suluk li-Ma'rifat Duwal al-Muluk* on the Ayyubids and Mamluks up to his own time. He also compiled a number of shorter works on various categories of important players in the history of the city, such as the viziers and the secretaries of

---

the closest of the Nasrallas to al-Maqrizi, was appointed teacher of the Hanbali *madhhab* at the Madrasa of al-Mu'ayyad, thus vacating the position of hadith teaching for al-Maqrizi according to the unsustainable report by Sakhawi, *Daw'*, 2: 22. But that must remain speculative for now.

3 There are many reasons for ascribing the plan to write the *Khitat* to the period between his last two stints as *muhtasib* between 1400 and 1405, as argued in Chapter 3.

4 For the known autograph copies of parts of the *Khitat*, see Al-Maqrizi, *Khitat2*, 1: 107°–22°, 2: 50°–70°, 4: 119°–47°; Frédéric Bauden, "al-Maqrizi," in *Christian–Muslim Relations: A Bibliographical History. Volume 5 (1350–1500)*, David Thomas and Alex Mallett, eds. (Leiden: Brill, 2013), 380–95, 388; Bauden, "al-Maqrīzī", *Medieval Muslim Historians*, 168–73.

sultans,[5] and a major biographical dictionary, *Kitab al-Muqaffa al-Kabir*, in which he wanted to group the biographies of all the important people who had lived in Egypt or visited it since the Islamic conquest, but he appears to have died before completing it.[6]

The *Khitat*: A Cumulative Book?

Throughout the period during which al-Maqrizi wrote all these books, he was often revisiting the *Khitat*, changing its framework and scope, adding to and modifying its content, but his additions seem to have slowed down after the 820s/1416–26, although they never stopped until very shortly before his death. The *Khitat* appears to have been, at the same time, the foundational text upon which al-Maqrizi constructed the rest of his historical works and the repository of condensed versions of data extracted from these same works and sometimes re-plugged back into the *Khitat* in summary form. This becomes clear if we compare the first draft (*musawwada*) of one of two volumes of the *Khitat* published by Ayman Fu'ad Sayyid in 2005 and the complete edition of Bulaq or the newer one also published by Sayyid, which is based on the last drafts or fair copies redacted by al-Maqrizi before his death.[7] The comparison not only shows the vast amount of data accumulated by al-Maqrizi in the interim, but also reveals something about the process by which the book took shape. The first draft consists of an appreciative though skeletal review of the Fatimid stage of Cairo's history and a hurried listing of the famous quarters and houses of the city in al-Maqrizi's time (i.e. early fifteenth-century). Its content is a first compilation of the material that will appear on pages 360–484 of the first Bulaq volume and pages 2–76 of the second (i.e. less than one sixth of the word count of the final draft that has reached us). Assuming that there was another volume of the first draft with roughly the same word count, we still have a final draft that is more than

[5] Although al-Maqrizi planned two books on viziers and *kuttab*, it is not clear that he ever completed them. The first, *Talqih al-'Uqul wa al-Ara' fi Tanqih Akhbar al-Jullat al-Wuzara'*, is mentioned in his *Khitat2*, 1: 443, but is nowhere listed in his publication inventories. The second, *al-Ta'rif fi man Wuliyya Wazifat al-Insha' wa Ktabat al-Sijillat fi Misr*, is mentioned on the margin of the manuscript of 'Ali ibn Sa'id al-Maghribi, *al-Mugharrib fi-Hilly al-Maghrib, al-Nujum al-Zahira fi-Hilly Hadrat al-Qahira*, H. Nassar, ed. (Cairo: 1970), 249, see Sayyid, *al-Muntaqa min Akhbar Misr*, n., where he identifies al-Maqrizi's sources for these two works as Ibn Muyassar and Ibn Sa'id.

[6] Sayyid, *Musawwadat*, 47–53; al-Shayyal, "Mu'allafat al-Maqrizi al-Saghira," 23–4; al-Maqrizi, *Muqaffa*, 1: 5–12.

[7] Beside Ayman Fu'ad Sayyid's comments in his edition of the *Khitat*, Frédéric Bauden in his series Maqriziana offers minutely detailed studies of several sources of al-Maqrizi's *Khitat*.

three times the size of the first draft. Some of the material of the first draft has clearly come from the draft of al-Awhadi's *Khitat* which al-Maqrizi acquired after his neighbor's death and directly incorporated in his draft, as proven by Frédéric Bauden.[8] But there is no way to tell whether al-Maqrizi's total first draft text depended on al-Awhadi's missing text.[9] Moreover, al-Maqrizi, as we saw in the discussion of the primary sources he used, has made an effort to directly quote the primary sources he was consulting rather than copying from al-Awhadi's citations from those same sources.[10]

With very few exceptions, the topographical and architectural information in this first volume of the *musawwada* focuses on the Fatimid period. The last draft added the Ayyubid and Mamluk stages of Cairo's history up until al-Maqrizi's time, augmented the Fatimid section, perhaps by incorporating material from sources that were not included in al-Awhadi's manuscript, and updated many of the individual entries to bring the description up to the time of writing (although he either missed or deliberately omitted some). The last draft also includes a structured history of the country, the city, and a survey of its various historical stages, from the pre-Islamic to the early Burji (Circassian) Mamluk, and the most important examples of its building types loosely arranged in chronological order and supplemented with short biographical notices on their patrons in numerous cases. The historical and geographical survey of pre- and early Islamic Egypt that occupies pages 1–348 of the first Bulaq volume may correspond to the missing "first volume" to which the discovered draft is a second volume, but this is impossible to ascertain until more material is discovered.[11]

Further examination of the last published draft we have, with all the addenda and loose inserts in the autograph volumes, reinforces the impression that it was far from being the final one, as planned by al-Maqrizi and stated in the book's introduction. The sixth section, for instance, which was supposed to deal with the Citadel of the Mountain and its kings (i.e. the

8 Bauden, "Maqriziana IX."

9 Sayyid, *Musawwadat*, 79, suggests that al-Awhadi's *Khitat* might have focused on the Fatimid stage and that it might have furnished the basis of al-Maqrizi's first draft, but we have no external evidence to support this suggestion. Bauden, on the other hand, argues for a much larger scope and a completer status of al-Awhadi's draft.

10 Frédéric Bauden, "Maqriziana XII," 59–60, shows that al-Maqrizi, in his collection of résumés from his sources, amended the quotations from his secondary source, Ibn 'Abd al-Zahir, when he had access to the original Ibn al-Ma'mun, and concludes that "al-Maqrīzī's intent was to quote his sources as faithfully as possible, a trait he already exhibited, especially in *al-Khiṭaṭ*." Bauden, "Maqriziana II," 91, presents another instance of al-Maqrizi's *modus operandi* when al-Maqrizi began by synthesizing information from his secondary source, al-Nuwayri's *Nihayat al-Arab*, but then returned to the original source, al-Jahiz's *Kitab al-Hayawan*, when he finally got hold of it.

11 Gardiner with Bauden, "A Recently Discovered Holograph," 123–31.

Ayyubids and Mamluks), is expanded to include the mosques, madrasas, *khanqahs*, *ribats*, *zawiyas*, *mashhads*, and other types of buildings in Cairo in addition to the synagogues, convents, and churches of Egypt and extended discussions of the Jewish and, especially, Christian sects in Egypt, festivals, and ecclesiastical history, and at least one elaborate discussion of a calamitous event in 721/1321 under Sultan al-Nasir Muhammad in which many Cairene churches were destroyed by a rabble. This large section—the most important in the book in my opinion, because it contains firsthand information collected by al-Maqrizi from contemporary documents or from direct observation—reads as a first draft of a section that al-Maqrizi tucked at the end of the sixth section in his original book structure but did not have the time to develop into a separate section on its own. Furthermore, the part dealing with the Jewish and Christian religions and structures is even more skeletal than the preceding part and does not seem to belong at the end of the section on the Islamic structures in Cairo, for the simple reason that it covers structures all over Egypt.

The book, in both its published Bulaq and Sayyid editions, ends abruptly with a short list of the churches of the Melkites in Cairo, followed by an uncommonly short and terse colophon that does not state dates, name of author, or place of writing.[12] The composition of the colophon itself implies that it was written by a copyist working with two separate volumes of the book, because it reads: "This is the end of the second volume of the book. With its completion, the book is completed . . ."[13] The seventh section, that was supposed to analyze the reasons for Cairo's decline in the author's time, is altogether missing, although the theme of decline is diffused throughout the book in the form of bitter comments added by al-Maqrizi to lament the disappearance or destruction of cities, buildings, habits, and practices in his own time.[14] Moreover, many of the individual entries are still not finished and the information in them is not always brought up to date. Sometimes, the text itself is not even edited: many sections still reveal the layers of their modification, at times with the dates on which new information was inserted into them. A good example is the tiny entry on the Mosque of al-Ashraf Barsbay, built during the period in which al-Maqrizi may have been writing his first draft of the *Khitat*, which covers only a couple of lines of basic information.[15]

[12] Sayyid, in his edition, al-Maqrizi, *Khitat2*, 4: 1087–8, adds a very short excursus on the reasons for decline that he glosses from the first draft, which does not even amount to a structure of a section but shows that al-Maqrizi was thinking of writing a section on decline from the first arrangement of the book.

[13] Al-Maqrizi, *Khitat1*, 2: 519.

[14] Examples in al-Maqrizi, *Khitat1*, 1: 60, 111, 128, 184, 227, 265, 305, 361, 365, 372–3, 405, 2: 98, 105, 119, 120, 132–8, 223, 232, 280, 283, 296, 311.

[15] Al-Maqrizi, *Khitat2*, 4: 348.

The brief section that follows on the mosques that have been "recently renovated" (*tajadadat*) seems to have been a later addition, still in the form of notes, which carry dates ranging from 830/1426–7 to Dhu al-Hijja 843/May 1440, two years before al-Maqrizi's death.[16] It is unclear whether he intended to go back to this and other similar sections and edit them as he had done with the material he had compiled for the first draft of the book, which went through several redactions.[17]

Obviously, extending the inquiry into his own time, which seems to have been a development that occurred at a later stage of his life, posed some methodical and organizational problems for al-Maqrizi, which he does not seem to have had the time to address in the introduction or to resolve in the text. This is clear from the fact both that he did not amend his introductory statement to include a reference to the buildings of his own time and that he did not add a heading to the large section on the various types of structures in Mamluk Cairo which occupies pages 244–519 of the second Bulaq volume (or all of Volume 4 of Sayyid's edition). This whole section may have constituted a fourth volume of the original book that was not included in the original structure. But at this stage of our knowledge it is difficult to reconstruct the exact and final structure of the book, except to conclude that it was rather fluid and changing over the long period of compilation and gestation to accommodate the growing data in al-Maqrizi's possession on the one hand and, on the other, his changing mood about the decline of the sultanate and the city (and the responsibility of his contemporary sultans for it), which seems to have been growing both darker and more daring in its frankness, and even derision, toward the sitting sultans.[18]

The book as it exists is a cumulative work, both in its scope and in its depth of treatment of the various topics it comprises. The different strata, in their

[16] Ibid., 4: 254, note 2. Sayyid notes that the date of death of al-Azrari on 12 Rabi' I 843/23 August 1439 is the last date mentioned in al-Maqrizi's *Khitat*.

[17] Ibid., 4: 352–60 and note 1, also 354, where Sayyid notes that this section was added after al-Maqrizi had returned from *mujawara* in Mecca, which Sayyid dates to 1430–35. Al-Maqrizi, as we saw, did more than one *mujawara* in the 1430s and he may have written this text after any of them.

[18] The scathing criticism and coarse language that marks the biographical entries on al-Maqrizi's contemporary sultans from Barquq to Barsbay in the *Suluk*, which were presumably composed when they died, has no equivalent in the *Khitat*, where these sultans are mentioned very briefly at the end of the section entitled "The Kings of Egypt since the Building of the Citadel of the Mountain," al-Maqrizi, *Khitat2*, 3: 780–8. Another clue that many sections of the book were not redacted is that the mention of the sultanates of al-Mu'ayyad to Barsbay is tucked at the end of the section on the Abbasid caliphs in Egypt. Al-Maqrizi does not even seem to have edited the section on the Mosque of al-Mu'ayyad for the floriated and flattering language it contains, *Khitat2*, 4: 338–40, as compared to the much stronger criticism he directs at al-Mu'ayyad in his obituary in the *Suluk*, 4: 550–1.

final form, reflect not only the growth and diversification of al-Maqrizi's data on Egypt during its long period of gestation and composition, but also his gradually darkening mood and circumstances, and his evolving views on the history and politics of his time. Its main motifs, however, seem to have been set from the beginning and maintained, if not reinforced, with every redaction. Three themes that come across clearly in the first draft, homage to the Fatimids and the grandeur of their caliphal capital, nostalgia for the bygone days of Cairo (including the early Mamluk period, especially the long reign of al-Nasir Muhammad), and persistent prediction of perdition under the Burji Mamluks anticipate the full-blown memorial and elegiac character of the last draft we now have. They in fact seem to have been among the most important motivations behind the writing of the book in the first place, which would have been further spelled out had al-Maqrizi had the time to complete the section on *kharab* that he promised in the introduction.[19] They all, however, stem from the one overwhelming emotion that animated al-Maqrizi's entire historical endeavor: his filial love of his country, and particularly his birth city Cairo. The *Khitat*, in fact, can be seen as an anxious love-letter from al-Maqrizi to his slowly crumbling city (at least as he sees it in his old-age pessimism) that recalls its better days, laments its current state of deterioration, and identifies and condemns its tormentors. In the process, al-Maqrizi also produces the most complete urban and architectural register we have, not only of Cairo but also of any medieval city before the fifteenth century, which is what had made his book famous in the first place.

Al-Mawaʿiz wa-l-Iʿtibar: What's in a Title?

Although the abbreviated title of al-Maqrizi's book, the *Khitat*, has almost always been taken as a straightforward description of its content, an analysis of the full title, *Kitab al-Mawaʿiz wa-l-Iʿtibar bi-Dhikr al-Khitat wa-l-Athar* (The Book of Moral Sermons and Lessons derived from the Remembrance of Cities' Traces and Building Remains), reveals the real scope of the book, which goes beyond the historical-topographical survey to subordinate that survey to greater moral and memorial aims.[20] The title clause delves straight into the reasons behind the writing of the book, and perhaps the reasons behind history writing itself from the perspective of the pious al-Maqrizi, a

19 See my "Maqrizi's *Khitat*: An Egyptian *Lieu de Mémoire*" in Behrens-Abouseif, *The Cairo Heritage*, 17–30.

20 In his partial translation of the book, Karl Stowasser, for instance, opted to keep the title as *Medieval Egypt: Al-Khiṭaṭ of Aḥmad ibn Alī Al-Maqrīzī* (Washington D.C.: Hans A. Stowasser, 2014), but in the text he offers this translation of the title: *The Book of Exhortations and Useful Lessons in Dealing with Topography and Historical Remains*.

perspective which, although familiar from other contemporary conceptions of the function and virtue of history writing, goes a step further in terms of method and, more importantly, criticism.[21] More than a century ago, Émile Galtier raised the same issue in an article that analyzed the meaning of every term in the book's title and concluded that its best translation into French would be "*Livre des enseignements et des leçons utiles que nous pouvons retirer de la description des quartiers successivement bâtis et des vestiges subsistants du passé.*"[22] Around the same time, Paul Casanova tried his hand at a translation of the *Khitat*, which never went beyond the Fatimid part of the original, and suggested as a title "*Livre des admonitions et de l'observation pour l'histoire des quartiers et des monuments, ou description historique et topographique de l'Égypte.*"[23] Both suggestions, the rhymeless (and clearly steeped in late nineteenth-century positivism) title of Galtier's translation and the direct and literal one of Casanova's, underscore the importance of capturing the meaning of every term in the title before attempting to understand its full implication.[24]

The use of the two terms *al-mawaʿiz* (moral sermons, exhortatory talks) and *al-iʿtibar* (deducing moral lessons) in Islamic historical writing has a long and venerated history. To begin with, its origin is Qur'anic. Throughout the sacred text, numerous historical examples (*qisas*, sg. *qissa*, story or tale) of the nations of yore are cited for believers as moral lessons (*ʿibar*) either to be emulated in order to win God's favor or to be avoided in order to avert God's

[21] Titles are not simple reflections of the content: they extend, modify, emphasize, and hint at motivations, intentions, and arguments, see Jerrold Levinson, "Titles," *The Journal of Aesthetics and Art Criticism* 44 (1985): 29–39; John Fisher, "Entitling," *Critical Inquiry* 11, 2 (December 1984): 286–98; Hazard Adams, "Titles, Titling, and Entitlement To," *The Journal of Aesthetics and Art Criticism* 46, 1 (Autumn 1987): 7–21. A discussion of the main arguments about the functions of titles in an Arabic context is Ibrahim Taha, "The Power of the Title "Why Have you Left the Horse Alone" by Maḥmūd Darwīsh," *JAIS* 3 (2000): 66–83.

[22] Émile Galtier, "Maqrizi a-t-il écrit une 'Description historique et topographique de l'Égypt et du Caire?,'" *Bulletin de l'IFAO* 5 (1906): 156–64 [reprinted in Fuat Sezgin et al., *Studies on Taqiyaddin al-Maqrizi (d. 1442): Collected and Reprinted*, 2 vols. (Frankfurt am Main: Institute for the History of Arabic-Islamic Science at the Johann Wolfgang Goethe University, 1992), 138–47.

[23] Al-Makrizi, *Kitab al-Mawaʿidh wa'liʿtibar bidhikr al-Khitat wa'l Athar, Livre des admonitions et de l'observation pour l'histoire des quartiers et des monuments, ou description historique et topographique de l'Égypte*, *MMAF* vols. 3–4, Paul Casanova, ed. (Cairo: IFAO, 1906), translation of v. 1, pp. 1–397 of the Bulaq edition.

[24] Loiseau, *Reconstruire la maison*, 1: 21–4, discusses the various possibilities of translating but also interpreting the significance of the term *khitat* as al-Maqrizi uses it. He notices that al-Maqrizi's employment of the term and his understanding of the genre differ from those of his contemporary *khitat* author Ibn Duqmaq.

punishment.[25] The *qisas* include the long and torturous history of the Banu Isra'il (the Israelites) path to monotheism, and other biblical and para-biblical examples of wicked nations such as 'Ad and Thamud (most probably Gog and Magog) and some non-biblical examples such as Bani Salih, who were all punished for their denial of divine messages and persecution of divine messengers by annihilation.[26] These examples furnished the foundation for the Islamic notion of history itself, and, more precisely, the sacred history of the relationship between God and humanity up to the final Muhammadan revelation.[27]

Following this venerated Qur'anic treatment of history, Muslim historians used the two terms or their derivations, especially *al-i'tibar*, which is the verbal noun of *'ibar*, in the titles of their books to express the same notion. One of the earliest examples we have is *Kitab al-I'tibar*, the famous autobiographical book of Usama ibn Munqidh (1095–1188), the Syrian prince from the castle of Shayzar, the stronghold of this feudal knightly family in Syria. Usama, who served the Fatimid Caliph al-Hafiz li-Din Allah (1076–1149), Nur al-Din of Syria, and Salah al-Din, and fought and interacted with the Crusaders, justifies his work by saying that he felt his life was worth reporting not because his own deeds were exceptional—although indeed they were in that crucial period of Islamic history—but because lessons could be learned from the events he had witnessed and recorded, hence the choice of the term *al-i'tibar*. He stresses this point further by stating that at the end of an exceptionally long and adventurous life, he realized that nothing could advance or delay death, the only unpredictable and unavoidable truth. He thus philosophically offers the story of his life as an illustration and confirmation of that

[25] Cf. Surat Yusuf, 12: 111; Hud, 11: 120; Al 'Imran, 3: 138. Also Ayman Fu'ad Sayyid, "Manahij al-Naqd al-Tarikhi 'ind al-Mu'rrikhin al-Muslimin," *AI* 32 (1998): 26–7; but see especially the collection of traditions on *'ibar* in Jamal al-Din Abi Ja'far al-Idrisi, *Anwar 'Uluwwy al-Ajram fi al-Kashf 'an Asrar al-Ahram*, ed. Ulrich Haarmann (Beirut: commissioned from Franz Steiner Verlag, Stuttgart, 1991), 5–11.

[26] A general study of the stories of the prophets in the Qur'an and early Islamic historiography is Roberto Tottoli, *Biblical Prophets in the Qur'an and Muslim Literature* (London: Routledge, 2002). See also Jane Dammen McAuliffe, "The Quranic Context of Muslim Biblical Scholarship," *Islam and Christian–Muslim Relations* 7, 2 (1996): 141–58. A recent exhaustive and systematic study of the concordance between the Qur'an and the Bible is Gabriel Said Reynolds, *The Qur'an and the Bible. Text and Commentary* (New Haven and London: Yale University Press, 2018).

[27] R. Stephen Humphreys, "Qur'anic Myth and Narrative Structure in Early Islamic Historiography," in *Tradition and Innovation in Late Antiquity*, F. M. Clover and R. S. Humphreys, eds. (Madison: WI: University of Wisconsin Press, 1989), 271–90; Fred Donner, *Narratives of Islamic Origins: The Beginnings of Islamic Historical Writing* (Princeton, N.J.: Darwin Press, 1998), 35–122, 291–5, provides a detailed study of how the Qur'an and the hadith functioned as the intellectual framework for early Islamic historical writing.

overarching conviction, which, even though it accepts the principle of personal will and hinges the notion of responsibility on it, still casts everything within the divine, omnipotent, and transcendent universal plan.[28] Usama's profound observations, rendered more melancholy and pessimistic by his frailty and advanced age, attracted many readers, including al-Maqrizi, who quotes Usama in his *al-Muqaffa* and *Itti'az al-Hunafa*.

The term *i'tibar* appears in the title of many books after Usama's, but none of them carries the same intimate emotional force that the knight's autobiography discharges.[29] They draw lessons from the actions of states or important public figures. Thus, for example, we have the long title of 'Abd al-Latif al-Baghdadi's short book, *al-Ifada wa-l-I'tibar fi al-Umur al-Mushahada wa-l-Hawadith al-Mu'ayana bi-Ard Misr* (The Benefit and Lessons [Deduced] from Things Observed and Events Witnessed in the Land of Egypt), which provides a firsthand and lively account of the flora, fauna, people, and monuments of Egypt, in addition to a chronicle of the years 'Abd al-Latif spent living there.[30] Here, the lessons are deduced from observation of events and happenings, not from personal experience: exactly how the notion is employed in several consequent books in the Mamluk period. These other examples, many almost contemporaneous with al-Maqrizi's *Khitat*, include the biographical dictionary of the famous Damascene historian Shams al-Din al-Dhahabi, *al-'Ibar fi Khabar man Ghabar* (Lessons Deduced from the Reports on Those Who Died) and the similarly-sounding title *Kitab al-'Ibar fi Khabar man Madha wa-Ghabar* (Book of Lessons Deduced from the Reports on those Who Died and Passed Away) of the Egyptian grammarian Muhammad ibn al-Naqqash (d. 1362), which is unknown or missing as it is only mentioned once by al-Maqrizi in his *Khitat*, but which seems to be a prosopographical book.[31]

Most important in relation to al-Maqrizi is the use of the term *'ibar* in Ibn Khaldun's own history, *al-'Ibar wa Diwan al-Mubtada' wa al-Khabar fi Akhbar al-'Arab wa al-'Ajam wa al-Barbar wa-man 'Asarahum min*

[28] Usama ibn Munqidh, *Kitab al-I'tibar*. Philip Hitti, ed. (Princeton, N.J.: Princeton University Press, 1930), 160–2; André Miquel, *Ousama, un prince syrien face au croisés* (Paris: Fayard, 1986), 7–11.

[29] Chase Robinson, *Islamic Historiography* (Cambridge: Cambridge University Press, 2003), 130.

[30] 'Abd al-Latif al-Baghdadi, *al-Ifada wa-l-I'tibar fi al-Umur al-Mushahada wa-l-Hawadith al-Mu'ayana bi-Ard Misr* (Cairo: Matba'at Wadi al-Nil, 1869), trans. as *Relations de l'Égypte* by Silvestre de Sacy (Paris: Imprimerie impériale, 1810), also trans. as *The Eastern Key: Kitab al-ifadah wa'l-l'tibar of 'Abd al-Latif al-Baghdadi* by Kamal Hafuth and John and Ivy Videan (London: Allen & Unwin, 1965).

[31] Al-Maqrizi, *Khitat2*, 4, 1: 118. The title does not appear in the biography of Ibn al-Naqqash that al-Maqrizi includes in his *Durar*, 3: 374–6; see also Bauden, "Maqriziana I, 2," 97–8.

Dhawi al-Sultan al-Akbar (Book of Lessons and Register of the Subject and Predicate Regarding the Days of the Arabs, the Foreigners, and the Berbers, and Those of Their Contemporaries who Possessed the Greatest Authority), a mouthful of a title that reflects a certain pride in the intended comprehensiveness of this universal historical survey of the Islamic world down to the author's time.[32] In Waseem El-Rayes's reading, Ibn Khaldun is using *ʿibar* in his title in an active form, as an invitation to his reader to partake in the deduction of lessons from history. Al-Maqrizi himself uses the verbal noun of the verb *waʿaza* (to preach, to teach) in the title of his Fatimid history, *Ittiʿaz al-Hunafa bi-Akhbar al-Aʾimma al-Fatimiyyin al-Khulafa*, which is, as we have seen in Chapter 1, both an exhortation and a plea to consider the rightfulness of the Fatimids' claim of descent from the Prophet Muhammad. In that sense it might have been deployed to serve a similar purpose to how Waseem El-Rayes reads *ʿibar* in Ibn Khaldun's title: an allusion, symbolic reference, parable, allegory that needs to be studied and reflected upon.[33] That drawing lessons from history requires the active participation of the reader is thus a goal that al-Maqrizi may have learned from his *shaykh* Ibn Khaldun and applied in his own work. This is, at least, what their choice of terms, and of verbal forms, for their titles hints at.

Al-Maqrizi's Notion of History

The full significance of the two terms *al-mawaʿiz* and *al-iʿtibar* in al-Maqrizi's title, however, cannot be grasped until we understand how they resonate with his comprehension of the import of history (*tarikh*) itself. To him, and to practically all medieval Muslim scholars, history writing exists not simply to report and present events for the pure purpose of knowing them, or the more modern one of interpreting them; it is also reportage with moral and social intentions.[34] In fact, history is, in al-Maqrizi's words but also in those of many of his contemporaries, first and foremost the reservoir of moral lessons. As such, it belongs to the domain of Islamic knowledge as understood by the

32 I am following, in this translation, with one significant difference, Waseem El-Rayes, "The Book of Allusions: A New Translation of the Title to Ibn Khaldun's Kitāb al-ʿIbar," *Religious Studies and Theology* 32, 1 (2013): 163–84, where he analyzes the title and its intentions. He also compares the three translations of the title by Franz Rosenthal, Muhsin Mahdi, and Nathaniel Schmidt and offers an elaborate, linguistically and historically compelling translation of the title as *Book of Allusions and Register of the Subject and Predicate Regarding the Days of the Arabs, the Foreigners, and the Berbers, and Those of Their Contemporaries Who Possessed the Greatest Authority*.

33 El-Rayes, "The Book of Allusions," 181–2.

34 Khalidi, *Historical Thought*, 215–19.

ulama of the period, although its origin was acknowledged by all Muslim historians to have been pre-Islamic and its position among the other religious sciences required of a true scholar was precarious.[35] Al-Maqrizi himself is fully aware of this Islamic dimension of the ethical purpose of history writing, which has its origins in the recording of the life and deeds of the Prophet Muhammad and his family and companions as the model for all Muslims to follow.[36] He presents it in summary form in the introductory remarks to his *Khitat*, and in fuller form in the preface to his *Durar*:

> Praise be to God who created all human beings and assigned to each of them a finite age, and endowed them with hearing, eyesight and conscience so they may thank Him. He entrusted them with His Earth so that He can judge their doing. He made them so that one generation would come after the other and each group follow in the footsteps of the former. The first ones would thus leave their stories to those after them as exhortations and moral examples [*Mawa'iz wa 'Ibar*], and the later ones would keep alive the memory and spread the fame of their predecessors. As a result, intelligent persons will be deterred from doing things which evoke criticism and which are recognized as evil. The educated will go after the best and finest character qualities. And when the time is over for life on Earth and the Day of Judgment is near, He will gather all humans to Him and revive them in His Presence to punish those who did evil and reward those who did good.[37]

The shorter version of al-Maqrizi's definition of history in the *Khitat* adds the ultimate Islamic exhortatory purpose: "to forewarn the reader of the ephemerality of this world as opposed to the next." But his definitive aim in stating this admittedly common opinion is less fatalistic than usual and more actively moral, for he goes on to list other benefits that rational men (*'uqala'*, sg. *'aqil*)

[35] Rosenthal, *Muslim Historiography*, 30–54; Makdisi, *The Rise of Humanism*, 163–70. See also Fu'ad Sayyid, "Shurut al-Mu'arrikh fi-Kitabat al-Tarikh: Khams Fatawa lam Tunshar li-Khamsa min A'lam al-Qarn al-Tasi' al-Hijri," *Majallat Ma'had al-Makhtutat al-'Arabiyya* 2, 1 (May 1956): 162–77, on five ulama opinions on the requirements to write history from the ninth century AH/sixteenth century CE.

[36] This is expressed very clearly in al-Maqrizi, *Imta'*, 1: 3, where he says, "It is outrageous for someone who calls himself a *'alim* and claims to be a person of understanding and knowledge to answer the question about the Prophets of God by listing names, which he does not understand. And what is worse is for the person who teaches, issues legal opinions, and sits as judge to be ignorant of the life of the Prophet (peace be upon him), or his genealogy, reputation, and high standing, and what he enjoyed of inherent and acquired merits, which is indispensable knowledge for anyone who believes in him, and which is necessary for anyone who claims to be a *'alim*" (my translation). See al-Sakhawi, *I'lan*, 64–5; Rosenthal, *Muslim Historiography*, 316. It is ironic that al-Sakhawi quotes al-Maqrizi here when he had accused him of having little knowledge of the history of early Islam and the first Muslims, see al-Sakhawi, *Daw'*, 2: 24.

[37] Mahmud al-Jalili, "Durar al-'Uqud al-Farida fi Tarajim al-A'yan al-Mufida li al-Maqrizi," *MMII* 13 (1965): 207. Trans. in Rosenthal, *Muslim Historiography*, 317.

can reap from studying history, "to appreciate the ethical criteria of their predecessors in order to follow them, and to distinguish their vile deeds in order to advise those in power against them."[38] This clearly resonates with the purpose and language of another genre of medieval Islamic writing, *nasa'ih al-muluk* (Mirror for Princes), which al-Maqrizi never directly used as a frame of any of his books, although, as we have seen, he often deploys an advisory tone in his policy-oriented treatises such as *Ighathat al-Umma* or *Shudhur al-'Uqud* or in his more polemical essays such as *al-Niza' wa al-Takhasum* or his passionate introduction to the *Itti'az al-Hunafa*.[39]

Al-Maqrizi provides another, more operative and culturally comparative definition of history in the body of the *Khitat*, which relies essentially on the established understanding of the term *tarikh* as it entered the Arabic language, most probably from Persian, and developed in the first few centuries of Islam.[40] He says:

> History is a day to which is ascribed what comes after it; it is also said that history is a known period that is determined from the beginning of an established time, through which one can know specific dates [relatively?]. There is a real need for history in all worldly and religious affairs. Every nation has its own history [in the sense of established chronology], which it needs in organizing its own activities and in identifying its own [important] dates, which distinguish it from other nations.[41]

He then adds the preamble that confirms his belonging to the established school of Islamic history by subscribing to its own creation timeline, even though he shows his willingness to discuss the stories of creation and timelines of other nations and religions, as is his wont in many aspects of the history of

[38] Al-Maqrizi, *Khitat1*, 1: 2; slightly different English translation in Stowasser, *Medieval Egypt*, 12. By *'uqala'*, al-Maqrizi most probably means "those who reason," a Qur'anically derived class of people that he seems to be addressing in most of his writing, but also other effective individuals in the society, especially ulama and advisors to rulers.

[39] On the *nasa'ih al-muluk* with an emphasis on the Arabic tradition see Louise Marlow, "Kings, Prophets and the 'Ulamā' in Mediaeval Islamic Advice Literature," *SI* 81 (1995): 101–20; idem, "Surveying Recent Literature on the Arabic and Persian Mirrors for Princes Genre," *History Compass* 7, 2 (March 2009): 523–38; Erik Ohlander, "Enacting Justice, Ensuring Salvation: The Trope of the 'Just Ruler' in Some Medieval Islamic Mirrors for Princes," *The Muslim World* 99, 2 (April 2009): 237–53.

[40] For the evolving definition and scope of *tarikh*, see the translation of al-Sakhawi, *I'lan*, in Rosenthal, *Muslim Historiography*, 249–61. See also H. A. R. Gibb, *Tarikh, Encyclopedia of Islam I Supplement* (Leiden: Brill, 1938), 233–45, reprinted in H. A. R. Gibb, *Studies on the Civilization of Islam*, Stanford Shaw and William Polk, eds. (Routledge and Kegan Paul, 1962), 108–33; R. S. Humphreys, art. "Tarikh, II. Historical Writing. I. In the Arab World," *EI*², 10: 271–80.

[41] Al-Maqrizi, *Khitat2*, 1: 677, my translation.

Egypt, where his openness to non-Islamic sources, including primary Jewish and Christian sources, is remarkable.[42] He states:

> And the first of the beginnings, and the most famous, is the beginning of the race of human beings. The People of the Book, Jews, Christians, and Magi, differ about its precise date of the First Man and about the recording of history from that beginning, which should not happen in history writing. Everything that relates to the beginning of creation and the events of ancient history is distorted by forgeries and myths because of the passage of time and the inability of those concerned to preserve its records over long stretches of time. God had said in the Qur'an, "Has there not reached you the news of those before you—the people of Noah and 'Ad and Thamud and those after them? No one knows them but God" [first half of Qur'an 9:14]. It is thus better to accept only what a Book revealed by God that can be trusted and that has not been changed or altered, or an account that is transmitted by the trustworthy. For if we look at [recorded] history, we will find vast discrepancies between the nations.[43]

Here, al-Maqrizi adheres to the traditional Islamic view of the accepted sources for transmission of historical reports, especially those related to the foundation stories of Islam and the life of its Prophet. For what other than the Qur'an, among the authorized revealed books, is free of alteration from an Islamic viewpoint? And what other than the sanctioned method of transmission (*isnad*) and verification (*jarh wa ta'dil*) of hadith would be considered valid from the perspective of the scholar/*'alim*? Both of these restrictions render the religious sources of other religions less reliable, even though al-Maqrizi, unveiling his unusual open-mindedness in comparison to his peers, will immediately delve into a detailed analysis of the kinds of dating

[42] Haggai Mazuz, "Post-Biblical Jewish Sources in al-Maqrizi's Historiography—Whence His Knowledge?" *JAIS* 17 (2017): 1–13, provides a preliminary analysis of al-Maqrizi's uses of Jewish sources and speculates about his possible informants. This is a first installment of Mazuz's research project on al-Maqrizi's Account on Jews and Judaism. Al-Maqrizi, *Khitat2*, 2: 409, specifies his source for a story about the Karaites' beliefs about the Mosque of Ibn a-Banna' as Ibrahim b. Faraj Allah b. 'Abd al-Kafi al-Dawudi al-'Anani (the Ananite, another name for Karaite), who he identifies as the "judge of the Jews." Another example that suggests that al-Maqrizi may have read the New Testament (the book of Matthew at least) in one of its available Arabic translations is the report inserted in the biography of one of his Sufi *shaykhs*, the Zahirite Ahmad bin 'Ali al-Tamimi al-Qassar, *Durar*, 1: 206–7. Al-Maqrizi states that he puzzled over an answer given by his *shaykh* until he read the New Testament and understood it. He then reproduces a correct Arabic translation of the verse (Matthew 23: 13, "But woe unto you, scribes and Pharisees, hypocrites! for ye shut up the kingdom of heaven against men: for ye neither go in yourselves, neither suffer ye them that are entering to go in," King James Version) while omitting the two terms *al-kataba* (clerks) and *al-farisiyyun* (Pharisees), but still retains the meaning by explaining that those addressed by the verse are the "Jewish scholars."

[43] Al-Maqrizi, *Khitat2*, 1: 677–8, my translation.

used by other nations, which comprises, beside the Jews and Christians, the Hindus, Kara Khitan, Uighur, and Chinese, for which he depended on Abu al-Rayhan al-Biruni's *al-Qanun al-Mas'udi* (*The Mas'udic Canon*), an encyclopedic work of astronomical knowledge that he dedicated to the Ghaznavid ruler Mas'ud ibn Mahmud (998–1040).[44] While explaining these different calendars, al-Maqrizi says, "I mentioned parts of the Hindu calendar calculation, and parts of those of the Uighur and Kara Khitan, which are derived from the Chinese calendar, so that the fair-minded will know that their wise men did not establish these timelines in vain. 'There is a reason behind Qasir's cutting off his nose,'[45] for how many ignorant of the wisdom of the ancients will deny their estimates of the age of the world without checking their evidence, when the right way would be to weigh the evidence of both sides of a problem before favoring one over the other. 'God knows and you do not' [last phrase of Qur'an 24:19]."[46]

This extremely revealing statement recalls al-Maqrizi's method of reasoning and his imploring his reader to use his/her own informed judgment when evaluating a historical report, as when he argued for the validity of the Prophetic genealogy of the Fatimids. Here, however, he rises above the controversy of a debated genealogy among Muslim scholars to urge his reader to weigh the evidence of authors of other cultures, including ones that were considered nonbelievers by Muslims, such as the Indian or Kara Khitan, before judging their reasoning. He goes even further by asking his reader to compare the various calendars of the different nations, without favoring any one over the others, giving them all equal weight in advancing their argument.[47] Moreover, he refrains from judging any of the stories of creation or the timelines based on them, even though he seems to doubt them all as a Muslim who believes in the Qur'anic admonition of those who pretend to know the story, which nonetheless does not establish any clear timeline of creation. But he does not categorically refute these other variants, leaving the possibility of their veracity open to evaluation. Here, again, he shows an openmindedness and a curiosity about the traditions of other cultures and other learned societies that far surpasses the norms of his time and his class, as we have already seen in other instances. Nevertheless, a certain hesitation,

[44] First published as Abu al-Rayhan al-Biruni, *al-Qanun al-Mas'udi (Canon Masudicus)*, 3 vols. M. Nizamu'd-Din et al. eds. (Hyderabad: Da'irat al-Ma'arif al-'Uthmaniyya, 1954–6).

[45] An Arabic proverb, said when a trick is suspected from an act of self-mutilation. The story of Qasir and his trick against Queen Zenobia of Palmyra, which explains the origin of the proverb, is related in al-Tabari, *History of al-Tabari, Vol. 4, The Ancient Kingdoms*, Moshe Perlmann trans. (Albany, N.Y.: State University of New York Press, 1987), 139–48.

[46] Al-Maqrizi, *Khitatz*, 1: 684, my translation.

[47] Compare to his method of reasoning concerning the validity of the Fatimid claim of descent from the Prophet, al-Maqrizi, *Itti'az*, 1: 44–54, discussed in Chapter 1.

or perhaps even an anxiety, transpires from al-Maqrizi's confirming his firm belief in the superiority of the Qur'anic telling of historical parables while maintaining his openness to other narrative possibilities as reasoned by other religious and cultural tradition. The intellectual uncertainty accentuated by his typical mild skepticism and his natural tendency to broad-mindedness shows itself here again, as it did in many controversial issues he discussed in his texts, such as the Fatimid genealogy, the struggle between the Umayyads, ʿAbbasids, and ʿAlids, and the many supranatural stories he delighted in reporting. But notwithstanding his unwavering belief in the rightfulness of the Orthodox Islamic interpretations, his partisanship for the family of the Prophet, and his typical siding with the underdog in major Islamic controversies, al-Maqrizi persistently maintains a healthy dose of inquisitiveness and a willingness to discuss multiple and contradictory stories, which distinguish him from many of his peers and bring him closer to Ibn Khaldun or to a much earlier generation of Islamic historians, like al-Tabari and al-Masʿudi, in his method of inquiry.[48]

Thus, it is not altogether surprising that al-Maqrizi's understanding of the historian's function appears to have been evolving throughout his career, although it would be impossible to follow its progress chronologically with the kind of dispersed and largely undated comments we have. One thing is clear, however: it did not stop at the operative level of his introductory statements in the *Khitat*, but grew and became more nuanced and sophisticated over time. It seems to have eventually reached rather supra-historic dimensions, not so different from that of the philosopher or the ethicist, if we are to believe a unique report by his nemesis al-Sakhawi. In his *al-'Iʿlan bi al-Tawbikh li man Zamma al-Tarikh*, al-Sakhawi records a hand-written definition of the historian copied by al-Maqrizi's most devoted companion, Najm al-Din Muhammad ibn Fahd, who, as we have seen, was a close companion of al-Maqrizi during the latter's various *mujawaras* in Mecca toward the end of his life, which places the statement late in al-Maqrizi's career.[49]

48 See the discussions on methods of history writing in Robinson, *Islamic Historiography*, 143–85; R. Stephen Humphreys, *Islamic History: A Framework for Inquiry* (Princeton: Princeton University Press, 1991), 104–47. On Ibn Khaldun's logical method see Muhsin Mahdi, *Ibn Khaldun's Philosophy of History* (London: Allen & Unwin, 1957), 172–87; Johan H. Meuleman, "La causalité dans la Muqaddimah d' Ibn Khaldun," *SI* 74 (1991): 105–39. For a sweeping critique of the Western historiographical neglect of the roots of Ibn Khaldun's method in Aristotelian logic, see Stephen Frederic Dale, "Ibn Khaldun: The Last Great Greek and the First *Annaliste* Historian," *IJMES* 38, 3 (2006): 431–51.

49 For the biography of Ibn Fahd see al-Sakhawi, *Daw'*, 6: 126–31. Ibn Fahd has an autograph on the cover of al-Maqrizi's oldest surviving manuscript of *Suluk* dated 846/1442, a year after al-Maqrizi's death. Muhammad Mustafa Ziyada, the editor of *Suluk*, noted that Ibn Fahd, according to al-Sakhawi, *Daw'*, 6: 128, was living in Mecca between 838/1435 and Jamada al-Akhar 850/ September 1446, which suggests that al-Maqrizi's book made it to

In that difficult-to-translate statement, al-Maqrizi defines the historian, or more correctly the chronicler, as the one who ontologically identifies with the time he is chronicling, and assigns to him the role of witness and guide to or mentor of future generations. He says:

> The person who writes the history [of his time] is tallying the days [i.e. time itself] on the days of his life [*hasaba al-ayyam 'ala 'umrihi*], and the one who writes the events of his time is making later generations witness his own age [*ashhada 'asruhu man lam yakun min ahl 'asrihi*]. He is presenting to the virtuous of the future additional lives to live and is opening to their eyes and ears places that had not been available to them. [poetry citation] I could not see the houses with my own eyes—maybe I will see them with my ears.[50]

> "من أرخ فقد حاسب الأيام على عمره ومن كتب حوادث دهره فقد أشهد عصره من لم يكن من أهل عصره فهو يهدي إلى الفضلاء أعماراً ويبوء أسماعهم وأبصارهم دياراً ماكانت دياراً. [وينهيها ببيت شعر للشريف الرضي] فاتني أن أرى الديار بعيني**فلعلي أرى الديار بسمعي"

With this statement, al-Maqrizi achieves an unprecedented lucidity in his understanding of the role of the historian as he must have honed it after many decades of thinking about and writing history books. His historian not only reports the events of his own time, he personifies his time and then transmits it to future generations in an almost corporeal manner that adds lives to their lives and allows them to experience the events of the past with their eyes and ears, not just their mind and abstract understanding. In his embodiment of history writing and transmission, the historian becomes a true witness (*shahid*) of his age. Thus, al-Maqrizi's use of the term "cause to witness" (*ashhada*) here acquires shades of transcendence as the term *shahid* has been developed in medieval Islamic literature, especially of the esoteric inclination.[51] Al-Maqrizi is obviously aware of this literature, and perhaps even versed in some of its genres. His use of the verb is thus intentional and significant. The citation of al-Sharif al-Radi's distich comes in to reinforce this reading by translating the intellectual grasp of historical reports into the ability to imagine the events and places described and by allowing one sense

---

Mecca after his death, see al-Maqrizi, *Suluk*, 1: 3. Ibn Fahd, *Mu'jam*, 64, does not indicate whether he read the *Suluk* in Mecca or Cairo but reveals a very close relationship with al-Maqrizi.

50 My translation; original quoted in al-Sakhawi, *I'lan*, 35, on the authority of Ibn Fahd; trans. differently in Rosenthal, *Muslim Historiography*, 316–17, who reads the first part as indicating the historian of the past, whereas I see it as speaking of the chronicler of his own time. Rosenthal identifies the poet cited as al-Sharif al-Radi (d. 1015), perhaps one of the most reflexive and philosophical medieval Arab poets, see al-Sharif al-Radi, *Diwan*, 2 vols., Yussef Shukri Farhat, ed. (Beirut: Dar al-Jil, 1995), 1: 598.

51 Nuha N. N. Khoury, "The Mihrab Image: Commemorative Themes in Medieval Islamic Architecture," *Muqarnas* 9 (1992): 11–28, and references in nos. 78 and 90.

(hearing) to substitute for another (seeing) in achieving the act of imagining, when the latter is unavailable because of the passage of time.[52]

Al-Maqrizi, in this definition, is also involving the reader in the act of experiencing past events through witnessing and imagining. He is in fact creating a dynamic relationship between the reporting historian and the receiving reader, whereby the former narrates from within the events he/she is living through whereas the latter is witnessing (*yashhadu*) history in both meanings of the word, to see and to testify, in order to share and to verify what the historian is reporting. With this definition, unfortunately unverifiable because it is reported only by al-Sakhawi, who had a very troubled relationship with al-Maqrizi, as we have seen, al-Maqrizi surpasses all understanding of history writing prevalent in his time and his milieu.[53] Not only does he appear to reject the passivity inherent in detached and purportedly objective reporting of events or in the lazy reception of only reading about these events. He is also endowing history writing with a certain phenomenological dimension, or at least a senses-based understanding, which brings it closer to literature as a form of embodied narrativity, one imbued with qualities that can be experienced with the senses.[54] His success in achieving that level of engagement in his own writing or chronicling of course varied, with some of his texts reverting back to the passive reporting, probably due to the weight of tradition and the prevalent modes of chronicling, which he followed. But a few other texts,

[52] It is tempting to read in al-Maqrizi's statement faint echoes of the historiographical debate around the spectator role of the Classical historian (exemplified by none other than Thucydides) who composes visual images of events for his readers and *enargeia* (vividness) as the perfect rhetorical tool of transmission of those historical events, see Andrew D. Walker, "*Enargeia* and the Spectator in Greek Historiography," *Transactions of the American Philological Association* 123 (1993): 353–77. In an unpublished piece, "Enargeia and Phantasia among the Arabic Aristotelians: Poetics, Politics and Prophecy from Farabi to Strauss," that he generously shared with me, Peter Makhlouf traces the correspondence between the function of *takhayul* in Arabic philosophical tracts on poetry and the Greek *enargeia*, which could be the indirect route through which the concept, filtered through centuries of Arabic philosophical and theological interpretation, made its way to al-Maqrizi's notice.

[53] Rosenthal, *Muslim Historiography*, 267–8, notes the problems with al-Sakhawi's method of quoting in his *I'lan*.

[54] Without attempting to cast al-Maqrizi in a presentist frame, it is difficult not to see in his definition parallels with contemporary theorizing of narrativity, as suggested, for example, by Marie-Laure Ryan: "narrative is a type of text able to evoke a certain type of image in the mind of the recipient," Marie-Laure Ryan, "Narrative," in *Routledge Encyclopedia of Narrative Theory*, David Herman, Manfred Jahn, and Marie-Laure Ryan, eds. (London and New York: Routledge, 2005), 347. See also Werner Wolf, "Narrative and Narrativity: A Narratological Reconceptualization and Its Applicability to the Visual Arts," *Word and Image* 19, 3 (2003): 180–97; Wendy Steiner, "Pictorial Narrativity," in *Narrative across Media: The Languages of Storytelling*, Marie-Laure Ryan ed. (Lincoln, N.E.: University of Nebraska Press, 2004), 145–77, for a wide-ranging discussion of narrativity in various media.

especially the *Khitat*, with its reliance on cities, topography, and buildings as visible and verifiable marks of past events and actions of people, undeniably attempts to move in the direction of engaging the reader in the narrative as an active participant in its unfolding.

Khitat and *Athar*: The Totality of the Urban Space

Based on his gradually evolving definitions of history writing, the use of the two terms *mawaʿiz* and *iʿtibar* in al-Maqrizi's *Khitat* can then be seen as a proposition to elevate the book's inquiry from the realm of the descriptive and reconstructive alone to that of the socially and ethically instructive and exhortative, and at times (and given al-Maqrizi's background and disposition), the religiously reprimanding and chastising as the limit of criticism as understood by a medieval ulama frame of mind. In other words, rhyme is not the main reason for the coupling of the two pairs of terms, *mawaʿiz* and *iʿtibar*, and *khitat* and *athar*, in al-Maqrizi's title. The aim is to link the purpose of the inquiry, which is ethical, moralistic, and explicitly argumentative, with the tools and physical embodiments of that inquiry, that is, the urban and architectural evidence of the *khitat* and *athar*, the "witnesses," as it were, to the story of decline that al-Maqrizi is telling.

Of course, there is nothing new in attempting to deduce moral lessons from historical inquiry. Most medieval Muslim historians, who had theological training as the basis of their education, come across as moralists in their historical treatises. In fact, modern disregard for medieval Islamic historical theorizing, or lack thereof, is almost totally predicated on the perception of an inherent teleological, divinely ordained trajectory to every medieval Islamic historical narrative. Even the great Ibn Khaldun, al-Maqrizi's teacher and later colleague, is accused of an underlying fatalism in his conception of history in his *Muqqadima*, and of strong, rigid determinism in his theory of historical cycles.[55] What is new in the scope and content of al-Maqrizi's book is the juxtaposition of the pedagogical and moral aims with the topographical, architectural (occasionally), and urban descriptions and the recounting of the city's history. This is in fact one of the main aspects that distinguishes al-Maqrizi from both historians and *khitat* authors of his tradition.[56]

[55] White, "Ibn Khaldun," 110–25. This notion was countered and debunked by Dale, "Ibn Khaldun." For a sustained critique of this stereotypical reading of Islamic historiography, see Mohammad R. Salama, *Islam, Orientalism and Intellectual History: Modernity and the Politics of Exclusion since Ibn Khaldun* (London: I. B. Tauris, 2011), 77–102.

[56] Sylvie Denoix, *Decrire le Caire Fustat-Misr d'apres Ibn Duqmaq et Maqrizi* (Cairo: IFAO, 1992), 15–16, sees in the invocation of the divine benediction of Egypt an attempt on al-Maqrizi's part to legitimize his writing of a history of the country. I think that it could be

Although the two terms *khitat* and *athar* retained several technical and physical denotations from earlier times, they appear to have acquired some connotative, period-specific meanings by the time al-Maqrizi was writing. *Khitat*, especially, is a word that has faded out of modern-day Arabic, probably because the legal and urban means by which settlements were established in classical and medieval Islamic history has changed so much as to not allow the word to easily migrate to the present with the new, and often imported, changes in the ways we think about and demarcate urban space. Originally, a *Khitta* was a piece of land acquired by a person or a group for the purpose of developing it for their dwelling or any other urban function.[57] As such, the *khitta* preserves the memory of its initial inhabitants, which in the case of Cairo meant that the names of tribes or individuals who had their own *khitat* at foundation time, when ʿAmru ibn al-ʿAs, the Arab general, divided the land among his army's constituent subdivisions, were preserved long after those tribes or individuals were gone in the designations of their *khitat*.[58] A *khitta*, thus, becomes the physical reminder of an act of building and the legal proof of a territorial claim of certain people, which is conserved in the act of naming itself. After the expiration of the legal claims by the disappearance of the initial claimants, the name of the *khitta* becomes a historical document, an index of a presence in the city at a certain point in its history. The accumulation of these memorial documents and the reconstruction of their peregrinations through time in order to reconstruct the history of the city and the people who built and inhabit it is what al-Maqrizi is trying to achieve in his book.

From this perspective, the term *athar* is both complementary to *khitat* and distinct from it. The basic meaning of *athar* is trace, mark, vestige, or effect.[59] In architecture, an *athar* is the remains of a building. It connotes erasure and incompleteness and requires a process of remembrance or mental reconstruction on the part of the historian wishing to use it in a historical inquiry. The word is also often invoked in classical Arabic poetry to describe the physical

---

better understood as an adherence to the convention that governed all writings on cities. Al-Maqrizi's originality, as I am arguing, lies elsewhere.

57 For a detailed discussion of the early uses of the terms *khitat* and *khitta* in the first Islamic *amsar*, see Jamel Akbar, "Khaṭṭa and the Territorial Structure of Early Muslim Towns," *Muqarnas* 6 (1989): 22–32.

58 The term *khitat* in relation to Egypt is studied in Jean-Claude Garcin, "Toponymie et topographie urbaines médiévales à Fustat et au Caire," *JESHO* 27 (1984): 113–17, 132; for a general discussion, see Patricia Crone, art. "Khitta," *EI*², 5: 23–4.

59 ʿAlaa el-Habashi, "Athar to Monuments: The Intervention of the Comité de conservation des monuments de l'art arabe," PhD Diss., University of Pennsylvania (2001), 7–12, reviews the changing meaning of the term *athar* after the Comité adopted it as the equivalent of "monuments." See https://repository.upenn.edu/dissertations/AAI3031658 (accessed August 8, 2017); see also Edward William Lane, 'Athar', in *An Arabic–English Lexicon*, 2 books (London: Williams and Norgate, 1863), book 1, part 1, 19.

traces of what has departed, be it the buildings of the ancients or just the disused scraps of the tribe of the beloved.[60] Both constituted favorite *topoi*, especially in the pre-Islamic and early-Islamic periods: one pensive, reflecting upon the inevitable effects of the passage of time, the other melancholic, lamenting the separation from the beloved.[61] Like all literati of his age, who memorized large corpuses of poetry as part of their education, al-Maqrizi was certainly aware of the emotional charge contained in these two connotations of the term *athar*.[62] He uses it to the same effect not only in the book title, but also twice in his introduction to indicate both the traces of ancient monuments and those not-so-old remains of the Fatimids in their al-Qahira. This statement, whose tone is explicitly and deliberately romantic and elegiac, uses the word *athar* as one of many words—such as *bala'* (erosion), *fana'* (anihilation)—that engender that melancholy feeling. It reads, "I wished to distill the reports on what is left in Egypt of the remains [*al-athar al-baqiyya*] of past nations and bygone centuries, and what is left in al-Fustat of institutions that are about to be erased by erosion and old age and have but a little time before they are engulfed by annihilation and nothingness, and to mention what is left in the city of al-Qahira of the remains [*athar*] of the luminous palaces [i. e. the Fatimid palaces] and what it comprised of *khitat* and areas [*asqa'*] and contained of finely designed buildings."[63]

[60] See the discussion and translation of some of the most famous examples in Jaroslav Stetkevych, "Najd and Arcadia: The Topology of Nostalgia," in *The Zephyrs of Najd* (Chicago: University of Chicago Press, 1993), 114–35; Sarah Savant, "Forgetting Ctesiphon: Iran's Pre-Islamic Past, c. 800–1100," in *History and Identity in the Late Antique Near East*, Philip Wood, ed. (Oxford: Oxford University Press, 2013), 169–86.

[61] The two topoi were related: the pensive developing out of the melancholic, as is apparent from the famous poem of al-Buhturi's in which he is inspired by the ruinous state of the Iwan Kisra to reflect on life, death, and vanity as opposed to the usual cliché of missing the beloved. See 'Abd al-Salam A. Fahmi, *Iwan al-Mada'in Bayn al-Buhturi wa-l Khaqani: Dirasa Adabiyya Muqarana bayn al-Qasidatayn al-'Arabiyya wa-l Farisiyya, Siniyyat al-Buhturi wa Nuniyyat al-Khaqani* (Jeddah: Dar al-Bayan al-'Arabi, 1983), 11–18; Richard A. Serrano, "Al-Buḥturī's Poetics of Persian Abodes," *JAL* 28, 1 (1997): 68–87; 'Izzat Hasan, *Shi'r al-Wuquf 'ala al-Atlal mina al-Jahiliyya ila Nihayat al-Qarn al-Thalith* (Damascus: Ministry of Culture, 1968), 109–15; Ahmad Hussein 'Abd al-'Ithawi, "Zahirat al-Atlal fi-al-Shi'r al-'Arabi qabl al-Islam," *Majallat al-Buhuth wal Dirasat al-Islamiyya* (2005): 29–59; Julie Meisami, "Places in the Past: The Poetics/Politics of Nostalgia," *Edebiyat* 8 (1998): 63–106; idem, "The Palace-Complex as Emblem: Some Samarran *Qasidas*," in *A Medieval Islamic City Reconsidered: An Interdisciplinary Approach to Samarra*, Chase Robinson, ed. (Oxford: Oxford University Press, 2001), 69–78; Sarah Cresap Johnson, "'Return to Origin Is Non-Existence': Al-Mada'in and Perceptions of Ruins in Abbasid Iraq," *IJIA* 6, 2 (2017): 257–83.

[62] See the various examples discussed in Martyn Smith, "Finding Meaning in the City: al-Maqrizi's Use of Poetry in the *Khitat*," *MSR* 16 (2012): 143–61.

[63] Al-Maqrizi, *Khitat2*, 1: 4.

But this is not the only meaning that the use of *athar* in al-Maqrizi's title signifies. As a correlate of *khitat* in the title, *athar* also means the actual remains of those *khitat*, which are by definition only spatial or even two-dimensional as traces on the ground. Thus, the two words together encompass the urban space in its totality: as a system of apportioning the city's territory among its different groups of inhabitants, both individuals and collective, and the establishing of legal claims over the land and property that can be transmitted over time, as well as the signs of that past human occupation, *athar*, in whichever state of preservation they might be. Coupling *khitat* and *athar* in the title is al-Maqrizi's way of indicating that he plans to cover both the urban and the architectural dimensions of the city in his book, which indeed he does. But his is a historical inquiry, aimed primarily at recovering the architecture of the past, the *athar*, not of the present, for which he would have used another term, such as *mabani* (buildings) or *'umran* (urbanism), even though he means it as a nagging antithesis to the sorry present state of urban affairs in his beloved city under the Burji sultans. It is also a didactic inquiry whose purpose is to deploy all sorts of ethical and exhortative lessons from the fate of past dynasties and rulers as they have been inscribed on the crumbling monuments and fading forms of the city, alerting the attentive observer to the role of buildings in both preserving and perpetuating the memory or their builders as well as demonstrating the inevitability of oblivion, as time will ultimately swallow every trace of even the mightiest building.

The Patriotic Impulse

In composing his *Khitat*—and presumably his other history of Egypt books—al-Maqrizi was driven by an emotion that cannot be described but as "patriotic," even though the word itself may be anachronistic. In his introduction, he stresses that impulse in a deeply felt lyrical language that borrows from several literary and poetic examples to construct an unusually passionate definition of what belonging to a homeland means to him. He says that he was drawn to the topic of *khitat* because of his filial attachment to his country, his city, and even his *hara* (neighborhood), Harat al-Burjuwan, that venerable *hara* in the heart of Fatimid al-Qahira, which had prompted him since his youth to collect every piece of information on its history that he came upon. He then delves into his declaration of love for his country:

> *Misr* [in this context meaning both the country and the city] is the place of my birth, the playground of my mates, the nexus of my society and clan, the home to my family and public [*'amma*], the bosom where I acquired my wings, and the niche I seek and yearn to. Ever since I sought knowledge and God gave me intelligence and understanding, I have wanted to know its events [*akhbaruha*], to draw

> from its wells [of information], and to question travelers on the inhabitants of its countries. So, over many years, I recorded in my own handwriting and collected many accounts that no book usually contains or that no cover can hold because of their large number and their wonder [*gharabatiha*].[64]

This statement deserves a thorough analysis for what it reveals not only about al-Maqrizi's attachment to his homeland and his emotional way of expressing it, but also the breadth of feelings of belonging that could have animated a fifteenth-century person to express what we, in our age of combative nationalism, have dubbed patriotism and reserved exclusively for the moderns.[65] First, al-Maqrizi firmly establishes his personal association with Egypt. He was born, raised, and grew up with his friends there. The country is the gathering place of his family, clan (*'ashira*), and close relatives (*hama*).[66] It is also the setting of his *'amma*, a term that was often applied to the common people, or even riff-raff, in the form *'awam*, in the Mamluk period and is today used to mean the general public. But according to medieval Arabic lexicons, the term could also mean people in the abstract, that is, those whom the individual does not know personally although he/she shares something with them, like belonging to a place, which is the conceptual basis of the anonymity implied today in designating the people belonging to a nation or a country.[67] Then comes a romantic clause, "the bosom where I acquired my wings," a hemistich that al-Maqrizi borrows from a poem on "love of country" (*hubb al-watan*) by the famous Andalusian vizier and litterateur Lisan al-Din Ibn al-Khatib, which he recited to his patron the Merinid sultan Abu Salem in Fez in 759/1359. Al-Maqrizi was definitely aware of the purpose of Ibn al-Khatib's poem as a poetic example of *hubb al-watan*, as he cites it on different occasions in a number of his own books.[68] That same feeling prompted

[64] Al-Maqrizi, *Khitat2*, 1: 3.

[65] See the discussion of "patriotism" and affiliation with one's homeland or one's city in the medieval Islamic period in Zayde Antrim, "*Waṭan* before *Waṭaniyya*: Loyalty to Land in Ayyubid and Mamluk Syria," *Al-Masaq* 22, 2 (2010): 173–90. More elaborate discussion in idem, *Routes and Realms: The Power of Place in the Early Islamic World* (Oxford: Oxford University Press, 2012), 11–29, 61–83.

[66] Though he was not a Bedouin or of Bedouin origin and had no clan of his own, al-Maqrizi uses *'ashira* figuratively as a term common in classical Arabic literature to designate one's own people.

[67] For the various meanings and cognates of the word *'amm* in Arabic see the collection from various Arabic lexica at https://www.almaany.com/ar/thes/ar-ar/عَام/ (last accessed August 6, 2018). In the NAS Old Testament Hebrew Lexicon, the word "'am" is translated as people, nation, members of one's people, compatriots, kinsmen: a bundle of meanings that seem to have been shared across the Semitic languages spectrum; see https://www.biblestudytools.com/lexicons/hebrew/nas/am.html (last accessed August 6, 2018).

[68] For the story of the poem's recitation see Nabil K. al-Khatib, *Lisan al-Din ibn al-Khatib (713–776–1313–1374): Nathruhu, Shi'ruhu wa Thaqafatuhu fi Itar 'Asrihi* (Beirut: Dar

Ibn al-Khatib to compose his famous paean to his own city Granada, *al-Ihata fi-Akhbar Gharnata*, the most encyclopedic book on the history and topography of the city and the biographies and literary production of its eminent citizens down to the author's time, which al-Maqrizi knew as well.[69] His borrowing of Ibn al-Khatib's hemistich, thus, is not only meaningful; it also opens an entire field of reference for the literary reader as it directly connects al-Maqrizi's brief prose proclamation to the poetic genre of *hubb al-watan*.[70] Tellingly, al-Maqrizi adds another clause to the hemistich, most probably of his own composition, that rhymes with it and complements and magnifies its meaning, "The niche I seek and yearn to." This entire heartfelt passage in fact suggests that al-Maqrizi intends to blend the idiom of *hubb al-watan* with the more historical scope and topographical content of the *khitat* genre to produce his own tribute to his city and country.

As numerous scholars have already noted, a certain aura of cosmocentricity had pervaded most Egyptian writing on the history of Egypt long before the advent of nationalism as we know it.[71] From as early as Pharaonic times,

al-Nahda al-'Arabiyya, 2013), 84–6, and no. 4. Al-Maqrizi certainly knew this poem, which is quoted in several sources with which he was familiar, such as Ibn Khaldun, *Kitab al-'Ibar*, 7: 307. He himself quotes the first distich in the biographical note he wrote on Ibn al-Khatib, most of which he copied from Ibn Khaldun, *Durar*, 3: 443–8. He then quotes the entire poem in the biography of the Merinid sultan Abu Salem, *Durar*, 1: 121, where he declares that his *shaykh* Ibn Khaldun recited this poem to him as he was recording it, another reference to the uninterrupted relationship of learning between al-Maqrizi and Ibn Khaldun.

69 Al-Maqrizi, *Durar*, 3: 448, mentions the book among the list of Ibn al-Khatib's compositions. The best available edition of the book is Ibn al-Khatib, *al-Ihata fi-Akhbar Ghurnata*, Muhammad 'Abdallah 'Inan, ed. 4 vols. (Cairo: Maktabat al-Khanji, 2nd edn., 1974–8). The book belongs, of course, to the genre Books of Cities (*kutub al-mudun*) and has as models *Tarikh Baghdad* of al-Khatib al-Baghdadi and the *Tarikh Madinat Dimashq* of Ibn 'Asakir. On the *Ihata*'s content see Saadeddine Bencheneb, "Mémoires, tableaux historique et portraits dans l'oeuvre de Lisan ad-Din Ibn al-Khatib," *Revue d'Histoire et de Civilisation du Maghreb* 2 (1967): 54–85.

70 For a review of the genre in classical literature, see Ibn al-Marzuban, *al-Hanin ila l-Awtan*, Jalil al-'Atiyyah, ed. (Beirut: 'Alam al-Kutub, 1987); Wadad al-Qadi, "Dislocation and Nostalgia: *al-Hanin ila l-awtan*. Expressions of Alienation in Early Arabic Literature," in *Myths, Historical Archetypes and Symbolic Figures in Arabic Literature: Towards a New Hermeneutic Approach; Proceedings of The International Symposium in Beirut, June 25th–June 30th, 1996*, Angelika Neuwirth, Birgit Embaló, Sebastian Günther, Maher Jarrar, eds. (Stuttgart: Franz Steiner Verlag [in Komm.], 1999), 3–31; Abu al-Faraj al-Isfahani (attributed), *The Book of Strangers: Medieval Arabic Graffiti and the Theme of Nostalgia*, Patricia Crone and Shmuel Moreh, trans. and eds. (Princeton: Markus Wiener, 2000), 8–15, 146–50; Beatrice Gruendler, "*Al-hanin ila l-awtan* and its Alternatives in Classical Arabic Literature," in *Representations and Visions of Homeland in Modern Arabic Literature*, Sebastian Günther and Stephen Milich, eds. (Hildesheim: Georg Olms Verlag, 2016), 1–42.

71 In addition to Antrim's studies, see Ulrich Haarmann, "Regional Sentiment in Medieval Islamic Egypt," *BSOAS* 43 (1980): 55–66; idem, "Al-Ummah wa-al-Watan fi al-'Usur

Egyptians are believed to have possessed a conception of their homeland with a distinct character, a single source of wealth, the Nile, and fixed natural boundaries formed by deserts to the east and west, obstructive cataracts in the Nile to the south, and the Mediterranean to the north. So solid was this notion that it outlasted all larger imperial formations that absorbed Egypt as a province from the Assyrian, Persian, and Macedonian Empires to the Arab Conquest of the seventh century C.E. and lived on in various religious, cultural, social, and artistic expressions, if not in political formation.[72] The particularist Egyptian cultural tendency was of course dampened after the seventh century C.E. by the universalist message of Islam and by the coming of Arabs as the new masters of the country and the imposition of Arabic as the language of all of the southern and eastern Mediterranean. But it never died out. It stayed near the surface throughout the first three centuries of Islamic rule, with noticeable surges during the Tulunid (868–905) and

al-Wusta al-Islamiyah wa-al-Urubbyah," *Dirasat Islamiyah* 2 (1987–8): 219–37; idem, "Watan," *EI*[2], Vol. II: 174–5; Wael Abu-'Uksa, *Freedom in the Arab World: Concepts and Ideologies in Arabic Thought in the Nineteenth Century* (Cambridge: Cambridge University Press, 2016), 135–7, and notes.

[72] The idea that Egypt had a specific character and was a clearly defined entity is the theme of many nationalist historical and analytical studies, especially in the 1990s. The pioneering study remains Jamal Hamdan, *Shakhsiyyat Misr, Dirasa fi 'Abqariyyat al-Makan*, 4 vols. (Cairo: 'Alam al-Kutub, 1980–4), passim; see also Ni'mat Ahmad Fu'ad, *Shakhsiyat Misr* (Cairo: al-Hay'a al-Misriyya al-'Amma lil-Kitab, 1968, reprinted 1978); Muhammad Nu'man Jalal and Majdi Mutawalli, *Hawiyat Misr* (Cairo: al-Hay'a al-Misriyya al-'Amma lil-Kitab, 1997); Muhammad Nu'man Galal, *Dynamics of the Egyptian National Identity* (Lahore: Sang-e-Meel, 1998); Rafiq Habib, *al-Shakhsiyya al-Misriyya: al-tatawwur al-nafsi fi khamsin qarnan* (Cairo: Markaz al-Mahrusa lil-Buhuth wa-al-Tadrib wa-al-Nashr, 1997); Milad Hanna, *al-A'mida al-sab'a lil-shakhsiyya al-Misriyya* (Cairo: Dar al-Hilal, 1990), trans. as *The Seven Pillars of the Egyptian Identity* (Cairo: General Egyptian Book Organization, 1994); 'Abd al-Latif Muhammad Khalifah and Sha'ban Jab Allah Radwan, *al-Shakhsiyya al-Misriyya: al-malamih wa-al-ab'ad: dirasah sikulujiyah* (Cairo: Dar Gharib, 1998); Tal'at Radwan and Fathi Radwan, *Ab'ad al-Shakhsiyya al-Misriyya: bayna al-madi wa-al-hadir* (Cairo: al-Hay'a al-Misriyya al-'Amma lil-Kitab, 1999). Ahmad 'Ashur and Subhi al-Sayyid 'Ashur, *al-Watan al-Umm: Dirarsa fi al-Thaqafa al-Qawmiyya al-Misriyya, Ta'sis Tarikhi* (Cairo: n.p., 1999), takes the Egypt-first argument to its extreme by casting the history of the country from 332 B.C.E. to 1952 C.E. as a long period of occupation and acculturation of Egypt by "foreigners" including the Arab conquerors from the Peninsula. To further appreciate the growing nativist tendency, see the changing views on Ibn Khaldun of one of Egypt's foremost medieval historians, Mahmud Isma'il 'Abd al-Razzaq, from his "Manhaj al-Mu'arrikh Ibn Taghri-Birdi fi Kitabihi *al-Nujum al-Zahira*," in *al-Mu'arrikh Ibn Taghri Birdi: Jamal al-Din Abu al-Mahasin Yusuf, 813–874 H.* (Cairo: al-Hay'a al-Misriyya al-'Amma lil-Kitab, 1974), 109–11 to his *Nihayat usturat nazariyat Ibn Khaldun: muqtabasa min rasa'il Ikhwan al-Safa* (al-Mansura: Amer lil-Tib'a wa-al-Nashr, 1996), where he coopts Ibn Khaldun's theories about the destructiveness of the Bedouin Arabs to explain the decline of Egypt under Islamic rule.

Ikhshidid periods (935–69), to burst out again in medieval times as a result of a number of historical and geopolitical developments. Chief among them was the establishment of the Fatimid Caliphate in the late tenth century, which created in Egypt a new state independent of Abbasid Baghdad and, later, the founding of the Mamluk military empire with its center firmly entrenched in Cairo, while its boundaries extended to the Upper Euphrates, Anatolia, and Hijaz. The Mamluk Sultanate undertook *jihad* as its mission and succeeded in halting and ultimately eliminating the threats from the invading Crusades and Mongols (and later Ilkhanid Mongols) in the early fourteenth century and in establishing itself as the premier Islamic empire of its times.[73]

The rise of the Mamluk Empire and its expansion into Syria, the Jazira, Anatolia, and the Hijaz, as well as its resurrection of a substitute Abbasid caliphate in Cairo, which lent it substantial prestige if not indisputable legitimacy, elicited a subtle yet significant shift in both the scope and character of the scholarly and artistic production of the time.[74] This was most palpable

[73] A passionate argument for the prevalence of the notion of homeland among Mamluk authors is Mustafa Abulhimal, "The Medieval Egyptian Homeland and Inhabitants: The Intelligentsia Speak," *International Journal of the Humanities* 8, 11 (2011): 81–93. For a historical analysis of the notion of the Mamluk Empire as the dominant Islamic empire in the fourteenth century, which was firmed up after the death of the Ilkhanid Abu Sa'id in 1335, see Anne F. Broadbridge, *Kingship and Ideology in the Islamic and Mongol Worlds* (Cambridge: Cambridge University Press, 2008), 138–67.

[74] See the analysis of Dorothea Krawulsky concerning the changing notion of belonging in historical production between the two ages of the Mamluk period, the Bahri and Burji, in "al-Intaj al-Thaqafi wa-Shar'iyat al-Sulta," her introduction to al-'Umari, *Masalik al-Absar fi-Mamalik al-Amsar, Dawlat al-Mamalik al-Ula* (Beirut: al-Markaz al-Islami lil-Buhuth, 1986), 15–45, reprinted in a volume of her collected articles, *al-'Arab wa Iran, Dirasat fi al-Tarikh wa al-Adab min al-Manzur al-Aydiologi* (Beirut: Dar al-Muntakhab al-'Arabi, 1993), 94–116. Krawulsky, on pp. 33–4, remarks that the pivotal role played by the Mamluks in defending Islam was, significantly, praised among some of the intellectuals who served in the court of their archenemies the Ilkhanid. Sharaf al-Din Wassaf (Vassaf) (1264–1330), the Persian historian who dedicated his treatise *Tajziyat al-Amsar wa Tazjiyat al-A'sar* to the Ilkhan Öljeytü (1304–17), dared in the same text to praise the Mamluks for their steadfastness in *jihad* and their adherence to the tenets of Islam, Vassaf, *Tajziyat al-Amsar wa Tazjiyat al-A'sar*, Muhammad Mahdi Isfahani, ed. (Bombay, 1853), 82–3. For Vassaf's book and his references to the Mamluks in it see Judith Pfeiffer, "A Turgid History of the Mongol Empire in Persia: Epistemological Reflections Concerning a Critical Edition of Vassaf's *Tajziyat al-Amsar fi Tazjiyat al-A'sar*," in *Theoretical Approaches to the Transmission and Edition of Oriental Manuscripts*, Judith Pfeiffer and Manfred Kropp, eds. (Wurzburg: Ergon Verlag, 2007), 109, no. 17, 110, no. 22; idem, "Confessional Ambiguity vs. Confessional Polarization: Politics and the Negotiation of Religious Boundaries in the Ilkhanate," in *Politics, Patronage and the Transmission of Knowledge in 13th–15th Century Tabriz*, Judith Pfeiffer, ed. (Leiden: Brill, 2014), 132 and note 8, sums up the other historiographical reaction shown in the Mamluk literature of the period to the Ilkhanid threat, including the adoption of a "golden age" polemic and the introduction of a notion of continuity from early Islam to the

in the geographical literature, namely the *al-masalik wa-l mamalik* genre (Routes and Realms), concerned as it is with land and territory. *Al-masalik wa-l mamalik* was essentially a loosely defined geographic *adab* type (the classical Arabic equivalent to the humanities) that was developed out of the combination of several scholarly, literary, and administrative pursuits including *futuh* (chronicles of the conquests), travel and *ziyarat* (pilgrimage to sacred sites) literature, chancery and *kharaj* (taxation) manuals, and *surat al-ard* (cartography).[75] Its framework was geographic, bordering on the cosmographical with a universalistic Islamic scope that rarely ventured outside the frontiers of the Islamic world. The genre began to take shape in the high caliphal period as a direct response to the administrative and management needs of the state. But its heyday was the ninth and tenth centuries, when a number of outstanding geographer-travelers crisscrossed the Islamic world, compiling their depictions of one Islamic world, after its political unity held together by the Abbasid caliphate had passed and its vast territory broke up into smaller political entities only loosely and symbolically connected to the center.[76]

In the thirteenth century, and after the startling early victories of the Mamluks against the Crusaders and the Mongols, the orientation of the classical genre of *al-masalik wal mamalik* moved toward the geopolitical.[77]

Mamluk period. In my "The Mosaics of the Qubba al-Zahiriyya in Damascus: A Classical Syrian Medium Acquires a Mamluk Signature," *Aram* 9–10 (1997–8 [1999]): 1–13 and "In Search of a Triumphant Image: the Experimental Quality of Early Mamluk Art," in *The Arts of the Mamluks in Egypt and Syria—Evolution and Impact*, Doris Behrens-Abouseif, ed. (Berlin: Bonn University Press, 2012), 21–35, I argue for a resurrected and deliberate continuity between the Umayyad art and architecture of Syria and the art and architecture of the Early Mamluks between Baybars and al-Nasir Muhammad. Finbarr Barry Flood, "Umayyad Survivals and Mamluk Revivals: Qalawunid Architecture and the Great Mosque of Damascus," *Muqarnas* 14 (1997): 57–79, reviews the same process with a special focus on the Umayyad Mosque of Damascus. For an archeological approach see Bethany J. Walker, "Commemorating the Sacred Spaces of the Past: The Mamluks and the Umayyad Mosque at Damascus," *Near Eastern Archaeology* 67, 1 (March 2004): 26–39; see also Hanna Taragan, "Sign of the Times: Reusing the Past in Baybars's Architecture in Palestine," *Mamluks and Ottomans. Studies in Honour of Michael Winter*, David J. Wasserstein and Ami Ayalon, eds. (London: Routledge, 2006), 54–66, with a focus on the Mamluk monuments in Palestine.

75 For a discussion of the classical genre of *al-masalik wal mamalik* see Charles Pellat, "al-Masālik Wa 'l-Mamālik," *EI*², 6: 639–40, http://dx.doi.org/10.1163/1573-3912_islam_SIM_4994 (last accessed August 6, 2018). See also André Miquel, *La géographie humaine du monde musulman jusqu'au milieu du 11e siècle* 3 vols. (Paris: Mouton, 1967–80), 1: 267–330.

76 For a fascinating analysis of the discursive origins of the genre in the tenth century, see Travis Zadeh, *Mapping Frontiers Across Medieval Islam: Geography, Translation, and the 'Abbasid Empire* (London: I. B. Tauris, 2011), 15–48.

77 Ulrich Haarman, "Auflösung und Bewahrung der klassischen Formen arabischer Geschichtsschreibung in der Zeit der Mamluken," *ZDMG* 121(1971): 46–60; idem, "Review

Moreover, a buoyant if not altogether triumphal tone pervaded other encyclopedic works that began to appear from as early as the reign of al-Zahir Baybars (1260–76) and peaked during the long, prosperous, and relatively peaceful reign of al-Nasir Muhammad (1293–1341, with two interruptions).[78] These enormous compendia broke the genre's boundaries and extended into cosmography, botany, zoology, history, biography, epistolary art and chancery protocols, and of course *adab*, with a focus on chronicling the most recent history under the Mamluks in the utmost detail. Between the late thirteenth and the end of the fourteenth century, a number of them were written by high-ranking scribes who were clearly conversant in more fields than a scribe needed to be. But for our purpose three major examples can illustrate the historiographical trend and its geopolitical underpinnings. They are: ʿIzz al-Din ibn Shaddad (1217–85), *al-Aʿlaq al-Khatira fi Dhikr Umaraʾ al-Sham wa-al-Jazira*; Shihab al-Din al-Nuwayri (1279–1333), *Nihayat al-Arab fī Funun al-Adab*; and Shihab al-Din ibn Fadhl Allah al-ʿUmari (1300–49), *Masalik al-Absar fi Mamalik al-Amsar*. The last two figure among al-Maqrizi's major sources for his *Khitat*.[79]

The first book, Ibn Shaddad's *al-Aʿlaq al-Khatira fi-Dhikr Umaraʾ al-Sham wa-l-Jazira*, is perhaps the least hybrid of these three compendia as it deals primarily with the geography, topography, architecture, and administrative divisions of Greater Syria, which was in the process of being absorbed into the Egyptian Mamluk sultanate. The book was composed around the year 1275 on the order of sultan al-Zahir Baybars, the true organizer of the Mamluk sultanate, probably to take advantage of Ibn Shaddad's knowledge

of Book: Weltgeschichte und Weltbeschreibung im mittelalterlichen Islam by Bernd Radtke," *JOAS* 115, 1 (1995): 133–5.

[78] Following the model of early modern Europe's drive to save the knowledge of the ancients from oblivion, historians of Islamic culture have long invoked a similar anxiety as the impulse behind the rise of encyclopedism in the early Mamluk period after the devastating Mongol conquest and the eradication of the Abbasid Caliphate in Baghdad. But as Elias Muhanna, *The World in a Book: Al-Nuwayri and the Islamic Encyclopedic Tradition* (Princeton: Princeton University Press, 2018), 16–19, argues, there seem to be few psychological effects of the Mongol invasions on the authors of the encyclopedias. In fact, he discerns a positive result of these invasions that facilitated the movement of people and ideas between the Iranian East and Mamluk Egypt and enhanced the cross-fertilization between the two intellectual traditions.

[79] A first attempt at gathering the sources of the *Khitat* is A. R. Guest, "A List of Writers, Books, and Other Authorities Mentioned by el-Maqrizi in his *Khitat*," *JRAS* (1902): 103–25. Bauden has meticulously reconstructed not only al-Maqrizi's uses of sources, but also the evolution of his use through the various iterations of the *Khitat* available to him, especially the notebook held at the Université de Liège (ms. 2232). For al-Maqrizi's use of Ibn Fadhl Allah al-ʿUmari's *Masalik al-Absar*, see Bauden, "Vers une archéologie," 109–10; idem, "Maqriziana II," 72–6, 117; on his use of al-Nuwayri's *Nihayat al-Arab*, idem, "Maqriziana I/2," 93–5, 108, 110; "Maqriziana II," 91.

of the various principalities of Syria.[80] Accordingly, the book is divided into sections on Aleppo and its environs, Damascus and its surrounding regions (including Lebanon, Jordan, and Palestine), and the Jaziran cities including Diyar Bakr and Diyar Mudhar, some of whose regions were never annexed by the Mamluks. Ibn Shaddad, an Aleppine scholar and *katib*, started his professional life as a high administrator in the court of Aleppo's last Ayyubid ruler, al-Nasir Salah al-Din Yusuf, but fled his native city ahead of the Mongol invasion in 1260 and joined the Mamluk court of Cairo in the entourage of al-Zahir Baybars's famous vizier Baha' al-Din Ibn Hinna. In this quite unprecedented geographic/urban history compendium, he does indeed discursively "make Syria Mamluk," as Zayde Antrim argues, after Baybars had achieved that on the ground by checking the Mongol expansion, confining the Crusaders to their anemic principalities, and wresting the various Syrian kingdoms (with the exception of Hama) from the bickering Ayybid princes to incorporate them into the Mamluk sultanate.[81]

Al-A'laq is, in fact, a learned exercise in the geographical and spatial organization of an entire country and its various cities, penned by an eager and consummate bureaucrat who was clearly cognizant of the classical genres of *al-masalik wal-mamalik* and *kutub al-mudun*, but who nonetheless brought to his own endeavor an unmatched urban and architectural attentiveness.[82] For the first time in Arabic geographic literature, the book includes a comprehensive list of major buildings—citadel, main mosque, madrasas, *khanqahs*, and caravanserais—for each city and, in the case of the major cities such as Damascus and Aleppo, the history of each structure in detail as well. As such, *al-A'laq al-Khatira* anticipates al-Maqrizi's *Khitat* in its orientation, structure, and appreciation of architecture, and perhaps in its pride of place, implicit in Ibn Shaddad's case, as he was now writing from Egypt about his native Syria as it was changing masters and forcibly becoming Mamluk after the shock of the devastating Mongol invasion. *Al-A'laq*, however, lacks

80 For an analysis of the book, see Muhammad Sa'id Rida, "Ibn Shaddad fi Kitabihi al-A'laq al-Khatirah, 'Qism al-Jazirah,'" *MMA* 14 (1980): 124–204. Ibn Shaddad, a typical sycophantic clerk, wrote a laudatory biography of al-Zahir Baybars, *Tarikh al-Malik al-Zahir*, Ahmad Hutait, ed. (Wiesbaden: Franz Steiner Verlag, 1983); Yoel Koch, "'Izz al-Din ibn Shaddad and his Biography of Baybars," *Annali: Istituto Universitario Orientale, Sezione Slava* 43 (1983): 249–87; P. M. Holt, "Three Biographies of al-Zahir Baybars," in *Medieval Historical Writing in the Christian and Islamic Worlds*, D. O. Morgan, ed. (London: School of Oriental and African Studies, 1982), 19–29; D. Sourdel, "Ibn Shaddad," *EI*^{2}, 3: 933.

81 Zayde Antrim, "Making Syria Mamluk: Ibn Shaddad's *Al-A'laq al-Khatirah*," *MSR* 11, 1 (2007): 1–18. On the various ways through which Baybars was symbolically appropriating Syria, see Anne Troadec, "Baybars and the Cultural Memory of Bilad al-Sham: The Construction of Legitimacy," *MSR* 18 (2014–15): 113–47; Denise Aigle, "Les inscriptions de Baybars dans le Bilad al-Sham: une expression de la légitimité du pouvoir," *SI* 96 (2003): 87–115.

82 See my "Perception of Architecture in Mamluk Sources," 168–70.

the emotional charge and personal investment that distinguish al-Maqrizi's *Khitat*. The detached and seemingly objective tone and the meticulous and exhaustive method of presentation of the book suggest the bureaucratic background of its author and his confidence in his expertise.

The second book is an *adab* encyclopedia of unprecedented breadth and syncretism composed between 1314 and 1333 by Shihab al-Din al-Nuwayri, an official in the Mamluk chancery of al-Nasir Muhammad who, like al-Maqrizi, withdrew from the administration in his forties to devote himself to the composition of his chef-d'oeuvre. He intended it to be the repository of all the knowledge needed by a learned scribe who might find himself close to the center of power both as an administrator and, possibly, as a courtier or a *nadim* (companion), a position which eluded al-Nuwayri in his own career and which al-Maqrizi briefly attained in the second reign of al-Zahir Barquq.[83] The *Nihayat al-Arab*'s thirty-three-volume compendium "expands a cosmographical model with the addition of a universal chronicle, an anthology of literary and ethical materials, and a voluminous treatment of secretaryship," then concludes with a huge chronicle, numbered Book 5 of the compendium's five books, that covers around 70 percent of the entire text and surveys the Islamic dynasties from the Prophet's to the author's time and stops in 1330.[84] This section undoubtedly underscores the centrality of history for al-Nuwayri, and perhaps for all the authors of his time, when a robust Mamluk school of history, which will peak in the fifteenth century with al-Maqrizi and his cohort, was taking shape in both Egypt and Syria (with significant differences in emphasis and perspective).[85]

The third book, composed by Ibn Fadhl Allah al-ʿUmari, a high administrator at the court of al-Nasir Muhammad who held the pivotal position of *katib al-sirr* to the Sultan between 1329 and 1332, is a truer amalgam of all the *adab* genres available to the late medieval Islamic literati, ranging from geography and cosmography to history, biography, and epistolary manuals, than its two predecessors. The *Masalik al-Absar* is a huge geographic/historical/biographical encyclopedia that surveys all the countries of the Islamic world and their direct neighbors, reviews their natural phenomena and flora and fauna, and offers topographic depictions of all the important Islamic cities and holy sites and firsthand information on the manners, customs, and

[83] Shihab al-Din al-Nuwayri, *Nihayat al-Arab fi Funun al-Adab*, 33 vols., various editors (Cairo: Dar al-Kutub, 1923–97). Selections were edited, translated, and annotated by Elias Muhanna as Shihab al-Din al-Nuwayri, *The Ultimate Ambition in the Arts of Erudition. A Compendium of Knowledge from the Classical Islamic World* (New York: Penguin, 2016).

[84] Muhanna, *The World in a Book*, 5–23, 38–55. Quotation, 49.

[85] Li Guo, "Mamluk Historiographic Studies: The State of the Art," *MSR* 1 (1997): 37–43, offers a full picture of the historiographic web of genealogies, interconnections, and chains of transmission that undergird Mamluk history.

duties of their rulers and lists of the ranks, functions, and protocols of their officials and caretakers. Buildings in these depictions are no longer identified only in terms of their locale as was the case with Ibn Shaddad's *al-A'laq*. They are seen in their sociopolitical context as expressions of dynastic and royal pride and splendor, and as positive material signs bestowing cultural distinction on their urban setting, whether royal, religious, pietistic, or educational.

A large portion of the collection (Volumes 5 to 19), however, is devoted to a systematic listing of various classes of people who by and large formed the learned, starting with the prophets and going through ulama, hadith scholars, Sufis, philosophers, and physicians to viziers, scribes, and poets across the Islamic world and beyond, and sometimes going back to the famous thinkers of antiquity to come down to the author's time. Egyptian groups and biographies, however, occupy the center of all these professional classifications, as does the country in the geopolitical survey of the countries of Islam in the first few volumes and in the final, chronicle part of the book down to the early Mamluk period. As such, this hybrid encyclopedia, which in the last count is only partially geographical, like al-Nuwayri's compendium, evinces a clear sense of confidence in the supremacy of the Mamluk sultanate in the Islamic world and beyond during his time.[86]

But, as Dorothea Krawulski and others have already noted, what began as an expression of pride of belonging to Egypt from a pan-Islamic and potentially universal perspective during the period of Mamluk ascendance, which carried echoes of an earlier period of Islamic political unity, reverted to a more local and introverted focus with the retreat of the sultanate in the fifteenth century from its leading role to mostly concentrate on defending its territorial integrity.[87] This is the political context within which the historical writing

[86] Krawulsky, "al-Intaj al-Thaqafi,"15–37; a nuanced discussion of al-'Umari and his book in the context of the Mamluk intellectual milieu is Muhanna, *The World in a Book*, 50–1, 90–1; see also Zayde Antrim, "The Politics of Place in the Works of Ibn Taymiyah and Ibn Fadl Allah al-'Umari," *MSR* 18, 1 (2014–15): 91–111, esp. 100–11.

[87] Krawulsky, "al-Intaj al-Thaqafi," 36–7. This state of affairs resembles the shift in the historical writing between the time of 'Abd al-Nasser, when the focus was on pan-Arabism and the centrality of Egypt in the Arab World, and Anwar al-Sadat, when the focus reverted to an introverted, and somewhat defiantly insular, Egyptian history. For a historical review of the various stages of history writing in Egypt during that period, see Yoav Di-Capua, *Gatekeepers of the Arab Past: Historians and History Writing in Twentieth-Century Egypt* (Berkeley: University of California Press, 2009), 282–336. See also Ulrike Freitag, "Writing Arab History: The Search for the Nation," *British Journal of Middle Eastern Studies* 21, 1 (1994): 19–37; Mona Arif, "Constructing the National Past: History-Writing and Nation-Building in Nasser's Egypt," *Shorofat* 1 (2017): 7–31, https://www.bibalex.org/Attachments/Publications/Files/2017121114173047484_ShorofatEnglish1.pdf (last accessed August 7, 2018).

centered exclusively on Egypt flourished in the first half of the fifteenth century. Scholars like Ibn Duqmaq, Ibn al-Furat, al-Qalqashandi, Badr al-Din al-ʿAyni, Ibn Hajar al-ʿAsqalani, Ibn ʿArab Shah, Ibn Taghri-Birdi, al-Sayrafi al-Jawhari, Abu Hamid al-Qudsi, Ibn Qadi-Shuhbah, al-Sakhawi, al-Suyuti, and al-Maqrizi himself all composed cosmocentric and regional histories and prosopographies. In their chronicles, they busied themselves with minutely chronicling the events of Mamluk Egypt, and to a much lesser extent Syria and other Islamic regions, sometimes beginning with a cursory run-down of Islamic history from the Prophet Muhammad to their own time, and sometimes adding the biographies of their contemporaries or immediate predecessors.[88] Likewise, their biographical dictionaries by and large focused on their contemporaries, especially those from Egypt or those who had come to live, work, or study in Egypt, or those Islamic figures who had some contact with Egypt. This was the case with al-Maqrizi's intimate account of the lives of people born during his lifetime, most of whom he personally knew, in *Durar al-ʿUqud*, as well as his larger dictionary *al-Muqaffa al-Kabir*, which he intended to cover only famous people who had something to do with Egypt in Islamic history. But it was also the case with the more comprehensive and less personal prosopography of Ibn Hajar al-ʿAsqalani, *al-Durar al-Kamina fi Aʿyan al-Miʾa al-Thamina*, which considered only the biographies of those important individuals who lived in the eighth century A.H., followed by the most famous Mamluk biographical dictionary written by Ibn Hajar's student al-Sakhawi, *al-Dawʾ al-Lamiʿ li-Ahl al-Qarn al-Tasiʿ*, which concentrated exclusively on those who lived in the ninth century A.H. and was an admiring if implicitly boastful continuation of his master's dictionary. The circumscribed coverage of all these historians, with its geographical or historical constrictions, resulted in the formation of an endogenous and insular school of historiography, in which every member was linked in more than one way to the others, and every member's work was inevitably and immediately measured against the works of others, who practically covered the same terrain and used the same sources, and sometimes appropriated each other's material. The situation encouraged intense scholarly and social competition, which at times escalated into fierce factionalism that affected the usual decorum maintained among historians, and found its way into their views of each other's work.[89]

[88] On Mamluk historiography, see Shakir Mustafa, *Tarikh*, 2: 139–304; all of vol. 3; 4: 7–227; Ulrich Haarmann, *Quellenstudien zur frühen Mamlukenzeit*; Rosenthal, *Muslim Historiography*, passim; Khalidi, *Historical Thought*, 182–231; Guo, "Mamluk Historiographic Studies."

[89] Muhammad Mustafa Ziada, *al-Muʾarrikhun fi Misr fi al-Qarn al-Khamis ʿAshar (al-Qarn al-Tasiʿ al-Hijri)* (Cairo: Lajnat al-Taʾlif wal Tarjama wal-Nashr, 1949), 81–105, is an early comparative study of the similarities between the Mamluk Egyptian historians of the

Al-Maqrizi's total historical oeuvre is the most representative illustration of that narrowing of perspective, with its resolute concentration on the land, history, cities, and people of Egypt. His books in fact feel like variations on one larger theme, Egypt, that try to cover all aspects of its history as encompassed by the literary genres available to the scholars of the time: chronicles, genealogy, biographical dictionaries, geography, and *khitat*.[90] His rebukes to the rulers of his time, scattered in the *Khitat* and *Durar*, but especially in the last sections of the *Suluk*, may reflect a nostalgic yearning for the days of the universal greatness of the state, when the Mamluk sultans acted as supreme rulers of the Islamic world.[91] But they are otherwise focused on the circumscribed affairs of Cairo and their mishandling by his contemporary sultans from Barquq to Jaqmaq. Although the tone, scope, and ire of his criticism vary from one sultan to the other, al-Maqrizi relentlessly stresses a number of shared flaws in their method of managing state affairs that al-Maqrizi considers detrimental to the wellbeing of the sultanate. Their greed, vanity, cruelty, and particularly their deviation from Islamic law are illustrated by examples and commented upon in the obituaries he appends to the chronicles of the years of their death in the *Suluk*, and to a lesser extent in the *Khitat* or the *Durar*.[92] The criticism is thus contextualized, dated, and essentially personal-

fifteenth century. Broadbridge, "Academic Rivalry," discusses the relationship between three of the main figures in Burji Mamluk historiography. Donald Little, *An Introduction to Mamluk Historiography: An Analysis of Arabic Annalistic and Biographical Sources for the Reign of al-Malik an-Nasir Muhammad ibn Qala'un* (Wiesbaden: F. Steiner, 1970), 73–99, is a limited comparative examination of the annals of six of these historians which shows their complicated patterns of interdependence; idem, "A Comparison of al-Maqrizi and al-ʿAyni," 205–15, applies his comparative method to the reporting on one year in the annals of al-Maqrizi and al-ʿAyni and concludes that al-Maqrizi was more critical and more attentive to detail than his rival.

[90] I am excluding here the books and essays on the Prophet and his family, which as I tried to argue earlier constitute another major theme for this dedicated historian, which may in fact resonate with the idea of reviving the model to which the current rulers should aspire. The two major and voluminous compendia of that group, *al-Khabar ʿan al-Bashar* and *Imtaʿ al-Asmaʿ*, though published in toto, still await a serious contextualizing study. *Al-Khabar ʿan al-Bashar* is being slowly published in a new, annotated and careful edition in the Bibliotheca Maqriziana.

[91] As discussed in the previous chapter, al-Maqrizi, *Khitat2*, 3: 693, in his most scathing criticism of the Mamluks of his own time, alludes to the days when their predecessors were "Masters who managed kingdoms, fighters in the name of God, and politicians who knew how to show both clemency and strength."

[92] Al-Maqrizi, *Suluk*, 3: 616–19 gives a generally positive report on the first reign of al-Zahir Barquq, which ended in 1389 with the revolt of Yalbugha al-Nasiri and Mintash, but ends it in ascribing three major vices to the departing sultan and likens him to a monkey in character and attributes. In al-Maqrizi, *Suluk*, 3: 943–7, in the obituary of Barquq after his death in 1399, al-Maqrizi retains only the positive attributes and achievements and voices only mild criticism of Barquq's insatiability for money, young slaves, and luxury items.

ized, even though the reprimands of the various sultans together amount to a general condemnation of the early Burji period, in which al-Maqrizi was an involved witness until his withdrawal in despair and disgust during the reign of al-Mu'ayyad Shaykh.[93]

It is in the *Khitat*, however, that his love of his country and pessimism about the sorry state of its affairs come through as framing devices as well as emotional charges imbuing the entire book with a political and memorial purpose. Having been long in gestation, the *Khitat* is not only the pivot around which al-Maqrizi's entire writing project revolved or the primal repository of information on the country, its topography, agricultural economy, history, urbanization, people, and merits, before some of that increasingly unwieldy amount of data was transferred to other chronicles, biographical dictionaries, or policy opinions where it was developed separately. It is also the manifestation of al-Maqrizi's abiding sense of belonging in the most tangible way: through the capturing of the historical narratives and the visual and spatial qualities of the land and cities of the country that in their totality make Egypt and that were threatened by the neglect and insatiability of its contemporary Mamluk rulers.

Structuring the *Khitat* on the Tempo of Ruination

In the introduction to his *Khitat*, al-Maqrizi describes his book as a "summary of the history of the monuments of Egypt from the earliest times,

Ibn Taghri-Birdi, *Nujum*, 11: 239–40, 15: 88–9, chastises al-Maqrizi for flip-flopping in his opinion of al-Zahir Barquq and reminds us that al-Maqrizi became close to the sultan during his second reign, hence his positive opinion of Barquq in the obituary, but he forgot to correct the negativity of his first biographical sketch in the chronicle of 1389. For al-Maqrizi's criticism of Faraj ibn Barquq, see *Suluk*, 4: 100, 105, 228–54; Ibn Taghri-Birdi, *Nujum*, 13: 108–10, again vehemently disagrees with his master. Al-Maqrizi, *Suluk*, 4: 487–8, 531–4, expresses a positive opinion of al-Mu'ayyad's piety, bonhomie, and humility, then in the obituary he penned, *Suluk*, 4: 550–1, he begins with the positive qualities, but then goes after al-Mu'ayyad for his corrupt policies and his causing of disorder (*fitna*) when he was a governor in Syria plotting against Faraj ibn Barquq. On al-Zahir Tatar, who ruled as sultan for less than a month, al-Maqrizi expresses a harsh opinion, *Suluk*, 4: 589, for which Ibn Taghri-Birdi, *Nujum*, 14: 199–200 rebukes him again. As for Barsbay, *Suluk*, 4: 1065–6, al-Maqrizi drops all restraints in his criticism, especially in the more elaborate biography in *Durar*, 1: 456–82, esp. 480–2, where he goes after every vice and every injustice of the sultan, to which Ibn Taghri-Birdi, *Nujum*, 15: 109–11, 189, 200–1 reacts very strongly, as we saw in Chapter 2.

93 See the discussion in Chapter 2. Questions have been raised about the absence of any criticism of Sultan Jaqmaq (r. 1438–53), who was reputed to be a pious sultan, in the *Suluk*. One possible reason is that al-Maqrizi was quite old by then and might have been already struggling with the malady that ultimately caused his death.

and of the surviving structures in Fustat, and the palaces, buildings, and quarters of al-Qahira with short biographies to their patrons and sponsors."[94] This is a definition of a *khitat* book that encompasses more than what the genre usually covers, as it recognizes the importance of knowing about the patrons as part of any assessment of architecture. It is also a rather truthful and accurate outlining of the scope of the book, regardless of the incomplete form in which it has reached us. Moreover, despite its topographical focus, the *Khitat* has lofty pedagogical or, more precisely, exhortative goals, albeit ones that are articulated through the moral prism of a strict medieval Muslim scholar. The book is highly opinionated and melancholy in its coverage, morally critical in its tone, and inherently teleological in its conclusions, which are dispersed throughout the text rather than at the end of the incomplete text. Its style is literary and legalistic, reflecting the educational and professional background of its author, although it is clear that al-Maqrizi is trying to keep his prose as direct and matter-of-fact as possible, avoiding intricate language and curtailing both the use of poetry and Qur'anic quotations, the two mainstays of medieval scholarly prowess and affectation.[95]

Al-Maqrizi states that he divided his book into seven sections, comprising a geographical survey of Egypt (with cosmographical overtones), a description of its people and many of its cities, a history of al-Fustat and its rulers, a chronicle of Cairo and its Fatimid caliphs, their pageantry, rituals, and the monuments they have left, a catalogue of the most important buildings in Cairo and its suburbs as he saw them, arranged by types, a history of the Citadel of the Mountain (the Cairo Citadel) with a rundown of its kings, and, finally, an analysis of the reasons for the *kharab* of Egypt. He maintained that order, for the most part, for the first four sections, which are the ones covering material before his time that depended mostly on his written sources rather than on his own observations. Sections five and six are incomplete and mixed up, whereas section seven, as we saw, is just missing.[96] Moreover, the text is speckled with copious entries on Cairo's wonders and religious merits and the ceremonies observed by its religious groups. Further digressions throughout add to the impression of a work-in-progress that was still in need of extensive

94 Al-Maqrizi, *Khitat2*, 1: 3–4.

95 For further analysis of the book's content see my "Al-Madina, al-Tarikh, wal-Sulta: al-Maqrizi wa Kitabuhu al-Ra'id 'al-Mawa'iz wa al-I'tibar bi Dhikr al-Khitat wa al-Athar," *AI* 35 (2001): 77–100; Jarrar, "Al-Maqrizi's Reinvention of Egyptian Historiography," 30–53.

96 Muhammad 'Abdallah 'Inan, *Misr al-Islamiyya wa-Tarikh al-Khitat al-Misriyya* (Cairo: Maktabat al-Khanji, 1969), 37–49; Sayyid, *Musawwadat*, Introduction, 6–22; Sayyid published a French summary of his introduction as "Remarques sur la composition des Hitat de Maqrizi d'après un manuscrits autographe," in *Hommages à la mémoire de Serge Sauneron, 1927–1976, II: Égypte post-pharaonique* (Cairo: IFAO, 1979), 231–58.

editing when its author stopped working on it, most probably because of his prolonged final illness.[97]

Overall, the *Khitat* is arranged in a chronological order which allows al-Maqrizi to expand his coverage in the sections where he has more information or where he deems the city's development momentous, such as in the Fatimid period and the early Bahri period. The book begins with the geographical survey of Egypt, in the tradition of *surat al-ard* (cartography) and geographical literature, especially as it had developed in the thirteenth and fourteenth centuries with the Mamluk encyclopedists such as Ibn Fadhl Allah al-ʿUmari and Shihab al-Din al-Nuwayri. Both were major sources for al-Maqrizi, as we saw. The geographical section understandably focuses on the Nile and its canalization and embankments over time as the historical sources of the prosperity of the country. It ends with a section on the merits (*fada'il*) of Egypt, which also depends on the material of earlier *khitat* authors and encyclopedists. The book then moves to Egypt's pre-Islamic history. Here, al-Maqrizi seems to be drawing on the two strings of accounts concerning its Pharaonic phase, identified by Michael Cook as the "traditionist" and the "Hermetic," which may have been, in the final account, an Islamic invention as well.[98] For Hellenistic, Roman, and Christian Coptic histories, al-Maqrizi cites the usual sources from within the established Islamic historiographic tradition which had subsumed many Jewish and Christian Coptic accounts, in addition to folktales adapted from other traditions, to explain those moments of intersection between the sacred histories of patriarchs and prophets of the Peoples of the Books and ancient Egyptian history. But he also seems to have had direct access to multiple Jewish (and probably Coptic) sources, as proven by Haggai Mazuz in a series of articles focused on the subject.[99] It is

[97] Al-Maqrizi, *Khitat2*, Introduction, 5: 15°–18°.

[98] Al-Maqrizi, *Khitat2*, 1: 105, raises the issue of the origin of the mummies by admitting that neither the Copts nor the Jews claim them as their ancestors, and that the Muslims know nothing about them. See the discussion by Michael Cook, "Pharaonic History in Medieval Egypt," *SI* 57 (1983): 67–103. The issue of Pharaonic history in Medieval Egypt has elicited much discussion, see Sandor Fodor, "The Origins of the Arabic Legends of the Pyramids," *Acta Orientalia Academiae Scientiarum Hungaricae* 23 (1970): 335–63; Ulrich Haarmann, "Die Sphinx: Synkretische Volksreligiositat im spatmittelalterlichen islamischen Agypten," *Saeculum* 29 (1978): 367–84; idem, "In Quest of the Spectacular Noble and Learned Visitors to the Pyramids Around 1200 AD," in *Islamic Studies Presented to Charles J. Adams*, Wael Hallaq and Donald Little, eds. (Leiden: Brill, 1991), 57–67; Ursula Sezgin, "Pharaonische Wunderwerke," *Zeitshcrift fur Geschichte der Arabische-Islamischen Wissenschaften* 9 (1994): 229–91.

[99] Beside the sources cited in note 41 above, Mazuz has continued his investigation of al-Maqrizi's Jewish and Islamic sources on the Jews in a number of articles: "From 'Moses' Mishnah' to Moses Maimonides' Mishneh Tōrah: The Development of the Jewish Oral Law according to al-Maqrizi," *Journal Asiatique* 306, 2 (2018): 201–7; "The

doubtful that al-Maqrizi read these sources directly, as we do not know him to have mastered any language other than Arabic. The information must have been communicated to him orally, as in the case of the Karaite Ibrahim b. Faraj Allah b. ʿAbd al-Kafi al-Dawudi, who he cites, but also other unnamed informants as claimed by none other than his nemesis al-Sakhawi.[100]

The urban history section begins with a succinct review of the major Egyptian cities. Only two receive more than cursory treatment: Alexandria, the Classical capital of the country for a millennium, and al-Fayyum, which was traditionally associated with the Patriarch Joseph, thus carrying a certain religious significance. After a concise index of the various calendars used by different nations from the sacred timeline of Creation to the Persians, al-Maqrizi turns his attention to the Coptic calendar, which still constitutes the basis for agricultural timetables in Egypt today. He supplements his discussion of the calendar with a survey of the Coptic holidays, festivals, and almanac in a tacit acknowledgment of their importance for understanding the history of the country, which still had a significant percentage of Copts during his lifetime.[101] Al-Maqrizi then moves to the site of the first Islamic capital, al-Fustat, and reviews its ancient history. He examines its establishment on the site of the ancient Roman fort of Babylon, its growth in the early medieval period, and its gradual ruin until what remained of it was eventually absorbed in the growing Cairo. Lingering on the theme of ruin (*kharab*), he delves into a detailed analysis of al-Shidda al-Mustansiriyya (the Calamity of Caliph al-Mustansir's time, 1065–72) in the middle of the Fatimid period, which resulted in the desertion of al-Fustat's northern half, and the burning of parts of the city by the Vizier Shawir at the end of the Fatimid rule when the Crusaders were threatening to occupy it in 1168. He also briefly reviews the history of al-Qata'iʿ, the magnificent urban settlement established by Ahmad

Jewish Calendar and Calendation according to al-Maqrīzī in *al-Khiṭaṭ*," *ZDMG* 169, 1 (2019): 77–96.

100 Al-Sakhawi, *Daw'*, 2: 24, states that "al-Maqrizi was knowledgeable about the creed of Ahl al-Kitab (Christians? Jews?) and that their notables used to visit him to learn from him." For the Karaite Ibrahim al-Dawudi, see note 41 above.

101 When Egypt became a majority Muslim country is still a subject of debate. Recent scholarship estimates that this did not happen until after the end of the Fatimid Caliphate in the twelfth century, and perhaps even later, although some argue that it was actually reached in the ninth century. For an examination of the various opinions about conversion to Islam in Egypt, see Shaun O'Sullivan, "Coptic Conversion and the Islamization of Egypt," *MSR* 10, 2 (2006): 65–79. See also Michael Brett, "Population and Conversion to Islam in Egypt in the Mediaeval Period," in *Egypt and Syria in the Fatimid, Ayyubid and Mamluk Eras*, IV, U. Vermeulen and J. van Steenbergen, eds. (Leuven: Peeters, 2005), 1–32, republished in his *The Fatimids and Egypt* (London: Routledge, 2019); Christian Décobert, "Sur l'arabisation et l'islamisation de l'Égypte médiévale," in Christian Décobert, ed., *Itinéraires d'Égypte. Mélanges offerts au Père Maurice Martin, SJ* (Cairo: IFAO, 1992), 273–300.

ibn Tulun north of al-Fustat in 868 as the seat of his semi-independent rule, which was spitefully destroyed in 905 by the ʿAbbasid army sent to wrest Egypt back from Ibn Tulun's descendants. Here, he cites thirteen poets who composed poems mourning the destruction of al-Qata'iʿ's palaces and Great Maydan, which he had painstakingly collected from several sources as a form of eulogy for the city and its celebrated builders.[102]

Al-Maqrizi bleakly prefaces this historical reporting on the Islamic capitals of Egypt before al-Qahira with a series of eschatological accounts of the preordained destruction of the various regions of the Islamic world leading up to the demise of al-Fustat. His main sources here are some of the most famous diviners in early Islam, notably Kaʿb al-Ahbar (d. 632) and Wahab ibn Munabbih (d. c. 725), who played crucial roles in the transmission of Biblical and para-Biblical prophecies and miracles to the nascent Islamic apocalyptic narratives.[103] He also ends this section with a listing of the succession of calamities that befell al-Fustat between the end of the Fatimid period and his own time, noting how reconstruction came back to renew the town after each instance of destruction. But he ominously closes his report with a matter-of-fact observation about the advanced state of the city's ruination after 790/1390 and a solemn Qur'anic warning: "And those cities, We destroyed them when they did evil, and appointed for their destruction a tryst" (Surat al-Kahf, 18:59).[104]

Next, al-Maqrizi moves to the Fatimid period, which he generally paints in a positive light, while making sure to keep his distance from the Ismaʿili creed. He analyzes the founding of Cairo as the center of the self-consciously proselytizing Fatimid caliphate in the 970s and spends a sizeable portion of the book describing the many spectacular structures and the order and

[102] Al-Maqrizi, *Khitat2*, 2: 85–112. The tradition of eulogizing departed kings through the description of their ruined palaces started in the Arabic tradition with al-Buhturi (821–97) and his famous poem on the ruins of Iwan Kisra in al-Mada'in (Ctesiphon), see Nasser Rabbat, "al-Iwan: Maʿnahu al-Faraghi wa Madluluhu al-Tazkari," *BEO* 49 (1997): 251–4; Anstas al-Karmali, "Salwan al-Asra fi-Iwan Kisra," *al-Mashriq* 5, 15 (August 1902): 673–81, 5, 16 (August 1902): 740–6, 5, 17 (September 1902): 780–6, 5, 18 (September 1902): 834–40.

[103] Kaʿb al-Ahbar was a Jewish convert to Islam to whom most of the traditions concerning the eschatological attributes of places were traced. See M. J. Kister, "Haddithu ʿan Bani Isra'ila wa-la Haraj," *Israel Oriental Studies* 2 (1972): 215–39; John C. Reeves, "Jewish Apocalyptic Lore in Early Islam: Reconsidering Kaʿb Al-Ahbar," in *Revealed Wisdom: Studies in Apocalyptic in Honour of Christopher Rowland*, John Ashton ed. (Leiden: Brill, 2014), 200–16. On Wahab ibn Munabbih, who was a Yemenite of Persian ancestry, see Nabia Abbott, "Wahb B. Munabbih: A Review Article," *Journal of Near Eastern Studies* 36, 2 (April 1977): 103–12; Alfred-Louis de Prémare, "Wahab ibn Munabbih: An Exceptional Figure of Early Islamic Scholarship," *Annales. Histoire, Sciences Sociales* 60, 3 (2005): 531–49.

[104] Al-Maqrizi, *Khitat2*, 2: 133–46. I am using Arthur John Arberry for the translation of the verse.

decorum the Fatimids established in Cairo and in Egypt in general. He also offers a full account of the Fatimid administration: its high offices, various divisions or *diwans*, chancery, and elaborate protocols. Furthermore, al-Maqrizi inserts a broad account of the Fatimid mission (*da'wa*) and its hierarchical structure, which is probably the most elaborate account of the subject we possess outside of the Isma'ili sources, while maintaining a balanced approach that neither condones nor condemns it. He had taken the same stand in his Fatimid-oriented *Itti'az al-Hunafa* (discussed in Chapter 1), in complete contrast to his contemporaries, who were by and large openly hostile to the Isma'ili Fatimids and their claim of descent from Fatima, the Prophet's daughter.[105] But the most meticulously elaborate description in this section is that of the Fatimid enclosure of al-Qahira with the various caliphal palaces inside the city and in its outskirts. This text is so detailed that it allowed the French Orientalist Paul Ravaisse to reconstruct the map of the Fatimid capital in the tenth to eleventh centuries, including a plan of the two Eastern and Western Palaces in its center, which had disappeared with no visible trace.[106] Throughout the Fatimid section, al-Maqrizi expends a great deal of care verifying and collating his sources, many of which are known to us solely through his thorough citations.[107]

Midway through his detailed narrative on the Fatimids, al-Maqrizi interjects a preamble on the *kharab* of al-Qahira which he ascribes to a mystical epic attributed to the master Sufi Ibn 'Arabi, which he clearly read about only through a commentary by an unknown author (although he was familiar with the more meditative Sufi writing of Ibn 'Arabi). Using a complicated astrological argument, the cryptic commentary asserts that the city will be destroyed between 780/1380 and 819/1416, that is, during al-Maqrizi's lifetime. But most importantly, this alleged timeframe allows al-Maqrizi to locate the *kharab* after the *mihna* of 806/1403–4, which is the event that triggered his critical project of history writing in the first place, first through the *Ighatha* and then the *Khitat*, before its expansion to narrating the entire history of Egypt as a means of preserving it. Not to miss the chance to vent his melancholy, al-Maqrizi states that the current situation (suggesting that he wrote this text before 1416), with widespread poverty and misery, the ruin of villages and farms, the crumbling structures, the extent of *kharab* in the city, the infighting between rulers, the nearness of the end of their state, and the inflation of

105 Al-Maqrizi, *Khitat2*, 2: 298–320. On the *da'wa*, see Samuel Stern, "Cairo as the Centre of the Isma'ili Movement," in *Colloque International sur l'Histoire du Caire*, 437–50, reprinted in his *Studies in Early Isma'ilism* (Leiden: Brill, 1983), 234–56.

106 Paul Ravaisse, *Essai sur l'histoire et la topographie du Caire d'après Maqrizi* (Palais des Khalifes Fatimites), 1ère et 2ème parties, *MMAF* vol. 1, parts 3 and vol. 3, part 4 (Cairo: IFAO, 1886–90).

107 Al-Maqrizi, *Khitat2*, Introduction, 2: 19°–49°.

all prices supports the mysterious prediction of his unknown source.[108] He returns to the theme of *kharab* once more at the end of the Fatimid section by citing a long, despondent poem by 'Umara al-Yamani, a pro-Fatimid poet, historian, and *faqih* from Yemen who was executed by Salah al-Din in 1174 on the accusation of taking part in a plot to restore Fatimid rule. The poem, clearly written shortly after the fall of the Fatimids, describes in mournful detail the first moment of desolation and emptiness that befell their palaces and the disappearance of their pomp and ceremony. Al-Maqrizi notes that it is rumored that this poem, which he, after Ibn Sa'id a-Maghribi, qualifies as the "best poem in lamenting the passing of a reign," was the reason for which 'Umara was killed after false allegations were concocted against him.[109] He then almost disparagingly records the hardships the Fatimid royal family endured and the humiliating seizure of their palaces under the Ayyubids until al-Zahir Baybars forced whoever was left of their descendants to transfer ownership of their remaining properties to the state treasury seventy years later.

The second half of the book, corresponding to the second volume of the Bulaq edition, covers Cairo in the Ayyubid and Mamluk period. It adopts a typological structure that moves from the urban unit, or quarters (*harat*), to the streets, divided into three categories depending on width and importance as *khitat* (sing. *khatt*), *durub* (sing. *darb*), and *aziqqa* (sing. *zuqaq*), to the small neighborhood gates named *khuwakh* (sing. *khukha*) and the city squares *rihab* (sing. *rahba*), before reaching the actual building categories. Starting with the famous mansions (*dur*, sing. *dar*), and palaces (*qusur* sing. *qasr*), al-Maqrizi proceeds to cover the bathhouses (*hamammat*, sing. *hammam*), the enclosed markets (*qayasir*, sing. *qaysariyya*), caravanserai (*khanat* and *fanadiq*, sing. *khan* and *funduq*), and markets (*aswaq*, sing. *suq*) and small, neighborhood markets (*suwayqat*, sing. *suwayqa*).[110] Following the survey of the residential and commercial architecture, al-Maqrizi ends this section with an interlude on the ceremonials and processions in the main avenue

[108] Al-Maqrizi, *Khitat2*, 2: 241–3.

[109] Al-Maqrizi, *Khitat2*, 2: 605–7; 'Umara al-Yamani, *Diwan* 'Abd al-Rahman 'Aryani and Ahmad Abd al-Rahman Mu'alimi, eds. (Damascus: 'Ikrima Press, 2000), 612–16. The poem is cited in Abu Shama, *Kitab al-Rawdatayn fi Akhbar al-Dawlatayn al-Nuriyya wa-l-Salahiyya* 2 vols., M. H. M. Aḥmad and M. M. Ziyada, eds. (Cairo: Matba'at Lajnat al-Ta'lif, 1956–62), 1, 2: 570–1. For an early and exhaustive study of 'Umara al-Yamani, see Hartwig Derenbourg, *'Oumara du Yémen. Sa vie et son oeuvre* (Paris: Ernest Leroux, 1909), https://gallica.bnf.fr/ark:/12148/bpt6k5439473v.r=omara%20yemen?rk=85837;2 (last accessed December 5, 2020). On the actions against the Fatimids taken by Salah al-Din, see Yaakov Lev, *Saladin in Egypt* (Leiden: Brill, 1999), 116–36; Fozia Bora, "Did Salah al-Din Destroy the Fatimids' Books? An Historiographical Enquiry," *JRASGBI* 25, 1 (2015), 21–39.

[110] Al-Maqrizi, *Khitat2*, 3: 1–354. Sayyid inserts a short passage on the mills of the city (p. 355), which he found in only one of his principal manuscripts. Its insertion actually breaks the structure of the book.

of al-Qahira, *al-Qasaba* (al-Mu'izz street of today) during both the Fatimid and early Mamluk periods. He then launches into a review of the outskirts of Cairo, moving counterclockwise from the area around the Khalij (Canal) to the west and further on to the two banks of the Nile, then to the south of al-Qahira outside of Bab Zuweila and beyond toward al-Fustat, and finally to the north beyond the two gates of al-Futuh and al-Nasr. He notes the topographic changes between the Fatimid and the Mamluk periods, especially the development of the marshland recovered from the westerly-receding Nile river, which peaked in the thirteenth to fourteenth centuries during the third reign of al-Nasir Muhammad.[111] When breaking the categories in this section down, al-Maqrizi focuses on the *ahkar* (urban zones, sing. *hukr*), which formed the main means of appropriating land by the state to develop it by distributing lots among the amirs and grandees.[112] Al-Maqrizi then turns his attention to listing the canals (*khiljan* sing. *khalij*), bridges (*qanatir* sing. *qantara*), ponds (*birak*, sing. *birka*), dikes (*jusur* sing. *jisr*), islands in the Nile, prisons (*sujun* sing. *sijn*), dockyards (*sina'a*), and hippodromes (*mayadin* sing. *maydan*).[113]

A review of the Citadel of the Mountain, the seat of the sultanate in Egypt since its first construction under Salah al-Din al-Ayyubi, is listed in the *Khitat*'s introduction as section six of the book's original structure right after the typological survey. But in the present form it bisects the topographical and architectural inventory, albeit falling into its logical place in the sequence after the section on the hippodromes. The analysis consists of an extensive but derivative architectural history of the citadel up to the fifteenth century, with an in-depth description of all the major structures within it, relying mostly on Ibn Fadhl Allah's *Masalik*. This is followed by succinct exposés on the origin and evolution of the various positions in the Mamluk court, army, and administration, and descriptions of the major royal ceremonies held in and around the citadel. Finally, al-Maqrizi provides short biographies of the Ayyubid and Mamluk sultans who had ruled Egypt since the building of the citadel. But he hastens to say that these biographical entries are succinct because he has provided elaborate versions for the same sultans in his two other books, *al-Muqaffa* and *al-Suluk*. The list stops with the accession of al-Ashraf Barsbay in April 1422, suggesting that al-Maqrizi did not revise this item as he was revising other sections of the book until shortly before his death in 1442.

[111] C. J. R. Haswell, "Cairo, Origin and Development. Some Notes on the Influence of the River Nile and Its Changes," *BSROGE* 11 (1922): 171–7.

[112] Al-Maqrizi, *Khitat2*, 3: 387, quotes Ibn Sidah, one of the major medieval lexicographers, in defining *hukr* as monopoly on land for building; ibid., 3: 378–403, lists 25 *hukrs* that were planned in the days of al-Nasir Muhammad.

[113] Ibid., 3: 402–636.

The last quarter of the book resumes the architectural/topographical survey, with a focus on religious buildings. The list comprises the congregational mosques (*al-masajid al-jami'a*), madrasas, hospitals (*bimaristans*), and neighborhood mosques (*masajid*), followed by three types of buildings for Sufis, *khanqahs*, *ribats*, and *zawaya* (sing. *zawiya*, Sufi shrines), then a very short list of *mashahid* (sing. *mashhad*, shrines named after descendants of the Prophets, a type popularized by the Fatimids). The survey then moves to the two main cemeteries, al-Qarafa al-Kubra (Great or Northern Qarafa) and al-Qarafa al-Sughra (Little or Southern) outside Cairo, enumerating their mosques and palaces (*jawasiq*, sing. *jawsaq*, usually used for visitations), tanks, wells, and oratories, and finally synagogues and convents and churches.[114] Each structure in this long list is recorded, dated, and its location described. The individual entries vary in length and scope, and many but not all end with brief biographies of the building's patron. The lists themselves are neither exhaustive nor complete, especially for the buildings erected during the last twenty years of al-Maqrizi's life, which implies that he either neglected to update the material during that period when he was busy with other major writing projects or that he was not done with the book's composition when he released the copy that was used by later copyists and taken as the fair copy of the book, as suggested by Ayman Fu'ad Sayyid. The latter is the explanation I am adopting in this book.[115]

Three major digressions in this final section on the various sects of the three religions practiced in Egypt are of particular interest as they underscore two aspects of al-Maqrizi's makeup that have been already mentioned: his theological knowledge and his ecumenical perspective, at least in his presentation of creeds to which he was fundamentally opposed. This is not to claim that al-Maqrizi was anything but a conservative, perhaps even textualist because of his Zahiri leanings, Shafi'i scholar with a pronounced veneration for the Prophet's family and salafist views. He was, of course, all of that. But his curiosity, erudition, and open-mindedness come across very clearly in his long review of the various sects and creeds in Islam as discussed in

114 Loiseau, *Reconstruire la maison*, 1: 23, note 35 tallies all the items mentioned by al-Maqrizi in this second half of the *Khitat*. The total is 1063 toponyms.

115 Al-Maqrizi, *Khitat2*, Introduction, 3: 70–81°, and Introduction, 4: 106°–18°. The second hypothesis is more plausible, giving how many *tayarat* were still loose between the pages of the autograph copies and how much empty space was left in various sections for later additions. In al-Maqrizi, *Khitat2*, Introduction, 4, 1: 150°, Ayman Fu'ad Sayyid also found out that al-Maqrizi did not copy twenty-seven entries on madrasas from his *musawwadat* to his assumed autograph copy, in addition to his failure to enlarge a two-page section on *kharab* which appears at the end of the *musawwadat* under the heading "On the causes of ruin" but consists of an interrupted first draft of an account of the failure of the state after Barquq to secure the land of Egypt against the Bedouins and assorted bandits.

Chapter 3, and more unusually in his concise but informed review of the beliefs and various sects of Judaism and Christianity. A conclusion to the review of Egypt's churches is missing as the book abruptly stops with a brief listing of the Melkite churches in Cairo. This is also the end of the *Khitat* as it has come down to us in the various complete manuscripts consulted by the book's editors. Evidently, this could not have been the intended conclusion, for as we know, a section on the *kharab* was promised in the introduction as the final chapter, and as Ayman Fuʿad Sayyid shows, such an embryonic and totally sketchy section did exist in the *musawwadat*. Why al-Maqrizi did not transfer it to his "autograph" copy (presumably the basis of the many copies dispersed around the world's libraries) remains an open question. It is hard to believe that he changed his plan and decided to forgo the originally planned conclusion on *kharab* to close his book with the list of churches, especially since the theme of ruin punctuates the whole narrative in an almost periodic fashion, whose frequency intensifies in the typological sections covering his own time. This alone strongly suggests that he was planning to bring his book to a climax of sorts about the utter ruination of his beloved city and country whose imminent onset was sadly inevitable as far as the pessimistic al-Maqrizi can tell.

Indeed, his anxiety, melancholy, and moral indignation at the general state of affairs suffuse his *Khitat* with an elegiac tone and a sense of urgency. Even in the seemingly dry and methodical toponymic lists, al-Maqrizi is trying to offset the decline he is noticing all around him by constituting what Pierre Nora, in a modern and excessively nationalistic context, termed a *lieu de mémoire* ("realm of memory").[116] His *Khitat* is thus the repository where memories surrounding the city, its people, topography, and architecture, can be recorded, saved, and later recalled. Al-Maqrizi, moreover, was vying with time. His Cairo, whose sad and accelerating degradation he was chagrined to witness in his mature years, was under a multi-pronged attack from neglect, economic strife, recurrent plagues, dissolution (*ikhtilal*) of the Mamluk order and the raging Mamluk venality. It was in fact at risk of no longer being the *milieu de mémoire* (environment of memory) it had been just a few years back as al-Maqrizi fondly remembers it throughout his text.[117]

116 Pierre Nora, "Between Memory and History: Les Lieux de mémoire," *Representations* 26 (Spring 1989), 7–25, is the theoretical introduction to his collaborative project on the national memory of France, published in 7 vols. as *Les Lieux de memoire*; vol. 1, trans. Arthur Goldhammer, *Realms of Memory: Rethinking the French Past* (New York: Columbia University Press, 1996).

117 Loiseau, *Reconstruire la maison*, 1: 27, note 52, referencing Gabriel Martinez-Gros's translation, notices that the same terms appear in Ibn Hazm, *Tawq al-Hamama* (*The Ring of the Dove*), in conjunction with the desolation of Cordoba after the Umayyads. Al-Maqrizi may have indeed read this work of Ibn Hazm, whom he revered as the second founder of

He recalls, perhaps a bit too theatrically, many mosques, madrasas, and palaces resplendent in all their opulence and their illustrious occupants, or streets filled with the bustle of city life where he played as a child and which no longer existed when he wrote his *Khitat*. In their place were empty alleys and vacant lots with the dilapidated remains of deserted structures.[118] Gone, too, in al-Maqrizi's words, were the manifestations of the leisurely and carefree life of the Mamluk capital of yesteryear, with its public festivities, religious processions, and markets stuffed with luxury goods brought from near and far.[119] This heightened notion of loss imbued him with an urgent need to capture cherished memories, both his own and the community's, as they had attached themselves to places and buildings before they slipped away with the disappearance of their settings. It also fired up his deep sense of right and wrong, which translated into vocal and unmitigated criticism, aimed at the main agents of decline as he sees it, the predatory Mamluks and their corrupt sultans, amirs, and officials, many of whom were personally known to him.

Al-Maqrizi and Khaldunian Cyclical History

As he was compiling his *Khitat* over the years, al-Maqrizi needed a malleable structure that would frame both his growing data and his mounting feelings of despondency and loss, while maintaining his overall historical perspective. This may have been furnished by the historical theory of his revered teacher, Ibn Khaldun, who, as I argued in Chapter 1, had a powerful influence on al-Maqrizi. A Khaldunian inspiration has been promulgated in at least two treatises of al-Maqrizi's, *Ighathat al-Umma* and *al-Niza' wal-Takhasum*. But it is in the *Khitat* that we can detect the subtle application of Ibn Khaldun's theory on the cyclical movement of history.[120] In his *Muqadimma*, Ibn

Zahirism and whose doctrinal book, *al-Fasl fi al-Milal*, he references heavily, as we saw in Chapters 2 and 3.

118 Examples are al-Maqrizi, *Khitat2*, 2: 225, where he laments the general ruination of the areas between Cairo and al-Fustat that had been developed in the Ayyubid and early Mamluk periods; *Khitat2*, 1: 346, where he reports that he used to go on promenade as a child in al-Rasd near the Nile, which was landscaped and provided with water under al-Nasir Muhammad, but was ruined later; al-Maqrizi, *Khitat2*, 4, 1: 129, on the Mosque of Rashida, which al-Maqrizi knew when it was in use, and the area around it built up before the crisis of 806/1403.

119 Al-Maqrizi, *Khitat2*, 3: 330–1, sounds like a kid in a candy store in his description of the abundance of marvels made out of sugar in the suq of the sweetmakers (*halawiyyin*), which dwindled over time to the point where nothing was made for the season of 'Id al-Fitr of 817/ November 1414 (indicating the date on which he is writing this report).

120 References to Ibn Khaldun in al-Maqrizi, *Khitat2*, 1: 130, 3: 605–6 and note 1, where he quotes a long passage from the *Muqaddima* on the Arabs' relationship to the sea;

Khaldun examines the political and environmental factors that contribute to the emergence and development of structured human societies, which he terms *'umran* (a concept whose meaning ranges between civilization and urbanization), and the causes of their decline. He devises a theoretical framework of cyclical change, reflecting the conflict between the two social groups he observed during his political career in North Africa, the nomads and the city dwellers. This cycle constitutes the major engine of history for him.[121] It goes roughly as follows. The nomads, united by kin solidarity (Ibn Khaldun's famous *'asabiyya*), conquer the softer city and establish a ruling dynasty. The first generation of rulers retains tribal virtues and solidarity as their main means of control. The second is forced to depend on bureaucrats and military recruits to manage its domain and preserve its hold on power. The third generation loses its social domination and succumbs to corruption, oppression, and the decadent luxuries of city life, which paradoxically energizes cultural and artistic production in the city. The ruling class's degradation finally leads to the ruin of the city and the fall of the dynasty with the fourth degenerate generation. Fresh new nomadic conquerors will start a new dynasty and will eventually experience the same cycle of gradual decline.[122]

In the *Khitat*, al-Maqrizi seems to have subsumed the overarching cycle of dynastic rise and fall of his master to organize the vast amount of topographical, urban, and architectural material he had collected over the years into a general discourse on Egypt's history. For that purpose, he seems to have devised an analogous cycle to frame his exposition of the fate of Cairo under the successive dynasties that ruled Egypt in the Islamic era. The political fortune of each ruling dynasty is plotted against the fluctuations of the urban and architectural prosperity of Cairo followed by decay and destruction in a way that echoes the Khaldunian view of historical movement. Al-Maqrizi, however, shifts the focus from the dynasty as the main unit of analysis to the city as the stage upon which history unfolds. Furthermore, his is a cycle of building to *kharab* rather than conquest to conquest. Thus, the establishment of al-Qata'i' marks the ascendance of Ibn Tulun's short-lived dynasty

---

the reference in 4, 2: 921 suggests that he was familiar with the *Muqaddima* and its propositions.

121 On Ibn Khaldun's cyclical movement of history see Ibn Khaldun, *The Muqaddimah: An Introduction to History*, trans. F. Rosenthal, 3 vols. (Princeton: Princeton University Press, 1967), Vol. 2, Chapter 3, Sections 33–50, 46–156; Tarif Khalidi, "Some Classical Islamic Views of the City," in *Festshrift for Ihsan 'Abbas*, 265–76; Robert Irwin, "Toynbee and Ibn Khaldun," *MES* 33, 3 (July 1997), 461–79; Dale, "Ibn Khaldun."

122 Akhtar Husain Siddiqi, "Ibn Khaldun's Concept of Urbanization," *International Journal of Islamic and Arabic Studies* 1, 2 (1984): 41–55; Manzoor Alam, "Ibn Khaldun on the Origin, Growth, and Decay of Cities," *Encyclopedic Survey of Islamic Culture*, 20 vols. Mohamed Taher, ed. (New Delhi: Islamic Book Service, 1997), 5: 229–47.

just as its destruction at the hands of the Abbasid army in 905 dates the dynasty's dissolution.[123] Al-Fustat undergoes two cycles of rise and ruination, one ending in the middle of the Fatimid period during the extended struggle under Caliph al-Mustansir's al-Shidda al-'Uzma (1065–72) and one occurring toward the end of the caliphate when Shawir burned the city in anticipation of a Crusader attack.[124] More elaborate is the cyclical history of Fatimid al-Qahira, possibly because of the availability of more source material, or because of nostalgia felt toward the Fatimids enhanced by al-Maqrizi's belief of belonging to their lineage. But here too al-Maqrizi arranges his material in a cyclical pattern that traces the ups and downs of the caliphate until its expiration in 1171.[125] The pattern is less noticeable in the section on the Ayyubids and the Bahri Mamluks, possibly because the Mamluks were first seen as a continuation of the Ayyubids and because the Mamluk system cannot be seen as a true dynastic one except for the case of the Qalawunids, of whom fifteen sultans from four generations succeeded one another.[126] Another reason for the lack of cyclicity in al-Maqrizi's story of Cairo under the early Mamluks may have been the nostalgia-induced bias he evinced toward them, which was noted by both his contemporaries and his modern critiques.[127]

But the main reason, in my opinion, is that the *Khitat* was not completed as al-Maqrizi had intended it. That promised section on the *kharab* as the end of the book would have provided the closure for the review of Cairo under the Ayyubids and Mamluks, as well as the conclusion of the book. The typological sections, already peppered with references to *kharab* and desolation, were supposed to culminate in the depiction of the most irreversibly devastating—according to the angry and pessimistic al-Maqrizi—ruin of the city and the country under the early Burji sultans, especially the ill-fated Faraj ibn Barquq, al-Mu'ayyad Shaykh, and al-Ashraf Barsbay, whom al-Maqrizi specifically and repeatedly blames for the sorry state of the city's and the sultanate's affairs.[128] To al-Maqrizi, the Mamluks of his age were no longer the deserving leaders their Bahri predecessors had once been, skillfully and thoughtfully managing a great empire and fighting for the cause of Islam. His deep

[123] Al-Maqrizi, *Khitat2*, 2: 80–114.

[124] Ibid., 2: 122–46.

[125] Ibid., 1: 360–5.

[126] Ibid., 3: 750–88 offers a brief chronology of the sultans from Salah al-Din to Barsbay about whom we have only the date of accession. Neither Barsbay's son al-Malik al-'Aziz Yusuf, who ruled for four months in 1438, nor al-Zahir Jaqmaq, who occupied the throne during the last four years of al-Maqrizi's life, is mentioned.

[127] Ibn Taghri-Birdi, *Nujum*, 11: 290–1, chastises his master for being blind to the excesses of al-Nasir Muhammad, which far exceeded the excesses of al-Zahir Barquq, whom al-Maqrizi severely censures. Irwin, "Al-Maqrizi and Ibn Khaldun," 228 picks up on the same point.

[128] Examples in al-Maqrizi, *Khitat2*, 1: 256, 4, 2: 456; see also idem, *Suluk*, 4: 1414.

disappointment translated into breaking all measures of caution and consideration in reporting their failings, especially after he withdrew from public life. From that date on, he unleashed his unmitigated hostility toward his contemporary sultans to the point where—as noted by Ibn Taghri-Birdi—he left no room for reconciliation or rapprochement.[129]

Al-Maqrizi's indignation at the state of affairs during his lifetime lends his otherwise nostalgic historical/topographic narrative of Ayyubid and Mamluk Cairo a sense of purpose. Chronicling the buildings and topography of the city was, in the final account, his way of drawing moral lessons from the actions of kings, amirs, and holy men as they were inscribed on the spaces and forms of the city, or its *khitat* and *athar*. This was a critical program, conceived and presented from within the epistemological framework of a medieval Muslim thinker, in other words, a pre-humanist and inherently teleological framework.[130] This is the same framework Hayden White critiqued Ibn Khaldun for adopting in his *Muqqadima*: an underlying fatalism in his conception of history and a strong, rigid determinism in his theory of recurrent cycles, totally ignoring the cultural milieu within which the two men were thinking and theorizing.[131]

Al-Maqrizi's historical theorizing deserves a more careful look than the one it has received so far, one that can transcend the biases of our rationalizing and thoroughly secularized and psychologized conception of history.[132] This way, we may be able to better appreciate the intellectual and emotional conditions under which this singular Mamluk historian reflected upon and wrote history. His narrative structures, conversational prose techniques, and even

[129] This is where Ibn Taghri-Birdi's repeated remarks on al-Maqrizi's hostility toward Barsbay gain their full meaning, see *Nujum*, 14: 200–1, 245, 310–11; 15: 109–10.

[130] See the discussion of Leonardo Capezzone, "Remembering, Knowing, Imagining: Approaches to the Topic of Memory in Medieval Islamic Culture," in *Texts in Transit in the Medieval Mediterranean*, Y. Tzvi Langermann and Robert G. Morrison, eds. (University Park, PA: Penn State University Press, 2016), 85–100, questioning the timeframe of humanism as a category of definition and opening the possibility of reading memory as a tool of another form of humanism.

[131] White, "Ibn Khaldun," 110–25. For an interpretation that insists on the role played by Ibn Khaldun's historiographic and intellectual context (and by extension al-Maqrizi's) in shaping but also in delimiting his theorizing see Aziz al-Azmeh, *Ibn Khaldun: An Essay in Reinterpretation* (London, Frank Cass, 1982), 145–63; idem, *Ibn Khaldun in Modern Scholarship: A Study in Orientalism* (London: Third World Centre for Research and Publishing, 1981), 67–149. Two books that place Ibn Khaldun in his historical context and assess his work accordingly are Abdesselam Cheddadi, *Ibn Khaldun: L'homme et le théoricien de la civilization* (Paris: Gallimard, 2006) and Gabriel Martinez-Gros, *Ibn Khaldun et les sept vies de l'islam* (Arles: Actes sud; Sindbad, 2006).

[132] As we are reminded by Michel de Certeau, *L'écriture de l'histoire* (Paris, Gallimard, 1975); trans. as *The Writing of History* by Tom Conley (New York: Columbia University Press, 1988), 19–55.

the religious underpinnings of his arguments could then unveil their relative significance for his history writing. The moralizing, the recurrent dwelling on *kharab*, and the gloomy outlook could then be seen for what they probably were meant to be: a critical apparatus brandished as the yardstick against which actions and decisions of influential people are measured and their consequences evaluated.

Al-Maqrizi's most impressive achievement in his *Khitat*, however, is primarily conceptual. Though his book focused on topography and buildings, he was consciously aware that the city is primarily a human artifact whose history is woven out of intentions, happenstances, strategies, competitions, intrigues, glorifications, vanities, good deeds, disjunctions, and, of course, failures and ruinations. This is why, as I argue in the next section, his book still resonates with modern Egyptian commentators on Cairo not just as an invaluable historical source, but also, and perhaps more powerfully, as a truly challenging and emotional discursive narrative.

PART 3

THE AFTERLIFE OF AL-MAQRIZI'S WRITING

CHAPTER 5

Al-Maqrizi and the Orientalists

When considered within his own intellectual tradition, al-Maqrizi appears almost as an anachronistic figure, both for his dedicated focus on the history of Islamic Egypt as a lifelong project (the Prophet Muhammad's life story being the second one) and for the critical stance displayed in most of his texts, especially the *Ighathat*, *Khitat*, and *Suluk*.[1] Certainly, no other Mamluk historian seems to have absorbed the Khaldunian perspective into his subject matter as al-Maqrizi did. Nor did any of his contemporaries capture the intensity of feelings displayed in his description of his country and city, his predictions of their ruination, or his persistent and steadily escalating denunciation of the Mamluk rulers of his time as primary responsible for that state of affairs. Nor was any other historian or *khitat* author creative enough to juxtapose the pedagogical and moral aims, common to all the period's historians, with the typographical and architectural descriptions as al-Maqrizi did in his *Khitat*. Top annalistic historians such as Ibn Taghri-Birdi, Ibn Hajar al-'Asqalani, al-Sakhawi, and even Ibn Khaldun himself sought their moral lessons in the actions of kings and holy men; al-Maqrizi located his in the marks of these actions on the face of the city, on its *khitat* and *athar*.[2] Other contemporaneous or slightly later Mamluk *khitat* authors, such as al-Suyuti, Abu Hamid al-Qudsi, Ibn Iyas, and the Damascene Ibn Tulun al-Salihi, stopped at the level of Galtier's utilitarian definition in their treatment of their material. They composed their books to preserve the actual memory of quarters and buildings.[3] They all drew up dispassionate inventories of quarters, streets,

[1] Characterized as "History in the Service of Faith," in Amalia Levanoni, "al-Maqrizi's Account of the Transition from Turkish to Circassian Mamluk Sultanate: History in the Service of Faith," in *The Historiography of Islamic Egypt*, 93–105.

[2] Loiseau, *Reconstruire la maison*, 1: 24, reaches the same conclusion by reading al-Maqrizi's method as reversing the usual annalistic mode whereby the events are attributed to their main actors.

[3] Al-Suyuti, *Husn al-Muhadara fi Tarikh Misr wa-l-Qahira* 2 vols., Muhammad Abu al-Fadhl Ibrahim, ed. (Cairo: Issa al-Babi al-Halabi, 1967); or Abu Hamid al-Qudsi (and not Ibn Zahira), *al-Fada'il al-Bahira fi Mahasin Misr wa-l-Qahira*, Mustafa al-Saqqa and Kamil al-Muhandis, eds. (Cairo: Dar al-Kutub, 1969); and his *al-Fawa'id al-Nafissa al-Bahira fi*

and buildings. But they did not use their compilations to advance a larger agenda, as al-Maqrizi did. Many, in fact, copied or summarized sections of al-Maqrizi's *Khitat* and commented on or added updated information to them, with no underlying historical awareness or emotive charge.[4] Their *khitat* books are informative, of course, but they deliberately—or, more likely, conformingly—stay at the level of documentary and descriptive presentations, dodging the engagement of their reader in their motivations, concerns, or agendas.

In contrast, al-Maqrizi's *Khitat* comes across not just as an invaluable historical source but also, and perhaps more powerfully, as an overtly emotional urban history laced with political innuendos, sociocultural proclamations, and an intense filial affinity with the city and the country. It actually anticipates—though in a less self-conscious way and in a clear gloomy tone—the problems Alois Riegl and other *fin-de-siècle* archeologists encountered as they tried to "historicize" by reconstituting as wholes the fragments of city spaces and structures.[5] As such, it may be considered a truly pioneering urban history, perhaps long-winded, cosmocentric, and depressed, but certainly methodical, reflective, and imbued with a strong sense of purpose.

The *Khitat* as Urban History

Al-Maqrizi might have thought that the voluminous biographical dictionary *al-Muqaffa al-Kabir*, or the large compendium on the cosmological history before the Prophet *al-Khabar 'an al-Bashar*, or the larger and minutely detailed biography of the Prophet and his family *Imta' al-Asma' bima lil-Rasul min al-Abna' wa al-Akhwal wa al-Hafada wa al-Mata'*, or

Bayan Hukm Shawari' al-Qahira fi Madhahib al-A'imma al-Arba'a al-Zahira, ed., Amal al-'Umari (Cairo: The Supreme Council of Antiquities, 1988); Ibn Iyas, *Nuzhat al-Umam fi'l-'Aja'ib wa'l-Hikam*, ed. Muhammad Zaynuhum M. 'Azab (Cairo: Madbouli, 1995); Ibn Tulun al-Salihi, *al-Qala'id al-Jawhariyya fi-Tarikh al-Salihiyya*, 2 vols., Muhammad Ahmad Duhman, ed. (Damascus: Maktabat al-Dirasat al-Islamiyya, 1949); Conermann, "Ibn Tulun," 115–40.

4 Surveyed by Sayyid in *Musawwadat*, Introduction, 24–7.

5 For the archeological dilemma in reconstructing cultural history, see Erika Naginski, "Riegl, Archaeology, and the Periodization of Culture," *Res: Anthropology and Aesthetics* 40 (Autumn 2001): 115–32. For a sweeping survey of the evolution of a concept of ruins in Western thought with a special focus on the positivistic attitude toward the nineteenth century exemplified by the German historian Johann Gustav Droysen (1808–84), who was "among the first to try to understand history in terms of a theory of remains," see Cornelia Vismann, "The Love of Ruins," *Perspectives on Science* 9, 2 (Summer 2001): 196–209. Another example of a similar influence, this time of Ibn Khaldun on Arnold Toynbee, is discussed in Irwin, "Toynbee and Ibn Khaldun," 461–79.

even the grander, incomplete, and missing encyclopedia *Kitab Mujama' al-Fara'id wa Manba' al-Fawa'id*, were his main contributions to scholarship. But it is the relatively small *Khitat* (only about 1200 letter-size printed pages) that made and ensured his reputation down to the present day and gave it a special twist and even a number of accusatory revisions in recent years. The reasons for this are many. Some are circumstantial. They have to do with issues of survival, popularity, and dissemination of the book, whose extant manuscripts surpass in number those of any other historical book from the middle Islamic period. Others relate to the book's translation and use outside Egypt, which started a century after its composition, first by the Ottomans, then by European orientalists from at least the middle of the seventeeth century. The orientalists saw in the *Khitat* a versatile source not only on the topography of Cairo, but also on a variety of subjects that it tangentially, and in some cases uniquely, treated, such as the churches and synagogues of Egypt, the history of the Copts, or the history of Damietta, the landing port of Louis IX's Crusade.[6] The early availability of the *Khitat* and its consequent indispensability for all later scholarly reconstructions of the history of medieval Egypt have furthermore initiated a secondary scholarship of historiographical analysis, verification, and appraisal of the book contents that culminated recently in the sustained critique by Frédéric Bauden in his Maqriziana series of articles.

But al-Maqrizi's *Khitat* should also have been recognized and celebrated for reasons that are scope- and method-related and less dependent on the completeness and factuality of its data or its relevance for the reconstruction of the history of Egypt or Cairo. These reasons range from the expansiveness of the *Khitat*'s coverage to encompass every aspect of the cosmography, geography, topography, and urban history of Egypt down to the fifteenth century to its unique blending of political and social history with detailed and comprehensive urban and (brief) architectural surveys. Indeed, every commentator on al-Maqrizi's *Khitat* agrees that it is the most complete premodern *khitat* book on the history of Cairo, containing as it does large segments from a variety of earlier and now-lost historical sources, sometime not found anywhere else. Hardly any researcher, however, notes that in his method and scope al-Maqrizi may have been probing new ways of writing about cities that preceded the efforts of the European Renaissance historians who revived the ancient genre of city history in the fifteenth century shortly after al-Maqrizi's death.[7] He thus should have been seen as a pioneer in the

6 See the fuller discussion in Chapter 4.

7 Humanist writings on cities come mostly in the form of orations and letters, like the *Laudatio Florentinae Urbis* by al-Maqrizi's almost exact contemporary Leonardo Bruni (1370–1444), see "Laudatio Florentinae Urbis," in *From Petrarch to Leonardo Bruni*,

study of urban history had it not been for the severe academic division that confines the Islamic production of knowledge, especially after the golden age of the Abbasid classical period, to its cultural and strictly religious boundaries, with very little impact on the worldwide epistemic evolution since the end of the European so-called Middle Ages and the advent of modernity.[8]

Hans Baron, ed. (Chicago: University of Chicago Press, 1968), 232–63. Another type is the antiquarian/topographical studies of Rome and other cities of Italy by scholars like Flavio Biondo (1392–1463) (*Roma triumphans*; *Italia illustrata*), Catherine J. Castner, "The Fortuna of Biondo Flavio's *Italia Illustrata*," in *A New Sense of the Past: The Scholarship of Biondo Flavio (1392–1463)*, Angelo Mazzocco and Marc Laureys, eds. (Leuven: Leuven University Press, 2016), 177–96, which summarizes the *Italia illustrata*'s relationship with classical models and its contribution to fifteenth-century humanist culture. For a collection on Quattrocento writings on the city of Florence, see *Images of Quattrocento Florence: Selected Writings in Literature, History, and Art*, Stefano Ugo Baldassarri and Arielle Saiber, eds. (New Haven: Yale University Press, 2000), 3–95. A major difference between Renaissance Europe and the Islamic Middle East is that maps of cities became a popular way of conveying topographic and architectural information on the city in humanist Europe. On the function of maps see Adam Drisin, "Intricate Fictions: Mapping Princely Authority in a Sixteenth-Century Florentine Urban Plan," *JAE* 57, 4 (May, 2004): 41–55. Another aspect of the humanist writing on the city is the political and moralistic one, illustrated graphically in the contrast between "good" and "bad" government and the effects on the city in Lorenzetti's fresco of 'Il Buon Governo' in the Palazzo Pubblico in Siena, made between 1338 and 1339, see Quentin Skinner, "Ambrogio Lorenzetti: The Artist as Political Philosopher," *Proceedings of the British Academy* 72 (1986) 1–56. This civic humanist ideology was influenced by the writing of the Ancient Roman historian Sallust (86–35 B.C.E.), who was called, in a fashion reminiscent of Irwin's characterization of al-Maqrizi, "the most obvious ancient model for historians of calamities" by Eric Cochrane, *Historians and Historiography in the Italian Renaissance* (Chicago: University of Chicago Press, 1981), 166, cited in Patricia J. Osmond "'Princeps Historiae Romanae': Sallust in Renaissance Political Thought," *Memoirs of the American Academy in Rome* 40 (1995): 112, n. 46. Osmond traces Sallust's influence, especially his explanation of the rise and decline of the Roman republic, which is largely moralistic but also attentive to political, social, and economic conditions, on a wide array of medieval and Renaissance historical and political thought, especially as a warning against the dangers of civil discord, particularly in the period from the medieval commune to Leonardo Bruni and Machiavelli (and beyond), Osmond "Princeps," 103–18. For the text of Sallust, see Sallustius Crispus, *Bellum Catilinae* (*The War With Catiline*), J. Rolfe trans., Loeb Classical Library (Cambridge, M.A.: Harvard University Press, 1921, rev. 1931), https://penelope.uchicago.edu/Thayer/E/Roman/Texts/Sallust/Bellum_Catilinae*.html (last accessed August 31, 2020). I am indebted to Patricia J. Osmond for many of these references.

8 This is a thorny subject that has recently begun to gain critical voices on both sides of the argument. For a sweeping and passionate call for an opening of the study of Islam to the long and complex Islamic history in all its rich intellectual diversity so as to recognize its interconnectedness as a complete epistemological whole see Shahab Ahmed, *What Is Islam?: The Importance of Being Islamic* (Princeton: Princeton University Press, 2015), 113–75. For a sustained critique of the discursive constitution of Orientalism, the field of knowledge primarily responsible for casting the Islamic epistemological tradition as outside

Hence, al-Maqrizi never made it into the modern study of urban history as a field of inquiry and remained a purveyor of specialized information in rather circumscribed fields: the history of Cairo and the study of the Islamic city, both of which belong almost exclusively to the Orientalist enterprise.[9] Even more unfortunate, fewer researchers notice how deftly al-Maqrizi was using the urban and architectural data he collected to advance his moral and political messages, ranging from his laments for the decline and destruction (*kharab*) of his city to his admonition of those who he believed caused it (i.e. the Mamluk ruling class) for having deviated from the proper Islamic system of rule. In fact, al-Maqrizi's *Khitat*, though not the first book to carry the term *khitat* in its title, is the first and possibly the only one to explore the full potential of the genre and to transcend its modest beginnings as a listing of a city's districts, streets, major monuments, and topographic markers, to reach the level not only of urban history, as far as we can apply the term to a premodern book, but that of an urban history with a critical aim. In that, al-Maqrizi's *Khitat* has remained a unique endeavor in the Arabic tradition of writing about cities, both before and after him, at least down to the mid-nineteenth century when the methods of modern history writing were introduced to the Arabic-speaking world.

Reclaiming this historiographical insight for al-Maqrizi has been one of the underlying arguments of this book. It has been articulated not only by analyzing the sequence, scope, and content of al-Maqrizi's Egyptian historical project, but also by reconstructing its formulation in connection with the author's family background, complex system of belief and notion of identity, intellectual formation and influences, career twists and turns, entanglement with patrons and peers, and final denouement when he decided to retreat from public life and spend the rest of his days writing. Carrying the narrative into al-Maqrizi's posthumous reputation and the afterlife of his historical work in the modern period is the objective of these last two chapters.[10] The

the dominant Western one, within the Western culture of modernity, see Wael B. Hallaq, "On Orientalism, Self-Consciousness and History," *Islamic Law and Society* 18, 3/4 (2011): 387–439; the themes discussed in that article were further elaborated in idem, *Restating Orientalism. A Critique of Modern Knowledge* (New York: Columbia University Press, 2018), 1–26.

[9] The renewed interest in chorography (or writing about place or region), a field of inquiry that went out of use with the advent of modern cartography and urban planning, could benefit from the inclusion of al-Maqrizi's *Khitat* (and the *khitat* genre in general) as a link between the classical tradition and the modern revival of the term and the practice. On the history and the revival of chorography with a focus on Scotland, see Darrell J. Rohl, "The Chorographic Tradition and Seventeenth- and Eighteenth-Century Scottish Antiquaries" *JAH* 5 (December 2011): 1–18, https://arthistoriography.files.wordpress.com/2011/12/rohl.pdf (last accessed November 30, 2020).

[10] See Menchinger, *First of the Modern Ottomans*, 260–7, where he analyzes the afterlife of the

aim is not only to provide a form of "closure" to the intellectual biography of this outstanding and unusual historian, but also to show how his reputation spread inside and outside Egypt beyond his time and how different contemporary audiences dealt with his legacy. The Ottomans were the first to translate excerpts of his *Khitat* and his *Shudhur al-ʿUqud* as sources for their own discussions on history and fiscal policy. Then the Orientalists discovered him when they were searching for Arab historians of the Crusades or those who narrated the history and geography of Egypt on the eve of the Napoleonic first colonial adventure there (1789–1801). The Mamlukists, this rather new specialized subgroup of Islamic historians, for whom he represented a major source on Egypt for generations, have recently taken to debate his trustworthiness and originality even though they still heavily depend on his material. To modern, nationalist Egyptian historians, however, he is not merely a more or less faithful recorder of Egyptian history, but also, and in ways closer to his spirit, a concerned son of Egypt whose entire historical project is a testimony to his worry for, and devotion and commitment to, his country. These qualities have provided for his memory to cross from scholarship to fiction and poetry, a fitting development for a historian who always wore his heart on his sleeve. Al-Maqrizi became an inspiration for novelists and poets who shared his love for Egypt or saw in his condemnation of the corruption and oppression of the Mamluks a model for them to follow, especially after the hardening of the 1952 Free Officers' "revolution" into an authoritarian regime, intolerant of any criticism or dissent.

Al-Maqrizi and the Ottomans

As the story of Shah Rukh's envoy asking for a copy of his *Suluk* in 1429 implies, al-Maqrizi was known outside Egypt during his lifetime. His reputation continued to grow after his death, as suggested by the profusion of manuscripts of his *Khitat* and their diverse locations around the Islamic world and beyond. When preparing his edition of the *Khitat* book in the late 1990s, Ayman Fu'ad Sayyid counted twenty-eight manuscripts in the Bibliothèque Nationale in Paris, fourteen in the British Library, fifteen in Dar al-Kutub (National Library) in Cairo, and thirty-five in Istanbul and other Turkish libraries, in addition to smaller numbers in various archives in Europe and the Arab world.[11] The numbers only grew in the interim with the

work of Ahmed Vasıf, the controversial Ottoman official, historian, and intellectual of the early nineeenth century; also Irwin, *Ibn Khaldun*, 162–203, which focuses on Ibn Khaldun's reception in scholarly circles from the Ottomans to the present.

11 Al-Maqrizi, *Khitat2*, 1: 107°–22°; Cahen, Claude. "Les chroniques arabes concernant la Syrie,

discovery of more manuscripts in those same depositories or in new ones.[12] It is safe to assume that the French and British copies (and other European specimens) were mostly acquired by diplomats, antiquarians, and Orientalists from Islamic repositories in Cairo and across the Ottoman Empire from at least the early eighteenth century. The Egyptian copies probably came from *waqfs* bequeathed to mosques and madrasas between al-Maqrizi's time and the mid-nineteenth century when the Dar al-Kutub was founded and started collecting manuscripts, or from the collections of Egyptian historians/collectors in the late nineteenth and early twentieth centuries, which were donated to or purchased by the Dar al-Kutub.[13] The Istanbul copies, however, were neither compiled in Turkey nor procured in modern times. Some of them were probably brought to Istanbul with the various artifacts and expensive colored marble revetments which Sultan Selim I (r. 1502–20) and his notables plundered from Mamluk Cairo after its conquest in 1517.[14] Others might have been brought later by Ottoman governors or officials in Egypt and Arab provinces and then have found their way either to the royal libraries in Istanbul or to Europe.[15]

But the sheer number and variety of dates of acquisition of *Khitat* manuscripts kept in Istanbul or acquired by Ottoman officials denote a more sustained interest in his work than just the possession of a trophy after a conquest or the endowment of a well-known book to a library. There clearly was an Ottoman readership in Istanbul, and possibly in other cities, drawn to

l'Égypte, et la Mésopotamie de la conquête arabe à la conquête ottomane dans les bibliothèques d'Istanbul," *REI* 4 (1936): 333–62.

[12] On the *Khitat* manuscript discovered in Michigan in 2010, see Gardiner with Bauden, "A Recently Discovered Holograph." Bauden in 2014 estimated the number of *Khitat* manuscripts to be more than 250.

[13] Di-Capua, *Gatekeepers*, 93–111, for the complex history of the *daftarkhane*, its expanded collection, and its organization.

[14] Ibn Iyas, *Bada'i'*, 5: 179, specifically lists the madrasas al-Mahmudiyya, al-Mu'ayadiyya and al-Sarghitmishiyya, among unnamed others, as having been robbed of their valuable books. See also Ayman Fu'ad Sayyid, "Intiqal al-Makhtutat al-'Arabiyya ila Turkiya wa-Atharuhu fi Tawtid al-Sabgha al-Islamiyya li-l Khilafa al-'Uthmaniyya," *Buhuth al-Mu'tamar al-Dawli hawl al-'Ilm wa-l Ma'rifa fi al-'Alam al-'Uthmani*, Salih Sadawi Salih, ed. (Istanbul: IRCICA, 2000), 293–302; Benjamin Lellouch, *Les Ottomans en Égypte. Historiens et conquérants au XVIe siècle* (Louvain: Peeters, 2006), 19–20. This is a neglected topic of research.

[15] See al-Maqrizi, *Khitat2*, 1: 119°, for a complete manuscript of four volumes that was endowed by Sultan Mahmud (r. 1730–54); idem, *Khitat2*, 2: 64°, for a collection of nineteen of al-Maqrizi's epistles, now at Leiden University, which was owned by the Sayyid Muhammad Pasha, governor of Egypt in 1785–6; ibid., 2: 67°, for a copy of the *Khitat* owned by Masih Pasha, governor of Egypt in 1574–80, which is now in the library of the Institute of Oriental Studies in St. Petersburg. See also Ahmed El Shamsy, *Rediscovering the Islamic Classics: How Editors and Print Culture Transformed an Intellectual Tradition* (Princeton: Princeton University Press, 2020), 19–23.

al-Maqrizi's writing on Egypt. This may have been instigated by the Ottomans' desire to understand the conditions of this rich and important province that they had recently added to their possessions. But there may have been an altogether different reason as well that stemmed from al-Maqrizi's clarion role as a critic of un-Islamic policies under the Mamluks, providing a model for both the admirers of the Ottoman rulers (in contrast to the Mamluks) and their budding reformists trying to understand the signs of slowdown appearing from as early as the late sixteenth century. The intersection of these two interests is suggested by the translation of some of al-Maqrizi's texts into Turkish, probably to ensure a better diffusion among Ottoman readers who did not read Arabic, that is, the administrative class, as opposed to the ulama who did.[16] The first instance of translation, so far as we know, happened in 1547, thirty years after the conquest of Egypt. This is when Celalzade Ṣaliḥ Çelebi (d. 1565), a scholar, judge, historian and poet and the younger brother of the more famous historian and statesman Nişancı Celalzade Mustafa Çelebi, wrote a book on the history of Egypt entitled *Tarih-i Mısr-ı Cedîd* (*New History of Egypt*).[17] Celalzade collected the material for his book while in Cairo on a mission to inspect the management of the Egyptian *waqfs* in 1547 and published it when he returned to Istanbul in the same year. He incorporated large sections from al-Maqrizi's *Khitat*, and from other Mamluk historians, including two books of al-Suyuti, and added his own observations

[16] A more sustained movement of translation occurred much later during the vizierate of Nevşehirli Damat Ibrahim Pasha (r. 1718–30) under sultan Ahmed III. Ibrahim Pasha, considered a progressive vizier, had many books translated from different languages, most notably Aristotle. Ironically, it was al-'Ayni, *'Iqd al-Juman*, which he chose to translate of the fifteenth-century Mamluk universal histories. See Ali Nihat Kundak, "The Influence of European Book Paintings on the Miniatures of Tercüme-i 'İkdü'l-cümân fî târîh-i ehli'z-zamân," *Proceedings of the Fourteenth International Congress of Turkish Art (2011)*, Frédéric Hitzel, ed. (Paris: Collège de France, 2013), 459–66. This translation carries echoes of the earlier report of al-'Ayni simultaneously translating his book into Turkish as he was reading it to Sultan Barsbay.

[17] Celalzade Ṣaliḥ Çelebi, *Tarih-i Mısr-ı Cedîd*, Tuncay Bülbül, ed. (Ankara: Grafiker Yayınları, 2011). A manuscript of the book in the British Library, Add 7849, is dated to the seventeenth century. Charles Bieu, *Catalogue of the Turkish Manuscripts in the British Museum* (London: the British Museum, 1888), 67–8, provides some information on the content of the manuscript and lists other manuscripts including an autograph one in Vienna, https://archive.org/details/catalogueofturkioobrituoft/page/66/mode/2up (last accessed December 1, 2020). For information about Celalzade, his book and its contents, I am indebted to Aleksandar Shopov, who shared with me his observations about the readership of al-Maqrizi in Istanbul and his dissertation "Between the Pen and the Fields: Books on Farming, Changing Land Regimes, and Urban Agriculture in the Ottoman Eastern Mediterranean ca. 1500–1700," PhD diss. Harvard University, 2016. On Celalzade's biography, see Tayyib Gökbilgin, "Celâl-zâde," *İslam Ansiklopedisi* 44 vols. (Eskişehir: Milli Eğitim Basımevi 1997), 3: 61–3.

on contemporary developments while in Cairo to bring the narrative to 1546. Celalzade says that of all the books he read on the history of Egypt he found al-Maqrizi's to be "the most beautiful, marvelous, and detailed," though he also benefited from the works of other Mamluk historians such as al-Suyuti.[18] His *Tarih-i Misr-i Cedîd*, which is highly autobiographical, enjoyed a degree of popularity among his peers and superiors, as evidenced by its numerous manuscript copies held in libraries in Istanbul, Cairo, and elsewhere. Celalzade was sent back to Cairo again in 1550, this time as a judge, probably because of his book and his success in his first mission as an inspector of *waqf*s. But he retired soon thereafter at an unknown date and returned to Istanbul to live in a small house next to his brother's mansion near the mosque of Eyup, devoting himself to writing in a pattern similar to al-Maqrizi's.[19]

There was another translation of al-Maqrizi's *Khitat* in the mid-sixteenth century, which has not been properly studied, and which I did not have the chance to consult. Three manuscripts are listed in Karatay's Catalogue of the Topkapi Museum Library (# R. 1394, R. 1395, and R. 1396) and each is labeled "Müntehab-ı Terceme-i Hitat-i Makrîzî" (sections of the translation of al-Maqrizi's *Khitat*).[20] Karatay states that the translation is of the third volume of the *Khitat*, presumably the section containing the typological surveys of the monuments of Cairo, but I could not find a more detailed description of the content. The first two manuscripts are tentatively dated to the sixteenth and seventeenth centuries respectively, while the third, R. 1396, is dated in the text to 975/1567–8. I cannot tell whether these are copies of the same text or sections of a continuous translation. If the latter, then this must be a substantial section of the original, as the total number of pages of the three manuscripts will amount to more than 1000 pages. Several names of translators are mentioned in various sources; none of them is a known figure.[21] The famous Ottoman encyclopedic bibliographer Kâtip Çelebi (Haji Khalifa), in his *Kashf al-Zunun*, mentions a translation of the *Khitat* which he dates to 969/1561–2 and ascribes to an unnamed scholar working for the

[18] Shopov, "Between the Pen and the Fields," 162–3, 219–20.

[19] Gökbilgin, "Celâl-zâde"; J. R. Walsh, "Djalālzāde Ṣāliḥ Čelebi", *EI*[2], 2: 400–1.

[20] Fehmi Edhem Karatay, *Topkapi Sarayi Müzesi Kütüphanesi türkçe yazmalar katalogu C. 1 Din, Tarih, Bilimler* (Istanbul: Topkapi Sarayi Müzesi, 1961), 191–2. I am indebted to Gül Kale for drawing my attention to this translation and for providing the references, a copy of the appropriate pages from Karatay's catalog, and translation from Turkish.

[21] Karatay, *Catalog*, 191 mentions that in Mehmed Tahir, *Osmanli Muellifleri* (Istanbul: Meral Yayınları, 1975), 3: 164, the translation was ascribed to someone called Zenbili-zade Abdulbaki, who is unknown. Karatay also notices that Tahir states on p. 159 that Zihni Mehmed Efendi (d. 1714), who was a court scribe, wrote a book on the history of Misru'l-Kahire, about which there is no additional information, https://archive.org/details/OsmanlMMellifleri3.Cild-BursalaMehmedTdhirEfendi/mode/2up (last accessed December 1, 2020).

Amir Ibrahim al-Daftari, who is also otherwise unidentified.[22] Charles Bieu, in his catalogue of the British Library Turkish manuscripts, lists a translation of al-Maqrizi's *Khitat*, Add. 7856, of 341 folios that covers the first half of the Arabic original from the introduction to the end of the Fatimid period (the first volume of the Bulaq edition).[23] The manuscript is dated to 970/1563, but the copyist mentions that he transcribed the manuscript from the autograph copy of the translator, Mawlana Yusuf b. Shukrallah b. Muhammad al-Ansari, who lived at the Citadel of the Mountain in Cairo and stated that he completed the translation on the 20th of Shawwal 969/June 23, 1562. This is most probably the translation mentioned by Haji Khalifa. But could the three manuscripts at the Topkapi have belonged to the same translation, since the date of Ms. R. 1396 is only slightly later and since it is a translation of the third volume of the original, which would have been logically undertaken after the completion of the first volume's translation? The hypothesis is tempting, but I cannot resolve it given my current inability to access the Topkapi library.

Another, more securely attributable, instance of translation from al-Maqrizi's corpus occurred thirty years later in 1599 when the judge of Thessaloniki, Kemalüddin Meḥmed Efendi (d. 1621), translated *Shudhur al-'Uqud fi Dhikr al-Nuqud*.[24] Kemalüddin, who would later become a judge in Damascus, Cairo, and Istanbul, and the military judge of Rumelia, is said to have decided to translate the book during a *majlis* (assembly) with the famous Grand Vizier Koca Sinan Pasha (d. 1596), who had twice served as governor of Egypt (1567–9, 1571–4) and had built there one of the most impressive Ottoman mosques in Cairo, the Sinan Pasha Mosque in Bulaq in 1573.[25] This connection may have provided the impetus for the translation of al-Maqrizi's

[22] Haji Khalifa, *Kashf al-Zunun 'an Asami al-Kutub wa-l Funun* 2 vols., Muhammad Şherefttin Yaltakaya and Rif'at Bilge al-Kilisli, eds. (Istanbul: Maarif Matbaasi 1941) (offset copy by Dar Ihya' al-Turath al-'Arabi, Beirut), 1: 715–16. The only reference to an Amir Ibrahim al-Daftari that I could find is in Muhibb al-Din al-Muhibbi, *Tarikh Khulasat al-Athar fi A'yan al-Qarn al-Hadi 'Ashar*, 4 vols., Muhammad Hasan Isma'il, ed. (Beirut: Dar al-Kutub al-'Ilmiyya, 2006), 4: 296. The Amir in question was the governor of Damascus for a few days in Jamada al-Akhira 1033/April 1624 after the appointed governor died suddenly and lasted until his replacement arrived. It is difficult to assume that this is the same Ibrahim al-Daftari who was patronizing translations more than sixty years earlier in Cairo.

[23] Bieu, *Catalogue of the Turkish manuscripts in the British Museum*, 65, https://archive.org/details/catalogueofturkioobrituoft/page/64/mode/2up (last accessed December 1, 2020).

[24] Shopov, "Between the Pen and the Fields," 239–40; see also Cemal Kafadar, "Les troubles monétaires de la fin du XVle siècle et la prise de conscience Ottomane du déclin," *Annales: Économies, Sociétés, Civilisations* 46, 2 (1991): 390–4.

[25] On Koca Sinan Paşa, see Nicolas Michel, "Les *waqf*-s d'un homme d'État ottoman dans la seconde moitié du XVIe siècle," *Turcica* 43 (2011): 276–80, for his endowments in Egypt and his reputation there as a great builder.

treatise on the monetary crisis in Mamluk Egypt and his sharia-based recommendations for solving it, but there is no way of proving it. What is more certain is that al-Maqrizi furnished the argument and the precedent for Kemalüddin Efendi to discuss in the introduction he wrote to the translation, which deals with the present Ottoman context, a similar problem to that diagnosed by his predecessor: the depreciation of defective akçe coinage, whose percentage of silver was less than required. Kemalüddin Efendi, like al-Maqrizi, attributed the crisis to deviation from silver and gold standards, the traditional Islamic currency. He further observed that tax collectors were benefiting from manipulating the exchange rate between Ottoman akçe coins and silver and gold and from channeling the defective coinage into government spending, thus costing the state treasury huge losses.[26] As Cemal Kafadar observed, however, there was in Kemalüddin Efendi's text a certain confidence in the ability of the treasury to overcome these financial troubles if it were to return to the proper standards.[27] It is interesting to note that of all al-Maqrizi's generally pessimistic works, *Shudhur al-'Uqud* is more upbeat as it was composed with an eye to gaining notice from the Sultan al-Mu'ayyad Shaykh during a similar financial crisis at the beginning of his reign. Later generations of Ottoman statesmen and historians from as early as the early eighteenth century were to become less convinced of the ability of the sultanate to transcend its chronic problems. They, as I have suggested was the case for al-Maqrizi, tried to find in Ibn Khaldun's cyclical interpretation of history and his theorization of the rise and fall of empires a framework for their own understanding of Ottoman history.[28]

Al-Maqrizi, Napoléon, and the Early Orientalists

It was around the same time that al-Maqrizi was discovered in Europe and treated essentially as a local informant on premodern Egyptian history and geography. Translations of some of his work started appearing with the rise

[26] Shopov, "Between the Pen and the Fields," 240.

[27] Kafadar, "Les troubles monétaires," 390.

[28] Cornell Fleischer, "Royal Authority, Dynastic Cyclism, and 'Ibn Khaldunism' in Sixteenth-Century Ottoman Letters," *Journal of Asian and African Studies* 18, 3–4 (1983): 198–220; Irwin, *Ibn Khaldun*, 162–4. These works include Katib Celebi (Hajji Khalifa), *Dustur al-Amal li Islah al-Khalal* (*Code of Practice for the Rectification of Defects*) (1652), which outlined the cycle of regimes following the Khaldunian pattern and suggested that the Ottoman Empire was in the early stages of old age. His disciple the historian Mustafa Na'ima, in his 1704 *Ta'riḫ-i Na'ima*, or *Rauḍat al-Ḥusain fi Hulaṣat Aḫbar al-Hafiqain*, 6 vols. (Istanbul: Maṭba'a-i 'Amira, 1864–6), 1: 33–46, starts with an exposé on the rise and fall of states that is based on Ibn Khaldun's cycle.

of colonial interest in the "Orient" and the beginning of the relentless movement of collecting Islamic manuscripts from mosques and madrasas, private collections, and booksellers in the great Arab cities by travelers, orientalists, and consuls-cum-antiquarians for European repositories in the eighteenth century.[29] Al-Maqrizi's first European editors and translators and their sponsors were predictably more interested in treatises and sections of his large historical compendia that were more relevant to European history or to current European interests in Egypt and beyond.

The first text by al-Maqrizi to appear in a European language, so far as I can ascertain, was the extracts related to Louis IX from the *Suluk* translated by the French orientalist and secretary-interpreter of the king Denis Dominique Cardonne, which he published in 1761 as part of his "Extraits des manuscripts arabes dans lesquels il est parlé des évènements historiques relatifs au règne de S. Louis," with other extracts on the same subject from other Mamluk historians such as Ibn Taghri-Birdi and Abu al-Fida.[30] This was followed by the first complete work of al-Maqrizi to appear in an edited Arabic text and a Latin translation: his treatise on Abyssinia (Ethiopia), *al-Ilmam bi-Akhbar man bi-Arḍ al-Ḥabash min Muluk al-Islam*, published with a chapter extracted from Abu al-Fida's famous geographical compendium, *Taqwim al-Buldan*, "Dhikr al-Janib al-Janubi min al-Arḍ wa-Huwa Bilad al-Sudan," also on the part of Africa south of the Sahara known to Muslim geographers.[31]

Translations and publications of further segments of the *Suluk* and the *Khitat* that would interest the European reader followed, especially right before and immediately after the short-lived but tremendously impactful Napoleonic invasion of Egypt (1798–1801), euphemistically called *L'expedition d'Égypte* in French.[32] One early example, and a clear sign of the

[29] Marina Tolmacheva, "The Medieval Arabic Geographers and the Beginnings of Modern Orientalism," *IJMES* 27 (1995), 141–56; Ina Baghdiantz McCabe, *Orientalism in Early Modern France: Eurasian Trade, Exoticism, and the Ancien Régime* (New York: Berg, 2008), 101–36.

[30] Denis Dominique Cardonne, "Extraits des manuscripts arabes dans lesquels il est parlé des évènements historiques relatifs au règne de S. Louis," as an addendum to a collection of treatises on St Louis, *Histoire de Saint Louis par Jehan Sire de Joinville, Les annals de son règne*, and *Sa vie et ses miracles* (Paris: Imprimerie royale, 1761), 525–45 (republished as Collection complète des mémoires relatifs à l'histoire de France; v. 3, 1819); Bauden, "al-Maqrīzī," 185.

[31] Al-Maqrizi, *Macrizi historia regum islamiticorum in Abyssinia. Interpretatus est et una cum Abulfedae descriptione regionum nigritarum e codd. biblioth. Leidensis*, Friedrich Theodor Rink, ed. and trans. (Leiden: Sam. et Joh. Luchtmans, 1790). The Arabic text was re-published a century later in Cairo as *al-Ilmam bi-Akhbar man bi-Arḍ al-Ḥabash min Muluk al-Islam* (Cairo: Matbaʿat al-Ta'lif, 1895).

[32] A recent wide-ranging study of the Napoleonic invasion of Egypt is Juan Cole, *Napoleon's Egypt: Invading the Middle East* (New York: Palgrave Macmillan, 2007); Geoffrey Symcox, "The Geopolitics of the Egyptian Expedition, 1797–1798," in *Napoléon in Egypt*, Irene

colonialist schemes to come, was the publication in 1799 by Louis Langlés, then keeper of Oriental manuscripts at the National Library, of al-Maqrizi's section on the ancient Red Sea Canal (Suez Canal) that connected the Nile to the Red Sea, followed in 1800 by another translated memorandum on various canals in Egypt, the Nilometer, the Pyramids, Alexandria and the oases, extracted from the *Khitat* and other Mamluk sources.[33] The timing and choice of translations from al-Maqrizi by Langlès, who otherwise was known as a translator and annotator of English and Persian travel texts in Persia and India and the redactor of a Manchu–French dictionary, do not seem to have been haphazard.[34] In an obituary of Langlés's in Britain's *The Asiatic Journal* of June 1824, he is said to have presented a lecture at the Institut National de France at an unspecified date, but probably around 1797–8, in which he persuasively demonstrated the "possibility of opening a passage to India through Egypt, and thereby striking a death-blow at British supremacy in the East."[35] Napoléon Bonaparte, who was a member of the Institut and present at that lecture, was very impressed by Langlès's argument. He requested a copy of the text, asked many questions, and "from that time turned his whole attention to the conquest of Egypt." Of course, this was not the first time that France pondered the occupation of Egypt or the digging of a canal that would connect

A. Bierman, ed. (Reading: Ithaca Press, 2003): 13–31; Henri Laurens, "Les Lumières et l'Égypte," in *Orientales I: Autour de l'expédition d'Égypte* (Paris: CNRS, 2004), 49–54.

33 Louis Langlès, "Histoire du Canal de Messr (vulgairement nommé Canal de Suez), tirée de la description historique 'Le Livre des avis et sujets de réflexions sur la description géographique et historique de l'Égypte par al-Maqryzy, et traduite,'" *Magasin Encyclopédique* 5 (1799): 289–310; idem, "Le Livre des avis et sujets de réflexions sur la description géographique et historique de l'Égypte par Ebn āl-Maqryzy, 1er extrait contenant la description historique du canal de l'Égypte (de Suez); II. Textes des différentes descriptions ou notices du canal de Messr, données par les auteurs arabes, [édité avec une traduction française]," *Notices et extraits des manuscrits de la Bibliothèque Nationale* 6 (1800/1801): 320–86. Both texts were reprinted in Sezgin, *Studies on al-Maqrizi*, 1: 1–89.

34 On Langlès's life and work (and some hints of plagiarism and defensiveness) see Abel Rémusat, *Notice sur la vie et les ouvrages de M. L.-M. Langlès* (Paris: Dondey-Dupré, 1824), https://gallica.bnf.fr/ark:/12148/bpt6k97669768.r=louis%20langles?rk=77 2536;0 (last accessed June 19, 2020); Bon-Joseph Dacier, "Notice historique sur la vie et les ouvrages de M. Langlès," *Histoire et mémoires de l'Institut royal de France* 9 (1831): 100–116, https://www.persee.fr/doc/minf1267-89961831num911258 (last accessed June 19, 2020).

35 *The Asiatic Journal and Monthly Register for British India and its Dependencies*, 17 (January–June 1824): 272–3, https://books.google.com/books?id=SYYAAAAYAAJ&pg=PA272&lpg=PA272&dq=Louis-Mathieu+Langlès+suez&source (last accessed June 18, 2020). It is interesting to note that the French obituaries omit this point, probably because they were written when France again had a royal regime and it would have been impertinent to emphasize the connection between the celebrated deceased and a defunct emperor, or because the animosity between the two had by then overshadowed any memory of a time in which the scholar and the general shared the same views.

the Mediterranean to the Red Sea. Leading scholarly and political figures such as the German philosopher Gottfried Leibniz, the traveler and scholar Comte de Volney (who knew Langlès), and the Directorate's redoubtable minister of foreign affairs Talleyrand had previously advised various French regimes to do just that.[36] Napoléon was definitely aware of that long history of colonial ambition and of its resurrection after the Revolution and under the Directorate. In fact, he was, along with Talleyrand, its main instigator. Article 2 of the directive he received from the Directorate on April 12, 1798, written by Talleyrand and authorizing the Egyptian expedition, stipulated that "The general in chief of the Army of the Orient will seize Egypt; he will chase the English from all their possessions in the Orient; and he will destroy all of their settlements on the Red Sea. He will then cut the Isthmus of Suez and take all the necessary measures in order to assure the free and exclusive possession of the Red Sea for the French Republic."[37] What is different in the intervention of Langlès is that it used concrete historic evidence to make the case for the viability of a canal. His translation of al-Maqrizi's collection of Arabic sources on the ancient Khalij Amir al-Mu'minin and its route offered tangible indications to Bonaparte about where to look for this long-lost waterway, which he promptly set out to search for shortly after his occupation of Cairo, managing to locate a few of its traces near the Bitter Lakes.[38] The irony is that Langlès refused all of Bonaparte's entreaties to accompany the *Expedition d'Égypte*, which earned him the ire of the general, who never forgave him for that rejection and never acknowledged him as one of the visionaries behind the Egyptian campaign.[39] The instrumentalization of al-Maqrizi's text

[36] The most exhaustive survey of the French obsession with Egypt and the Suez canal between the reign of Louis XIV and Napoleon is Jules-Charles Roux, *L'isthme et le Canal de Suez: Historique—État Actuel*, 2 vols. (Paris: Hachette, 1901), 1: 55–125; for a brief recounting see Zachary Karabell, *Parting the Desert: The Creation of the Suez Canal* (New York: Knopf, 2003), 12–21; see also the discussion by Thierry Hentsch, *Imagining the Middle East*, Fred Reed trans. (Montréal: Black Rose, 1992), on Leibniz's project 94–8, and Volney's, 123–30.

[37] Roux, *L'isthme*, 1: 128; Karabell, *Parting the Desert*, 20.

[38] Roux, *L'isthme*, 1: 139, Napoléon left Cairo on December 24, 1798 (Christmas Eve!) with several of his generals and savants.

[39] Nonetheless, his translations of al-Maqrizi appear in the *Descriptions de l'Égypte* (see note below). Although the list of Langlès's publication is digitized online, I could not find a separate text of a lecture on Egypt and the Suez Canal given at the Institut National de France, where Langlès was a prominent member. It is interesting to note that the publication date of al-Maqrizi's text on the canal, 1799, makes it very plausible that the lecture that Napoléon attended was either the draft of al-Maqrizi's published text or a portion of it with remarks on the current situation with the British controlling India and many ports in the Red Sea that were omitted from the published text. Langlès, who generally shunned politics, seems to have been a virulent nationalist and a critic of the British. In his *Catalogue des principaux ouvrages de M. Langlès* (Paris: Le Normant Imprimeur-Librairie, 1811), https://gallica.bnf.fr/ark:/12148/bpt6k93111127.r=louis%20langles?rk=21459;2 (last accessed June 20, 2020), two

in the service of colonial aims, however, was not to bear immediate results. Napoléon entrusted the reconstruction of the ancient channel's route and the study of the feasibility of digging a canal between the Mediterranean and the Red Sea to the engineer J. M. Le Père, who wrote an extensive report where he incorrectly concluded that there is a ten-meter difference between the Red Sea level and the Nile level, making it very costly and risky to build a canal connecting the two.[40] This risible technical error delayed the actual construction of a canal at the Isthmus of Suez for fifty years, when another Frenchman, Ferdinand de Lesseps, received the concession for the Suez Canal from Saïd Pasha in 1854.

Evidently, not all translations of al-Maqrizi (or other medieval Islamic authors) at the time had a direct bearing on the imperial project, although the interest in Arabic and other "Oriental" languages and history was definitely bolstered by the budding colonial enterprise and its mounting need for officers, advisors, and administrators conversant with the languages, mores, and cultures of those soon to be colonized. This is how the establishment and expansion of instruction in oriental languages at the university level in European capitals should be contextualized, and this is exactly how Langlès presented his case for the creation of a special school for the "living" oriental languages in front of the Assemblée Nationale in 1790, a mere year after the French Revolution and only eight years before the dawn of France's colonial forays into the Arab world.[41] The École spéciale des langues orientales vivantes

lectures are listed: *Observations sur les relations politiques et commerciales de l'Angleterre avec la France*, whose text is unavailable, and *Observations sur les relations politiques et commerciales de l'Angleterre et de la France avec la Chine, par L. Langlès* (Paris: impr. de Delance et Lesueur, an XIII–1805), https://catalogue.bnf.fr/ark:/12148/cb323465077 (last accessed June 20, 2020), which starts with a diatribe against Lord [*sic*] Robert Clive, the first British Governor of the Bengal Presidency, moves on to praise the expansionist commercial policy of the British and chastises the French, and ends with an expected note on the necessity to train French traders in the languages and cultures of the countries in which they conduct their business. Langlès here reveals a side of his personality and interest that contradicts the general tenor of reports about his reluctance to indulge in politics and corresponds instead to what the British obituary ascribes to him—patriotism and a sharp sense of competitiveness with the British—while maintaining his priorities as a scholar concerned with the propagation of the study of Oriental languages and cultures.

40 See J. M. Le Père, "Mémoire sur la communication de la mer des Indes à la Méditerranée par la mer Rouge et l'Isthme de Sueys," *Descriptions de l'Égypte*, Vol. 11 (État Moderne) (Paris: L'imprimerie impériale, 1809), 11: 21–186, pp. 49–51, for the report he sent to Napoléon informing him of the results of his measurements, and pp. 84, 180–5, where he quotes Langlès' translation of al-Maqrizi and copies large sections of both publications cited above. On Le Père's error, see Roux, *L'isthme*, 1: 147–50; Charles Coulston Gillispie and Michael Dewachter, eds., *Monuments of Egypt. The Napoleonic Edition: The Complete Archaeological Plates from la Description de l'Égypte* (Princeton: Princeton University Press, 1987), 10–12.

41 Louis Langlès, "De l'importance des langues orientales pour l'extension du commerce, le

was finally founded in 1795, and Langlès became its first administrator and Professor of Persian. But the most prominent scholar at this new school, and the one who will lead the consistent effort to translate classical Arabic texts as a method of inquiry, was Langlès's colleague and teacher Antoine Isaac Silvestre de Sacy (1758–1838). This prodigious editor of Arabic and Persian texts, archivist, translator, state official and one of the principal founders of modern Orientalism as a discipline became the first Arabic teacher at the École spéciale (to which he added Persian in 1806), where he taught an entire generation of French Orientalists and Egyptologists.[42] For the benefit of his students, he edited and translated sections from various Mamluk historical works and published them in three large volumes under the rhyming Arabic title *Kitab al-Anis al-Mufid lil-Taleb al-Mustafid wa Jamiʿ al-Shuzur min Manzum wa Manthur* (The Pleasant and Profitable Companion for the Studious Pupil and the Collector of fragments of both Poetry and Prose), and the French subtitle *Chrestomathie arabe, ou, Extraits de divers écrivains arabes, tant en prose qu'en vers, avec une traduction française et des notes, à l'usage des élèves de l'École royale et spéciale des langues orientales vivantes* (1806).[43] Fragments from al-Maqrizi's *Khitat* and *Suluk*, with no clear order or chronology, occupy a large portion of De Sacy's anthologies, along with shorter fragments from Ibn Khaldun's *Kitab al-ʿIbar* and others, mostly Mamluk historians.[44] Since the *Chrestomathie arabe* became the premier Arabic text-

progrès des lettres et des sciences, adresse à l'Assemblée nationale, par L. Langlès" (Paris: Champigny, 1790), https://gallica.bnf.fr/ark:/12148/bpt6k8524044.r=louis%20langles?rk=214593;2 (last accessed June 19, 2020).

42 For a critical assessment of De Sacy's career, methods, and output, see Edward Saïd, *Orientalism* (New York: Pantheon, 1978), 122–31; for a less negative review, see Christian Décobert, "L'orientalisme, des Lumières à la Révolution, selon Silvestre de Sacy," *Revue du monde musulman et de la Méditerranée* 52, 1(1989): 49–62. Also Ian Coller, *Arab France: Islam and the Making of Modern Europe, 1798–1831* (Berkeley: University of California Press, 2011), 110–12. A broader evaluation of de Sacy's contribution to Orientalism is Alain Messaoudi, "Figures d'un père de l'orientalisme moderne: Les représentations de Silvestre de Sacy à travers ses biographes," in Nora Lafi, Michel Espagne and Pascale Rabault-Feuerhahn, eds., *Silvestre de Sacy. Le projet européen d'une science orientaliste* (Paris: Éditions du Cerf, 2014), 23–40.

43 The more common, and appropriate, title for the anthologies is *Chrestomathie arabe, ou, Extraits de divers écrivains arabes, tant en prose qu'en vers, avec une traduction française et des notes, à l'usage des élèves de l'École royale et spéciale des langues orientales vivantes*, 3 vols. (Paris: Imprimerie impériale, 1806). See François Déroche, "La 'Chrestomathie arabe' de Silvestre de Sacy," in Lafi et al., *Silvestre de Sacy*, 61–71. The relevant translations from al-Maqrizi in the *Chrestomathie* were reprinted in Sezgin, *Studies on al-Maqrizi*, 1: 91–243.

44 Saïd, *Orientalism*, 128–30, argues that incoherent fragments are essentially the building blocks of the Orientalist's métier, who with his scholarly work will endow them with a new rationality appropriate for the new field of learning, Orientalism, which was being developed then.

book for all orientalists under training throughout Europe in the first half of the nineteenth century, al-Maqrizi's name and work became even more familiar and interest in editing and translating fragments of his books more widespread. The most important of these translations and editions is the systematic translation of a sizeable chunk of the *Suluk* with profuse annotation by the French Orientalist Étienne Quatremère, *Histoire des sultans mamlouks de l'Égypte, écrite en arabe par Taki-eddin-Ahmed-Makrizi*, between 1837 and 1845. The translation covers the reigns of the Mamluk sultans from Aybak to al-Nasir Muhammad, and is still consulted today by historians of Mamluk Egypt. Quatremère also offers the first complete biography of al-Maqrizi in a Western language.[45]

Some European scholars translated their chosen sections under different titles from that of the entire book from which they were excerpted. This led later editors to sometimes mistake them as separate works by al-Maqrizi. This is the case, for example, with the texts on the Christians (Copts) and Jews of Egypt, extracted from the *Khitat* and published as separate tracts by several scholars before more systematic and complete translations were attempted by prominent orientalists.[46] The Arabic texts were re-published several times as independent titles, with the collection on the Copts of Egypt acquiring the authenticating rhyming title *Qawl al-ibrizi lil-ʿallamah al-Maqrizi* (The

[45] Étienne Quatremère, *Histoire des sultans mamlouks de l'Égypte, écrite en arabe par Taki-eddin-Ahmed-Makrizi*, 2 vols. in four sections (Paris: Oriental Translation Fund of Great Britain and Ireland, 1837–45). For the biography of al-Maqrizi, see vol. 1, t. 1, I–XIX. For a contemporary review of the book, see William M. de Slane, "Compte-rendu, Étienne Quatremère, *Histoire des sultans mamlouks de l'Égypte.*" *Journal asiatique* (3rd ser.) 6 (1838): 615–20.

[46] The first such publication consisted of the extracts translated by Heinrich Joseph Wetzer and added to a book on church history by Leander van Ess, *Restitutio veræ chronologiæ rerum ex controversiis Arianis inde ab anno 325 usque ad annum 350 exortarum contra chronologiam hodie receptam exhibita, una cum specimine historiæ Coptorum a Makrisio Arabice scriptæ* (Frankfurt am-Main, Sumptibus et Typis H. L. Brœnneri, 1821), republished separately with further notes as *Taki-eddini Makrizii historia Coptorum Christianorum in Aegypto Arabice*, ed. and trans. Heinrich Joseph Wetzer (Sulzbach, Germany: in Libraria J. E. de Seideliana, 1828). This was followed by a German translation by the famous orientalist Ferdinand Wüstenfeld, *Geschichte der Copten: aus den Handschriften zu Gotha und Wien mit Übersetzung und Ammerkungen* (Göttingen: Dieterichschen Buchhandlung, 1845), and an English translation by the Rev. S. C. Malan, *A Short History of the Copts and of Their Church* (London: D. Nutt, 1873). More systematic translations were later published in French: L. Leroy, trans., "Les synagogues des juifs (Moïse et Élie d'après les traditions arabes)," *ROC* 11 (2nd ser., vol. 1) (1906): 149–62, 371–402; idem, "Les églises des chrétiens: traduction de l'arabe d'al-Makrizi," *ROC* 12 (2nd ser., vol. 2) (1907): 190–208, 269–79; idem, "Les couvents des chrétiens: traduction de l'arabe d'al-Makrizi," trans. L. Leroy, *ROC* 13 (2nd ser., vol. 3) (1908): 33–46, 192–204; Leroy's three studies are reprinted in Sezgin, *Studies on al-Maqrizi*, 2: 147–251.

Golden Saying by the Learned Scholar al-Maqrizi), further lending it the semblance of a distinct work, to the point where it was published several times in Egypt by Egyptian editors as a discrete work of al-Maqrizi.[47] Paradoxically, the reverse also happened in the early days of translation of al-Maqrizi's oeuvre in Europe. An Arabic extract of the *Khitat* on Damietta, the Niletic city that witnessed several Crusader attacks, was translated into Latin as a separate title.[48] The Arabic text was most probably redacted in 1567 by a certain Ahmad ibn 'Uthman, possibly as a way of emphasizing the importance of the city as a *thaghr* (frontline city) and enhancing its reputation.[49] Frédéric Bauden suggested that the extracts functioned as a treatise of *fada'il* and noticed that the translator, Hamaker, did not translate the entire tract but stopped the history before the crusade of Louis IX, because he discovered that al-Maqrizi's text was copied from the earlier historians Ibn Wasil and Ibn al-Furat.[50] All in all, the early European interest in al-Maqrizi and the pioneering efforts of various Orientalists to bring his historical testimonies to bear on the reporting on European history or European geographic, economic, and political objectives in Egypt and the Orient, while valuable in bolstering al-Maqrizi's reputation or in making well-redacted editions of many of his texts available to a wider readership, led nonetheless to further confusion both about the exact number and titles of his works and about the historiographic context in which he worked in fifteenth-century Cairo.

Arabic Editions of al-Maqrizi's *Khitat*

The publication of the full text of al-Maqrizi's *Khitat* by the Amiri Press (Bulaq Press) in two volumes in 1853 marked a watershed in the study of

[47] Al-Maqrizi, *Qawl al-ibrizi* (Cairo: Matba'at al-Tawfiq, 1898), recently republished with the rising interest in Islamic titles as al-Maqrizi, *Tarikh al-Aqbat al-maruf bi-al-Qawl al-ibriz lil 'Allama al-Maqrizi*, 'Abd al-Majid Diyab, ed. (Cairo: Dar al-Fadila, 1998); also idem, *Tarikh al-Yahud wa-atharuhum fi Misr*, 'Abd al-Majid Diyab, ed. (Cairo: Dar al-Fadila, 1997).

[48] Al-Maqrizi, *Takyoddini Ahmedis al-Makrizii, Narratio de expeditionibus, a Graecis francisque adversus Dimyatham, ab A. C. 708 ad 1221 susceptis, e codicibus bibliothecae Lugduno-Batavae excerpsit*, Hendrik Arent Hamaker, ed. and trans. (Amsterdam: Pieper et Ipenbuur, 1824).

[49] Harvard University, Houghton Library, MS Arab 357, *Tarjamat thaghr Dimyāṭ wa-mā waqa'a bihā min 'ahd Nūḥ 'alayhi al-salām ilá ākhir dawlat al-Turk*, attributed to an unknown book, *al-'Anasir li-Majalis al-Malik al-Nasir*, f. 170-f. 196, bound with *Kitāb Ṭabaqāt al-aqṭāb fī dhikr awliyā' Allāh ta'ālá wa-aqwālihim wa-aḥwālihim ilá intihā' ājālihim*. Hamaker reports a different Arabic title, *Dhikr Ḥurūb al-Rūm wa-al-Firanj 'alá Dimyāṭ min Sanat Tis'īn ilá Sanat Thamānī 'Ashrat wa-Sittmāyah min al-Hijrah*.

[50] Bauden, "al-Maqrīzī," 173–4.

Cairo's history. The publication seems to have been privately sponsored by Raphael 'Ubaid (d. 1866), a little-known patron of education in Khedivial Egypt who, along with his brother, in 1860 established the 'Ubaydiyya School (today the Greek school Ubaydi Foundation in Hada'iq al-Qubba), which was an endowed primary and secondary school for boys, especially Greek Orthodox.[51] 'Ubaid is thanked in the colophon at the end of the second printed volume for "causing the circulation of the book and its apperception and utilization everywhere," a prescient statement that could have not predicted the popularity that this edition would enjoy.[52] 'Ubaid, who hailed from a Damascene family of the Greek Orthodox denomination which had settled in Egypt a generation earlier, was not an unusual publishing patron in Cairo at the time. Many philanthropists, motivated by a nationalist sense that sought to recover the Arabic heritage in the face both of Turkish Ottoman chauvinism and the growing European knowledge hegemony, have sponsored the publication of major classical Arabic sources in various fields.[53] What is remarkable about 'Ubaid is that he was the only non-Muslim patron in this gallery of philanthropists, and that he chose to sponsor a book of *Khitat*, probably as a token of his strong sense of belonging to Egypt despite being of *Shami* (Christian Syrian) extraction. That feeling comes through very clearly in the charter of the 'Ubaydiyya School he founded, in whose beautiful classical Arabic composition 'Ubaid was directly involved.[54]

The *Khitat* was compiled from an unknown number of manuscripts and edited and corrected by Muhammad ibn 'Abd al-Rahman Qutta al-'Adawi (1795–1864), a graduate of al-Azhar who was the head copy editor of the

51 On Raphael 'Ubaid, his family, wealth and philanthropy and his establishment of the 'Ubaydiyya School and its Christiano-Egyptian nationalist charter, see Na'um Chocair, *Tarikh Sina al-Qadim wa-l Hadith wa-Jughrafiyataha. Ma'Khulasat Tarikh Misr wa-l Sham wa-l'Iraqwa-Jazirat a-'Arabwa ma kanabaynaha min al-'Ala'iq al-Tijariyya wa-l Harbiyya wa-Ghayraha 'an Tariq Sina' min-Awal 'Ahd al-Tarikh ila al-Yawm* (Cairo: Dar al-Ma'arif, 1916), 267–78. Viewed via the electronic edition of the Hindawi Organization, https://www.hindawi.org/books/91480429/ (last accessed June 29, 2020).

52 Al-Maqrizi, *Khitat1*, 2: 521; the colophon states the date of publication as Monday 19th of Safar 1270/ 21 November 1853. Sayyid, *Musawwadat*, 91, n. # 1 notes that this edition was published before the establishment of the Egyptian National Library in 1870, and that the manuscripts of historical books, al-Maqrizi's included, were still dispersed in madrasas and mosques and private libraries without any indexing or numbering systems, which means that there was no systematic way of identifying the manuscripts used. For the later editions, see Sayyid, *Musawwadat*, 92–3; idem, *Khitat2*, 1: 100°–2°.

53 On the history of the publication of major Arabic sources in Egypt, see Mahmud Muhammad al-Tanahi, *Fi al-Lugha wa-l Adab: Buhuth wa-Dirasat*, 2 vols. (Beirut: Dar al-Gharb al-Islami, 2002), 2: 640–9; On the motivation behind the publication of classical sources, see 'Abd al-Salam Harun, *Qutuf Adabiyya: Dirasat Naqdiyya fil-Turath al-'Arabi. Hawl Tahqiq al-Turath* (Cairo: Maktabat al-Sunna, 1988), 76–92.

54 Chocair, *Tarikh Sina*, 268–75.

publishing house, and who, among more than 300 other books, corrected and edited the original manuscripts of *Kalila wa-Dimna* and *One Thousand and One Nights* in 1857 and 1862/63 respectively.[55] Despite the effort that this pioneering editor expended in verifying his text, the published *Khitat* is extremely flawed, with countless typographical errors, misspellings, and whole sections omitted due to its reliance on a limited number of secondary manuscripts.[56] Yet this edition remained for more than a hundred and fifty years the only available complete text of the book, used by countless scholars. It will, in fact, be impossible to discard it totally, as any verification of sources for more than a century of scholarship on Egypt's history will have perforce to depend on its pagination. A second edition, which followed in 1908 in Cairo, this time in three volumes, was based on the Bulaq edition and was equally devoid of any mention of manuscript and redaction strategy.[57] Several editions have since been reprinted in offset form from one or other of the early editions, once in each of Beirut (1959), Cairo (1967–8), Baghdad (1970), and Damascus (1987), without any real editorial corrections, collation of variant readings from the numerous manuscripts available, or redaction.[58] An edition published in three volumes in 1998, and touted as a new edited version by its publisher, Madbuli of Cairo, totally depends on the old Bulaq edition and only adds slapdash and unnecessary comments and biographical notes while the text remains unaltered with all of its mistakes and even typos and its variants unverified.[59]

It was not until Ayman Fu'ad Sayyid embarked on a new critical edition of the *Khitat*, which he published in five volumes and one volume of indexes,

[55] On Qutta al-ʿAdawi's biography, see Muhammd Kamil al-Fiqqi, *al-Azhar wa Atharuhu fi al-Nahda al-Adabiyya al-Haditha*, 3 vols. (Cairo: Majmaʿ al-Buhuth in al-Azhar, 1982), 1: 123–6; Jean-Claude Garcin, *Pour une lecture historique des Mille et Une Nuits* (Paris: Actes Sud, 2013), 23–4.

[56] See Étienne-Marc Quatremère, "Compte rendu," *Journal des Savants* (1856): 321–37; reprinted in Sezgin, *Studies on al-Maqrizi*, 1: 333–49.

[57] Al-Maqrizi, *al-Mawaʿiz wa-al Iʿtibar bi-Dhikr al-Khitat wa-al-Athar, al-Mʿaruf bi-al-Khitat al-Maqriziyya* 3 vols. (Cairo: Matbaʿat al-Nil, 1908).

[58] The Beirut edition (Shiyyah, Lebanon: Matbaʿat al-Sahil al-Janubi, 1959) was published in three volumes after the 1908 Cairo edition as stated in the colophon at the end of its third volume. The 1967–8 Cairo edition follows the three-volume format and is prefaced by a study by Muhammd Mustafa Ziada on al-Maqrizi (Cairo: Dar al-Tahrir, 1967–8). The Baghdad edition is an offset copy of the 1853 Bulaq edition in 2 vols. (Baghdad: Maktabat al-Muthanna, 1970). The Damascus edition is not complete: it is presented as selections based on the Bulaq edition, *Min Kitab al-Mawaʿiz wa al-Iʿtibar bi Dhikr al-Khitat wa al-Athar li al-Maqrizi*, 4 vols., Zuhair Humaidan, ed. (Damascus: Ministry of Culture, 1987).

[59] Al-Maqrizi, *al-Mawaʿiz wa-al Iʿtibar bi-Dhikr al-Khitat wa-al-Athar, al-Mʿaruf bi-al-Khitat al-Maqriziyya*, Madihah Sharqawi and Muhammad Zaynuhum, eds., 3 vols. (Cairo: Maktabat Madbuli, 1998); see the devastating but justified review by Frédéric Bauden, *MSR* 8, 1 (2004): 299.

between 2002 and 2004, that a more reliable text of this crucial source was made available to researchers, although many still rely on the old Bulaq edition and some reviewers of the new edition still have substantial reservations about its structure and content.[60] This new edition came on the heels of a critical edition of an incomplete early draft of the *Khitat* by Sayyid as well in 1995. The manuscript of this early draft, written in al-Maqrizi's hand and dubbed "the second volume" by him (no first volume has been found), is 179 pages long, that is, less than one sixth of the Bulaq edition in length. Its unfinished status is evident from the many blank sections—whole pages at times—purposely left by the author to fill out with data he planned to collect, and from the many addenda in the margins or in the form of detached scraps of paper of different sizes and forms which were inserted among its pages. These loose sheets contain bits of historical, topographic, and biographical raw data collected from older sources and inserted in their appropriate place in the manuscript with a view to their being reworked and transferred to the text in a later draft. As we have seen, this incomplete draft of the *Khitat*, which Sayyid dates between 818 and 827/1415–24, provides a rare opportunity to assess the development of the book during its long period of gestation.[61] Together with the autographed notebook discovered by Frédéric Bauden, this draft has also allowed a fuller review of al-Maqrizi's use of sources and method of compilation and redaction, which is being revealed incrementally in Bauden's Maqriziana articles.

Translating al-Maqrizi's *Khitat*

Despite its importance, al-Maqrizi's *Khitat*, however, was never fully translated into any European language. This may be because of its length or its circumscribed focus on the specialized topic of Egypt's cities, or because of the difficulty in collating the vast number of its holographs and early manuscripts. The first to announce his intention to translate the full text was none other than the famed Arabist Étienne-Marc Quatremère. To prove his resolve, he affixed to the end of his critical review of the Bulaq edition a translation of al-Maqrizi's Introduction.[62] Yet, he never had the chance to move beyond that introduction, as we learn from the preface of another partial translation

[60] Al-Maqrizi, *Khitat2*. Frederic Bauden gave a mixed review of the first two volumes of this edition in *MSR* 11, 2 (2007): 169–76; Jean-Claude Garcin's review, *JESHO* 48, 1 (2005): 125–31, is more expansive but still as critical as Bauden's, yet it more generously recognizes the efforts of Sayyid.

[61] Sayyid, *Musawwadat*, 100.

[62] Quatremère, "Compte rendu," 327–37, where he announces that he was about to start his own translation of the *Khitat*.

of the *Khitat* by Urbain Bouriant, an Egyptologist by training who was then the director of the recently renamed Institut Français d'archéologie orientale du Caire (IFAO). Bouriant reproduced Quatremère's introduction at the beginning of the two volumes of translation he published in 1895 and 1900, that covered the first 250 pages of the Bulaq edition down to the section on the city of al-Nahririyya.[63] Although he too declared his intention to translate the entire *Khitat* in his preface, he never completed his project because of a long illness that led to his premature death in 1903.[64] His second volume was seen through publication by his colleague the Arabist Paul Casanova, who undertook the continuation of the project and published a third volume of translation in 1906 covering pp. 250–347 of the first volume of the Bulaq edition. Another volume of translation by Casanova, which came out in 1920, covered pp. 348–97.[65] In the preface to this fourth volume, Casanova defensively explained that his involvement in other research projects and teaching at the Collège de France, in addition to his own illness, had prevented him from moving faster with his translation.[66] He did not publish another volume.

Around the same time, Gaston Wiet, a young Arabist and epigraphist who had just landed in Cairo as an intern at the IFAO, began a critical Arabic edition of the *Khitat* on the recommendation of his director to supplant the unreliable Bulaq edition.[67] The first volume came out in 1911. But Wiet had to stop his edition in 1927 after he had published five large volumes of text and extensive commentaries.[68] He had concluded that the completion of the project required a large team of scholars to sift through the large number of

63 Urbain Bouriant, trans. *Maqrizi. Description topographique et historique de l'Égypte*, *MMAF* vol. 17, part 1 and 2 (Paris: Ernst Leroux, 1895 and 1900), I–XIV. The first part corresponds to pp. 1–128 of Bulaq's edition, the second to 128–250.

64 Pierre Bouriant, "Notice sur Urbain Bouriant," *Recueil de travaux relatifs à la philologie et à l'archéologie égyptiennes et assyriennes* 26, 1, 2 (1904), 29–32.

65 Casanova, trans. *Makrizi*. *MMAF* vols. 3 and 4.

66 Casanova, *Makrizi*, vol. 4, I–III.

67 Al-Maqrizi, *El-mawaiz wal-itibar fi dhikr el-khitat wal-athar*, ed. Gaston Wiet, *MMAF* vols. 30, 33, 46, 49, 53 (Cairo: IFAO, 1911–27). See Carl Heinrich Becker, "Review of al-Maqrizi's al-Mawa'iz wa-al-I'tibar, Edited by Gaston Wiet," *Der Islam* 2 (1911): 405–7. On the life and work of Gaston Wiet see M. Rosen-Ayalon, "Gaston Wiet 1887–1971," *Kunst des Orients* 8, 1/2 (1972): 155–9; André Parrot, "Gaston Wiet (1887–1971)," *Syria* 48, 3/4 (1971): 531–2. Rosen-Ayalon, 156, quotes a letter from Wiet to his mentor, the famous epigraphist Max van Berchem, dated to March 3, 1909, right after his arrival in Cairo in which he states, "I am disoriented. I will probably engage the text of al-Maqrizi that Chassinat [then director of the IFAO, where Wiet was a resident researcher] wants re-edited because of all the errors marring the Bulaq edition. But this is a truly redoubtable task" (my translation).

68 In the preface to the fourth volume, Wiet mentions that he is well advanced in his preparation of volume 6, but this was never published, Gaston Wiet, *El-Mawâ'iz wa'l I'tibar fî Dhikr el-Khitat wa'l-Âthâr, tome quatrième, deuxième partie, chapitres L–XCIV* (Cairo: IFAO, 1924), Avant-propos.

extant manuscripts of the book, which were constantly on the rise with the discovery of new copies. When Wiet started his work, he surveyed the known manuscripts of the *Khitat* and found 164 of them dispersed around the world. He had access to forty-six manuscripts for his first volume and forty-nine for his second, then stopped mentioning his manuscript numbers for the three following volumes.[69] The five volumes he published cover pages 1–322 of the first volume of the Bulaq edition, about one third of the total page count of the *Khitat*, leaving out the important material on Fatimid and Mamluk Cairo. The fifth volume, published in 1927, has no introduction at all and stops abruptly in the middle of a sentence describing the sacking of al-Qata'i', the Tulunid capital, by the Abbasid general Muhammad ibn Sulayman in 292/905, indicating either the frustration of the editor with the enormity of the work or the sloppiness of the publisher, who had already decided to give up on the project.

During his long and very successful career, however, Wiet was involved in at least two more collaborative projects of partial translations from al-Maqrizi's *Khitat* and one detailed translation of al-Maqrizi's first treatise, *Ighathat al-Umma*, published in 1962.[70] The first translation based on al-Maqrizi's *Khitat* was a co-authored geographical dictionary, *Matériaux pour servir à la géographie de l'Égypte*, published in 1919 with ample annotations, cross-referencing, and etymological research going back to the Greek sources of the Byzantine period.[71] Wiet's partner was the papyrologist and Byzantinist Jean Maspero, the son of the famous Egyptologist Gaston Maspero, who was both the director-general of excavations and of the antiquities of Egypt and the founding director of the IFAO. Jean Maspero died young in action during the Great War in 1915 before the completion of the book, but his mark is evident in the profusion of Greek origins in reconstructing the place names of Egypt. There is no doubting the erudition and wide-ranging scope of the etymological and orthographic analysis in this publication, but it remains strange that Bouriant's translation of the same material from the *Khitat*, published a mere fifteen years before, receives no acknowledgment and only three corrective notes in the text. The second partial translation from the *Khitat*, *Les marchés du Caire*, came out in 1979, eight years after Wiet's passing, thanks to the diligence of his collaborator André Raymond, who later became the dean of French Islamic urban historians. He saw the publication through while serving as the director of the Institut français d'études arabes in Damascus

69 Wiet, *El-Mawâ'iz*, vol. 1 (30), v; vol. 2 (33), iii, iv.

70 Wiet, "Traité des famines."

71 Jean Maspero and Gaston Wiet, *Matériaux pour servir à la géographie de l'Égypte*. *MMAF* vol. 36 (Cairo: IFAO, 1919). See the review by A. R. Guest, *JRASGBI* 4 (October 1921): 624–7.

(IFEAD).[72] The book brings together four important texts in the *Khitat* dealing with the markets and caravanserais and *wikala*s, translated and annotated by Wiet, with Raymond furnishing the appendices and corresponding maps of the commercial spaces and structures in Cairo.[73] This was the first French translation from the *Khitat* of material from al-Maqrizi's own time, which derives mostly from his own observations and experience of Cairo's markets and commerce as a *muhtasib* in the early fifteenth century, one of the most original aspects of the book.

Parallel to the on-and-off efforts to edit and translate al-Maqrizi's *Khitat*, another endeavor was under way at the IFAO to study Cairo's urban history. Encouraged by the charge of the Institute's remarkable founding director Gaston Maspéro (served 1880–1) to "Arabists" to combine archeology with philology, a number of French scholars translated sections of the *Khitat* as integral parts of their research on various aspects of Cairo's urban history, that also involved surface archeology and surveying.[74] Three of them, Paul Ravaisse, Paul Casanova, and Georges Salmon, who knew each other as residents at the IFAO, conceived of their projects as complementary and interconnected.[75] Ravaisse was the pioneer. He used the *Khitat*'s section on the Fatimid palaces of Cairo for his *Essai sur l'histoire et sur la topographie du Caire d'après Makrizi (Palais des Khalifes Fatimites)*, in which he reconstructed the topography of the central part of the Fatimid capital in the tenth

[72] André Raymond and Gaston Wiet, *Les marchés du Caire: Traduction annotée du texte de Maqrizi* (Cairo: IFAO, 1979). See the review by R. Stephen Humphreys, *Middle East Studies Association Bulletin* 15, 2 (December 1981): 63–5. Raymond continued to use al-Maqrizi's *Khitat* in his urban history studies, see his "La localisation des bains publics au Caire au quinzième siècle d'après Les Ḫiṭaṭ de Maqrīzī," *BEO* 30 (1978): 347–60.

[73] Raymond had already established himself as the premier student of Cairo's economy during the Ottoman period with the publication of his massive Doctorat d'État, *Artisans et commerçants au Caire au XVIIIe siècle* (Damascus: IFEAD, 1973), where he came to appreciate al-Maqrizi as a major source for Cairo's urbanism, economy, and social structure in the period right before the one covered in the book.

[74] Donald Malcolm Reid, *Whose Pharaohs? Archaeology, Museums, and Egyptian National Identity from Napoleon to World War I* (Berkeley: University of California Press, 2002), 247 and note 100, quotes a letter from Maspero to Max van Berchem in which he clearly admonishes his own Arabists to follow van Berchem's model of combining "archeology" (really here surveying and documenting) with philology: "More and more I have been thinking that the Arabist school up to now has taken the wrong path in refusing to see in Arabic more than a grammar and literature to study in the *cabinet*. Your studies in Cairo show what there is to be done in archaeology and what reality the history of the Muslim Orient will take on if it draws on the still surviving monuments." Quoted from Solange Ory, "Max Van Berchem, Orientaliste," in Marie-Claude Burgat, ed., *D'un Orient l'autre. Les métamorphoses successives des perceptions et connaissances*, 2 vols. (Paris: éditions CNRS, 1991), 2: 13.

[75] Georges Salmon, "Progrès des études arabes," *Archaeological Report 1902–1903*, F. L. Griffith, ed. (London: Egypt Exploration Fund, 1902–3), 69.

to eleventh centuries.[76] Casanova, while engaged in the translation of the *Khitat* after Bouriant's death, published two volumes in the same *Mémoires* series, one on the Citadel of Cairo, in which the *Khitat*'s text constitutes the main source, and the second a reconstruction of the topography of Misr al-Fustat that depended to a large extent on the texts of al-Maqrizi and (the recently edited) Ibn Duqmaq on this first Islamic Egyptian capital.[77] Salmon did the same for the part of Cairo that belonged to the vanished Tulunid city of al-Qata'i', the Qal'at al-Kabsh (the Castle of the Ram) and the Birkat al-Fil (the Elephant's Pond).[78] A later map of Cairo at the time of al-Maqrizi (1442), which has not received any critical review, was drawn by Moustafa Munir Adham and presented at the First International Geographic Conference in Cairo in 1925. The map was accompanied by a lecture in Arabic that described a walk through fifteenth-century Mamluk Cairo whose details were extracted from al-Maqrizi's *Khitat*.[79]

The situation is not better regarding the translation of the *Khitat* into English. Various scholars translated fragments in their publications on diverse aspects of Egypt's history or topography or Cairo's urbanism and architecture. But only one attempt was made to translate the text in its entirety, and that too was abruptly halted by the inability of the translator, Karl Stowasser, to find a publisher before his death in 1997. Part of Stowasser's manuscript, covering the first 128 pages of the first volume of the Bulaq edition and stopping at the description of al-Fustat's suburb of al-Rasd, was finally published through the efforts of a former colleague of Stowasser's, Clopper Almon, in 2014 with the copious notes Stowasser added.[80] In the introduction to

76 Ravaisse, *Essai*; reprinted in Sezgin, *Studies on al-Maqrizi*, 2: 1–81.

77 Paul Casanova, *Histoire et déscription de la citadelle du Caire. MMAF* vol. 6, part 4–5 (Cairo: IFAO, 1894–7); idem, *Essai de reconstitution topographique de la ville d'al Foustat ou Misr. MMAF* vol. 35, parts 1 and 2 (Cairo: IFAO, 1913–19).

78 M. Georges Salmon, *Études sur la topographie du Caire, la Kal'at al-Kabch et la Birkat al-Fil, MMAF* vol. 7 (Cairo: IFAO, 1902).

79 Moustafa Bey Munir Adham, "Le Caire au XV siècle d'après les données de Maqrizi," *BSROGE* 13 (1924–5): 131–80; reprinted in Sezgin, *Studies on al-Maqrizi*, 2: 271–322. Adham specifies that he is following in the footsteps of Ravaisse and Casanova for the sections on the Mamluk palaces and al-Fustat and Creswell for the enclosure of the Citadel. I could not find much information on Adham (d. 1927), except that he worked for the Maslahat al-Tanzim (Planning Department in Cairo) and was clearly interested in historic Cairo. He is the author of a booklet (46 pp.) on the journey of Imam al-Shafe'i to Egypt in Arabic (Cairo: Amin 'Abd al-Rahman Press, 1930), at least four articles on Cairene landmarks in the famous cultural journal *al-Muqtataf* between 1922 and 1927 (https://archive.alsharekh.org/AuthorArticles/21524), and a list of the historic names of Cairo's streets which he presented to King Fu'ad sometime before the geographic conference.

80 Stowasser, *Medieval Egypt*. Almon, who sat in on one of Stowasser's courses, performed what is termed a "book rescue" when Stowasser's papers were left in the estate of his wife, Barbara, after her death in 2012. He tracked down the print-out of the whole three-volume

the privately published book, Almon, identified as the Publishing Helper, informs the reader that what he has managed to edit and publish covers one third of the material left by Stowasser.[81] Thus, assuming that the three parts are of equal size, Stowasser might have managed to translate most of the first volume of the *Khitat*. Several attempts by Mamlukists in the US, led by the Middle East Documentation Center (MEDOC) at the University of Chicago which publishes the *Mamluk Studies Review*, have been made to issue the rest of his translation and to complete it. But by now there is little hope that it will see the light of day any time soon.

Re-editing al-Maqrizi

Recently, Frédéric Bauden started a very ambitious project to produce "definitive critical edition[s] of the Arabic text and annotated translation[s] (on facing pages) of a number of al-Maqrizi's important opuscules and major works."[82] The series is appropriately named Bibliotheca Maqriziana and is undertaken under the imprimatur of the acclaimed publisher E. J. Brill. Between 2014 and the fall of 2020, six heavily annotated editions and translations of a number of epistles and sections of one of al-Maqrizi's large compendia were released. They include the critical editions of two previously published tractates, *al-Ḏahab al-masbūk fī ḏikr man ḥağğa min al-ḫulafā' wa-l-mulūk* and *Ḍaw' al-sārī li-ma'rifat ḫabar Tamīm al-Dārī*.[83] Another edition and German translation of the little-noticed opuscule on minerals *Kitāb al-Maqāṣid al-saniyyah li-ma'rifat al-ağsām al-ma'diniyyah* was completed in 2015,[84] whereas three volumes by three separate scholars/translators of the enormous universal history *al-Ḫabar 'an al-bašar (al-Khabar 'an al-Bashar)*, covering four sections of Volume 5 and dealing with foreign nations (Persia and Western nations from the Greeks to the Goths) and pre-Islamic Arab "Thieves," have come out between 2017 and November of 2020.[85] The website promises ten more opuscules as parts of an Opera minora

work in the Georgetown University Library Special Collections, obtained scans of it, corrected all the special characters made by an optical character recognition macro he had developed initially for Stowasser, and gave the result to Stowasser's son, who published it via Amazon. Information obtained from https://bsos.umd.edu/featured-content/book-rescuer, and from a discussion published by Jane Jakeman on Thursday April 3, 2014, https://networks.h-net.org/node/20229/pdf (both last accessed June 27, 2019).

81 Al-Maqrizi, *Medieval Egypt*, 7–8.

82 https://brill.com/view/serial/BIMA (last accessed June 23, 2020).

83 Van Steenbergen, *Caliphate and Kingship*; Frenkel, *Daw' al-Sari*.

84 Käs, *al-Maqrizi's Traktat über die Mineralien*.

85 Jaakko Hämeen-Anttila, *al-Maqrizi's al-Ḫabar 'an al-bašar*, Vol. V, section 4: *Persia*

under preparation. An even more impressive Opera maiora is announced that comprises ten more volumes of *al-Ḫabar ʿan al-Bašar*, in addition to four sections from *al-Sulūk li-Maʿrifat Duwal al-Mulūk* (minus the parts about the long and crucial reign of al-Nasir Muhammad ibn Qalawun and those on the sultans ruling during the last thirty years of al-Maqrizi's life). A new edition of the *Ittiʿaz al-Hunafa bi-Akhbar al-A'imma al-Fatimiyyin al-Khulafa*, of an unspecified number of volumes to be edited by the prominent Fatimid scholar Paul Walker, is also listed. Although rumor has it that a new edition of the *Khitat* has been contemplated (alluded to in the review by Bauden of Sayyid's edition),[86] no mention of that is officially made on the website. In fact, at the rate of publication thus far, it will be many years before new titles, potentially from the *Khitat*, could be added to the series.

Thus, al-Maqrizi's oeuvre, unavailable to non-Arabic readers (at least for now), has remained the domain of the professional Arabists and Arab scholars who mined it essentially as a fount of primary reports, some his, others preserved from older and sometimes lost sources. They turned to his chronicles, and more frequently his unique *Khitat*, as sources of information in the reconstruction of both the history of Islamic Egypt and the urban and architectural history of Cairo, but hardly ever as discursive texts replete with personal, ideological, or critical input that needed to be studied. Al-Maqrizi himself was seen until recently as a compiler extraordinaire: an indefatigable collector and organizer of texts on the history of Egypt and an avid chronicler of the annals of its successive Islamic periods. He was granted the highest position among the historians of his period, the Burji period, in Orientalist historiography. But when scholars could not ignore the idiosyncratic and opinionated remarks strewn among his historical writings, they explained them away as reflections of a hurt ego, strict religiosity, or even an exceedingly gloomy personality, aggravated by a slew of personal tragedies and setbacks that afflicted al-Maqrizi throughout his life from his unstable status in the court of Barquq to the loss of his last daughter in 1423.[87]

Furthermore, the steady publication in the 1960s and 1970s of the chronicles of other historians of the Burji period, many of them contemporaries of al-Maqrizi covering the same timeframe as he does, began to shake his historiographical supremacy. Several comparisons between his material and that of other contemporaneous or earlier historians yielded results that indicated his overwhelming reliance on the work of others, sometimes without any

---

and Its Kings, part I (Leiden: Brill, 2017); Peter Webb, *al-Maqrizi's al-Ḫabar ʿan al-bašar* Vol. V, sections 1–2: *The Arab Thieves* (Leiden: Brill, 2019); Mayte Penelas, *al-Maqrizi's al-Ḫabar ʿan al-bašar* Vol. V, section 6: *The Greeks, the Romans, the Byzantines, the Franks, and the Goths* (Leiden: Brill, 2020).

86 See note 45 above.

87 Broadbridge, "Academic Rivalry," 87–90; Irwin, "al-Maqrizi and Ibn Khaldun."

acknowledgment. This was exacerbated by al-Maqrizi's method of abridging and rearranging copied reports so that they succinctly fitted into his larger discourse, and possibly lost their textual connection to their original reports.[88] Thus, even when Islamic historians turned to source criticism, most of those who worked on al-Maqrizi focused on his shortcomings as a recorder of events or his sloppy referencing habits, bordering, in many instances, on what we would today call plagiarism (although the question is far from being settled).[89] Articles started to appear that raised doubts about the veracity of his reporting in a vast array of areas, from Mongol history to economy and even the affairs of the court in Cairo.[90] The clincher came with the sustained criticism mounted by Frédéric Bauden in his series of numbered articles entitled Maqriziana, which, even though they tremendously enriched our knowledge of al-Maqrizi's method of working, gleaned from the unique manuscript of his preparatory drafts at the Library of Liège, dealt a serious blow to his reputation, especially the handling of the *khitat* manuscript of his neighbor al-Awhadi.[91]

Missing from most of these new judgmental studies of al-Maqrizi's writing is any sustained attention to the other facets of his personality and scholarship—his beliefs, biases, social standing, politics, wide source material that includes non-Islamic sources, personal tragedies, feelings toward his contemporaries, fundamentalist religiosity, ideological agenda, and even his own pronouncements about his own writing—precisely what gives his work its special flavor and endows it with a consciousness of mission.[92] The extensive

88 Little, *Mamluk Historiography*, 76–80; idem, "A Comparison of al-Maqrizi and al-ʿAyni"; Massoud, *Chronicles and Annalistic Sources*, 48–53; on page 53 he concludes that al-Maqrizi had "recourse to devices smacking of literary license to recreate historical facts."

89 The first to my knowledge to use the term "plagiarism" in relation to al-Maqrizi's *Khitat* is Qautremére in the copious biography he penned as the preface to his *Histoire des Sultans Mamlouks*, XIII.

90 David Ayalon, "The Great Yāsa of Chingiz Khān. A Reexamination (Part C2): al-Maqrizi's Passage on the *Yasa* under the Mamluk," *SI*, 38 (1973): 107–56; Bora, "A Mamluk Historian"; Amitai, "Historiographical Villain?"; Bauden, "al-Maqrizi," 1074; idem, "Maqriziana VII: Al-Maqrizi and the *Yāsa*: New Evidence of His Intellectual Dishonesty," was supposed to be published in *The Mamluk Sultanate of Egypt and Syria: Aspects of a Medieval Muslim State*, ed. Reuven Amitai and Amalia Levanoni in 2018, but the book was canceled and I could not gain access to this text.

91 Bauden, "Maqriziana IX." For a different, idiosyncratic, meditative, but thought-provoking interpretation of authorship, forgery, plagiarism, and copying in classical and medieval Arabic literature see Abdelfattah Kilito, *The Author and His Doubles: Essays on Classical Arabic Culture*, Michael Cooperson, trans. (Syracuse, N.Y.: Syracuse University Press, 2001).

92 Meloy, "Economic History," 203, mentions al-Maqrizi's political orientation; Massoud, "al-Maqrizi as a Historian," 127–9, notes that al-Maqrizi was the only historian of his time to describe the predatory fiscal practices of the Mamluks as the root cause of both internal ruin and external defeat, but pronounces his tone "alarmist."

biography of al-Maqrizi and the historicization of his total oeuvre which form the core of this book aim at providing a corrective perspective on his historical project, and at repositioning him in his rightful place as a pioneer in the study of urban history and a critical premodern historian who was overly disturbed by the conditions of his city and country. The following concluding chapter will analyze his standing in modern Egyptian historiography and the reception of his *Khitat* in modern Egyptian creative writing. It will show that his strong filial passion for Egypt and sharp alertness to the causes of its troubles were not lost on his modern and contemporary Egyptian interpreters and admirers. The historians saw in him a medieval model for their nationalist brand of proud history during the hopeful moments of post-independence and the early years of Gamal ʿAbd al-Nasser's presidency (before the 1967 war), when national fervor was at a high pitch. The creative writers, who discovered him a bit later, focused primarily on his relentless critique of the Mamluk rulers, cameoed in their narratives as prototypical of the present authoritarian rulers of Egypt, especially during Anwar al-Sadat's and Husni Mubarak's period (1970–2011). Some of the novelists and poets picked up on his ardent feelings of belonging and profound expression of loss of urbanity in his city, two sentiments shared by many of them, especially during the bumpy early days of Anwar al-Sadat's forced *infitah* (economic opening up) in the late 1970s. Others imaginatively employed him as a transhistorical and cogent voice of discontent, and, with a bit of a lyrical license, a symbol of resistance to despotism then and now.

CHAPTER 6

Reading al-Maqrizi in Modern Egypt

As a premier source for the urban history of Egypt, al-Maqrizi's *Khitat* stood unrivaled for well over 400 years, a scholarly feat that would not be contested until the beginning of the nineteenth century with the appearance of the monumental *Description de l'Égypte*, ordered by Napoléon Bonaparte immediately after his army took Cairo in 1798. Only the *Description* was no real sequel to the literary *Khitat* tradition of medieval Egypt, although al-Maqrizi's *Khitat* constituted one of its principal sources.[1] It was instead an imposing herald of another intellectual tradition that will dominate the modern study of history: the empirical method of visual and textual documentation, archival research, and analysis. Following the model of Diderot's and d'Alembert's *Encyclopédie*, the *Description de l'Égypte* was the cumulative effort of more than a hundred and fifty scientists, scholars, engineers, and students recruited by Napoléon to accompany his expedition to Egypt (1798–1801). They systematically collected, studied, classified, and graphically represented everything known and knowable about Egypt, its geography and topography, its flora and fauna, its Pharaonic and Islamic patrimony as well as its contemporary conditions. The product of their labor was published in Paris between 1809 and 1828 after many difficulties in nine volumes of text and fourteen grand volumes of illustrations.[2] A catalogue raisonné of prodigious proportions that formed the basis of the modern understanding of Egypt, the *Description de l'Égypte* was nonetheless a paradigmatic Enlightenment project both in its methods and in its epistemological principles of exhaustive coverage and scientific accuracy, as well as in its conjectures, biases, and goals. It brought back a sufficiently exhaustive and scientifically ordered body of knowledge about Ancient Egypt that helped establish and justify its foun-

[1] Bouriant, *Maqrizi. Description topographique et historique de l'Égypte*, part 1, Preface, I; André Raymond, "La population du Caire, de Maqrizi à la 'Description de l'égypte,'" *BEO* 28 (1975): 207–9.

[2] There exist two editions of the *Description de l'Égypte*. The first is the édition Imprimerie Nationale (Paris, 1809–28), the second is the édition dite Panckoucke, twenty-six octavo vols. of text and twelve folio vols. of illustrations (Paris, 1821–9). For a review of the *Description*'s history, see Gillispie and Dewachter, *Monuments of Egypt*, 1–29.

dational place in the history of Western civilization as we know it today. Conversely, it reinforced the prejudiced and negative opinions on the conditions of contemporary Egypt, and the whole "Orient" by extension, and presented nineteenth-century Europe with rationalized pretexts for intervention there on the eve of its grand colonial project.[3]

In Egypt, the Napoleonic occupation had several long-lasting consequences despite its brevity.[4] On the political level, it opened the way for the rise of the semi-independent and hugely ambitious regime of Muhammad 'Ali Pasha (1805–48), who strove with varying degrees of success to carve an empire out of the Ottoman province he maneuvered to control. He ultimately had to settle on a hereditary rule for perpetuity in his family in Egypt, only after European powers ganged up against him and forced his army out of Syria and Anatolia in 1840. In pursuing his project of building a modern state, army, and economy, Muhammad 'Ali relied heavily on French military, managerial, educational, agricultural, and planning expertise. One of his main contacts in France was none other than Edme-François Jomard, one of Napoléon most energetic savants and the main author and editor of the *Description de l'Égypte*.[5] Jomard recruited a number of French experts from diverse disciplines to work for Muhammad 'Ali in Egypt and supervised the Egyptians sent for training to France in successive missions.[6] Many of these students ended up becoming the leaders of modernization (*tajdid*) and its internalization of westernization as the surest way to burn the stages toward measuring up to the West. This was seen as the prelude to the late

3 For the various assessments of the role of the *Description de l'Égypte* in shaping the image of the Orient, see Henry Laurens, *Les origines intellectuelles de l'expedition d'Égypte: l'orientalisme islamisant en France (1698–1798)* (Istanbul: Isis, 1987); Hentsch, *Imagining the Middle East*, 119–23; David Prochaska, "Art of Colonialism, Colonialism of Art: the Description de l'Égypte," *L'esprit créateur* 34 (1994): 69–91.

4 For a French view of the effects of the expedition on Egypt, see Edouard Driault, "La Renaissance de l'Égypte," *Napoléon* 14, 1 (January–February 1925): 5–22; Louis Hautecoeur, "L'expedition d'égypte et l'art français," *Napoléon* 14, 1 (January–February 1925): 81–7. For a collection of Arabic views, see Ra'if Khuri, *Modern Arab Thought: Channels of the French Revolution to the Arab East*, Ihsan 'Abbas, trans. (Princeton, N.J.: The Kingston Press, 1983). Modern historiography claims that the Napoleonic invasion represented the first brush that Egypt had with (European) modernity. For critical evaluations of that claim, see Saïd, *Orientalism*, 76–88; Anwar Louca, "La renaissance égyptienne et les limites de l'œuvre de Bonaparte," *Cahiers d'histoire égyptienne* 7 (1955): 1–20; Henry Laurens, *L'expédition d'Égypte 1798–1801* (Paris: Seuil, 1997); Elliott Colla, "'Non, non! Si, si!': Commemorating the French Occupation of Egypt (1798–1801)," *Modern Language Notes* 118, 4 (September 2003): 1043–69.

5 Patrice Bret, "L'Égypte de Jomard: la construction d'un mythe orientaliste, de Bonaparte à Méhémet-Ali," *Romantisme* 120 (2003): 5–14.

6 Alain Silvera, "The First Egyptian Student Mission to France under Muhammad Ali," *MES* 16, 2 (May, 1980): 1–22.

nineteenth-and early twentieth-century *Nahda* (Renaissance, named in hopeful expectation after its European precedent) that flavored intellectual production in Egypt (and Greater Syria) with an unmistakably Western orientation, method, and look while insisting on reviving the glorious roots of an Arabic national culture within the confines of an Ottoman Empire steadily moving toward Turkification.[7]

Al-Maqrizi's Readers on the Eve of the *Nahda*: al-Jabarti and Hasan al-'Attar

Recent critical scholarship has rejected the facile model of modernization by imitation that still informs many commentaries on the *Nahda* and proposed instead a much more complex and long-brewing process of cultural renewal that preceded, confronted, appropriated, translated, and ultimately survived the encounter with European modernity during the colonial interventions.[8] From this new perspective, the Napoleonic French invasion is no longer seen as a rupture with the past or a herald of a novel mode of cultural

[7] *Tajdid*, a term used in the nineteenth century to signify modernization, was equally applied to designate the renovation of any old building. This semantic correlation reveals something about the notion of modernization in the mind of most nineteenth-century reformers: they were renovating an existing system, not remaking it, see Jacques Berque, *Egypt: Imperialism and Revolution*, J. Stewart, trans. (London: Faber, 1972), 76–83. A turning point in the study of the *Nahda* in English is Albert Hourani, *Arabic Thought in the Liberal Age, 1798–1939* (Cambridge: Cambridge University Press, 2nd edn., 1983), 34–102. See also Khaled El-Rouayheb, "Opening the Gate of Verification: The Forgotten Arab-Islamic Florescence of the 17th Century," *IJMES* 38, 2 (May 2006): 263–81, for the postulation of an Arab renascence before the Napoleonic occupation; Stephen Sheehi, "Towards a Critical Theory of al-Nahḍah: Epistemology, Ideology and Capital," *JAL* 43, 2/3 (2012): 269–98, for a synthesis of interpretations of the *Nahda*.

[8] Tarek el-Ariss, *Trials of Arab Modernity: Literary Affects and the New Political* (New York: Fordham University Press, 2013), 19–87, discusses Rifa'a Rafi' al-Tahtawi's first-hand account of his five years in Paris, *Takhlis al-Ibriz fi-Talkhis Bariz*, and Ahmad Faris al-Shidyaq's *al-Saq 'ala al-Saq* (Leg over Leg); Stephen Sheehi, *Foundations of Modern Arab Identity* (Gainesville, FL: University Press of Florida, 2004), 107–34; Shaden M. Tageldin, *Disarming Words: Empire and the Seductions of Translation in Egypt* (Berkeley: University of California Press, 2011), 108–51; Dahlia E. M. Gubara, "al-Azhar in the Bibliographic Imagination," *JAL* 43, 2/3 (2012): 299–335, esp. 317–22, debunks the persistent theme of Arab/Muslim incredulity at Western intellectual, scientific, and technological accomplishments using none other than al-Jabarti; Mustafa Riyadh, "al-Tarjama wa-Bina' al-Dawla al-Haditha fi-Misr," *Alif* 38 (2018): 1–34, esp. 1–4. Recently, Peter Gran has proposed a new interpretation of the roots of modernization under Muhammad 'Ali, ascribing it to a possible Albanian conection, and has criticized the persistence of a Western-instigated paradigm for the *Nahda* in his *The Persistence of Orientalism: Anglo-American Historians and Modern Egypt* (Syracuse: Syracuse University Press, 2020), 11–27, 110–46.

expression. Rather, it is considered both a catalyst that energized the emerging voices of reform and a challenge that provoked them to more carefully weigh the tools at their disposal, some of which were thought to be hidden in plain sight in the neglected intellectual Arabo-Islamic heritage, or to seek new ones. Indeed, some contemporary Egyptian intellectuals, most of whom had traditional ulama training, were taken aback by the ease with which the French defeated the Ottomans and the Mamluk Beys in 1798. They were, moreover, impressed by various aspects of the French military discipline and administrative efficiency without necessarily abandoning their opposition to, or at least their privately expressed rejection of, the French presence as a Christian power ruling an Islamic country. A select few of these leading ulama who were invited to the Institut d'Égypte in Cairo were fascinated by displays of French science and technology designed with that purpose in mind, although they were equally repelled by spectacles of French cruelty, licentiousness, and generally profligate behavior.[9]

These mixed feelings come through very clearly in the writing of 'Abd al-Rahman al-Jabarti (1753–1825), the celebrated Egyptian chronicler of the French occupation and the rise of Muhammad 'Ali, who represents the epistemic link between the premodern Islamic Egyptian school of history writing and the nationalist modern one of the late nineteenth and early twentieth centuries.[10] Trained at al-Azhar and writing in the traditional annalistic method and language, he perceptively, even critically, recorded the momentous events he witnessed up to the middle of Muhammad 'Ali's reign and unsparingly reported on the shortcomings of the powerful among his contemporaries. In the Introduction to his main chronicle, *'Aja'ib al-Athar fi-l-Tarajim*

9 For a straightforward analysis of the views of the French as expressed by our main Arabic source of the period, 'Abd al-Rahman al-Jabarti, see Shmuel Moreh, "Napoleon and the French Impact on Egyptian Society in the Eyes of al-Jabarti," in *Napoleon in Egypt*, Irene A. Bierman, ed. (Reading: Ithaca Press, 2003), 77–98; also, J. W. Livingston, "Shaykhs Jabarti and 'Attar: Islamic Reaction and Response to Western Science in Egypt," *Der Islam* 74 (1997): 92–106, on the two poles of such reaction represented (exaggeratedly, I should add) by the two shaykhs.

10 David Ayalon, "The Historian al-Jabarti and his Background," *BSOAS* 23, 2 (1960): 217–49; Jane Murphy, "Locating the Sciences in Eighteenth-century Egypt," *The British Journal for the History of Science* 43, 4 (December 2010): 557–71, esp. 565–70, offers a more nuanced reading of al-Jabarti's reaction to institutions of learning under the French and Muhammad 'Ali; Lars Bjørneboe, *In Search of the True Political Position of the 'Ulama: An Analysis of the Aims and Perspectives of the Chronicles of Abd al-Rahman al-Jabarti (1753–1825)* (Aarhus: Aarhus University Press and the Danish Institute, Damascus, 2007) is a close reading of al-Jabarti's writing that contextualizes it in a changing sociopolitical setting; Mario M. Ruiz, "Orientalist and Revisionist Histories of 'Abd al-Rahman al-Jabarti," *Middle East Critique* 18, 3 (2009): 261–84 meticulously reviews the scholarship on al-Jabarti since his main chronicle *'Aja'ib al-Athar* was first published in 1878.

wa-l-Akhbar, he explicitly situates his text in the long line of annalistic history writing from al-Tabari in ninth-century Abbasid Baghdad to the Mamluk fifteenth-century school and laments the dearth of texts of a similar caliber from the Ottoman period.[11] His disorderly list of precedents, however, suggests that he might not have had access to many of the titles he mentions, most of whose manuscripts, according to him, had been dispersed and sold by the *waqf* supervisors of mosques and madrasas where they had been kept or collected by the French and shipped back to France. One exception, however, was al-Maqrizi's books, which he lists correctly, even referring to the lost Fatimid sources that al-Maqrizi used, mostly in the *Khitat*, implying that he had read the full book. Ayman Fu'ad Sayyid in fact discovered that volumes two and three of a manuscript of the *Khitat* copied either in the late sixteenth or the seventeenth century were owned by al-Jabarti until at least 1814, eleven years before his death, when they inexplicably entered the library of the Coptic Patriarchate in Cairo.[12] Volume one of that same manuscript is today in the British Museum (Add. 25741). It too belonged to al-Jabarti, and has an added page with a biography of al-Maqrizi written by al-Jabarti himself.[13]

It is tempting to wonder whether al-Jabarti saw any parallel between himself and al-Maqrizi or between his writing and that of his Mamluk predecessor. After all, he, like al-Maqrizi, was a rather strict religious scholar at odds with the authority of his time: Burji Mamluk sultans in the case of al-Maqrizi and, in the case of al-Jabarti, the French occupiers first but then, and much more pronouncedly, Muhammad 'Ali, who prevented the printing of his history and may have caused him much more harm according to some reports.[14] Al-Jabarti, like al-Maqrizi again, was scathingly critical of the Pasha's

[11] 'Abd al-Rahman al-Jabarti, *'Aja'ib al-Athar fi-l-Tarajim wa-l-Akhbar*, 4 vols. (Cairo: Bulaq Press, 1879–80), 1: 5–6; Ayalon, "The Historian al-Jabarti," 219–22.

[12] Al-Maqrizi, *Khitat2*, 2: 69°. Al-Jabarti clearly had a manuscript library, perhaps inherited from his father, and may even have been a dealer in books, hence he might have sold his *Khitat* to the Coptic Patriarchate. Butrus Abu-Manneh, "Four Letters of Šayḫ Ḥasan al-'Aṭṭār to Šayḫ Ṭāhir al-Ḥusaynī of Jerusalem," *Arabica* 50, 1 (January 2003): 79–95, esp. 84 and 91–3, reproduces a letter from Hasan al-'Attar to Tahir al-Husayni, the Hanafi Mufti of Jerusalem, dated June 1814, in which al-'Attar reports on the failure of the negotiation with al-Jabarti to sell al-Husayni two compendia on law of several volumes each because they could not agree on the price.

[13] Al-Maqrizi, *Khitat2*, 2: 69°. I could not examine the manuscript, but the British Museum, Department of Oriental Printed Books and Manuscripts' catalogue *Catalogus codicum manuscriptorum orientalium qui in Museo britannico asservantur* (London: impensis Curatorum Musei britannici, 1871), 681, has a short description of Add. 25741 that indicates that al-Jabarti gathered information on al-Maqrizi from several listed sources, https://books.google.com/books?id=oZYsnh9boLgC&source=gbsbookotherversions (last accessed July 1, 2020).

[14] Ayalon, "The Historian al-Jabarti," 229–30, 247–8.

policies and actions as he was maneuvering toward the total control of Egypt. His objections resonate with those of al-Maqrizi in their insistence on the perils of deviating from Islamic norms and precedents or the introduction of novel and questionable procedures, as Muhammad 'Ali was certainly doing.[15] Finally, al-Jabarti spent the last part of his life in (probably forced) seclusion, where he was working on his history until he died blind and heartbroken two years after the tragic assassination of his son in 1823. Al-Maqrizi had made the same decision, although his retreat, equally fraught with personal tragedies, was more productive and lasted far longer than al-Jabarti's. But with the absence of any comments on al-Maqrizi in al-Jabarti's text other than the staid references to the *Khitat* and the mentions of contemporary notables who bought copies of this most popular of Mamluk histories, the possibility of an imagined affinity with al-Maqrizi will unfortunately have to remain hypothetical.[16]

On the other hand, another eminent early nineteenth-century scholar, Hasan al-'Attar (1766–1835), has left us a few remarks handwritten on the margins of an autograph yet incomplete manuscript of al-Maqrizi's *Muqaffa*, which insinuate a dialogue with the text that goes beyond appreciation of its informative content.[17] Al-'Attar, a *'alim* with a penchant for *adab*, an

[15] El-Ariss, *Trials of Arab Modernity*, 33–4; Ayalon, "The Historian al-Jabarti," 234–5 emphasizes the hatred of Muhammad 'Ali expressed by al-Jabarti, but does not cast it in any critical stance, even if it was traditionalist and defensive as al-Jabarti's was.

[16] Ayalon, "The Historian al-Jabarti," 220, note 2.

[17] Al-Maqrizi, *Khitat2*, 2: 51°–7°. The manuscript is now owned by the library of the University of Leyden, under the call number Or. 14.533. It was bought by Jan Just Witkam, then the curator of Oriental manuscripts at Leiden, at an auction at Christie's in London in 1978 without an established provenance. Sayyid, 56°, wonders if the manuscript came from the library of Rifa'a al-Tahtawi in Sohag, but then decides against that hypothesis, remarking that the manuscript was not photographed in 1948 when the Institute of Arab Manuscripts documented al-Tahtawi's collection. Witkam, "Reflections on al-Maqrizi's Biographical Dictionary," tells the story of the acquisition and raises the question of provenance. On p. 105, he reports that Mahmud al-Jalili (the owner of the unique complete manuscript of *Durar al-'Uqud al-Farida*) had approached him a couple of months before the auction at Christie's and told him that he owned an autograph manuscript of al-Maqrizi, which I think was most probably *Durar al-'Uqud*, not the one about to be auctioned. Witkam then (pp. 108–10) states that Sayyid drew his attention in 2012 (ten years after the publication of his *Khitat*, where he had initially speculated about the provenance of this manuscript from Sohag) to a report written in 1958 about al-Tahtawi's library with the description of a manuscript that is most probably the same as Or. 14.533. Witkam cannot fully confirm the correspondence, but to me it is undoubtedly the same manuscript. It cannot have passed unnoticed to al-Jalili's collection in Mosul between 1958 and 1978, and we also now know that when he visited Witkam al-Jalili was most probably talking about *Durar al-'Uqud*, which he will publish in 2002. So the riddle of provenance is still unsolved, like many issues of provenance in recent auctions of Oriental artifacts, and the manuscript must have been smuggled out of Egypt illegally, to end up in London between 1958 and 1978.

accomplished poet, and a keen observer of the French occupation, was a close friend of and an occasional collaborator with al-Jabarti. He taught at al-Azhar for many years and became its rector at the end of his life (1831–5).[18] In this last position, he initiated the pedagogical reform promoted by Muhammad 'Ali, earning himself a reputation as a "reformist" in the subsequent binary portrayal of ulama as either modernizers or conservatives, which in many orientalist and nationalist phrasings uncritically translates into another neat dichotomy of collaborators versus resisters (of colonial authority).[19] Al-'Attar, like al-Jabarti, who is usually relegated to the old-fashioned side, does not fit either category. His life story encapsulates that stance of uncertainty between the pressure exerted by the forces of imposed, top-down change, exemplified by the French occupation and Muhammad 'Ali's rule, and the opposition, if not to change altogether, at least to its pace and scope, embodied in institutions like al-Azhar and the ulama class in general, although of course he ultimately took the side of unreserved reform. He first escaped the French for a couple of months; came back and collaborated with them; was fascinated by their scholarship and science; may even have indulged in (possibly imagined) homoerotic relationships with some of them; mysteriously relocated to Albania, Syria, and Istanbul for more than twelve years after their departure; came back and resumed his life at al-Azhar as if nothing had happened; drew the attention of Muhammad 'Ali Pasha for his reformist mind; was appointed as editor of the first Egyptian newspaper, *al-Waqa'i' al-Misriyya*, established by Muhammad 'Ali in 1828; and became al-Azhar's rector at the age of sixty-five three years later and strove to reform its curriculum. Yet he remained, throughout, moored in the milieu of his received traditional knowledge. He composed many tractates on various Islamic religious disciplines, as

[18] On the unusual life and career of al-'Attar, see the pioneering study of Peter Gran, *Islamic Roots of Capitalism: Egypt, 1760–1840* (Austin: University of Texas Press, 1979), 76–106; Peter Gran, "Ḥasan al-'Aṭṭār," *Essays in Arabic Literary Biography: 1350–1850* J. E. Lowry and D. Stewart, eds. (Wiesbaden: Harrasowitz Verlag, 2009) 56–68; see also the review of the book and the rebuttal by the author, where Gran expounds on his interpretive method in reading al-'Attar's life, F. De Jong and P. Gran, "On Peter Gran, Islamic Roots of Capitalism: Egypt, 1760–1840: A Review Article with Author's Reply," *IJMES* 14, 3 (August 1982): 381–99. See also a much-expanded revisionist reading of al-'Attar's career and its wider implications in Gran, *The Persistence of Orientalism*, 111–23, where Gran, following a little-read article by Muhammad al-Arna'ut, places much importance on al-'Attar's possible stay in Scutari in Albania during the reign of the reformist Bushatli brothers, Mustafa and Ibrahim (d. 1810). See also Abu-Manneh, "Four Letters," 79–87. For a critical analysis of the contrast between the traditional and new methods of education in al-Azhar, see Timothy Mitchell, *Colonizing Egypt* (Berkeley: University of California Press, 1988), 74–92.

[19] Livingston, "Shaykhs Jabarti and 'Attar," 93–8; for a sustained critique of that division in the particular case of al-'Attar and al-Jabarti, see Colla, "Non, non! Si, si!" 1052–6; Gubara, "al-Azhar," 318–22.

well as on Arabic language and on rational sciences, that followed the established norms of composition and style, even when he dealt with new scientific subjects. He also penned numerous classically-inspired poems, though often spiced with colloquial expressions, which his friend al-Jabarti quotes at length in his *'Aja'ib al-Athar*.[20]

Unlike the majority of his contemporaries, who contented themselves with reading abridgments and commentaries on the large medieval masterworks, al-'Attar was known for his insistence on going to the original sources and for his habit of notating the books he read. His notes on the margins of al-Maqrizi's manuscript span more than twelve years (from 1823 to 1835, the year he died). Three of them announce al-'Attar completing the reading of the collection (which was not bounded as a book yet) at three equal intervals (1823, 1828, and 1833) as if part of a lifetime program. The last remark adds a curious twist: "I read it a third time in 1833 when my worries were accumulating and my concerns adding up, so I used this book as a distraction from these things and I pray to God that I will obtain satisfaction."[21] The date of the remark is quite revealing: al-'Attar had been rector of al-Azhar for two years by then, and was facing stiff resistance to his reforms from his own colleagues on top of the constant pressure from Muhammad 'Ali to deliver palpable results. It is puzzling for us today to imagine that a collection of biographies of dead people could be a diversion from anxiety, but in an age in which history was still seen as a moral lesson, reading about the lives of others might indeed have brought solace at the realization of how they had faced similar problems and overcome obstacles. Another remark indicates the point in the text at which al-'Attar was able to identify the author as al-Maqrizi (as the cover page was missing). Still another long note on the margin, dated to 1830 and proving that al-'Attar was always consulting al-Maqrizi's text, is attached to the biography of a Nubian ruler.[22] In it al-'Attar attempts to bridge the historical distance by offering a mini-narrative of Muhammad 'Ali's annexation of Sudan all the way to the borders of Ethiopia and his adoption of the same modernization measures there as he had already enacted in Egypt, so that the Sudan began to look like the Egyptian countryside. There is a discernible whiff of pride in this remark, both at the Pasha's expansionist project, but also at Egypt's

[20] More recent scholarship has recognized this ambiguity and ascribed to al-'Attar more subversive interactions with the colonial interlocutor, see 'Abu-Manneh, "Four Letters," 79–85; Colla, "Non, non! Si, si!" 1061–6; Tageldin, *Disarming Words*, 66–107. This role is suggestively captured in a felicitous sentence by Sunil Agnani as the "Alice in Wonderland perspective on colonial culture" in his "For the Love of Lost Sovereignty: Egypt and Postcolonial Thought. Review of Disarming Words: Empire and the Seductions of Translation in Egypt by Shaden M. Tageldin," *Cultural Critique* 89 (Winter 2015): 211–21, quotation p. 219.

[21] Al-Maqrizi, *Khitat2*, 2: 51°–2°.

[22] Al-Maqrizi, *Khitat2*, 2: 52°–6°.

transformation under him, a sort of modern nationalism in formation, albeit showing signs of imperialist aspirations that are more commensurate with fully-formed colonial nation-states.

The one remark that truly implies a dialogue between al-ʿAttar and al-Maqrizi's text is a short plea that reminds us of the admonitions al-Maqrizi had added on the frontispieces of his autograph books like *al-Suluk* about the vagaries of fate (see Chapter 2). Al-ʿAttar uses the tale of how an aide to Khumarawayh (r. 884–96) betrayed his master, recounted by al-Maqrizi, to reflect on the duplicity of one's own associates, which he bemoans having experienced several times and which he asks for God's grace in avoiding.[23] Not only the exhortative tone but also the stoic and devout feel of this remark suggest an approach to reading that connects to the text at several levels. This goes beyond the cognitively defined registers of reading for comprehension, from inspection to analysis, or even the traditional moralistic reading of history in the Islamic tradition, to an identificatory engagement. Al-ʿAttar, in this sentence, begins with a nod to drawing moral lessons familiar from countless Islamic commentators on the purpose of history. But then, he pulls the comment toward his own experience as if both to personalize it and to insert himself, or at least his observation, into the narrative, which recalls one of al-Maqrizi's definitions of the historian as the one who embodies his time (Chapter 4). This fluidity between original text and marginal note may have something to do with the scriptural mode of *writing* in Arabic manuscripts, as Timothy Mitchell has noted, that allows various bits of text to coexist on the surface of the page with few restrictive regulators like punctuation marks or strict writing orientation.[24] But whether that fluidity seeped into the scriptural mode of *reading* prior to the transformation wrought by the introduction of the printing press into Egypt is an open question.[25] One thing is for sure: al-ʿAttar, whether because of cultural or personal style, clearly treats the text as a contemporaneous interlocutor rather than an inert and distant reservoir of historical knowledge. This perhaps explains how he can seek and enjoy rereading a bunch of biographies, which is what the book is about, repeatedly and on different occasions and testify to his delight at doing this.

[23] Al-Maqrizi, *Khitat2*, 2: 56°.

[24] Mitchell, *Colonizing Egypt*, 146–8.

[25] Ibid., 92, in accord with the general theme of his book, asserts that in the traditional system of al-Azhar "writing had never formed its own realm of representation, meaning, or culture; there had been no fundamental division between 'text' and 'real world.'" Although I question the strictness of the first binary, I will retain the insight that text and real world were much more intimately intertwined in that mindset, as I am trying to argue with al-ʿAttar's notes.

Publishing al-Maqrizi's *Khitat*

Al-ʻAttar and al-Jabarti belonged to the last generation to read al-Maqrizi only in manuscript form, as the *Khitat* was finally published in its totality in 1853. Shifting from a manuscript culture to the printed book is usually presented both as a sign of modernization and as one of the main foundations of the impending *Nahda*. Printing is purported to have had a profound effect on the availability of books to a general readership, on habits of reading and writing, on the scholarly prestige and hierarchy of the learned, and on the methods by which textual accuracy was verified.[26] But the shift was not as drastic as was alleged by an earlier generation of modernization scholars, nor was it immediate.[27] Egyptian scholars continued to copy and use manuscripts in their study for the first fifty years after the establishment of the Bulaq Amiri Press in 1820, but the topography of the learning environment was nonetheless slowly and irrevocably changing.[28] In the case of al-Maqrizi's *Khitat*, its publication had several noticeable effects. The first stems from its early date. Appearing just as the idea of a geographically and politically delineated Egypt was settling in the Egyptian imagination after the failure of the grand adventure of Muhammad ʻAli at founding a new empire in the Arab Ottoman territories, it was the perfect text to consolidate that notion and to give it historical legitimacy. As such, the *Khitat* was bound from the outset to become a foundational text in the rising national school of history and historical geography. Moreover, the significant delay in the publication of al-Maqrizi's other major compendia on Egypt (*al-Suluk*, for instance, was published between 1934 and 1972, *Ittiʻaz al-Hunafa* between 1967 and 1973, and of course the complete *Durar* not until 2002) meant that for generations of Arabic readers his reputation rested essentially on the *Khitat*.[29] Thus he is more frequently

[26] Needless to say, the most influential such study, although it only deals with the Arabic case in passing, is Benedict Anderson, *Imagined Communities: Reflections on the Origin and Spread of Nationalism* (New York: Verso, 1983). See Geoffrey Roper, "The Printing Press and Change in the Arab World," *Agent of Change: Print Culture Studies After Elizabeth Eisenstein* (Boston: University of Massachusetts Press, 2007), 251–67; El Shamsy, *Rediscovering the Islamic Classics*, 31–91. Mitchell, *Colonizing Egypt*, 146–54, on the changing significance of the language itself when forced into printing.

[27] Dana Sajdi, "Print and Its Discontents. A Case for Pre-Print Journalism and Other Sundry Print Matters," *The Translator* 15, 1 (2009): 105–38 offers a sustained argument against every aspect of the supposed revolution wrought by print in the Arabic context from classes of producers and consumers of texts to genres of publication.

[28] Abu al-Futuh Radwan, *Tarikh Matbaʻat Bulaq wa-Lamha ʻan Tarikh al-Tibaʻa fi-Buldan al-Sharq al-Awsat* (Cairo: al-Matbaʻa al-Amiriyya, 1953). Hala Auji, *Printing Arab Modernity. Book Culture and the American Press in Nineteenth Century Beirut* (Leiden: Brill, 2016), 3–16.

[29] Earlier, and in most cases incomplete, editions of these books were published by Orientalists

cast as the historian of Egyptian space and place rather than as a historian of Egypt *tout court*, or at least an annalist among many Mamluk annalists competing to tell the story of their time. But more importantly from this book's perspective, his fully-fledged criticism of the Mamluk sultans for the undoing of both the state and the city, which is unique to him and appears more explicitly in the *Suluk*, *Ighathat*, and *Durar*, was not available to the early commentators on al-Maqrizi among the nationalist and orientalist historians. They undoubtedly saw his gloomy side, abundantly captured in the theme of *kharab* sprinkled throughout the *Khitat*, without its staunchly articulated causal explanation loudly injected into the biographies of the Mamluk sultans and corrupt officials in the *Suluk* and *Durar*, as analyzed in Chapter 3.

Sociologically, the publication of the *Khitat* made its text available to a wider readership, including a group that was emerging at the time from the ranks of those returning from their studies in Europe or those graduating from the newly-installed non-traditional educational system, which expanded significantly under Khedive Isma'il (r. 1863–79). Still taking shape in the 1850s and 1860s, the group, which will often be later called the *effendiyya* (an Ottoman term of Greek origin that was generally applied to Western-educated professionals in modern Egypt), will soon replace the ulama in leading cultural life in Egypt.[30] Many of the early *effendiyya* who studied in Europe were impressed to varying degrees by the culture they glimpsed through their strictly regimented life in their missions. Yet upon returning home and assuming their new responsibilities in the administration and the educational system, they by and large strove to find a way of reviving their Arabic and Islamic intellectual heritage and reconciling it with the culture of modernity they learned to admire, rather than unconditionally embracing the European model.[31] The

in Europe and were generally not available to researchers in Egypt or the rest of the Arab world. Smaller epistolary treatises were of course available, but they are too specific and circumscribed to define a historian's reputation.

30 On the *effendiyya*, see Israel Gershoni and James P. Jankowski, *Redefining the Egyptian Nation, 1930–1945* (Cambridge: Cambridge University Press, 1995), 7–22; Michael Eppel, "Note about the Term *Effendiyya* in the History of the Middle East," *IJMES* 41, 3 (2009): 535–9, for a critical review of the term's use over time; Lucy Ryzova, *The Age of the Efendiyya: Passages to Modernity in National-Colonial Egypt* (Oxford: Oxford University Press, 2014), 9 succinctly demarcates the *Efendiyya* as a "social group defined by its claim on publicly defined signs of modernity"; Di-Capua, *Gatekeepers*, 143–4.

31 This is still the subject of heated debate in today's scholarship. See, for instance, *The Making of the Arab Intellectual. Empire, Public Sphere and the Colonial Coordinates of Selfhood*, Dyala Hamzah, ed. (London: Routledge, 2014), 1–10; Aziz al-Azmeh, "The Reformist State and the Universalist Orientation," in his *Secularism in the Arab World: Contexts, Ideas, and Circumstances* (Edinburgh: Edinburgh University Press, 2019), 85–179; Ruiz, "Orientalist and Revisionist Histories," *passim*; Michael Eppel, "The Elite, the *Effendiyya*, and the Growth of Nationalism and Pan-Arabism in Hashemite Iraq, 1921–1958," *IJMES* 30, 2 (May

accelerated pace of publication of key Arabic and Islamic sources, both religious and secular, in the second half of the nineteenth century, possibly under the influence of Rifa'a al-Tahtawi, is one direct outcome of this revivalist impulse. Complemented by an active movement in scholarship, but also in the nascent realm of cultural journalism, to comment on, abridge, debate, diffuse, and build upon the substance of these sources, the endeavor gained a more focused nationalist flavor by the end of the century after the British occupied Egypt in 1882.

One of the first *effendiyya* to adopt, incorporate, update, and attempt to modernize a medieval source, al-Maqrizi's *Khitat* in this case, was 'Ali Pasha Mubarak (1824–93), a French-trained engineer, educator, author, and minister who assumed many ministerial portfolios under 'Abbas Pasha (r. 1849–54), Khedive Isma'il, and his son Tawfiq (r. 1879–92).[32] By students of urban history, Mubarak is often celebrated (or maligned) as the true brain and managerial force behind the aggressive modernization of Cairo initiated by Isma'il. When he visited the Paris Exposition Universelle in 1867, Khedive Isma'il greatly admired the new imperial capital that Baron Haussmann was busy molding in the 1860s despite a major uproar from the Parisians. Isma'il ordered Mubarak, who was not part of the official delegation but was asked to join Isma'il at the Exhibition, to model the new Cairo after Haussmann's Paris.[33] Hiring designers from all over Europe and Istanbul and spending huge sums of money (mostly borrowed from European banks at exorbitant rates), he fashioned an alluring architectural spectacle fronting the old city, complete with all the accouterments of modern urban living.[34] The original

---

1998): 227–50, argues for an important role of the *Effendiyya* in the emergence of Arab nationalism in twentieth-century Iraq.

32 On Mubarak's unusual life story, see 'Ali Pasha Mubarak, *al-Khitat al-Tawfiqiyya*, 9: 37–61; Elias al-Ayyubi, *Tarikh Misr fi 'Ahd al-Khidiwi Isma'il Pasha*, 2 vols. (Cairo: Madbouli, 2nd edn., 1994), 1: 172–97, which copies most of his material from Mubarak but adds a number of revealing observations; Lorne M. Kenny, "'Ali Mubarak: Nineteenth Century Egyptian Educator and Administrator," *MEJ* 21, 1 (Winter, 1967): 35–51, which offers a modern English translation of parts of Mubarak's autobiography; Jack A. Crabbs, Jr., *The Writing of History in Nineteenth-Century Egypt* (Detroit: Wayne State University Press, 1984), 109–29; Wen-chin Ouyang, "Fictive Mode, 'Journey to the West,' and Transformation of Space: Discourses of Modernization in 'Ali Mubarak's *'Alam al-Din*," *Comparative Critical Studies* 4, 3 (December 2007): 331–58.

33 Khaled Fahmy, "Modernizing Cairo: A Revisionist Narrative," *Making Cairo Medieval*, 173–99, esp. 176–7. Fahmy, using Egyptian archives, shows that the efforts to modernize Cairo predate both Mubarak and the Khedival visit to the Exposition Universelle. Yet, there is no denying that that visit and the desire of Isma'il to modernize and Europeanize his capital before the inauguration of the Suez Canal (delayed by one year) were the true boosters of Cairo's architectural and urban boom.

34 Janet Abu-Lughod, *Cairo, 1001 Years of the City Victorious* (Princeton: Princeton University Press, 1971), 98–117; Berque, *Egypt*, 84–102; André Raymond, *Cairo*, W. Wood,

master plan would have crisscrossed the old city with diagonal and peripheral boulevards that would have demolished entire historical neighborhoods. Mubarak, who faced stiff opposition from the steadily organizing movement to conserve the Islamic heritage of Cairo, argued that the old city needed this intervention to provide it with better circulation, hygienic standards, and infrastructural services.[35] But the demolition work proceeded very slowly despite Mubarak's enthusiasm and his ability to survive the various reshuffles in the Egyptian cabinet. By 1874, only two new boulevards, al-Sikka al-Gadida (the New Street) and Muhammad ʿAli Street, had been cut in the dense fabric of the old city. The project came to a halt after the British landed in 1882.

Mubarak's appropriation of al-Maqrizi's *Khitat* as the core of his own *al-Khitat al-Tawfiqiyya al-Jadida* came on the tail-end of his actual incisive interventions in the urban fabric of old Cairo and as a way of contextualizing and historicizing them. Published in twenty volumes in 1888–9, the compendium incorporated most of al-Maqrizi's material and built upon his entries to document the changes wrought on the monuments and sites in the interim between the fifteenth century and Mubarak's own time.[36] As such, the book epitomized the pros and cons of the revivalist intellectual project, oscillating as it did between Western-style modernization and an informed return to traditional knowledge values. But, from the perspective of this book, Mubarak's *al-Khitat al-Tawfiqiyya* played a decisive role in the reception of al-Maqrizi's text in modern Egyptian scholarship and national literature in general. It actually opened the door for its constitution as the incontestable foundation of the academic study of Egypt's urban and architectural history, which picked up speed in the twentieth century with the formation of the field of Islamic architecture, on the one hand, and the rise of Egyptian nationalism on the other.

---

trans. (Cambridge, M.A.: Harvard University Press, 2000), 309–38; Nezar AlSayyad, *Cairo: Histories of a City* (Cambridge, M.A.: Belknap Press of Harvard University Press, 2011), 199–228.

[35] The conservation of the Islamic heritage became official policy with the establishment by Khedive Tawfiq in December of 1881 of the Comité de Conservation des Monuments de l'Art Arabe, in which Mubarak served ex-officio until he resigned. See Alaa el-Habashi, "The Preservation of Egyptian Cultural Heritage through Egyptian Eyes: The Case of the Comité de Conservation des Monuments de l'Art Arabe," *Urbanism: Imported or Exported?* Joe Nasr and Mercedes Volait, eds. (Chichester, England; Hoboken, N.J.: Wiley-Academy, 2003), 160–2.

[36] Di-Capua, *Gatekeepers*, 48–50. I am less convinced by his argument that Egypt before the end of the nineteenth century was not as clearly delineated in the mind of Egyptians as it became later with the rise of nationalism and that the word *misr* in *khitat* literature, for instance, referred essentially to Cairo than I am by his depiction of the romantic Egyptian historicism of the late nineteenth century.

Reviving the *Khitat* Genre: 'Ali Mubarak and Muhammad Kurd'ali

Mubarak, an unabashed modernizer who loudly proclaimed that the old has to give way to the new, enthusiastically carried out radical changes in the three areas he oversaw as a minister: the planning and extension of the city, the development of railroads and canals, and the reform of the education system.[37] He famously expounded his ideas about education, hygiene, economic growth, reform, progress, modernization, and westernization in his two major publications: *'Alam al-Din*, a didactic *Weltanschauung*-ish novel of almost 1500 pages, and the equally extensive *al-Khitat al-Tawfiqiyya al-Jadida*. The first was written when Mubarak assumed his first cabinet appointment as minister of education between 1867 and 1871. The second was compiled toward the end of his ministerial career when he was out of the government between 1883 and 1888, before his last return to the ministry of education (1888–91). Scholars have sometimes treated these two works in different ways, although they have recognized their underlying and unifying drive to both educate and modernize by example. Some saw them as nodes in a continuum of instructive writing, couched in unevenly grasped and loosely differentiated literary genres ranging from fictive autobiography to classificatory, historical topography.[38] Others considered them as two distinct stages in a civil servant's evolving understanding of progress. The early stance was articulated in *'Alam al-Din* at the exuberant start of Mubarak's ministerial career when he was still totally taken with the Western model (it is not clear how much he distinguished between the British and the French varieties) and eager to apply it to all aspects of society and government. The second, embodied in *al-Khitat al-Tawfiqiyya*, brought his years of bureaucratic experience and accumulated knowledge of the minutiae of modern urban management to an elaborate and wide-ranging historical geography of Egypt, and in particular Cairo.

'Alam al-Din tells the story of a trip from Cairo to Paris via Alexandria and Marseille undertaken by an Azharite sheikh and his son with an unnamed English orientalist who had hired the sheikh to help him edit a major medieval Arabic lexicon. The setting allowed Mubarak to arrange his

[37] Bassim Musallam, "The Modern Vision of Ali Mubarak," *The Islamic City*, R. B. Serjeant, ed. (Paris: Unesco, 1980): 183–99, emphasizes Mubarak's modernization efforts in both education and city planning.

[38] Nezar AlSayyad, "Ali Mubarak's Cairo: Between the Testimony of *'Alamuddin* and the Imaginary of the *Khitat*," in Alsayyasd, Bierman, and Rabbat, eds., *Making Cairo Medieval*, 49–66; Wen-chin Ouyang, *Politics of Nostalgia in the Arabic Novel: Nation-State, Modernity and Tradition* (Edinburgh: Edinburgh University Press, 2013), 147–61, for an analysis of both works as expressions of budding modernization and nationalism.

text in overtly instructive dialogues called *musamarat* (conversations, 125 in total) between the two main protagonists about the various characteristics of modern civilization, understood to be European, and how best to implement them in the Orient (reduced in most instances to Egypt), which is the main purpose of the book. The narrative, ending abruptly in Paris before the group reaches its final destination in England and with no conclusion, suggesting that it was not completed, is acknowledged today as a pioneering work of fiction in Arabic literature.[39] Stylistically and conceptually meandering between the modern genres of autobiography, confessions, and travelogue, *'Alam al-Din* is most clearly indebted to *adab al-rihla* (travel literature) as it had reemerged in the early nineteenth century in the form of books on the "discovery of the West" theme, one of which, Rif'at Rifa'a al-Tahtawi's famous *Takhlis al-Ibriz fi Talkhis Bariz*, is mentioned several times in the narrative. For that reason, the correspondence between *'Alam al-Din*'s literary form and typological models and its message of westernization is unambiguous even if its language remains beholden to the more floriated style of traditional *adab*.

Al-Khitat al-Tawfiqiyya al-Jadida, on the other hand, inexplicably adapts a literary genre whose last great example, al-Maqrizi's *Khitat*, was more than 400 years old, and deploys structuring strategies adopted from its premodern predecessor. Purportedly undertaken to update al-Maqrizi's topographic, geographic, and historical data and highlight the recent planning and infrastructural developments in Cairo and Egypt in general that 'Ali Mubarak had overseen, *al-Khitat al-Tawfiqiyya* is strident about the urgent need to reform and improve the built environment and other facets of communal life.[40] For him, it seems that, beside al-Maqrizi's *Khitat* content, which formed the pre-history of his *al-Khitat al-Tawfiqiyya*, the framework and scope of his predecessor's work offered an appropriate and flexible vehicle for the conveyance of his modernization musings. Like the didactic mock-autobiography he had employed in *'Alam al-Din*, the *khitat* form allowed Mubarak to expand and update his analytical and structural toolkit without having to abandon his tried-and-tested literary framework or to stretch it beyond recognition. Thus, while building on the *khitat* scaffolds throughout his text, he was able to very deftly incorporate the modern tool of statistics, draw extensively from European sources, particularly from the *Description de l'Égypte*, and insert

[39] Wadad al-Qadi, "East and West in Ali Mubarak's *Alamuddin*," in Marwan R. Buheiry, ed., *Intellectual Life in the Arab East, 1890–1939* (Beirut: AUB Press, 1981) 21–37; Wen-chin Ouyang, *Poetics of Love in the Arabic Novel* (Edinburgh: Edinburgh University Press, 2012), 147–57, reconstructs the quality of the book as a novel and uncovers its main political and cultural messages.

[40] Ouyang, *Poetics of Love*, 47–8, notices that, as a genre that depends on topographical accuracy, *khitat* studies need to be constantly rewritten.

official documents and reports to supplement and validate his empirical observations.

Yet, despite its implementation of all these modern analytical devices, *al-Khitat al-Tawfiqiyya* has no illustrations whatsoever. Neither maps, nor architectural drawings, not even that most modern instrument of representation, photography, made their way into the pages of this detailed study of cities, topography, architecture, and infrastructure. This is perplexing, since Mubarak was known to have studied drafting and used it in his planning work, and one of his main sources, the *Description de l'Égypte*, heavily depends on figures, both as illustrations and as carriers of meaning in their own right. Yet, in his *Khitat*, Mubarak exclusively uses textual techniques reminiscent of those *waqf*-inspired, annalistically-imbued descriptions of cities, neighborhoods, and buildings used in the premodern *khitat* tracts. The absence of illustrations seems to be more a function of *al-Khitat al-Tawfiqiyya*'s composition and means of signification than a reflection of the difficulty of printing figures in Egypt when the book was published. Nor does that absence seem to be an attempt on the part of Mubarak to adhere to the expectations of his presumed audience, most of whom would in fact have had a similar background to his (i.e. a westernized education), which would have taught them to appreciate the instructive value of images.

The main reason for the absence of figures seems to lie in the strong grip on Mubarak's conceptualization and arrangement of his own *khitat* book of his intellectual paradigm, al-Maqrizi's *Khitat*. *Al-Khitat al-Tawfiqiyya al-Jadida* was indeed consciously modeled and named after al-Maqrizi's *Khitat*, and relied heavily on al-Maqrizi's data for its discussion of Medieval Cairo.[41] It even reflected al-Maqrizi's idiosyncrasies and closely followed his organizational scheme when adding sections on the urban developments in Cairo and Egypt between the fifteenth and nineteenth centuries. Mubarak, moreover, lucidly understood the link between space and politics and space and history, two of the main interpretive axes that guided al-Maqrizi's *Khitat*. His focus on the modernization of Cairo is animated by similar concerns, if opposite in intention, to those of al-Maqrizi's. Where al-Maqrizi decries the effects bad Mamluk politics had on the city space and wellbeing, Mubarak by contrast, in a mixture of subservience and self-congratulation, was praising

[41] Mubarak, *al-Khitat al-Tawfiqiyya*, 1: 65–77; Crabbs, *Writing of History*, 114–19, where Mubarak is rightly dubbed an encyclopedist, perhaps in reference to his medieval predecessors, al-'Umari and al-Qalqashandi. A systematic study of the frame and purpose of Mubarak's *Khitat* is Stephan Fliedner, *Ali Mubarak und seine Hitat: kommentierte Ubersetzung der Autobiographie und Werkbesprechung* (Berlin: K. Schwarz, 1990); Musallam, "The Modern Vision of Ali Mubarak"; Nadia al-Bagdadi, "The Invisible-Visible City: Topography, History and the Mind of Ali Mubarak," *Beiruter Texte Und Studien* 64 (1999): 539–51.

the impact of good (modern) politics on the appearance and functioning of the city. And if al-Maqrizi was lamenting the decline of the city, and the state, under the corrupt and lax rule of his contemporary Mamluk sultans, Mubarak was documenting the advances in planning, hygiene, services, and building in the city, in which he himself played a major role under his two patrons Khedive Isma'il and Khedive Tawfiq, the monarch to whom the book is somewhat self-consciously dedicated. Perhaps it is because of that contrast between al-Maqrizi's pessimism and Mubarak's buoyancy in using architecture as a tool of sociopolitical commentary that the latter's text does not match the intensity and passion of the former's hermeneutic, mantra-like theme of *kharab* wielded to illuminate the memories of bygone eras and their venerable historical figures.[42]

The rebirth of the *khitat* genre proved to be short-lived in an age of immense strides in intellectual exploration that extended both back in time to unearth the Arabic literary legacy and across the Mediterranean toward modern Europe and its irresistible epistemological advances. Certainly, Mubarak's *Khitat* provided a bridge between the venerable school of Mamluk history whose conceptualization of identity was largely city-based and the nascent national history predicated on the modern notion of the territory-defined nation-state.[43] But it could not, or perhaps did not even attempt to, transpose the sense of intimate belonging that al-Maqrizi expressed in his attentive descriptions of the urban spaces with which he was personally familiar to the new expanded canvas, encompassing an abstracted territory that from now on will make up the Egyptian nation. Mubarak did adopt the framework of the *khitat* genre to organize his narrative of urban modernization. And, along with its ample topographic and architectural material, al-Maqrizi's *Khitat* did prove its adaptability to his expectation of conceptualizing a spatial and historical continuity from the visible and appreciable Mamluk built heritage to the new Khedivial city under construction. But, in the end, *al-Khitat al-Tawfiqiyya* was a revivalist experiment undertaken out of necessity by a

42 Ouyang, *Poetics of Love*, 49–54, notices the difference between the two and analyzes it in light of their understanding of the construction of power in time and space (i.e. in the history of *khitat*).

43 On the notion of belonging in Medieval Egypt see Ulrich Haarmann, "Regional Sentiment in Medieval Islamic Egypt," *BSOAS* 43 (1980): 55–66; idem, "Glaubensvolk und Nation im islamischen und lateinischen Mittelalter," *Berichte und Abhandlungen/ Berlin-Brandenburgische Akademie der Wissenschaften* 2 (1996): 161–99; Antrim, "Waṭan before Waṭaniyya," 173–90; Petra M. Sijpesteijn, "Building An Egyptian Identity," in *The Islamic Scholarly Tradition: Studies in History, Law, and Thought in Honor of Professor Michael Allan Cook*, Asad Q. Ahmed, Michael Bonner, and Behnam Sadeghi, eds. (Leiden: Brill, 2011), 85–105. Di-Capua, *Gatekeepers*, 36–46, 51–2, argues for a rambling process of transition between the traditional and modern ways of writing history in late nineteenth-century Egypt that followed the evolution of the idea of an Egyptian nation.

French-trained engineer whose intellectual roots were still firmly planted in the traditional education he had received in Egypt before his mission to Paris. A new generation of historians were emerging who were trained in the new methods and concepts of history writing, which began to be taught in the recently-established Egyptian University in 1908. Only one other *khitat* compendium was composed after Mubarak's and in direct dialogue with it before the genre was abandoned altogether in favor of more nimble modes of framing and recounting national history.[44]

That second *khitat* book was Muhammad Kurd'ali's *Khitat al-Sham* (Khitat of Syria), written more than thirty years after Mubarak's *al-Khitat al-Tawfiqiyya* and published in six volumes in Damascus between 1925 and 1928.[45] Kurd'ali, a Damascene intellectual coming of age in the twilight years of the Ottoman Empire and suffering the absurdities of its endgame erratic policies, was a reformer and a prominent revivalist of the Arabic language and heritage.[46] He in fact edited a number of classical masterpieces of *adab* and founded the Academy of the Arabic Language in Damascus in 1919, whose aim was the modernization of the Arabic language, and proudly served as its president until his death in 1953. His appropriation of the *khitat* genre, though directly informed by the same revivalist considerations that prompted Mubarak's earlier decision, differs from it in the clarity of its underlying political reasons. Unlike Mubarak, Kurd'ali had no urban modernization project to peddle or to nestle in the city's glorious urban past. Instead, his was a more urgent drive to outline a definition of modern Syria—the land, its people,

[44] A much later book with the term *khitat* in its title, Salih Ahmad al-'Ali's *Khitat al-Basra wa-Mantiqataha: Dirasa fi-Ahwaliha al-'Imranyya wa-l Maliyya fi al-'Uhud al-Islamiyya al-Ula* (Baghdad: al-Majma' al-'Ilmi al-'Iraqi, 1986), can hardly be considered a conventional *khitat* book. It is, rather, a modern historical topography of the city and its surroundings equipped with all the modern tools of study from maps and plans to source criticism. Al-'Ali was most probably using the term *khitat* as a genuine Arabic term for topographic studies. He used it also in the title of a book he translated from English, Jacob Lassner's *Topography of Baghdad in the early Middle Ages: Text and Studies by Jacob Lassner* (Detroit: Wayne State University Press, 1970), which he published as *Khitat Baghdad fi al-'Uhud al-'Abbasiyya al-Ula* (Baghdad: al-Majma' al-'Ilmi al-'Iraqi, 1984).

[45] Muhammad Kurd'ali, *Khitat al Sham*, 6 vols. (Damascus, Matba'at al-Taraqqi, 1925–8). There is another small book (148 pp.) by another Syrian scholar that also uses the term *khitat* in its title. This is Salah al-Din al-Munajjid, *Khitat Dimashq: Nusus wa-Dirasat fi Tarikh Dimashq al-Toboghrafi wa Athiaraha al-Qadima* (Beirut: Catholic Press, 1949). Al-Munajjid, one of the great editors of historical Arabic manuscripts in the twentieth century, gathered here fourteen articles, initially published in the journal *al-Mashriq*, on various aspects of Damascus's topography and historical architecture. Like al-'Ali, al-Munajjid is clearly using the term as the authentic Arabic term for topographic studies.

[46] Kurd'ali, *Khitat*, 6: 333–47, for his autobiography; Samir Seikaly, "Damascene Intellectual Life in the Opening Years of the Twentieth Century," *Intellectual Life in the Arab East*, 125–53, for a biography cast within the intellectual context of his times.

and their history—which had emerged fragmented after the dissolution of the Ottoman Empire and the subsequent forcible imposition of a dividing European colonialism.[47] Kurd'ali, who, like many Arab intellectuals of his generation, had wavered between pan-Ottomanism and Arabism before settling on the notion of an Arab Syrian nation, was writing at the depressing moment that saw Palestine and Jordan relinquished to Great Britain while France proceeded to sever Lebanon from the motherland and split the rest of Syria into four statelets.[48] His *Khitat* was thus a *cri de coeur* of a nationalist who had witnessed the shattering of his dreams of a unified Syria, fleetingly assembled under King Faisal in the form of the Arab Kingdom of Syria in 1919–20. In his encyclopedic book, Kurd'ali was recreating that Syrian nation: independent, modern, and molded over a long and brilliant history, which actually never materialized.[49] To structure his vast material, he overextended the *khitat* genre to its methodological limits, pushing it to both embody and express a territorial nationalism despite its traditional city-geared framework. But the genre was, at the same time, the closest approximation to political geography available to this reformist keen on reviving the intellectual contours of an Arabic epistemology that had been active at least five centuries in the past. That is why he so wholeheartedly embraced it. However, as with the case of Mubarak's *Khitat*, Kurd'ali's genre restoration did not have any takers among the professional Syrian historians of the next generation, who, as in Egypt, turned to the modern, European-inspired history writing.[50]

[47] Ouyang, *Poetics of Love*, 48–61, offers a comparison between the two *khitat*s and underscores the more urgent task of Kurd'ali, worrying about the fragmentation of Bilad al-Sham.

[48] The most penetrating analysis of Muhammad Kurd'ali's shifting politics and intellectual views during the last days of the Ottoman empire is Salim Tamari, "A 'Scientific Expedition' to Gallipoli: The Syrian-Palestinian Intelligentsia and the Ottoman Campaign Against Arab Separatism," *Jerusalem Quarterly* 56 (Winter/Spring 2014): 6–28, repub. as "Muhammad Kurd'ali and the Syrian-Palestinian Intelligentsia in the Ottoman Campaign Against Arabic Separatism," in *Syria in World War I: Politics, Economy and Society*, M. Talha Çiçek, ed. (London: Routledge, 2016), 37–60, then again in Tamari's collection of essays as "A 'Scientific Expedition' to Gallipoli: The Syrian-Palestinian Intelligentsia Divided," in *The Great War and the Remaking of Palestine* (Berkeley: University of California Press, 2017), 67–87.

[49] See Heghnar Watenpaugh, "An Uneasy Historiography: The Legacy of Ottoman Architecture in the Former Arab Provinces," *Muqarnas* 24 (2007): 34–7, for the discussion of the *Khitat al-Sham*'s scope and aim in redrawing a Syrian nation; Joseph H. Escovitz, "Orientalists and Orientalism in the Writings of Muhammad Kurd'ali," *IJMES* 15, 1 (1983): 95–109, for a review of Kurd'ali's possibly earliest critique in Arabic of orientalist views on the subject of Arab history and the conception of an Arab nation, which will become standard stance in later pan-Arabist writings of the 1960s.

[50] It was severely and negatively reviewed by the dean of American Arabists Philip K. Hitti, "*Kitab Khiṭaṭ al-Sham* by Muḥammad Kurd'ali," *JOAS* 51, 2 (June 1931), 178–9.

Architectural History Comes to Egypt: From Coste to Creswell

The dependence of the *khitat* genre on textual descriptions of spaces and places without graphic representation did not allow it to become the organizational vehicle of another emerging discipline, architectural history, even one that covers the same terrain (i.e. the Islamic architecture of Egypt). The Western paradigm of architectural knowledge, which started to take shape in the Renaissance with the publication of large, illustrated treatises surveying the architecture of the ancients (Greeks and Romans), fundamentally relied on codified architectural representation.[51] The method arrived in Egypt with the savants of the Napoleonic invasion, who based their study of the Islamic monuments of Cairo and the rest of Egypt on measured plans, perspective drawings, and analytical details. Magnificently printed in grand format in the *Description de l'Égypte*, these drawings were backed up by textual descriptions that borrowed heavily from al-Maqrizi. The section of the *Description* in which they were published in a travelogue-like order, the two volumes of illustrations of the *état moderne*, marked the emergence of the modern study of Islamic architecture in general, and its Egyptian subfield in particular, as a part of a totalizing colonial project. Several European architects, especially French, followed in the footsteps of the *Description*'s savants: encouraged by the openness of Muhammad ʿAli and his eagerness to recruit European experts to help in his modernization project, they traveled to Egypt to measure and record buildings and ruins and depict them using various representational techniques.[52] Some of these architects also ferreted through the limited available written sources to verify the historical details about the structures they drew: date, provenance, patron, cost, and the like. They then published their finds in impressive architectural catalogs that introduced to the European architectural profession the rich Islamic heritage of Cairo, which was hitherto almost totally unknown and untapped. In the process, the extant *khitat* books, particularly al-Maqrizi's *Khitat*, were reduced to repositories of textual

[51] A concise overview of the evolution of architectural drawings is François Bucher, "Medieval Architectural Design Methods 800–1560," *Gesta* 11, 2 (1972): 37–51. On the Renaissance transformation of the architect, see Leopold D. Ettlinger, "The Emergence of the Italian Architect during the Fifteenth Century," in *The Architect: Chapters in the Hisotry of a Profession*, Spiro Kostof, ed. (New York: Oxford University Press, 1977), 96–123; also Catherine Wilkinson, "The New Professionalism in the Renaissance," in Kostof, *The Architect*, 124–60. An alternative view focused on the case of Egypt is Nasser Rabbat, "Design Without Representation in Medieval Egypt," *Muqarnas* 25 (2008): 147–54.

[52] There were earlier travelers who attempted to architecturally capture some of Egypt's Islamic monuments before the French Occupation in less systematic ways. For a survey of these travelers/illustrators, see Doris Behrens-Abouseif, "Islamic Architecture from Travelogue to Survey. The Discovery of Islamic Cairo," *Lexico: Storie e architettura in Sicilia e nel Mediterraneo* 28 (2019): 7–26.

information on buildings and their urban surroundings that can be plucked as primary material to complete the architectural evidence collected in situ and verify and contextualize its graphic representation.

The immediate successor to the *Description de l'Égypte*'s groundbreaking codification of the Islamic architecture of Cairo was the work of a French architect from Marseille, Pascal-Xavier Coste (1787–1879). Between 1817 and 1827, Coste worked for Muhammad ʿAli Pasha as the designer and supervisor of large engineering projects and as an architect of palaces and commemorative structures. After his return to France, he published his impressive compendium, *L'Architecture Arabe ou monuments du Kaire mesurés et dessinés de 1818 à 1826*, which, as the title indicates, focuses exclusively on (a selection of) the Islamic monuments of Cairo. The book is conceived and presented in the grand tradition of the Beaux-Arts, where Coste was trained.[53] Every example is depicted in plan, sections, elevations, interior and exterior perspectives, and what used to be called "analytiques," that is, various details rendered in different scales and format, in addition to short, descriptive paragraphs to explain the drawings. A concise historical introduction, indirectly influenced by al-Maqrizi probably via the *Description de l'Égypte*, sums up Coste's knowledge of the Islamic architecture of Egypt and contextualizes the architecture of the "Arabs" in general in relation to medieval Western architecture. Despite its limited coverage, the book ratifies the notion of an endogamous Egyptian architectural tradition first implied by the *Description*'s practical focus on Egypt to the exclusion of its surrounding cultural milieu. Coste, in fact, was the first to establish and order a basic vocabulary for a Cairene Mamluk style, which he considered the most representative of the architecture of Cairo. After Coste, several books on Cairo's architecture and geometric ornament were published in the nineteenth century furthering the construct of a stand-alone architectural tradition in the city. Chief among them were the two manuals on Islamic Cairene ornaments by Émile Prisse d'Avennes in 1847 and Jules Bourgoin in 1879.[54] One study, Martin S. Briggs's

[53] Pascal-Xavier Coste, *Architecture Arabe ou monuments du Kaire mésurés et dessinés de 1818 à 1826* (Paris: Firmin-Didot, 1839). Coste's work has received critical attention in the last few decades. See, for example, the articles collected in Daniel Armogathe and Sylviane Leprun, *Pascal Coste ou l'architecture cosmopolite* (Paris: Éditions l'Harmattan, 1990); my "The Formation of the Neo-Mamluk Style in Modern Egypt," in Martha Pollak, ed., *The Education of the Architect: Historiography, Urbanism and the Growth of Architectural Knowledge. Essays Presented to Stanford Anderson on His Sixty-Second Birthday* (Cambridge, MA: MIT Press, 1997), 363–86. See also *Pascal Coste, toutes les Égypte* (Marseille: Parenthèses, 1998), published on the occasion of an exhibition organized by the Bibliothèque municipale de Marseille June 17–September 30, 1998 as part of the national observance "France-Égypte, horizons partagés."

[54] Émile Prisse d'Avennes, *Monuments Egyptiens, bas-reliefs, peintures, inscriptions etc., d'après les dessins exécutés sur les lieux, par E. Prisse d'Avennes* (Paris: Firmin Didot fréres, 1847); Jules

Muhammadan Architecture in Egypt and Palestine, published in 1924, stands out for its unprecedented conscious attempt to explore the links between the architecture of Cairo and the Syro-Palestinian cities which were historically and culturally associated with it, like Jerusalem, Damascus, and Aleppo.[55]

Then came the most comprehensive and architecturally astute study, the lifetime's work of an English technical draftsman turned architectural historian, K. A. C. Creswell (1879–1974). Diligent and dogged, Creswell measured, photographed, researched, and drew all known Cairene monuments up to the Sabil of Sultan al-Nasir Muhammad constructed in 1326, and published them in two heavy volumes as the *Muslim Architecture of Egypt*. With their predecessors on early Muslim architecture, these two volumes played an important role in establishing the field of Islamic architecture on solid, definite grounds.[56] Creswell's systematic technique of documentation, thorough measurement, and quantitative accuracy were bolstered by his extensive perusal of the primary textual sources, which he unfortunately read only in translation, in search for any reference to the building under study.[57] With every entry on a building, he methodically listed the primary sources he used from the earliest to the newest. Naturally, al-Maqrizi's *Khitat* was one of his main sources, which he quoted verbatim countless times, though either from Casanova's and Wiet's incomplete editions or from translations supplied by unnamed assistants since he did not know Arabic. But for Creswell, al-Maqrizi, like all other Islamic sources, was only a purveyor of information that needed to be checked against empirical research and was never seen as an interpretive or discursive source. This strictly positivistic approach was adequate for the formal evaluation of buildings; several scholars have adopted it since, most notably Jacques Revault and Michael Meinecke, with spectacular

Bourgoin, *Les éléments de l'art arabe: le trait des entrelacs* (Paris: Firmin Didot, 1879). For a contextualization of this series of manuals, see Mercedes Volait, "History or Theory? French Antiquarianism, Cairene Architecture, and Enlightenment Thinking," *Ars Orientalis* 39 (2010): 231–54.

55 Martin S. Briggs, *Muhammadan Architecture in Egypt and Palestine* (Oxford: Clarendon Press; 1924). Briggs, p. 47, uniquely critiques the Orientalists of his time in their denigration of any "Arabic" contribution to the development of Islamic architecture, a widely held assumption among those who studied Islamic architecture at the time.

56 K. A. C. Creswell, *Early Muslim Architecture*, 2 vols. (Oxford: Oxford University Press, 2nd edn., 1969), and *Muslim Architecture of Egypt*, 2 vols. (Oxford: Oxford University Press, 1959). A volume of *Muqarnas*, vol. 8 (1991) was devoted to Creswell and his legacy.

57 For a critique of Creswell's methods and obsessions see the analysis of J. M. Rogers, "Architectural History as Literature: Creswell's Reading and Methods," *Muqarnas*, 8 (1991): 45–54; Julian Raby, "Reviewing the Reviewers," *Muqarnas*, 8 (1991): 4–11. Neither author evaluates the effects of Creswell's conservative imperial politics or his pronounced contempt for modern Egypt and Egyptians on his studies.

documentary results.[58] Yet, although his plans and architectural descriptions still furnish the basis for any study of early Islamic or Egyptian architecture, Creswell's deterministic proclamations have been superseded by subsequent and more empathetic scholarship that probes the full range of signification offered by the available sources.

Moreover, Creswell's neglect of the architectural heritage of the eastern half of the Islamic world, his uncritical acceptance of linear architectural chronology, and his strict adherence to a stringent imperial stratification of cultures have relegated the utility of his monumental work to that of a reference book that is consulted for details but not engaged with in an interpretive historical debate.[59] His narrow definition of a culture's territory unintentionally but effectively provided an imposing precedent for later contentions of an endogenic and seemingly insular Egyptian architectural tradition that were motivated by another kind of passion. This impression is what one actually gets out of Creswell's own text, which, despite a fanatical preoccupation with "architectural origins," precedents, and formal analogy between buildings across (certain) cultures and geographies, constructed an imaginary Egypt severed from its Mediterranean, African, and Islamic extensions, thus hindering any meaningful crosscultural analysis.

Ironically, Creswell, the ex-colonial officer who lived and worked in Cairo for more than fifty years, never warmed to the culture whose built environment he was so obsessively studying.[60] His haughty detachment not only hampered his full understanding of the architecture in its context, leading him to overlook or misread many of its sociocultural subtleties. It also severely limited his interaction with the nationalist scholarly milieu burgeoning around him, in whose formation he was paradoxically involved as the first professor of Islamic architecture at the Egyptian University. In fact, his unguarded scorn extended to his contemporary Egyptian architectural historians, although some of them were his erstwhile students, helpers, and

[58] Jacques Revault produced or supervised at least a dozen books on Islamic residential architecture in several Arab capitals, Tunis, Fez, Cairo, and Algiers, with detailed measured drawings of the houses, their plans, sections, elevations, and ornaments. Michael Meinecke's *opus magnum* was his exhaustive *Die Mamlukische Architektur in Ägypten und Syrien (648/1250 bis 923/1517)* 2 vols. (Glückstadt: Verlag J. J. Augustin, 1992), in which he reproduced plans of most Mamluk structures in the same scale in addition to all the primary and secondary sources references related to them.

[59] Raby, "Reviewing the Reviewers," 10, quotes Eric Schroeder's review in which he bitingly opines that Creswell's book is not a classic in the sense of possessing great human interest.

[60] Donald Malcolm Reid, "Cultural Imperialism and Nationalism: The Struggle to Define and Control the Heritage of Arab Art in Egypt," *IJMES* 24, 1 (February 1992): 57–76, p. 70, no. 71, quoting R. W. Hamilton, "Keppel Archibald Cameron Creswell, 1879–1974," *Proceedings of the British Academy* 60 (1974): 1–20, pp. 15–16, reprinted in *Muqarnas* 8 (1991): 128–36.

collaborators, even though they at times went unacknowledged in his published books. They, in turn, had their muffled misgivings about this strange and unlikely father figure of the study of the Islamic architecture of Egypt. They certainly appreciated his exhaustive method of collecting references and visual evidence, his straightforward and precise writing style, and his dedication to accuracy in representation. But they were wary of his highhandedness and colonial disdain of Egyptian living culture and its corollary: his stubborn refusal to learn Arabic, even though his research depended to a large extent on Arabic primary texts.

This strained relationship between Creswell and the Egyptian architectural historians was but one particularly pronounced manifestation of a general pattern of scholarly separation that originated under colonial rule but remained effective until today. There was and still are in Egypt two research apparatuses, one Egyptian and the other Western but specializing in Egyptian history. Both work on the same subjects, including Islamic Egyptian architecture, with minimal interaction. Their scant relationship is, moreover, fraught with mutual suspicion, scholarly disdain, and frequent accusations of plagiarism. Analyzing the reasons for these hostile attitudes requires grounding the argument within the larger issue of the intellectual split in Islamic studies between the Islamic world and the West, an Orientalist predicament loaded with overtones of elitism, cultural and religious misgivings, and a perverse nostalgia for the colonial age.[61]

Nationalist Architectural History: 'Abdel-Wahab, Maher, Fikri, and Shafe'i

While Creswell was diligently working on his enormous tomes in colonial Cairo, a new generation of native architectural historians who had pursued

[61] An honest and unwaveringly blunt assessment with a rather heavy-handed suggestion for a remedy is Stephan Conermann's review of N. Mahmud Mustafa, *al-'Asr al-Mamluki*, in *MSR* 4 (2000): 257–60; see also Nasser Rabbat, "Review of Fahmi 'Abd al-'Alim, *Al-'Imara al-Islamyah fi 'Asr al-Mamalik al-Jarakisa: 'Asr al-Sultan al-Mu'ayyad Shaykh* (Cairo: Wizarat al-Thaqafa, al-Majlis al-A'la lil-Athar, 2003)," *MSR* 10, 2 (2006): 210–13. Di-Capua, *Gatekeepers*, in reviewing the collapse of an authoritative historiography on modern Egypt in the period 1970–2000, ascribes it to the move toward a security state, the rise of Islamist historiography, and what he terms authoritarian pluralism, 311–36. On page 335 6 he concludes with an ominous pronouncement that "Not only has the Egyptian scholarly community not entered a dialogue with the Western historical method and striven to influence it from the stance of an Egyptian experience, but also, for the most part, that community has become entirely removed from what seems to be an emerging global historiographical field." From his perspective this seems to be the fault of the Egyptian side only. No Western responsibility for this state of affairs is mentioned.

their higher education in various European universities was setting the stage for an Egyptian school of architectural history. Laboring in an ardent nationalist ambiance in which the cultural identity of Egypt was hotly debated, these historians were trying to fashion from a number of competing historical frames of reference—Pharaonic, Islamic, Arabic, modern, or strictly vernacular—a coherent Egyptian whole.[62] In their pursuit, they were greatly influenced by three authoritative and exclusivist scholarly discourses that considerably shaped the contours of their field of inquiry. One was disciplinary; the two others were linked to the Egyptian context. The disciplinary discourse derived from the peculiar historiography of the study of Islamic history in the West that came to be called Orientalism and its various peregrinations over time. Orientalism, as Edward Said observed, formed a discursive and intricate network of scholarly and cultural conventions that used, produced, and controlled knowledge about the Islamic world. But its scope also reflected the dominant paradigm of traditional Western scholarship, which affirms a self-conscious and historically evolving cultural identity for the West from Classical origins to its triumphant culmination in modern times while relegating other cultures to marginal places in its ordered chronology.[63] This historiographical framework, which depended on imperial postures (and some twisting of the historical record)[64] rather than historical facts or scholarly reflections, divided history into specialized subfields confined within clearly proscribed and exclusive time, space, and culture, with no interaction with or influence on the master Western narrative.[65]

In art and architectural history, the most graphic illustration of this hierarchy is the infamous "Tree of Architecture" of the two Banister Fletchers

[62] Di-Capua, *Gatekeepers*, 219–37, reviews the partisan historiography of the 1940s–50s and assesses the national allegory aspects of Egyptian nationalist texts of the period.

[63] Marshall Hodgson, *Rethinking World History: Essays on Europe, Islam, and World History* edited with introduction and conclusion by Edmund Burke III (Cambridge: Cambridge University Press, 1993), 97–299, offers the most lucid analysis of the rigid structure of history and proposes a method in world history that he calls the interregional approach to counter it; Nasser Rabbat "The Hidden Hand: Edward Said's Orientalism and Architectural History," in *the Journal of the Society of Architectural Historians* 77, 4 (December 2018): 388–96.

[64] Martin Bernal, *Black Athena: The Afroasiatic Roots of Classical Civilization*, 2 vols. (New Brunswick, N.J.: Rutgers University Press, 1987), 1: 121–226, offers an extensive review of blatant instances of historiographical dishonesty in nineteenth-century Europe.

[65] This is the main argument of Edward Said, *Culture and Imperialism* (New York: Vintage, 1993), 1–18; Hentsch, *Imagining the Middle East*, 119–38, contextualizes the historiographical redefinition of the Orient in the age of modernity and colonialism. Garth Fowden, *Empire to Commonwealth: Consequences of Monotheism in Late Antiquity* (Princeton, 1993), 9, picked up on the same point by asserting that "There are roads out of antiquity that do not lead to the Renaissance." His book offers a historical reconceptualization of the antiquity-to-Islam continuum that challenges previous frameworks.

(father and son), which appeared as frontispiece in all seventeen editions of their influential book *A History of Architecture on the Comparative Method for the Student, Craftsman, and Amateur*, published between 1896 and 1954. This unabashed yet fanciful Eurocentric diagram, conceived of at the height of the colonial age, reserved the living trunk and the upper, healthy branches of the tree for an uninterrupted succession of Western styles from ancient Greece to modern America (dubbed historical styles) and demoted the architecture of all other cultures (labeled nonhistorical styles) to dead-end branches functioning primarily as stylistic curiosities.[66] This strict scheme, which was very problematic on its own, had an indelible effect on the conceptualization of all non-Western architectural cultures, including Islamic architecture. It reduced it to a set of prevalent characterizations—static, sensual, and ornamental being the favorite among them—that stood in stark contrast to the historically evolving attributes frequently portrayed as specific to Western architecture.[67]

The practice of hierarchical demarcation survived in academe and scholarship far longer than its biased and compromised source, the bluntly Eurocentric cultural stratification of the triumphant colonial age. It even affected the writing of most of the post-independence historians and theorists in the sometimes hastily formed nations of the Islamic world, not the least the writing of the tiny scholarly community of Egyptian architectural history. As Franz Fanon succinctly noted at the outset of the postcolonial age, the nationalists' heartfelt resistance to a hegemonic intellectual construct did not prevent their falling into the trap of its conceptual dichotomous substratum.[68] In their zeal to purge their emerging national identity of any potentially

[66] For a critical discussion of Fletcher's structure, see Gulsum Baydar Nalbantoglu, "Toward Postcolonial Openings: Rereading Sir Banister Fletcher's *History of Architecture*," *Assemblage* 35 (1998): 6–17.

[67] Sibel Bozdoğan and Gülru Necipoğlu, "Entangled Discourses: Scrutinizing Orientalist and Nationalist Legacies in the Architectural Historiography of the 'Lands of Rum,'" *Muqarnas* 24 (2007): 1–6; Gülru Necipoğlu, "The Concept of Islamic Art: Inherited Discourses and New Approaches," *JAH* 6: special issue, "Islamic art historiography", http://arthistoriography.wordpress.com/, originally published in Benoît Junod, Georges Khalil, Stefan Weber and Gerhard Wolf, eds., *Islamic Art and the Museum* (London: Saqi, 2012), 57–76; Heghnar Watenpaugh, "Resonance and Circulation: The Category 'Islamic Art and Architecture,'" in Finbarr Barry Flood and Gülru Necipoglu, eds., *A Companion to Islamic Art and Architecture*, 2 vols. (Hoboken, N.J.: John Wiley, 2017), 2: 1223–41.

[68] Franz Fanon, *The Wretched of the Earth*, trans. Constance Farrington (New York: Grove Press, 1963), "On National Culture," 167–99, for a no-holds-barred analysis of the paradoxical psychological and epistemological consequences of colonial corruption on the construction of a postcolonial national culture. See the elaborate analysis of Saïd, *Culture and Imperialism*, 191–280, focusing on the rise of a postcolonial literature and its entanglement with the literature of the metropolis. For a discussion of the relationship between culture and ideology see Clifford Geertz, "Ideology as a Cultural System," *The Interpretation of Cultures* (New York: Basic Books, 1973), 193–229.

damning colonial influence, they ended up structuring and categorizing the history of "their" architecture, "their" cities, and "their" culture in general from an exclusive and ultimately narrowly defined national, religious, or cultural perspective.[69]

Two locally grown particularist currents bolstered the impact the Orientalist framework had on the orientation and purview of the emerging Egyptian architectural history. First was the long and undeniably Egyptian tradition of *khitat*, exemplified by al-Maqrizi's foundational work and Mubarak's updating of it. Second was the idiosyncratic but authoritative Creswellian paradigm, which was Egyptocentric for reasons stemming from its Orientalist roots rather than any particular identification with Egypt on the part of the author. Until very recently, Egyptian histories of architecture reflected this mixed conceptual lineage in varying combinations. The art/architectural history's stratified structure imposed on them the cultural limits of their investigation, confining it to Egypt and, at best, its Arab-Islamic milieu. This was also the frame implemented by a large number of Orientalist studies on the Islamic architecture of Egypt that went back, as we saw, to Pascal Coste and that constituted a solid and indispensable set of reference works. Their number and reach grew in the twentieth century. Their authors were primarily Europeans (and later Americans) who resided and worked in Egypt, either in Western research centers or in Egyptian cultural institutions under the auspices of the colonial authorities. They thus had access to the historical architecture of the country that was equal to that of the recently minted native historians, if not greater. This was especially the case for the members of the Comité de Conservation des Monuments de l'Art Arabe, who enjoyed the backing of the authorities and the exclusive access to monuments under conservation. They by and large had a complicated relationship with their Egyptian counterparts that ranged from amicable collaboration to professional disparagement, sometimes coupled with underhanded exploitation.[70] Creswell of course, by virtue of his unconventional personality, manifest colonial mentality, and long stay in Egypt, was both a peculiar and a typical example of that relationship. His massive survey of Islamic Egyptian monuments, which benefited from the contributions of many, often unnamed

[69] Several recent studies in Egypt picked up on Fanon's observation to examine the consequences of the orientalist roots of national culture: cf. Muhammad Khalifah Hasan Ahmad, *Athar al-fikr al-istishraqi fi al-mujtama'at al-Islamiyya* (Cairo: 'Ayn lil-Dirasat wa-al-Buhuth al-Insaniyya wa-al-Ijtima'iyya, 1997); Ahmad Shaykh, *Hiwar al-istishraq: min naqd al-istishraq ila naqd al-istighrab* (Cairo: al-Markaz al-'Arabi lil-Dirasat al-Gharbiyya, 1999).

[70] El-Habashi, "The Preservation of Egyptian Cultural Heritage through Egyptian Eyes"; Reid, "Cultural Imperialism and Nationalism," 64–73, traces the episodes of that competition in relation to the comité and the Museum of Arab [later Islamic] Art.

Egyptians, was both an extreme representative of the Orientalist tradition and a precedent that cannot be ignored despite its underlying biases.

But if the Orientalist legacy and Creswell's towering presence embodied the colonial influence in the endogamous framing of the Egyptian architectural history, al-Maqrizi's *Khitat* constituted the opposite referent. Not only its scope and fullness, striving to cover the entire urban history of Egypt up to the fifteenth century, but also al-Maqrizi's ardent passion and filial affinity with Egypt made his book the most powerfully felt formative discourse of the national (architectural) history. Many modern Egyptian historians in fact reproduced his feelings not only for their historical significance but also—ignoring possible anachronism—as exemplary patriotic proclamations from a "true Egyptian citizen."[71] Thus, if the Western academic field of architectural history and Creswell "orientalized" Egyptian architectural history, al-Maqrizi's *Khitat* offered Egyptian historians the historical justification to nationalize it. Ideologically, al-Maqrizi's *Khitat* represented a model national history—before the corrupting colonial influence, and even before the "long decline" under the Ottomans, as it were[72]—and therefore a positive example to follow. Historically, the cosmocentric framework of the *Khitat* legitimized similar particularist treatments in modern, nationalistically driven studies, which prevailed until the rise of a vocal, state-sponsored cultural pan-Arabism under Gamal 'Abd al-Nasser in the 1960s. Scholarly emphasis then shifted to Egypt's Arabic milieu as the context of its own architectural development.[73]

Some Egyptian studies went a step further in their identification with the framework and focus of al-Maqrizi's *Khitat* so that they come across

[71] A tone of suprahistorical fellowship with al-Maqrizi emanates from the collection of studies in Ziyada et al., *Dirasat 'an al-Maqrizi*, where al-Maqrizi is repeatedly called a "true Egyptian citizen" and a "patriot." The same kind of feeling must have influenced the choice of Salah 'Issa's book title, *Hawamish al-Maqrizi, Hikayat min Misr* (*The Margins of al-Maqrizi, Stories from Egypt*), two collections (Cairo: Dar al-Qahira, 1983). The book is a collection of populist essays in which history and sociology are rhetorically conscripted to advance an ardent nationalistic message. For the author, al-Maqrizi's name seems to have presented a model both of a historian and a nationalist to whom he can relate.

[72] Di-Capua, *Gatekeepers*, 340, points to the consequences of ignoring 400 years of Ottoman rule in modern Egyptian historiography.

[73] The 1960s witnessed the rise of romantic pan-Arabist (and Baathist) art history, which saw a continuous genealogy in the arts of the various pre-Islamic cultures of the "Arabs," leading to the Islamic art of the Umayyads with its pronounced Arabic character, and somehow bypassing the encounter with classicism during the Hellenistic, Roman, and Byzantine periods. Cf. 'Afif al-Bahnasi, *al-Fann al-Islami* (Damascus: Dar Talas, 1986), 38–40 and a more elaborate discussion in idem, *al-Sham: Lamahat Athariyy wa-Fanniyya* (Baghdad, Dar al-Rashid, 1980), 10–37. It is also possible that the model appears inadvertently in some Arabic studies simply because they were copying from European sources. This seems to be the case with Tharwat Ukashah, *al-Taswir al-Islami: al-Dini wa-al-'Arabi* (Beirut: al-Mu'assasa al-Arabiyya lil-Dirasat wa-al-Nashr, 1977).

as essentially modern renditions with a visually oriented outlook and more extensive and architecturally precise verbal descriptions. 'Ali Mubarak might be considered an early example of this affinity, although in his case the identification with al-Maqrizi was more inclusive as he adopted his text verbatim, probably in accordance with the established traditional scholarly norms with which he grew up. But in the twentieth century, pioneering art historians like Hasan 'Abdel-Wahab (1898–1967) in his *Tarikh al-Masajid al-Athariyya allati salla fiha faridhat al-jum'a hadhrat sahib al-jalala al-malik al-salih Farouq al-Awwal* (*The History of Heritage Mosques in which his Majesty King Faruk I Performed the Friday Prayer*), and Su'ad Maher (1917–96) in her *Masajid Misr wa Awliya'uha al-Salihun* (*The Mosques of Egypt and its Pious Saints*), did something similar, albeit with a more professional art-historical language all their own.[74] 'Abdel-Wahab's book, as the title indicates, deals with the distinguished mosques of Cairo and Alexandria in which King Farouq prayed up to 1946. This clever ploy to attract royal patronage to the mosques and the book at the same time may be seen as an already circumscribed criterion without the superimposition of al-Maqrizi's framework. And in fact, it is. But a careful examination of the entries on the individual mosques themselves shows how much they owe to al-Maqrizi's method of weaving the history of the structure with anecdotal biographies of its patrons, users, and builders when they are known ('Abd a-Wahab is credited with discovering the name of the building supervisor of the Mosque of Sultan Hasan).[75] This method insures the primacy of a vertical (chronological or diachronic) historical investigation in constructing any building's architectural history rather than a horizontal or synchronic comparative probe, which would have extended the analysis beyond the building under study to other comparable buildings in the city or in a wider environment, thus establishing norms, inventions, variations, and deviations from dominant styles at any given moment. Su'ad Maher's book deals with the Islamic religious structures all over Egypt, and as such, her framework is closer to that of al-Maqrizi's *Khitat* than 'Abdel-Wahab's book, and still betrays the same primacy of Cairo in thinking about Egypt noticed in the outlook of the fifteenth-century historian as in the framework of a twentieth-century art historian. But like

[74] Hasan 'Abdel-Wahab, *Tarikh al-Masajid al-Athariyya allati salla fiha faridhat al-jum'a hadret sahib al-jalala al-malik al-salih Farouq al-Awwal*, 2 vols. (Cairo: Dar al-Kutub, 1946 and reprint 1994); Su'ad Maher, *Masajid Misr wa Awliya'uha al-Salihun*, 3 vols. (Cairo, 1971). An earlier French survey of Cairo's mosques may have supplied another frame of reference for these and similar later books: Louis Hautecœur and Gaston Wiet, *Les mosquées du Caire*, 2 vols. (Paris: Ernest Leroux, 1932).

[75] 'Abdel-Wahab, *Tarikh al-Masajid*, 1: 176. See Abdallah Kahil, *The Sultan Ḥasan Complex in Cairo 1357–1364: A Case Study in the Formation of Mamluk style* (Würzburg, Germany: Ergon-Verlag, 2008), 169–80, for a discussion of the attribution.

'Abdel-Wahab's, and ultimately like al-Maqrizi's, her investigation is more diachronic than synchronic on all scales, from the single edifice to the architectural type, and, like the two other authors', her book's cosmocentrism is literally built into its structure, language, and scope.

The Free Officers' coup/revolution in 1952 that removed the king and established a new republican regime let by Gamal 'Abd al-Nasser (r. 1954–70) ushered in a reorientation of the state's political identity toward an outspoken pan-Arabism and instituted a more intrusive control of cultural life.[76] These changes altered the tone and range of historical writing, now promoted by the state as part of its vast new propaganda apparatus.[77] But many historians enthusiastically espoused the state-sanctioned direction: they were cultural pan-Arabists themselves who bore their ideological stance in their teaching and scholarship even before 'Abd Nasser's political realignment. For those working on architectural history, this meant widening their purview to encompass a broad terrain that extended to North Africa, Bilad al-Sham, and beyond. Conceptually, they turned to interculturality as a framework and wielded a comparative lens to explain the interaction between the architecture of Egypt and Arabic architectural traditions around the Mediterranean and other Islamic regions. Although they still depended on the *khitat*'s data and sometimes language, their works diverged from the diachronic order of *khitat*-inspired analysis and adopted one of two more inclusive methods current in contemporary art-historical studies. This allowed them to transcend the cosmocentrism embedded in the *khitat*'s structure and historiography, even though their work still conveyed a heavy emphasis on the centrality of Egypt, and Cairo in particular, in the development and understanding of Arabic architecture, an assertion that might have been more influenced by the political maneuvering of the 'Abd Nasser's regime to lead the Arab world than by any direct residue of the *khitat* genre.

The first method is the typologically structured survey, and its most distinct representative is *Masajid al-Qahira wa Madarisaha* (*The Mosques and Madrasas of Cairo*) by Ahmad Fikri (1904–75), a distinguished professor of

[76] Judiciously analyzed in Richard Jacquemond, *Conscience of the Nation: Writers, State, and Society in Modern Egypt*, David Tresilian, trans. (Cairo: AUC Press, 2008), 1–21.

[77] Louis 'Awad, "Cultural and Intellectual Developments in Egypt since 1952," *Egypt since the Revolution*, P. J. Vatikiotis, ed. (2nd edn., Routledge, 2013), 143–61; Joel Gordon, *Nasser: Hero of the Arab Nation* (Oxford: Oneworld, 2006), 50–78; Mona Arif, *Constructing the National Past: History Writing and Nation-Building in Nasser's Egypt* (Alexandria, Egypt: Bibliotheca Alexandrina, Futuristic Studies Unit, 2017), 13–24; Di-Capua, *Gatekeepers*, 256–7 and notes 32, and 340 and 4, asserts that Pan-Arabism hardly left any historiographical mark. Perhaps his focus on modern histories of Egypt did not allow him to see the tremendous changes post-1952 toward a pan-Arab scope and orientation in histories of Egyptian architecture.

Islamic civilization at the University of Alexandria.[78] Exhaustive, theoretically alert, and argumentative, the book is divided into three volumes each covering a period of Egypt's medieval Islamic history—the Fatimid, Ayyubid, and Bahri Mamluk—with a long introductory essay that tackles the formative period of Islamic architecture between the Islamic conquests and the arrival of the Fatimids in the tenth century and that extends beyond Egypt to encompass the eastern part of the Arab world, where the early centers of Islamic culture developed. The book's clearly stated agenda is to counter the claims that Islamic architecture owes many of its achievements to influences from the non-Arabic cultures it appropriated through conquest and that the Arabs played a negligible role in its evolution. Accordingly, Fikri situates his book both in opposition to and in dialogue with the Orientalists, praising their meticulous efforts at reconstructing the history of Islamic architecture (primarily in Egypt) but methodically debunking their theories about the origins and development of various elements of Islamic architecture by pointing out their biases and their seemingly received ideas about the Arabic culture under Islam. Unsurprisingly, his main *bête noire* is Creswell, who he accuses of arrogance, pugnacity, and antagonism, to the point of accusing him of altering the translation from an Arabic source to serve his ideological agenda, which seems indeed to be the case.[79]

The second method is writing architectural history as an unbroken narrative that weaves architectural analysis together with political, cultural, and religious history. A good example of this type is the weighty book of Farid Shafeʿi (1907–85), *al-ʿImara al-ʿArabiyya fi-Misr al-Islamiyya, al-Mujallad al-Awwal, ʿAsr al-Wulat (31–358/639–969)* (*Arabic Architecture in Islamic Egypt, Tome 1, The Age of the Governors, 31–358/639–969)*, which unfortunately remained without a sequel that would take the narrative into the Fatimid period.[80] Shafeʿi, who was trained as an architect before earning a graduate degree in Islamic architecture under Creswell's supervision, made a name for

[78] Ahmad Fikri, *Masajid al-Qahira wa Madarisaha*, 3 vols. with an introductory essay (Cairo: Dar al-Maʿarif, 1962–9).

[79] Fikri, *Masajid al-Qahira, Introductory Essay*, 18–19, vol. 2: 6, 130. Fikri points out that al-Maqrizi's text on the building of the gates of Cairo under Badr al-Jamali mentions only three brothers who came from al-Ruha (Odessa or Urfa) to build them (al-Maqrizi, *Khitat2*, 2: 269–70); Creswell, *Muslim Architecture of Egypt*, 1: 162 adds the word "Christian" to the text. Creswell does not quote Abu Salih al-Armani, who is the only source that references a person with a Christian name, Yuhanna al-Rahib (the Priest), as the builder of Cairo's gates, Al-Maqrizi, *Khitat2*, 2: 269, note 2.

[80] Farid Shafeʿi, *al-ʿImara al-ʿArabiyya fi Misr al-Islamiyya, ʿAsr al-Wulat* (Cairo: al-Hay'a al-Misriyya al-ʿAmma li-l-Ta'lif wa-l-Nashr, 1970, reprinted 1994), and the more general *al-ʿImara al-ʿArabiyya al-Islamiyya, Madiha wa-Hadiraha wa-Mustaqbalaha* (Riyadh: Jamiʿat al-Malik Saʿud, 1982), published when Shafeʿi served as a professor of Islamic architecture in Saudi Arabia.

himself as a designer of many neo-Islamic structures in Egypt, Libya, and Saudi Arabia. In this book, he poured his pan-Arabist sentiments not only into his language but also in organizing his narrative around the idea of a continuous and productive Arabic cultural presence before and throughout the early Islamic period in which Egypt came to play a vital role, albeit toward the end of the formative Islamic period. As Fikri did in his introductory volume, which covers the same historical ground, Shafe'i sets his study against the Orientalists' denigration of the Arabs' cultural role in the formation of Islamic architecture. And like Fikri, he engages in elaborate critiques of his former tutor Creswell, challenging his interpretations on both factual and ideological grounds while at the same time recognizing his pioneering role in the study of Islamic architecture and his meticulous documentation method.[81]

Fikri and Shafe'i are but two outstanding examples of an entire school of interpretation that dominated the study of Islamic architecture in Egypt (and the history of Egypt in general) during the Pan-Arabism heyday, which lasted into the mid-1970s.[82] Upbeat, defiant, and hopeful like the majority of intellectuals who believed in the progressive march of pan-Arabism, they celebrated the political, cultural, and social gains and endured the numerous strategic blunders, economic setbacks, and human rights abuses made in its name in the eventful 1950s and 1960s.[83] But their aspirations came crashing down with the humiliating defeat in the 1967 war with Israel, which marked the end of 'Abd al-Nasser's grand scheme of building a modern state that would lead a triumphant Arab Nation with him at the helm. A mood of melancholy and wounded ego pervaded the intellectual and literary response to the crushing military defeat (delusionally called *naksa*, or "setback," by the regime) that was manifested in fiction, poetry, art, and even religious

[81] Shafe'i, *al-'Imara al-'Arabiyya*, 40–46; Farid Shafe'i, "The Mashhad al-Juyushi (Archaeological Notes and Studies), in *Studies in Islamic Art and Architecture in Honour of Prof. K. A. C. Creswell*, C. L. Geddes ed. (Cairo, AUC Press, 1965), 237–252, p. 246 refutes the interpretation offered by Creswell of this enigmatic Fatimid monument. Yusuf Ragib, "Un oratoire fatimide au sommet du Muqaṭṭam," *SI* 65 (1987): 51–67, pp. 57–8 summarizes the debate over the attribution of the tomb of al-Juyushi between Creswell and Shafe'i, then refutes Shafe'i's refutation of Creswell.

[82] Examples include 'Abd al-Rahman Zaki, *al-Qahira, Tarikhuha wa-Atharaha* (Cairo: al-Hay'a al-Misriyya al-'Amma li-l-Ta'lif wa-l-Nashr, 1966) and *Mawsu'at Madinat al-Qahira fi Alf 'Am* (Cairo: Maktabat al-Anjlo al-Misriyah, 1969); Ahmad 'Abd al-Razzaq Ahmad, *Tarikh wa Athar Misr al-Islamiyya* (Cairo: Dar al Fikr al-'Arabi, 1977, reprinted 1993). Amal al-'Umari and 'Ali Tayish, *al-'Imara fi Misr al-Islamiyya: (al-'Asrayn al-Fatimi wa-al-Ayyubi)* (Cairo: Maktabat al-Safa wa-al-Marwa, 1996) postdates the age of pan-Arabism but carries echoes of its concerns and orientations.

[83] Eugene L. Rogan, *The Arabs: A History* (New York: Basic Books, 2009), 277–318; Youssef M. Choueiri, *Arab Nationalism: a History. Nation and State in the Arab World* (Oxford: Blackwell, 2000), 65–100; Jacquemond, *Conscience of the Nation*, 22–33.

and historical studies.[84] 'Abd al-Nasser's successor, Anwar al-Sadat (r. 1970–81), while maintaining the military grip on political life in Egypt, drastically reoriented the country's direction on both the internal and external fronts. He began by planning a war with Israel in collaboration with Syria to restore the bruised national morale and to seek a return of the occupied territories. The war, launched in October 1973, was inconclusive, even though it was later celebrated as a victory. Sadat then shifted gears toward the West and toward political retrenchment and even retraction from a leading role in Arab affairs, especially after his controversial decision to recognize Israel in 1979 in exchange for the return of Sinai to Egypt.[85] He also introduced a statist form of neoliberalism that intensified under his successor Hosni Mubarak (r. 1981–2011), who clung to power for thirty years against rising challenges from a reinvigorated militant Islamism until he was deposed by the army after a popular uprising in 2011. Egypt's prominence in its geopolitical milieu shrank under Sadat and Mubarak, and the country experienced more acute problems of political repression and corruption, urban and rural degradation, population explosion, and socioeconomic ailments than it had done during the last few years of 'Abd al-Nasser, without the allure of a national mission that he had kept alive by dint of his popularity and charisma.[86] This left many people, but especially the nationalist and pan-Arabist intellectuals and cultural producers nostalgic for the pre-1967 days of confidence and shared purpose, reeling at the dismal state of affairs, with little freedom to openly and candidly criticize it.

It was during these trying times that al-Maqrizi acquired a new array of roles in the national discourse as the Egyptian intellectuals and literati struggled to respond to the new political, economic, and cultural realities. To

[84] Trevor J. LeGassick, "Some Recent War-Related Arabic Fiction," *MEJ* 25, 4 (Autumn, 1971): 491–505; Michael B. Oren, *Six Days of War: June 1967 and the Making of the Modern Middle East* (Oxford: Oxford University Press, 2002), 305–30; Jacquemond, *Conscience of the Nation*, 88–107.

[85] The question of the Arab identity and leading role of Egypt became a subject of debate immediately after Sadat's visit to Israel. An interesting article by the scion of a political Coptic family and brother of Boutros-Boutros Ghali, the architect of Sadat's reconciliation with Israel, is Mirrit Boutros Ghali, "The Egyptian National Consciousness," *MEJ* 32, 1 (Winter, 1978): 59–77, which sums up the reorientation away from the Arabs and toward the West and gives it a historical and moral twist.

[86] Clement Henry Moore, "Authoritarian Politics in Unincorporated Society: The Case of Nasser's Egypt," *Comparative Politics*, 6, 2 (January 1974): 193–218; Roger Owen, "Socio-economic Change and Political Mobilization: the Case of Egypt," *Democracy Without Democrats?: The Renewal of Politics in the Muslim World*, Ghassan Salamé, ed. (London: I. B. Tauris, 1994), 183–99; Relli Shechter, "The Cultural Economy of Development in Egypt: Economic Nationalism, Hidden Economy and the Emergence of Mass Consumer Society During Sadat's Infitah," *MES* 44, 4 (2008): 571–83.

many of them, al-Maqrizi became a voice of the undying spirit of Egypt and a parable of resistance to corruption and oppression. His *Khitat* obviously remained a major source of information in academic fields for any urban or architectural history of Egypt, written by either Egyptians or Orientalists.[87] This status will not be changed any time soon, despite the mounting critical revisions of al-Maqrizi's scholarship and the probing of his indebtedness to other contemporary *khitat* authors in the last two decades, for we simply have no broader or more comprehensive source than his book. But it was in literature, especially the critical, engaged, and veiled political kind, that al-Maqrizi was adopted once more as a powerful pivot of a reawakened national consciousness.[88]

Al-Maqrizi in Modern Narratives of Cairo

Al-Maqrizi's modern literary incarnation begins, probably only on a subliminal level, with Naguib Mahfuz (1911–2006), the most famous Egyptian novelist of the twentieth century. A prodigiously prolific novelist whose career spans almost seventy years and more than thirty novels, Mahfouz is best known for his *Trilogy*, *Bayn al Qasrayn*, *Qasr al Shawq*, and *al-Sukkariya*

[87] This is especially true for surveys of Mamluk architecture, for which al-Maqrizi is obviously the main historical source. Examples of outstanding surveys of the period include Michael Meinecke's *Die Mamlukische Architektur*; Doris Behrens Abouseif, *Cairo of the Mamluks: A History of Architecture and its Culture* (London: I. B. Tauris, 2008); Bernard O'Kane, *The Mosques of Egypt* (Cairo: AUC Press, 2017).

[88] History, the Mamluks, and the city have played significant roles in modern Egyptian fiction. On Cairo and its spaces as literary tropes, see Samia Mehrez, "From the Hara to the Imara: Emerging Urban Metaphors in the Literary Production on Contemporary Cairo," in idem, *Egypt's Culture Wars: Politics and Practice* (London: Routledge, 2008), 144–68, republished in *Cairo Contested: Governance, Urban Space, and Global Modernity* Diane Singerman, ed. (Cairo: AUC Press, 2009), 145–73. On history in the work of some of the most prominent contemporary Egyptian novelists, see Samia Mehrez, *Egyptian Writers between History and Fiction: Essays on Naguib Mahfouz, Sonallah Ibrahim, and Gamal al-Ghitani* (Cairo: AUC Press, 1994). On the Mamluks in modern Egyptian narratives (not "Mind," as the title says), see Il Kwang Sung, *Mamluks in the Modern Egyptian Mind: Changing the Memory of the Mamluks 1919–1952* (New York: Palgrave Macmillan 2017), 59–121 for an overview of the Mamluks as they appear in Egyptian fiction during the colonial period. Sung particularly analyzes the work of early Egyptian novelists and their use of Mamluk themes during the period of consolidation of nationalist history. His main examples are Jurji Zaydan and his novel *al-Mamluk al-Sharid* (*The Runaway Mamluk*) (1891) on the period of Muhammad 'Ali, and Muhammad Farid Abu Hadid, *Ibnat al-Mamluk* (*The Mamluk's Daughter*) (1925), on a love story between an Egyptian and the daughter of a Mamluk amir at the time of Muhammad 'Ali, and Muhammad Sa'id al-'Aryan, *'Ala Bab Zuywila* (*On the Gate of Zuweila*) (1947) on the tragic end of the last Mamluk sultan, Tuman Bay.

(all names of neighborhoods in historic Cairo), completed in 1957, that won him the Nobel Prize for Literature in 1988.[89] Realist with an artfully disguised autobiographical coming-of-age core, this saga spans the life and times of three generations of a Cairene family as they negotiated the changes that their city and country were thrust into in the eventful first half of the twentieth century, from the Egyptian revolution against British occupation in 1919 to the end of World War II. Mahfuz deftly enlists the city in which he grew up as both the setting of his narrative and an allegory of the awakened nation (condensed into a web of interconnected urban characters) as it struggles to find a way forward between traditions and modernity. The oscillation between the two modes of social existence is cast onto the binary spatial and architectural distinction between the two halves of Cairo: the historical core where Mahfouz was born and brought up, and the modern extensions of Khedivial Cairo where his family moved when he was a teenager and where he lived for the rest of his life.[90] He, however, perceptively shows that the boundaries between the two halves were becoming increasingly porous, not only outwardly in the intermingling of architectural styles, but also in the penetration of modern mores and behavioral patterns, not without fierce resistance, into the traditional society of the historic core and vice versa.

Mafhouz considered the *Trilogy* one of his favorite works and the only one in which he tried his hand at writing a modern-day historical novel (in his early days he published three novels set in Pharaonic Egypt).[91] There are

[89] *Al-Thulathiyya, Bayn al Qasrayn, Qasr al Shawq,* and *al-Sukkariya* (Cairo: Dar Rose al-Youssef, 1956–57), is available in an English edition as *The Cairo Trilogy: Palace Walk, Palace of Desire, Sugar Street,* trans. William M. Hutchins et al. (New York: Everyman's Library, 2001). See a critical overview of the Trilogy in Karim Mattar, *Specters of World Literature: Orientalism, Modernity, and the Novel in the Middle East* (Edinburgh: Edinburgh University Press 2020), 183–91.

[90] Mehrez, *Egyptian Writers*, 59 calls Ghitani and Mahfouz "architects of the history of Cairo." Sabry Hafez, "The New Egyptian Novel: Urban Transformation and Narrative Form," *New Left Review* 64 (July–August 2010): 58–9 calls Mahfouz and others the product of the "passage between the two worlds of the two cities, with their contrasting rhythms and visions."

[91] Gamal al-Ghitani, ed., *Naguib Mahfouz Yatadhakkar* (Beirut: Dar al-Masira, 1980), 43–4, 58–72; trans. Humphrey Davis as *The Mahfouz Dialogs* (Cairo: AUC Press, 2007), 75–85 and 93–8. On p. 68 of the Arabic text, Mahfouz says, "The Trilogy and Awlad Haritna (trans. as Children of Gebelawi) and al-Harafish are my favorite books. In the Trilogy there is a great part of me, represented in the character of Kamal Abdel Jawad. But Kamal did not enter the narrative haphazardly, nor because he is part of me, but because his character is an inseparable component of the novel." Ouyang, *Poetics of Love*, 47–8 accepts Mehrez's definition of Mahfouz as a historian of the city, but adds to the analysis that ascribes Mahfouz's fiction to historical narrative a layer of deconstruction of power as it unfolds in the spaces of the city, a function that she then proceeds to read more fully in al-Ghitani's fiction. She then goes back to analyzing the intertwined movements of power on the political scale of

passages in the narrative that recall in their intensity and intimate knowledge of historic Cairo similar sections in al-Maqrizi's *Khitat*, particularly where al-Maqrizi lets his feelings take over his normally staid scholarly documentation. But neither al-Maqrizi nor his book is mentioned in Mahfouz's discussion of the sources of his *Trilogy*'s thick descriptions of the city and its people, which seem to be primarily projections of lived experiences shaped by decades of keen observation. If anything, Mahfouz may be read as channeling al-Maqrizi's spirit in his existential identification with his city and its changing spaces as it may have echoed in the reality of life in the dual city and in popular literature at the time, when the Mamluk center of Cairo was still the beating heart of the native city and the abode of many of its notable citizens. Unlike al-Maqrizi, however, Mahfouz enjoyed the malleability of a modern genre, the novel, which allowed him the freedom of fiction to construct his image of the city; whereas indeed, the nostalgia that al-Maqrizi expressed toward the bygone Cairo of the Fatimids and early Mamluks has provoked exacting modern historians to accuse him of sentimentalism.

But if al-Maqrizi's impact is only conjectured in the novels of Mahfouz, it is much more pronounced in the work of many luminaries among the next generation of *udaba'*, the generation of 1967. His figure and life work, but more directly his *Khitat* and *Ighathat*, inspired some of the most intensely particularist, painfully soul-searching, and deeply patriotic works of the late twentieth-century generation, which range from historical novels to fictional autobiographies to time-travel and daring poetical manifestos. He even personally appears in some of these texts as a paradigmatic authoritative and erudite character: guiding, commenting, correcting mistakes in history and attribution of events and buildings, and even instigating rebellion against tyranny and oppression, an action that he would have been very hesitant to advocate during his lifetime. He has, however, clearly achieved the transformation from history to historical fiction without losing any of the attributes that attracted Mustafa Ziyada and other Egyptian historians to him in the first place. In fiction as in scholarship, it is his "Egyptianness" and "patriotism" that are rhapsodized as true and cogent emotions expressed by this fifteenth-century nationalist forerunner before the terms themselves became meaningful identity framers.

The one author who so thoroughly identifies with al-Maqrizi's love and care for Cairo is none other than Mahfouz's close associate and presumptive literary heir, Gamal al-Ghitani (1945–2015). More than Mahfouz, al-Ghitani,

---

the nation in Mahfouz's *Arabian Nights*-inspired novel *Layali Alf Layla*, which brings his allegory down to the age of Anwar al-Sadat, during whose rule the novel was published, pp. 127–39. Ouyang, pp. 131–2, even detects a certain intertextuality between Mahfouz's *Layali* and al-Maqrizi's *Ighathat al-Umma*.

who was born in a small town in Upper Egypt but grew up in the same neighborhood described in his mentor's *Trilogy*, seems to have never left the spaces of the old city behind even when he moved to a newer section of town. He had his favorite spots—alleyways, houses, shops, and cafés—to which he frequently and leisurely returned. They deeply informed his creative writing, some of which in fact devolves into pure urban and architectural sketches that he used to frame his narrative.[92] Moreover, al-Ghitani, probably as part of a generational reaction to the shock of the 1967 defeat and the faltering project of westernized modernization that led to it, turned to the Arabic classical literary tradition and Sufi heritage. Beside historical inspiration, he was seeking models of belle-lettrist and mystical writing styles that he could adopt and that he would increasingly deploy in his own fiction after an earlier brush with more Western genres.[93] He pioneered, in the words of the noted translator Humphrey Davies, who had translated texts by both Mahfouz and al-Ghitani, "a kind of magic realism but an intensely Egyptian sort, with roots in both the history of Arabic literature but also areas such as Sufism and magic."[94] The *khitat* genre, with its Egypt-centric focus, was definitely one of the main historical literary forms that al-Ghitani embraced. It actually influenced his novelistic project on two levels: as a guide to the history and geography of the city, which undergird the structure of many of his novels, and as authentic and stylistically succinct and elegant textual renditions of places and spaces that he explicitly incorporated in his evolving style.[95]

Al-Ghitani even wrote his own fictionalized *khitat*, titled *Khitat*

[92] Nasser Rabbat, "Dala'il al-'Imran fi- *Asfar al-Bunyan*: al-'Imara fi Kitabat Jamal al-Ghitani," *al-Hilal* 107, 1 (January 1999): 152–9. On Cairo and its spaces as literary tropes, see Samia Mehrez, "From the Hara to the Imara," 144–68; Mara Naaman, *Urban Space in Contemporary Egyptian Literature: Portraits of Cairo* (New York: Palgrave Macmillan US, 2011), 1–35.

[93] Gamal al-Ghitani, *Munataha al-Talab ila-Turath al-'Arab: Dirasat fi al-Turath* (Cairo: Dar al-Shuruq, 1997), 5–16, is a concise introduction to al-Ghitani's engagement with the Arabic literary heritage.

[94] Humphrey Davies in an interview after al-Ghitani's passing, https://apnews.com/77de7116 33cd48109acb1c4860c9bb8c (last accessed August 6, 2020).

[95] Al-Ghitani, *Munataha al-Talab*, 7, lists al-Maqrizi and his *Khitat* (as well as those of Mubarak and Kurd'ali) among his sources for new narrative modes; he develops that style in books dedicated to Cairene landmarks such as *Malamih al-Qahira fi 1000 sana* (Cairo: Dar al-Hilal, 1983) and *Qahiriyat: Asbilat al-Qahira* (Cairo: Madbuli, 1984). Mehrez, *Egyptian writers*, 58–63, and Ouyang, *Poetics of Love*, 47–68, thoroughly analyze the evolution of the *khitat* genre from al-Maqrizi to al-Ghitani, passing by Mubarak and Kurd'ali. For later Egyptian novelists, al-Ghitani himself achieves the status of a model for *khitat* writing, perhaps eclipsing al-Maqrizi's primacy, see Paul Starkey, "Strange Incidents from History: Youssef Rakha and his Sultan's Seal," in *Studying Modern Arabic Literature: Mustafa Badawi, Scholar and Critic*, Roger Allen and Robin Ostle, eds. (Edinburgh: Edinburgh University Press, 2015), 165–72.

al-Ghitani (1980). An Orwellian tale of sorts, the novel cunningly wields the term *khitat* as its title and as a proper name for the otherwise unspecified but recognizable locus of the action, Cairo, as well as a referent that signifies the topographic configuration that frames and loosely steers the narrative. The story, which develops in a linear temporality from the near past to a potential near future but with multiple spatial nodes, has two main sections, differentiated by their topographic settings. The first takes place in Khitat itself, a densely built city that intermingles the old and traditional with the new and modern architecture, not so dissimilar to contemporary Cairo. It recounts the travails of a mysterious, unnamed leader and his posse of aides who control the city (and the country, since no distinction between the two is discernible) primarily by means of news, rumors, and surveillance. The command operation is concentrated in an imposing building named simply *al-anba'* (the news), probably a reference to one of the behemoth modern media buildings in Cairo, like al-Ahram and al-Akhbar Headquarters or the TV Maspero Building, in which al-Ghitani spent his professional career, or possibly as a faint echo of Orwell's Ministry of Truth.[96] The narrative flows through a series of numbered topographic markers, streets, walls, and a maydan, which intentionally recall the structure of al-Maqrizi's *Khitat*. The landscape changes with the disappearance of the leader and the dispersal of his assistants. The action moves to two suburbs, controlled by two rival successors of the Leader, and the desert, where the rebels are building their strength, while the city recedes in significance without totally exiting the stage. Corruption mounts, enemies are invited to the city, while the historic artifacts, perhaps symbolizing the heritage (*turath*), are sold off.[97] Here, it is difficult to ignore the Khaldunian backdrop of the conflict between the desert and the city, in which nomadic power comes from the desert to conquer the city and then in time is sapped by the degrading urban pleasures so that the city becomes anew the prey of the next unadulterated desert power lurking beyond the horizon.[98]

In his *Khitat*, al-Ghitani appropriated the subject, form, language, and structure of the genre as it was elaborated by his two great precursors, al-Maqrizi and 'Ali Mubarak (though he was critical of Mubarak's urban modernization).[99] He, however, extended their temporal limits, confined to

[96] In "Jadaliyyat al-Tannas (Intertextual Dialectics): An Interview with Gamal al-Ghitani," *Alif: Journal of Comparative Poetics* 4 (1984): 74, he mentions that Orwell's *1984* still impressed him twenty-five years after he had first read it.

[97] For two synopses of the novel with an emphasis on the role of the *khitat* genre in its conception, see Mehrez, *Egyptian writers*, 58–76; Ouyang, *Poetics of Love*, 58–66.

[98] On Ibn Khaldun's views on the city and the desert, see Khalidi, "Classical Islamic Views," 265–76; Siddiqi, "Ibn Khaldun's Concept of Urbanization," 41–55.

[99] Al-Ghitani, *Munataha al-Talab*, 14; Ouyang, *Poetics of Love*, 48–9; idem, *Politics of*

the past and present by the constraints of the historical genre, to include projections into or imaginations of the future. He also stretched, enhanced, and reimagined the social reality in the service of the fantastic narrative partly because of the license of fiction, especially the kind of magic realism with which he was experimenting. But as Samia Mehrez has noted, al-Ghitani, in his use of the structure and nomenclature of the *khitat* genre, was deliberately confounding history and fiction or imagination and reality.[100] By deploying the very real markers of topography and architecture—buildings, streets, open spaces—he was actually plotting another, intentionally muddled hyper-reality, at the same time familiar and strange to anyone who knows Cairo, the unnamed but recognizable site of the novel. In the process, he blended the purpose of his precursors' *khitat*s, nostalgia for an inflated prosperous past of the city in the case of al-Maqrizi and celebration of an overstated present transformation of the city in the case of ʻAli Mubarak, to create what can be termed nostalgia for a possible utopian future that is very much rooted in the past. This is most evident at the end of the novel, where al-Ghitani delivers prophetic signs of rescue, return, resurrection, and possible efflorescence for the wretched city of Khitat although the hope remains inconclusive. Such multi-directional nostalgia, as Wen-chin Ouyang, quoting Svetlana Boym, observed in relation to Arabic modernist writings in general,

> "is not merely an expression of local longing", of national imagining of community and nationalisation of modernity, but is also "a rebellion against the modern idea of time, the time of history and and progress. The nostalgic desires to obliterate history and turn it into private or collective mythology, to revisit time as space, refusing to surrender to the irreversibility of time that plagues the human condition", as well as [a rebellion] against the Western history of civilisation. Its "affective yearning for a community with a collective memory, a longing for continuity in a fragmented world" is its defensive mechanism not only to the "accelerated rhythms of life and historical upheavals" that is modernity but also to the overwhelming presence of the cultural other in Arab modernity.[101]

The intertextuality in al-Ghitani's text, though multi-layered, draws on the same range of feelings as his ubiquitous yet implicit model, al-Maqrizi, did. First is the intense filial identification with Cairo, distilled in al-Ghitani's *Khitat* from what is left of the habits, lifestyle, and social atmosphere of old

Nostalgia, 160.

100 Mehrez, *Egyptian writers*, 64–5.

101 Ouyang, *Politics of Nostalgia*, 51; pp. 50–4, Ouyang invokes Svetlana Boym, *The Future of Nostalgia* (New York: N.Y.: Basic Books, 2001), xiii–xvi, in discussing the novel *Ibn Fattouma* by Mahfouz and *Mihyar al-Dimashqi* by Adonis, the noted Syrian poet. Her discussion is relevant to the interpretation I am offering here of al-Ghitani's *Khitat* as well. The passage quoted is especially revealing.

Cairo, where he himself roamed in modern days in search of inspiration and solace. Second is the anxiety the entire 1967 generation felt at the rapid changes in Egypt's vision, its outlook, and commitment to its Arabic and Islamic heritage following the *infitah*, or the economic, political, and ultimately cultural opening toward the West instituted by President Anwar al-Sadat in 1976. Finding refuge, among many other tools of remembrance, in the symbols of architectural ingenuity and affinity with the land and the city is a reaction not so different from that of al-Maqrizi reminiscing about the merry life of his youth when describing the *kharab* in the city of his late adulthood. It is probably even consciously modeled after it, for the same reason more prosaic architectural and urban historians modeled their writing after al-Maqrizi's *Khitat*. He provides the only authentic and extensive link with all that is antediluvian Cairo, that is, the City Victorious (al-Qahira) before it was reduced to an Ottoman provincial capital and then transmogrified into the modern, run-down, and identityless metropolis suffering now under the double threat of heedless development and omnivorous capitalist greed.

Al-Ghitani, as a historically-oriented narrator, was associated primarily with the style of Ibn Iyas (1448–1522), the late Mamluk chronicler of the end of the Mamluk Sultanate and the beginning of the Ottoman rule in Egypt who paid more attention to quotidian events than his peers. Al-Ghitani used him to great effect in many of his famous early works, especially in *al-Zayni Barakat* (1971), his most historical yet transparently allegorical rendering of the hopes, horrors, and contradictions of the ʿAbd al-Nasser era, set in the safely distant period that Ibn Iyas covered in his chronicle, that is, the late fifteenth century.[102] Later in his career, al-Ghitani, under the double trauma of a generational defeat extending into the confusion of the *infitah* and the sudden death of his father in 1980, turned to Sufi spiritual literature. He sub-

[102] Gamal al-Ghitani, *al-Zayni Barakat* (Damascus: Wizarat al-Thaqafah wa-al-Irshad al-Qawmi, 1st edn., 1974); English edition, *Zayni Barakat*, Farouk Abdel Wahab, trans. (London: Viking, 1988). See Edward Said, "Foreword," to the 2004 edition (Cairo: AUC Press, 2004), vii–ix. On the historical figure of Zayni Barakat in Ibn Iyas' chronicle, see Carl Petry, *Protectors or Praetorians: The Last Mamluk Sultans and Egypt's Waning as a Great Power* (New York: State University of New York Press, 1994), 145–7. See also al-Ghitani, "Jadaliyyat al-Tannas," 79–80, where he explains how and why he appropriated the style of Ibn Iyas in his *Waqāʾiʿ Ḥārat al-Zaʿfarānī* (*The Zafarani Files*), Farouk Abdel Wahab, trans. (Cairo: AUC Press, 2009); also al-Ghitani, *Munataha al-Talab*, 148, for his appreciative analysis of Ibn Iyas's chronicle. Christina Phillips, *Religion in the Egyptian Novel* (Edinburgh: Edinburgh University Press 2019), 129, note 20, invokes Linda Hutcheon's concept of parody as repetition with critical distance to explain al-Ghitani's use of topography and the period's writing styles as exemplified by Ibn Iyas. Ouyang, *Poetics of Love*, 18–24, analyzes the torturous path al-Ghitani followed and the critical challenges he faced as he developed his style of reviving narrative traditions while revising (mostly recent) history, as she titled her section.

limated the language and images of several Sufi masters, particularly 'Abd al-Karim al-Gilani or al-Gili (1365–1428) and Muhiyy al-Din Ibn 'Arabi (1165–1240), perhaps the greatest Sufi mystic of medieval Islam. Ibn 'Arabi's profound and cryptic style inspired al-Ghitani's prose in his trilogy *al-Tajaliyyat* ("Epiphanies," 1983–7), a thinly ficitionalized autobiography in which Ibn 'Arabi himself (among other historical figures) appears as the spiritual and fantastic guide of the narrator, pointedly named Gamal.[103] The Sufi stylistic bent remained palpable in al-Ghitani's later writing. It even intensified in his last publications. But his continuous fascination with al-Maqrizi's *Khitat* led him to develop a blend of "Sufisized" architectural/topographic style to address philosophical and meditative issues after he suffered a scary health episode in the mid-1990s. Nostalgia then became a strategy for personal survival as much as for retelling collective history. Al-Ghitani subsequently published several lyrical studies on Islamic Cairo that more directly invoke the city's neighborhoods or landmarks that enchanted him throughout his life.[104] This is clearly how his introspective novel *Safr al-Bunyan* (*The Book of Building*, 1997) was conceptualized. From Pharaonic Egypt to modern-day Cairo, this collection of transcendental moments in the urban history of the country uses builders, buildings, and architectural elements to weave together his pensive and melancholy reflections on time, life, eternity, belonging, and remembrance.[105] Al-Maqrizi, the archetypical lover of Cairo, would have greatly approved of this lyrical, philosophical evolution in topographical/historical writing.

Al-Maqrizi in the Egyptian Consciousness

Perhaps the most extraordinary indication of al-Maqrizi's enduring status as an über-Egyptian is how he himself became a character in several works of fiction and poetry in the post-1967 period. Although he was transposed across time to bear witness or provide an opinion, he maintained his integral personality as a fifteenth-century historian throughout these literary resurrections.

[103] Gamal al-Ghitani, *Kitab al-Tajalliyat*, three parts (Cairo: Dar al-Mustaqbal al-Arabi, 1983–7), translated in an unfortunately abbreviated form as *The Book of Epiphanies*, Farouk Abdel Wahab, trans. (Cairo: AUC Press, 2012). On the impetus behind the novel, see al-Ghitani, "Jadaliyyat al-Tannas," 80–2. Gamal 'Abd al-Nasser also plays a major role in these epiphanies, see Omar Khalifah, *Nasser in the Egyptian Imaginary* (Edinburgh: Edinburgh University Press 2017), 96–101.

[104] Gamal al-Ghitani, *The Cairo of Naguib Mahfouz* (Cairo: AUC Press, 1999); idem, *Isti'adat al-Musafir Khana: Muhawala lil-Bina' min al-Dhakira* (Cairo: Dar al-Shuruq, 2007). See also the analysis of Samia Mehrez, *Egyptian writers*, 58–76.

[105] Gamal al-Ghitani, *Sifr al-bunyan* (Cairo: Dar al-Hilal, 1997). See my analysis of the architectural metaphors in his writing in "Dala'il al-'Imran," 152–9.

This image comes across most vividly in the highly ambitious time-travel novel *Rihalat al-Turshaji al-Halwaji* (1991), published in English as *The Time-Travels of the Man who Sold Pickles and Sweet* (2016), by Khayri Shalabi (1938–2011).[106] This farcical, ironic, and ultimately pessimistic time-travel tale by one of the paragons of the Neo-Realist wave in Egyptian fiction deals irreverently yet lovingly with Cairo's historical experience. In it, the narrator Ibn Shalabi (i.e. the author himself) is uncontrollably tossed through time, but without ever leaving the circumscribed space of Islamic Cairo. The ostensible aim of this is to get to the table of the Fatimid Caliph, al-Mu'izz li-Din Allah, where Ibn Shalabi is invited to celebrate the first Ramadan after the founding of the new capital of al-Qahira. But he ends up spending most of the novel going in and out of the turbulent years in the mid-fourteenth century, when he becomes directly involved in the succession struggles after the death of Sultan al-Nasir Muhammad. The novel ends with Ibn Shalabi barely escaping imprisonment and possibly execution in 1343 by zooming back to his own time, to discover that he has actually landed in the future, in 2077.

It is noteworthy that Ibn Shalabi keeps the position of an observer throughout his time-travel. He does not try to influence the historical events he witnesses, even though he comes too close to the centers of power in some cases and his counsel is sought by some major historical actors, who at times appear to implement the recommendations of this man from the future. It is also revealing that Ibn Shalabi travels only in the past, with the exception of the last instance, which tantalizingly closes the narrative without any suggestion of where the author would have gone with this reversal of temporal direction. He also skips the Ottoman period altogether, possibly because of the limitations of his sources, but probably also because the Ottoman period is still considered a period of foreign occupation in the post-Nasserist national imagination.[107] Ibn Shalabi's obsession with a spatially and historically confined past (Fatimid, Ayybid, but mostly Mamluk), however, has an underlying motive. His time-travel is actually a rescue mission. Its deeper intention is to conscript the entire Egyptian Islamic history in order to recuperate the authentic Egyptian national character. For that purpose, Shalabi parades a large number of minor characters representing the various walks of life in the city, especially the common, marginal, and shady classes. Some of them appear only to throw a one-liner; others belabor, engage in conversation, or

[106] Khayri Shalabi, *Rihlat al Turshaji al Halwaji* (Cairo: Akhbar al-Yawm, 1983, 1st edn.); idem, *The Time-Travels of the Man who Sold Pickles and Sweets*, Michael Cooperson, trans. (Cairo: AUC Press, 2010). On Khayri Shalabi, see Naaman, *Urban Space*, 71–104, pp. 72–5 for a brief assessment of Shalabi's place in modern Egyptian fiction.

[107] Michael J. Reimer, "Egyptian Views of Ottoman Rule: Five Historians and Their Works, 1820–1920," *Comparative Studies of South Asia, Africa and the Middle East* 31, 1 (2011): 149–63.

explain awkward situations that Ibn Shalabi bumps into with witticisms and jokes. All together are meant to exemplify an eternal Egyptian persona of bonhomie, openness, quick humor, and tolerance. The reconfirmation of this time-honored type is desperately needed to counter the otherwise bleak observation repeatedly made by the author that contemporary Egypt is falling prey to fanaticism, dogmatism, and chaos.[108]

Ibn Shalabi also meets a number of apparently more informed fellow time-travelers such as the historians Ibn ʿAbd al-Hakam (803–71) and Ibn Taghri-Birdi (1411–70), the Orientalist Stanley Lane-Poole (1854–1931), Naguib Mahfuz, and al-Maqrizi. These famous historical figures are obviously selected for the purpose of guiding the protagonist in his flipping through time in the space of Cairo.[109] They also provide him with the historical authority necessary to anchor his various encounters in their proper and recognizable historical contexts. And they all are the right, if idiosyncratic, choices for the purpose. But what is important here is how al-Maqrizi in particular is presented among this group. Whereas all others are made to tell the protagonist about some historical event or figure, al-Maqrizi is distinguished as the recorder and transmitter of Cairo's urban and topographic episodes. Throughout the novel, he is portrayed in a respectful and adoring way as the meticulous researcher always preoccupied with the correct information regardless of the circumstances. When Ibn Shalabi first meets him, al-Maqrizi, an old man with the mien of an *ʿalim*, is surrounded by soldiers shoving him around, but he is nonetheless busy recording the changes in the topography around him. Even when Ibn Shalabi halfheartedly asks him if he needs any help, al-Maqrizi inquires only about the spot upon which they were standing, saying "I have kept track of everyone who's set foot here going back as many years as I can count, but it never hurts to double-check."[110]

[108] See the analysis of Michael Cooperson, "Remembering the Future: Arabic Time-Travel Literature," *Edebiyat* 8 (1998): 179–84.

[109] It is unlikely that Khayri Shalabi read Flann O'Brien's last novel *The Dalkey Archive*, published posthumously in 1964 after the author's death, and it is probably impossible to find out. O'Brien's novel too had the protagonist meet historical figures, James Joyce and St. Augustine, in his fantastic wanderings. The setting and purpose of the resurrection of these figures for O'Brien is very different from how they are for Shalabi. They are sarcastic, confrontational, and ultimately psychologically loaded. See M. Keith Booke, "The Dalkey Archive: Flann O'Brien's Critique of Mastery," *Irish University Review* 23, 2 (Autumn/Winter, 1993): 269–85; Ronald L. Dotterer, "Flann O'Brien, James Joyce, and 'The Dalkey Archive,'" *New Hibernia Review/Iris Éireannach Nua* 8, 2 (Summer 2004): 54–63. I am thankful to Finbarr Barry Flood for the reference. There is of course a whole genealogy of fiction writing that enlists dead people for the purpose of the narrative, going back to Dante in the Western tradition and to Abu al-ʿAla' al-Maʿrri in the Arabic tradition.

[110] Shalabi, *Rihalat*, 9; idem, *The Time-Travels*, 4. Al-Maqrizi will appear no fewer than seven more times.

In another instance, al-Maqrizi shows his vast knowledge by describing to the narrator the layout of the Fatimid Palace and its transformation in the Mamluk period. This passage is lifted verbatim from the *Khitat* and put to use in the novel to allow Ibn Shalabi to find his way in space to the dinner table of al-Muʿizz. When Ibn Shalabi explains to al-Maqrizi what happened to the site of the *funduq* of al-Khalili after his time (the modern-day Khan al-Khalili), al-Maqrizi exclaims, "Nothing has remained but the name. O *Misr* [the Arabic term for Egypt, but used by Egyptians for Cairo as well], how many names has your memory retained."[111]

This brief sentence epitomizes in a few words how al-Maqrizi, as the author of the most extensive and heartfelt *khitat* book, has become lodged in modern Egyptian consciousness as the true keeper of Cairo's history across the ages. He is the one who in his book saved most place-names, long after the places themselves and their contemporary records have vanished. He is also the one who preserved the descriptions of these places and gathered the stories of their names as they dissipated over time.[112] In the identity narratives of our queasy nationalist age, he thus provides two indispensable and interconnected mainstays of belonging: the history of the place and the history of the people who occupied that place, at least until his death in the middle of the fifteenth century. As such, his *Khitat* has become the most significant repository of Cairo's medieval heritage in its most expansive sense as defined by David Lowenthal, a total historical narrative and total material history, when most of the true material history (i.e. buildings and streets and objects) has effectively disappeared.[113] Stated differently, al-Maqrizi's *Khitat* has come be to the closest manifestation of a "cultural memory" as elaborated by the Egyptologist Jan Assman, that is, a narrative of the past appropriated and curated by the nation (or its narrators) as part of its identity formation.[114] It has thus transcended its original role as an intentionally constructed *lieu de mémoire*, where al-Maqrizi collected the textual descriptions of places and the biographies of the people associated with them as a means of countering the accelerated ruination

[111] Shalabi, *Rihalat*, 20–2, the citation is from p. 21; idem, *The Time-Travels*, 15–17, citation 17, my translation differs from Cooperson's here.

[112] Vismann, "The Love of Ruins," 196–209 cites Ernst Kantorowicz's essay "The Problem of Medieval World Unity," pp. 199–200, stating that "Fragments contain an imperative for the historian to tell the story of a former completeness. Just as the archaeologist who finds the broken pieces assumes a pot whose original form his job is to reconstruct, the historian who imagines the past as a collection of fragments assumes a past unity that needs to be put back together again."

[113] Lowenthal, *Possessed by the Past*, 127–72.

[114] Jan Assmann, "Collective Memory and Cultural Identity," *New German Critique* 65 (1995): 125–33.

of these places he was bitterly observing and predicting to be irreparable. Shalabi's novel is but an advanced phase of the metamorphosis of al-Maqrizi himself as well as his *Khitat* in modern Egyptian narratives that started with 'Ali Mubarak.[115] Through the agency, creativity, and imagination of various nationalist authors, the man and his book now metonymically stand for something that could not have been conceived in the fifteenth century: the memory of the nation.

But al-Maqrizi's reincarnation in modern Egyptian literature did not stop at the level of national memory as it unfolds in the built heritage. There was another register that his moral rectitude, audacious stand against corruption and injustice, and sad and gloomy demeanor definitely qualified him to occupy. This was the voice of the nation's conscience and the witness to its suffering at the hands of despotic rulers, then and now. These attributes drew many intellectuals disillusioned with the deteriorating conditions in Egypt under Sadat to al-Maqrizi, but none captured his anguished morality more ardently than the late activist, poet, and playwright Naguib Surur (1932–78).[116] Angry, intense, defiant, sarcastic and morose all at once, this most expressive literary virtuoso was deeply disturbed by the heavy-handed policies of the Egyptian regimes under both 'Abd al-Nasser and Sadat, which he often felt personally targeted him. He wrote musicals and plays and composed poetry, ballads, and *mawawil* (sing *mawwal*, a traditional and popular form of vocal music) that dug deep into the vernacular poetic and musical reservoir of the country, adopted melodies, folktales, and songs known to everyone, and infused them with new lyrics loaded with his unabashed rants and revolutionary zeal.[117] His leitmotif was Egypt

[115] Khayri Shalabi published another novel, *Batn al-Baqara* (Cairo: Dar al-Ma'arif, 1995), which is directly inspired by al-Maqrizi's *Khitat*. Shalabi called it a geo-novel since it deals with the topography of three of the most popular neighborhoods in Old Cairo and uses the books of *khitat*, namely al-Maqrizi's and Mubarak's, as characters in the narrative. Shalabi explains his indebtedness to al-Maqrizi on the dedication page of the book, addressed to his late cousin the *shaykh* 'Ali Muhammad 'Ukasha in whose library the boy Shalabi discovered the coverless first volume of al-Maqrizi's *Khitat*. Shalabi then says, "the book enchanted me so that I gave it a title I derived from its topic as I understood it, 'the history of houses and streets.' The emotive spontaneity in that title still frames my approach to this unique genre, the *khitat*, i.e. the history of place."

[116] On Naguib Surur and his tormented life and work see Mahmoud El-Lozy, "Rebel with a cause," *al-Ahram Weekly* 400 (October 22–8, 1998), archived at http://web.archive.org/web/20100314025621/http://wadada.net/surur/delirium.htm (last accessed August 12, 2020); Benjamin Koerber, "Naguib Surur: The Poetics and Politics of Niyāka," *Conspiracy in Modern Egyptian Literature* (Edinburgh: Edinburgh University Press, 2017), 59–68. There is also an imaginary biographical novel on Naguib Surur that I was not able to consult, Talal Faysal, *Surur* (Cairo: Kutub Khan, 2015).

[117] Pierre Cachia, "Folk Themes in the Works of Najib Surur," in his *Exploring Arab Folk Literature* (Edinburgh: Edinburgh University Press, 2011), 203–13.

itself, which he passionately loved and sometimes desperately hated. He relentlessly denounced the rapacity of the regime, the greed of the new business class, the duplicity of the intellectuals, and the inertia of the people. His sharp and often insulting words offended many, even some of those who took his side in his sundry quixotic battles.[118] He died alone in his native village, relatively young, depressed, paranoid, and shunned by friends and foes alike.[119]

In one of his most melancholic poems, *Tada'iyyat al-Sukr wa-l-Dayya'* (lit. "Ramifications of Being Drunk and Wasted" but sensibly translated as *Drink Delirium*), Surur casts al-Maqrizi as a drink companion, a category of interlocutor familiar from classical Arabic history and poetry.[120] Written in one bout on September 22, 1977 at the height of President Anwar al-Sadat's megalomaniacal redefinition of himself as the "Devout Leader" (*al-Ra'is al-Mu'min*), the poem is a truly tormented soliloquy against tyranny, cowardice, and indifference.[121] Utterly desperate and suicidally defiant at the same time (the poem is actually subtitled *qasida intihariyya*, or "suicidal poem"), Surur directly addresses the silent al-Maqrizi several times. But instead of waiting for his replies, Surur thrice glosses al-Maqrizi's critical passages from

118 See the analysis of Surur's use of a profane language, diatribes, and enraged anti-Western in Benjamin Koerber, "Naguib Surur," 68–93.

119 His work was neglected for two decades and was rediscovered in the early 2000s, after his son Shuhdy developed a website devoted to the memory of his father and uploaded many journalistic articles on Surur as well as some of his poems and texts, including the controversial *Kuss Ummiyyat* (*Quatrains of Mother's Cunt*). Shuhdi was preposterously sentenced to one year in prison for publishing "indecent material." He escaped to Russia, his mother's homeland, then relocated to India where he died in 2019 without being able to return home to Cairo. His website, http://www.wadada.net/surur, was de-activated, but is now archived at http://web.archive.org/web/20100329025336/http://www.wadada.net/surur (last accessed August 12, 2020).

120 *Al-nadim*, the boon-companion, was an institutionalized character in the Abbasid court, which made it into Abbasid poetry and later as a proverbial interlocutor of the narrator, see Anwar G. Chejne, "The Boon-Companion in Early 'Abbāsid Times," *JOAS* 85, 3 (1965): 327–35. Al-Maqrizi himself, as we have seen, was for a while a *nadim* to Sultan Barquq (Chapter 2).

121 Naguib Surur, *Tada'iyyat al-Sukr wa-l-Dayya'*, extracted from *Faris Akhir Zaman* (Knight of Our Time), a collection of poetry written in the year of his death (1978) but published twenty years later in Naguib Surur, *Complete Works*, 4 vols. (Cairo: General Egyptian Book Organization, 1997), 4: 135–58. Questions of social justice, resistance against repressive state power and revolutionary ideas were lifelong issues for Surur, see Ahmad Saqr, "Qira'a naqdiyya tahliliyya fi masrah Najib Surur," *al-Hiwar al-Mutamaddin*, published online March 5, 2011, http://www.ahewar.org/debat/show.art.asp?aid=249140&r=0، (last accessed August 16, 2020). The poem was partially translated by Mona Anis and Nour Elmessiri as *Drink Delirium, Al-Ahram Weekly* 400 (October 22–8, 1998) and is archived at http://web.archive.org/web/20100314025621/http://wadada.net/surur/delirium.htm (last accessed August 12, 2020).

his small, early treatise *Ighathat al-Umma bi Kashf al-Ghumma*, with its very suggestive title "Helping the Nation in Dissipating the Crisis," about the abuse of power.[122] He also reworks some of al-Maqrizi's images from the *Khitat* in his lines to dramatic effect. To him, al-Maqrizi appears to be both an alter ego and the antithesis to the contemporary intelligentsia: the phony, self-appointed guardian of liberation and progress, whom he despises and repeatedly disparages. Al-Maqrizi, by contrast, is an honest interpreter of the dire conditions in Egypt and their victim at the same time, just as Surur painfully sees himself as being. An intellectual as well as existential identification with al-Maqrizi is palpable throughout the poem. Surur says:

> There will be anger
> Followed by the deluge.
> We know we will be among the drowned.
> But we will take the devil with us down
> To the deepest of deeps:
> Our end will be his . . .
> But slowly . . . What will be said
> Of us when they look back on it all?
> What will be said
> Of us after the deluge,
> After the coming drowning, after the coming anger,
> What will be said of us poets and writers?
> [. . .]

122 Of all al-Maqrizi's books, his voice is especially poignant in *Ighathat al-Umma*, which, as we saw, he wrote after the crisis of 806/1403–4 to analyze the causes of famine and to connect them to corruption, mismanagement of agricultural land, and misguided monetary policies. The treatise was reprinted several times, particularly in recent years, and often in popular and cheap editions. The number and frequency of editions, which are very difficult to establish, deserves an elaborate study that will connect their dates of publication to external factors such as the *infitah*, the January 25 Revolt of 2011, or the coronavirus pandemic of 2020; see the article by Sayyid Mahmoud on the website al-ʿAyn al-Ikhbariyya, March 22, 2020, https://al-ain.com/article/read-book-sale (last accessed August 14, 2020). The earliest Egyptian edition came out in 1940 from Dar al-Kutub in Cairo and was edited by M. Mustafa Ziyada and Jamal al-Din al-Shayyal, two of the most dedicated editors of al-Maqrizi's work. That edition was reprinted in 1957. The book was edited again by Badr al-Din al-Sibaʿi (Homs, Syria: Dar Ibn al-Walid, 1957); Gaston Wiet published his translation in 1962. Then in recent years, *al-Hilal*, a popular cultural journal, printed the book in the Kitab al-Hilal series in 1990. The English translation by Adel Allouche came out in 1994 from the University of Utah Press. Makatabat al-Usra (the Family Library), of the Egyptian General Organization of Books put out its popular edition in 1999, reprinted in 2017; Dar al-Watha'iq a-Qawmiyya in Cairo, the official publisher of heritage books, published another edition in 2002. Dar al-Mada in Baghdad published yet another popular edition in 2003. Dar ʿAyn, a small publishing house in Cairo, published a further edition in 2018. Finally, a Kindle edition came out in 2018 from al-Karma Mass Market Paperbacks.

O Maqrizi,
You who always come after the deluge:
A plague is a plague—
It always comes on the tail of a famine.
It snatched your daughter, and many other daughters
As the wolf was standing guard.

But Surur does not stop at summoning al-Maqrizi from his hideout in the past, or bemoaning the tragedy that struck him when he lost the person dearest to him (his daughter Fatima, who died in 1423). The interaction could have ended there, and al-Maqrizi would have been a reminder of a causal dynamic between disaster and suffering. Surur, however, has another reason for needing al-Maqrizi: the failure of poetry to capture the rot of the moment. To fully convey his rage and defiance, Surur needs another form of textuality: one that does not mince words or embellish a narrative, one that tells it like it is. More precisely, Surur enlists al-Maqrizi's candor and clarity to write his own "*Khitat* al-Maqrizi," as the book has become lodged in the Egyptian imagination as a referent to a specific kind of political criticism and a roadmap to guide all those concerned about the fate of their beloved country:

[. . .]
I hereby solemnly swear, Maqrizi,
Not to leave this world
Without scandal.
I ask no one for justice:
True justice is not to be begged.
Our judges are high priests,
Our high priests are distant
And all are traitors.
Let someone else write poetry,
I am writing the *Khitat* of Maqrizi.
His roadmap is my guide in the Sea of Darkness,
I am looking for my homeland in my homeland,
But I do not lose my way in the plunge,
Or the noise, or the shouting, or the violence.
Let others write poetry.
I will not pen down
A single line, or a single verse
For the sake of poetry.
[. . .]

After a very dark passage, Surur returns to invoking al-Maqrizi as the conscience of the nation. Then, the words of the sensitive and distressed medieval historian and the angry Marxist poet merge together in one seamless, cross-historical admonition on the venality of the rulers, and their corruption, oppression, and injustice. What al-Maqrizi starts, with his pointing the finger at the widespread corruption and the role of bribery in ruining the structure of government in Mamluk times, Surur brings to the present by adding the effect of the commodification of every value at the hands of a new class that did not exist in the fifteenth century: the businessmen. Surur, self-deprecatingly, acknowledges the pervasiveness of capitalism: he too has become a commodity in the marketplace and he will be bought by whoever pays the highest price. But then he pauses, regains his defiance, and ends his poem by asserting that his flesh is bitter—nothing will eat it but the worms of the earth:[123]

> Maqrizi's daughter is lost
> In the plague
> And the plague always comes on the tail of a famine,
> When prices are measured against a kilo of meat,
> Even the price of writers, novelists, poets,
> Artists and scientists,
> When the stuff of the dreams of the poor is meat;
> And *foul* beans,
> Fruit for the masters.
> And fruit for the commoners, the lower classes
> When anger consumes the monkeys
> And the mice[124]
> And the lice
> Then the deluge will come
> And what is the main reason O Maqrizi:

> "The Main reason, which is the root of this corruption, is the selling of appointments in the sultanian administration and the religious positions, like the vizirate, the judgeships, the governorships, the *muhtasib*, and all other positions, so that no one has to pay a lot to attain any of them. This way many corrupt, unjust, oppressive, and tyrannical people acquired positions they could have not dreamt of save

[123] This last line recalls the often-repeated aphorism that the "ulama's flesh is poisonous," meaning that whoever dares to punish them will be divinely punished in retribution, an aphorism that in fact encapsulates the contrasting sentiments of defiance and helplessness. The aphorism is ascribed to Ibn 'Asakir, *Tabyin Kadhib al-Muftari Fima Nusiba ila Abi al-Hasan al-Ash'ari* M. Zahid al-Kawthari, ed. (Damascus: Matba'at al-Tawfiq, 1928), 29; repeated in Taj al-Din al-Subki, *Mu'id al-Ni'am wa Mubid al-Niqam*, M. A. al-Najjar, A. Z. Shalabi, and M. A. al-'Uyun, eds. (Cairo: Dar al-Kitab al-'Arabi, 1993), 47–9. The same aphorism is inserted in two verses by the poet Ibn al-'Attar al-Misri (1346–94), see al-Maqrizi, *Durar*, 1: 206, where he tells us that he knew the poet well.

[124] These lines, and a few before them, evoke al-Maqrizi, *Khitat2*, 3: 692–4, where he says about the Mamluks that "they became more lustful than monkeys, more ravenous than rats, and more harmful than wolves."

for their connection with some courtiers and their promise of paying heavily to the sultanian purse."[125]

Maqrizi's daughter is lost
In the plague
In a deluge of money
She was lost in the jaws of businessmen
[. . .]

It seems clear here that Naguib Surur, with his obsessive criticality and high moral commitment, found in al-Maqrizi a soulmate, a companion in his uncompromising struggle, and a paradigmatic example to follow.[126] Conversely, in Surur, al-Maqrizi completed a transhistorical cycle of sorts. From being a historian of Egypt, with or without a nationalist edge, he crossed into fiction and poetry, where he was more imaginatively and lyrically assimilated to "speak for Egypt," as it were, assuming a transhistorical persona that transcended all of his previous manifestations in Egyptian historiography in its authoritative judgment, interpretive reach, and embodied representativeness.[127]

125 Quoted verbatim from *Ighathat al-Umma*, 61.

126 Surur's poetry witnessed a revival after the January 25 Revolution in 2011 when a young generation of revolutionaries discovered his anti-establishment stance, see Atef Botros, "Rewriting Resistance: The Revival of Poetry of Dissent in Egypt after January 2011 (Surūr, Najm and Dunqul)," in *Commitment and Beyond: Reflections on/of the Political in Arabic Literature since the 1940s*, Yvonne Albers, Georges Khalil and Friederike Pannewick, eds. (Wiesbaden: Ludwig Reichert Verlag, 2015), 50–60.

127 One area that could not be covered in this book is whether al-Maqrizi achieved any standing in extremist Islamist writing in the last couple of decades. With the rise of tenaciously militant Islamist movements in Egypt and across the Islamic world, I had assumed that al-Maqrizi made his way into their discourse as a conservative historical commentator with an exacting adherence to Islamic tenets. But having scanned the online polemical historical revisionism put out on the Web by various fundamentalist Islamist thinkers, I found no indications that his writing had made any impact. One clue, however, arose from the name of a mysterious research center, al-Maqreze (notice the strange transliteration) Center for Historical Research, allegedly established in London by the fundamentalist Egyptian cleric Hani al-Siba'i. Considered by many a façade for extremist activities, the Center no longer has any presence on the Internet. But in earlier captures of the defunct site dating to 2011, I recorded a posted mission statement that included the following points: 1 – a revisionist re-writing of Islamic history to cleanse it from "impurities"; 2 – adapting history writing to hadith methodology; 3 – restoring the legacy of the leaders of the Islamic *umma*; 4 – debunking the "lies" of the Orientalists and secular historians working on Islamic history. I found no publications from the Center online that would have allowed any assessment of its success in pursuing its stated goals. Many web searches for the Center or its publications led me to spurious anti-terrorism and intelligence pages. There is, however, an English entry on Hani al-Siba'i on Wikipedia, https://en.wikipedia.org/wiki/Hanial-Sibai (last accessed August 16, 2020), that reviews his career but does not mention the al-Maqreze Center.

In the Guise of a Conclusion: Becoming the Greatest Historian of Egypt

In a review of a biography of Susan Sontag in *The New Yorker* entitled "The Unholy Practice of Biography," Janet Malcolm wrote:

> Biographers often get fed up with their subjects, with whom they have become grotesquely overfamiliar. We know no one in life the way biographers know their subjects. It is an unholy practice, the telling of a life story that isn't one's own on the basis of oppressively massive quantities of random, not necessarily reliable information. The demands this makes on the practitioner's powers of discrimination, as well as on his capacity for sympathy, may be impossible to fulfill.[1]

I should know. Al-Maqrizi's project stayed with me for too many years, during which I frustratingly decided to drop it several times. Then something would happen that would trigger my interest again. Finding more information about the man, his social milieu, his views and beliefs, and the aims of his history writing became a chronic passion. It required sifting through many thousands of pages of his vast historical oeuvre and of the texts of his many contemporary chroniclers and biographers as well as those writing about him in the modern period. Most offered only canned portrayals limited to a set of categories: places and dates of birth and death, teachers, books composed, positions held, patrons, etc. Some gossiped, but even the gossip was impersonal, skin-deep, and, naturally, often malicious. Even the most important junctures in his life, such as his switching *madhhab* upon reaching majority, his relationship with his patrons and peers, and his withdrawal and retreat to his family home, which were matter-of-factly reported, remained unexplained and uncontextualized. This dearth of personal material was not surprising, though. It was the norm in medieval Arabic historiography to avoid what we today crave and value, intimate details, except in the very rare cases when some idiosyncratic author, like Usama

[1] Janet Malcolm, "Susan Sontag and the Unholy Practice of Biography: A New Book Is As Unillusioned About the Writer As She Was About Herself," *The New Yorker* (September 23, 2019), https://www.newyorker.com/magazine/2019/09/23/susan-sontag-and-the-unholy-practice-of-biography (last accessed December 17, 2020).

ibn Munqidh or Abu Shama, decides to hint at his inner life, thoughts, and feelings.

Al-Maqrizi, from the scattered bits about him we have in his historical work, was definitely such a singular character who marched to his own tune and did not shy away from expressing his controversial opinions. He nonetheless left no autobiography, not even a *mashikhat* as many of his famous colleagues did. Any modern reconstruction of his biography (many have been written since Quatremère published his in 1837) had perforce to depend primarily on the obituary notices penned by his many admirers and detractors among his peers and near-contemporaries. Then, the publication in 2002 of the complete text of his *Durar al-ʿUqud al-Farida*, ostensibly a biographical dictionary of his contemporaries, revealed that al-Maqrizi sprinkled his own autobiography in the biographies of others. The stories of their lives offered him many opportunities to insert references about himself, the circumstances of his life, and his various social, political, and moral views in the guise of conversations, dreams, compliments, and admonitions. He is a devoted son, husband, and friend, a devout and proud scholar, and a scathing critic of those he deems corrupt, though he is never unduly rude. He is a passionate son of Egypt, and Cairo in particular, pained by what he sees as an irrevocable calamity that has befallen his city and destroyed its once-prosperous ways of life. He is also an indignant observer of his society and its ruling class, which he blames for the decline he detects in every aspect of city life, economy, and civic stability. The book proved to be both a treasure trove and a game-changer for my book project. I was now able not only to sketch a more rounded image of the man and the historian than the one we had until then, but also to better reconstruct how his lifelong endeavor to write the history of Egypt both reflected and expressed his background, social network, strong convictions, uncompromising morality, and quirks. The second major project, of writing an extensive hagiography of the Prophet Muhammad, that moved up in time to Adam through the patriarchal lineage and down to his family and descendants, which al-Maqrizi undertook later in life, denotes his growing religiosity and intensifying devotion to the *Al al-Bayt* (who he passionately, albeit discreetly, believed to be his ancestors through the Fatimids) as he neared his death.

Despite the long time it took me to rebuild al-Maqrizi's biographical narrative, I did not become fed up with him. Instead, the man himself, or what I could grasp of the self of a person who died almost 600 years ago, grew on me. I began to imagine his appearance, voice, gaze, gait, and snappy character. My appreciation of his rectitude, tenacity, and stoicism rose with every new story I found where he laid bare his feelings as if he were writing for himself. I also began to see his unequivocal naiveté vis-à-vis the supernatural and wondrous, his deepening melancholy, and the ire that breathes in his obituaries of the Mamluk grandees of his time, in a different light. He may have been growing angrier and more paranoid as he aged, but the concrete evidence of *kharab* around him in his beloved city had been visibly increasing in the mid-Burji period. Thus, I found myself sympathizing with his arguments, disputes, and unyielding, strict religious opinions, although most of them paradoxically resemble views and attitudes that I oppose in my own life. I would even wonder sometimes, when reflecting on particularly vexing moments of social, moral, and political failure in our times, how al-Maqrizi would have reacted. This is how I began to discern the shades of Malcolm's title about the unholiness of the biographer's practice and the impossibility of reaching a balance between critical judgment and empathy under the weight of prolonged but never fully complete familiarity with the subject. A partial remedy was for me to dissect the bias resulting from overexposure. Another was to critically reevaluate what others who were closer in time to al-Maqrizi, both known friends and confirmed detractors, had to say about him, and why. Still another was to let the man's historical writing disclose his qualities and peculiarities through a careful analysis of his organizing methods, patterns of referentiality, text structure, phraseology and word choice. I interwove all three lines of inquiry into the narrative of my book.

I was concerned, though, that I might be standing alone in my admiration of al-Maqrizi at a time in which most of my Mamlukist colleagues, brandishing the metric of objectivity, went after his honesty, veracity, and historical robustness and found them all wanting. Only a few among them, notably the late Ulrich Haarmann, Ayman Fu'ad Sayyid, Julien Loiseau, and Jo Van Steenbergen, looked in his texts for the same kind of emotional and intellectual subjectivity in the service of a larger goal that I was highlighting. To me, this made his writing multi-layered and distinct from the norms of his time. Casting a wider net that went beyond the Orientalists of the nineteenth and twentieth centuries and the close-knit Mamlukist community of my peers, however, I realized that many modern Egyptian scholars understood al-Maqrizi for what his oeuvre represented more than for what it documented and recorded. To them, he was an Egyptian citizen before the term, loving his country and fearing for its future, which prompted him to dutifully record every shred of its history on which he could lay his hands. Finally, shifting my attention from the historians, I discovered in the works of a few novelists and a poet inspired by al-Maqrizi the fulfillment of a role that I guessed he tacitly aspired to in his lifetime but could not attain. Writing during a turbulent period in Egypt's modern history when the country had to endure several major military defeats, flipflopping socioeconomic experiments, and a hardening authoritarian regime, these imaginative modern storytellers found in al-Maqrizi a distant soulmate. To them, he was not just a historian but the keeper of Egypt's history who, more than anyone else, saved its memories, written and built, from the worst possible fate: oblivion. In his words, they spotted the clarion call for resistance to the forces of erasure, and they made sure that it still resounds today.

Bibliography

Primary Sources

Abu Hamid al Qudsi (1997). *Kitab Duwal al-Islam al-Sharifah al-Bahiyah: wa-Dhikr ma Zahara li Min Hikam Allah al-Khafiyah fi Jalb Ta'ifat al-Atrak ila al-Diyar al-Misriyah*. Ulrich Haarmann and Subhi Labib, eds. Beirut: al-Sharika al-Muttahida.

Abu Hamid al-Qudsi (1969). *Al-Fada'il al-Bahira fi Mahasin Misr wa-l-Qahira*, Mustafa al-Saqqa and Kamil al-Muhandis, eds. Cairo: Dar al-Kutub.

Abu Hamid al-Qudsi (1988). *Al-Fawa'id al-Nafissa al-Bahira fi Bayan Hukm Shawari' al-Qahira fi Madhahib al-A'imma al-Arba'a al-Zahira*. Amal al-'Umari, ed. Cairo: The Supreme Council of Antiquities.

Abu Shama, Shihab al-Din (1949). *Al-Dhayl 'ala-al-Rawdatayn*. M. Zahed al-Kawthari, ed. Cairo: Dar al-Kutub al-Malikiyya.

Abu Shama, Shihab al-Din (1956–62). *Kitab al-Rawdatayn fi Akhbar al-Dawlatayn al-Nuriyya wa-l-Salahiyya*. 2 vols. M. H. M. Aḥmad and M. M. Ziyada, eds. Cairo: Matba'at Lajnat al-Ta'lif.

Al-'Ayni, Badr al-Din (1985). *'Iqd al-Juman fi Tarikh Ahl al-Zaman*. 'Abd al-Razzaq al-Ṭanṭawi al-Qarmūṭ, ed. Cairo: Maṭba'at 'Alā'.

Al-'Ayni, Badr al-Din (2010). *'Iqd al-Juman fi Tarikh Ahl al-Zaman*. 9 vols. Mahmud Rizq Mahmud and Muhammad Muhammad Amin, eds. Cairo: Dar al-Kutub, 2nd edn.

Al-'Ayni, Badr al-Din (1962). *Al-Rawḍ al-Zahir fi-Sirat al-Malik al-Ẓahir Tatar*. Hans Ernst, ed. Cairo: Dar Ihya' al-Kutub al-'Arabiyya.

Al-'Ayni, Badr al-Din (1966). *Al-Sayf al-Muhannad fi Sirat al-Malik al-Mu'ayyad Shaykh al-Mahmudi*. Fahim M. Shaltut and Muhammad M. Ziyada. eds. Cairo: Dar al-Kitab al-'Arabi.

Al-Baghdadi, 'Abd al-Latif (1869). *al-Ifada wa-l-I'tibar fi al-Umur al-Mushahada wa-l-Hawadith al-Mu'ayana bi-Ard Misr*. Cairo: Matba'at Wadi al-Nil.

Al-Baha' Zuhair (1977). *Diwan al-Baha' Zuhair*. Muhammad Abu al-Fadl Ibrahim and Muhammad Taher al-Gabalawi, eds. Cairo: Dar al-Ma'arif.

Al-Bakri al-Andalusi, Abu 'Ubayd (1992). *Kitab al-Masalik wal Mamalik*. 2 vols. Adrian van Leeuwen and André Ferré, eds. Carthage: Bayt al-Hikma.

Al-Biruni, Abu Rayhan (1954–6). *Al-Qanun al-Mas'udi (Canon Masudicus)*, 3 vols. M. Nizamu'd-Din et al. eds. Hyderabad: Da'irat al-Ma'arif al-'Uthmaniyya.

Al-Buqa'i, Ibrahim b. Hasan (2001). *'Unwan al-Zaman bi-Tarajim al-Shuyukh wal-Aqran*. Hasan Habashi, ed. Cairo: Dar al-Watha'iq al-Qawmiyya.

Al-Dhahabi, Shams al-Din (1988). *Mu'jam al-Shuyukh*. 2 vols. Muhammad Habib al-Hailai, ed. Ta'if, Saudi Arabia: Maktabat al-Siddiq.

Al-Ghazzi, Najm al-Din (1997). *Al-Kawakib al-Sa'ira fi A'yan al-Mi'a al-'Ashira*. 3 vols. Khalil Mansur, ed. Beirut: Dar al-Kutub al-'Ilmiyya.

Al-Hanbali, Ibn al-'Imad (1931). *Shadharat al-Dhahab fi Akhbar Man Dhahab*. Cairo: Maktabat al-Qudsi.

Al-Idrisi, Jamal al-Din (1991). *Anwar 'Uluwwy al-Ajram fi al-Kashf 'an Asrar al-Ahram*. Ulrich Haarmann, ed. Beirut: commissioned from Franz Steiner Verlag, Stuttgart.

Al-Isfahani, Abu al-Faraj (2008). *Kitab al-Aghani*. 25 vols. Ihsan 'Abbas et al., eds. Beirut: Dar Sader, 2008.

Al-Jabarti, 'Abd al-Rahman (1879–80). *'Aja'ib al-Athar fi-l-Tarajim wa-l-Akhbar*. 4 vols. Cairo: Bulaq Press.

Al-Jawhari al-Sayrafi, Ali ibn Dawud (1970). *Inba' al-Hasr bi-Abna' al-'Asr*. Hasan Habashi, ed. Cairo: Dar al-Kutub.

Al-Jawhari al-Sayrafi, Ali ibn Dawud (1970). *Nuzhat al Nufus wa-l-Abdan fi Tawarikh al-Azman*. 4 vols. Hasan Habashi, ed. Cairo: Dar al-Kutub.

Al-Kirmani, Hamid al-Din (1953). *Rahat al-'Aql*. Muhammad Kamil Hussein and Muhammad Mustafa Hilmi, eds. Cairo: Dar al-Fikr al-'Arabi.

Al-Kutubi, Muhammad ibn Shakir (1973). *Fawat al-Wafiyyat wa-l-Zayl 'Alyha*. 4 vols. Ihsan 'Abbas, ed. Beirut: Dar Sader.

Al-Makrizi (1906). *Kitab al-Mawa'idh wa'li'tibar bidhikr al-Khitat wa'lAthar, Livre des admonitions et de l'observation pour l'histoire des quartiers et des monuments, ou description historique et topographique de l'Égypte*, Paul Casanova, ed., vols. 3–4, *MMFA*. Cairo: IFAO.

Al-Maqqari, Ahmad ibn Muhammad (1997). *Nafh al-Tib min Ghusn al-Andalus al-Ratib wa Zikr Waziraha Lisan al-Din Ibn al-Khatib*. 8 vols. Ihsan 'Abbas, ed. Beirut: Dar Sader, 2nd edn.

Al-Maqrizi, Taqiyy al-Din (1955). *al-Dhahab al-Masbuk fi Dhikr man Hajja min al-Khulafa' wa al-Muluk*. Jamal al-Din Shayyal, ed. Cairo: Maktabat al-Khanji, 1955.

Al-Maqrizi, Taqiyy al-Din (1895). *Al-Ilmam bi-Akhbar man bi-Arḍ al-Ḥabash min Muluk al-Islam*. Cairo: Matba'at al-Ta'lif.

Al-Maqrizi, Taqiyy al-Din (2002–4). *Al-Mawa'iz wa-al-I'itbar fi Dhikr al-Khitat wa-al-Athar*. 4 vols. in 5 tomes. Ayman Fu'ad Sayyid, ed. London: al-Furqan Foundation.

Al-Maqrizi, Taqiyy al-Din (1853). *Al-Mawa'iz wa-l-I'tibar bi-Dhikr al-Khitat wa-l-Athar* 2 vols. Ahmad Qitta al-'Adawi, ed. Cairo: al-Matba'a al-Amiriyya.

Al-Maqrizi, Taqiyy al-Din (1981). *Al-Muntaqa min Akhbar Misr li ibn Muyassar*, also *Choix de passages de la chronique d'Égypte d'Ibn Muyassar*. Ayman Fu'ad Sayyid, ed. Cairo: IFAO.

Al-Maqrizi, Taqiyy al-Din (1934–72). *Al-Suluk li-Ma'rifat Duwal al-Muluk*. 4 vols. Muhammad Mustafa Zyada et al., eds. Cairo: Dar al-Kutub.

Al-Maqrizi, Taqiyy al-Din (1983). *Book of Contention and Strife Concerning the Relations between the Banu Umayya and the Banu Hashim*. C. E. Bosworth, ed. and trans. Manchester: University of Manchester.
Al-Maqrizi, Taqiyy al-Din (2002). *Durar al-'Uqud al-Farida Fi Tarajim al-A'yan al-Mufida*. 4 vols. Mahmud al-Jalili, ed. Beirut: Dar al-Gharb al-Islami.
Al-Maqrizi, Taqiyy al-Din (1992). *Durar al-'Uqud al-Farida Fi Tarajim al-A'yan al-Mufida*. 2 vols. Muhammad Kamal al-Din 'Izz al-Din, ed. Beirut: 'Alam al-Kutub.
Al-Maqrizi, Taqiyy al-Din (1995). *Durar al-'Uqud al-Farida Fi Tarajim al-A'yan al-Mufida: Qit'a Minhu*. 2 vols. 'Adnan Darwish and Muhammad al-Masri, eds. Damascus: Ministry of Culture.
Al-Maqrizi, Taqiyy al-Din (1911–27). *El-mawaiz wal-itibar fi dhikr el-khitat wal-athar*. Gaston Wiet, ed. *Memoires publies par les membres de l'IFAO*, vols. 30, 33, 46, 49, 53. Cairo: IFAO.
Al-Maqrizi, Taqiyy al-Din (1957). *Ighathat al-Umma bi-kashf al-Ghumma, aw Tarikh al-Maja'at fi Misr*. Badr al-Din al-Siba'i, ed. Homs, Syria: Dar Ibn al-Walid.
Al-Maqrizi, Taqiyy al-Din (1999). *Imta' al-Asma' bima lil-Rasul min al-Abna' wa al-Akhwal wa al-Hafada wa al-Mata '*. 15 vols. Muhammad 'Adb al-Hamid al-Namisi, ed. Beirut: Dar al-Kutub al-'Ilmiyya.
Al-Maqrizi, Taqiyy al-Din (1967). *Itti'az al-Hunafa bi-Akhbar al-A'imma al-Fatimiyyin al-Khulafa*. 4 vols. Jamal al-Din Shayyal, ed. Cairo: Supreme Council of Islamic Affairs.
Al-Maqrizi, Taqiyy al-Din (1991). *Kitab al-Muqaffa al-Kabir*. 8 vols. Muhammad Ya'lawi, ed. Beirut: Dar al-Gharb al-Islami.
Al-Maqrizi, Taqiyy al-Din (1888). *Kitab Al-Niza' wa-al-Takhasum fi-ma Bayn Bani Umayyah wa-Bani Hashim, Kampfe Und Streitigkeiten Zwischen Den Banu Umajja Und Den Banu Hasim; Eine Abhandlung von Takijj Ad-Din al-Makrizijj*. Geerhardus Vos, trans. Leiden: Brill.
Al-Maqrizi, Taqiyy al-Din (1993). *Kitab al-Witr*. Muhammad A. 'Ashur and Jamal 'A. al-Kumi, eds. Cairo: Dar al-I'tisam.
Al-Maqrizi, Taqiyy al-Din (1790). *Macrizi historia regum islamiticorum in Abyssinia. Interpretatus est et una cum Abulfedae descriptione regionum nigritarum e codd. biblioth. Leidensis*. Friedrich Theodor Rink, ed. and trans. Leiden: Sam. et Joh. Luchtmans.
Al-Maqrizi, Taqiyy al-Din (2014). *Medieval Egypt: al-Khitat, Part I*, trans. and annotated by Karl Stowasser. CreateSpace Independent Publishing Platform.
Al-Maqrizi, Taqiyy al-Din (1994). *Mukhtasar al-Kamil fi al-Du'afa wa-'Ilal al-Hadith li-Ibn 'Adi*. Ayman ibn 'Arif al-Dimashqi, ed. Cairo: Maktabat al-Sunna.
Al-Maqrizi, Taqiyy al-Din (1988). *Mukhtasar Qiyam al-Layl wa Qiyam Ramadhan wa Kitab al-Witr lil Imam Abi 'Abdallah Muhammad b. Nasr al-Marwazi*. Faysalabad, Pakistan: Hadith Academy.
Al-Maqrizi, Taqiyy al-Din (1995). *Musawwadat Kitab al-Mawa'iz wa-al-I'itbar fi Dhikr al-Khitat wa-al-Athar*. Ayman Fu'ad Sayyid, ed. London: al-Furqan Foundation.
Al-Maqrizi, Taqiyy al-Din (1898). *Qawl al-ibrizi*. Cairo: Matba'at al-Tawfiq.

Al-Maqrizi, Taqiyy al-Din (1988). *Rasail al-Maqrizi*. Ramadan al-Safanawi Badri and Ahmad Mustafa Qasim, eds. Cairo: Dar al-Hadith.

Al-Maqrizi, Taqiyy al-Din (1990). *Shudhur al-ʻUqud Fi Dhikr al-Nuqud*. Muhammad ʻAbd al-Sattar Uthman, ed. Cairo: Dar al-Maʻarif.

Al-Maqrizi, Taqiyy al-Din (1998). *Tarikh al-Aqbat al-maʻruf bi-al-Qawl al-ibriz lil ʻAllama Al-Maqrizi*. ʻAbd al-Majid Diyab, ed. Cairo: Dar al-Fadila.

Al-Maqrizi, Taqiyy al-Din (1997). *Tarikh al-Yahud wa-atharuhum fi Misr*, ʻAbd al-Majid Diyab, ed. Cairo: Dar al-Fadila.

Al-Muhibbi, Muhibb al-Din (2006). *Tarikh Khulasat al-Athar fi Aʻyan al-Qarn al-Hadi ʻAshar*. 4 vols., Muhammad Hasan Ismaʻil, ed. Beirut: Dar al-Kutub al-ʻIlmiyya.

Al-Muqqadasi, Shams al-Din (1906). *Ahsan al-Taqasim fi-Maʻrifat al-Aqalim*. M. J. de Goeje, ed. Leiden: Brill.

Al-Musabbihi, ʻIzz al-Mulk (1980). *Akhbar Misr fi Sanatayn (414–415)*. William G. Millward, ed. Cairo: General Egyptian Book Organization.

Al-Nuʻaymi, ʻAbd al-Qadir (1990). *Kitab al-Daris fi Tarikh al-Madaris*. 2 vols. Ibrahim Shams al-Din, ed. Beirut: Dar al-Kutub al-ʻIlmiyya.

Al-Nuwayri, Shihab al-Din (1923–97). *Nihayat al-Arab fi Funun al-Adab*. 33 vols. Various editors. Cairo: Dar al-Kutub.

Al-Qalqashandi, Shihab al-Din (1913–19). *Subh al-Aʻsha fi-Sinaʻat al-Insha*, 14 vols. Cairo: al-Matbaʻa al-Amiriyya.

Al-Safadi, Khalil ibn Aybak (1931–2013). *Kitab al-Wafi bi-al-Wafayat*. 30 vols. plus 2 index vols. Various eds. Leipzig; Wiesbaden: Deutsche Morgenlandische Gesellschaft.

Al-Sakhawi, Shams al-Din (1935). *al-Daw' al-Lamiʻ li-Ahl al-Qarn al-Tasiʻ*. 12 vols. Cairo: Maktabat al-Qudsi.

Al-Sakhawi, Shams al-Din (1930). *al-Iʻlan bi-al-Tawbikh li-man Dhamma al-Tarikh*. Damascus: Maktabat al-Qudsi.

Al-Sakhawi, Shams al-Din (2002). *Kitab al Tibr al-Masbuk fi Dhayl al-Suluk*. Najwa Kamil and Labiba Mustafa, eds. Cairo: Dar al-Watha'iq al-Qawmiyya.

Al-Sakhawi, Shams al-Din (1896). *Kitab al Tibr al-Masbuk fi Dhayl al-Suluk*. Cairo: al-Matbaʻa al-Amiriyya.

Al-Shahrastani, ʻAbd al-Karim (1956). *Kitab al-Milal wa-l Nihal*. 2 vols. Muhammad b. Fath-Allah Badran, ed. Cairo: Anglo-Egyptian Library.

Al-Shawkani, Muhammad ibn ʻAli (1930). *Al-Badr al-Taliʻ bi Mahasin man Baʻd al-Qarn al-Sabiʻ*. 2 vols. Cairo: Dar al-Saʻada.

Al-Subki, Taj al-Din (1983). *Muʻid al-Niʻam wa Mubid al-Niqam*, M. A. al-Najjar, A. Z. Shalabi, and M. A. al-ʻUyun, eds. Cairo: Dar al-Kitab al-ʻArabi.

Al-Subki, Taj al-Din (1964). *Tabaqat al-Shafiʻyyah al-Kubra*. 10 vols. Mahmud Muhammad al-Tanahi and ʻAbd al-Fattah Muhammad Huluw, eds. Cairo: Dar Ihya' al-Kutub al-Arabiyya.

Al-Suyuti, Jalal al-Din (1967). *Husn al-Muhadara fi Tarikh Misr wa-l-Qahira*. 2 vols. Muhammad Abu al-Fadhl Ibrahim, ed. Cairo: Issa al-Babi al-Halabi.

Al-Suyuti, Jalal al-Din (1952). *Tarikh al-Khulafa'*. Muhammad Muhiyy al-Din ʻAbd al-Hamid, ed. Cairo: Dar al-Saʻada.

Al-Tabari, Muhammad ibn Jarir (1987). *History of al-Tabari, Vol. 4, The Ancient Kingdoms*. Moshe Perlmann, trans. Albany, N.Y.: State University of New York Press.

Al-Yusufi, Musa ibn-Muhammad (1986). *Nuzhat al-Nazir fi-Sirat al-Malik al-Nasir*. Ahmad Hutait, ed. Beirut: ʻAlam al-Kutub.

Al-Ẓahiri, ʻAbd al-Basit b. Khalil b. Shahin al-Zahiri (2011). *Al-Mujmaʻ al-Mufanan Bil-Muʻjam al-Muʻanwan*. 2 vols. ʻUmar ʻAbd al-Salam Tadmuri, ed. Beirut: al-Maktaba al-ʻAsriyya.

Al-Ẓahiri, Khalil ibn Shahin (1894). *Kitab Zubdat Kashf al-Mamlik wa Bayan al-Turuq wa-l-Masalik*. Paul Ravaisse, ed. Paris: Imprimerie Nationale.

Celalzâde Ṣaliḥ Çelebi (2011). *Tarih-i Mısr-ı Cedîd*, Tuncay Bülbül, ed. Ankara: Grafiker Yayınları.

Çelebizâde İsmail Âsım Efendi (2013). *Târih-i Râşid ve Zeyli*. Abdülkadir Özcan, ed. İstanbul: Klasik.

Haji Khalifa, Kâtip Çelebi (1941). *Kashf al-Zunun ʻan Asami al-Kutub wa-l Funun*. 2 vols. Muhammad Şherefttin Yaltakaya and Rifʻat Bilge al-Kilisli, eds. Istanbul: Maarif Matbaasi.

Ibn ʻAbd al-Zahir, Muhiyy al-Din (1996). *Al-Rawda al-Bahiyya fi Khitat al-Qahira al-Muʻizziyya*. Ayman Fu'ad Sayyid, ed. Cairo: al-Dar al-ʻArabiyya li-l-Kitab.

Ibn ʻAbd al-Zahir, Muhiyy al-Din (1961). *Tashrif al-Ayyam wa-l-ʻUsur fi-Sirat al-Malik al-Mansur*. Murad Kamil, ed. Cairo: Ministry of Culture.

Ibn ʻAbd-al-Zahir, Muhiyy al-Din (1976). *Al-Rawd al-Zahir fi-Tarikh al-Malik al-Zahir*. ʻAbd al-ʻAziz al-Khuwaiter, ed. Riyadh: Mu'assasat Fu'ad.

Ibn ʻAsakir, ʻAli ibn al-Hasan (1928). *Tabyin Kadhib al-Muftari Fima Nusiba ila Abi al-Hasan al-Ashʻari*. M. Zahid al-Kawthari, ed. Damascus: Matbaʻat al-Tawfiq.

Ibn al-ʻAdim, Kamal al-Din (1951–68). *Zubdat al-Halab min Tarikh Halab*, 3 vols. Sami al-Dahhan, ed. Damascus: IFEAD.

Ibn al-Ahmar, Ismaʻil ibn Yusuf (1967). *Nathir Fara'id al-Juman fi Nazm Fuhul al-Zaman*. Muhammad Radwan al-Daya, ed. Beirut: Dar al-Thaqafa.

Ibn al-Furat, Nasir al-Din (1939–42). *Tarikh al-Duwal wa-l-Muluk*. 3 vols. K. Zurayk and N. Izzedine, eds. Beirut: AUB Press.

Ibn al-Khatib, Lisan Al-Din (1974–8). *Al-Ihata fi-Akhbar Ghurnata*. 4 vols. Muhammad ʻAbdallah ʻInan, ed. Cairo: Maktabat al-Khanji, 2nd edn.

Ibn al-Marzuban, Muhammad ibn Sahl (1987). *Al-Hanin ila l-Awtan*, Jalil al-ʻAtiyyah, ed. Beirut: ʻAlam al-Kutub.

Ibn Duqmaq, Ibrahim ibn Muhammad (1893). *Al-Intisar li-Wasitat ʻAqd al-Amsar*. Vols. 4 and 5. Karl Vollers, ed. Cairo: al-Matbaʻa al-Amiriyya.

Ibn Duqmaq, Ibrahim ibn Muhammad (1982). *Al-Jawhar al-Thamin fi-Siar al-Khulafa' wa-l-Muluk wa-l-Salatin*. 3 vols. S. A. F. ʻAshur, ed. Mecca: Umm-al-Qura University.

Ibn Fadhl Allah al-ʻUmari, Shihab al-Din (1986). *Masalik al-Absar fi Mamalik al-Amsar: Dawlat al-Mamalik al-Uwla*. D. Krawulsky, ed. Beirut: al-Markaz al-Islami lil-Buhuth.

Ibn Fadhl Allah al-ʿUmari, Shihab al-Din (2010). *Masalik al-Absar fi Mamalik al-Amsar*. 27 vols. Kamil Salman al-Jabburi and Mahdi al-Najm, eds. Beirut: Dar al-Kutub al-ʿIlmiyya.

Ibn Fadhl-Allah al-ʿUmari, Shihab al-Din (1997). *Al-Taʿrif bi-l-Mustalah al-Sharif.* Muhammad Hussein Shams al-Din, ed. Beirut: Dar al-Kutub al-ʿIlmiyya.

Ibn Fahd, Najm al-Din Umar (1982). *Muʿjam al-Shuyukh*. Muhammad al-Zahi ed. Riyadh: Dar al-Yamamah.

Ibn Hajar al-ʿAsqalani, Shihab al-Din (1929–32). *Al-Durar al-Kamina fi Aʿyan al-Miʾa al-Thamina*, 4 vols. Hyderabad: Daʾirat al-Maʿarif al-Uthmaniyya.

Ibn Hajar al-ʿAsqalani, Shihab al-Din (1992). *Al-Majmaʿ al-Muʾassis li al-Muʿjam al-Mufahris, Mashikhat Ibn Hajar*. 4 vols. Yusif ʿAbd al-Rahman al-Marʿashli, ed. Beirut: Dar al-Maʿrifa.

Ibn Hajar al-ʿAsqalani, Shihab al-Din (1967). *Inbaʾ al-Ghumr bi-ʾAnbaʾ al-ʿUmr.* 5 vols. Hyderabad: Daʾirat al-Maʾarif al-Uthmaniyya.

Ibn Hajar al-ʿAsqalani, Shihab al-Din (1957). *Rafʿ al-Isr ʿan Qudat Misr*. 2 vols. Hamid ʿAbd al-Majid and Muhammad Abu Sinna, eds. Cairo: Ministry of Education.

Ibn Hazm, ʿAli ibn Ahmad (1996). *al-Fasl fi al-Milal wa-al-Ahwaʾ wa-al-Nihal.* 5 vols. Muhammad Ibrahim Nasr and Abdul-Rahman ʿAmira, eds. Beirut: Dar al-Jil.

Ibn Iyas al-Hanafi, Muhammad ibn Ahmad (1960–75). *Badaʾiʿ al-Zuhur fi-Waqaʾiʿ al-Duhur*. 5 vols. in 6 books. Muhammad Mustafa, ed. Wiesbaden: Franz Steiner.

Ibn Iyas al-Hanafi, Muhammad ibn Ahmad (1995). *Nuzhat al-Umam fiʾl-ʿAjaʾib waʾl-Hikam*. Muhammad Zaynuhum M. ʿAzab, ed. Cairo: Madbouli.

Ibn Kathir, Ismaʿil ibn ʿUmar (1988). *Al-Bidaya wal-Nihaya*. 14 vols. ʿAli Shiri, ed. Beirut: Dar Ihyaʾ al-Turath al-ʿArabi.

Ibn Khaldun, ʿAbd al-Rahman (1960). *Al-Muqaddima*. 4 vols. ʿAli A-W Wafi, ed. Cairo: Lajnat al-Bayan al-ʿArabi.

Ibn Khaldun, ʿAbd al-Rahman (2005). *Al-Muqaddima*. 5 vols. Abdessalam M. Cheddadi, ed. Casablanca: Bayt al-Funun wal-ʿUlum wal-Adab.

Ibn Khaldun, ʿAbd al-Rahman (1967). *The Muqaddimah: An Introduction to History*. 3 vols. Franz Rosenthal, trans. Princeton: Princeton University Press.

Ibn Manzur, Jamal al-Din (1984–90). *Mukhtasar Tarikh Dimashq l-Ibn ʿAsakir*. 29 vols. Ruhiyya al-Nahhas, M. Mutiʿ al-Hafiz, et al., eds. Damascus: Dar al-Fikr.

Ibn Munqidh, Usama (1930). *Kitab al-Iʿtibar*. Philip Hitti, ed. Princeton: Princeton University Press.

Ibn Qaḍi Shuhbah, Abu Bakr ibn Ahmad (1977). *Tarikh Ibn Qaḍi Shuhbah*. 4 vols. Adnan Darwish, ed. Damascus: IFEAD.

Ibn Saʿid al-Maghribi, Nur al-Din (1970). *Al-Mugharrib fi-Hilly al-Maghrib: al-Nujum al-Zahira fi-Hilly Hadrat al-Qahira*. H. Nassar, ed. Cairo: Dar al-Kutub.

Ibn Saʿid al-Maghribi, Nur al-Din (1953). *Al-Mugharrib fi-Hilly al-Maghrib: al-Juzʾ al-Awwal min al-Qism al-Khāṣṣ bi-Miṣr [al-Ightibat fi Ḥula Madinat al-Fusṭaṭ]*. Shawqi Dhayf et al., eds. Cairo: Fuʾad al-Awwal University.

Ibn Shaddad, ʿIzz al-Din (1953). *Al-Aʿlaq al-Khatira fi-Dhikr Umaraʾ al-Sham wa-l-Jazira, Tarikh Halab*. Vol. 1, pt. 1. Dominique Sourdel, ed. Damascus: IFEAD.

Ibn Shaddad, 'Izz al-Din (1956–64). *Al-A'laq al-Khatira fi-Dhikr Umara' al-Sham wa-l-Jazira, Tarikh Dimashq*. Vol. 2. Sami al-Dahhan, ed. Damascus: IFEAD.

Ibn Shaddad, 'Izz al-Din (1978–91). *Al-A'laq al-Khatira fi-Dhikr Umara' al-Sham wa-l-Jazira*. 3 vols. 6 pts. Yahya 'Abbara, ed. Damascus: Ministry of Culture.

Ibn Shaddad, 'Izz al-Din (1983). *Tarikh al-Malik al-Zahir*. Ahmad Hutait, ed. Wiesbaden: Franz Steiner Verlag.

Ibn Taghri-Birdi, Abu al-Maḥasin (1956–93). *Al-Manhal al-Safi wa-al-Mustawfi ba'da al-Wafi*. 7 vols. Ahmad Najati, Muhammad Muhammad Amin et al., eds. Cairo: Dar al-Kutub.

Ibn Taghri-Birdi, Abu al-Maḥasin (1930–56). *Al-Nujum al-Zahira fi-Muluk Misr wa-l-Qahira*. 16 vols. Ahmad Ramzi, ed. Cairo: Dar al-Kutub.

Ibn Taghri-Birdi, Abu al-Maḥasin (1990). *Hawadith al-Duhur fi Mada al-Ayyam wa-al-Shuhur*. 2 vols. Muhammad Kamal 'Izz al-Din, ed. Beirut: 'Alam al-Kutub.

Ibn Taghri-Birdi, Abu al-Maḥasin (1958). *History of Egypt, 1382–1469* A.D. *(Part IV, 1422–1438 A. D.)*. William Popper, trans. Berkeley: University of California Press.

Ibn Tawit al-Tanji, Muhammad (1951). *Al-Ta'rif bi Ibn Khaldun wa-Rihlatahu Gharban wa Sharqan*. Cairo: Lajnat al-Ta'lif wa-l Tarjama wa-l Nashr.

Ibn Tulun al-Salihi, Shams al-Din (1929–30). *Al-Fulk al-Mashhun fi Ahwal Muhammad ibn Tulun*. Damascus: Maktabat al-Qudsi wa Budayr.

Ibn Tulun al-Salihi, Shams al-Din (1949). *Al-Qala'id al-Jawhariyya fi-Tarikh al-Salihiyya*. 2 vols. Muhammad Ahmad Duhman, ed. Damascus: Maktabat al-Dirasat al-Islamiyya.

Na'ima, Mustafa (1866). *Ta'riḫ-i Na'ima*, or *Rauḍat al-Ḥusain fi Ḫulaṣat Aḫbar al-Ḫafiqain*. Istanbul: Maṭba'a-i 'Amira.

Sibt Ibn al-'Ajami, Muhammad ibn Ibrahim (1996). *Kunuz al-Dhahab fi Tarikh Halab*. 2 vols. Shawqi Sha'ath and Falih Bakkour, eds. Aleppo: Dar al-Qalam.

Vassaf al-Hazrat, 'Abdallah ibn Fadhl-Allah (1853). *Tajziyat al-Amsar wa Tazjiyat al-A'sar*. Muhammad Mahdi Isfahani, ed. Bombay.

Secondary Sources

'Abd al-Razzaq, Mahmud Isma'il (1996). *Nihayat usturat nazariyat Ibn Khaldun: muqtabasa min rasa'il Ikhwan al-Safa*. Al-Mansura: Amer lil-Tib'a wa-al-Nashr.

'Abdel-Wahab, Hasan (1946, reprinted 1994). *Tarikh al-Masajid al-Athariyya allati salla fiha faridhat al-jum'a hadret sahib al-jalala al-malik al-salih Farouq al-Awwal*, 2 vols. Cairo: Dar al-Kutub.

'Ashur, Ahmad, and Subhi al-Sayyid 'Ashur (1999). *al-Watan al-Umm: Dirarsa fi al-Thaqafa al-Qawmiyya al-Misriyya, Ta'sis Tarikhi*. Cairo: n.p.

'Ashur, Sa'id 'Abd al-Fattah (1983). "Adwa' Jadidah 'Ala al-Mu'arrikh Ahmad Ibn 'Ali al-Maqrizi Wa-Kitabatihi." *'Alam al-Fikr* 14, 2: 453–98.

'Asi, Husayn (1992). *al-Maqrizi, Taqiyy al-Din Ahmad ibn Ali ibn Abd al-Qadir al-Ubaydi, 766–845 H-1366–1441 M: Mu'arrikh al-Duwal al-Islamiyah fi Misr*. Beirut: Dar al-Kutub al-'Ilmiyya.

'Awad, Louis (2013 [1968]). "Cultural and Intellectual Developments in Egypt since 1952." In P. J. Vatikiotis, ed., *Egypt since the Revolution*, 2nd edn. London: Routledge, 143–61.

'Inan, Muhammad 'Abdallah (1969). *Misr al-Islamiyya wa-Tarikh al-Khitat al-Misriyya*. Cairo: Maktabat al-Khanji.

'Issa, Salah (1983). *Hawamish al-Maqrizi, Hikayat min Misr*. Cairo: Dar al-Qahira.

'Izz al-Din, Muhammad Kamal al-Din (1990). *Al-Maqrizi: Mu'arrikhan*. Beirut: 'Alam al-Kutub.

'Ukashah, Tharwat (1977). *Al-Taswir al-Islami: al-Dini wa-al-'Arabi*. Beirut: al-Mu'assasa al-'Arabiyya lil-Dirasat wa-al-Nashr.

'Umara al-Yamani (2000). *Diwan*. 'Abd al-Rahman 'Aryani and Ahmad Abd al-Rahman Mu'alimi, eds. Damascus: 'Ikrima Press.

Abbott, Nabia (1977). "Wahb B. Munabbih: A Review Article." *Journal of Near Eastern Studies* 36, 2 (April): 103–12.

Abu-'Uksa, Wael (2016). *Freedom in the Arab World: Concepts and Ideologies in Arabic Thought in the Nineteenth Century*. Cambridge: Cambridge University Press.

Abu-Lughod, Janet (1971). *Cairo, 1001 Years of the City Victorious*. Princeton: Princeton University Press.

Abu-Manneh, Butrus (2003). "Four Letters of Šayḫ Ḥasan al-'Aṭṭār to Šayḫ Ṭāhir al-Ḥusaynī of Jerusalem." *Arabica* 50, 1 (January): 79–95.

Abulhimal, Mustafa (2011). "The Medieval Egyptian Homeland and Inhabitants: The Intelligentsia Speak." *International Journal of the Humanities* 8, 11: 81–93.

Adams, Hazard (1987). "Titles, Titling, and Entitlement To." *The Journal of Aesthetics and Art Criticism* 46, 1 (Autumn): 7–21.

Adham, Moustafa Bey Munir (1924–5). "Le Caire au XV siècle d'après les données de Maqrizi." *BSROGE* 13: 131–80.

Agnani, Sunil (2015). "For the Love of Lost Sovereignty: Egypt and Postcolonial Thought. Review of Disarming Words: Empire and the Seductions of Translation in Egypt by Shaden M. Tageldin." *Cultural Critique* 89 (Winter): 211–21.

Ahmad, 'Abd al-Raziq, Ahmad (1977). "La Hisba et le Muhtasib en Égypte au Temps des Mamluks." *AI* 13: 115–78.

Ahmad, 'Abd al-Raziq, Ahmad (1977, reprinted 1993). *Tarikh wa Athar Misr al-Islamiyya*. Cairo: Dar al-Fikr al-'Arabi.

Ahmad, Muhammad Khalifah Hasan (1997). *Athar al-fikr al-istishraqi fi al-mujtama'at al-Islamiyya*. Cairo: 'Ayn lil-Dirasat wa-al-Buhuth al-Insaniyya wa-al-Ijtima'iyya.

Ahmed, Shahab (2015). *What Is Islam? The Importance of Being Islamic*. Princeton: Princeton University Press.

Aigle, Denise (2003). "Les inscriptions de Baybars dans le Bilad al-Sham: Une expression de la légitimité du pouvoir." *SI* 96: 87–115.

Akbar, Jamel (1989). "Khaṭṭa and the Territorial Structure of Early Muslim Towns." *Muqarnas* 6: 22–32.

Aksan, Virginia. (2002). "The Question of Writing Premodern Biographies of the Middle East." In Mary-Ann Fay, ed., *Auto/Biography and the Construction of Identity and Community in the Middle East*. New York: Palgrave, 191–200.

Al-'Ali, Salih Ahmad (1986). *Khitat al-Basra wa-Mantiqataha: Dirasa fi-Ahwaliha al-'Imranyya wa-l Maliyya fi al-'Uhud al-Islamiyya al-Ula*. Baghdad: al-Majma' al-'Ilmi al-'Iraqi.

Al-'Ithawi, Ahmad Hussein (2005). "Zahirat al-Atlal fi-al-Shi'r al-'Arabi qabl al-Islam." *Majallat al-Buhuth wal Dirasat al-Islamiyya*: 29–59.

Al-'Umari, Amal, and Ali Tayish (1996). *al-'Imara fi Misr al-Islamiyya: al-'Asrayn al-Fatimi wa-al-Ayyubi*. Cairo: Maktabat al-Safa wa-al-Marwa.

Al-Ayyubi, Elias (1994). *Tarikh Misr fi 'Ahd al-Khidiwi Isma'il Pasha*, 2 vols. Cairo: Madbouli, 2nd edn.

Al-Azmeh, Aziz (1981). *Ibn Khaldun in Modern Scholarship: A Study in Orientalism*. London: Third World Centre for Research and Publishing.

Al-Azmeh, Aziz (1982). *Ibn Khaldun: An Essay in Reinterpretation*. London: Frank Cass.

Al-Azmeh, Aziz (2019). *Secularism in the Arab World: Contexts, Ideas, and Circumstances*. Edinburgh: Edinburgh University Press.

Al-Bagdadi, Nadia (1999). "The Invisible-Visible City: Topography, History and the Mind of Ali Mubarak." *Beiruter Texte Und Studien* 64: 539–51.

Al-Baghdadi, 'Abd al-Latif (1869). *al-Ifada wa-l-I'tibar fi al-Umur al-Mushahada wa-l-Hawadith al-Mu'ayana bi-Ard Misr*. Cairo: Matba'at Wadi al-Nil.

Al-Bahnasi, 'Afif (1986). *al-Fann al-Islami*. Damascus: Dar Talas.

Al-Bahnasi, 'Afif (1980). *al-Sham: Lamahat Athariyy wa-Fanniyya*. Baghdad, Dar al-Rashid.

Al-Basha, Hasan (1957). *al-Alqab al-Islamiyya Fi-l-Tarikh Wa-l-Watha'iq Wa-l-Athar*. Cairo: Maktabat al-Nahda.

Al-Fiqqi, Muhammd Kamil (1982). *Al-Azhar wa Atharuhu fi al-Nahda al-Adabiyya al-Haditha*, 3 vols. Cairo: Majma' al-Buhuth in al-Azhar.

Al-Ghitani, Gamal (1984). "Jadaliyyat al-Tannas (Intertextual Dialectics): An Interview with Gamal al-Ghitani," *Alif: Journal of Comparative Poetics* 4: 71–82.

Al-Ghitani, Gamal (1974). *Al-Zayni Barakat*. Damascus: Wizarat al-Thaqafah wa-al-Irshad al-Qawmi.

Al-Ghitani, Gamal. ed. (1980). *Naguib Mahfouz Yatadhakkar*. Beirut: Dar al-Masira.

Al-Ghitani, Gamal (2007). *Isti'adat al-Musafir Khana: Muhawala lil-Bina' min al-Dhakira* (*Remembering the Musafi Khana: An Attempt to Reconstruct from Memory*). Cairo: Dar al-Shuruq.

Al-Ghitani, Gamal (2012). *Kitab al-Tajalliyat*, 3 parts. Cairo: Dar al-Mustaqbal al-'Arabi, 1983–7. Trans. as *The Book of Epiphanies*, Farouk Abdel Wahab, trans. Cairo: AUC Press.

Al-Ghitani, Gamal (1983). *Malamih al-Qahirah fi 1000 Sanah*. Cairo: Dar al-Hilal.

Al-Ghitani, Gamal (1997). *Munataha al-Talab ila-Turath al-'Arab: Dirasat fi al-Turath*. Cairo: Dar al-Shuruq.

Al-Ghitani, Gamal (1984). *Qahiriyat: Asbilat al-Qahirah*. Cairo: Madbuli.

Al-Ghitani, Gamal (1997). *Sifr al-Bunyan*. Cairo: Dar al-Hilal.

Al-Ghitani, Gamal (1999). *The Cairo of Naguib Mahfouz*. Cairo: AUC Press.

Al-Ghitani, Gamal (2007). *The Mahfouz Dialogs*. Humphrey Davis, trans. Cairo: AUC Press.

Al-Ghitani, Gamal (1988). *Zayni Barakat*. Farouk Abdel Wahab, trans. London: Viking.

Al-Isfahani, Abu al-Faraj (attributed) (2000). *The Book of Strangers: Medieval Arabic Graffiti and the Theme of Nostalgia*. Patricia Crone and Shmuel Moreh, trans. and eds. Princeton: Markus Wiener.

Al-Jalili, Mahmud (1965). "Durar al-'Uqud al-Farida fi Tarajim al-A'yan al-Mufida li al-Maqrizi." *Majallat al-Majma' al-'Ilmi al-'Iraqi* 13: 201–14.

Al-Karmali, Anstas (1902). "Salwan al-Asra fi-Iwan Kisra." *al-Mashriq* 5, 15 (August): 673–81; 5, 16 (August): 740–6; 5, 17 (September): 780–6; 5, 18 (September): 834–40.

Al-Khatib, Nabil K. (2013). *Lisan al-Din ibn al-Khatib (713-776-1313-1374): Nathruhu, Shi'ruhu wa Thaqafatuhu fi Itar 'Asrihi*. Beirut: Dar al-Nahda al-'Arabiyya.

Al-Munajjid, Salah al-Din (1949). *Khitat Dimashq: Nusus wa-Dirasat fi Tarikh Dimashq al-Toboghrafi wa Atharaha al-Qadima*. Beirut: Catholic Press.

Al-Nuwayri, Shihab al-Din (2016). *The Ultimate Ambition in the Arts of Erudition. A Compendium of Knowledge from the Classical Islamic World*. Elias Muhanna, ed. and trans. New York: Penguin Books.

Al-Qadi, Wadad (1999). "Dislocation and Nostalgia: al-Hanin ila l-Awtan. Expressions of Alienation in Early Arabic Literature." In Angelika Neuwirth, Birgit Embaló, Sebastian Günther, and Maher Jarrar, eds. *Myths, Historical Archetypes and Symbolic Figures in Arabic Literature: Towards a New Hermeneutic Approach*. Stuttgart: Franz Steiner Verlag, 3–31.

Al-Qadi, Wadad (1981). "East and West in Ali Mubarak's Alamuddin." In Marwan R. Buheiry, ed., *Intellectual Life in the Arab East, 1890–1939*. Beirut: AUB Press, 21–37.

Al-Sharif al-Radi (1995). *Diwan*. 2 vols. Yussef Shukri Farhat, ed. Beirut, Dar al-Jil.

Al-Tanahi, Mahmud Muhammad (2002). *Fi al-Lugha wa-l Adab: Buhuth wa-Dirasat*. 2 vols. Beirut: Dar al-Gharb al-Islami.

Alam, Manzoor (1997). "Ibn Khaldun on the Origin, Growth, and Decay of Cities." In Mohamed Taher, ed., *Encyclopedic Survey of Islamic Culture*, 20 vols. New Delhi: Islamic Book Service, 5: 229–47.

Alleaume, Ghislaine, et al. (1998). *Pascal Coste, toutes les Égypte*. Marseille: Parenthèses.

Allouche, Adel, trans. and ed. (1994). *Mamluk Economics: A Study and Translation of al-Maqrizi's Ighathat al-Ummah bi-Kashf al-Ghummah*. Salt Lake City: University of Utah Press.

AlSayyad, Nezar, Irene A. Bierman, and Nasser Rabbat, eds. (2005). *Making Cairo Medieval*. Lanham: Lexington Books.

AlSayyad, Nezar (2011). *Cairo: Histories of a City*. Cambridge, M.A.: Belknap Press of Harvard University Press.

Amin, Muhammad, M. (1980). *Al-Awqaf Wa-l-Hayyat al-Ijtima'iyya Fi-Misr, 684–923 A.H./1250–1517 A.D.* Cairo: Dar al-Nahda al-'Arabiyya.

Amitai, Reuven (2003). "Al-Maqrizi as a Historian of the Early Mamluk Sultanate (or: Is al-Maqrizi an Unrecognized Historiographical Villain?)." *MSR* 7, 2: 99–118.

Amitai, Reuven (2016). "Egypt: 4. Late Medieval (including Syria: Ayyubid, Mamluk)." In *The Encyclopedia of Empire*. 4 vols. N. Dalziel and J. M. MacKenzie, eds. London: John Wiley, 2: 779–86.

Anawati, Georges C. (1969). "Un aspect de la lutte contre l'hérésie au XVeme siècle d'aprés un inédit attribué à Maqrizi." In André Raymond et al., eds., *Colloque International sur l'Histoire du Caire (27 Mars–5 Avril 1969)*. Cairo: Ministry of Culture, 23–31.

Anderson, Benedict (1983). *Imagined Communities: Reflections on the Origin and Spread of Nationalism*. New York: Verso.

Antrim, Zayde (2007). "Making Syria Mamluk: Ibn Shaddad's *Al-A'laq al-Khatirah*." *MSR* 11, 1: 1–18.

Antrim, Zayde (2014–15). "The Politics of Place in the Works of Ibn Taymiyah and Ibn Fadhl Allah al-'Umari." *MSR* 18, 1: 91–111.

Antrim, Zayde (2010). "*Waṭan* before *Waṭaniyya*: Loyalty to Land in Ayyubid and Mamluk Syria." *Al-Masaq* 22, 2: 173–90.

Antrim, Zayde (2012). *Routes and Realms: The Power of Place in the Early Islamic World*. Oxford: Oxford University Press.

Ariès, Philippe and Georges Duby, eds. (1999). *A History of Private Life, Volume II: Revelations of the Medieval World*. Arthur Goldhammer, trans. Cambridge, M.A.: Harvard University Press.

Arif, Mona (2017). "Constructing the National Past: History-Writing and Nation-Building in Nasser's Egypt," *Shorofat* 1: 7–31, also published as *Constructing the National Past: History Writing and Nation-Building in Nasser's Egypt* (Alexandria: Bibliotheca Alexandrina).

Armogathe, Daniel, and Sylviane Leprun, eds. (1990). *Pascal Coste ou l'architecture cosmopolite*. Paris: Éditions l'Harmattan.

Assmann, Jan (1995). "Collective Memory and Cultural Identity." *New German Critique* 65: 125–33.

Auji, Hala (2016). *Printing Arab Modernity. Book Culture and the American Press in Nineteenth Century Beirut*. Leiden: Brill.

Ayalon, David (1973). "The Great Yasa of Chingiz Khan. A Reexamination (Part C2): al-Maqrizi's Passage on the *Yasa* under the Mamluk." *SI*, 38: 107–56.

Ayalon, David (1960). "The Historian al-Jabarti and his Background." *BSOAS* 23, 2: 217–49.

Aydüz, Salim (2000). "Bilimsel Faaliyetler Açısından Lâle Devri." In Mustafa Armağan, ed., *İstanbul Armağanı: Lâle Devri*. Istanbul Büyüksehir Belediyesi Kültür Isleri Dairesi, 159–93.

Bacharach, Jere (1975). "Circassian Mamluk Historians and Their Quantitative Economic Data." *JARCE* 12: 75–87.

Bacharach, Jere (1973). "The Dinar versus the Ducat." *IJMES* 4, 1: 77–96.

Badawi, 'Abd al-Rahman (2006). *Mu'allafat Ibn Khaldun*. Cairo: al-Majlis al-A'la lil-Thaqafa, 2nd edn.

Baghdiantz-McCabe, Ina (2008). *Orientalism in Early Modern France: Eurasian Trade, Exoticism, and the Ancien Régime*. New York: Berg.

Baldassarri, Stefano Ugo, and Arielle Saiber, eds. (2000). *Images of Quattrocento Florence: Selected Writings in Literature, History, and Art*. New Haven: Yale University Press.

Banister, Mustafa (2014–15). "'Naught Remains to the Caliph but his Title': Revisiting Abbasid Authority in Mamluk Cairo." *MSR* 18: 219–45.

Bauden, Frédéric (2009). "De la codicologie à l'archéologie du savoir. Le cas particulier du carnet de notes de l'historien égyptien al-Maqrīzī (m. 845/1442)." In Renaud Adam and Alain Marchandisse, eds., *Le livre au fil de ses pages, actes de la 14e journée d'étude du Réseau des Médiévistes belges de Langue française, Archives et Bibliothèques de Belgique=Archief en Bibliotheekwezen in Belgie* 87: 29–47.

Bauden, Frédéric (2003). "Maqriziana IV: Le carnet de notes d'al-Maqrizi: l'apport de la codicologie à une meilleure compréhension de sa constitution," *Manuscripta orientalia* 9: 24–36.

Bauden, Frédéric (2014). "Taqi al-Din Ahmad b. 'Ali al-Maqrīzī." *Medieval Muslim Historians and the Franks in the Levant*. Alex Mallett, ed. Leiden: Brill, 161–99.

Bauden, Frédéric (2004). "The Recovery of Mamluk Chancery Documents in an Unsuspected Place." In Michael Winter and Amalia Levanoni, eds., *The Mamluks in Egyptian and Syrian Politics and Society*. Leiden: Brill, 59–76.

Bauden, Frédéric (2009). "Vers une archéologie du savoir en Islam: la méthode de travail d'al-Maqrīzī, historien du XVe siècle." *Comptes rendus des séances de l'Académie des Inscriptions et Belles-Lettres* 153, 1: 97–110.

Bauden, Frédéric (2013). "Al-Maqrizi." In David Thomas and Alex Mallett, eds., *Christian-Muslim Relations: A Bibliographical History. Volume 5 (1350–1500)*. Leiden: Brill, 380–95.

Bauden, Frédéric (2010). "Al-Maqrīzī." In R. G. Dunphy, ed., *Encyclopedia of the Medieval Chronicle*. Leiden: Brill, 1074.

Bauden, Frédéric (2003). "Maqriziana I: Discovery of an Autograph Manuscript of al-Maqrīzī: Towards a Better Understanding of His Working Method, Description: Section 1." *MSR* 7: 21–68.

Bauden, Frédéric (2006). "Maqriziana I: Discovery of an Autograph Manuscript of al-Maqrizi: Towards a Better Understanding of His Working Method Description: Section 2." *MSR* 10, 2: 81–139.

Bauden, Frédéric (2008). "Maqriziana II: Discovery of an Autograph Manuscript of al-Maqrīzī: Towards a Better Understanding of His Working Method, Analysis." *MSR* 12, 1: 51–118.

Bauden, Frédéric (2010). "Maqriziana IX: Should al-Maqrizi Be Thrown out with the Bath Water? The Question of his Plagiarism of al-Awhadi's *Khitat* and the Documentary Evidence." *MSR* 14: 159–232.

Bauden, Frédéric (2020). "Maqriziana X. Al-Maqrizi and His al-Tarih al-Kabir al-Muqaffa li-Miṣr. Part 1: An Inquiry into the History of the Work." *Studies in Islamic Historiography: Essays in Honour of Professor Donald P. Little*, Sami G. Massoud, ed. Leiden: Brill, 66–123.

Bauden, Frédéric (2010). "Maqriziana XII: Evaluating the Sources for the Fatimid Period: Ibn al-Ma'mūn al-Baṭā'iḥī's History and Its Use by al-Maqrīzī (with a Critical Edition of His Résumé for the Years 501–515 A.H.)." In Bruce D. Craig, ed., *Islamic and Fatimid Studies in Honor of Paul E. Walker*. Chicago: Middle East Documentation Center, 33–85.

Bauden, Frédéric (2017). "Maqriziana XIII: An Exchange of Correspondence between al-Maqrīzī and al-Qalqashandī" In Yuval Ben-Bassat, ed., *Developing Perspectives in Mamluk History Essays in Honor of Amalia Levanoni*. Leiden: Brill, 201–29.

Bauden, Frédéric (2004). "Review of al-Maqrizi, *al-Mawa'iz wa-al I'tibar bi-Dhikr al-Khitat wa-al-Athar, al-M'aruf bi-al-Khitat al-Maqriziyya*, Madihah Sharqawi and Muhammad Zaynuhum, eds." *MSR* 8, 1: 299.

Bauden, Frédéric (2007). "Review of al-Maqrizi, *al-Mawa'iz wa-al-I'itbar fi Dhikr al-Khitat wa-al-Athar*, Ayman Fu'ad Sayyid, ed." *MSR* 11, 2: 169–76.

Baydar Nalbantoglu, Gulsum (1998). "Toward Postcolonial Openings: Rereading Sir Banister Fletcher's *History of Architecture*." *Assemblage* 35: 6–17.

Becker, Carl Heinrich (1911). "Review of al-Maqrizi's al-Mawa'iz wa-al-I'tibar, edited by Gaston Wiet." *Der Islam* 2: 405–7.

Behrens Abouseif, Doris (2019). "Islamic Architecture from Travelogue to Survey. The Discovery of Islamic Cairo." *Lexico: Storie e architettura in Sicilia e nel Mediterraneo* 28: 7–26.

Behrens Abouseif, Doris (2008). *Cairo of the Mamluks: A History of Architecture and Its Culture*. London: I. B. Tauris.

Behrens-Abouseif, Doris (1992). "The Façade of the Aqmar Mosque in the Context of Fatimid Ceremonial." *Muqarnas* 9: 29–38.

Behrens-Abouseif, Doris (1987). *Fatḥ Allāh and Abū Zakariyya: Physicians under the Mamluks*. Cairo: IFAO.

Bencheneb, Saadeddine (1967). "Mémoires, tableaux historique et portraits dans l'oeuvre de Lisan ad-Din Ibn al-Khatib." *Revue d'Histoire et de Civilisation du Maghreb* 2: 54–85.

Berkey, Jonathan (1992). "Mamluks and the World of Higher Education in Medieval Cairo, 1250–1517." In Hassan Elboudrari, ed., *Modes de transmission de la culture religieuse en Islam*. Cairo: IFAO, 93–116.

Berkey, Jonathan (2003). "The *Muhtasib*s of Cairo Under the Mamluks: Toward an Understanding of an Islamic Institution." In Michael Winter and Amalia Levanoni, eds., *The Mamluks in Egyptian and Syrian Politics and Society*. Leiden: Brill, 245–76.

Berkey, Jonathan (1992). "Women and Islamic Education in the Mamluk Period." In Nikki Keddie and Beth Baron, eds., *Women in Middle Eastern History: Shifting Boundaries in Sex and Gender*. New Haven: Yale University Press, 143–57.

Berkey, Jonathan (2017). *The Transmission of Knowledge in Medieval Cairo: A Social History of Islamic Education*. Princeton: Princeton University Press.

Bernal, Martin (1987). *Black Athena: The Afroasiatic Roots of Classical Civilization*. 2 vols. Brunswick, N.J.: Rutgers University Press.

Bernheimer, Teresa (2012). "Genealogy, Marriage, and the Drawing of Boundaries among the 'Alids (8th–12th Centuries)." In Kazuo Morimoto, ed., *Sayyids and Sharifs in Muslim Societies: The Living Links to the Prophet*. London: Routledge, 75–91.

Berque, Jacques (1972). *Egypt: Imperialism and Revolution*. J. Stewart, trans. London: Faber.

Bieu, Charles (1888). *Catalogue of the Turkish Manuscripts in the British Museum*. London: the British Museum.

Bjørneboe, Lars (2007). *In Search of the True Political Position of the 'Ulama: An Analysis of the Aims and Perspectives of the Chronicles of Abd al-Rahman al-Jabarti (1753–1825)*. Aarhus: Aarhus University Press and the Danish Institute, Damascus.

Booke, M. Keith (1993). "The Dalkey Archive: Flann O'Brien's Critique of Mastery." *Irish University Review* 23, 2 (Autumn/Winter): 269–85.

Bora, Fozia (2012). "A Mamluk Historian's Holograph: Messages from a Musawwada of Tārīkh." *Journal of Islamic Manuscripts* 3: 119–53.

Bora, Fozia (2015). "Did Salah al-Din Destroy the Fatimids' Books? An Historiographical Enquiry." *JRASGBI* 25, 1: 21–39.

Boswell, James (1791). *The Life of Samuel Johnson, LL.D.* Reprint. 2 vols. London: J. M. Dent & Sons.

Bosworth, Clifford Edmund (1979). "Al-Maqrizi's Exposition of the Formative Period in Islamic History and Its Cosmic Significance: The Kitab al-Niza' Wa-al-Takhasum." In Alford T. Welch and Pierre Cachia, eds., *Islam: Past Influence and Present Challenge: In Honour of William Montgomery Watt*. Edinburgh: Edinburgh University Press, 93–104.

Bosworth, Clifford Edmund (1981). "Al-Maqrizi's Epistle Concerning What Has Come Down to Us About the Banu Umayya and the Banu l-'Abbas." In Wadad al-Qaḍi, ed., *Studia Arabica and Islamica: Festshrift for Ihsan 'Abbas*. Beirut: AUB Press, 39–45.

Bosworth, Clifford Edmund (1982). *Medieval Arabic Culture and Administration*. London: Variorum Reprints.

Botros, Atef (2015). "Rewriting Resistance: The Revival of Poetry of Dissent in Egypt after January 2011 (Surūr, Najm and Dunqul)." In Yvonne Albers, Georges Khalil, and Friederike Pannewick, eds., *Commitment and Beyond: Reflections on/of the Political in Arabic Literature since the 1940s*. Wiesbaden: Ludwig Reichert Verlag, 45–62.

Bourgoin, Jules (1879). *Les éléments de l'art arabe: le trait des entrelacs*. Paris: Firmin Didot.

Bouriant, Pierre (1904). "Notice sur Urbain Bouriant." *Recueil de travaux relatifs à la philologie et à l'archéologie égyptiennes et assyriennes* 26, 1 and 2: 29–32.

Bouriant, Urbain, trans. (1895, 1900). *Maqrizi. Description topographique et historique de l'Égypte, MMAF*, vol. 17, part 1 and 2, Paris: Ernst Leroux.

Boutros Ghali, Mirrit (1978). "The Egyptian National Consciousness." *MEJ* 32, 1 (Winter): 59–77.

Boym, Svetlana (2001). *The Future of Nostalgia*. New York: N.Y.: Basic Books.

Bozdoğan, Sibel, and Gülru Necipoğlu (2007). "Entangled Discourses: Scrutinizing Orientalist and Nationalist Legacies in the Architectural Historiography of the 'Lands of Rum.'" *Muqarnas* 24: 1–6.

Braunstein, Philippe (1999). "Toward Intimacy: The Fourteenth and Fifteenth Centuries." In Philippe Ariès and Georges Duby, eds., trans. Arthur Goldhammer, *A History of Private Life, Volume II: Revelations of the Medieval World*. Cambridge, M.A.: Harvard University Press, 536–56.

Bret, Patrice (2003). "L'Égypte de Jomard: la construction d'un mythe orientaliste, de Bonaparte à Méhémet-Ali." *Romantisme* 120: 5–14.

Brett, Michael (2005). "Population and Conversion to Islam in Egypt in the Mediaeval Period." In U. Vermeulen and J. van Steenbergen, eds., *Egypt and Syria in the Fatimid, Ayyubid and Mamluk Eras*, IV. Leuven: Peeters, 1–32.

Brett, Michael (1983). "Review of *Choix de passages de la chronique d'Égypte d'Ibn Muyassar Tāǧ ad-Dīn Muḥ. b. 'Alī b. Yūsuf b. Ǧalab Rāǧib m. 677 H.*, sélection faite par Taqiyy ad-Dīn Aḥmad b. 'Alī al-Maqrīzī en l'année 814 H. by Ayman Fu'ād Sayyid." *JRASGBI* 2: 293–5.

Brett, Michael (2019). *The Fatimids and Egypt*. London: Routledge.

Brett, Michael (2001). *The Rise of the Fatimids: The World of the Mediterranean and the Middle East in the Fourth Century of the Hijra, Tenth Century CE*. Leiden: Brill.

Briggs, Martin S. (1924). *Muhammadan Architecture in Egypt and Palestine*. Oxford: Clarendon Press.

Broadbridge, Anne (1999). "Academic Rivalry and the Patronage System in Fifteenth-Century Egypt: Al-'Ayni, al-Maqrizi, and Ibn Hajar al-'Asqalani." *MSR* 3: 85–107.

Broadbridge, Anne (2007). "Diplomatic Conventions in the Mamluk Sultanate." *AI* 41: 97–118.

Broadbridge, Anne (2003). "Royal Authority, Justice, and Order in Society: The Influence of Ibn Khaldun on the Writings of al-Maqrizi and Ibn Taghribirdi." *MSR* 7, 2: 231–45.

Broadbridge, Anne (2008). *Kingship and Ideology in the Islamic and Mongol Worlds*. Cambridge: Cambridge University Press.

Brogan, Olwen and David Smith (1957). "The Roman Frontier Settlement at Ghirza: An Interim Report." *The Journal of Roman Studies* 47, 1: 173–84.

Bruni, Leonardo (1968). "Laudatio Florentinae Urbis," In Hans Baron, ed., *From Petrarch to Leonardo Bruni*. Chicago: University of Chicago Press, 232–63.

Bucher, François (1972). "Medieval Architectural Design Methods 800–1560." *Gesta* 11, 2: 37–51.

Buheiry, Marwan R., ed. (1981). *Intellectual Life in the Arab East, 1890–1939*. Beirut: AUB Press.

Busch, Briton Cooper (1968). "Divine Intervention in the 'Muqaddimah' of Ibn Khaldūn." *History of Religions* 7, 4 (May): 317–29.

Cachia, Pierre (2011). *Exploring Arab Folk Literature*. Edinburgh: Edinburgh University Press.

Cahen, Claude (1936). "Les chroniques arabes concernant la Syrie, l'Égypte, et la Mésopotamie de la conquête arabe à la conquête ottomane dans les bibliothèques d'Istanbul." *Revue des Études Islamiques* 4: 333–62.

Caldwell, Malcolm (2002). "Group Think." *New Yorker*, December 2, 102–7.

Capezzone, Leonardo (2016). "Remembering, Knowing, Imagining: Approaches to the Topic of Memory in Medieval Islamic Culture." In Y. Tzvi Langermann and Robert G. Morrison eds., *Texts in Transit in the Medieval Mediterranean*, University Park: Penn State University Press, 85–100.

Cardonne, Denis Dominique (1761). "Extraits des manuscripts arabes dans lesquels il est parlé des évènements historiques relatifs au règne de S. Louis." In *Histoire de Saint Louis par Jehan Sire de Joinville, Les annals de son règne*, and *Sa vie et ses miracles*. Paris: Imprimerie royale, 525–45 (republished as Collection complète des mémoires relatifs à l'histoire de France; v. 3, 1819).

Casanova, Paul, trans. (1906, 1920). *Makrizi: Description historique et topographique de l'Égypte*. *MMAF* vols. 3 and 4. Cairo: IFAO.

Casanova, Paul (1913–19). *Essai de reconstitution topographique de la ville d'al Foustat ou Misr*. *MMAF* vol. 35, parts 1 and 2. Cairo: IFAO.

Casanova, Paul (1894–7). *Histoire et déscription de la citadelle du Caire*. *MMAF* vol. 6, pt. 4–5. Cairo: IFAO.

Cassarino, Mirella (2018). "Between Function and Fiction: The Representation of Women in al-Ibshīhī's al-Mustaṭraf." *MSR* 21: 1–20.

Castner, Catherine J. (2016). "The Fortuna of Biondo Flavio's *Italia Illustrata*." In Angelo Mazzocco and Marc Laureys, eds., *A New Sense of the Past: The Scholarship of Biondo Flavio (1392–1463)*. Leuven: Leuven University Press, 177–96.

Chamberlain, Michael (1994). *Knowledge and Social Practice in Medieval Damascus, 1190–1350*. Cambridge: Cambridge University Press.

Cheddadi, Abdesselam (2006). *Ibn Khaldun: L'homme et le théoricien de la civilization*. Paris: Gallimard.

Chejne, Anwar G. (1965). "The Boon-Companion in Early ʿAbbāsid Times." *JOAS* 85, 3: 327–35.

Chocair, Naʿum (1916). *Tarikh Sina al-Qadim wa-l Hadith wa-Jughrafiyataha. Maʿ Khulasat Tarikh Misr wa-l Sham wa-l'Iraq wa-Jazirat al-ʿArab wa ma kana baynaha min al-ʿAlaʾiq al-Tijariyya wa-l Harbiyya wa-Ghayraha ʿan Tariq Sinaʾ min-Awal ʿAhd al-Tarikh ila al-Yawm*. Cairo: Dar al-Maʿarif.

Choueiri, Youssef M. (2000). *Arab Nationalism: A History. Nation and State in the Arab World*. Oxford: Blackwell.

Clauson, Gerard (1972). *An Etymological Dictionary of Pre-13th Century Turkish*. Oxford: Clarendon Press.

Clifford, Winslow W. (1977). "*Ubi Sumus?* Mamluk History and Social Theory." *MSR* 1: 45–62.

Cobb, Paul (2003). "Al-Maqrizi, Hashimism, and the Early Caliphates." *MSR* 7, 2: 69–81.

Cochrane, Eric (1981). *Historians and Historiography in the Italian Renaissance*. Chicago: University of Chicago Press.

Cole, Juan (2007). *Napoleon's Egypt: Invading the Middle East*. New York: Palgrave Macmillan.

Colla, Elliott (2003). "'Non, non! Si, si!': Commemorating the French Occupation of Egypt (1798–1801)." *Modern Language Notes* 118, 4 (September): 1043–69.

Coller, Ian (2011). *Arab France: Islam and the Making of Modern Europe, 1798–1831*. Berkeley: University of California Press.

Colquhoun, Keith, and Ann Wroe, eds. (2008). *The Economist Book of Obituaries*. New York: Bloomberg Press.

Conermann, Stephan, ed. (2018). *Mamluk Historiography Revisited—Narratological Perspectives*. Goettingen: V&R Unipress with Bonn University Press.

Conermann, Stephan, ed. (2013). *Ubi Sumus? Quo Vademus? Mamluk Studies, State of the Art*. Göttingen: V&R Unipress with Bonn University Press.

Conermann, Stephan (2004). "Ibn Tulun (d. 955/1548): Life and Works." *MSR* 8, 1: 115–40.
Conermann, Stephan (2000). "Review of N Mahmud Mustafa, *al-'Asr al-Mamluki*." *MSR* 4: 257–60.
Conermann, Stephan (2014). *Mamlukica: Studies on the History and Society of the Mamluk Period*. Goettingen: V&R Unipress with Bonn University Press.
Cooperson, Michael (1998). "Remembering the Future: Arabic Time-Travel Literature." *Edebiyat* 8: 171–89.
Cooperson, Michael (2005). "Probability, Plausibility, and 'Spiritual Communication' in Classical Arabic Biography." In Philip Kennedy, ed., *On Fiction and Adab in Medieval Arabic Literature*. Wiesbaden: Harrassowitz, 69–84.
Corbin, Henry (1966). "The Visionary Dream in Islamic Spirituality." In Gustave E. von Grunebaum and Roger Caillois, eds., *The Dream and Human Societies*. Berkeley: University of California Press, 381–408.
Coste, Pascal-Xavier (1839). *Architecture Arabe ou Monuments du Kaire mésurés et dessinés de 1818 à 1826*. Paris: Firmin-Didot.
Crabbs, Jr., Jack A. (1984). *The Writing of History in Nineteenth-Century Egypt*. Detroit: Wayne State University Press.
Creswell, K. A. C. (1969). *Early Muslim Architecture*. 2 vols. Oxford: Clarendon Press, 2nd edn.
Creswell, K. A. C. (1959). *Muslim Architecture of Egypt*. 2 vols. Oxford: Oxford University Press.
Dacier, Bon-Joseph. (1831). "Notice historique sur la vie et les ouvrages de M. Langlès." *Histoire et mémoires de l'Institut royal de France* 9: 100–16.
Daftary, Farhad (2004). *Ismaili Literature: A Bibliography of Sources and Studies*. London: I. B. Tauris.
Daftary, Farhad (1990). *The Isma'ilis: Their History and Doctrines*. Cambridge: Cambridge University Press.
Dale, Stephen Frederic (2006). "Ibn Khaldun: The Last Great Greek and the First *Annaliste* Historian." *IJMES* 38, 3: 431–51.
Darraj, Ahmad (1961). *L'Égypte Sous Le Règne de Barsbay, 825–841/1422–1438*. Damascus: IFEAD.
De Certeau, Michel (1988). *The Writing of History*. Tom Conley trans. New York: Columbia University Press.
De Jong, F. and P. Gran (1982). "On Peter Gran, Islamic Roots of Capitalism: Egypt, 1760–1840: A Review Article with Author's Reply." *IJMES* 14, 3 (August): 381–99.
De Prémare, Alfred-Louis (2005). "Wahb ibn Munabbih: An Exceptional Figure of Early Islamic Scholarship," *Annales. Histoire, Sciences Sociales* 60, 3: 531–49.
De Slane, William MacGuckin (1838). "Compte-rendu, Etienne Quatremère, *Histoire des sultans mamlouks de l'Égypte*." *Journal asiatique* (3rd ser.) 6: 615–20.
Décobert, Christian (1989). "L'orientalisme, des Lumières à la Révolution, selon Silvestre de Sacy." *Revue du monde musulman et de la Méditerranée* 52, 1: 49–62.
Décobert, Christian (1992). "Sur l'arabisation et l'islamisation de l'Égypte médiévale." In Christian Décobert, ed., *Itinéraires d'Égypte. Mélanges offerts au Père Maurice Martin, SJ*. Cairo: IFAO, 273–300.

Denny, Frederick Mathewson (1977). "Some Religio-Communal Terms and Concepts in the Qur'ān." *Numen* 24, 1 (April): 26–59.

Denoix, Sylvie (1992). *Decrire le Caire Fustat-Misr d'apres Ibn Duqmaq et Maqrizi*. Cairo: IFAO.

Derenbourg, Hartwig (1909). *Oumara du Yémen. Sa vie et son oeuvre*. Paris: Ernest Leroux.

Déroche, François (2014). "La 'Chrestomathie arabe' de Silvestre de Sacy." In Nora Lafi, Michel Espagne and Pascale Rabault-Feuerhahn, eds., *Silvestre de Sacy. Le projet européen d'une science orientaliste*. Paris: Éditions du Cerf, 61–71.

Di-Capua, Yoav (2009). *Gatekeepers of the Arab Past: Historians and History Writing in Twentieth-Century Egypt*. Berkeley: University of California Press.

Donner, Fred (1998). *Narratives of Islamic Origins: The Beginnings of Islamic Historical Writing*. Princeton: Darwin Press.

Dotterer, Ronald L. (2004). "Flann O'Brien, James Joyce, and "The Dalkey Archive." *New Hibernia Review/Iris Éireannach Nua* 8, 2 (Summer): 54–63.

Driault, Edouard (1925). "La Renaissance de l'Égypte." *Napoléon* 14, 1 (January–February): 5–22.

Drisin, Adam (2004). "Intricate Fictions: Mapping Princely Authority in a Sixteenth-Century Florentine Urban Plan." *JAE* 57, 4 (May): 41–55.

Du Grandlaunay, René Guérin (2013). "Le Milieu Familial de Šams Al-Dīn al-Saḫāwī. Quelques Aspects d'une Lecture Autobiographique." *AI* 47: 283–306.

El Shamsy, Ahmed (2020). *Rediscovering the Islamic Classics: How Editors and Print Culture Transformed an Intellectual Tradition*. Princeton: Princeton University Press.

El-Ariss, Tarek (2013). *Trials of Arab Modernity: Literary Affects and the New Political*. New York: Fordham University Press.

El-Bahi, Ahmed (2008). "Feriana (Furriyana) à l'époque médiévale: questions de toponyme." *Actes du 5ème colloque international sur l'histoire des steppes tunisiennes* Fathi Bejaoui, ed. Tunis: Institut National du Patrimoine, 249–58.

El-Habashi, 'Alaa (2001). "Athar to Monuments: The Intervention of the Comité de Conservation des Monuments de l'Art Arabe." PhD diss., University of Pennsylvania.

El-Habashi, 'Alaa (2003). "The Preservation of Egyptian Cultural Heritage through Egyptian Eyes: The Case of the Comité de Conservation des Monuments de l'Art Arabe." In Joe Nasr and Mercedes Volait, eds., *Urbanism: Imported or Exported?* Chichester, England: Wiley-Academy, 155–83.

El-Kadi, Galila and Alain Bonnamy (2007). *Architecture for the Dead: Cairo's Medieval Necropolis*. Cairo: AUC Press.

El-Leithy, Tamer (2005). "Coptic Culture and Conversion in Medieval Cairo, 1293–1524 A.D." PhD diss., Princeton University.

El-Lozy, Mahmoud (1988). "Rebel with a Cause," *al-Ahram Weekly* 400 (October 22–8), archived at http://web.archive.org/web/20100314025621/http://wadada.net/surur/delirium.htm

El-Rayes, Waseem (2013). "The Book of Allusions: A New Translation of the Title to Ibn Khaldun's Kitāb al-'Ibar." *Religious Studies and Theology* 32, 1: 163–84.

El-Rouayheb, Khaled (2006). "Opening the Gate of Verification: The Forgotten Arab-Islamic Florescence of the 17th Century." *IJMES* 38, 2 (May): 263–81.
Encyclopaedia of Islam I.
Encyclopaedia of Islam II.
Encyclopaedia of Islam III.
Eppel, Michael (2009). "Note about the Term *Effendiyya* in the History of the Middle East." *IJMES* 41, 3 535–9.
Eppel, Michael (1998). "The Elite, the *Effendiyya*, and the Growth of Nationalism and Pan-Arabism in Hashemite Iraq, 1921–1958." *IJMES* 30, 2 (May): 227–50.
Escovitz, Joseph H. (1983). "Orientalists and Orientalism in the Writings of Muhammad Kurd ʻAli." *IJMES* 15, 1: 95–109.
Escovitz, Joseph H. (1976). "Vocational Patterns of the Scribes of the Mamluk Chancery." *Arabica* 23: 42–62.
Esposito, John L. ed. (1995). *The Oxford Encyclopedia of the Modern Islamic World*. 4 vols. New York: Oxford University Press.
Ettlinger, Leopold D. (1977). "The Emergence of the Italian Architect during the Fifteenth Century." In *The Architect: Chapters in the History of a Profession*. Spiro Kostof, ed. New York: Oxford University Press, 96–123.
Fahd, Toufic (1966). "The Dream in Medieval Islamic Society." In Roger Caillois and Gustave E. von Grunebaum, eds., *The Dream and Human Societies*. Berkeley: University of California Press, 351–63.
Fahmi, ʻAbd al-Salam A. (1983). *Iwan al-Mada'in Bayn al-Buhturi wa-l Khaqani: Dirasa Adabiyya Muqarana bayn al-Qasidatayn al-ʻArabiyya wa-l Farisiyya, Siniyyat al-Buhturi wa Nuniyyat al-Khaqani*. Jeddah: Dar al-Bayan al-ʻArabi.
Fanon, Franz. (1963). *The Wretched of the Earth*. Constance Farrington, trans. New York: Grove Press.
Fay, Mary Ann, ed. (2002). *Auto/Biography and the Construction of Identity and Community in the Middle East*. New York: Palgrave.
Fernandes, Leonora (1987). "Mamluk Politics and Education: The Evidence from Two Fourteenth Century Waqfiyya." *AI* 23: 87–98.
Fikri, Ahmad (1962–6). *Masajid al-Qahira wa Madarisaha*, 3 vols. Cairo: Dar al-Maʻarif.
Firanescu, Daniela Rodica (2018). "Medieval Arabic Islam and the Culture of Gender: Feminine Voices in al-Suyūṭī's Literature on Sex and Marriage." *MSR* 21: 69–86.
Fischel, Walter (1967). *Ibn Khaldun in Egypt; His Public Functions and his Historical Research, 1382–1406; a Study in Islamic Historiography*. Berkeley: University of California Press.
Fisher, John (1984). "Entitling." *Critical Inquiry* 11, 2 (December): 286–98.
Fleischer, Cornell (1983). "Royal Authority, Dynastic Cyclism, and 'Ibn Khaldunism' in Sixteenth-Century Ottoman Letters." *Journal of Asian and African Studies* 18, 3–4: 198–220.
Fleischer, Cornell (1986). *Bureaucrat and Intellectual in the Ottoman Empire the Historian Mustafa Âli (1541–1600)*. Princeton: Princeton University Press.
Fliedner, Stephan (1990). *Ali Mubarak und seine Hitat: kommentierte Ubersetzung der Autobiographie und Werkbesprechung*. Berlin: K. Schwarz.

Flood, Finbarr Barry (1997). "Umayyad Survivals and Mamluk Revivals: Qalawunid Architecture and the Great Mosque of Damascus." *Muqarnas* 14: 57–79.

Fodor, Sándor (1970). "The Origins of the Arabic Legends of the Pyramids." *Acta Orientalia Academiae Scientiarum Hungaricae* 23: 335–63.

Fowden, Garth. (1993) *Empire to Commonwealth: Consequences of Monotheism in Late Antiquity*. Princeton: Princeton University Press.

Freitag, Ulrike (1994). "Writing Arab History: The Search for the Nation." *British Journal of Middle Eastern Studies* 21, 1: 19–37.

Frenkel, Yehoshua (2008). "Dream Accounts in the Chronicles of the Mamluk Period." In Louise Marlow, ed., *Dreaming Across Boundaries: The Interpretation of Dreams in Islamic Lands*. Cambridge, M.A.: Harvard University Press, 202–20.

Frenkel, Yehoshua (2014). *Daw' al-Sari li-Ma'rifat Habar Tamim al-Dari. On Tamim al-Dari and his Waqf in Hebron*. Leiden: Brill.

Fu'ad, Ni'mat Ahmad (1968, reprinted 1978). *Shakhsiyat Misr*. Cairo: al-Hay'a al-Misriyya al-'Amma lil-Kitab.

Galal, Muhammad Nu'man, and Majdi Mutawalli (1997). *Hawiyat Misr*. Cairo: al-Hay'a al-Misriyya al-'Amma lil-Kitab.

Galal, Muhammad Nu'man (1998). *Dynamics of the Egyptian national identity*. Lahore: Sang-e-Meel.

Galtier, Émile (1906). "Maqrizi a-t-il écrit une 'Description historique et topographique de l'Égypt et du Caire?'" *Bulletin de l'IFAO* 5: 156–64.

Garcin, Jean-Claude (1984). "Toponymie et topographie urbaines médiévales à Fustat et au Caire," *JESHO* 27: 113–55.

Garcin, Jean-Claude (2001). "Outsiders in the City." In Doris Behrens-Abouseif, ed., *The Cairo Heritage Papers in Honor of Layla Ali Ibrahim*. Cairo: AUC Press, 7–15.

Garcin, Jean-Claude (2005). "Review of al-Maqrizi, *al-Mawaiz wa-al-I'itbar fi Dhikr al-Khitat wa-al-Athar*, Ayman Fu'ad Sayyid, ed." *JESHO*, 48, 1: 125–31.

Garcin, Jean-Claude (2013). *Pour une lecture historique des Mille et une Nuits*. Paris: Actes Sud.

Gardiner, Noah, with Frédéric Bauden (2011). "A Recently Discovered Holograph Fair Copy of al-Maqrīzī's al-Mawā'iz wa-al-i'tibār fī dhikr al-khitat wa-al-āthār: University of Michigan Islamic MS 605." *Journal of Islamic Manuscripts* 2: 123–31.

Gardiner, Noah (2014). "Esotericism in a Manuscript Culture: Aḥmad al-Būnī and His Readers through the Mamlūk Period." PhD diss., University of Michigan.

Geertz, Clifford (1973). *The Interpretation of Cultures*. New York: Basic Books.

Gershoni, Israel, and James P. Jankowski (1995). *Redefining the Egyptian Nation, 1930–1945*. Cambridge: Cambridge University Press.

Gharaibeh, Mohammad (2018). "Narrative Strategies in Biographical Dictionaries: The Ad-Durar al-Kāmina of Ibn Ḥağar al-'Asqalānī—A Case Study." In Stephan Conermann, ed., *Mamluk Historiography Revisited: Narratological Perspectives*. Göttingen: V&R Unipress with Bonn University Press, 51–75.

Ghersetti, Antonella (2018). "The Representation of Slave Girls in a Physiognomic Text of the Fourteenth Century." *MSR* 21: 21–46.

Gibb, H. A. R. (1962). "Islamic Biographical Literature." In Bernard Lewis and Peter

Holt, eds. *Historians of the Middle East*. Oxford: Oxford University Press, 54–58.
Gibb, H. A. R. (1962). *Studies on the Civilization of Islam*. Stanford Shaw and William Polk, eds. London: Routledge and Kegan Paul.
Gibb, H. A. R. (1938). *Tarikh, Encyclopedia of Islam I Supplement*. Leiden: Brill, 233–45.
Gillispie, Charles Coulston, and Michael Dewachter, eds. (1987). *Monuments of Egypt. The Napoleonic Edition: The Complete Archaeological Plates from la Description de l'Égypte*. Princeton: Princeton University Press.
Goldziher, Ignaz (1971). *The Ẓahiris: Their Doctrine and Their History. A Contribution to the History of Islamic Theology*. Wolfgang Behn, ed. and trans. Leiden: Brill.
Gordon, Joel (2006) *Nasser: Hero of the Arab Nation*. Oxford: Oneworld.
Gran, Peter (2009). "Ḥasan al-'Aṭṭār." In J. E. Lowry and D. Stewart, eds., *Essays in Arabic Literary Biography: 1350–1850*. Wiesbaden: Harrasowitz Verlag, 56–68.
Gran, Peter (1979). *Islamic Roots of Capitalism: Egypt, 1760–1840*. Austin: University of Texas Press.
Gran, Peter (2020). *The Persistence of Orientalism: Anglo-American Historians and Modern Egypt*. Syracuse: Syracuse University Press.
Green, Nile (2003). "The Religious and Cultural Roles of Dreams and Visions in Islam." *JRAS* 13, 3: 287–313.
Griffith, Sidney Harrison (2010). *The Church in the Shadow of the Mosque: Christians and Muslims in the World of Islam*. Princeton: Princeton University Press.
Gruendler, Beatrice (2016). "*Al-hanin ila l-awtan* and its Alternatives in Classical Arabic Literature." In Sebastian Günther and Stephen Milich, eds., *Representations and Visions of Homeland in Modern Arabic Literature*. Hildesheim: Georg Olms Verlag, 1–42.
Gubara, Dahlia E. M. (2012). "Al-Azhar in the Bibliographic Imagination." *JAL* 43, 2/3: 299–335.
Guest, A. R. (1902). "A List of Writers, Books, and Other Authorities Mentioned by el-Maqrizi in his Khitat." *JRAS*: 103–25.
Guest, A. R. (1921). "Review of Jean Maspero and Gaston Wiet, *Matériaux pour servir à la géographie de l'Égypte*." *JRASGBI* 4 (October): 624–7.
Guo, Li (1997). "Mamluk Hisotorigraphic Studies: The State of the Art." *MSR* 1: 15–43.
Haarmann, Ulrich (2000). "Al-Maqrizi, the Master, and Abu Hamid al-Qudsi, the Disciple—Whose Historical Writing Can Claim More Topicality and Modernity?" In Hugh Kennedy, ed., *The Historiography of Islamic Egypt, c. 950–1800*. Leiden: Brill, 59–75.
Haarmann, Ulrich (1987–8). "Al-Ummah wa-al-Watan fi al-'Usur al-Wusta al-Islamiyah wa-al-'Urubbyah." *Dirasat Islamiyah* 2: 219–37.
Haarmann, Ulrich (1971). "Auflösung und Bewahrung der klassischen Formen arabischer Geschichtsschreibung in der Zeit der Mamluken." *ZDMG* 121: 46–60.
Haarmann, Ulrich (1978). "Die Sphinx: Synkretische Volksreligiositat im spatmittelalterlichen islamischen Agypten." *Saeculum* 29: 367–84.

Haarmann, Ulrich (1991). "In Quest of the Spectacular: Noble and Learned Visitors to the Pyramids around 1200 AD." In Wael Hallaq and Donald Little, eds., *Islamic studies presented to Charles J Adams*. Leiden: Brill, 57–67.
Haarmann, Ulrich (1980). "Regional Sentiment in Medieval Islamic Egypt." *BSOAS* 43: 55–66.
Haarmann, Ulrich (1995). "Review of Weltgeschichte und Weltbeschreibung im mittelalterlichen Islam by Bernd Radtke," *JOAS* 115, 1: 133–5.
Haarmann, Ulrich (1988). "Arabic in Speech, Turkish in Lineage: Mamluks and Their Sons in the Intellectual Life of Fourteenth-Century Egypt and Syria." *Journal of Semitic Studies* 33: 81–114.
Haarmann, Ulrich (1996). "Glaubensvolk und Nation im islamischen und lateinischen Mittelalter." *Berichte und Abhandlungen/Berlin-Brandenburgische Akademie der Wissenschaften* 2: 161–99.
Haarmann, Ulrich (1988). "Rather the Injustice of the Turks than the Righteousness of the Arabs: Changing 'Ulamā' Attitudes towards Mamluk Rule in the Late Fifteenth Century." *SI* 68: 61–77.
Haarmann, Ulrich (1991). "The Plight of the Self-Appointed Genius: Muṣṭafā 'Ālī." *Arabica* 38, 1: 73–86.
Haarmann, Ulrich (1970). *Quellenstudien zur frühen Mamlukenzeit*. Freiburg: Klaus Schwartz.
Habib, Rafiq (1997). *Al-Shakhsiyya al-Misriyya: al-Tatawwur al-Nafsi fi Khamsin Qarn*. Cairo: Markaz al-Mahrusa lil-Buhuth wa-al-Tadrib wa-al-Nashr.
Hafez, Sabry (2010). "The New Egyptian Novel: Urban Transformation and Narrative Form." *New Left Review* 64 (July–August): 47–62.
Hafuth, Kamal, John and Ivy Videan (1965). *The Eastern Key: Kitab al-ifadah wa'l-l'tibar of 'Abd al-Latif al-Baghdadi*. London: Allen & Unwin.
Halbwachs, Maurice (1980). *The Collective Memory*. Francis J. Ditter Jr. and Vida Yazidi Ditter, trans. New York: Harper Colophon Books.
Hallaq, Wael B. (2011). "On Orientalism, Self-Consciousness and History." *Islamic Law and Society* 18, 3/4: 387–439.
Hallaq, Wael B. (2018). *Restating Orientalism: A Critique of Modern Knowledge*. New York: Columbia University Press.
Hamdan, Jamal (1980–4). *Shakhsiyyat Misr, Dirasa fi 'Abqariyyat al-Makan*. 4 vols. Cairo: 'Alam al-Kutub.
Hämeen-Anttila, Jaakko (2017). *Al-Maqrīzī's al-Ḫabar 'an al-bašar*, Vol. V, section 4: *Persia and Its Kings*, part I. Leiden: Brill.
Hamilton, R. W. (1974). "Keppel Archibald Cameron Creswell, 1879–1974." *Proceedings of the British Academy* 60: 1–20.
Hamilton, R. W. (1978). "Khirbat Al Mafjar: The Bath Hall Reconsidered." *Levant* 10, 1: 126–38.
Hamzah, Dyala, ed. (2014). *The Making of the Arab Intellectual. Empire, Public Sphere and the Colonial Coordinates of Selfhood*. London: Routledge.
Hanna, Milad (1990). *Al-A'mida al-sab'a lil-shakhsiyya al-Misriyya*. Cairo: Dar al-Hilal. Trans. as *The Seven Pillars of the Egyptian Identity*. Cairo: General Egyptian Book Organization, 1994.

Harun, ʿAbd al-Salam (1988). *Qutuf Adabiyya: Dirasat Naqdiyya fil-Turath al-ʿArabi. Hawl Tahqiq al-Turath.* Cairo: Maktabat al-Sunna.

Hasan, ʿIzzat (1968). *Shiʿr al-Wuquf ʿala al-Atlal mina al-Jahiliyya ila Nihayat al-Qarn al-Thalith.* Damascus: Ministry of Culture.

Hasebe, Fumihiko (2003). "'Yalbugha al-Salimi—Koki Mamluk-Cho Ustadar No Shogai (2)' (The Career of Yalbugha al-Salimi al-Ustadar [2])." *Keio Gijuku Daigaku Gengo Bunka Kenkyujo Kiyo* (*Reports of the Keio Institute of Cultural and Linguistic Studies*) 35: 133–45.

Hassan, Mona (2016). *Longing for the Lost Caliphate: A Transregional History.* Princeton: Princeton University Press.

Haswell, C. J. R. (1922). "Cairo, Origin and Development. Some Notes on the Influence of the River Nile and Its Changes." *BSROGE* 11: 171–7.

Hautecœur, Louis (1925). "L'expedition d'Égypte et l'art français." *Napoléon* 14/1 (January–February): 81–7.

Hautecœur, Louis, and Gaston Wiet. (1932). *Les mosquées du Caire*, 2 vols. Paris: Ernest Leroux.

Hentsch, Thierry (1992). *Imagining the Middle East.* Fred Reed, trans. Montréal: Black Rose Books.

Hirschler, Konrad (2013). "Studying Mamluk Historiography: From Source-Criticism to the Cultural Turn." In Stephan Conermann, ed., *Ubi Sumus? Quo Vademus? Mamluk Studies, State of the Art.* Göttingen: V&R Unipress with Bonn University Press, 159–86.

Hitti, Philip K. (1931) "*Kitab Khiṭaṭ al-Sham* by Muḥammad Kurdʿali." *JOAS* 51, 2 (June): 178–9.

Hitzel, Frédéric, ed. (2013). *Proceedings of the Fourteenth International Congress of Turkish Art (2011).* Paris: Collège de France.

Hodgson, Marshall (1993). *Rethinking World History: Essays on Europe, Islam, and World History.* Edmund Burke III, ed. Cambridge: Cambridge University Press.

Hodgson, Marshall (1974). *The Venture of Islam.* 3 vols. Chicago: University of Chicago Press.

Holt, P. M. (1982). "Three Biographies of al-Zahir Baybars." In D. O. Morgan, ed., *Medieval Historical Writing in the Christian and Islamic Worlds.* London: School of Oriental and African Studies, 19–29.

Holt, P. M. (1998). "Literary Offerings: A Genre of Courtly Literature." In Thomas Philipp and Ulrich Haarmann, eds., *The Mamluks in Egyptian Politics and Society.* Cambridge: Cambridge University Press, 3–16.

Hourani, Albert (1983). *Arabic Thought in the Liberal Age, 1798–1939.* Cambridge: Cambridge University Press, 2nd edn.

Humphreys, R. Stephen (1989). "Qur'anic Myth and Narrative Structure in Early Islamic Historiography." In F. M. Clover and R. S. Humphreys, eds., *Tradition and Innovation in Late Antiquity.* Madison: Wis.: University of Wisconsin Press, 271–90.

Humphreys, R. Stephen (1981). "Review of André Raymond and Gaston Wiet, *Les marchés du Caire*," *MESAB* 15, 2 (December): 63–5.

Humphreys, R. Stephen (1991). *Islamic History: A Framework for Inquiry*. Princeton: Princeton University Press, rev. edn.

Hurvitz, Nimrod (1997). "Biographies and Mild Asceticism: A Study of Islamic Moral Imagination." *SI*, 85: 41–65.

Ibn al-Burhan, Ahmad (attributed to the Imam Abi Hashim?) (2019). *Kitab Tariq al-Istiqama li-Ma'rifat al-Imama*. 'Aqil Jasim Dahsh and 'Abd al-Hadi 'Abd al-Rahman al-Shawi, eds. *Kufa Studies Center Journal* 1, 55: 115–76.

Ibrahim, Laila and Bernard O'Kane (1988). "The Madrasa of Badr al-Dīn al-'Aynī and its Tiled Miḥrāb." *AI* 24: 253–68.

Ibrahim, Najiyya 'Abdallah, and Nada 'Abd al-Razzaq al-Jilawi (2015). "Ibn Tulun's Personal and Scientific Biography: Shams id-Din Mohammad Ibn Ali al-Dimashqi al-Salihi (953 A.H./A.D. 1546)." *Journal of College of Education for Women* 26, 4: 1057–75.

Irwin, Robert (1997). "Toynbee and Ibn Khaldun." *MES* 33, 3 (July): 461–79.

Irwin, Robert (2003). "Al-Maqrizi and Ibn Khaldun, Historians of the Unseen." *MSR* 7, 2: 217–30.

Irwin, Robert (2018). *Ibn Khaldun: An Intellectual Biography*. Princeton: Princeton University Press, 2018.

Isma'il, 'Abd al-Razzaq Mahmud (1974). "Manhaj al-Mu'arrikh Ibn Taghri-Birdi fi Kitabihi al-Nujum al-Zahira." In *al-Mu'arrikh Ibn Taghri Birdi: Jamal al-Din Abu al-Mahasin Yusuf, 813–874 H.* Cairo: al-Hay'a al-Misriyya al-'Amma lil-Kitab, 109–22.

Jacquemond, Richard (2008). *Conscience of the Nation: Writers, State, and Society in Modern Egypt*. David Tresilian, trans. Cairo: AUC Press.

Jarrar, Sabri (2001). "Al-Maqrizi's Reinvention of Egyptian Historiography." In Doris Behrens-Abouseif, ed., *The Cairo Heritage: Essays in Honor of Laila Ali Ibrahim*. Cairo: AUC Press, 30–53.

Jenkins, Jr., Everett (2000). *The Muslim Diaspora: A Comprehensive Reference to the Spread of Islam in Asia, Africa, Europe and the Americas. Volume 2, 570–1799*. Jefferson, N.C.: McFarland.

Jiwa, Shainool, trans. (2013). *The Founder of Cairo: The Fatimid Imam-Caliph al-Mu'izz and His Era: An English Translation of the Text on al-Mu'izz from Idrīs 'Imād al-Dīn's 'Uyūn al-Akhbār*. London: I. B. Tauris.

Jiwa, Shainool, trans. (2009). *Towards a Shi'i Mediterranean Empire: Fatimid Egypt and the Founding of Cairo: The Reign of the Imam-Caliph al-Mu'izz from Taqī al-Dīn Aḥmad b. 'Alī al-Maqrīzī's Itti'āẓ al-Ḥunafā' Bi-Akhbār al-A'imma al-Fāṭamiyyīn al-Khulafā'*. London: I. B. Tauris.

Johnson, Sarah Cresap (2017). "'Return to Origin Is Non-Existence': Al-Mada'in and Perceptions of Ruins in Abbasid Iraq." *IJIA* 6, 2: 257–83.

Kafadar, Cemal (1991). "Les troubles monétaires de la fin du XVIe siècle et la prise de conscience Ottomane du déclin." *Annales: Économies, Sociétés, Civilisations* 46, 2: 381–400.

Kahil, Abdallah (2008). *The Sultan Ḥasan Complex in Cairo 1357–1364: A Case Study in the Formation of Mamluk Style*. Würzburg: Ergon-Verlag.

Karabell, Zachary (2003). *Parting the Desert: The Creation of the Suez Canal*. New York: Knopf.

Karatay, Fehmi Edhem (1961). *Topkapi Sarayi Müzesi Kütüphanesi türkçe yazmalar katalogu C. 1 Din, Tarih, Bilimler*. Istanbul: Topkapi Sarayi Müzesi.

Käs, Fabian (2016). Al-Maqrīzīs *Traktat Uber Die Mineralien: Kitāb Al-Maqāṣid Al-Saniyyah Li-Ma'rifat Al-Aǧsām Al-Ma'diniyyah*. Leiden: Brill.

Kazi, A. K., and J. G. Flynn, trans. (2013). *Muslim Sects and Divisions. The Section on Muslim Sects in Kitab al-Milal wa 'l-Nihal*. London, Kegan Paul International 1984, reprint, New York: Routledge.

Keddie, Nikki, and Beth Baron, eds. (1992). *Women in Middle Eastern History: Shifting Boundaries in Sex and Gender*. New Haven: Yale University Press.

Kenny, Lorne M. (1967). "'Ali Mubarak: Nineteenth Century Egyptian Educator and Administrator." *MEJ* 21, 1 (Winter): 35–51.

Khalidi, Tarif (1981). "Some Classical Islamic Views of the City." In Wadad al-Qadi, ed., *Studia Arabica and Islamica: Festshrift for Ihsan 'Abbas*. Beirut: AUB Press, 265–76.

Khalidi, Tarif (1994). *Arabic Historical Thought in the Classical Period*. Cambridge: Cambridge University Press.

Khalifah, 'Abd al-Latif Muhammad, and Sha'ban Jab Allah Radwan (1998). *al-Shakhsiyya al-Misriyya: al-malamih wa-al-ab'ad: dirasah sikulujiyah*. Cairo: Dar Gharib.

Khalifah, Omar (2017). *Nasser in the Egyptian Imaginary*. Edinburgh: Edinburgh University Press.

Khoury, Nuha N. N. (1992). "The Mihrab Image: Commemorative Themes in Medieval Islamic Architecture." *Muqarnas* 9: 11–28.

Khuri, Ra'if (1983). *Modern Arab Thought: Channels of the French Revolution to the Arab East*, trans. I. 'Abbas. Princeton: The Kingston Press.

Kilito, Abdelfattah (2001). *The Author and His Doubles: Essays on Classical Arabic Culture*. Michael Cooperson, trans. Syracuse, N.Y.: Syracuse University Press.

Kinberg, Leah (1985). "What Is Meant by Zuhd." *SI* 61: 27–44.

King, G. R. D. (1989). "Islamic Archaeology in Libya, 1969–1989." *Libyan Studies* 20: 193–207.

Kister, M. J. (1972). "Haddithu 'an Bani Isra'ila wa-la Haraj." *Israel Oriental Studies* 2: 215–39.

Koch, Yoel (1983). "'Izz al-Din ibn Shaddad and his Biography of Baybars," *Annali: Istituto Universitario Orientale, Sezione Slava* 43: 249–87.

Koerber, Benjamin (2017). *Conspiracy in Modern Egyptian Literature*. Edinburgh: Edinburgh University Press.

Kramer, Martin, ed. (1991). *Middle Eastern Lives: The Practice of Biography and Self-Narrative*. Syracuse: Syracuse University Press.

Krawulsky, Dorothea (1993). *Al-'Arab wa Iran, Dirasat fi al-Tarikh wa al-Adab min al-Manzur al-Aydiologi*. Beirut: Dar al-Muntakhab al-'Arabi.

Krawulsky, Dorothea (1986). *Al-'Umari, Masalik al-Absar fi-Mamalik al-Amsar, Dawlat al-Mamalik al-Ula*. Beirut: al-Markaz al-Islami lil-Buhuth.

Kundak, Ali Nihat (2013). "The Influence of European Book Paintings on the

Miniatures of Tercüme-i 'İkdü'l-cümân fî târîh-i ehli'z-zamân." In Frédéric Hitzel, ed., *Proceedings of the Fourteenth International Congress of Turkish Art (2011)*. Paris: Collège de France, 459–66.

Kurd'ali, Muhammad (1925–8). *Khitat al Sham*. 6 vols. Damascus: Matba'at al-Taraqi.

Kwang Sung, Il. (2017). *Mamluks in the Modern Egyptian Mind: Changing the Memory of the Mamluks 1919–1952*. New York: Palgrave Macmillan.

Lane, Edward William. (1863) *An Arabic–English Lexicon*, 2 books. London: Williams & Norgate.

Langlès, Louis (1790). "De l'importance des langues orientales pour l'extension du commerce, le progrès des lettres et des sciences, adresse à l'Assemblée nationale, par L. Langlès." Paris: Champigny.

Langlès, Louis (1799). "Histoire du Canal de Messr (vulgairement nommé Canal de Suez), tirée de la description historique "Le Livre des avis et sujets de réflexions sur la description géographique et historique de l'Égypte par al-Maqryzy, et traduite." *Magasin Encyclopédique* 5: 289–310.

Langlès, Louis (1800/1). "Le Livre des avis et sujets de réflexions sur la description géographique et historique de l'Égypte par Ebn āl-Maqryzy, 1er extrait contenant la description historique du canal de l'Égypte (de Suez); II. Textes des différentes descriptions ou notices du canal de Messr, données par les auteurs arabes [édité avec une traduction française]." *Notices et Extraits des manuscrits de la Bibliothèque Nationale* 6: 320–86.

Langlès, Louis (1811). *Catalogue des principaux ouvrages de M. Langlès*. Paris: Le Normant Imprimeur-Librairie.

Lassner, Jacob (1970). *Topography of Baghdad in the Early Middle Ages: Text and Studies by Jacob Lassner*. Detroit: Wayne State University Press. Trans. as *Khitat Baghdad fi al-'Uhud al-'Abbasiyya al-Ula*. Baghdad: al-Majma' al-'Ilmi al-'Iraqi, 1984.

Laurens, Henri (1997). *L'expédition d'Égypte 1798–1801*. Paris: Éditions du Seuil.

Laurens, Henri (1987). *Les origines intellectuelles de l'expedition d'Égypte: l'orientalisme islamisant en France (1698–1798)*. Istanbul: Isis.

Laurens, Henri (2004). *Orientales I: Autour de l'expédition d'Égypte*. Paris: éditions CNRS.

Le Père, J. M. (1809). "Mémoire sur la communication de la mer des Indes à la Méditerranée par la mer Rouge et l'Isthme de Sueys," *Descriptions de l'Égypte*. 23 vols. Paris: L'imprimerie impériale, 11: 21–186.

LeGassick, Trevor J. (1971). "Some Recent War-Related Arabic Fiction." *MEJ* 25, 4 (Autumn): 491–505.

Lellouch, Benjamin (2006). *Les Ottomans en Égypte. Historiens et conquérants au XVIe siècle*. Louvain: Peeters.

Lev, Yaakov (1999). *Saladin in Egypt*. Leiden: Brill.

Levanoni, Amalia (2001). "Al-Maqrizi's Account of the Transition from Turkish to Circassian Mamluk Sultanate: History in the Service of Faith." In Hugh Kennedy, ed., *The Historiography of Islamic Egypt (c. 950–1800)*. Leiden: Brill, 93–105.

Levanoni, Amalia (2003). "'Sīrat al-Mu'ayyad Shaykh' by Ibn Nāhid." In Chase

Robinson, ed., *Texts, Documents and Artefacts: Islamic Studies in Honour of D. S. Richards*. Leiden: Brill, 211–33.

Levanoni, Amalia (2010). "Who Were the 'Salt of the Earth' in Fifteenth-Century Egypt?" *MSR* 14: 63–83.

Levinson, Jerrold (1985). "Titles." *The Journal of Aesthetics and Art Criticism* 44: 29–39.

Lewis, Bernard and Peter Holt, eds. (1962). *Historians of the Middle East*. Oxford: Oxford University Press.

Little, Donald (2003). "A Comparison of al-Maqrizi and al-ʿAyni as Historians of Contemporary Events." *MSR* 7, 2: 205–15.

Little, Donald (1976). "Coptic Conversion to Islam under the Bahrī Mamlūks, 692–755/1293–1354." *BSOAS* 39: 552–69.

Little, Donald (1970). *An Introduction to Mamluk Historiography: An Analysis of Arabic Annalistic and Biographical Sources for the Reign of al-Malik an-Nasir Muhammad ibn Qalawun*. Wiesbaden: Franz Steiner Verlag.

Livingston, J. W. (1997). "Shaykhs Jabarti and ʿAttar: Islamic Reaction and Response to Western Science in Egypt." *Der Islam* 74: 92–106.

Loiseau, Julien (2013). "Les événements de l'année 806. Ou comment al-Maqrizi a pensé une rupture majeure dans l'histoire de l'Égypte." *Médiévales* 64 (Spring): 119–34.

Loiseau, Julien (2010). *Reconstruire la Maison du sultan, 1350–1450: ruine et décomposition de l'ordre urbain au Caire*, 2 vols. Cairo: IFAO.

Loiseau, Julien (2014). *Les Mamelouks. Xiiie–XVIe siècle*. Paris: Éditions du Seuil.

Louca, Anouar (1989). "Pèlerinage a trois voix: lecture d'un texte de Maqrīzī." *Arabica* 36, 1: 93–108.

Louca, Anwar (1955). "La renaissance égyptienne et les limites de l'œuvre de Bonaparte." *Cahiers d'histoire égyptienne* 7: 1–20.

Lowenthal, David (1997). *Possessed by the Past: The Heritage Crusade and the Spoils of History*. London: Viking.

Lowry, Joseph E. (1996). "Time, Form and Self: The Autobiography of Abu Shama." *Edebiyat* 7, 2 (Autumn): 313–25.

Mahdi, Muhsin (1957). *Ibn Khaldun's Philosophy of History*. London: Allen & Unwin.

Maher, Suʿad (1971). *Masajid Misr wa Awliya'uha al-Salihun*, 3 vols. Cairo: al-Majlis al-Aʿla li-l Shu'un al-Islamiyya.

Mahfuz, Naguib (2001). *The Cairo Trilogy: Palace Walk, Palace of Desire, Sugar Street,* William M. Hutchins et al., trans. New York: Everyman's Library.

Mahfuz, Naguib (1956–7). *Thulathiyyat al-Qahira, Bayn al Qasrayn, Qasr al Shawq*, and *al-Sukkariya*. Cairo: Dar Rose al-Youssef.

Makdisi, George (1990). *The Rise of Humanism in Classical Islam and the Christian West*. Edinburgh: Edinburgh University Press.

Makhlouf, Peter (n.d.). "Enargeia and Phantasia among the Arabic Aristotelians: Poetics, Politics and Prophecy from Farabi to Strauss," unpublished paper.

Malti-Douglas, Fedwa (1989). "Mentalités and Marginality: Blindness and Mamluk Civilization." In Clifford Edmund Bosworth et al., eds., *The Islamic World from*

Classical to Modern Times: Essays in Honor of Bernard Lewis. Princeton: Darwin Press, 211–37.

Marimoto, Kazuo (2014). "Keeping the Prophet's Family Alive: Profile of a Genealogical Discipline." In Sarah Bowen Savant and Helena de Felipe, eds., *Genealogy and Knowledge in Muslim Societies: Understanding the Past*. Edinburgh: Edinburgh University Press, 11–23.

Marlow, Louise (1995). "Kings, Prophets and the 'Ulamā' in Mediaeval Islamic Advice Literature." *SI* 81: 101–20.

Marlow, Louise (2009). "Surveying Recent Literature on the Arabic and Persian Mirrors for Princes Genre." *History Compass* 7, 2 (March): 523–38.

Martel-Thoumian, Bernadette (1992). *Les civils et l'administration dans l'état militaire mamluk (IXe/XVe Siècle)*. Damascus: IFEAD.

Martinez-Gros, Gabriel (2006). *Ibn Khaldun et les sept vies de l'islam*. Arles: Actes sud; Sindbad, 2006.

Maspero, Jean, and Gaston Wiet (1919). *Matériaux pour servir à la géographie de l'Égypte*. *MMAF* vol. 36. Cairo: IFAO.

Massignon, Louis (1983). *Parole Donnée*. Vincent Monteil, ed. 3rd ed. Paris: Seuil.

Massingberd, Hugh (1995). *The Daily Telegraph Book of Obituaries: A Celebration of Eccentric Lives*. London: Macmillan.

Massoud, Sami (2003). "Al-Maqrizi as a Historian of the Reign of Barquq." *MSR* 7, 2: 119–36.

Massoud, Sami (2007). *The Chronicles and Annalistic Sources of the Early Mamluk Circassian Period*. Leiden: Brill.

Mattar, Karim (2020). *Specters of World Literature: Orientalism, Modernity, and the Novel in the Middle East*. Edinburgh: Edinburgh University Press.

Mazuz, Haggai (2018). "From 'Moses' Mishnah' to Moses Maimonides' Mishneh Tōrah: The Development of the Jewish Oral Law according to al-Maqrīzī." *Journal Asiatique* 306, 2: 201–7.

Mazuz, Haggai (2017). "Post-Biblical Jewish Sources in al-Maqrīzī's Historiography—Whence His Knowledge?" *JAIS* 17: 1–13.

Mazuz, Haggai (2019). "The Jewish Calendar and Calendation according to al-Maqrīzī in *al-Khiṭaṭ*," *ZDMG* 169, 1: 77–96.

McAuliffe, Jane Dammen (1996). "The Quranic Context of Muslim Biblical Scholarship." *Islam and Christian-Muslim Relations* 7, 2: 141–58.

McDonald, William, ed. (2011). *The Obits 2012: The New York Times Annual*. New York: Workman.

Mehrez, Samia (2008). *Egypt's Culture Wars: Politics and Practice*. London: Routledge.

Mehrez, Samia (1994). *Egyptian Writers between History and Fiction: Essays on Naguib Mahfouz, Sonallah Ibrahim, and Gamal al-Ghitani*. Cairo: AUC Press.

Meinecke-Berg, Viktoria (1977). "Quellen zu Topographie und Baugeschichte in Kairo unter Sultan an-Nasir b. Qala'un." *ZDMG* supplement 3: 539–50.

Meinecke, Michael (1992). *Die Mamlukische Architektur in Ägypten und Syrien (648/1250 bis 923/1517)* 2 vols. Glückstadt: Verlag J. J. Augustin.

Meisami, Julie (1998). "Places in the Past: The Poetics/Politics of Nostalgia." *Edebiyat* 8: 63–106.

Meisami, Julie (2001). "The Palace-Complex as Emblem: Some Samarran *Qasidas*." In Chase Robinson, ed., *A Medieval Islamic City Reconsidered: An Interdisciplinary Approach to Samarra*. Oxford: Oxford University Press, 69–78.

Meloy, John (2003). "The Merits of Economic History: Re-Reading al-Maqrizi's Ighathah and Shudhur." *MSR* 7, 2: 183–203.

Melvin-Koushki, Matthew (2017). "In Defense of Geomancy: Šaraf al-Dīn Yazdī Rebuts Ibn Ḫaldūn's Critique of the Occult Sciences." *Arabica* 64, 3/4: 346–403.

Menchinger, Ethan (2017). *The First of the Modern Ottomans: The Intellectual History of Ahmed Vasif*. Cambridge: Cambridge University Press.

Mercer, John (1979). "The Canary Islanders in Western Mediterranean Politics." *African Affairs* 78, 311 (April): 159–76.

Messaoudi, Alain (2014). "Figures d'un père de l'orientalisme moderne: Les représentations de Silvestre de Sacy à travers ses biographes." In Nora Lafi, Michel Espagne and Pascale Rabault-Feuerhahn, eds., *Silvestre de Sacy. Le projet européen d'une science orientaliste*. Paris: Éditions du Cerf, 23–40.

Meuleman, Johan H. (1991). "La causalité dans la Muqaddimah d' Ibn Khaldun." *SI* 74: 105–39.

Michel, Nicolas (2011). "Les *wafq*-s d'un homme d'état ottoman dans la seconde moitié du xvie siècle," *Turcica* 43: 269–308.

Miquel, André (1967–80). *La géographie humaine du monde musulman jusqu'au milieu du 11e siècle*. 3 vols. Paris: Mouton.

Miquel, André (1986). *Ousama, un prince syrien face au croisés*. Paris: Fayard.

Mitchell, Timothy (1988). *Colonizing Egypt*. Berkeley: University of California Press.

Moore, Clement Henry (1974). "Authoritarian Politics in Unincorporated Society: The Case of Nasser's Egypt." *Comparative Politics* 6, 2 (January): 193–218.

Moreh, Shmuel (2003). "Napoléon and the French Impact on Egyptian Society in the Eyes of al-Jabarti." In Irene A. Bierman, ed., *Napoléon in Egypt*. Reading: UK: Ithaca Press, 77–98.

Moritz, Bernhard (1905). *Arabic Paleography: A Collection of Arabic Texts from the First Century of the Hidjra till the Year 1000*. Cairo: Khedivial Library.

Mubarak, 'Ali Pasha (1882). *'Alam al-Din*. 4 vols. Alexandria: Jaridat al-Mahrusa.

Mubarak, 'Ali Pasha (1888–9). *al-Khitat al-Tawfiqiyya al-Jadida*, 20 vols. Cairo: Bulaq.

Muhanna, Elias (2018). *The World in a Book: Al-Nuwayri and the Islamic Encyclopedic Tradition*. Princeton: Princeton University Press.

Murphy, Jane (2010). "Locating the Sciences in Eighteenth-century Egypt." *The British Journal for the History of Science* 43, 4 (December): 557–71.

Musallam, Bassim (1980). "The Modern Vision of Ali Mubarak." In R. B. Serjeant, ed., *The Islamic City*. Paris: Unesco, 183–99.

Mustafa, Shakir (1978). *Al-Tarikh al-'Arabi Wa-l-Mu'arrikhun: Dirasa Fi Tatawwur 'Ilm al-Tarikh Wa-Rijaluhu Fi-l-Islam*. 4 vols. Beirut: Dar al-'Ilm li'l Malayin.

Muth, Franz-Christoph (2005). "A Globe-Trotter from Maghrib in al-Maqrīzī's booklet on Ethiopia: A Footnote from Some Arabic Sources," *Afrique & histoire*, 4, 2: 123–31.

Myrne, Pernilla (2018). "Women and Men in Al-Suyūṭī's Guides to Sex and Marriage." *MSR* 21: 47–68.

Naaman, Mara (2011). *Urban Space in Contemporary Egyptian Literature: Portraits of Cairo*. New York: Palgrave Macmillan US.

Naginski, Erika. (2001) "Riegl, Archaeology, and the Periodization of Culture." *Res: Anthropology and Aesthetics* 40 (Autumn): 115–32.

Necipoğlu, Gülru (2012). "The Concept of Islamic Art: Inherited Discourses and New Approaches." In Benoît Junod, Georges Khalil, Stefan Weber and Gerhard Wolf, eds., *Islamic Art and the Museum*. London: Saqi Books, 57–76.

Nora Lafi, Michel Espagne and Pascale Rabault-Feuerhahn, eds. (2014). *Silvestre de Sacy. Le projet européen d'une science orientaliste*. Paris: Éditions du Cerf.

Nora, Pierre (1989). "Between Memory and History: Les Lieux de mémoire." *Representations* 26 (Spring): 7–25.

Nora, Pierre (1996). *Realms of Memory: Rethinking the French Past*. Arthur Goldhammer, trans. New York: Columbia University Press.

Nuwaysir, Husni Muhammad (1996). *Al-'Imara al-Islamiyya fi-Misr: 'Asr al-Ayyubiyyin wa-l Mamalik*. Cairo: Maktabat Zahra' al-Sharq.

O'Boyle, Jane (2001). *Cool Dead People: Obituaries of Real Folks We Wish We'd Met a Little Sooner*. New York: Plume.

O'Kane, Bernard (2017). *The Mosques of Egypt*. Cairo: AUC Press.

O'Sullivan, Shaun (2006). "Coptic Conversion and the Islamization of Egypt." *MSR* 10, 2: 65–79.

Ohlander, Erik (2009). "Enacting Justice, Ensuring Salvation: The Trope of the 'Just Ruler' in Some Medieval Islamic Mirrors for Princes." *The Muslim World* 99, 2 (April): 237–53.

Onimus, Clément (2017). "Réforme des monnaies et spéculation dans le sultanat mamlouk au début du ixe/xve siècle: al-Maqrīzī et la question de la responsabilité de l'élite mamlouk dans l'instabilité monétaire." *Arabica* 64, 2: 213–36.

Oren, Michael B. (2002). *Six Days of War: June 1967 and the Making of the Modern Middle East*. Oxford: Oxford University Press.

Ory, Solange (1991). "Max Van Berchem, Orientaliste," in Marie-Claude Burgat, ed., *D'un Orient l'autre. Les métamorphoses successives des perceptions et connaissances*, 2 vols. Paris: éditions CNRS, 2: 11–24.

Osmond, Patricia J. (1995) "'Princeps Historiae Romanae': Sallust in Renaissance Political Thought." *Memoirs of the American Academy in Rome* 40: 101–43.

Ouyang, Wen-chin (2007). "Fictive Mode, 'Journey to the West,' and Transformation of Space: Discourses of Modernization in 'Ali Mubarak's *'Alam al-Din*." *Comparative Critical Studies* 4, 3 (December): 331–58.

Ouyang, Wen-chin (2012). *Poetics of Love in the Arabic Novel*. Edinburgh: Edinburgh University Press.

Ouyang, Wen-chin (2013). *Politics of Nostalgia in the Arabic Novel: Nation-State, Modernity and Tradition*. Edinburgh: Edinburgh University Press.

Owen, Roger (1994). "Socio-economic Change and Political Mobilization: The Case of Egypt." In Ghassan Salamé ed., *Democracy Without Democrats? The Renewal of Politics in the Muslim World*. London: I. B. Tauris, 183–99.

Parrot, André (1971). "Gaston Wiet (1887–1971)," *Syria* 48, 3/4: 531–2.

Penelas, Mayte (2020). Al-Maqrīzī's *al-Ḫabar ʿan al-bašar* Vol. V, section 6: *The Greeks, the Romans, the Byzantines, the Franks, and the Goths*. Leiden: Brill.

Perho, Irmeli (2013). "Ibn Taghrībirdī's Voice." In Sylvia Akar, Jaakko Hämeen-Anttila, and Inka Nokso-Koivisto, eds., *Travelling Through Time: Essays in Honour of Kaj Öhrnberg*. Helsinki: Finnish Oriental Society, 135–46.

Petry, Carl (2002). "Educational Institutions as Depicted in the Biographical Literature of Mamluk Cairo: The Debate over Prestige and Venue." *Medieval Prosopography* 23: 101–23.

Petry, Carl (1993). "Scholastic Stasis in Medieval Islam Reconsidered: Mamluk Patronage in Cairo." *Poetics Today* 14, 2: 323–48.

Petry, Carl (1981). *The Civilian Elite of Cairo in the Later Middle Ages*. Princeton: Princeton University Press.

Pfeiffer, Judith (2007). "'A Turgid History of the Mongol Empire in Persia': Epistemological Reflections Concerning a Critical Edition of Vassaf's *Tajziyat al-Amsar fi Tazjiyat al-Aʿsar*." In Judith Pfeiffer and Manfred Kropp, eds., *Theoretical Approaches to the Transmission and Edition of Oriental Manuscripts*. Wurzburg: Ergon Verlag, 107–29.

Pfeiffer, Judith (2014). "Confessional Ambiguity vs. Confessional Polarization: Politics and the Negotiation of Religious Boundaries in the Ilkhanate." In Judith Pfeiffer, ed., *Politics, Patronage and the Transmission of Knowledge in 13th–15th Century Tabriz*. Leiden: Brill, 129–68.

Phillips, Christina (2019). *Religion in the Egyptian Novel*. Edinburgh: Edinburgh University Press.

Prisse d'Avennes, Émile (1847). *Monuments Egyptiens, bas-reliefs, peintures, inscriptions etc., d'après les dessins exécutés sur les lieux, par E. Prisse d'Avennes*. Paris: Firmin Didot.

Prochaska, David (1994). "Art of Colonialism, Colonialism of Art: The Description de l'Égypte." *L'esprit créateur* 34: 69–91.

Quatremère, Étienne-Marc (1856). "Compte rendu." *Journal des Savants*: 321–37.

Quatremère, Étienne-Marc (1837–45). *Histoire des sultans mamlouks de l'Égypte, écrite en arabe par Taki-eddin-Ahmed-Makrizi*, 2 vols. in 4 sections. Paris: Oriental Translation Fund of Great Britain and Ireland.

Rabbat, Nasser (1999). "Dala'il al-ʿImran fi- *Asfar al-Bunyan:* al-ʿImara fi Kitabat Jamal al-Ghitani." *al-Hilal* 107, 1 (January): 152–9.

Rabbat, Nasser (2001). "Maqrizi's *Khitat:* An Egyptian *Lieu de Mémoire*." In Doris Behrens-Abouseif, ed., *The Cairo Heritage. Papers in Honor of Layla Ali Ibrahim*. Cairo, AUC Press, 17–30.

Rabbat, Nasser (1996). "My Life with Salah al-Din: The Memoirs of ʿImad al-Din al-Katib al-Isfahani." *Edebiyat* 7: 2 (Fall 1996): 61–81.

Rabbat, Nasser (1997). "The Formation of the Neo-Mamluk Style in Modern Egypt." In Martha Pollak, ed., *The Education of the Architect: Historiography, Urbanism and the Growth of Architectural Knowledge. Essays Presented to Stanford Anderson on His Sixty-Second Birthday*. Cambridge, MA: MIT Press, 363–86.

Rabbat, Nasser (1997–8 [1999]). "The Mosaics of the Qubba al-Zahiriyya in Damascus: A Classical Syrian Medium Acquires a Mamluk Signature." *Aram* 9–10: 1–13.

Rabbat, Nasser (2006). "'Ajīb and Gharīb: Artistic Perception in Medieval Arabic Sources." *The Medieval History Journal* 9, 1: 99–113.

Rabbat, Nasser (1996). "Al-Azhar Mosque: An Architectural Chronicle of Cairo's History." *Muqarnas* 13: 45–67.

Rabbat, Nasser (1997). "al-Iwan: Ma'nahu al-Faraghi wa Madluluhu al-Tazkari." *BEO* 49 (1997): 249–67.

Rabbat, Nasser (2001). "Al-Madina, al-Tarikh, wal-Sulta: al-Maqrizi wa Kitabuhu al-Ra'id 'al-Mawa'iz wa al-I'tibar bi Dhikr al-Khitat wa al-Athar.'" *AI* 35: 77–100.

Rabbat, Nasser (2014). "Al-Maqrīzī's Connection to the Fatimids." In Farhad Daftary and Gurdofarid Miskinzoda, eds., *The Study of Shi'i Islam: History, Theology and Law*. London: I. B. Tauris, 67–75.

Rabbat, Nasser (2008). "Design without Representation in Medieval Egypt." *Muqarnas* 25: 147–54.

Rabbat, Nasser (2012). "In Search of a Triumphant Image: the Experimental Quality of Early Mamluk Art." In Doris Behrens-Abouseif, ed., *The Arts of the Mamluks in Egypt and Syria—Evolution and Impact*. Berlin: Bonn University Press, 21–35.

Rabbat, Nasser (2002). "Perception of Architecture in Mamluk Sources." *MSR* 6: 155–76.

Rabbat, Nasser (2006). "Review of Fahmi 'Abd al-'Alim, *Al-'Imara al-Islamyah fi 'Asr al-Mamalik al-Jarakisa: 'Asr al-Sultan al-Mu'ayyad Shaykh*." *MSR* 10, 2: 210–13.

Rabbat, Nasser (2018). "The Hidden Hand: Edward Said's Orientalism and Architectural History." *Journal of the Society of Architectural Historians* 77, 4 (December): 388–96.

Rabbat, Nasser (2003). "Who Was Al-Maqrizi? A Biographical Sketch." *MSR* 7, 2: 1–19.

Rabbat, Nasser (2010). *Mamluk History through Architecture: Building, Culture, and Politics in Mamluk Egypt and Syria*. London: I. B. Tauris.

Rabbat, Nasser (1995). *The Citadel of Cairo: A New Interpretation of Royal Mamluk Architecture*. Leiden: Brill.

Raby, Julian (1991). "Reviewing the Reviewers." *Muqarnas*, 8: 4–11.

Radwan, Abu al-Futuh (1953). *Tarikh Matba'at Bulaq wa-Lamha 'an Tarikh al-Tiba'a fi-Buldan al-Sharq al-Awsat*. Cairo: al-Matba'a al-Amiriyya.

Radwan, Tal'at, and Fathi Radwan (1999). *Ab'ad al-Shakhsiyya al-Misriyya: bayna al-madi wa-al-hadir*. Cairo: al Hay'a al-Misriyya al-'Amma lil-Kitab.

Ragib, Yusuf (1987). "Un oratoire fatimide au sommet du Muqaṭṭam." *SI* 65: 51–67.

Ramadan, Sa'ida Muhammad (1982). *Baha'al-Din Zuhair al-Hijazi al-Makki al-Qusi, Hayatuhu wa Shi'ruhu*. Cairo: Dar al-Ma'arif.

Rapoport, Yossef (2013). "Ibn Ḥağar Al-'Asqalānī, His Wife, Her Slave-Girl: Romantic Triangles and Polygamy in 15th Century Cairo." *AI* 47: 327–52.

Ravaisse, Paul (1886–90). *Essai sur l'histoire et la topographie du Caire d'après Maqrizi (Palais des Khalifes Fatimites)*, 1ère et 2ème parties. *MMAF* vol. 1, pt. 3 and vol. 3, pt. 4. Cairo: IFAO.

Raymond, André, and Gaston Wiet (1979). *Les marchés du Caire: Traduction annotée du texte de Maqrīzī*. Cairo: IFAO.

Raymond, André (1975). 'La population du Caire, de Maqrīzī à la "Description de l'égypte."' *BEO* 28: 201–15.

Raymond, André (1978). "La localisation des bains publics au Caire au quinzième siècle d'après Les Ḫiṭaṭ de Maqrīzī." *BEO* 30: 347–60.

Raymond, André (1973). *Artisans et commerçants au Caire au XVIIIe siècle*. Damascus: IFEAD.

Raymond, André (2000). *Cairo*. W. Wood, trans. Cambridge, M.A.: Harvard University Press.

Reeves, John C. (2014). "Jewish Apocalyptic Lore in Early Islam: Reconsidering Ka'b Al-Ahbar." In John Ashton ed., *Revealed Wisdom: Studies in Apocalyptic in Honour of Christopher Rowland*. Leiden: Brill, 200–16.

Régnier-Bohler, Danielle (1999). "Imagining the Self: Exploring Literature." In Philippe Ariès and Georges Duby, eds., trans. Arthur Goldhammer, *A History of Private Life, Volume II: Revelations of the Medieval World*. Cambridge, M.A.: Harvard University Press, 373–82.

Reid, Donald Malcolm (1992). "Cultural Imperialism and Nationalism: The Struggle to Define and Control the Heritage of Arab Art in Egypt." *IJMES* 24, 1 (February): 57–76.

Reid, Donald Malcolm (2002). *Whose Pharaohs? Archaeology, Museums, and Egyptian National Identity from Napoléon to World War I*. Berkeley: University of California Press.

Reimer, Michael J. (2011). "Egyptian Views of Ottoman Rule: Five Historians and Their Works, 1820–1920." *Comparative Studies of South Asia, Africa and the Middle East* 31, 1: 149–63.

Reisman, David C. (1998). "A Holograph MS of Ibn Qadi Shuhbah's *'Dhayl'*." *MSR* 2: 19–45.

Rémusat, Abel (1824). *Notice sur la vie et les ouvrages de M. L.-M. Langlès*. Paris: Dondey-Dupré.

Reynolds, Dwight F. (2005). "Symbolic Narratives of Self: Dreams in Medieval Arabic Autobiographies." In Philip Kennedy, ed., *On Fiction and Adab in Medieval Arabic Literature*. Wiesbaden: Harrassowitz, 261–86.

Reynolds, Dwight F. ed. (2001). *Interpreting the Self: Autobiography in the Arabic Literary Tradition*. Berkeley: University of California Press.

Reynolds, Gabriel Said (2018). *The Qur'an and the Bible. Text and Commentary*. New Haven and London: Yale University Press.

Reza'i, Muhammad Javad, and Mahdi Dasht Bozorgi (2009). "A Study of the Verses of Mubāhalah." *Journal of Shi'a Islamic Studies* 2, 1: 69–83.

Richards, Donald (1972). "The Coptic Bureaucracy under the Mamluks." In *Colloque International sur l'histoire du Caire, 27 Mars–5 Avril 1969*. Cairo: Ministry of Culture, 373–81.

Rida, Muhammad Sa'id (1980). "Ibn Shaddad fi Kitabihi al-A'laq al-Khatirah, 'Qism al-Jazirah.'" *Majallat al-Mu'arrikh al-'Arabi* 14: 124–204.

Riegl, Alois (1982). "The Modern Cult of Monuments: Its Character and Its Origin." Diane Ghirardo and Kurt Forster, trans. *Oppositions* 25: 21–51.

Riyadh, Mustafa (2018). "Al-Tarjama wa-Bina' al-Dawla al-Haditha fi-Misr." *Alif* 38: 1–34.

Robinson, Chase (2003). *Islamic Historiography*. Cambridge: Cambridge University Press.

Rogan, Eugene L (2009). *The Arabs: A History*. New York: Basic Books.

Rogers, J. M. (1991) "Architectural History as Literature: Creswell's Reading and Methods." *Muqarnas* 8: 45–54.

Rohl, Darrell J. (2011). "The Chorographic Tradition and Seventeenth- and Eighteenth-Century Scottish Antiquaries." *Journal of Art Historiography* 5 (December): 1–18, https://arthistoriography.files.wordpress.com/2011/12/rohl.pdf.

Roper, Geoffrey (2007). "The Printing Press and Change in the Arab World." In Sabrina Alcorn Baron, Eric N. Lindquist, and Eleanor F. Shevlin, eds., *Agent of Change: Print Culture Studies After Elizabeth Eisenstein*. Boston: University of Massachusetts Press, 251–67.

Rosen-Ayalon, Miriam (1972). "Gaston Wiet, 1887–1971," *Kunst des Orients* 8, 1/2: 155–9.

Rosenthal, Franz (1981). "'Blurbs' (Taqrīẓ) from Fourteenth-Century Egypt." *Oriens* 27–28: 177–8.

Rosenthal, Franz (1968). *A History of Muslim Historiography*. Leiden: Brill, 2nd edn.

Roux, Jules-Charles (1901). *L'isthme et le Canal de Suez: Historique—État Actuel*. 2 vols. Paris: Hachette.

Ruiz, Mario M. (2009). "Orientalist and Revisionist Histories of 'Abd al-Rahman al-Jabarti." *Middle East Critique* 18, 3: 261–84.

Ryan, Marie-Laure (2005). "Narrative." In David Herman, Manfred Jahn, and Marie-Laure Ryan, eds., *Routledge Encyclopedia of Narrative Theory*. London and New York: Routledge, 344–8.

Ryzova, Lucy (2014). *The Age of the Efendiyya: Passages to Modernity in National-Colonial Egypt*. Oxford: Oxford University Press.

Saïd, Edward (1993). *Culture and Imperialism*. New York: Vintage Books.

Saïd, Edward (1978). *Orientalism*. New York: Pantheon.

Sajdi, Dana (2009). "Print and Its Discontents. A Case for Pre-Print Journalism and Other Sundry Print Matters." *The Translator* 15, 1: 105–38.

Salama, Mohammad R. (2011). *Islam, Orientalism and Intellectual History: Modernity and the Politics of Exclusion since Ibn Khaldun*. London: I. B. Tauris.

Saleh, Walid (n.d.). "A Rebel and his Treatise: On Revolutionary Religious Language in a Medieval Society." Unpublished lecture.

Salih, Salih Sadawi. ed. (2020). *Buhuth al-Mu'tamar al-Dawli hawl al-'Ilm wa-l Ma'rifa fi al-'Alam al-'Uthmani*. Istanbul: IRCICA.

Sallustius Crispus (1921, rev. 1931). *Bellum Catilinae* (*The War with Catiline*). J. Rolfe, trans. Cambridge, M.A.: Harvard University Press.

Salmon, M. Georges (1902–3). "Progrès des études arabes." *Archaeological Report 1902–1903*, F. L. Griffith, ed. London: Egypt Exploration Fund, 68–73.

Salmon, M. Georges (1902). *Études sur la topographie du Caire, la Kal'at al-Kabch et la Birkat al-Fil. MMAF* vol. 7. Cairo: IFAO.

Savant, Sarah (2013). 'Forgetting Ctesiphon: Iran's Pre-Islamic Past, c. 800–1100.' In Philip Wood, ed., *History and Identity in the Late Antique Near East*. Oxford: Oxford University Press, 169–86.

Sayyid, Ayman Fu'ad, and Thierry Bianquis (1978). *Al-Juz' al-arba'un min Akhbar Misr lil-Musabbihi*. Cairo: IFAO.

Sayyid, Ayman Fu'ad (1998). "Manahij al-Naqd al-Tarikhi 'ind al-Mu'rrikhin al-Muslimin." *AI* 32: 1–40.

Sayyid, Ayman Fu'ad (1979). "Remarques sur la composition des Hitat de Maqrizi d'après un manuscrit autographe." In J. Vercoutter, ed., *Hommages à la mémoire de Serge Sauneron, 1927–1976, II: Égypte post-pharaonique*. Cairo, IFAO, 231–58.

Sayyid, Ayman Fu'ad (2000). "Intiqal al-Makhtutat al-'Arabiyya ila Turkiya wa-Atharuhu fi Tawtid al-Sabgha al-Islamiyya li-l Khilafa al-'Uthmaniyya." In Salih Sadawi Salih, ed., *Buhuth al-Mu'tamar al-Dawli hawl al-'Ilm wa-l Ma'rifa fi al-'Alam al-'Uthmani*. Istanbul: IRCICA, 293–302.

Sayyid, Ayman Fu'ad (1997). *Al-Kitab al-'Arabi al-Makhtut wa 'Ilm al-Makhtutat*. 2 vols. Cairo: al-Dar al-Misriyya al-Lubnaniyya.

Sayyid, Fu'ad, et al. (1954–60). *Fihrist al-Makhtutat al-Musawwara, Ma'had al-Makhtutat al-'Arabiyya*. 3 vols. Cairo: Dar al-Riyadh.

Sayyid, Fu'ad (1956). "Shurut al-Mu'arrikh fi-Kitabat al-Tarikh: Khams Fatawa lam Tunshar li-Khamsa min A'lam al-Qarn al-Tasi' al-Hijri." *Majallat Ma'had al-Makhtutat al-'Arabiyya* 2, 1 (May): 162–77.

Seikaly, Samir (1981). "Damascene Intellectual Life in the Opening Years of the Twentieth Century." In Marwan R. Buheiry, ed., *Intellectual Life in the Arab East, 1890–1939*. Beirut: AUB Press, 125–53.

Serrano, Richard A. (1997) "Al-Buḥturī's Poetics of Persian Abodes." *JAL* 28, 1: 68–87.

Sezgin, Fuat et al., eds. (1992). *Studies on Taqiyaddin al-Maqrizi (d. 1442): Collected and Reprinted*. 2 vols. Frankfurt am Main: Institute for the History of Arabic-Islamic Science at the Johann Wolfgang Goethe University.

Sezgin, Ursula (1994). "Pharaonische Wunderwerke." *Zeitshcrift fur Geschichte der Arabische-Islamischen Wissenschaften* 9: 229–91.

Shafe'i, Farid (1965). "The Mashhad al-Juyushi (Archaeological Notes and Studies). In C. L. Geddes, ed., *Studies in Islamic Art and Architecture in Honour of Prof. K. A. C. Creswell*. Cairo, AUC Press, 237–52.

Shafe'i, Farid (1982). *Al-'Imara al-'Arabiyya al-Islamiyya. Madiha wa-Hadiruha wa-Mustaqbaluha*. Riyadh: Jami'at al-Malik Sa'ud.

Shafe'i, Farid (1970, reprinted 1994). *Al-'Imara al-'Arabiyya fi Misr al-Islamiyya, 'Asr al-Wulat*. Cairo: al-Hay'a al-Misriyya al-'Amma li-l-Ta'lif wa-l-Nashr.

Shalabi, Khayri (1995). *Batn al-Baqara*. Cairo: Dar al-Ma'arif.

Shalabi, Khayri (1983). *Rihlat al-Turshaji al-Halwaji*. Cairo: Akhbar al-Yawm.
Shalabi, Khayri (2010). *The Time-Travels of the Man who Sold Pickles and Sweets*, Michael Cooperson, trans. Cairo: AUC Press.
Shaykh, Ahmad (1999). *Hiwar al-istishraq: min naqd al-istishraq ila naqd al-istighrab*. Cairo: al-Markaz al-ʿArabi lil-Dirasat al-Gharbiyya.
Shechter, Relli (2008). "The Cultural Economy of Development in Egypt: Economic Nationalism, Hidden Economy and the Emergence of Mass Consumer Society during Sadat's Infitah," *MES* 44, 4: 571–83.
Sheehi, Stephen (2012). "Towards a Critical Theory of al-Nahḍah: Epistemology, Ideology and Capital." *JAL* 43, 2/3: 269–98.
Sheehi, Stephen (2004). *Foundations of Modern Arab Identity*. Gainesville, FL: University Press of Florida.
Shopov, Aleksandar (2016). "Between the Pen and the Fields: Books on Farming, Changing Land Regimes, and Urban Agriculture in the Ottoman Eastern Mediterranean ca. 1500–1700," PhD diss., Harvard University.
Shukri, Iman Omar (2003). *Al-Sultan Barquq, Mu'asis Dawlat al-Mamalik al-Jarakisa Min Khilal Makhtut ʿIqd al-Juman fi Tarikh Ahl al-Zaman*. Cairo: Madbuli.
Siddiqi, Akhtar Husain (1984). "Ibn Khaldun's Concept of Urbanization." *International Journal of Islamic and Arabic Studies* 1, 2: 41–55.
Siegel, Marvin, ed. (1997). *The Last Word: The New York Times Book of Obituaries and Farewells: A Celebration of Unusual Lives*. New York: William Morrow.
Sijpesteijn, Petra M. (2011). "Building an Egyptian Identity." In Asad Q. Ahmed, Michael Bonner, and Behnam Sadeghi, eds., *The Islamic Scholarly Tradition: Studies in History, Law, and Thought in Honor of Professor Michael Allan Cook*. Leiden: Brill, 85–105.
Silvera, Alain (1980). "The First Egyptian Student Mission to France under Muhammad Ali," *MES* 16, 2 (May): 1–22.
Silvestre de Sacy, Antoine Isaac (1806). *Chrestomathie arabe, ou, Extraits de divers écrivains arabes, tant en prose qu'en vers, avec une traduction française et des notes, à l'usage des élèves de l'École royale et spéciale des langues orientales vivantes*. 3 vols. Paris: Imprimerie impériale.
Silvestre de Sacy, Antoine Isaac (1810). *Relations de l'Égypte*. Paris: Imprimerie impériale.
Singerman, Diane, ed. (2009). *Cairo Contested: Governance, Urban Space, and Global Modernity*. Cairo: AUC Press.
Sirriyeh, Elizabeth (2015). *Dreams and Visions in the World of Islam: A History of Muslim Dreaming and Foreknowing*. London: I. B. Tauris.
Skinner, Quentin (1986). "Ambrogio Lorenzetti: The Artist as Political Philosopher." *Proceedings of the British Academy* 72: 1–56.
Smith, Martyn (2012). "Finding Meaning in the City: al-Maqrizi's Use of Poetry in the *Khitat*." *MSR* 16: 143–61.
Spence, Jonathan (2001). *Treason by the Book*. New York: Viking.
Starkey, Paul (2015). "Strange Incidents from History: Youssef Rakha and his Sultan's

Seal." In Roger Allen and Robin Ostle, eds., *Studying Modern Arabic Literature: Mustafa Badawi, Scholar and Critic*. Edinburgh: Edinburgh University Press, 159–77.

Steiner, Wendy (2004). "Pictorial Narrativity." In Marie-Laure Ryan, ed., *Narrative across Media: The Languages of Storytelling*. Lincoln, N.E.: University of Nebraska Press, 145–77.

Stern, Samuel (1972). "Cairo as the Centre of the Isma'ili Movement," in *Colloque international sur l'histoire du Caire*. Cairo: Ministry of Culture, 437–50.

Stern, Samuel (1983). *Studies in Early Isma'ilism*. Leiden: Brill.

Stetkevych, Jaroslav (1993). *The Zephyrs of Najd: The Poetics of Nostalgia in the Classical Arabic Nasib*. Chicago: University of Chicago Press.

Stowasser. Karl, ed. and trans. (2014). *Medieval Egypt: Al-Khiṭaṭ of Aḥmad ibn Alī Al-Maqrīzī*. Washington, D.C.: Hans A. Stowasser.

Symcox, Geoffrey (2003). "The Geopolitics of the Egyptian Expedition, 1797–1798." In Irene A. Bierman, ed., *Napoléon in Egypt*, Reading: Ithaca Press, 13–31.

Tageldin, Shaden M. (2011). *Disarming Words: Empire and the Seductions of Translation in Egypt*. Berkeley: University of California Press.

Taha, Ibrahim (2000). "The Power of the Title 'Why Have you Left the Horse Alone' by Maḥmūd Darwīsh." *JAIS* 3: 66–83.

Tahir, Mehmed. (1975) *Osmanli Muellifleri*. Istanbul: Meral Yayınları.

Tamari, Salim (2017). "A 'Scientific Expedition' to Gallipoli: The Syrian-Palestinian Intelligentsia Divided." In *The Great War and the Remaking of Palestine*. Berkeley: University of California Press, 67–87.

Tamari, Salim (2014). "A 'Scientific Expedition' to Gallipoli: The Syrian-Palestinian Intelligentsia and the Ottoman Campaign Against Arab Separatism." *Jerusalem Quarterly* 56 (Winter/Spring): 6–28.

Tamari, Salim (2016). "Muhammad Kurd'ali and the Syrian-Palestinian Intelligentsia in the Ottoman Campaign Against Arabic Separatism." In M. Talha Çiçek, ed., *Syria in World War I: Politics, Economy and Society*. London: Routledge, 37–60.

Taragan, Hanna (2006). "Sign of the Times: Reusing the Past in Baybars's Architecture in Palestine." In David J. Wasserstein and Ami Ayalon eds., *Mamluks and Ottomans. Studies in Honour of Michael Winter*. London: Routledge, 54–66.

Tolmacheva, Marina (1995). "The Medieval Arabic Geographers and the Beginnings of Modern Orientalism." *IJMES* 27: 141–56.

Tomar, Cengiz (2008). "Between Myth and Reality: Approaches to Ibn Khaldun in the Arab World." *Asian Journal of Social Science* 36, 3: 590–611.

Tottoli, Roberto (2002). *Biblical Prophets in the Qur'an and Muslim Literature*. London: Routledge.

Troadec, Anne (2014–15). "Baybars and the Cultural Memory of Bilad al-Sham: The Construction of Legitimacy." *MSR* 18: 113–47.

Van Ess, Leander (1821). *Restitutio veræ chronologiæ rerum ex controversiis Arianis inde ab anno 325 usque ad annum 350 exortarum contra chronologiam hodie receptam exhibita, una cum specimine historiæ Coptorum a Makrisio Arabice script*. Frankfurt-am-Main, Sumptibus et Typis H. L. Brœnneri.

Van Steenbergen, Jo (2011). "The Amir Yalbughā Al-Khāṣṣakī, the Qalāwūnid

Sultanate, and the Cultural Matrix of Mamlūk Society: A Reassessment of Mamlūk Politics in the 1360s." *JOAS* 131, 3: 423–43.

Van Steenbergen, Jo (2016). *Caliphate and Kingship in a Fifteenth-Century Literary History of Muslim Leadership and Pilgrimage. al-Ḏahab al-Masbūk Fī Ḏikr Man Ḥağğa Min al-Ḫulafā' Wa-l-Mulūk. Critical Edition, Annotated Translation, and Study*. Leiden: Brill.

Vesely, Rudolf (1999). "Ibn Nāhiḍ's as-Sīra aš-Šaykhīya (Eine Lebensgeschichte Des Sultans al-Mu'ayyad Šaykh): Ein Beitrag Zur Sīra-Literatur." *Archiv Orientalni* 67: 149–220.

Vismann, Cornelia (2001). "The Love of Ruins," *Perspectives on Science* 9, 2 (Summer): 196–209.

Volait, Mercedes (2010). "History or Theory? French Antiquarianism, Cairene Architecture, and Enlightenment Thinking." *Ars Orientalis* 39: 231–54.

Von Grunebaum, Gustave E., and Roger Caillois, eds. (1966). *The Dream and Human Societies*. Berkeley: University of California Press.

Walker, Andrew D. (1993) "*Enargeia* and the Spectator in Greek Historiography." *Transactions of the American Philological Association* 123: 353–77.

Walker, Bethany J. (2004). "Commemorating the Sacred Spaces of the Past: The Mamluks and the Umayyad Mosque at Damascus." *Near Eastern Archaeology* 67, 1 (March): 26–39.

Walker, Bethany (2004). "Ceramic Evidence for Political Transformations in Early Mamluk Egypt." *MSR* 8, 1: 54–114.

Walker, Paul (2003). "Al-Maqrizi and the Fatimids." *MSR* 7, 2: 83–97.

Walker, Paul (1999). *Hamid al-Din al-Kirmani: Ismaili Thought in the Age of al-Hakim*. London: I. B. Tauris.

Watenpaugh, Heghnar (2007). "An Uneasy Historiography: The Legacy of Ottoman Architecture in the Former Arab Provinces." *Muqarnas* 24: 27–43.

Watenpaugh, Heghnar (2017). "Resonance and Circulation: The Category 'Islamic Art and Architecture.'" In Finbarr Barry Flood and Gülru Necipoglu, eds., *A Companion to Islamic Art and Architecture*, 2 vols. Hoboken, N.J.: John Wiley, 2: 1223–41.

Webb, Peter (2019). *Al-Maqrīzī's al-Ḫabar 'an al-bašar* vol. V, sections 1–2: *The Arab Thieves*. Leiden: Brill.

Wetzer, Heinrich Joseph, ed. and trans. (1828). *Taki-eddini Makrizii historia Coptorum Christianorum in Aegypto Arabice*. Sulzbach, Germany: In Libraria J. E. de Seideliana.

White, Hayden (1959–60). "Ibn Khaldun in World Philosophy of History (Review Article)," *Comparative Studies in Society and History* 2: 110–25.

Wiederhold, Lutz (1999). "Legal-Religious Elite, Temporal Authority, and the Caliphate in Mamluk Society: Conclusions Drawn from the Examination of a 'Zahiri Revolt' in Damascus in 1386." *IJMES* 31, 2: 203–35.

Wiet, Gaston (1962). "Le traité des famines de Maqrizi," *JESHO* 5: 1–90.

Wilkinson, Catherine (1977). "The New Professionalism in the Renaissance." In Spiro Kostof, ed., *The Architect: Chapters in the History of a Profession*. New York: Oxford University Press, 124–60.

Williams, John Alden (1984). "Urbanization and Monument Construction in Mamluk Cairo." *Muqarnas* 2: 33–45.

Witkam, Jan Just (1994). "Les autographes d'al-Maqrizi." In Ahmed-Chouqui Binebine, ed., *Le manuscrit arabe et la codicologie*. Rabat: Publications de la Faculté des Lettres et des Sciences Humaines, 89–98.

Witkam, Jan Just (2014). "Reflections on al-Maqrizi's Biographical Dictionary." In Obada Kohela, ed., *In the History and Islamic Civilization: Essays in Honour of Ayman Fu'ad Sayyid*. Cairo: al-Dar al-Misriyya al-Lubnaniyya, 93–114.

Wolf, Werner (2003). "Narrative and Narrativity: A Narratological Reconceptualization and Its Applicability to the Visual Arts." *Word and Image* 19, 3: 180–97.

Yarbrough, Luke (2019). "Medieval Sunni Historians on Fatimid Policy and Non-Muslim Influence." *Journal of Medieval History* 45, 3: 331–46.

Zadeh, Travis (2011). *Mapping Frontiers Across Medieval Islam: Geography, Translation, and the 'Abbasid Empire*. London: I. B. Tauris.

Zaki, 'Abd al-Rahman (1966). *al-Qahira, Tarikhuha wa-Atharaha*. Cairo: al-Hay'a al-Misriyya al-'Amma li-l-Ta'lif wa-l-Nashr.

Zaki, 'Abd al-Rahman (1969). *Mawsu'at Madinat al-Qahira fi Alf 'Am*. Cairo: Maktabat al-Anjlo al-Misriyah.

Ziyada, Muhammad Mustafa, et al. (1971). *Dirasat 'an al-Maqrizi*. Cairo: Egyptian Historical Society.

Ziyada, Muhammad Mustafa (1949). *Al-Mu'arrikhun fi Misr fi al-Qarn al-Khamis 'Ashar (al-Qarn al-Tasi' al-Hijri)*. Cairo: Lajnat al-Ta'lif wal Tarjama wal-Nashr.

Index of Books Cited in the Text

General Index